Vintage Southern Cookbook

THE LOCHLAINN SEABROOK COLLECTION

AMERICAN CIVIL WAR
Abraham Lincoln Was a Liberal, Jefferson Davis Was a Conservative: The Missing Key to Understanding the American Civil War
Confederacy 101: Amazing Facts You Never Knew About America's Oldest Political Tradition
Confederate Blood and Treasure: An Interview With Lochlainn Seabrook
Everything You Were Taught About African-Americans and the Civil War is Wrong, Ask a Southerner!
Everything You Were Taught About the Civil War is Wrong, Ask a Southerner!
Give This Book to a Yankee! A Southern Guide to the Civil War For Northerners
Heroes of the Southern Confederacy: The Illustrated Book of Confederate Officials, Soldiers, and Civilians
Lincoln's War: The Real Cause, the Real Winner, the Real Loser
The Great Yankee Coverup: What the North Doesn't Want You to Know About Lincoln's War!
The Ultimate Civil War Quiz Book: How Much Do You Really Know About America's Most Misunderstood Conflict?
Women in Gray: A Tribute to the Ladies Who Supported the Southern Confederacy

CONFEDERATE MONUMENTS
Confederate Monuments: Why Every American Should Honor Confederate Soldiers and Their Memorials

CONFEDERATE FLAG
Confederate Flag Facts: What Every American Should Know About Dixie's Southern Cross
What the Confederate Flag Means to Me: Americans Speak Out in Defense of Southern Honor, Heritage, and History

SECESSION
All We Ask Is To Be Let Alone: The Southern Secession Fact Book

SLAVERY
Everything You Were Taught About American Slavery is Wrong, Ask a Southerner!
Slavery 101: Amazing Facts You Never Knew About America's "Peculiar Institution"

CHILDREN
Honest Jeff and Dishonest Abe: A Southern Children's Guide to the Civil War
Saddle, Sword, and Gun: A Biography of Nathan Bedford Forrest For Teens

NATHAN BEDFORD FORREST
A Rebel Born: A Defense of Nathan Bedford Forrest - Confederate General, American Legend (winner of the 2011 Jefferson Davis Historical Gold Medal)
A Rebel Born: The Screenplay (film about N. B. Forrest)
Forrest! 99 Reasons to Love Nathan Bedford Forrest
Give 'Em Hell Boys! The Complete Military Correspondence of Nathan Bedford Forrest
I Rode With Forrest! Confederate Soldiers Who Served With the World's Greatest Cavalry Leader
Nathan Bedford Forrest and African-Americans: Yankee Myth, Confederate Fact
Nathan Bedford Forrest and the Battle of Fort Pillow: Yankee Myth, Confederate Fact
Nathan Bedford Forrest and the Ku Klux Klan: Yankee Myth, Confederate Fact
Nathan Bedford Forrest: Southern Hero, American Patriot - Honoring a Confederate Icon and the Old South
Saddle, Sword, and Gun: A Biography of Nathan Bedford Forrest For Teens
The God of War: Nathan Bedford Forrest As He Was Seen By His Contemporaries
The Quotable Nathan Bedford Forrest: Selections From the Writings and Speeches of the Confederacy's Most Brilliant Cavalryman

QUOTABLE SERIES
The Alexander H. Stephens Reader: Excerpts From the Works of a Confederate Founding Father
The Quotable Alexander H. Stephens: Selections From the Writings and Speeches of the Confederacy's First Vice President
The Quotable Jefferson Davis: Selections From the Writings and Speeches of the Confederacy's First President
The Quotable Nathan Bedford Forrest: Selections From the Writings and Speeches of the Confederacy's Most Brilliant Cavalryman
The Quotable Robert E. Lee: Selections From the Writings and Speeches of the South's Most Beloved Civil War General
The Quotable Stonewall Jackson: Selections From the Writings and Speeches of the South's Most Famous General
The Unquotable Abraham Lincoln: The President's Quotes They Don't Want You To Know!

CIVIL WAR BATTLES
Encyclopedia of the Battle of Franklin - A Comprehensive Guide to the Conflict that Changed the Civil War
Nathan Bedford Forrest and the Battle of Fort Pillow: Yankee Myth, Confederate Fact
The Battle of Franklin: Recollections of Confederate and Union Soldiers
The Battle of Nashville: Recollections of Confederate and Union Soldiers
The Battle of Spring Hill: Recollections of Confederate and Union Soldiers

CONSTITUTIONAL HISTORY
America's Three Constitutions: Complete Texts of the Articles of Confederation, U.S. Constitution, and C.S. Constitution
The Articles of Confederation Explained: A Clause-by-Clause Study of America's First Constitution
The Constitution of the Confederate States of America Explained: A Clause-by-Clause Study of the South's Magna Carta

VICTORIAN CONFEDERATE LITERATURE
Rise Up and Call Them Blessed: Victorian Tributes to the Confederate Soldier, 1861-1901
Support Your Local Confederate: Wit and Humor in the Southern Confederacy
The God of War: Nathan Bedford Forrest As He Was Seen By His Contemporaries
The Old Rebel: Robert E. Lee As He Was Seen By His Contemporaries
Victorian Confederate Poetry: The Southern Cause in Verse, 1861-1901

ABRAHAM LINCOLN
Abraham Lincoln: The Southern View - Demythologizing America's Sixteenth President
Lincolnology: The Real Abraham Lincoln Revealed in His Own Words - A Study of Lincoln's Suppressed, Misinterpreted, and Forgotten Writings and Speeches
Lincoln's War: The Real Cause, the Real Winner, the Real Loser
The Great Impersonator! 99 Reasons to Dislike Abraham Lincoln
The Unholy Crusade: Lincoln's Legacy of Destruction in the American South
The Unquotable Abraham Lincoln: The President's Quotes They Don't Want You To Know!

NATURAL HISTORY
North America's Amazing Mammals: An Encyclopedia for the Whole Family
The Concise Book of Owls: A Guide to Nature's Most Mysterious Birds
The Concise Book of Tigers: A Guide to Nature's Most Remarkable Cats

PARANORMAL
Carnton Plantation Ghost Stories: True Tales of the Unexplained from Tennessee's Most Haunted Civil War House!
UFOs and Aliens: The Complete Guidebook

FAMILY HISTORIES
The Blakeneys: An Etymological, Ethnological, and Genealogical Study - Uncovering the Mysterious Origins of the Blakeney Family and Name
The Caudills: An Etymological, Ethnological, and Genealogical Study - Exploring the Name and National Origins of a European-American Family
The McGavocks of Carnton Plantation: A Southern History - Celebrating One of Dixie's Most Noble Confederate Families and Their Tennessee Home

MIND, BODY, SPIRIT
Autobiography of a Non-Yogi: A Scientist's Journey From Hinduism to Christianity (Dr. Amitava Dasgupta, with Lochlainn Seabrook)
Britannia Rules: Goddess-Worship in Ancient Anglo-Celtic Society - An Academic Look at the United Kingdom's Matricentric Spiritual Past
Christ Is All and In All: Rediscovering Your Divine Nature and the Kingdom Within
Christmas Before Christianity: How the Birthday of the "Sun" Became the Birthday of the "Son"
Jesus and the Gospel of Q: Christ's Pre-Christian Teachings As Recorded in the New Testament
Jesus and the Law of Attraction: The Bible-Based Guide to Creating Perfect Health, Wealth, and Happiness Following Christ's Simple Formula
Seabrook's Bible Dictionary of Traditional and Mystical Christian Doctrines
The Bible and the Law of Attraction: 99 Teachings of Jesus, the Apostles, and the Prophets
The Book of Kelle: An Introduction to Goddess-Worship and the Great Celtic Mother-Goddess Kelle, Original Blessed Lady of Ireland
The Goddess Dictionary of Words and Phrases: Introducing a New Core Vocabulary for the Women's Spirituality Movement
Vintage Southern Cookbook: 2,000 Delicious Dishes From Dixie

WOMEN
Aphrodite's Trade: The Hidden History of Prostitution Unveiled
Princess Diana: Modern Day Moon-Goddess - A Psychoanalytical and Mythological Look at Diana Spencer's Life, Marriage, and Death (with Dr. Jane Goldberg)
Women in Gray: A Tribute to the Ladies Who Supported the Southern Confederacy

REPRINTS
A Short History of the Confederate States of America (author Jefferson Davis; editor Lochlainn Seabrook)
Prison Life of Jefferson Davis (author John J. Craven; editor Lochlainn Seabrook)
Life of Beethoven (author Ludwig Nohl; editor Lochlainn Seabrook)
The New Revelation (author Arthur Conan Doyle; editor Lochlainn Seabrook)

Lochlainn Seabrook does not author books for fame and fortune, but for the love of writing and sharing his knowledge.

SeaRavenPress.com

Vintage Southern Cookbook

2,000 Delicious Dishes From Dixie

CONCEIVED, COLLECTED, EDITED, & ARRANGED, WITH AN INTRODUCTION BY THE AUTHOR,
"THE VOICE OF THE TRADITIONAL SOUTH," COLONEL

Lochlainn Seabrook

JEFFERSON DAVIS HISTORICAL GOLD MEDAL WINNER

Diligently Researched and Generously Illustrated
by the Author for the Elucidation of the Reader

2021

Sea Raven Press, Nashville, Tennessee, USA

VINTAGE SOUTHERN COOKBOOK

Published by
Sea Raven Press, Cassidy Ravensdale, President
PO Box 1484, Spring Hill, Tennessee 37174-1484 USA
SeaRavenPress.com • searavenpress@gmail.com

Copyright © text and illustrations Lochlainn Seabrook 2021
in accordance with U.S. and international copyright laws and regulations, as stated and protected under the Berne Union for the Protection of Literary and Artistic Property (Berne Convention), and the Universal Copyright Convention (the UCC). All rights reserved under the Pan-American and International Copyright Conventions.

1st SRP paperback edition, 1st printing, September 2021 • ISBN: 978-1-955351-06-5
1st SRP hardcover edition, 1st printing, September 2021 • ISBN: 978-1-955351-07-2

ISBN: 978-1-955351-06-5 (paperback)
Library of Congress Control Number: 2021946020

This work is the copyrighted intellectual property of Lochlainn Seabrook and has been registered with the Copyright Office at the Library of Congress in Washington, D.C., USA. No part of this work (including text, covers, drawings, photos, illustrations, maps, images, diagrams, etc.), in whole or in part, may be used, reproduced, stored in a retrieval system, or transmitted, in any form or by any means now known or hereafter invented, without written permission from the publisher. The sale, duplication, hire, lending, copying, digitalization, or reproduction of this material, in any manner or form whatsoever, is also prohibited, and is a violation of federal, civil, and digital copyright law, which provides severe civil and criminal penalties for any violations.

Vintage Southern Cookbook: 2,000 Delicious Dishes From Dixie, by Lochlainn Seabrook. Includes an introduction, illustrations, index, endnotes, appendices, and a bibliography.

ARTWORK
Front and back cover design and art, book design, layout, and interior art by Lochlainn Seabrook
All images, image captions, graphic design, & graphic art copyright © Lochlainn Seabrook
All images selected, placed, manipulated, and/or created by Lochlainn Seabrook
Image cleaning, coloration, & tinting by Lochlainn Seabrook
Cover layout and graphic art by Lochlainn Seabrook copyright © 2021
Cover art, "Southern Smorgasbord," copyright © DiViArts

All persons who approve of the authority and principles of Colonel Lochlainn Seabrook's literary work, and realize its benefits as a means of reeducating the world about the South and the Confederacy, are hereby requested to avidly recommend his books to others and to vigorously cooperate in extending their reach, scope, and influence around the globe.

The views on the American South documented in this book are those of the publisher.

PRINTED & MANUFACTURED IN OCCUPIED TENNESSEE, FORMER CONFEDERATE STATES OF AMERICA

Dedication

To an Anglo-Celtic goddess and the world's best cook.

Epigraph

"To be a good cook means the knowledge of all fruits, herbs, balms and spices, and of all that is healing and sweet in field and groves, and savory in meats. It means carefulness, inventiveness, watchfulness, willingness and readiness of appliance. It means the economy of your great-grandmothers and the science of modern chemists. It means much tasting and no wasting. It means English thoroughness, French art and Arabian hospitality. It means, in fine, that you are to . . . always . . . see that every one has something nice to eat."

John Ruskin
(1819-1900)

Contents

Notes to the Reader - 11
How to Use This Book - 12
Disclaimer - 15
Introduction, by Lochlainn Seabrook - 17

The Recipes

1 BEVERAGES - 21
2 BREADS - 43
3 CANDIES - 70
4 CEREAL GRAINS - 81
5 CHEESE DISHES - 86
6 CROQUETTES - 95
7 DESSERTS - 100
8 DUMPLINGS - 192
9 EGGS - 197
10 ENTREES - 209
11 FRITTERS - 221
12 FRUITS - 226
13 HEALING RECIPES - 234
14 JELLIES AND PRESERVES - 247
15 MEATS - 265
16 PANCAKES AND WAFFLES - 313
17 PASTAS - 321
18 PASTRIES, PIES, AND CUSTARDS - 328
19 PICKLING & CATSUPS - 353
20 SALADS - 365
21 SALAD DRESSINGS - 378
22 SANDWICHES - 383
23 SAUCES - 392
24 SCHOOL AND BUSINESS LUNCHES - 404
25 SEAFOODS - 408
26 SNACKS - 429
27 SOUPS - 433
28 VEGETABLES - 458

Notes - 481
Bibliography - 519
Index - 521
Appendix A: Vintage Weights and Measures - 573
Appendix B: Things to Remember - 575
Appendix C: Table Etiquette - 577
Appendix D: French Words in Cooking - 580
Appendix E: Housekeeper's Alphabet - 581
Appendix F: How to Cook Husbands - 582
Appendix G: Contributors to the Vintage Southern Cookbook - 583
Meet the Author - 586
Learn More - 587

"Books invite all; they constrain none."
Hartley Burr Alexander (1873-1939)

Notes to the Reader

TEXT AND FORMATTING
☞ In the interest of historical preservation I have made very few alterations to the text and formatting of the original cooking material. In several instances I have added or subtracted a word of text or changed paragraph indents (to better fit the page). Additionally, I sometimes reworded recipe titles (such as changing "Pears Preserved" to "Preserved Pears") for clarity's sake, or to differentiate them from similar recipes. I have also corrected obvious typos that were missed in the original manuscripts of the authors, such as "pwdered" ("powdered"). Lastly, brackets contain my comments.

FOOD SUBSTITUTION
☞ With our modern emphasis on whole organic foods and quality nutritional supplements, many of the ingredients used in these old Southern recipes will stand out as "unhealthy." Whether this is scientifically accurate or not I will leave to the reader to decide. However, at the same time one must bear in mind that, as any good cook knows, one ingredient may always be substituted for another. Thus, one can use healthy or natural alternatives to those called for in any recipe.

Health begins in the kitchen. — L.S.

Examples: butter, olive oil, avocado oil, or coconut oil can be exchanged for lard, shortening, and bacon grease; fresh vegetables for canned vegetables; organic for inorganic; whole grains can replace denatured "enriched" grains; rice, almond, chickpea, or potato flour can take the place of wheat flour; honey or raw, coconut, beet, or date sugar can be used instead of white sugar; tofu and tempeh replace meat; freshly squeezed juices can be substituted for artificially processed juices; almond, soy, coconut, oat, quinoa, cashew, hemp, or rice milk instead of cow's milk; soy or rice cheese for dairy cheese; and so on.

Just remember that ingredient substitution will change the taste, texture, and color of a dish, and even affect the measurements of other ingredients—which in turn may affect cooking time—so it is best to proceed with caution.

RECIPE SOURCES
☞ The original source of each recipe is indicated in its accompanying endnote.

CONTINUE YOUR EDUCATION ON SOUTHERN CULTURE
☞ This book is not only meant to be a genuine, practical, very serviceable cookbook, as a gastronomical record of the Old South it is also meant to preserve an important piece of Southern culture for future generations. Those who are interested in learning about the lives, beliefs, and accomplishments of the amazing people behind the recipes in *Vintage Southern Cookbook* must, of course, study Southern history.

Not just any Southern history. One must study the *true* history of the American South, and this can only come from books penned by writers and historians sympathetic to and educated in *authentic* Southern history.

I call upon those of my readers who are interested in what the South has to say about her own history to peruse the list of my books on pages 2 and 3 of this work. I have authored a wide variety of volumes on nearly every aspect of Southern culture, society, and history, all meant to establish and preserve the facts while educating the inquisitive and enlightening the open-minded.

How to Use This Book

AS A PERUSAL OF A dozen random cookbooks will attest, there is no consensus among cooks on how to best categorize recipes or even foods themselves. For example, is a bowl of pudding a type of custard, an appetizer, an entree, a dessert, part of the main meal, or a side dish? Is it a breakfast food, a dish for brunch, lunch, or dinner, or even a nighttime snack? The answer is that it all depends on the cook's personal views and intentions.

It is for these reasons that, while keeping my readers foremost in mind, I have organized the recipes herein according to what I consider the most efficacious system: grouping recipes together according to either their predominant ingredient or the primary food category they belong to.

Thus, my "Beef Steak Pie" recipe does not appear in the Pastries, Pies, and Custards section, but rather in the Meats section. "Vegetable Soup" is not listed in the Vegetables section, but in the Soup section. "Anchovy Sauce" is not included in the Seafoods section, but in the Sauce section. "Pickled Eggs" are not listed in the Eggs section, but rather in the Pickling and Catsups section. "Apple Sauce" does not appear in the Sauce section but instead in the Fruit section. "Stonewall Jackson Pudding" is not listed in the Pastries, Pies, and Custards section, but in the Desserts section.

Dinnertime!

As there is no solution to this problem that will appeal to everyone (after all, food preparation spans all seven continents and thousands of different cultures, regions, languages, ethnicities, and societies), before embarking on your initial gastronomical journey I advise first familiarizing yourself with the general Contents (at the front of the book) and afterward the detailed Index (at the back of the book).

If a recipe calls for a prepared food or ingredient that you are not familiar with, check for it in the appropriate category in the Index, where you are quite likely to find a recipe or more information regarding that particular item. For instance, many dishes call for white sauce, the recipe for which may be found in the Sauces section.

Keep Your Body, Mind, & Spirit Vibrating at Their Highest Level

YOU CAN DO SO BY READING THE BOOKS OF

SEA RAVEN PRESS

There is nothing that will so perfectly keep your body, mind, and spirit in a healthy condition as to think wisely and positively. Hence you should not only read this book, but also the other books that we offer. They will quicken your physical, mental, and spiritual vibrations, enabling you to maintain a position in society as a healthy erudite person.

KEEP YOURSELF WELL-INFORMED!

The well-informed person is always at the head of the procession, while the ignorant, the lazy, and the unthoughtful hang onto the rear. If you are a Spiritual man or woman, do yourself a great favor: read Sea Raven Press books and stay well posted on the Truth. It is almost criminal for one to remain in ignorance while the opportunity to gain knowledge is open to all at a nominal price.

We invite you to visit our Webstore for a wide selection of wholesome, family-friendly, well-researched, educational books for all ages. You will be glad you did!

Five-Star Books & Gifts From the Heart of the American South

SeaRavenPress.com

LochlainnSeabrook.com
BestCivilWarBookEver.com
NathanBedfordForrestBooks.com

Some 2,000 gastronomical delights for the young and old are contained within this book!

Disclaimer

WE AT SEA RAVEN PRESS invite you to enjoy the intriguing and tasty victuals found in this volume of Old South Southern recipes: Lochlainn Seabrook's *Vintage Southern Cookbook*. However, please note the following 12 pieces of important information:

1. Sea Raven Press and the author-editor Lochlainn Seabrook are not responsible for the outcome of any recipe you try from this book.
2. We cannot guarantee that acceptable or favorable results will be obtained from the use of these recipes. In utilizing this book make sure you have both the proper culinary skill set and experience to match a specific recipe.
3. The many variations in recipe elements such as ingredients, cooking temperatures, and individual cooking ability, as well as typos, errors, and omissions in the original recipe sources, may also cause unexpected or undesirable results.
4. We assume no obligation or liability, and make no warranties with respect to these recipes. It is up to you to determine their value.
5. You should always take great care when cooking with raw ingredients such as eggs, chicken, or seafood and seek expert advice before beginning if in doubt.
6. You should always use proper judgment when handling sharp instruments, electrical machinery, or other potentially dangerous cooking implements. To guard against hazards to yourself and others, please take extra precautions while cooking, especially around hot surfaces.
7. Please review all ingredients prior to using a recipe to make sure they do not contain any substances that might cause an adverse reaction in those who will be consuming them, or even those who might consume them.
8. Recipes in this book may not have been tried or tested by us or for us, and we do not provide any assurances nor accept any responsibility or liability with regard to their originality, quality, nutritional value, safety, etc.
9. All of the information contained in this cookbook is provided on an "as is" basis with no guarantees of health benefits, completeness, accuracy, usefulness, or timeliness.
10. Neither Sea Raven Press or Lochlainn Seabrook are responsible for any domestic accidents, fires, or food poisoning that could or may result from the preparation of the recipes, or the eating of raw vegetables, eggs, meat, fish, etc. We are also not responsible for any kind of food borne disease or anything else dangerous or damaging that might arise as a consequence of using these recipes.
11. Pertaining to Chapter 13, "Healing Recipes," in particular: While these antique American recipes were presumably used and found safe in the 19th and early 20th Centuries, they are not intended to diagnose, treat, cure, or prevent any illness, disease, or health condition. No actual cure or even improvement is implied by the use of the word "healing" in the title of Chapter 13—whose recipes are presented for historical purposes only.
12. You *always* use these recipes and their ingredients *at your own risk and discretion.*

> Owning, possessing, borrowing, reading, or using this book or its contents in any manner whatsoever infers that you have read, understand, and agree to this Disclaimer and all of the terms and conditions contained therein—without exception.

Thank You!

Introduction

THOUGH I THOROUGHLY ENJOY AN occasional culinary adventure in the kitchen, I am not a chef, nor even what could be considered a mediocre cook. What then is a historian without a background in gastronomy doing writing and editing a cookbook?

This is not just a cookbook. It is a *Southern* cookbook. And it is not just a Southern cookbook. It is a *vintage* Southern cookbook, one steeped in the traditions of the Old South, the home of my ancestors dating back to the founding of Jamestown in 1607. I am very proud of my Southern heritage and this book is just one way I am helping to preserve it, while simultaneously honoring the cradle of my being: Dixie, and in particular, Kentucky, Virginia, West Virginia, Tennessee, and North Carolina—from whence most of my Southern forebears originated.

Yet, there is more to it than that.

In one form or another I have been involved in health, nutrition, exercise, and diet for many decades, and even helped found and operate a natural foods store in my youth. I did much of the ordering, reordering, advertising, customer service, and artistic designs for our small fledgling company—which went on to become a great success even before I departed to travel across America and concentrate on my writing, music, photography, and art.

Thus my interest in putting together a *vintage Southern cookbook* did not come about by accident or as the result of an idle whim. This volume encompasses many of the interests of which I am most passionate and which have the deepest personal meaning to me: the South, my Southern ancestry, healthy food, and healthy living.

Though Southern at their heart, the recipes in this cookbook derive from a wide variety of influences that traverse international cookery, and more specifically the time period from 1838 to 1924—nearly 100 years. Many of these recipes derive from sources far older, of course, dating back hundreds of years. This means that this work chronicles cooking instructions that not only predate the founding of the U.S.A. (1776), but which have roots in the medieval world.

In short, one will find here recipes from European American Southerners, Latin American Southerners, Native American Southerners, African American Southerners, Jewish American Southerners, and Asian American Southerners, the same Conservative people who fought in their hundreds of thousands for the Confederacy and the Constitution during the War for Southern Independence.[1]

As such, I have purposefully chosen Southern recipes that cater to as many tastes and proficiency levels as possible, from the traditional (e.g., fried chicken) to the exotic (e.g., roast opossum and sweet potatoes), from simple beginner recipes (e.g., corn fritters) to complex advanced ones (e.g., roast veal fillet). As a result, I believe there is something here for nearly everyone, whether they are a carnivore, an omnivore, a flexitarian, a vegetarian, an ovolacto vegetarian, a lacto vegetarian, a pescatarian, a fruitarian, or a vegan.

My collection of antique recipes will be of interest to a number of other demographics as well: old school individuals, farming families, outdoorsy types, and back-to-the-land folks, or anyone merely interested in learning the traditional ways in which Old South Southerners prepared their food. For myself and my Southern readers, these include our grandparents, great grandparents, second great grandparents, third great grandparents, and so on.

Some of the 19th- and early 20th-Century Southern men and women who participated in the early Dixie-oriented cookbooks that I researched for this volume did not create the recipes they contributed. In many cases they took them from non-Southern sources, including from areas such as New England and the West Coast, and even as far away as Europe, Russia, and India. Despite this, I have included these types of recipes because they were borrowed, given the stamp of approval, Southernized, and regularly used by Southerners. In a sense then, this makes these particular non-Southern recipes "Southern." Not in origin, but in adoption, acceptance, and usage. For example, in most early Southern cookbooks one will find at least one recipe for "Boston baked beans."

As referenced in my "Notes to the Reader," while some of the recipes in this book use ingredients that are not considered healthy today, I have included them nonetheless. I do not allow presentism to taint my history books, and I did not allow it to taint my cookbook, despite its purely epicurean subject matter. For it is my intent to not only record old Southern recipes, but also to preserve the thinking, beliefs, and attitudes of the people who invented and used them. In any event, experienced cooks and readers know how to substitute a recipe's original ingredients—if that is of interest to them.

In perusing this volume, modern cuisiniers will notice the casual manner in which most of the recipes are presented. This is due to the fact that they retain a time and place when food preparers approached their craft in a more intuitive fashion rather than an intellectual one. Thus in most instances one will find few exact measurements, temperatures, amounts, or specific cooking times. Numbers were not considered as essential to cooking in days of old as they are in our modern science-obsessed world.

As one who enjoys both cooking and observing the cooking talents of others, I mark this as a positive. Early chefs understood that this type of informality gives one enormous creative freedom in the garden, at the market, and in front of the stove, allowing one to add his or her own unique personality to their dishes. The original Southern creators of these recipes would heartily approve, for if there is one thing the South is well-known for it is the hearty individualism of its inhabitants.

May my *Vintage Southern Cookbook* inspire and entertain, and more importantly, nourish the bodies, minds, and spirits of those who try the delightful Old South recipes I have painstakingly hand-selected for inclusion. They were created (or adopted) with love by 19th- and 20th-Century Southerners and were compiled with love by a 21st-Century Southerner. Experiment. Eat. Enjoy!

Lochlainn Seabrook
Nashville, Tennessee, USA
September 2021
"When it comes to cooking, the best is none too good."

Vintage Southern Cookbook

The Recipes

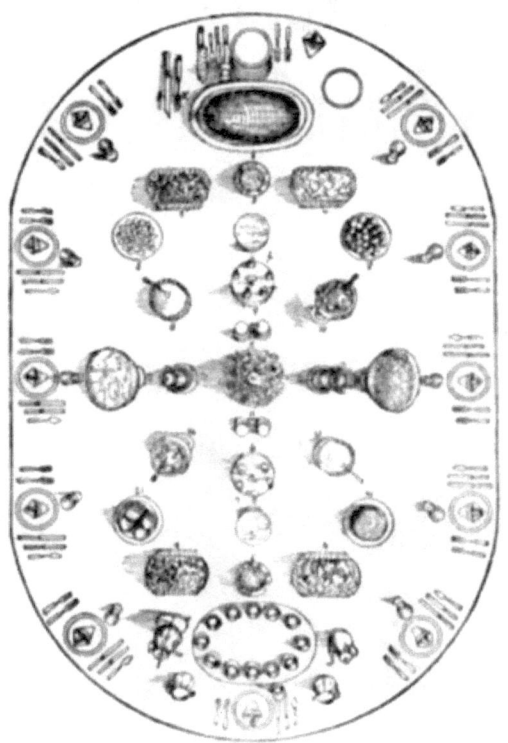

Summer breakfast table setting for 12.

1. Beverages

DRINKING WATER

☞ As the human body is composed of two-thirds its weight in water, so upon the liquid we drink depends, to a large degree, health and long life. Through it, the blood receives new life and discharges the worn-out substances. In this way it becomes a part of the human frame, and is derived principally from the outside, in the form of drinks and food. Great care, therefore, should be exercised as to the sort of water we drink as well as to the food we eat.

Water, when pure, is a colorless, transparent liquid. Rain water is the best example of pure water known, but when it stands in cisterns it is liable to become contaminated by neighboring sinks and vaults and rendered unfit to drink.

Spring water is the nearest approach to perfect water that we have. This is particularly so when it flows through rocky or sandy soil. A "living spring" is a boon to humanity, and how beautiful that our country is blessed with them.[2]

FILTERED WATER

☞ The functions of water are so important to the human race that where the least suspicion occurs as to its purity, it should be either filtered or boiled before using. Many people in cities take the double precaution. They first filter the water, then boil it. In boiling, the insoluble lime which the water takes up in its passage through the air and soil is precipitated to the bottom of the kettle, thus the impurities are eliminated, and the water becomes soft. Filters are procurable at a slight cost. They are valuable in taking sediment out of water, but they do not remove germs. Boiling must do this.[3]

FRUIT JUICES

☛ The juice of oranges, strawberries, currants, or any fruit makes a delicious first course for luncheon in summer time or the fruit season, when properly prepared. It is served cold in small glasses and eaten with a spoon. Take a quart of fruit-juice; this will require about a dozen oranges, or two quarts of strawberries or other juicy fruit; strain it through filter paper to make it clear; put it in an earthenware or porcelain-lined saucepan on the fire, and as soon as it steams, stir in three teaspoonfuls of arrowroot moistened in a little cold water. Cook it until clear; then add a half cupful of sugar (or more if an acid fruit), and as soon as the sugar is dissolved turn it into a bowl to cool. At the moment of serving put a piece of ice in each glass.[4]

MINT JULEP

☛ These are some essentials:

1st. Fine, straight, old Kentucky Bourbon whisky—blended whiskies do not give good results.

2nd. An abundant supply of freshly cut sprigs of mint—preferably young shoots—no portion of which has been bruised.

3rd. Dry, cracked flint ice. A glass will answer the purpose, but a silver mug is preferable. Keep your silver cups on ice. A syrup of sugar and water is also kept on hand.

Mint juleps.

The silver cup is first filled with the ice, and then the desired quantity of fine whisky poured in and thoroughly shaken with a spoon or shaker until a heavy frost forms on the mug. The desired amount of syrup is then poured in and stirred enough to be mixed.

The mint is then carefully placed in the mugs with the stems barely sticking in the ice and the tops projecting 2 inches above the top of the cup. Straws are then placed in the cup, reaching from the bottom to about 1 inch above the top, and the sooner one sticks one's nose in the mint and begins drinking through the straws the better.

There is no flavor of mint, merely the odor. *Any stinting in quality or quantity* materially affects the result.[5]

PINEAPPLE JULEP
☞ Pare a very ripe pineapple with as little waste as possible, and cut it into thin slices. Lay these in a large bowl and strain over them the juice of two sweet oranges.

Pour in one-quarter of a pint of raspberry syrup and mix thoroughly. Just before serving add a tumblerful of shaved ice.[6]

BEER
☞ Two quarts of wheat bran, two and a half gallons of water, a few hops, one pint of molasses, and one pint of yeast.[7]

BLUE GRASS APPLE TODDY
☞ Dissolve 2 lumps of sugar in 1 ounce of hot water. Add a hot baked apple and 1½ ounces of good high-proof old Kentucky whisky.[8]

OLD-FASHIONED KENTUCKY TODDY
☞ ¼ glass of water,
¼ glass of good whisky,
2 lumps of loaf sugar.

Dissolve sugar in water thoroughly, add whisky and 1 lump of ice, not crushed, as it melts rapidly and spoils proportions of drink.[9]

PUNCH
☞ 1 quart claret,
1 pint sherry,
½ dozen lemons,
8-10 oranges,
1 can pineapple,
½ pint whisky,
(Champagne, if you like.)

If served frozen, add claret, sherry, whisky, and champagne after it is frozen.[10]

CAROLINA PINEAPPLE PUNCH
☞ Pull to pieces with a fork one pineapple and soak in one quart of French brandy for twenty-four hours in a covered bowl, then strain.

Punch.

Make a rich syrup of one pound of sugar and one cupful of water. Mix with the brandy and dilute it with one quart of freshly drawn cold tea.

When ready to serve add one syphon of Shasta water, a few cubes of pineapple, and a block of ice. Sprinkle a large handful of wild rose leaves on top.

This can be bottled, and if corked tightly will keep indefinitely.[11]

APPLE WINE

☞ Take cider, fresh from the press, and to each gallon add two pounds of good brown sugar; after dissolving the sugar, strain it and put in a new cask (one that had held brandy or whisky should not be used); tack a piece of muslin or perforated tin over the bung, and let it thus stand for one week. After this, put in the cork lightly and let it remain thus two weeks longer, then fasten it tightly, to exclude the air. The vessel should not be filled—at least one eighth of the space should be left. It is not fit for use under two or three months; then it should be drawn off, bottled, and sealed. This recipe makes wine equal to catawba.[12]

BOURBON WHISKY PUNCH

☞ Squeeze 10 lemons and stir the juice in 3 pints of water. Add 1 quart of Jamaica rum and 1 gallon of Bourbon whisky and sweeten to taste. Let it simmer slowly for 20 minutes. Cover till cold and then bottle. Drink either cold or hot, and add water if too strong.[13]

CONFEDERATE COFFEE

☞ Allow a tablespoonful of ground coffee for each cup, and 1 extra spoonful for good measure. For 6 cups take 7 tablespoons of coffee and stir into it the white of 1 egg and ½ cup of cold water. To each spoonful add 1 cup of boiling water and let all boil 10 minutes. Pour off and serve. Use only the best fresh-roasted coffee; 1 pound of Java to ⅓ of Mocha make a good combination.[14]

BLACK COFFEE

☞ Take six light tablespoons coffee beans, grind them neither too coarse nor too fine, put the coffee in strainer with the small strainer over; pour over one half pint boiling water, little by little. The water must be boiling or it is useless to attempt it; always use water at the first boil or it becomes insipid. After all the water is used, put on cover and let it infuse slightly, but on no account let it boil again. Never prepare coffee more than five minutes in advance.[15]

Tea and coffee strainer.

CONFEDERATE ARMY COFFEE

☞ Coffee or tea may be made quickly by placing the required quantity of cold water in the pot, and adding the coffee, tied up in a sack of fine gauze, or piece of muslin; bring to boiling point, boil five minutes and serve. Make tea in the same way, except that the tea is put loose in the water, and simply allowed to boil up once.[16]

LOUISIANA COFFEE

☞ One heaping tablespoonful of coffee, a little white of egg, one cup of boiling water (allow this quantity for each person). Scald the coffee pot, add the coffee, egg, and sufficient cold water to moisten. Mix well, add the boiling water and cook five minutes. Then place where it will keep hot, but not cook, for fifteen minutes. It is then ready to serve.[17]

BLOCKADE COFFEE

☞ Scald some rye in boiling water, and let it simmer for twenty minutes until it is slightly soft. Then remove from the fire and wash it in cold water, and parch as brown as coffee. To three tablespoonfuls of the ground rye take one tablespoonful of coffee, or a saltspoonful of the essence of coffee, and put into a tin pot, and pour over a quart of boiling water, and let it boil slowly for more than an hour. Let it settle and pour off, and you will find it quite clear without eggs, and very good. Okra seeds parched and ground, and mixed with coffee, in the proportion of one-fourth coffee to three-fourths of okra, is a very nice beverage, and a good substitute for coffee.[18]

Tea/coffee can.

ACORN COFFEE

☞ Acorn coffee is much used in Germany as a substitute for ordinary coffee. It is said to be strengthening to consumptive persons. Acorns are very astringent in their raw state, but they lose this quality when roasted. Delicate children are benefitted by this method of preparing acorns. They are always gathered in autumn when they are ripe, shelled and cut into pieces the size of coffee berries when they are thoroughly dried in a cool oven. They are then roasted like ordinary coffee, until they become a cinnamon-brown. After roasting, the acorns are ground or pounded in a mortar, to prevent their becoming tough; a very little butter is added and the coffee is then placed in air-tight bottles. Prepare in the same way as ordinary coffee.[19]

CHOCOLATE COFFEE

☞ Take 6 tablespoons grated chocolate, twice the amount of sugar, and mix together. Boil 1 qt. each of milk and water together, or 1 more water than milk, stir in the mixture and let it come to a boil, then serve. Cocoa can also be made after this recipe, and is more delicate than chocolate. Cocoa shells are still more delicately flavored, and some people much prefer them to any other drink. Cocoa and cocoanut are two different articles of commerce. Cocoa is the seed of a small tropical tree, growing something like beans. There are several forms in which it is sold. The ground bean is simply cocoa; ground fine and mixed with sugar, it is chocolate. Shells are the coverings of the beans, generally removed without grinding. The beans are roasted like coffee, and ground between hot rollers. Some prefer to boil the chocolate in water first and let it stand over night and skim off what oil rises to the top; then add the milk and sugar, boil up and serve.[20]

TEA
☞ The water should be freshly boiled, scald and heat the tea pot, (never use tin) allow one teaspoon tea to each cup boiling water, reduce the proportions if several cups are required, put the tea in a strainer, pour boiling water through them, then put in the teapot and pour on the boiling water, cover closely and keep hot, but not boil. In five minutes serve with cold milk.[21]

SOUTHERN TEA
☞ Take one-half teaspoonful of tea to one cup of boiling water. Put the tea in the pot, pour the boiling water upon it and let stand where it will keep hot for five minutes. Then serve. Tea should never be boiled for it makes it bitter.[22]

ICED TEA

Iced tea.

☞ Make the tea, strain it and let cool, when ready to serve put in two cups of sugar in a glass, some ice, a slice of lemon and fill with cold tea.[23]

MINT PUNCH
☞ Chop fine one dozen large stalks of mint, add half cup powdered sugar, the juice of two lemons, let stand one hour stirring occasionally, strain pressing hard, add the strained juice of four more lemons, make a syrup of half cup sugar one pint water boiled together with the sliced yellow rind of two lemons, stir well, add one quart shaved ice and two bottles of ginger ale. Serve.[24]

CRANBERRY PUNCH
☞ 3 pints of cranberries,
6 lemons.

Make quite sweet. Boil cranberries in ½ gallon of water till tender. Strain through a sieve to get all the pulp, holding back the skins. Add the lemon juice and make as sweet as you would sherbet. Put in freezer and freeze well. Then take 1 wineglassful of fine whisky, ½ wineglass of old Jamaica rum, and beat in thoroughly, and pack in freezer till ready to serve.[25]

LEMON BRANDY

☛ Slice half a dozen fresh lemons, put them in a quart of peach brandy, cover the jar securely, and let it sit till the flavor of the lemons is extracted: then strain it, and to each pint of the liquid add half a pound of powdered loaf sugar. When the sugar is completely dissolved, put it up in small bottles, cork them securely, dipping the necks into melted rosin, and keep them in a cool place. A few spoonfuls of this will give an excellent flavor to puddings, mince pies, etc.[26]

Utensils for boiling sugar: thermometer, cup, saucepan, spatula, marble slab, brushes, skewer, and candy wire.

LEMONADE

☛ Take ripe lemons, roll them under your fingers on a table till they appear like they are full of juice; then squeeze the juice into a bowl, to each pint of which allow three pints of water, or if in summer, allow two and a half pints of water and a lump of ice equal to the other half pint. Sweeten it to your taste with loaf sugar, and serve it up in small glasses.[27]

ORANGE-ADE

☛ May be made in every respect by the receipt written for lemonade above.[28]

SWANNEE FRUIT PUNCH

☛ Two cups of sugar,
One cup of water,
One cup of tea,
One pint of strawberry syrup,
Juice of ten lemons,
Juice of six oranges,
Two cans of grated pineapple,
One large bottle of Maraschino cherries.

Make syrup by boiling sugar and water together for ten minutes. Add the tea, fruit juices, pineapple, and strawberry syrup. Let stand thirty minutes, strain and add enough iced water to make one or one and one-half gallons of liquid. Turn into large punch bowl over a piece of ice and lastly add cherries. This quantity will serve about ten people.[29]

TO MAKE APPLE CIDER

Pressing out grape juice by hand.

☞ The following recipe if given due attention will secure a fine quality of this delightful beverage. Much of the excellence of cider depends upon the temperature at which the fermentation is conducted; as soon as pressed from the fruit, it should be strained into sulphured casks, and placed in a cool situation, where the temperature does not exceed 50 deg. Fahr., if left in the heating sun, much of the sugar is converted into vinegar by the absorption of atmospheric oxygen, and thus the liquor becomes acid and rough. If the fermentation be conducted at a low temperature, nearly the whole of the sugar is converted into alcohol, and remains in the liquor instead of undergoing the process of acidification; this is the principal cause of the superiority of the cider made by one person over another living in the same neighborhood, independent of differences in the quality of the fruit, the one having a cooler cellar or barn than the other to store his cider in. Sour and rough apples are thought to produce the best cider, they contain less sugar, and more malic acid, the latter quality impedes the conversion of alcohol into vinegar; but cider made with such apples cannot equal in quality that prepared at a low temperature from fruit abounding in sugar, which, if properly strained, or racked at every indication of fermentation, will keep good for 20 years.[30]

FRUIT PUNCH

☞ One cup water, two cups sugar, one cup tea, infusion one quart apollinaris, two quarts strawberry juice or syrup, juice of five lemons, five oranges, one can grated pineapple, one cup maraschino cherries, make a syrup of the sugar and water, add all the fruit juices, let stand half hour, strain and add water enough to make one and a half gallons, then add cherries and apollinaris, serve in punch bowl with a large piece of ice.[31]

CLARET PUNCH

☞ Three gallons St. Julian claret, two gallons sherry, one half gallon whiskey, half gallon Jamaica rum, one pint green tea infusion, one box guava jelly, one quart maraschino cherries, six lemons, sweeten to taste makes ten gallons; ice to suit.[32]

SHERRY COBBLER

☞ 3 lemons,
   3 oranges,
   6 slices of ripe pineapple,
   1 large cup of powdered sugar.

Slice the fruits very thin and put them in a bowl or pitcher, cover with the sugar and crushed ice and let it stand for 15 or 20 minutes. Then pour over it 2 large glasses of water. Add more crushed ice and season highly with sherry. Serve in glasses with slices of the fruit and strawberries.[33]

LEMON CORDIAL

Summer zephyrs.

☛ Cut six fresh lemons in thin slices, put them into a quart and a half of milk, boil it until the whey is very clear, then pass it through a sieve; put to this whey, one and a half quarts of French brandy, and three pounds of powdered loaf sugar; stir it till the sugar is dissolved—let it stand to refine, and bottle it; pare some of the yellow rind of the lemons very thin, and put a little in each bottle.[34]

STRAWBERRY CORDIAL

☛ Pick your strawberries when very ripe, and make the cordial by the preceding receipt. Never boil delicate fruit for cordial, or the flavor will be injured.[35]

TOM AND JERRY

☛ 1 dozen eggs,
1 tablespoon sugar,
1 tablespoon ground cloves,
1 tablespoon allspice,
1½ tablespoons cinnamon,
1 wineglass of Jamaica rum.

Beat the eggs separately. Mix the sugar with the yolks, then add the whites. Add the spices and rum last.
To serve it take:
1 tablespoon of mixture and add 1 wineglass of old whisky and same amount of hot water. Grate a little nutmeg on top and serve. The mixture will keep many days.[36]

VIENNA HOT CHOCOLATE

☛ Use four ounces of vanilla chocolate, one quart of milk, three tablespoonfuls of hot water and one tablespoonful of sugar. Cut the chocolate in fine bits. Put the milk on the stove in the double boiler and when it has been heated to the boiling point, put the chocolate, sugar and water in a small iron or graniteware pan and stir over a hot fire until smooth and glossy. Stir this mixture into the hot milk and beat well with a whisk. Serve at once, putting a tablespoonful of whipped cream in each cup and then filling up with the chocolate. The plain chocolate may be used instead of the vanilla, but in that case use a teaspoonful of vanilla extract and three generous tablespoonfuls of sugar instead of one.[37]

CHAMPAGNE
☛ Dissolve twelve pounds of loaf and ten of brown sugar in nine gallons of water, mix in the whites of four eggs, boil it gently and skim it well, add concrete acid of lemons, or crystalized acid of tartar, six drachms, and before it gets entirely cold, mix in a pint of good yeast and ferment. When it is nearly done working, add one gallon of perry, three pints of brandy, and bung it up for three months: then draw out a quart, dissolve in it one ounce of isinglass, pour it again in the cask, to clear it, and in two weeks it will be ready to bottle. If a red color is desired, mix in an ounce of cochineal before it is first bunged.[38]

Champagne tap.

XALAPA PUNCH
☛ ½ gallon of strong tea,
Grated rind of 1 lemon.
Let it stand a few minutes and strain.
Add 1 pound of loaf sugar.
Equal parts of Syracuse rum, apple brandy, and claret wine to suit the taste. Serve with ice and thinly sliced lemon.[39]

OYSTER COCKTAIL
☛ For each person the strained juice of half a lemon, half teaspoonful of vinegar, eight drops tabasco sauce, half teaspoonful horse radish, half teaspoonful tomato catsup; add eight small oysters; let stand five minutes and serve.[40]

GINGER ALE
☛ 2 gallons of water, 2 pounds of brown sugar, 1 dessertspoon of cream of tartar, 2 tablespoons of the fibrous part of whole ginger, ½ of a lemon sliced; when milk warm, put in ½ pint of patent yeast, and bottle it when it begins to ferment. After putting in the yeast do not put it again on the fire.[41]

GINGER POP
☛ Put into a 3 gallon stone jar 3 pounds of brown sugar, the rind and juice of 1 lemon, 1 handful of bruised race ginger. Then fill up the jar with boiling water, and let it stand until nearly cool; then add a tea-cup

of home made yeast; cover it up tightly for 3 hours; then bottle it. The corks must be hammered in the bottles, and then tied down.⁴²

GINGER BEER

Method of tying down corks on bottles.

☛ 13 gallons of water, 13 pounds of loaf sugar, 3 ounces of bruised ginger; boil it all for 1 hour; skim it, and put in it the beaten whites of 8 eggs to clarify it. When boiled, strain it into a tub; let it become cold; then pour it into a barrel, with the thin peel and juice of 13 lemons, and put on the top ½ teaspoon of yeast; stop the cask close; in 3 days bottle it, and in a week after it will be fit for use.⁴³

CONFEDERATE MILK SHAKE

☛ Fill a glass two-thirds full of milk; sweeten it to taste with any fruit syrup or with sugar and then flavor with vanilla or orange water. Fill up glass with cracked ice and shake together until well mixed.⁴⁴

EGG NOG

☛ Six eggs beaten separately very light, nine tablespoonfuls of sugar beaten with the yolks, nearly a cup of whiskey and rum mixed, the stiff whites folded in. A cup of cream or milk may be added. Grate nutmeg over.⁴⁵

VERY FINE EGG NOG

☛ 1 gallon of cream,
   24 eggs, using only the yolks,
   26 tablespoons of sugar,
   ½ grated nutmeg,
   8 wineglasses of rum,
   10 wineglasses of brandy,
   8 wineglasses of whisky.

Beat the eggs till very light, adding the sugar as you beat, then add the liquor, beating all well together. Then add the cream, except 1 quart, which whip to a stiff froth, and stir in gradually and lightly. Add the nutmeg.

After adding the liquor to the eggs, it is well to let it stand for a while before adding the cream, as it cooks the eggs.⁴⁶

CONFEDERATE EGG NOG

☛ Break six eggs, separating the whites from the yolks; beat the whites to a stiff froth, put the yolks in a bowl and beat them light. Stir into it slowly, that the spirits may cook the egg, half a pint of rum, or three gills of common brandy; add a quart of rich sweet milk and half a pound of powdered sugar; then stir in the egg froth, and finish by grating nutmeg on the top.[47]

BONNIE BLUE EGG NOG

☞ Beat the yolk of one egg and a teaspoonful of sugar to a light cream; whip the white of the egg to a stiff froth; mix them together; turn them into a glass; add one teaspoonful of rum or brandy and as much milk as the glass will hold. Stir or shake it well together; add more sugar and rum if desired. Grate a dash of nutmeg over the top; whipped cream may be used instead of milk, and will give more nourishment when it is used for an invalid.[48]

FROZEN EGG NOG

☞ For 4 eggs use 1 pint of hot milk, in which a small stick of cinnamon has been boiled. Beat the yolks of the eggs and add slowly the hot milk, stirring continually. Sweeten to taste with powdered sugar, add a half pint of brandy, and the well beaten whites of the eggs. When quite cold freeze and serve with macaroons.[49]

GADSDEN FLAG EGG NOG

☞ 5 eggs.
4 tablespoons sugar.
1 pint cream.
1 teaspoon vanilla.

Beat eggs separately. Whip cream stiff and combine with egg yolks, folding in whites last. Serves 8 people.[50]

ALEXANDER H. STEPHENS EGG NOG

☞ Beat separately the yolks and whites of six eggs, and stir into the yolks sufficient powdered loaf-sugar to make it pleasantly sweet, and beat them till very light, and flavor with a little lemon-juice and nutmeg. Beat in six tablespoonfuls of brandy. Boil a quart of thin cream or new milk. Fill the goblets half full of the sugar and eggs, after stirring in the beaten whites just before putting into the glasses. Put a teaspoon in each goblet, and place them on a waiter so they can be distributed immediately after the milk is poured in. Pour the boiling milk into a pitcher, and fill up the goblets with as you hand them around. Stir the milk and egg well together before drinking.[51]

Ginger ale, ice cream, and preserved ginger.

CONFEDERATE FROZEN EGG NOG

☛ Yolks of 12 eggs,
 1 pound of sugar,
 1 pint of brandy,
 1 pint of Jamaica rum,
 1 gallon of cream.

Beat the yolks very light and add the sugar, then the whipped cream. Freeze till firm, and then add the brandy and rum, and turn freezer rapidly a few times to mix well. Ready to serve.[52]

CHERRY SHRUB

☛ To 1 pint of juice add ¼ pound sugar,
 Brandy to taste.

Put the cherries in a stone jar and set in kettle of cold water. Let the water boil till the cherries burst, strain, sweeten, and add the brandy. Bottle till ready to use.[53]

ROOT BEER 1

☛ Wild cherry bark, ½ oz., the same of coriander, ¼ oz. hops, 3 qts. molasses, and 1 oz. each sassafras, allspice, yellow-dock, and wintergreen. Put the above into a crock, over which pour 5 gals. boiling water. Allow it to remain 24 hours, then strain, and add ½ pt. yeast. Let stand another twenty-four hours, when it is ready for use.[54]

ROOT BEER 2

☛ Pour boiling water on sassafras 2½ ounces; wild cherry bark, 1½ ounce; allspice, 2½ ounces; wintergreen bark, 2½ ounces; hops, one-half ounce; coriander seed, one-half ounce; molasses, two gallons. Let the mixture stand one day. Strain and add yeast, one pint; water enough to make 15 gallons. May be bottled the following day.[55]

Utensil for driving corks into bottles.

ROOT BEER 3

☛ To five gallons of boiling water add 1½ gallon of molasses. Allow it to stand for three hours, then add one-fourth pound each of bruised sassafras bark, wintergreen bark and sarsaparilla root, also one-half pint of fresh yeast, and water enough to make 15 to 17 gallons. After this has fermented for 12 hours it can be drawn off and bottled.[56]

ROOT BEER 4

☛ For each gallon of water used take hops, burdock, yellow dock, sarsaparilla, dandelion and spikenard roots bruised, of each one-half ounce. Boil about 20 minutes and strain while hot. Add eight or 10 drops of oil of spruce and Sassafras mixed in equal proportions. When cool enough not to scald your hand, put in two or three tablespoons of yeast, two-thirds of a pint of molasses or one-half pound white sugar. Keep these proportions for as many gallons as you wish to make. It is best to get the dry roots or dig them and let them dry. You can add any other root known to possess medicinal properties desired. After all is mixed let it stand in a jar with a cloth thrown over it, to work, about two hours, then bottle and set in a cool, place. When unable to obtain all the roots normally required, you may add root beer extract, which improves the beer.⁵⁷

Shakers for mixing iced drinks.

ROOT BEER 5

☞ Yellow birch twigs, about one-half inch at the large end, remove leaves and cut in six-inch lengths. Same of spruce, about six quarts of each, one pound yellow dock root, one pound burdock root, half pound Sarsaparilla root, half pound pressed hops. Boil three hours, strain and add one quart potato yeast and put in five-gallon keg. Fill with water, let stand 10 days with bung open to work out sediment.⁵⁸

SASSAFRAS MEAD

☞ Mix carefully one quart of boiling water and one and one-half pounds of light brown sugar; add to it one-half pint of good New Orleans molasses and one-eighth of a pound of tartaric acid. Stir well and when cool strain into a granite pitcher. When cool add a small one-half teaspoonful of essence of sassafras. Put in bottles, cork tightly with new corks and keep in a cool place. To make a glass of sassafras mead for drinking, put a large tablespoonful of the mead into a tumbler one-half full of ice-water, stir into it one-half teaspoonful of carbonate of soda and it will immediately foam to the top. The essence of sassafras and tartaric acid can be obtained at the druggist's.⁵⁹

FRUIT NECTAR

☞ Remove the rind of three lemons, and put it in an earthenware jar with one pound of chopped raisins and one and one-half pounds of sugar. Pour over these ingredients two gallons of boiling water, let the liquid stand until cold, then add the strained juice of the lemons and leave it in a cool place for a week, stirring it every day. Strain it through a jelly bag until quite clear, and bottle.⁶⁰

CORN BEER

☞ Take a pint of corn, boil it until soft, and add to it a gallon of water sweetened with a pint of brown sugar. Cork it tightly and set it in a warm place, and put into it a small quantity of yeast if the weather is cold. In warm weather omit the yeast. Add a few roots of bruised ginger, and a few sliced lemons. The same corn will answer for a year. When you pour out a pitcherful of beer, put in one of sweetened water.[61]

MEAD
☛ Take sweet cider, just from the press, and boil and skim it well. Mix with each gallon one quart of clarified honey, put it in a cask, and leave the bung loose till it is done fermenting, and becomes clear. Then mix with it a quart of the best white brandy or rectified spirits to each gallon of the fermented mixture, and cork it up for use. It will keep well, and is very much liked.[62]

SCUPPERNONG WINE
☛ Gather very ripe grapes. Press the juice from them at once. Use one and a half pounds of sugar to each gallon of juice. Put in a vessel and keep it full enough to let the scum run off four or five days. When fermenting, keep vessels full as directed, in making grape wine. Then stop it loosely. Allow to stand five days or more, after which cork and keep in a cool dark place for three months; bottle and seal. To make dry, omit the sugar.[63]

Paper for filtering fruit juices.

GRAPE FRUIT COCKTAILS
☛ Cut the grape fruit in halves, scoop out the pulp without any of the inner white skin, then clean out the shells and throw them into cold water. Hull a pint strawberries, mix them with the grape fruit pulp, add two tablespoonsful sugar and stand the mixture on ice. At serving time dry the shells and fill them with the mixture, add a tablespoonful rum or sherry and a tablespoonful shaved ice. Stand the shells on a paper mat or on a spray of fern and serve at once. (Orange cocktails are made just the same.)[64]

FROZEN PUNCH
☛ For one-hundred people, seven quarts water, three and a half quarts of sugar boiled, add the juice of thirteen lemons and twelve oranges to it, two quarts claret wine, half box gelatine swollen then dissolved, will give it more body. Fine.[65]

BRANDY PEACHES
☛ Peel your peaches. Put in a jar a layer of fruit and a layer of sugar, cover with good corn whiskey, let stand ten days, then drain every drop of the liquor off and cover with California brandy. The liquor need not be wasted, but used for other purposes. This is the only way I can keep them, by using two liquors.[66]

BLACKBERRY CORDIAL

☛ Mash and strain the berries through a sieve. To 1 gallon of juice, put 1 pound of sugar. Boil and add
　1 tablespoon of allspice,
　1 tablespoon of cloves.
Cook till thick. When nearly cold add 1 quart of whisky or brandy. Bottle and seal.[67]

MINT CORDIAL

☛ Gather some young tender stalks of mint early in the morning; pick off the leaves, put them in a jar, pour on enough rectified whiskey to cover them, close the jar, and set it by for two days. Then squeeze out the mint, and fill up the jar again with fresh mint. Repeat this the third and fourth time; lastly, strain it, add two pounds of sugar to each gallon of the brandy, and bottle and cork it up for use. When you wish to make use of it, dilute it to the proper strength with water, and add more sugar.[68]

WILD PLUM CORDIAL

☛ Get ripe plums, stick them with a fork, put in a jar and cover with alcohol diluted, say two quarts of alcohol to two quarts water, let stand four days, then strain. To every quart of the liquor use three-fourths pound of sugar. Dissolve the sugar in just as little water as it will bear; stir over the stove, but never let it boil. When dissolved, mix with the plum liquor and bottle. Now ready for use.[69]

CHAMPAGNE ICE

☛ Make a syrup of 1 pound sugar, 1 quart water, and add juice of 3 oranges and 1 lemon. Boil a few minutes and strain into the freezer. When it begins to thicken, flavor with a small bottle of champagne.[70]

Lemon squeezer.

GRAPE ICE

☛ 1 quart of juice from fresh grapes,
　4 lemons, juice only,
　1 tablespoon of gelatine, dissolved in water.
Sweeten to taste. Mix well and freeze.[71]

MADEIRA ICE

☛ 1 quart Madeira wine,
　1 pint water,
　pound sugar,
　Juice of 1 lemon.

Make a syrup of sugar and water and add lemon juice. When cool, strain and put in freezer. When it begins to thicken, add 1 quart Madeira wine and freeze hard.[72]

SANGAREE

☞ Sangaree is a mixture of clear, cold water and wine, porter, or ale, sweetened in glasses with lumps of loaf sugar, and crowned lightly with grated nutmeg.

A very good proportion is two measures of water to one of spirits. In warm weather, a small lump of ice in each glass improves it.[73]

ORANGE ICE

☞ 6 oranges,
2 lemons,
1 quart of water,
1 pint sugar.

Squeeze the fruit, being careful to remove the seed. Boil the water and pour over the sugar. When dissolved, let the water stand on the fruit for ½ hour. Strain and mix with the juice and freeze.

This will make 2 quarts.[74]

RASPBERRY ICE

☞ Take enough berries to make a quart of juice. Add juice of 3 lemons and 1 pound sugar.

Pour over 1 quart boiling water and let it stand 1 hour, and then strain into freezer and freeze hard.[75]

STRAWBERRY ICE

☞ Mash the berries and have 1 quart juice. Add juice of 2 lemons, 1 pound sugar. Pour over 1 quart boiling water and let it stand an hour. Strain and pour in freezer and freeze quite hard.[76]

RASPBERRY CORDIAL

☞ Gather ripe fruit, cover with good corn whiskey, let stand four days, then strain. Use three pounds of sugar to each gallon of the strained liquor. Let heat until the sugar is dissolved. For blackberries put one teaspoonful each of mace, allspice and cloves.[77]

CONFEDERATE BRANDY PEACHES

☞ Select clingstone peaches of good size, wash off as much fuzz as possible, put in a kettle, cover with cold water; let scald, but not boil. When the skin is tender enough for the head of a pin to penetrate, remove, place under the hydrant and let cold water run over them.

Then rub off again and put in the sun to bleach all day.

Then put them in two quart jars and put about one-third full of sugar and fill with good whiskey or California brandy. It is the same price.[78]

BLACKBERRY WINE

☛ To one quart of blackberries, mashed, add one quart water and two to three pounds sugar, according to taste; place in an open vessel and let it ferment four to six days, then strain through a coarse cloth; put in a jug, keg or barrel, according to quantity, and let fermentation continue through a siphon, under water, until it stops; then close air-tight. Larger quantities may be made in the same proportions as above. Very fine.[79]

Crown tea/coffee pot stand.

DANDELION WINE

☛ One quart blossom dandelion, pour in 1 gallon boiling water and let stand 3 days. Strain and add juice of 2 lemons, 2 oranges and 3 pounds coffee sugar, 1 yeast cake; let ferment, keep jug full and when it stops fermenting, bottle.[80]

GINGER WINE

☛ To three gallons of water, put three pounds of sugar, and four ounces of race ginger, washed in many waters to cleanse it; boil them together for one hour, and strain it through a sieve; when lukewarm, put it in a cask with three lemons cut in slices, and two gills of beer yeast; shake it well, and stop the cask very tight; let it stand a week to ferment; and if not clear enough to bottle, it must remain until it becomes so; it will be fit to drink in ten days after bottling.[81]

HOT CHOCOLATE

☛ 3 ounces chocolate,
2 teaspoons cornstarch,
1 quart milk,
1 quart water,
½ pound sugar.

Melt chocolate and starch and add sugar and 1 pint milk. Let it boil up once, then add rest of milk and water and boil 20 minutes. If wanted very good and rich, add 2 beaten eggs with last milk.[82]

COCOA

☛ Dissolve a teaspoonful of cocoa in half a cupful of boiling water; then add a half cupful of boiling milk and boil it for one minute, stirring vigorously all the time. Sweeten to taste. Brioche or Bath buns are good to serve with chocolate or cocoa for a light lunch.[83]

TO KEEP CREAM

☛ Take cream that is thick and perfectly sweet, boil it gently for a few minutes, and skim it well: stir in a pound of powdered loaf sugar to each quart of cream, and simmer it over a few coals for three quarters of an hour, stirring it very frequently. When it gets entirely cold, put it in bottles, cork them securely, dipping the necks in melted rosin, and keep them in a cool place. It is said it will keep well for several months, and may be used for many purposes when fresh cream cannot be obtained.[84]

MILK
☛ The receipt written for butter will suffice for the management of milk. As soon as you are done churning, pour the buttermilk into a jar, cover it closely, set it in the spring house, and each time, before you take any out for the table, churn it up well for a few minutes with a small dash, made for the purpose, that the thick part of the milk may be well mixed with the whey. Buttermilk is very much liked when rich and new, but it is seldom eaten with any thing else than warm bread and butter. Nice sweet clabber is also fine. When the milk begins to turn sour, put it in a large tureen or bowl, and set it in a cool place. After it is clabbered, do not break it up, but send it to table whole, in the tureen or bowl in which it turned, as the whey will rise on the top very soon after it is broken up, and of course it is not so good. Sprinkle on the top of the clabber a handful of powdered sugar, and provide it with a large spoon to list it at table. Do not stir it, but take it out by large spoonfuls without breaking what is left in the bowl. Set by it a bowl of powdered sugar and some mixed cinnamon and nutmeg, that the company may season it to suit their own taste. It is eaten as a dessert with sweet-cakes, etc. A little lemon juice mixed in just as it is beginning to turn improves the taste.

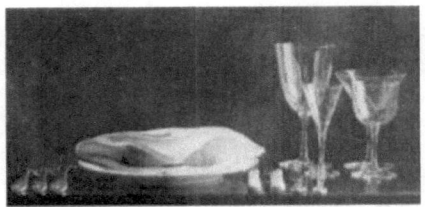
Detail of one cover.

Never skim the cream from sweet milk, that is to set before company; keep it in the spring house or some other cool place till a few minutes before it is sent to table; then pour it with the cream into a pitcher, drop in it a small lump of ice, and with a bunch of hickory rods or wires, whirl it round and round near the top for a few minutes till a rich froth rises, and send it immediately to the table. It is eaten with pies, tarts, etc.[85]

MILK SHAKE
☛ Fill a glass two thirds full of milk; sweeten it to taste with any fruit syrup, or with a syrup made of boiled sugar flavored with vanilla, orange-flower water, or any liqueur; strained preserve of any kind or liquefied jelly may be used.

Fill up the glass with cracked ice and shake together until well mixed.[86]

STRAWBERRY WINE

☞ Crush the berries and add 1 quart of water to a gallon of berries and let it stand 24 hours. Strain and add 2½ pounds of white sugar to a gallon of juice. Put in a cask, with thin muslin tacked over the bunghole, and let it ferment, keeping it full from a quantity reserved for the purpose. If a small quantity is made, use jugs or bottle.

When fermentation ceases, add 1 pint of good whisky to the gallon, and bottle and seal securely. Ready for use in six weeks.[87]

SOUTHERN NEGUS

☞ Take one quart of red cherries, three pounds of black heart cherries and four pounds of currants; mash and mix all together, and stand away in a cool place for three or four days; strain and boil juice; to every pint add half a pound of sugar; let cool and bottle. Add two or three tablespoonfuls to a glass of ice water.[88]

GRAPE WINE

☞ Crush the grapes and let them stand 1 week. Draw off the juice, strain; add 1 quart of water and 3 pounds of sugar to each gallon. Put in a barrel or cask, with a thin piece of muslin tacked over the bunghole, and let it stand till fermentation stops. Put in a cask and seal securely and let it stand for six months. Then bottle and seal and keep in a cool place.[89]

RASPBERRY WINE

☞ Select the finest raspberries, which are ripe, and full of juice. Pick them carefully, crush them to pieces, squeeze out the juice, and measure it. Pour as much boiling water on the mashed berries as you have juice, let it stand a few hours, to extract from them the remaining juice, and then mix all the liquid together, and strain it. Dissolve in it three pounds of loaf sugar to each gallon, mixing in the white of one egg to every two quarts, and boil and skim it, till the scum ceases to rise.

When it is cold, put it in a keg till it is done fermenting, leaving the bung quite loose; then put it in bottles, scaling the corks, and keep them in a cool place, buried in a box of dry saw dust. With these proportions, no brandy is necessary.[90]

ORANGE WINE

☞ Dissolve fourteen pounds of sugar in five gallons of water, mix in the whites of three eggs, boil, skim it, and pour it while boiling upon the parings of fifty oranges.

Squeeze the juice from the oranges, and when the liquid is nearly cold, mix them together, adding a pint of good yeast. Let it ferment three or four days; then strain it into a barrel and bung it loosely. In a month add a quart of brandy, and in three months more it will be fit for use.[91]

RAISIN WINE

☛ Chop sixty pounds of raisins, put them in a cask with fifteen gallons of water, and let them remain for two weeks, stirring them every day: then press them out, put the liquid into a clean cask, leaving the bung loose till it is done hissing. Afterwards add four pints of brandy and bung it up closely. Some use nearly double this quantity of raisins: it makes the wine much richer to be sure, but it is quite extravagant.[92]

BLACK CURRANT WINE

☛ Take the currants when ripe, pick them and bruise them, and to every twenty pounds add a gallon of brandy, twelve gallons of water and a gill of good yeast. Let it stand to ferment for eighteen days; then filter, bottle and cork it securely. It yields a thick, purplish colored wine.[93]

ELDERBERRY WINE

☛ Take the berries when ripe, press out the juice, and to each gallon add a gallon and a half of water, stirring in three pounds of brown sugar to each gallon after it is mixed, and a pint of brandy to every five gallons; put it in a cask with the bung put in loosely, let it stand for six or eight days to ferment, and then close the bung very tight. At the end of six months draw off a quart of it, mix in the whites of a few eggs that have been beaten to a froth, or a little dissolved isinglass, pour it again into the cask, mix it well, let it stand two weeks longer to refine, and then bottle it.[94]

ALMOND MILK

☛ Blanch the almonds, and take their weight in sugar; pound in a mortar to a paste, the almonds, and pour on it boiling milk. After it is cold, strain it, and it is a pleasant drink for invalids.[95]

RICE MILK

☛ Boil ½ pint of rice in water until tender; pour off the water, and add 1 pint of milk with 2 eggs, well beaten; boil all together for 3 minutes; serve it hot; eat with butter, sugar, and nutmeg. It can be sweetened and cooled in molds, and turned out and surrounded with milk, and eaten with preserves. Wine is an improvement, if added.[96]

Sliced oranges.

2. Breads

BREAD MAKING RULES

☞ Sift soda with flour for all things.
 Sift flour before measuring.
 Soda, salt and spices are measured level full.
 Use a level teaspoonful of soda to a pint of sour milk.
 Use soft, light brown sugar for fruit and molasses cake. Don't use black molasses.
 In mixing cake, after creaming butter and sugar, first put in a little milk, then a little flour.[97]

HOW TO MAKE YEAST

☞ ½ gallon of water,
 4 large potatoes,
 ½ cup of salt,
 ½ cup of sugar,
 1 tablespoon of hops,
 1 cup of yeast.

Put the sugar and salt in the water and put hops in a little muslin bag and drop in the water. Let it boil, then grate potatoes and stir in. Let it simmer till it thickens. Remove from stove, and when it is milk cold add 1 cup of good yeast. Let it remain near the fire to rise. Keep in glass jar in a cool place. Use ½ cup of yeast to 1 quart of flour.[98]

Forms of growth of the yeast plant.

DRY YEAST

☞ 1 quart of water; put it on to boil with a handful of hops, and let it boil for half an hour. When done, strain the boiling hop water on 1 quart of flour; let it stand until quite cold; then add 1 teacup of brisk yeast, and 2 quarts of sifted corn meal; make a stiff dough; then squeeze it through

Farina balls.

your fingers into a dish, and put it to dry in the sun, or in cool weather near the stove. When used, soak it in a little water. Some persons prefer this kind of yeast in warm weather, as it is not apt to sour. But liquid yeast, if kept in a cool place, and the mouth of the jug covered only with a piece of muslin, is quite as easily kept. Take ⅓ of a cup of dry yeast; fill the cup with milk-warm water; let it stand for 6 hours, and then pour off and use the water only. This will give the strength of the yeast without using the corn meal.[99]

HOW TO MAKE BREAD

☛ 1 cup of yeast,
1 quart of flour,
1 teaspoon of lard,
1 teaspoon of salt,
1 teaspoon of granulated sugar,
½ pint of water.

Put the yeast, lard, salt, and sugar in the flour, then the water. Work till it blisters, which will take from 15 to 20 minutes. Put in a little lard on top and put in a wooden bowl. Let it rise from 5 to 6 hours, then make out into rolls. Let them rise for 1½ hours, then bake in a quick oven. If for loaves, they will require 2 hours for second rising and a moderate oven for baking.[100]

TO TOAST BREAD

☛ Bread for toasting should be rather stale; cut the slices evenly, and a third of an inch in thickness; put each piece separately upon the toasting fork, turning it as it becomes of a nice brown color. As the pieces are toasted put them upon a plate in front of the fire and cover them over, unless they are required to be buttered, in which case each piece should be buttered as it is toasted. Lay one upon another. Keep covered until ready to serve.[101]

SOUTHERN BUTTERED TOAST

☛ Although toast is commonly used, few know how to prepare it nicely. Take bread not too fresh, cut thin and evenly, trim off the crust-edges for the crumb-jar; first warm each side of the bread, then present the first side again to the fire until it takes on a rich, even, brown color; treat the other side in the same way; butter and serve immediately. The coals should be bright and hot. Toast properly made is very digestible, because all the moisture is extracted, and the bread has become pure farina of wheat; but when it is exposed to a hot fire and the outside charred, the inside remains as moist as ever, and butter applied to it while warm does not penetrate, but floats on the surface in the form of rancid oil.

Or, beat one cup of butter and three tablespoons flour to a cream, pour over this one and a half pints boiling water; place over a kettle of boiling water for ten minutes, dip into it the toast, and serve hot.

Or, dip each slice of toast in boiling hot water (slightly salted), spread with butter, cover and keep hot.[102]

CINNAMON TOAST
☛ Cut stale bread into thin slices, remove crusts, and cut in halves; toast evenly, and spread first with butter, then with honey, and dust with cinnamon. Serve very hot.[103]

CROUTONS
☛ Cut bread in slices about one-fourth of an inch thick, remove crusts and cut in small cubes or finger length cubes; fry in hot butter or spread with butter and brown in the oven.[104]

MILK TOAST
☛ Is made similar to the above, only just before sending to table, pour enough boiling milk upon the toast to cover it. To butter the toast makes it richer than to melt the butter in the milk.[105]

Tins for bread and rolls.

DRY TOAST
☛ Cut light bread in thin slices, place in the oven; brown a light brown on both sides, then butter and return to the oven for a few minutes to melt the butter. Serve on plate covered with napkin.[106]

DIXIE BISCUITS
☛ 3 pints of flour,
2 eggs,
1 small cup of yeast,
1 cup of sweet milk,
2 tablespoons lard,
1 teaspoon of salt.

Mix up the bread at eleven o'clock and let it rise. At four o'clock roll out and cut into biscuits two sizes, putting the small one on top and let it rise till supper. Bake twenty minutes.[107]

OLD SOUTH BISCUITS
☛ One pint of milk,
One teaspoonful of lard,
Two teaspoonsful of butter,

Two teaspoonsfuls of sugar,
One heaping teaspoonful of salt,
One-half yeast cake,
Six cupfuls of flour.

Put milk on stove in double boiler with butter, salt, lard and sugar. When milk becomes scalded, let it cool until blood heat. Dissolve yeast and stir it into the scalded milk. Then add to milk when cooled two and a half cups of flour and mix to a stiff batter. Next add an egg well beaten to the batter and put the batter in a warm place to rise. Let it rise about five hours and then knead as for ordinary biscuit using three and a half cups of flour. Knead until dough can be handled easily, then roll out to one-half inch thickness. Rub each biscuit with melted butter, put two biscuits together and place in pans far enough apart not to touch. Bake fifteen or twenty minutes in hot oven.[108]

Oatmeal biscuits.

JOHNNY REB CAKE

☛ 2 cupsful of flour,
1 cupful of yellow meal,
4 tablespoonsful of sugar,
½ teaspoonful of salt,
1 teaspoonful of Cream of Tartar,
½ teaspoonful of soda,
   or,
2 teaspoonsful of baking-powder.

Add enough milk or water to make a thin batter, and bake.[109]

CONFEDERATE CRACKERS

☛ Mix two teaspoonfuls of cream of tartar, and three-fourths of a teaspoonful of soda, with one quart of flour, and a piece of butter the size of a goose-egg. Make these ingredients into a stiff dough with cold water, and beat and work the dough well. Roll it out, and cut into cakes with a tumbler.[110]

SECESSION WHEAT CRACKERS

☛ Mix fresh-ground wheat-meal with pure soft water into a stiff dough. Roll out and cut the mass into thin crackers . . . and bake in a brick oven. Be very cautious and not over-cook or burn them.[111]

CONFEDERATE CINNAMON ROLLS

☛ When yeast bread is ready to knead into loaves, take as much of the dough as is needed and roll out about two-thirds of an inch thick. Spread on top a thin layer of butter, then sugar, and upon this sprinkle cinnamon. Roll the dough as you would for a jelly-cake roll, and slice off as many rolls as you want. Put these in a pan to rise as you would light biscuits. When raised, bake a nice brown. [Before they cool, cover the rolls with a thick layer of white icing—the editor, L.S.]¹¹²

SECOND AMENDMENT CINNAMON ROLLS
☛ Make a biscuit dough of one pint of flour, one and one-half teaspoonfuls of baking-powder, one-half teaspoonful of salt and a full tablespoonful each of butter and lard. Rub the shortening into the flour, having first thoroughly mixed in the salt and baking-powder. Use enough new milk to make a soft dough. Roll it out very thin and sprinkle on a cupful of granulated sugar well mixed with one teaspoonful of cinnamon. Then roll up tightly and cut across in slices from three-quarters of an inch to an inch thick. Lay upon a biscuit pan and bake quickly. Try these and see if they are not good.¹¹³

CHEESED CRACKERS
☛ Take fresh snow-flake or butter thin crackers; butter and grate cheese lightly over them. Put in oven and toast.¹¹⁴

MARYLAND BEAT BISCUIT
☛ Take one quart of flour, add one tea spoonful of salt, one tablespoonful of lard, half tablespoonful of butter. Dry rub the lard and butter into the flour until well creamed; add your water gradually in mixing so as to make dough stiff, then put the dough on pastry board and beat until perfectly moist and light. Roll out the dough to thickness of third of an inch. Have your stove hot and bake quickly. To make more add twice the quantity.¹¹⁵

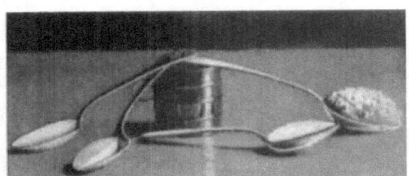
Measuring cup and measuring spoons.

GRAHAM BREAD
☛ 1 quart of new milk, ½ cup of new yeast, and ½ cup of molasses, or 1 pint of bread sponge, with milk and molasses. Stir in Graham meal until stiff; let it rise, and bake it for ¾ of an hour; never mold as for fine flour bread. When the meal is coarse, as is best for pudding, stirring in a cup of shorts or fine flour will make it less harsh. This is an excellent bread for dyspeptics, wholesome and easily digested.¹¹⁶

CONFEDERATE GRAHAM CRACKERS
☛ Mix one cup of graham flour, with one cup of fine bran or two cups of graham flour may be used instead—just add two cups of white flour,

sifted with two teaspoonfuls of salt, and one-fourth a cup of sugar. Dissolve one-fourth a teaspoon of baking soda in one cup of water, add three tablespoons of butter, or a substitute, then turn in the dry ingredients all at once before the water has lost its heat, and mix quickly to a dough.

Let this cool, then roll out, as thin as possible, on a lightly floured board, cut into squares, prick each of these all over with a fork, and place on a baking sheet, thinly dredged with flour, in a moderate over for ten minutes, or until done.[117]

LAPLANDS

☞ 1 pint milk,
½ pint flour,
2 eggs,
1 dessertspoon lard.
Beat separately and light as for cake. Bake in small shallow pans.[118]

KENTUCKY CORN DODGERS

☞ Sift the best meal made from the white corn, any quantity desired. Salt to taste. Mix with cold water into stiff dough and form into round, long dodgers with the hands. Take the soft dough and form into shape by rolling between the hands, making the dodgers about 4 or 5 inches long and 1½ inches in diameter.

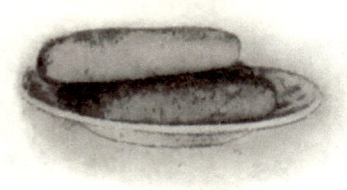

CORN DODGERS.

Have a griddle hot, grease a little with lard, and put the dodgers on as you roll them. Put in oven and bake thoroughly, when they will be crisp and a rich brown. This bread does not rise.[119]

TEA BISCUIT

☞ Sift a quart of flour, mix with it two ounces of sugar, two of butter, and make it into good paste with sweet cream. Knead it well, roll it out into a thin sheet, cut it into cakes with a biscuit cutter or the edge of a tumbler, pierce the tops with a fork, and bake them in a brisk oven. Send them to table warm.[120]

EGG CRACKERS

☞ Beat an egg with ¼ cup of cold water. Sift ½ teaspoon of salt and 1 teaspoon of baking powder with a cup of white flour. Mix all, and add more flour if necessary to make a dough which can be rolled out thin. Knead smooth, roll out as thin as can be handled, cut out with a small biscuit cutter and bake brown quickly. Prick each round with a fork before baking. Very nice with salad or cheese.[121]

SODA BISCUIT

☛ Dissolve a teaspoonful of soda in two spoonfuls of boiling water, and mix it with a pint of sour milk, pour it on two pounds of flour, add four ounces of powdered sugar and four of butter, knead it well, roll it into a sheet about half an inch thick, and cut it out with the edge of a tumbler, pierce the tops with a fork, and bake them in a quick oven. Send them to the tea-table warm.[122]

SOUTHERN SWEET POTATO BISCUITS

☛ Two cups flour,
One cup of mashed boiled sweet potatoes,
Two tablespoonsful of lard,
One teaspoonful of salt,
One and one-half teaspoonfuls of baking powder,
One-half teaspoonful of soda.
Enough buttermilk to make soft dough. Mix flour, salt, soda and baking powder together. Add sweet potatoes and work the lard in lightly. Mix with milk to make soft dough, roll thin cut into biscuits and bake in quick oven.[123]

MILK BISCUIT

☛ Rub a spoonful of butter into three pints of flour, sprinkle in a large teaspoonful of salt, and make it into a stiff dough with cold sweet milk. Roll it thin, put on a spoonful of butter, broken up in small bits, dust on a little flour, fold it up and roll it out again; put on another spoonful of butter in the same manner; fold it up again, and roll it into a sheet about half an inch thick; cut it out with a biscuit cutter, and bake it hastily. Do not split them with a knife, but break them open with your hands, butter them and eat them warm.[124]

Chocolate bread.

ELEGANT ROLLS

☛ Put half a cup of milk in a bowl, pour over half a cup of boiling water, let stand until tepid; then put in half a cake of Fleischmann's yeast. When dissolved, put in a cup of flour, let stand two hours, then add a tablespoonful of sugar, one teaspoonful of salt, one-fourth cup of softened lard, the white of an egg beaten stiff and flour enough to make a dough that won't stick to your hands or board when worked. Then, and not until then, has it flour enough. Put in a greased bowl to rise. In three hours it will be ready to mold into rolls. It must not be worked at all then, but pinch off pieces and roll them in any shape you prefer. In an hour they will be light enough to put in a hot oven. Grease over the top when half done.[125]

PIZZA OF THE CONFEDERACY

☛ Pizza means pie, so saying "pizza pie" is like saying "pie pie." The Italian pizza is made of a thin round of leavened dough worked up after leavening with a small amount of olive oil. On this round, small depressions are made, and the whole is covered with a variety of mixtures. These may only be tomatoes and oregano or may include grated cheese, anchovies, or ground meat. Sometimes one-half of the round is covered with one mixture and the other with a different one. Then the round of dough is placed in a hot oven and baked until the dough has become crusty. This, with a green salad, makes a good snack or lunch.[126]

PRETZELS

☛ Into two cupfuls of flour put one-third of a cup of butter, the yolks of two eggs and one whole egg, a pinch of ginger, one teaspoonful of salt, one-half of a yeast cake; then stir in enough milk to form a very stiff dough; turn the dough on a board and pound with the rolling-pin; let rise. Cut off small pieces, roll between the hands into strips, pinch the ends together to form small rings and let rise. Put them, a few at a time, into boiling water previously salted. Let cook until they begin to come to the surface. Take out quickly, sprinkle with salt, arrange in a greased baking-pan and bake a light brown.[127]

JOHNNY CAKE

☛ 1 quart corn meal,
1 pint warm water,
1 teaspoon salt.

Sift meal in a pan and add water and salt. Stir it until it is light, and then place on a new, clean board and place nearly upright before the fire. When brown, cut in squares, butter nicely, and serve hot.[128]

GEORGE WASHINGTON'S BREAKFAST CAKES

☛ Make a thick mush with corn meal and water, add some salt and a little butter, and drop in little cakes half an inch thick on a hot griddle.[129]

INDIAN BREAD

☛ There is no bread so healthy as good Indian bread. Take three pints of rye-meal, three of Indian-meal; mix with this two tablespoonfuls of salt, one tablespoonful of soda, one cupful of molasses and one-half of a cup of yeast.

Scald the meal. When that is cool add the rest. Let it rise four hours, then bake three or more.[130]

INDIAN MUFFINS
☛ Beat five eggs light, stir them into a quart of milk, with a small handful of flour and a teaspoonful of salt; then stir in as much fine Indian meal as will make it a tolerably thick batter. Having buttered some little scalloped muffin pans, place them in an oven that is moderately heated, put in each a small ladleful of the batter, and bake them a nice brown; then take them from the pans, arrange them neatly in a plate, lay on the top of each a slice of firm butter, and eat them warm.[131]

INDIAN FLAPPERS
☛ Sift a quart of fine Indian meal, mix with it a small handful of flour, three beaten eggs, a teaspoonful of salt, three spoonfuls of good yeast, and enough warm sweet milk to make it a tolerably thin batter; set it by the fire till it looks light, and then bake them on a clean, hot griddle, that is well buttered. Allow a large ladleful to each cake, making them quite thin, round, and the edges smooth, and as soon as they are a light brown on both sides, stack them in a plate, lay a slice of firm butter between each cake, cut them across, dividing each one into four, and send them to table warm.[132]

KENTUCKY BUTTERMILK BISCUITS
☛ 1 quart flour.
   1 teaspoon soda.
   1 teaspoon salt.
   2 tablespoons lard.
Sift flour, mix soda and salt well with flour, work in lard, pour in buttermilk to make soft dough. Roll thin, cut and bake in hot oven.[133]

OATMEAL MUFFINS
☛ To one egg, beaten well, add one teacup of sweet milk and a half teaspoonful of salt; then one teacup of oatmeal flour, in which a teaspoonful of baking powder has been sifted. Bake in hot, well greased muffin pans.[134]

BLUEBERRY MUFFINS
☛ 2 cups flour.
   3 teaspoons Royal baking powder.
   3 tablespoons sugar.
   3 tablespoons shortening.
   1 cup milk.
   1 egg.
   1½ cups blueberries.
   ½ teaspoon salt.
Sift dry ingredients together; add beaten egg and enough milk to make stiff batter; beat well, add melted shortening and blueberries which have been carefully picked over and dusted with flour. Bake in greased

muffin tins in hot oven 20 to 30 minutes.[135]

BANNOCK

☛ Sift a quart of fine Indian meal, mix with it a salt-spoonful of salt, two large spoonfuls of butter and a gill of molasses; make it into a common dough with scalding water, or hot sweet milk, mixing it well with a spoon; put it in a well buttered skillet, make it smooth, and bake it rather briskly. When it is done, cut it in thin smooth slices, toast them lightly, butter them, stack them and eat them warm.[136]

PREMIUM CRACKERS

☛ Rub one tablespoonful of butter into one pint of flour to which has been added one teaspoonful of salt; then work up with enough sweet milk to make stiff dough; roll very thin; cut into three inch squares and bake on writing paper.[137]

WHOLE WHEAT BREAD

☛ 2 cups of milk scalded.
1 cup white flour.
1 tablespoonful sugar.
5 or 6 cups of whole wheat flour or enough to knead.
2 teaspoonfuls salt.
1 yeast cake.
Make the same as milk bread with sponge.[138]

LIGHT INDIAN BREAD

Bread cooler (and roast dripper).

☛ Having ready a pot of boiling water, throw in a small handful of fine salt, and make it into a common bread dough, with sifted Indian meal. Stir it very hard with a wooden paddle or spaddle, till well mixed; sprinkle on the top a handful of dry meal, cover it and set it in a warm place to rise. In a few hours it will look very light and crack on the top; then heat your oven as for other Indian bread, grease it with a little lard, rub it with a handful of dry Indian meal, and bake your bread with common heat. It will keep moist for several days, and will be found quite convenient, being always in readiness.[139]

CREAM SCONES

☛ 2 cups flour.
2 tablespoonfuls butter.
2 eggs.
2 teaspoonfuls baking powder.
¼ teaspoonful salt.

⅓ cup cream.

Sift dry materials together, work in the butter with the fingers, beat eggs well and add to the cream. Stir this into the dry materials and butter. Roll out three-fourths inch thick. Cut in diamond shape; brush over with white of egg, slightly beaten, sprinkle with powdered sugar. Bake ten minutes in hot oven.[140]

SCOTTISH SCONES

☛ Two cupfuls of flour, two teaspoonfuls of baking-powder, one-half of a teaspoonful of salt, one-third of a cup of sugar, three tablespoonfuls of butter, one egg, currants if desired. Add enough milk to make a soft dough, divide in half, flatten with the hand into a round cake the thickness of a biscuit, mark with a knife into four scones and bake quickly.[141]

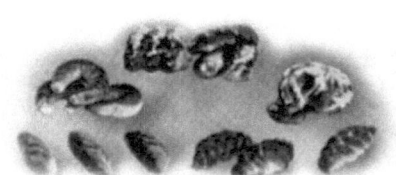

Rolls, pretzels, coffee cake, etc.

SOUTHERN CORN BREAD

☛ 1 quart meal.
1 teaspoon salt.
3 tablespoons lard.
1½ cups butter milk.
¼ teaspoon soda.
1 cup water.

Dissolve soda in buttermilk, add to meal with lard and salt—then add water to right consistency (add more water if necessary). Cook in hot oven.[142]

PLANTATION CORN BREAD (OR HOE CAKE)

☛ Half tablespoonful of lard to a pint of meal, one teacup of boiling water; stir well and bake on a hot griddle. Sift in meal one teaspoonful of soda.[143]

ALABAMA HOE CAKE

☛ One pint corn-meal, one-half table-spoonful salt, and cold water to make a stiff batter; beat well; sprinkle a hot griddle with meal, let brown; then spread "hoe cake" half an inch thick, let brown on both sides. Good for dyspeptics.[144]

GEORGIA HOE CAKE

☛ One quart of meal, a teaspoonful of salt; mix with cold water, or buttermilk and soda if preferred. Make a very stiff batter; spread half an inch thick on griddle. Bake over quick fire.[145]

CLABBER CAKES

☞ 1 pint of clabber, 1 teaspoon of saleratus, 1 tablespoon of butter, 1 pint of flour; if not stiff enough add a little more flour to the batter. Bake in muffin-rings and let them remain in the oven until soaked, or they will be clammy. 1 teaspoon of salt. Bake in a quick oven.[146]

NUT BREAD

☞ Make a regular light bread; at the second rising work in some English walnuts broken in small pieces, then make into loaves; when risen, bake. You may use chopped almonds if you prefer. This bread is so nice for sandwiches cut thin.[147]

NEW ORLEANS NUT BREAD

☞ ¼ cup of sugar,
¾ cup hot water,
½ cup molasses,
¼ cup milk,
2 cups entire wheat flour,
1 cup bread flour,
5 teaspoons baking powder,
1½ teaspoons salt,
½ teaspoon soda,
¾ cup nut meats, finely chopped.

Mix in order given, sifting dry materials together before adding. Turn into a greased bread pan, let stand fifteen minutes, and bake in a moderate oven one hour.[148]

SOUR MILK BISCUITS

☞ One pint of flour, half a level teaspoonful of soda, same of baking powder, little salt, a small teaspoonful of sugar, two level tablespoonfuls of lard, about half a cup of buttermilk. Sift soda and baking powder with the flour, put in salt, sugar and lard.

Now mix with the milk. Make a smooth dough, let stand some time before using. In winter let stand all night; in summer, an hour. Roll thin and cut small.[149]

CONFEDERATE ZWIEBACK

☞ Make the receipt for rusks in one large loaf the same shape as the rusks, or two loaves can be made from it, if liked small. Rise and bake well. When cold, cut in half-inch slices and dry them in a very slow oven, until dried through and of a deep yellow.[150]

CONFEDERATE WAFERS

☞ Two teacupfuls of flour, two eggs, one tablespoonful melted butter, sweet milk to make a rather stiff batter; add a level teaspoonful of salt, beat thoroughly and bake in hot, slightly greased wafer irons.[151]

ROLLS

☛ 1 quart of flour, 1 tablespoon of butter and lard mixed, 2 tablespoons of yeast, ½ pint of water. Work all well together; set in a warm place to rise; use only 1 pint of flour to mix with at night, and work in the other pint in the morning. Do not work the dough much in the morning. Roll it out on the board, and cut into shapes. Bake in a moderate oven.[152]

LIGHT ROLLS

☛ 2 pints flour,
1 tablespoon of sugar,
1 teaspoon salt,
2 eggs,
½ cup of lard,
½ cup of home-made yeast.

First mix lard, flour, and sugar. Then stir in other ingredients. Add enough milk and warm water to make thin batter. Set in warm place to rise, and then work in flour to make pretty stiff dough and very smooth. If put to rise at 12, will be ready at 6. Don't work much last time. Make out in pretty shape and put to rise, and bake in quick oven.[153]

RICE BREAD

☛ Mix with one cup of cold rice, three well beaten eggs, and one and a half cups of sweet milk, salt and white pepper to taste, and one teaspoonful of butter. Pour into a baking dish or pan and bake until a light brown. Add teaspoonful of baking powder if preferred. Serve at once.[154]

SWEET ROLLS

☛ 2 quarts of flour, 2 tablespoons of fine white sugar, a little salt, 3 tablespoons of butter. Melt it in 1 pint of milk, a sponge made of 2 tablespoons of corn meal made into a thin gruel. Boil the gruel, and then add the pint of milk—the milk must be new—4 tablespoons of yeast to be added when the milk and gruel are cooled. Add 2 well beaten eggs. Make into rolls in the morning, and set them to rise. Add the sugar in the morning.[155]

MT. AIRY BEATEN BISCUITS

Beaten biscuits.

☛ 3 pints of flour sifted, 1 large kitchen spoon of lard, 1 teaspoon salt. Have the lard well chilled on ice. Rub the lard into two pints of the flour. Make this into a stiff dough with ice water and a very little milk. Work through a kneader 150 times, gradually adding the other pint of flour, or till the dough is perfectly smooth. Roll out one-half inch thick, cut into biscuits, stick with a fork, and bake in a moderate oven till light brown. Serve hot.[156]

HOT CROSS BUNS

☞ Sift and set before the fire, 2½ pounds of flour, not near enough to scorch. When warmed through, mix with it ½ pound of sugar, ½ pound of butter, melted in ½ pint of milk, ½ teaspoon of powdered cinnamon, ½ teaspoon of coriander seed. These ingredients must be well stirred together, and then stir in 2 tablespoons of yeast. Set to rise; when risen, handle lightly as you form the dough into buns; on each bun cut a cross, it can be done with the back of a knife. Serve them while hot. These buns are made for "Good Friday."[157]

Universal dough mixer and kneader.

NORWEGIAN SWEET BREAD

☞ 1 cake fresh yeast.
1 cup of sugar.
2 tablespoons of sugar.
Season well with cinnamon.
3 teaspoons of salt.
1 fresh egg well beaten.
1 large tablespoon of lard.
Half a citron cut in medium size pieces.
4 cups of water.
Flour enough to make stiff dough.
A handful of large raisins cut in half.
When risen work over and add, 1 tablespoon full of butter or lard.

This takes longer to rise than plain bread. When about to brown, brush with lard, and sprinkle with sugar and cinnamon. This is a delicious bread and a favorite in Norway. When stale may be toasted and served for breakfast.[158]

VIENNA ROLLS

☞ Have ready in a bowl a table-spoon of butter or lard, made soft by warming a little, and stirring with a spoon. Add to one quart of unsifted four two heaping tea-spoons baking powder; mix and sift thoroughly together, and place in a bowl with butter. Take more or less sweet milk as may be necessary to form a dough of usual stiffness, according to the flour (about three-fourths of a pint), put into the milk half a tea-spoon of salt, and then stir it into the flour, etc., with a spoon, forming the dough, which turn out on a board and knead sufficiently to make smooth. Roll out half an inch thick, and cut with a large round cutter; fold each one over to form a half round, wetting a little between the folds to make them stick together; place on buttered pans, so as not to touch, wash over on top with milk to give them a gloss, and bake immediately in a hot oven about twenty minutes. It will do them no harm to stand half an hour before baking, if it is desired.[159]

YORKSHIRE PUDDING
☞ Sift one pint of flour and add to it one-half pint of milk; beat milk into flour with a large spoon until very light; then beat four eggs yolks and whites together very light, and add to flour and milk, and then beat the whole, adding one tablespoonful of butter, salt to taste. Put to bake in a dish; twenty minutes will bake it. When done send to table with roast beef, in same dish it is baked in.[160]

LIGHT BREAD
☞ Half yeast cake to two quarts of flour, teaspoonful of salt, one dessertspoonful of butter or lard. Dissolve yeast in warm water; make up over night at 10 o'clock; make dough soft and spongy, and set to rise in a warm place. Next morning work the dough over until it be comes perfectly light, adding flour so as to keep it from sticking to the hands, then put to rise in your baking pan, and when it rises bake in a hot oven until thoroughly done.[161]

HANOVER ROLLS
☞ Sift twice 2 quarts of flour,
Add 4 tablespoons yeast,
Add 1 tablespoon lard or butter,
1 tablespoon sugar,
1 dessertspoon salt and a pinch of soda.
Use enough lukewarm water to make the mass soft enough to knead well, and put where it will rise. When light, grease the hands and make into rolls. Let it rise again and then bake.[162]

SOUTH CAROLINA BISCUITS
☞ One quart sweet cream or milk, one and a half cups butter or fresh lard, two tablespoons white sugar, one good teaspoon salt; add flour sufficient to make a stiff dough, knead well and mold into neat, small biscuit with the hands, as our grandmothers used to do; add one good teaspoon cream tartar if preferred; bake well, and you have good sweet biscuit that will keep for weeks in a dry place, and are very nice for traveling lunch. They are such as we used to send to the [Confederate] army, and the "boys" relished them "hugely."[163]

OLD VIRGINIA CORN BATTER-BREAD
☞ Take 1 pt. corn-meal, and pour over it 1 pt. very hot water; add ½ teaspoon salt and heaping tablespoon butter. Stir well and when cool add 3 well beaten eggs and 1 qt. sour milk with 1 teaspoon soda dissolved in it. Bake in deep pan and serve quickly.[164]

APPLE ROLLS

☛ To one quart of flour add a tablespoonful each of butter and lard (or two of butter, if preferred,) and one teaspoonful of fine salt. Work the lard or butter into the flour dry until it is thoroughly mixed, then add salt and a teacupful of water, a little at a time, and mix until the dough is sufficiently thick to roll on the pastry block. Always sprinkle dry flour on the block to keep the dough from sticking. Use one and one-half pounds of mellow apples, peeled and cut very thin. Roll your dough out as thin as pie crust, eighteen by ten inches in size. Have three pieces of this size, and lay one sheet of it down and cover it with apples; then lay the second and third sheets down, covering each with apples. Roll the whole up together as you would a towel, then wet a white cloth in cold water and wrap it around the roll, sewing it tightly; then put into a pot of boiling water. Sprinkle dry sugar over each layer of apples before rolling in the cloth. Do not cook over twenty minutes. Put in water enough to cover the roll.[165]

Fontage iron and bread cups formed in hot fat.

CHEESE BISCUITS

☛ ⅝ cup milk.
2 teaspoons Royal baking powder.
6 tablespoons grated cheese.
1½ cups flour.
1 teaspoon shortening.
¼ teaspoon salt.

Sift together baking powder, salt and flour: add shortening and cheese; slowly just enough milk to hold the dough together. Roll on flour board ½ inch thick; cut with small biscuit cutter and bake 15 minutes.[166]

SOUTHERN BEATEN BISCUIT

☛ One lb. flour, 2¼ oz. lard; stir 1 teaspoon salt and lard into flour and add enough water or sweet milk to make a very stiff dough, beat this dough until it blisters (or knead it with the hands until it blisters) adding a little flour occasionally; roll out ½ in. thick and cut into biscuit and bake rather slowly.[167]

RUSKS

☛ 3 pounds of flour, 1¼ pounds of sugar, 6 ounces of lard, 1 egg, ½ pint of yeast, ½ pint of milk, 1 nutmeg, 1 teaspoon of allspice, 4 tablespoons of rose water. Beat the egg; add the sugar and yeast; rub the flour, sugar, and spice together. Mix them well, and then add the milk and rose water. Stir it smooth; cover with flour as when you set bread to rise; in the morning when bubbles break through the flour, work it into rolls; let them rise, and when light, bake them.[168]

LOUISIANA RICE PONE

☛ One pint of boiled rice stirred in one pint of milk with a small teacupful of corn-meal (white corn-meal preferable), four well-beaten eggs, a large tablespoonful of butter and lard melted together, one small teaspoonful of salt, all well mixed; beat in three heaping teaspoonfuls of baking-powder; bake and serve in ordinary pans well greased.[169]

SOUTHERN BROWN BREAD

☛ 1 cup corn meal.
　1 teaspoon salt.
　2 cups Graham flour.
　2 teaspoons soda.
　¾ cup sorghum.
　1 cup chopped raisins.
　1 cup buttermilk.
Mix and sift soda with dry ingredients, add molasses and milk, add raisins last, turn into well greased pound molds filled ⅔ full; steam three hours.

For steaming, place mold on trivet in kettle containing water, boiling hot, allowing water to come up around mold; cover and steam, adding water as needed.[170]

SAUCE FOR APPLE ROLLS

☛ Two tablespoonfuls of butter and one and one-half teacupfuls of powdered sugar rubbed together until as light as cream, one-half of a grated nutmeg, one wineglassful of brandy beaten into the creamed butter and sugar.[171]

BEATEN BISCUIT

☛ One pound of flour, three ounces lard, little salt, cold or ice water to make a very stiff dough. Beat until pliable and you see the dough blister, roll thin, cut with a small cutter, bake quick, and let dry in oven until hard and crisp. When done rub with a cloth.[172]

MUFFINS

☛ 4 eggs,
　1 quart sweet milk,
　1 quart flour,
　1 tablespoon melted butter,
　A little salt.
Beat the eggs separately. Add milk and butter to yolks and then the flour. Add whites last and bake in hot muffin-irons.[173]

CORN MUFFINS

☛ One quart sifted Indian meal, a heaping tea-spoon butter, one quart milk, a salt-spoon salt, a third cup yeast, a table spoon of molasses; let it rise four or five hours, and bake in muffin-rings.[174]

DROP MUFFINS

☛ 2 eggs, 1⅓ pints of milk or water, 1 teaspoon of butter, 1 of salt, 1 tea-cup of yeast. Stir 2 quarts of flour into this mixture, after having beaten the eggs.

In the morning don't stir the batter, but drop it a spoonful at a time in a dripping pan and bake. Use 2 light quarts of flour, or the muffins will be too stiff, when baked. Bake them in rather a quick oven for half an hour.[175]

ENGLISH MUFFINS

☛ Take 1 qt. flour, ½ teaspoon sugar, 1 teaspoon salt, 2 large teaspoons baking powder, 1¼ pts. milk. Sift together flour, sugar, salt, and powder; add milk, and mix into smooth batter, a trifle stiffer than for griddle-cakes.

Artificial stone griddle.

Have griddle heated regularly all over, grease it, and lay on muffin-rings, half fill them, and when risen well up to top of rings, turn over gently with cake-turner. They should not be too brown, just a buff color.

When all cooked, pull each open in half, toast delicately, butter well, serve on folded napkin, piled high, and very hot.[176]

LONDON CRUMPETS

☛ Take 1½ lbs. flour, 1 qt. warm water, a cup yeast, 1 tablespoon melted butter, and 1 of syrup, 1 teaspoon salt; mix all together.

Set at night, or six hours before baking. Beat well at time of mixing, and also just before baking.[177]

CHEESE STRAWS

☛ ¼ lb. flour.
Pinch of salt.
2 oz. grated cheese.
2 oz. butter.
1 egg yolk.
Dash of cayenne pepper.

Combine above ingredients to a paste with egg yolk. Roll thin one-third inch wide from three to five inches long. Straws may be twisted if desired. Place on hot baking pan, cook in moderate oven light brown.[178]

BREAKFAST CORN BREAD

☞ One tea-cup of rice boiled nice and soft, to one and a half tea-cupful of corn meal mixed together, then stir the whole until light; one teaspoonful of salt, one tablespoonful of lard or butter, three eggs, half tea-cup of sweet milk.

The rice must be mixed into the meal while hot; can be baked either in muffin cups or a pan.[179]

AUNT SALLY'S CRACKLING BREAD

☞ Take as many cracklings as you wish, crush with your hands, add some corn meal, salt and warm water, Make into small pones and bake.[180]

CORN BREAD

☞ 1 cup of boiled rice,
1 pint of sifted corn meal,
2 well-beaten eggs,
A little salt,
Small piece of melted butter or lard,
1 teaspoon baking-powder,
Sweet milk to make a rather thin batter.

Pour in a well-greased earthen baking dish and bake a half hour or more in a hot oven.[181]

BATTER BREAD

☞ One pint of sweet milk put on to boil. When boiling sprinkle in with one hand and stir with the other one cup of sifted meal.

As soon as it will pour remove and stir in a tablespoonful of lard, salt. When cool put in two or three yolks of eggs, half a teaspoonful of baking powder. Bake in a greased dish. Serve with a spoon. The whites beaten stiff are added last.[182]

Toast rack.

VIRGINIA BATTER BREAD

☞ One-half cup rice, ½ cup cornmeal, 1 egg, 1 pint of sweet milk, 1 teaspoon baking powder, ½ teaspoon salt. Boil rice until soft, sift the cornmeal on the rice, add the baking powder and salt.

Beat egg well, stir the milk and egg in gradually. Bake in a buttered dish one-half hour in a moderate oven.[183]

GRAHAM MUFFINS

☞ Two cupfuls of graham flour, one cupful of wheat flour, three table spoonfuls of sugar, two teaspoonfuls of baking-powder, a pinch of salt, one egg beaten well, one cup of milk. Last add about one-half of a cup more of milk.[184]

CORN CAKES

☞ 1 quart of meal, 4 eggs, 1 pint of milk, ½ pint of water, 1 tablespoon of lard, or butter. Beat the eggs; add the milk and water; stir in the meal slowly; mix in the butter; 1 teaspoon of salt. Bake on a heated griddle.[185]

RICE CAKES

☞ Cook 1 cup of rice, and add to it ½ cup of cream, 1 teaspoon baking-powder, 2 tablespoons flour, 2 eggs, well beaten. Fry in lard or butter just enough to grease skillet.[186]

SPOON BREAD

☞ One cup of sweet milk, two cups of butter milk, two eggs beaten separately, four tablespoonfuls corn meal, one level teaspoonful soda, little baking powder, salt.[187]

BRAN BREAD

☞ Of unbolted wheat flour, 3 pints. Mix with warm water, 1 gill of yeast, 1 teaspoon of salt. Mix as for wheat bread, and bake according to directions given. Rye bread is made in the same manner.[188]

RYE BREAD

☞ When making the regular supply of bread reserve one pint of very light wheat flour sponge, add a level teaspoonful of salt, a heaping teaspoonful of brown sugar and rye flour to permit kneading. Knead well. When light, mold into loaves; let rise again till more than double its first size, brush the top with melted butter and bake one hour in a moderate oven. A delicious bread, with a crust as tender as cake.[189]

SALT RISING BREAD

☞ Scald one teacupful of sweet milk; stir in half a level teaspoonful of salt and a heaping tablespoonful of corn meal. Put in a warm place to stay over night. Next morning stir into this a light pint of flour, using a little warm water to make the yeast the consistency of cake batter. Let this rise. This should not take more than an hour and a half. Sift six pints of flour. Reserve one quart of this to work up with. Work into the rest of the flour lard the size of a hen egg, then pour in the yeast. If while mixing the dough seems to be getting stiff, work in a little warm water. (The dough for salt risen bread must never be stiff). Now work hard for half an hour, make into pones and set to rise in a warm place, being careful not to expose to draughts. This should rise in half, or three quarters of an hour. Bake quickly.[190]

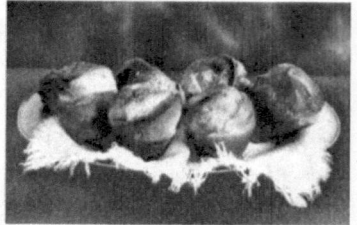

Rye popovers.

OWENDEN BREAD

☛ One cup hot boiled hominy, put in a small tablespoonful lard; next, one cup of sweet milk stirred in gradually, half a cup corn meal, two well beaten eggs. Should be the consistency of boiled custard. Bake as a whole or as muffins. Elegant.[191]

POPOVERS

☛ Two eggs, one cup sifted flour, one cup milk, one saltspoonful of salt. Beat the eggs without separating until they are well mixed, but not light. Add to them the milk. Put in another bowl the flour, add the salt, and pour into it gradually the eggs and milk. Strain through a sieve into the first bowl. Have heated greased iron gem pans. Fill two-thirds full of batter and bake in a moderate oven forty minutes. They must be baked until perfectly light in weight.[192]

Popover cups.

HOT CORN BREAD

☛ Scald one quart of meal; add to it while hot, a tablespoonful of butter. Beat two eggs, separately. Dissolve one teaspoonful of soda in two tablespoonfuls of warm water; then add it to one pint of sour milk, or buttermilk; add it to meal, beat; add next the yolks, then whites of eggs and one teaspoonful of salt and bake in shallow pans for forty minutes.[193]

WHEAT GEMS

☛ Two and one-half cupfuls of sifted flour, one and one-fourth cupfuls of milk, three eggs, sugar to sweeten, one tablespoonful of melted butter and two teaspoonfuls of baking-powder. Bake in gem-pans.[194]

HOMINY MUFFINS

☛ Stir 1 table-spoon of butter in 2 tablespoons of hot hominy, 4 tablespoons of flour, ½ teaspoon of salt. Mix with milk to a batter; bake in greased tins, in a quick oven. Mix the hominy, butter, and flour into a paste; beat up 2 eggs, and add them; then beat in the milk.

HOMINY CAKES

☛ 1 pint of cold boiled hominy, 1 pint of flour, 2 eggs, 1 quart of milk, 1 tablespoon of lard or butter. Mash the hominy, mix in the flour, then the eggs and milk. Mash the butter with the hominy. Beat all well together, and add 2 tablespoons of yeast. Set to rise, and bake on the heated griddle.[195]

RICE MUFFINS

☛ 3 eggs, 1½ pints of flour, 2 pints of milk, 1 pint of boiled rice, stir in the rice while it is hot, 1 tablespoon of butter, ½ teaspoon of salt, 2 tablespoons of yeast. Let the rice cool before mixing with the other ingredients. Beat all well together, and set to rise. Bake in greased tins.[196]

FLANNEL CAKES
☛ One pint of sifted flour, one pint of butter milk, add half the milk to the flour, break in an egg, little salt, the rest of the milk, two full tablespoons melted butter, one rounded teaspoonful of soda in a little water. Have griddle hot and only grease the first time. Fine.[197]

ABBY'S FLANNEL CAKE
☛ One quart of flour, quarter tea-cup of yeast, make into a batter, with one teaspoonful of salt; make up over night and put to rise. Just before baking on a nicely greased griddle, for breakfast, add one level teaspoonful of soda, and stir it well into the batter.[198]

BUTTERMILK MUFFINS
☛ 1 quart of flour, mix in it 1 teaspoon of cream of tartar, 1 quart of buttermilk, mix with it 1 teaspoon of soda, 1 tablespoon of butter. Mix the butter in the flour, then beat in the buttermilk, beat it all well together; 1 teaspoon of salt. Bake in greased tins or muffin-rings. Serve while hot, or they will be clammy.[199]

BUTTERMILK CAKES
☛ 1 quart of flour, 1 teaspoon of soda, 1 of salt, 1 tablespoon of butter, or lard. Mix with buttermilk to a soft dough; work it until the dough is smooth; roll them out about an inch thick; cut out with the top of the dredging box; prick with a fork, and bake them in a quick oven.[200]

MRS. MATHEWS' BATTER CAKES
☛ One quart sour or butter milk, one teaspoonful soda put in the milk and one teaspoonful of salt, two eggs broken in, flour enough for a batter that will run off the spoon. Grease the griddle with scraps of beef suet.[201]

EGG BREAD
☛ 1 quart of flour, 1 egg, 2 tablespoons of yeast, 1 tablespoon of butter. Mix into a dough with milk; work into a loaf; set it to rise, and then bake it.[202]

QUICK MUFFINS
☛ Two teacupfuls of buttermilk, one teacupful of thick cream, or three even tablespoonfuls of melted butter, four eggs, one half teaspoonful of soda. Thicken to the consistency of waffle batter.[203]

SODA BISCUITS
☛ Mix
  1 quart flour,

1 pint of buttermilk,
1 tablespoon lard,
½ teaspoon soda,
½ teaspoon salt,
Make into biscuits and bake quickly.[204]

PONE CORN BREAD
☞ One quart sifted water ground meal, one tablespoon of lard rubbed in two teaspoonfuls of salt, one pint of sweet milk. Mold with the hands in small pones.[205]

CORN EGG BREAD
☞ Two eggs, one pint of meal, half pint of sour milk, one teaspoonful of soda—beat eggs very light,—one tablespoonful of melted lard or butter, mix all together, well stirred or beaten. Bake in an ordinary pan.[206]

NUT CAKES WHEN WE WERE CHILDREN

Cake tins and baking sheet.

☞ Heat a pint of milk just lukewarm. Stir into it a teacupful of lard. (The lard should be melted.) Stir in flour till it is a thick batter, then add a teacupful of liquid yeast. Set it in a warm place. When light, work in two and one half teacupfuls of powdered sugar, four eggs beaten to a froth, two teaspoonfuls of cinnamon and one of salt. Knead into it sufficient flour to roll it out; put in a warm place to rise again. When it appears of a spongy lightness, roll out about half an inch thick. Cut into cakes with a wine glass and set aside. Now put in a porcelain-lined pot over a brisk fire two pounds of lard; when this is boiling hot a blue smoke will rise; the cakes will now be ready to cook; drop in a few at a time and when they are a light brown, take out with a wire dipper. If liked, as they are removed from the lard dip them in powdered sugar. The lard must not be allowed to burn; a piece of Irish potato dropped in occasionally will help to keep the lard clear, and will not affect the taste of the cakes.[207]

MAMMY'S GRAHAM MUFFINS
☞ 1 pint of Graham flour,
½ cupful of molasses,
½ teaspoonsful of salt,
½ pint of white flour,
1 teaspoonsful of soda.

Put the salt into the flour and soda into the molasses. Stir all together and mix with milk or water. Drop into muffin tins and bake twenty minutes.[208]

BREAD CAKES

All kinds of white bread.

☞ Take 1 quart of sweet stale loaf bread, and cover it with either milk or water; let it soak over night; in the morning beat 2 eggs, and stir in it. Beat all well together; if too thin, add a little flour to make it the proper consistency for baking. Bake on a heated griddle. If nicely made, these cakes are superior to flannel cakes.[209]

SALLY LUNN

☞ On quart of flour, one half pound butter, two eggs, one teaspoonful of salt, one half teacupful of sweet milk, and good yeast sufficient to mix the dough to a proper consistency. Make it up about nine o'clock in the morning in winter, and eleven o'clock in summer; work it over about four o'clock, and make it in a round shape into pans and bake for seven o'clock tea. Butter, before sending it to the table.[210]

SALLY LUNN BREAD CAKE

☞ Two well beaten eggs, three-fourths of a cup of sugar, one cup of sweet milk, one tablespoonful of butter, three teaspoonfuls baking powder, nearly one pint of flour.[211]

OLD VIRGINIA LOAF BREAD

☞ Boil one large, Irish potato until done, peel and mash fine; add a little cold water to soften it, stir into it a teaspoonful of brown sugar, a tablespoonful of lard, and three tablespoonfuls of liquid hop yeast. Mix all the ingredients thoroughly and put the sponge in a close jar; cover and let stand several hours to rise.

Sift into the tray three pints of flour, to which add a teaspoonful of salt, then pour the sponge in, with enough tepid water to work into a stiff dough; knead until smooth and let stand over night to rise. In the morning, make into loaves, allow it to rise one hour and bake.[212]

SALT-RISING BREAD

☞ ⅔ pint of milk,
2 tablespoons of corn meal,
1 teaspoon of salt,
1 tablespoon of lard,
1 tablespoon of white sugar.

Pour boiling milk over salt and meal and stir well. Set to rise at night.

Next morning add hot water to warm it; then flour enough to make it thick. Then add sugar and melted lard. Mold in loaves and put to rise in a warm place. When risen, bake in moderately hot oven.[213]

BOILED, BAKED OR STEAMED ROLL

☛ One pint of flour, lard the size of an egg, salt. Take half the flour and half the lard, and make a dough with cold water, roll very thin and spread over the remaining lard and sift over the rest of the flour; fold up and roll out again quite thin; spread with stewed and sweetened fruit; roll it up. If steamed, lay a piece of cheesecloth on the steamer; then lay on the roll. If boiled, roll in a well floured cloth and tie. If baked, put in a pan; pour in water, sugar and butter. The paste must be rolled very thin. Serve with hard sauce.[214]

BUCKWHEAT CAKES

☛ Put a large spoonful of yeast and a little salt, into a quart of buckwheat meal; make it into a batter with cold water; let it rise well, and bake it on a griddle it turns sour very quickly, if it be allowed to stand any time after it has risen.[215]

FRENCH ROLLS

☛ Sift a quart of flour, add a little salt, a spoonful of yeast, two eggs well beaten, and half a pint of milk—knead it, and set it to rise: next morning, work in an ounce of butter, make the dough into small rolls, and bake them. The top crust should not be hard.[216]

CRUMPETS

☛ Take a quart of dough from your bread at a very early hour in the morning; break three fresh eggs, separating the yolks from the whites—whip them both to a froth, mix them with the dough, and add gradually milk-warm water, till you make a batter the thickness of buckwheat cakes: beat it well, and set it to rise till near breakfast time; have the griddle ready, pour on the batter to look quite round: they do not require turning.[217]

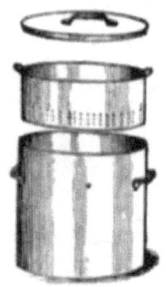

Steaming kettle.

POTATO BREAD

☛ Boil 6 large Irish potatoes, peel and mash them through a sieve or colander, add to them while hot twice the quantity of flour, and ½ pint of milk and 1 egg, well beaten. Knead it into a smooth dough, rather stiff. 2 tablespoons of yeast. Set it to rise; in the morning work it again and mold into loaves or rolls; let them rise, and then bake them. If sugar is liked in this bread it can be added. 1 tablespoon of powdered white sugar.[218]

KENTUCKY BATTER BREAD

☛ 1 pint meal,
   3 eggs,
   1 teaspoon salt,

1 tablespoon melted butter.

Make a thin batter with sweet milk. Pour in a baking-dish and bake ¾ of an hour, or till it is a rich brown.[219]

STEAM PONE

1 teacup New Orleans molasses,
5 teacups corn meal,
2 teacups brown flour, 1 teaspoon salt,
1 quart buttermilk,
2 teaspoons soda.

Mix thoroughly and place in air-tight bucket. Set in kettle of boiling water and boil for 6 hours. Then take from bucket, put in pan and bake slowly for 2 hours till a rich brown.[220]

PARKER HOUSE ROLLS

Two quarts of flour, half a cup of sugar, half a cup of butter, half a cup of liquid yeast. Mix these ingredients with fresh, sweet milk until you have a nice, light dough, about the same consistency of bread dough.

Grandmother's brown bread.

Let them stand in a warm place; if made after dinner, and to be used at tea time, four hours will be a sufficient length of time for them to rise.

Let them stand in a cooler place if made over night to be used for breakfast.

When the dough is light, take about as much as for an ordinary biscuit and roll it out in any desired size, spread on one half of the piece of dough a little soft butter, lap over the other half, and when they have risen again, and are baked in a "quick oven" they are delicious, making the famous "Parker House Rolls."[221]

WASHINGTON BREAKFAST CAKES

3 eggs, 1 pint of milk, 1 pint of flour, 1 teaspoon of butter. Beat all well together and add 2 tablespoons of yeast.

Set to lighten in a warm place. Put in greased tins and bake in a quick oven. Beat the eggs light before adding them to the other ingredients.[222]

MUSH CAKES

1 pint of corn-meal, boil half of it to a mush; when nearly cold, add 2 eggs beaten light, 1 tablespoon of butter, 1 gill of milk, and then the rest of the meal.

Drop a tablespoonful at a time on the griddle, or bake them in greased tins.[223]

Bottom: Steps in shaping a loaf of bread.

3. Candies

CANDY MAKING TIPS

☛ 1ˢᵗ In making candy use the finest granulated sugar and cold water.
2ⁿᵈ Dissolve the sugar and water before it goes over the fire.
3ʳᵈ Butter should not be added until candy is nearly done.
4ᵗʰ Cream and flavoring should be added after the candy is taken from the fire. I mean when only a small quantity of cream is used. Cream or butter should be used in preference to milk.

FRENCH FONDANT

☛ One cup granulated sugar, ¾ cup cold water, as much cream tartar as you can take up on end of a teaspoon, stir well, wipe down sides of kettle and cover closely and let cook over a hot fire until you see the steam coming out freely, remove cover, put in thermometer and cook to exactly 240 or if you have no thermometer cook until a little dropped in cold water will make a soft ball, dampen your slab or dish with your wet hand and be very careful in pouring it out so as not to disturb it and never scrape the kettle.

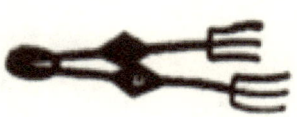
Candy Tongs.

Let stand until perfectly cold, then beat it until it commences to thicken, then work with your hand as you would dough until too stiff to work, then put in a bowl and wring a cloth out of cold water until quite dry; cover over the fondant and set away for future use.

(Tip: Let the syrup boil from the center and not from the sides; it prevents its graining.)²²⁴

NUT CREAMS

☛ Grind some walnut meats, work some into the fondant, make into balls and roll in the dry nut meats. You can chop raisins and citron fine and add to the fondant in the same way.²²⁵

CHOCOLATE CARAMELS

☞ One-half cup cold water, ⅓ cup milk, ⅔ cup molasses, 3 cups brown sugar, ¼ lb. butter, ¼ lb. chocolate, put on in one pan ½ lb. almonds (in shell) blanched and chopped.

Put in the first 4 ingredients, when hot put in the chocolate, in a short while put in the butter, boil until a very stiff jelly and almost to the crack. Flavor, pour out in a thin layer one-half of it, cover with the chopped almonds, then pour over the rest of the candy, when cold cut in squares.[226]

NUT FRITTERS

☞ Melt some fondant, stir in grated chocolate and nuts, flavor and drop out in cakes.[227]

GROUND PEA CANDY

☞ Dissolve 1 lb. of sugar in a cup of cold water, pinch cream tartar, stir until dissolved, then boil until it will form a soft ball when dropped in water. Have ready 1 lb. of parched peanuts broken by rolling. Remove from fire, stir in peanuts and sift in a level teaspoon soda. Pour up in a square buttered pan, cut in strips. You can use pecans.[228]

Caramels.

ALICE PEANUT CANDY

☞ One and ½ pints sugar house syrup, ¼ lb. brown sugar, a teaspoon butter, boil until hard when dropped in cold water, just before pouring out stir in a pint of parched peanuts rolled to break them, stir well, pour in a battered pan and cut while warm. One qt. peanuts will make a pint.[229]

WHITE CANDY

☞ Put into a kettle 1¾ lbs. white sugar, ¾ pt. water, and ½ teaspoon cream tartar. Boil over a quick fire, and carefully watch that it does not burn. Test, and when sufficiently brittle to snap off, pour into a buttered tin, and proceed as in the above recipe. Before commencing to pull the candy, drop on some flavoring of lemon or vanilla.[230]

ALICE MOLASSES CANDY

☞ Two cups sugar house syrup, 2 tablespoons white sugar. When near done add a full teaspoon butter, stir often and cook until it will snap between the teeth, cook slowly, by thermometer 275. Pull rapidly and straight down.[231]

BUTTERSCOTCH

☛ Three pounds "coffee A" sugar, fourth pound butter, half teaspoon cream tartar, eight drops extract of lemon; add as much cold water as will dissolve the sugar; boil without stirring till it will easily break when dropped in cold water, and when done, add the lemon; have a dripping-pan well buttered and pour in one-fourth inch thick, and when partly cold, mark off in squares. If pulled, when partly cold, till very white, it will be like ice-cream candy.[232]

NEW ORLEANS PRALINES

☛ Is made of brown sugar, and water cooked to 280, then stir in tablespoon butter to every 2 cups sugar and a cup of pecan meats, stir rapidly and dip out with a spoon about the size of a small saucer on wax paper.[233]

ALICE SUGAR CANDY

☛ One lb. sugar, 1 cup cold water, dissolve, wipe down sides of kettle, put on a cover and cook until you see steam coming from the sides, after it steams well remove cover and put in gently 3 tablespoons vinegar. Put in thermometer and cook to 275 or a hard ball when dropped in cold water, pour out and pull it just as hot as you can handle to be porous.[234]

ALICE CHOCOLATE CANDY

☛ One and ½ lbs. brown sugar, ¼ lb. chocolate, cut small, 1 tablespoon each of vinegar and syrup, dessert spoon butter, 1 cup sweet milk. When it commences to boil cook by the clock 20 minutes or until quite thick, stirring all the while, set off, add vanilla and beat until it just commences to grain, pour up very quickly or it will get too hard in a buttered pan and cut in squares. Should your milk or cream curdle in making candy stir rapidly a little while and it will be smooth and be sure you don't allow it to stick to the kettle. When a receipt calls for water use cold water.[235]

FUDGE

☛ 3 cups of brown sugar,
Just enough cream to wet the sugar,
1 pinch of salt,
1 pinch of soda,
1 teaspoonful of vanilla,
Butter size of a hen's egg,
⅓ cake of chocolate.

Stir the cream well into the sugar; then place it on the stove. Watch carefully, so it cannot burn; then, when it begins to boil, add salt and soda. Later, put in the chocolate and butter. Take it off before it is quite done; then add the vanilla. Beat it until it creams; then pour in a dish. Put out to cool and cut in squares.[236]

CHOCOLATE FUDGE

☞ Two and ½ lbs. sugar, ½ lb. glucose, 1 qt. cream, 1 tablespoon butter. I find water can be used in place of cream, but cream is better. Put it all in a large kettle to allow for boiling, stir constantly until it comes to a good boil then put in thermometer and cook to 236 or 238, being careful to stir under the thermometer or it will stick. Set off the fire and cream it against side of kettle until you see it just commences to grain a little, then pour it out quickly or it will set on you. It is best to pour it out on a shallow pan lined with wax paper. Chocolate Fudge is made adding ¼ lb. cut fine chocolate to kettle when it comes from the fire and flavor with vanilla. Black walnuts are fine in this.[237]

COCOANUT KISSES

☞ One and ½ lbs. sugar, 1 fresh grated cocoanut or ½ lb. desiccated, ¼ teaspoon cream tartar. Dissolve the sugar in as little cold water as it will bear, ¼ teaspoon cream tartar, stir until it boils, then add the fresh cocoanut and continue stirring until it will spin a thread by taking a little between your thumb and forefinger and pull apart it has cooked enough. Set off, if dry cocoanut is used put in ½ lb. with ½ lb, of fondant, beat until stiff, and with a fork dip out in kisses, if you don't find it stiff enough work in more fondant; always dip from around the edges, flavor, after dipping some white, color the batch pink and flavor with strawberry, make some of this color thin, color the rest chocolate and flavor with vanilla.[238]

Small kisses (left) and iced Madeleines (right) in various shapes.

COCOANUT CANDY

☞ Three-fourths cup sugar, ¼ teaspoon cream tartar, enough water to dissolve. Cook to a golden brown, then pour in the milk of a cocoanut if the fresh is used and dissolve, if not use water, 3 more cups sugar, cook and just before it is done put in the meat of a grated cocoanut and a little salt. Cook to the soft ball stage, set off, use no flavor, beat until it commences to grain and pour out on butterer or wax paper. Cut in squares; if desiccated cocoanut is used put in after it comes from fire.[239]

OLD VIRGINIA MOLASSES TAFFY

☞ Put a pint of New Orleans molasses over the fire in a saucepan and boil for twenty minutes. Stir in a quarter teaspoon of baking soda and boil fifteen minutes longer, or until a little, dropped into cold water, becomes brittle. This candy must be stirred constantly while it is cooking or it will scorch. When it reaches the brittle stage, add a teaspoon of vinegar and a tablespoon of butter and pour into well-buttered pans. Mark into shape with a buttered knife after the candy begins to form and before it is really hard.[240]

SALT WATER TAFFY

☛ Two and ½ lbs. sugar, 1 lb. glucose, 1 tablespoon glycerine, 1 heaping tablespoon butter, 1 teaspoon salt, 1 pt. water. Put sugar, glucose and water on the fire and cook to 256 or 258 then add salt and glycerine, stir it well in and pour on a greased slab and when cool enough pull over a hook. Flavor and color when pulling as desired, cut in small pieces and wrap in waxed paper.[241]

BROWN TAFFY

☛ 3 pounds sugar,
½ pound butter,
1 teaspoon cream of tartar.

Put in pan and dissolve with water. Boil till it cracks. Flavor with vanilla. Pour on marble slab and when cool enough to pull, pull till light, and arrange in long strips and cut any length desired.[242]

MARSHMALLOWS

☛ Soak four ounces of gum arabic in a cupful of water until it is dissolved. Strain it to take out any black specks that may be in the gum. Put the dissolved gum arabic into a saucepan with a half pound of powdered sugar. Place the saucepan in a second pan containing boiling water. Stir until the mixture becomes thick and white. When it begins to thicken, test it by dropping a little into cold water. When it will form a firm ball remove it from the fire, and stir into it the whites of three eggs whipped to a stiff froth. This will give it a spongy texture.

Lastly, flavor it with two teaspoonfuls of orange-flower water. Turn the paste into a pan covered thick with corn-starch. The layer of paste should be one inch thick. Too large a pan must not be used, or it will spread and make a thin layer. After the paste has stood twelve hours, turn it onto a slab and cut it into inch squares, dust them well with corn-starch or with confectioner's sugar, and pack in boxes. As the paste is more or less cooked, it will be more or less stiff. Marshmallows become harder the longer they are kept, but are best when as soft as they can be handled.[243]

PINOCHI

☛ Three cups sugar, 1 cup pecan meats, a full tablespoon butter, ¼ teaspoon cream tartar. Take 1 cup of the sugar, the cream tartar and enough water to dissolve, put on and cook to a golden brown, then pour it up in a shallow buttered pan. When cold take half of it and break it up to put in the candy, the rest put in your chocolate candy. Take the other 2 cups sugar, the water, the caramel and butter, cook to a soft ball 238, remove, put in pecans and teaspoon vanilla, beat until it commences to thicken. Dip out by spoonfuls on a buttered pan.[244]

CRYSTALIZED POPCORN

☛ One cup sugar, enough water to dissolve it, and a piece of butter as large as an English walnut. Boil until it strings from the spoon, then stir quickly into about 3 qts. nicely popped corn, stirring well so that each kernel may be covered with the candy.[245]

LEMON DROPS

☛ Dissolve a coffee-cupful of powdered sugar with lemon juice. Boil till it is brittle when a little is plunged into cold water. Butter plates and let the candy fall on them in drops. Set away to get hard.[246]

COCOANUT DROPS

☛ Grate a cocoanut, add one-half of its weight of sugar and the white of an egg beaten to a stiff froth. Mix thoroughly and drop on buttered white paper or tin plates. Bake fifteen minutes.[247]

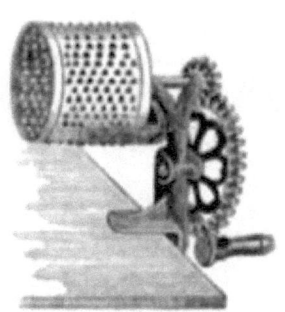
Revolving grater.

PEPPERMINT DROPS

☛ Take one cupful of sugar and let it come to a boil with one-half cupful of water. Take it from the fire as soon as it comes to this degree of heat. Stir all the time and add one-half teaspoonful of essence of peppermint and drop the candy on an oiled slab. Pour it from the spout of the pan else the liquid will grain before the drops are molded.[248]

EGG KISSES

☛ Whites of 3 eggs,
1 pint sugar.
Put the sugar in a bowl and pour the whites over and beat 20 minutes. With a dessertspoon drop the mixture on paper an inch or more apart. Do not let them touch. Put on a board or an inverted bread-pan, and put enough layers of paper to keep the bottom from burning. Bake in a moderate oven till brown. Let the mixture rise and then bake, or they will not be light. Remove with a knife and put on a dish.[249]

CONFEDERATE COCOANUT DROPS

☛ Whites of 2 eggs beaten very stiff, add 1 cup granulated sugar, 1 tablespoon flour, 2 cups grated cocoanut. Butter a baking pan, cover with greased paper. Drop on the cake or make in small balls, sift over granulated sugar, and bake to a nice brown crust.[250]

COCOANUT BALLS
☛ One lb. grated cocoanut, ½ lb. powdered sugar, whites 4 or 5 eggs, mix sugar and cocoanut together, add the whites beaten, mix the whole together, shape with the hand in small round balls the size of a walnut. Bake a light brown slowly.[251]

POPCORN BALLS
☛ Pop the corn in an iron vessel in very hot lard that has been salted. Dip off the popped grains into a bowl or pan. Make a syrup of 1½ cups of granulated sugar and ¼ cup of water. Let this boil until a soft ball forms when dropped into cold water. Pour the syrup over the popped corn, stirring the corn all the time. Then, with the hands, form the corn into balls.[252]

CREAM CANDY
☛ Put in a kettle 4 cups sugar and 3 cups cold water, stir until dissolved and commences to boil, put in a tablespoon butter and cook until it hardens in water about 270, pour out and when cool enough pull until white, cut in small pieces, don't use until next day, it will then be as soft as velvet.[253]

PEANUT BRITTLE
☛ 1 pint brown sugar,
1 pint shelled peanuts.
Melt the sugar in a pan till it boils and turns color; then pour over the nuts, which have been scattered on a well-buttered slab. Cut in squares or break in pieces.[254]

PEPPERMINT CANDY
☛ 2 teacups white sugar,
1 tablespoon butter,
1 tablespoon vinegar and J teaspoon soda,
½ cup of boiling water.
Set on stove and stir till thoroughly dissolved. Cook till brittle. Remove from the stove, flavor with 3 or 4 drops of oil of peppermint, and beat till creamy. Pour on slab and cut in squares.[255]

MOLASSES TAFFY
☛ Two lbs. sugar, ½ lb. glucose, 1 pt. molasses, 1 tablespoon butter, ⅔ pt. water. Cook sugar, glucose and water to 245 steaming a short while, put in thermometer when it reaches 245 put in the butter and pour in the molasses slowly and stir constantly until it reaches 260. Pour on a greased slab and pull until white. If you wish nuts in it sprinkle them over before pulling.[256]

SUGARED ALMONDS

☛ Put a cupful of granulated sugar in a saucepan with a little water. Stir until it is dissolved, then let it cook to the ball stage without touching except to test. Turn in a half cupful of blanched almonds and stir off the fire until the nuts are well covered with the granulated sugar, but turn them out before they become one mass. Boil another cupful of sugar to the ball, turn in the coated almonds and stir again in the same way, giving them a second coating of sugar, but not leaving them in the pan until they are all stuck together. The nuts may be given a third coating in the same way, if a larger size is wanted. For pink almonds, add a little carmine to the sugar just before putting in the almonds for the last coating. Any flavoring desired may also be added at this time.[257]

Candies and nuts.

PEPPERMINTS

☛ One and ½ cups sugar, ½ cup boiling water, 6 drops oil of peppermint. Dissolve the sugar and water, put on and boil 10 minutes, remove and when cool add the peppermint, beat until it commences to get cloudy, then drop out as rapidly as possible before it sets on buttered paper.[258]

CARAMEL CANDY

☛ ¼ pound chocolate,
1 pound brown sugar,
1 cup of sweet cream,
1 tablespoon of butter.
Boil till thick and flavor with vanilla. Beat till creamy. Pour on slab and cut in squares.[259]

PEANUT BRITTLE 1

☛ Have some roasted peanuts broken by rolling with a rolling pin. Melt your sugar (use no water), stir in the peanuts, pour out on an oiled slab, have an iron hot and greased, iron out the candy until as thin as you wish. Fine.[260]

PEANUT BRITTLE 2

☛ Two and ½ lbs. sugar, 1 lb. glucose, 1 ½ cups water, dissolve and then cook to 240 or it will make a soft ball when dropped in cold water, then add ¼ lbs. shelled peanuts (raw), stir almost constantly until a golden brown, just before you take it off add 2 or 3 tablespoons butter, when it comes from the fire add ½ teaspoon soda and turn on an oiled slab, when cool enough to handle turn the batch over and pull it out as thin as possible. The peanuts will pop when done.[261]

COCOANUT BRITTLE

☛ Is exactly the same [as peanut brittle above] only put in the shredded cocoanut when it comes from the fire.²⁶²

MAMMY'S PEANUT CANDY

☛ Two cups of brown sugar,
One cup of chopped peanuts,
One cup of water,
Butter the size of an egg.

Cook about twenty minutes, beat until creamy, and pour into buttered plates. When cold cut into squares.²⁶³

DIVINITY CANDY

☛ Three cups of white sugar,
Three-fourths cup of white Karo syrup,
Whites of two eggs,
Three-fourths cup of water,
One teaspoonful of vanilla.

Put sugar, syrup and water on to cook. Let it cook until it will form a hard ball when tried in cold water. Remove from stove and pour gradually over stiffly beaten whites. Add vanilla and one cup of nuts and beat until creamy. Pour into buttered plates and cut into squares when cold.²⁶⁴

CANDIED ORANGE AND LEMON PEEL

☛ Take the peel from 2 large oranges, drop in cold water and boil until quite tender, then scrape the white soft part out. Take a cup of sugar and a cup of water, let come to a boil, put in the peel and cook until very thick. Pour what syrup is left and let dry. Nice for flavoring puddings and cake.²⁶⁵

CHOCOLATE DROPS

☛ 2 pounds of powdered sugar,
Whites of 2 eggs,
⅓ cup of sugar,
1 tablespoonful of vanilla,
1½ pounds of grated pecans.

Beat the whites of 2 eggs. Sift the sugar; then pour gradually into the eggs, stirring rapidly. Put in the vanilla; then the grated nuts; then pour in the cream.

Add the rest of the sugar until it can be worked as dough; then roll out in any shape, and put on a dish to cool.

Take ¾ cake of chocolate (melted); then drop them in, taking out with a toothpick on either side. Place them on buttered paper; then put a pecan on top.

Set out to cool; then put them on a dish.²⁶⁶

SUGAR PLUMS

☛ Take small pieces of fondant, flavored and colored to taste; form it into olive-shaped balls. Hold one in the palm of the hand, cut it half through and press into it an almond; form the fondant around it, leaving a narrow strip of the nut uncovered, giving the appearance of a shell cracked open, showing the kernel. If chocolate color is used the almond should be blanched, but with light colors the skin is left on to give contrast. When green color is used it represents a green almond.[267]

Plums.

MAPLE CANDY

☛ To two cupfuls of maple syrup add one cupful of granulated sugar and butter the size of a walnut. Cook until it hardens. Pour into buttered pan and set away to cool.[268]

Square-cornered dinner-table with fourteen covers and white decorations.

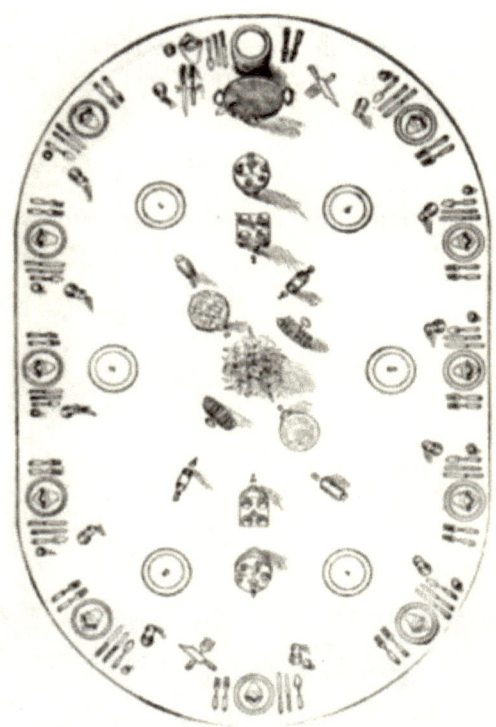

Dinner table setting of five courses for 12.

4. Cereal Grains

(Wheat, corn, rice, oats, barley, sorghum, millet, rye)

DELICIOUS WAY TO COOK RICE

☞ ½ cup of rice,
2 quarts of boiling water,
2 teaspoons of salt.

Wash the rice through two waters. Put the rice in the boiling water gradually, so as not to stop the boiling, and let it boil 20 minutes without stirring. Then drain through colander, rinse with cold water, and shake free from water. Put back in saucepan and let it stand on back of stove for 5 minutes.[269]

SOUTHERN RICE

☞ After thoroughly washing and rubbing the rice, put it in salted water enough to cover it twice over, in a custard-kettle, or tin pail set in a kettle of boiling water; cover the whole closely for fifteen or twenty minutes, until the grains of rice are full and plump but not "mushy;" drain off all the water possible, and replace rice in the kettle, allowing it to cook for half an hour longer, when it is ready to serve.

The grains should be full and soft, and each one retain its form perfectly. During the last half hour it should be occasionally stirred lightly with a fork, and it is improved by standing on the back of the stove a few minutes before serving.[270]

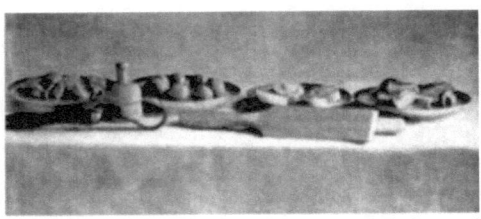

Utensils and molds used to make pats, balls, and shells out of butter.

SOUTH CAROLINA RICE

☞ Pick and wash through three waters, one pint of rice; add one teaspoonful of salt. Then place in a boiler with three pints of water. Bring slowly to a boil; then simmer gently until a grain taken between the fingers yields to the slightest pressure. The large supply of water is the secret of successfully cooked rice, keeping the grains distinct. When done enough drain through colander, shake gently before a hot fire until quite dry. Then serve in a hot, covered.[271]

CREAM OF WHEAT

☞ ½ cup cream of wheat.
3 cups boiling water.
½ teaspoon salt.

Add salt to boiling water, stir in cream of wheat and continue stirring a few moments to prevent lumping. Cook slowly over direct heat 20 minutes or more, or in double boiler one hour or more. Can be placed in fireless cooker three or four hours. Serve with cream and sugar.[272]

POLENTA

☞ Put a large spoonful of butter in a quart of water, wet your corn meal with cold water in a bowl, add some salt, and make it quite smooth, then put it in the buttered water when it is hot, let it boil, stirring it continually till done; as soon as you can handle it, make it into a ball, and let it stand till quite cold then cut it in thin slices, lay them in the bottom of a deep dish as to cover it, put on it slices of cheese, and on that a few bits of butter; then mush, cheese and butter, until the dish is full; put on the top thin slices of cheese and butter, put the dish in a quick oven; twenty or thirty minutes will bake it.[273]

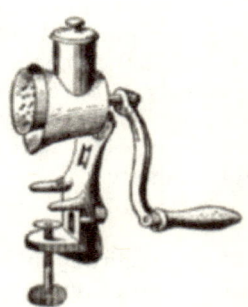

A bread, cheese, cocoanut, and corn grater.

RISOTTO

☞ Boil rice until tender, but not soft. The Italian rice must be used, as it does not get soft like the Carolina rice; when the rice is done, drain off the water and steam it dry; then add, while the rice is still on the fire, some mixed grated Parmesan and Swiss cheese. Turn them together lightly until the cheese has softened, then put it into the hot serving-dish, and cover with sauce.[274]

CONFEDERATE OATMEAL

☞ Wash well in cold water to get out all trash. To one teacup of oatmeal add two even teaspoonfuls of salt and one quart of water, hot or cold.

Place in a porcelain-lined kettle, or boiler if possible. When it begins to thicken, stir well; then let boil for three hours without further attention, except to see that it does not scorch, keeping it closely covered. Serve when done in a covered dish; and at table with milk and sugar if liked, or butter.[275]

ROLLED OATS
☛ Put two teacupfuls of rolled oats in a double boiler; add one teaspoonful of salt and four teacupfuls of boiling water; boil half hour and serve with cream or sweet milk and sugar, or with butter.[276]

OATMEAL FRIED
☛ Put oatmeal, which has been cooked, into a mold wet with cold water. Let it stand until thoroughly cold; slice and roll in egg and bread crumbs and fry in boiling lard. Serve with butter and sugar or syrup.[277]

OATMEAL PORRIDGE

Oatmeal with dates.

☛ Oatmeal is ground in different grades of coarseness, and some brands are partly cooked before they are put up for sale; therefore the time for cooking varies, and it is better to observe the directions given on the packages. Oatmeal requires to be cooked until very soft, but should not be mushy. The ordinary rule is to put a cupful of meal into a quart of salted boiling water (a teaspoonful of salt), and let it cook in double boiler the required time. It is well to keep the pan covered until the oatmeal is cooked, then remove the cover and let the moisture evaporate until the oatmeal is of the right consistency. It should be moist enough to drop but not run from the spoon. It should be lightly stirred occasionally to prevent its sticking to the pan, but carefully so as not to break the grains. If carefully cooked, the sides of the pan will not be covered with burned oatmeal, and so wasted. Oatmeal is very good cold, and in summer is better served in that way. It can be turned into fancy molds or into small cups to cool, and will then hold the form and make an ornamental dish.[278]

CRACKED WHEAT
☛ Add to three cupfuls of water a half teaspoonful of salt; when it boils add a half cupful of cracked wheat, and let it cook uncovered until the water is nearly evaporated; then add three cupfuls of hot milk; cover and cook until the wheat is soft; then uncover and cook to the right consistency. It should be quite moist. Stir it carefully from time to time while it is cooking, but with care not to break the grains. Turn into molds to harden, and serve cold with sugar and milk.[279]

STEAMED RICE

☛ Pick and wash in three waters one pint of rice; place in a steamer over a pot of boiling water; cover closely and let it remain until a grain will easily mash between the fingers. Salt and serve hot. Each grain will stand to itself.[280]

CORN MEAL SHORT CAKE

☛ Stir into a pint of sweet milk three well beaten eggs; add a little salt and a half cup of butter, with sifted corn meal to make a stiff batter. Drop it from a large spoon upon buttered tins. Bake them in a quick oven. When they are a little browned they are done. Send them to the table hot and eat with butter.[281]

SPANISH RICE

Kitchen lantern.

☛ Chop one white onion fine, brown it in two tablespoonfuls of lard, then add one pepper chopped fine and a half pound of well-washed rice; stir constantly until the rice is slightly brown, then add three cupfuls of bouillon, one heaping spoonful of salt, a dash of cayenne pepper and a pinch of Spanish saffron. Boil until the stock is quite absorbed by the rice, which should be rather dry.[282]

CORNMEAL MUSH

☛ Sprinkle with the hand a pint of cornmeal into rapidly boiling salted water, stirring all the time. Cook for half an hour; or mix the cornmeal with a pint of milk and teaspoonful of salt and turn it slowly into a quart of boiling water; cook for half an hour, stirring constantly. This may be eaten cold or hot, with milk, with butter and sugar, or with syrup. When cold it can be cut into slices and browned on both sides in a saute-pan, and used as a vegetable dish, or as a breakfast dish, and may be eaten with syrup.[283]

HOMINY

☛ Wash them nicely, and let them soak in the water it is to be boiled in, for 30 minutes; put it on to boil for 1 hour; let it boil stiff. Be careful that it does not burn. When ready to serve, stir a small piece of butter in it; boil slowly, so as to give the grits time to swell.[284]

SAMP

☛ This is cracked corn, or very coarse hominy. As it usually comes to the purchaser, it needs thorough washing in two or three waters, to remove the hulls. It is cooked like the cracked wheat, requiring about the same length of time. It may also be cooked in a bag, (allowing room to swell) suspended in a kettle of water, not allowing it to touch the kettle.[285]

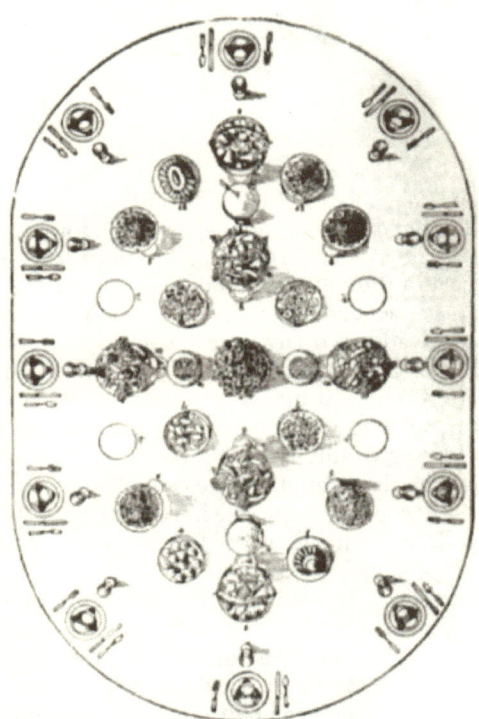
Dinner dessert table setting for 12.

5. Cheese Dishes

TO MAKE CHEESE

☛ If you have the preparation of rennet, it will be found very convenient to use that in the place of dried rennet, allowing a large spoonful of the liquid to each quart of the milk. If you use dried rennet, cut a piece four or five inches square, according to its strength; pour on a gill and a half of lukewarm water, add two large table spoonfuls of brandy, cover it securely, and set it by to steep till next morning: then, having your milk fresh from the cows, strain it into a large pot or kettle; throw round it a few embers to make it about blood warm, and stir into it the prepared rennet water, allowing a table-spoonful to each quart of milk.

Much depends on the strength of the rennet, some having double the gastric juice that others of the same size have: therefore if the milk should not conglomerate and form a firm curd in half an hour, mix in more of the rennet water.

As soon as the whole is formed into a firm curd, press out as much of the water as you can conveniently with a saucer, put the curd on a large cloth over a sieve to drain, having first wet the cloth in cold water, to prevent the card sticking to it; season it lightly with salt, and put it

with the cloth into a cheese-hoop; place it in a cheese-press or on a smooth plank, lay a bit of plank on the cheese, putting one corner of the cloth smoothly between, and having the plank cut exactly to fit the inside of the hoop; put a small weight on the top, and press it lightly for several hours; then increase the weight, and let it remain untouched till next morning; then take it out of the hoop, dip the cloth in water, wring it tolerably tight, spread it smoothly over the cheese, and invert it in the hoop: lay the plank again on the top, put on the weight, and let it sit till next day; then take it from the cloth, rub it evenly over with butter, and put it in a wire safe on a smooth plank, where it will be exposed to the air.

Turn it over once a day till the outside becomes firm, brushing it each time with a soft cloth and occasionally a little butter. If you press your cheese too hard, it will be dry and crumbly, and if you use too much rennet, it will be tough and porous: therefore both of these extremes should be carefully avoided.[286]

TO MAKE CREAM CHEESE

☛ Having kept your night's milk perfectly sweet, skim it, and mix the cream with the morning's; make it lukewarm over a few embers, and stir into it enough of the preparation of rennet, to turn it to a curd in twenty or thirty minutes, adding half a pint of wine to each gallon of the milk, a little rose water, and a small portion of salt.

When a firm curd is formed, drain the whey from it, put it in wet cloths, place them smoothly in small cheese hoops, and press them lightly: next day turn them, wetting the cloth, and press them lightly again for twenty-four hours; then brush them over well with butter, using a soft cloth; place them in a wire safe, or some other convenient place where the air will have free admission to them, taking care to turn them over every morning, and brush them lightly with a soft cloth, and a little butter.

In one week they will be fit for use. Scrape and brush the outsides neatly, and send them to table whole, as they should be quite small. They are eaten at tea, and are considered very fine. They look very pretty pressed in hoops of a conical shape, and sent whole to be sliced at table. When you press them in such hoops, you must have a small hole made in the top, or pinnacle of each hoop for the whey to escape, and place the small ends downwards while pressing.[287]

TO MAKE COTTAGE CHEESE

☛ Take a large bowl of milk that is just beginning to turn sour, cover it and set it in the corner where it will keep lukewarm till it forms a curd. Then place a linen cloth over a sieve; put in your curd, fold over the corners of the cloth to keep out the dust, and let it drain till next morning, without pressing it in the least. Then turn it in an earthen dish, add as much rich, sweet cream as will make it a little soft; add a large spoonful of butter to each pint of the curd, mixing in a very little salt, and work it with a spoon till the whole is very smoothly mixed. Then put it in a china bowl, and set it in a cool place till the tea-table is ready.

Large grater.

This kind of cheese may be made of entire sweet milk, by turning it with a little preparation of rennet, but you must not make near as stiff a curd as for cinnamon cheese.[288]

GRATED CHEESE

☛ Of course there can be no great art in grating cheese. The prime reason why I give a receipt for it, as well as many others, is because it is a fashionable mode of serving it. Take cheese that are well dried; remove the hard peeling; grate the cheese fine, and serve it in small plates.

A very common way to serve cheese, is to peel and slice them neatly, and lay them on a glass or china plate.[289]

CHEESE MACARONI

☛ Never wash maccaroni. Break in short lengths and boil in a large kettle of salted water. When done put in a warm place to swell for fifteen or twenty minutes; then drain and put in butter, pepper, cream, and only use enough to prevent its sticking together, not a gravy. Serve with grated cheese.[290]

CHEESE FONDU 1

☛ Quarter of a pound of cheese, half a cup of milk, one saltspoonful of soda, two saltspoons of mustard, little pepper, little cayenne, a grating of nutmeg, two tablespoonfuls fresh bread crumbs, one tablespoonful of butter, three beaten eggs. Mix soda, mustard and pepper together. Melt the cheese and butter together over hot water.

When melted add the soda mixture, pour over the milk, and stir until the froth disappears; add the bread crumbs; when soft, the butter, nutmeg and beaten eggs.

Butter a baking dish, pour in the fondu, strew the bread crumbs over the top and bake in rather a quick oven. Serve at once, it soon falls. Fine.[291]

CHEESE FONDU 2

☛ Melt a rounding tablespoonful of butter and put into it a pint of milk. Dissolve two tablespoonfuls of flour in a little cold milk. Pour in the boiled milk and let it cook. Beat the yolks of four eggs, add a teaspoonful of salt, half a teaspoonful of pepper and five ounces of grated cheese. Beat the whites stiff, add them. Pour in a deep pan and bake twenty minutes. Fine.[292]

CHEESE FONDU 3

☛ To 2 ounces of butter, put 1 tablespoon of flour, ½ tea-cup of water. Drop the flour and butter into water, boiling hot; stir it until it thickens, and then stir in it; pound of grated Parmesan cheese.

Take it off, and let it stand until nearly cool; beat separately the whites and yolks of 3 eggs; stir in the yolks, and then stir in the whites; put the mixture immediately into paper cases, only filling them half full, as they rise in baking.

The oven must only be of a moderate heat, as they bake quickly; they take ¼ of an hour to bake. Serve hot upon a napkin.[293]

CHEESE PUDDING

☛ Remove the crusts, break stale bread in small pieces, put a layer in your baking dish, a layer of cheese broken small, salt and pepper. Continue until you have two layers, putting bits of butter between and over. Beat two eggs, add a pint of milk and pour over the bread; let stand awhile, then bake till firm; bake slowly.[294]

CHEESE SALAD

☛ 1 pint stiff whipped cream.
1 cup grated cheese.
1 package gelatine.
½ pimento.
½ green pepper.
Juice of 1 lemon.
¼ teaspoon salt.

Soak gelatine in a little cold water, then mix all together. Place in mold to congeal. Turn out on platter of lettuce. Serve with mayonnaise.[295]

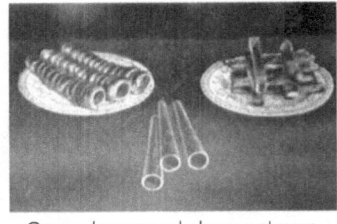

Cream horns and cheese straws.

CHEESE BALLS

☛ One cup of grated cheese, season with salt, cayenne and Worcester sauce, one teaspoonful of flour in the cheese. Beat two whites stiff to moisten the mixture. Make into small balls, roll in bread crumbs and drop in deep boiling fat. They swell very much. Fine.[296]

CONFEDERATE CHEESE PIE

☛ Put a small cupful of grated cheese into a sauce pan with a cupful of milk and a small piece of butter. When melted, add a cupful of bread crumbs, two beaten eggs, and a little salt. Pour into a buttered pie plate and bake until brown.[297]

CHEESE OMELET

☛ Stir 1 teacup of bread-crumbs into 1 pint of scalded milk. Add butter the size of an egg, a little salt, and ½ cup grated cheese. Then add 3 eggs beaten separately. Bake 15 or 20 minutes in a hot oven.[298]

CHEESE SOUFFLE

☛ ½ pound of cheese, grated,
3 eggs,
1 cup of milk,
2 even tablespoons of butter,
1 heaping tablespoon of flour,
½ teaspoon of salt.

Make a sauce of the butter, flour, and milk. Add the cheese and salt; lastly, the yolks of the eggs, well beaten. When cold, and just before baking, add the well beaten whites; put into small buttered shells, and place in shallow pans with water. Bake 20 minutes.[299]

CHEESE AND EGG TOAST
☛ Put one cupful cheese crumbs in half pint of sweet milk and boil until melted; add two eggs well beaten, with butter, pepper and salt to taste. Stir rapidly a few minutes; take from the fire; have ready the bread toasted, and the slices cut in quarters. Pour the cheese on and serve at once.[300]

CHEESE TOAST
☛ Crumb three biscuits, or slices of light bread in a baking dish. Break over it a quarter of a pound of nice fresh cheese.

Pour over it one cup of boiling water, slightly salted, and bake quickly.[301]

CONFEDERATE CHEESE TOAST
☛ Dissolve a half pound of cheese in a teacup of hot water; grate a quarter of a pound of stale bread over the cheese and bake ten minutes.[302]

CHEESE TOAST WITH MILK
☛ Place alternate layers of grated cheese and bread in a baking dish, pour over it fresh sweet milk to cover and break over the top a teaspoonful of butter. Bake ten minutes. Serve hot.[303]

REBEL CHEESED CRACKERS
☛ Snow flakes, or any other dry crackers can be made more palatable this way: Spread the butter on them and sprinkle with grated cheese; put in a hot oven and slightly brown. Serve cold. They are nice with after dinner coffee, or for lunch.[304]

CHEESE STICKS
☛ Make the finest pastry—1 pound of flour makes a good-sized dish. Roll the pastry about ⅓ or ½ inch thick. Cut accurately in sticks 5 inches long and ⅔ of an inch wide. Sprinkle heavily with finely grated cheese and bake a light brown.[305]

CHEESE STRAWS
☛   8 tablespoons of flour,
    8 tablespoons of grated cheese,
    4 tablespoons of butter,
    1 teaspoon of baking-powder,
    1 egg,
    Pinch of cayenne pepper and salt.
    Roll *very thin* and cut into straws.[306]

SARDINE RAREBIT

☞ Drain and broil sardines carefully, arrange on slices of bread toasted on one side. Melt two tablespoonfuls of butter and half a pound of cheese broken in bits and stir constantly. Beat the yolk of an egg, dilute with two-thirds of a cup of cream, add to the cheese and stir until smooth and slightly thickened. Season with salt, paprika and a little Tabasco sauce. Pour over the sardines and serve at once.[307]

WELSH RAREBIT 1

☞ Half a pound of cream cheese cut in small pieces. Put a large tablespoonful of butter in your chafing dish. When hot put in the cheese and put over the cover. Have ready a beaten egg. Put a teaspoonful of Worcester in a wine glass, fill with ale or beer. When the cheese melts turn in the beer; stir until smooth, and let cook until a little thick. Pour on toasted bread.[308]

WELSH RAREBIT 2

☞ To ½ pound of cheese, cut fine, add 1 dessertspoon of butter; let it melt in a chafing-dish; add dust of nutmeg, cayenne pepper, mustard, ⅔ of a wine-glass of wine. Toast the bread on one side, and spread with the rarebit while hot.[309]

FROZEN CHEESE

☞ Two Neuchatel cheese mashed to a smooth paste with a cup of whipped cream, add half a cup of chopped olives, Spanish pimentos, salt and lemon juice to season. Dissolve a teaspoonful of granulated gelatine and add to the mixture. Pour in a baking powder tin can, cover with a piece of paper, put on top and bury in ice and salt. Let stand several hours. Serve with a vegetable salad and toasted wafers.[310]

Ice shaver.

MASSA'S CHEESE CROQUETTES

☞ 3 tablespoonsful shortening,
   ¼ teaspoon paprika,
   ⅓ cup bread flour,
   ¼ teaspoon mustard,
   1 cup hot milk,
   Few grains cayenne,
   ¼ teaspoon salt,
   1 cup cheese cut fine.

Melt shortening, add flour; add hot milk, and stir until smooth and thick; add seasonings and cheese, and pour into a shallow dish to cool. Shape into small pyramids, roll in sifted crumbs, dip in egg, and again in crumbs, and fry in deep fat until brown. Serve immediately.[311]

CHEESE CHIPS

☛ One full cup grated American cheese, butter size of an egg, pinch of salt and cayenne pepper to taste. One cup of flour, sufficient water to make into pastry. Roll very thin, cut in narrow strips and bake in a hot oven on tins or buttered paper.[312]

CHEESE MOUSSE

☛ 1 pint cream.
1 package gelatine.
1 lemon (juice).
Salt to taste.
1 cup grated cheese.
Cayenne pepper to taste.
2 green peppers.
Whip cream and when nearly stiff add lemon juice; then whip stiff. Put in peppers ground fine (through meat chopper) and cheese; add salt and pepper to taste. Then fold in gelatine (softened in a little cold water and dissolved over hot). Set in ice box to cool, serve with mayonnaise and lettuce.[313]

MEXICAN ENCHILADAS

☛ First: To make the tortillas for the enchiladas, take 1 qt. blue corn meal mixed with water and salt, making a batter stiff enough to flatten out into round cakes, and bake on the bare hot lid. Second: To make the chili sauce: 1 cup tepid water, 3 tablespoons ground chili; let boil down to a batter. Third: To make filling: grated cheese and chopped onions very fine. Dip into a pan of boiling hot lard 1 tortilla, then dip this tortilla into the Chili batter, then sprinkle with the filling, first the cheese and then the onion; then put on 1 spoon Chili batter, and lay like a layer cake as many cakes as desired, then pour over the Chili batter. Cut like cake and serve hot.[314]

CHEESE RAMEQUINS

☛ Four tablespoons grated cheese, ½ cup milk, 2 ounces bread (two slices), yolks of 2 eggs, 1 tablespoon butter, 1 teaspoon mustard, ½ teaspoon salt, pinch of cayenne, whites of 2 or 3 eggs, boil milk and bread till smooth, add cheese and butter and cook 1 minute. Remove from fire, season, add yolks and whites which have been beaten to a stiff froth. Put into a greased baking dish, or individual ones, bake 15 min. in quick oven.[315]

CHEESE BLOCKS

☛ Two ounces of cheese, grated, two ounces of butter, fresh, two ounces of flour, season to taste with salt, cayenne, pounded mace and form a stiff paste. Roll out thin as possible, then cut part of it into strips, or straws, about four inches long and not more than the third of an inch wide, and stamp out the remainder into rings about an inch in diameter. Place both straws and rings on a greased baking tin and bake for a few minutes in a brisk oven until colored. When quite cold, put into each ring as many straws as each will hold, and serve tastefully arranged on a pretty dish paper, and garnished here and there with tiny sprigs of fresh parsley.[316]

"He who works with all his strength on the development of our knowledge of food and nutrition, and who also persistently strives to apply the results of investigation, is working on a broad basis for the development of mankind."

Franciscus Cornelius Donders
Dutch physician, 1818-1889

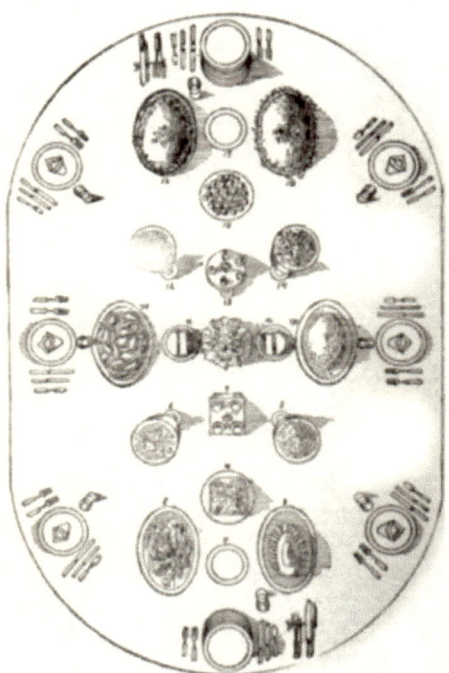

Winter lunch table setting for eight.

6. Croquettes

CROQUETTE MAKING TIPS

☞ In frying croquettes and things of a similar nature Wesson oil is very satisfactory. It can be raised to a high degree of heat without burning and strained and used again and again. It comes in quart cans. All croquettes are practically the same, made of thick white sauce. Use bread crumbs, not crackers, for crumbing, and to each egg to dip them in add one tablespoonful of hot water.[317]

CROQUETTES

☞ This receipt will answer for all kinds of croquettes. Never grind the meat, but chop fine sufficient cold meat to make a quart. Rub together two tablespoonfuls of butter and four rounding tablespoonfuls of flour; add them to a pint of hot milk or use half stock, the water the chicken was boiled in. Stir and cook to a smooth thick paste. Then take from the fire and add the meat. Season with two level teaspoonfuls or more of salt, a teaspoonful of white pepper, dash of cayenne, two tablespoonfuls of chopped parsley, a little nutmeg, one tablespoonful of onion juice. Mix thoroughly with the cream sauce before adding the meat, and turn on a flat dish to cool. When cold and stiff make as directed.

Croquettes.

In making sauces always put in your liquid cold to prevent lumping.[318]

CHICKEN CROQUETTES

☞ Cook a four pound fowl in boiling water salted, with four slices of carrot, four slices of onion, sprig of parsley, half a bay leaf, piece of lemon rind. Cook the fowl until tender, remove the chicken and strain the stock; then boil stock down to three cups, cool, and remove fat. Remove the flesh from the bones, discarding skin, and chop very fine and mix with white sauce. Season with salt, cayenne and a little nutmeg. Finish as directed.[319]

SWEETBREAD AND CHICKEN CROQUETTES

☛ For nine croquettes and one and a half pints chicken salad, or thirteen croquettes, take one four pound chicken, one small onion, one bay leaf, one pair sweetbreads, four whole cloves, one sprig of parsley. Put the chicken on in boiling water, add the above seasonings, cover and cook slowly until the meat is very tender. While this is cooking prepare the sweetbreads, trimming the fat and pipes off, soak fifteen minutes in cold water, drain, and cover with boiling water. Add one teaspoonful of salt and let simmer twenty minutes. Never let them boil; it ruins them. When done throw in cold water, remove the fibrous skin and pull in small pieces. When the chicken is done remove skin and bones, put back in the kettle, add salt, and simmer longer. Then chop very fine. Mix with the sweetbreads. Then mix with a white sauce and finish as directed.[320]

Chestnut croquettes.

SWEETBREAD AND MUSHROOM CROQUETTES

☛ Simmer a pair of sweetbreads, chop fine with a silver knife (steel spoils flavor), two tablespoonfuls of mushrooms chopped very fine. Mix with this sauce: One tablespoonful of butter, two of flour, cooked together. Add half a cup of cream. When very thick remove, add five drops of onion juice, little nutmeg, little chopped parsley, salt and pepper to season. Add sweetbreads and mushrooms. Let get very cold and mold. Blanched almonds may be added. Serve with French peas.[321]

CHEESE CROQUETTES

☛ Make a white sauce of one cup of milk, one tablespoonful each of flour and butter. When thick add a cup of grated cheese, salt and cayenne. Now add half a cup of cheese cut in small pieces, yolks of two eggs. Put in the saucepan. Finish as directed. Serve with a green vegetable.[322]

EGG CROQUETTES

☛ For 6 croquettes take
    6 eggs,
    1 pint milk,
    1 tablespoon butter,

1 tablespoon flour,
1 tablespoon chopped parsley,
10 drops onion juice,
1 teaspoon salt,
1 teaspoon pepper.

Boil eggs hard and drop in cold water, and, after removing shells, squeeze through potato-masher. Boil the milk, and add the flour and butter, which have been well mixed, then add other ingredients. Turn in a platter to cool. Let the mixture stand 3 hours. Shape and drop in egg and breadcrumbs and fry in boiling fat.[323]

OYSTER CROQUETTES

☛ Parboil and drain one pint of oysters. Cut them in quarters and mix in a cream sauce enough to hold them together. Season with salt and pepper. Finish as directed.[324]

Wire oyster fork.

FISH CROQUETTES

☛ Some cold boiled fish, from which all bone, skin and fat has been removed, chopped fine, one-third as much mashed Irish potatoes rubbed to a cream with a little butter; some thick white sauce with an egg in it; season with salt, pepper and anchovy sauce. Mix thoroughly, roll into shape, and finish as all croquettes.[325]

HAM CROQUETTES

☛ To each cup of cold ham chopped very fine take a cup of milk and two tablespoonfuls of bread crumbs. Cook to a smooth paste. Season with grated onion and chopped parsley. Add the yolk of an egg. When cold finish as other croquettes.[326]

POTATO CROQUETTES 1

☛ Two cups of seasoned and mashed potatoes. Add one and a half tablespoonfuls of butter, yolk of two eggs, one tablespoonful of chopped parsley, a little nutmeg and cayenne. Stir over the fire until it leaves the sides of the pan. Let get cold and form into small cylinder croquettes. Egg and crumb. Then fry in hot fat.[327]

POTATO CROQUETTES 2

☛ Two cups of mashed potatoes, two tablespoonfuls of cream, one teaspoonful of grated onion, salt to season, grating of nutmeg, yolks of two eggs, one tablespoonful chopped parsley, small tablespoonful of butter, dash of cayenne. Add the beaten yolks to the potatoes; then add the other ingredients; mix and turn into a saucepan. Stir over the fire until it leaves the sides. Set aside to cool; then form into cylinders. Roll first in egg, then in crumbs, and fry in very hot fat.[328]

PLAIN RICE CROQUETTES

☛ One and a half cups of rice; cover with cold water and bring quickly to the boiling point; let boil five minutes; drain; put in a double boiler with a cup each of hot water and hot milk; cook until the liquid is absorbed; stir in the beaten yolks of two eggs or one whole egg, little salt and two tablespoonfuls of butter. Let get cold and finish as other croquettes.[329]

POTATO CROQUETTES STUFFED

☛ Boil eight Irish potatoes, drain and mash, put in two yolks, a little salt and nutmeg, one teaspoonful of butter. Mix altogether thoroughly. Form into round balls. Make a hole in the center with your finger and fill with thick tomato sauce or asparagus tips. Close the openings and roll in egg batter, then in crumbs. Fry in very hot fat.[330]

Horse-powered gin distillery.

Icing decoration ideas for desserts.

7. Desserts

CONFEDERATE JUMBLES
☞ One and a half cups white sugar, three-fourths cup butter, three eggs, three table-spoons sweet milk, half tea-spoon soda and one of cream tartar; mix with sufficient flour to roll; roll and sprinkle with sugar; cut out and bake.[331]

NASHVILLE PEPPER-NUTS
☞ One pound sugar, five eggs, half pound butter, half tea-cup milk, two tea-spoons baking powder, flour enough to roll.[332]

DIXIE PUDDING
☞ 1 pint bread-crumbs,
   1 quart milk,
   1 tablespoon sugar,
   Yolks of 6 eggs.

Stir the bread-crumbs into the boiling milk, add the sugar and well-beaten yolks. Flavor with vanilla and bake till it begins to thicken. Add 2 cups of sugar to the 6 whites which have been well beaten. Cover the top of pudding with acid jelly and spread on the meringue and stick almonds here and there on the top. Let it brown and serve cold with cream or sauce. A little wine may be used by leaving out the same quantity of milk.[333]

Cornstarch pudding garnished with pansies.

CONFEDERATE CAKES
☞ One pound of flour mixed with a quarter of a pound of butter. Three quarters of a pound of sugar beaten with two eggs. Flavor with rose-water and brandy and spice. Make the whole into a soft dough, and bake in small cakes.[334]

DIXIE CREAM PUFFS
☞ Five eggs, whites and yolks beaten separately, one and a half cups each of white sugar and sifted flour, two tea-spoons baking powder in the flour; bake in tea-cups, filling about half full. The cream is prepared by placing a small tin pail containing a pint sweet milk in a kettle of boiling water; beat the whites and yolks of two eggs separately; stir in the milk while boiling, a half tea-cup sugar, a large table-spoon corn starch dissolved in a little sweet milk, then the beaten yolks and a piece of butter the size of a large walnut; flavor with lemon or vanilla. When done, cut the cakes open, put in a spoonful of the cream, place together again, roll in the whites, and then in coarse granulated sugar.[335]

JEFF DAVIS PUDDING
☞ 3 eggs,
2½ teacups of sugar,
1 teacup of cream,
1 small cup of butter,
3 tablespoons of flour.
Season with lemon or nutmeg.[336]

JEFFERSON DAVIS JUMBLES
☞ One teacupful of grated loaf-sugar, one cup of butter, and the white of one egg beaten light. Mix to a tolerably stiff dough with flour, and if you like, add a tablespoonful of thick cream, and as much soda as will lie on a sixpence. Roll the dough in thin sheets, and cut in round cakes or rings. Dip the cakes in grated loaf-sugar before baking.[337]

GENERAL STONEWALL JACKSON JUMBLES
☞ A teacupful of sugar, one of butter, one of sour cream, three eggs, and a teaspoonful of soda, stirred into sufficient flour to make a soft dough. Bake in a quick oven.[338]

STONEWALL JACKSON PUDDING
☞ Pare, core and slice in a deep pudding dish a thick layer of juicy, tart apples; cover with a layer of sugar, then a layer of cake sliced thin (stale cake is best); continue alternating apples, sugar and cake until the dish is heaping full, having a layer of apples on top. Pour on a cup of cold water and cover with rich pie crust. Bake in a slow oven until the apples are thoroughly cooked; turn out on a platter so that the crust is underneath; put small lumps of butter over top of pudding and serve hot with hard sauce or sweetened cream.[339]

LADY LEE PUDDING
☞ 1 cup of suet, chopped fine,
1 cup of molasses,
1 cup of milk, with teaspoon of soda,

1 cup of raisins, currants, and citron, mixed,
2½ cups of flour.
Boil 3 hours.[340]

UNITED DAUGHTERS OF THE CONFEDERACY PUDDING
☛ One cup of finely chopped crystallized pineapple,
One cup of finely chopped crystallized cherries,
One cup of finely chopped nuts,
Six eggs.
Add a tablespoonful of sugar to each egg, beat well, leaving out the whites. To the yolks and sugar add one cup of sherry wine and cook to a thick custard in double boiler. To the custard while hot add one tablespoonful of gelatine dissolved in one-half cup of water, then whip in lightly the beaten whites. Roll out macaroons or Social Teas into dust. Into a bowl begin to lay cracker dust, pineapple, nuts and cherries. When you have used half the ingredients, pour over it the other half of the

Pudding molds.

fruits and custard, sprinkling the top with cracker dust. Put into refrigerator to congeal. Serve with whipped cream (no sugar or flavoring in cream).[341]

SONS OF CONFEDERATE VETERANS BLUEGRASS CAKE
☛ Two cups each of butter and corn-starch, three of sugar, one of sweet milk, six of flour, whites of fourteen eggs, one tea-spoon soda, two tea-spoons cream of tartar. Cream the butter and sugar well, add the milk, then the corn-starch, sift the cream of tartar in the flour (stirring it well together), add the flour and well-beaten whites alternately, bake in a loaf. When it is done and cold, with a long knife cut it through the middle, make an icing of one-half cup of sugar and just enough water to dissolve sugar, boil until it will spin a thread in dropping from a spoon, then stir in the well-beaten whites of four eggs, flavor to taste; take one pound of fresh figs, one pound of raisins, and one pound of almonds or hickory-nuts, chop the fruit very fine, blanch the almonds or prepare the hickory-nut meats, chop slightly, and stir all in the icing; put a layer between the cake, and on top and all over the side. This is a delicious cake.[342]

SOUTHERN RIGHTS CAKE
☛ Three eggs, one tea-cup sugar, one of butter, two of flour, scant half cup New Orleans molasses, half a table-spoon each of cinnamon, sifted ginger and allspice, half a tea-spoon soda, half a wineglass brandy, cream, sugar and butter; beat spices and yolks of eggs together, dissolve soda in

molasses, whip whites to a froth, and add last, a little at a time, alternating with the flour. (Best baked in small pans and frosted.)[343]

SOUTHERN SEED CAKE
☛ Cream, one cup sugar, and one-third cup butter; add yolks of two eggs, one-half cup sweet milk, two tea-spoons baking-powder sifted in two cups flour, one table-spoon caraway seed, one grated nutmeg and well-beaten whites. This has been tried and approved in our family for years.[344]

NORTH CAROLINA JUMBLES
☛ One pound of flour, the same of sugar, and an equal quantity of butter. Mix these ingredients with three well-beaten eggs, a wineglassful of rose-water, and some essence of lemon.
Roll into thin sheets, and cut in rings, and dip in loaf-sugar before baking.[345]

MAMMY'S SWEET POTATO PUDDING
☛ Grate three medium sized potatoes. Beat together one cup of sugar, three eggs, one tablespoonful of butter, one pint of milk, and add to the grated potato.
Pour in a buttered pan, drop bits of butter on top and bake one hour in a moderate oven. Flavor with one teaspoonful of vanilla.[346]

UNITED CONFEDERATE VETERANS CHOCOLATE
☛ Brake up two squares of Bakers Chocolate in a sauce pan with one cup boiling water, third cup sugar, let it melt, then add another cup of water and one pint milk, put in a double boiler and let boil, mix a teaspoon corn starch in half cup milk and when chocolate is boiling mix in the corn starch and let boil again, beat an egg with the Dover and half cup hot water, but not hot enough to cook, and beat until it foams well, place half in a pitcher with three drops vanilla, strain in the chocolate slowly, add remaining foam and serve with ginger nuts or light cake.[347]

The Dover egg beater.

ICED CHOCOLATE
☛ Is made of all milk, fill glasses half full of crushed ice, pour in the cold chocolate, and put whipped cream on top, serve with light cake.[348]

GRANOLA CAKE
☛ Take 1½ cups granola; 2 cups milk, yolk of 1 egg, 1 teaspoon sugar, little salt. Beat well before baking.[349]

BIVEAU CREAM

☛ Boil
1 pint of water,
1 ounce of gelatine,
¼ of a vanilla bean,
½ pound of sugar.
When the mixture is almost cold, stir in 3 pints of thick cream, whipped to a stiff froth.[350]

ITALIAN CREAM

☛ Beat the yolks of six eggs till very light and smooth; stir into them gradually a pint of wine, and let it set for hall an hour; then stir in half a pound of powdered sugar, the juice and grated peel of one orange and one lemon, and let it again for half an hour, after which stir in a quart of rich sweet cream, beat it light, serve it in glasses, and crown them with whipped cream. These cold creams, as they are called, are plain, nice, fashionable and easily prepared. They are eaten with tarts, sweetmeats and cake.[351]

BREAKFAST CREAM CAKE

☛ Four eggs beat light, one gill of cream to a tea-cup of sweet milk, one pint of four, sifted, half teaspoonful of salt; mix cream, milk, and eggs together, well stirred, then add flour gradually until thoroughly mixed. Have your baking cups hot when put to bake. Requires ten minutes to bake in hot oven.[352]

GENERAL LEE JELLY CAKE

☛ 10 eggs, 1 pound of sugar, ½ pound of flour, the grated rind of 1 lemon and half the juice; mix as for sponge cake, and bake in jelly tins. Take the whites of 2 eggs, 1 pound of sugar, the grated rind and juice of 1 orange, and half of the juice of the lemon. Stir the eggs around one way very briskly; when light, add the sugar by degrees, until it is all mixed; then put in the orange and the lemon. Before the cakes are perfectly cold, spread them with this icing, putting one layer of cake on another. This quantity will make 2 cakes.[353]

CAKE PYRAMID

☛ A pyramid of cake is introduced only at the finest suppers. Make them all of common poundcake, or have every cake of a different quality, if you choose. The pans in which they are baked should all be of a circular form, gradually diminishing in circumference, from the largest to the smallest size. Ice them very white, and when they get about half dry, put

Cake spoon.

round each a decorament of devices and borders in white sugar, or a very delicate garland or festoon. When the icing gets perfectly dry, stack them regularly, putting the largest at the bottom, and the smallest on the top, and stick a small bunch of real or artificial flowers on the pinnacle, or top cake.[354]

PEACH COBBLER

☛ Peel the peaches (freestones) and make a pastry the same way as for pie, and roll out the dough as thin as for pie crust. Put one layer at the bottom of the dish, and cut the peaches into pieces the size of a plum and fill the dish with them, sprinkling them freely with fine sugar. Cover them over with another layer of pastry, cut with a knife two or three air-holes on the top and put to bake. Let it bake brown. It makes a delicious luncheon or dessert. Season the peaches with powdered cinnamon to taste.[355]

"When mother bakes strawberry shortcake."

HOW TO MAKE FROSTING

☛ Two cups of sugar and water to moisten. Let stand till it dissolves; boil slowly without stirring until it threads from the spoon. Beat the whites of two eggs to a stiff froth, when syrup is slightly cooled, stir in gradually, and beat until cold; season to taste with vanilla, lemon or what you prefer.[356]

TENNESSEE CAKE

☛ One pint sifted meal, half a pint flour, eight eggs, half a pound each butter and sugar; nutmeg and cinnamon to taste. Beat butter and sugar together, add eggs, then meal and flour gradually. Beat all well, and bake an hour and a half. To be eaten soon after baking.[357]

STRAWBERRY SHORT CAKE

☛ For the pastry: One pint of flour, sifted with one light teaspoonful of baking powder; quarter pound of lard, level teaspoonful salt, and cold water to make a moderately soft dough, mixing quickly with a spoon and working as little as possible. The lard and flour should be rubbed together until smooth before mixing. Divide the dough in two parts, roll out thin, and bake in square or long pans. Remove carefully from the pans to cool.

Or, make the pastry without baking powder as follows: sift half pound of flour with level teaspoonful salt; add a quarter pound of lard, cutting it in and mixing it thoroughly with a spoon, then enough ice water to make a stiff dough. Roll out thin, fold and roll again. Divide and bake in two crusts, using a square or long pan, and letting the dough come up on the sides of the pans an inch, to form a rim on the crust.

Cap, wash and sweeten to taste two quarts of ripe berries.

Whip to a froth with a syllabub churn, one quart of cream sweetened with a teacupful of sugar, removing the whipped cream as it rises to a sieve over another vessel.

When ready to serve, place a crust on a flat surface and spread with half the berries; on top of this place the other crust, and spread with the rest of the berries; cut into four inch squares; place each square on a dessert or tea plate, and cover the top with a large spoonful of whipped cream.[358]

DANISH PUDDING

☛ One cup tapioca, 3 pts. water, ½ teaspoon salt, ½ teacup sugar, 1 tumbler of any kind bright jelly.

Wash the tapioca, soak over night in the water; in the morning put on in the double boiler, cook 1 hour, stir often; add the salt, sugar, and jelly and mix thoroughly; turn into a mold that has been dipped in cold water and set aside to harden; serve with cream and sugar.[359]

SOFT MOLASSES COOKIES

☛ One cup of molasses, one tablespoonful of ginger, one teaspoonful of soda, two tablespoonfuls warm water, half a cup of creamed butter, flour for a soft dough. Mix in the order given. Dissolve the soda in the water. Roll one-third of an inch thick, cut and bake.[360]

MOLASSES PIE

☛ One teacupful of sugar, one teacupful of molasses, four eggs beaten separately, two table-spoonfuls of butter.[361]

BUTTERMILK ICE CREAM

☛ Equal quantities of fresh buttermilk (which has had no water added to it in churning) and sweet milk, sweetened to taste and flavored with vanilla. Freeze until hard.[362]

CHOCOLATE SYRUP FOR VANILLA ICE CREAM

☛ One ounce of chocolate, three tablespoonfuls of sugar, one cup of boiling water, two inches of stick cinnamon, two cups of sugar less the three tablespoonfuls put in the chocolate, one teaspoonful of vanilla. Melt the chocolate over hot water; add three tablespoonfuls of sugar and slowly the cup of boiling water.

When smooth and glossy, add the rest of the sugar and cinnamon. Stir until it boils.

Let boil five minutes, strain and cool; then add the vanilla. Serve with ice cream.[363]

ENGLISH CHRISTMAS PUDDING

☛ One and one-half cups Graham flour, ½ cup brown sugar, ¼ cup butter, ½ cup sweet milk, 1 egg, 1 teaspoon baking powder, 1 cup raisins seeded. Flavor to taste and steam 2 hours.[364]

CHOCOLATE BAVARIAN CREAM

☛ Cover ½ box of gelatine with ½ teacup of water and let it soak 20 minutes. Whip 1 pint of cream. Grate ounces of chocolate and boil in 1 pint of sweet milk. Add the gelatine and stir till dissolved. Take from the fire and sweeten with ½ cup of sugar; flavor with vanilla and turn into a pan to cool. Stir till it begins to thicken, then add the whipped cream. Stir till mixed, and pour in a bowl to harden. Serve with whipped cream.[365]

BAVARIAN CREAM WITH ALMONDS

☛ Blanch 3 ounces of sweet and 1 ounce of bitter almonds, and skin them. Put them in a pan on a moderate fire, stirring constantly. As soon as they have acquired a fine yellow color, take off and let get cold. Pound them into fine pieces. Then add 1 pint of cream, nearly boiling, 2 or 3 tablespoons of sugar, ½ package of gelatine, previously washed in cup of cold water. Put upon the ice, and when ready to thicken stir till smooth. Have ready 1 pint of cream; whip and then stir it in; put into a mold and surround with ice.[366]

Ice cream molds.

CHEESE ICE CREAM

☛ Take 3 cream cheeses and mix thoroughly with 1 quart of cream, adding 1 tablespoon vanilla and 10 heaping tablespoons sugar. Then freeze like ice cream. If not liked so rich take 1 pint cream and 1 pint milk, in place of all cream.[367]

SCOTCH CAKES

☛ Sift into a deep pan three pints of flour, sprinkle in a salt-spoon of salt, a spoonful of powdered cinnamon, one of mace, and three quarters of a pound of powdered sugar. Cut up three quarters of a pound of butter into small bits, and rub them into the flour, etc., with your hands, till it is completely saturated. Dissolve a teaspoonful of saleratus in a large spoonful of boiling vinegar, pour in enough sour milk to make the whole into good paste. Mix it very well, and knead it a little. Put it on your paste board, roll it into a round or circular form, about an inch thick; cut it across into four equal parts, crimp or notch them neatly round the edges; ice them with tart icing, and bake them in rather a quick oven.[368]

SCOTCH PUDDING

☞ 12 small sponge cakes, grated,
5 eggs,
1 teacup of currants,
1 teacup of raisins, cut fine,
1 teacup of sugar,
1 tablespoon of butter,
3 tablespoons of marmalade,
1 teacup of cream.

Cook 15 or 20 minutes. When pudding is nearly done, stick it with a knife in several places, and pour over it a glass of wine. To be served with or without sauce.[369]

SOUTHERN FRUIT CAKE

☞ One cupful each of butter, sugar and molasses, one-half cupful of sour cream, three cupfuls of flour, three eggs, yolks and whites beaten separately, one teaspoonful of cinnamon, one-half teaspoonful each of cloves and allspice, and one-fourth of a nutmeg, grated, one-half pint of seeded raisins, one-half cup of currants, one-half teaspoonful of soda. Mix in order named; dissolve soda in one tablespoonful of hot water and add last. Bake in slow oven. Delicious.[370]

WHITE CHARLOTTE

Charlotte mold.

☞ One quart of heavy cream, one quart of sweet milk, whites of eight eggs, two teacupsful of sugar, one half ounce of gelatine, one half teacupful of sherry wine, and teaspoonful each of vanilla and lemon. Soak the gelatine in half teacupful of cold water, half an hour, then set the vessel containing the gelatine on the cap of the stove or range, and when it is thoroughly dissolved, set aside to cool.

Add the wine, extract and one cup of sugar to the milk and cream, and churn as for syllabub, removing the whipped cream to another vessel as it rises. Beat the whites of the eggs to a stiff froth and add to them the other cup of sugar. When the gelatine is nearly congealed mix the eggs and whipped cream, then add the gelatine; whip just enough to mix, pour in molds, and keep in a cool place until ready to serve.[371]

THANKSGIVING FRUIT CAKE

☞ Six pounds flour, three of butter, three and a half of sugar, an ounce mace, two glasses wine, two glasses brandy, four pounds raisins, half pound citron, six eggs, one pint yeast, small tea-spoon soda put in at last moment. After tea, take all the flour (except one plate for dredging raisins), a small piece butter, and a quart or more of milk, and mix like biscuit; then mix butter and sugar, and at nine o'clock in the evening, if sufficiently light, put one-third of butter and sugar into dough; at twelve add another third, and very early in the morning the remainder; about eleven o'clock, if light enough, begin kneading, and continue for an hour, adding meanwhile all the other ingredients. This will make seven loaves.[372]

CHARLOTTE RUSSE PUDDING

☞ Five eggs beaten separately, one pint of milk, half a cup of flour. Beat the yolks; add the flour and milk alternately; then stir in the stiff whites and a little salt. Serve hot with hard sauce.[373]

LADIES' CAKE

☞ Two pounds of flour, half a pound of sugar, half a pound of butter, one pint of milk, three eggs, and a little yeast. Mix part of the flour, milk, and yeast together, and let them stand till light; then stir in the butter, eggs, and sugar, and let them rise till very light. This cake will require five hours to rise. Bake in pans.[374]

SCOTCH CAKE

☞ Make into a dough three-quarters of a pound of butter, a pound of sifted flour, a pound of sugar, and three well-beaten eggs; flavor with cinnamon. Roll into small, thin sheets, and cut into round cakes, and bake in a quick oven.[375]

ORDER OF CONFEDERATE ROSE SPONGE PUDDING

Charlotte russe made with lady's fingers.

☞ Boil one pint of sweet milk, thicken with two ounces of flour wet in a little cold milk. When the mixture becomes thick stir in two ounces of sugar and two ounces of butter. Remove and put in six eggs beaten separately. Put in a baking dish and set in a dish of water and bake until firm; it takes three-fourths of an hour. Serve with liquid or cocoanut snow sauce. Fine.[376]

CREAM BOULET

☞ Take 5 pts. new milk, 6 eggs; beat the yolks, add 2 cups brown sugar, brown 1 cup sugar, stirring until all is dissolved; add the milk to the burnt sugar, let it come to a boil, beat the whites to a stiff froth and add to the beaten yolks and sugar, let all boil up once and pour off; dissolve 2 tablespoons gelatine, and put in; season with vanilla; when cool freeze.[377]

WHITE SPONGE CAKE

☛ Whites of twenty eggs, two goblets of flour, three of sugar, two teaspoonfuls of lemon, one of cream of tartar; barely stir flour in; bake quickly. This is the premium cake at the Bourbon [Kentucky] fair.[378]

SOUTHERN HERITAGE CORN PUDDING

☛ Take one dozen ears of corn and grate from the cob. Beat four eggs light and add a pint of sweet milk and a tablespoonful of butter, salting and peppering to taste. Beat lightly, place in a deep dish and bake in a hot oven. Ten minutes will bake it. Grease the dish with butter before putting pudding into it, and send to table in the dish it is baked in.[379]

Cornstarch pudding in layers.

BLUE GRASS CORN PUDDING

☛ 8 ears of corn,
1 tablespoon of butter,
1 teacup of milk,
1 teaspoon of flour,
Salt and pepper to taste,
3 eggs.

Grate the corn and scrape cob with a knife. Beat the eggs light and stir in cream, butter, and flour, and mix with the milk and add the corn. Season and bake ¾ of an hour.[380]

AUGUSTA PUDDING

☛ Nine tablespoonfuls of flour, ten eggs, and one quart of milk. Boil the milk, and pour over the flour, and let it stand till it is cool, and then put in the eggs, which have been beaten separately and very light. Bake it in a tin mold or dish, and in a quick oven. Serve with cream sauce.[381]

MONTGOMERY PUDDING

☛ Take thin slices of sponge cake, and put into a deep dish until it is half full. Grate over the cake the rind of a lemon, squeeze the juice into the dish, and put in wine or brandy enough to moisten the cake well. Then make a custard, with milk, eggs, and sugar, and fill the dish, and set into a moderate oven and bake a light brown.

When it is done and cold, make an icing of whites of eggs and sugar, as for cake, and spread over the top of the pudding thickly, and brown it in the oven. Serve cold.[382]

BANANAS AND CREAM

☛ An especially nice way to serve bananas is to cut them in thin round slices; pour over them whipped cream, unflavored.[383]

CHOCOLATE ECLAIRS

☞ Make sponge cake and flavor with lemon,
Make a filling of 1 quart of new milk,
Yolks of 4 eggs.
Boil the milk and add the yolks with 4 tablespoons sugar. When the milk has boiled, pour it on the yolks, stirring rapidly all the time. After well mixed return to the fire. Make a paste of 3 spoons cornstarch and cold milk and stir into the custard. Cook till well thickened. Flavor with vanilla. Put a layer of this custard between the layers of cake. Cover the top with an icing made of 3 tablespoons chocolate, 6 of sugar, 2 of sweet cream, and a little butter.[384]

SPONGE CAKE

☞ Take one dozen eggs and put in scales as the balance for weighing an equal quantity of sugar. Then balance flour to the weight of six eggs. Beat the yolks of the dozen eggs with the sugar very light, then beat the whites very light and add to the other. Grate the peel of one lemon into it also, squeezing the juice in, and then stir the flour in lightly. Have your pans in readiness, grease with butter, and place white paper at bottom of pan. This should be done for all cakes. A sponge cake should not stand a second after made before it is baked. Bake in a medium oven, keeping heat at bottom.[385]

BLACK PUDDING

☞ 4 yolks of eggs,
1 teacup of sugar,
2 teacups of flour,
1 teacup of butter,
½ teacup of sour cream,
1 teacup of blackberry jam,
½ teaspoon soda,
Cinnamon, allspice, and cloves to taste.
Bake in pudding-pan or steam. Eat with white sauce seasoned with whisky.[386]

FLUMMERY

☞ One measure of jelly, one of cream, and half a one of wine; boil it fifteen minutes over a slow fire, stirring all the time; sweeten it, and add a spoonful of orange flower or rose water; cool it in a mold, turn it in a dish, and pour around it cream, seasoned in any way you like.[387]

BLUE GRASS PUDDING

☞ 1 coffeecup of molasses,
1 coffeecup of sour cream,
1 full teaspoon of soda,
1 coffeecup of beef suet,

4 cups of flour,
1 pound of raisins,
¼ pound of citron,
1 pound of apples, chopped fine,
½ nutmeg,
2 teaspoons of cinnamon, or spices to taste.

Mix molasses, cream, and soda and let it foam. Add suet, flour, raisins, citron having dredged them with flour apples, and spices. Grease mold well and let it steam 3 hours. Leave room for swelling. This quantity makes 2 puddings. Serve with sauce.[388]

STRAWBERRY PARFAIT
☛ Whip a quart of cream to a froth; add half a pint of strawberry juice and a cupful of sugar; turn carefully into an ice cream mold, press the lid down tightly, pack in salt and ice, and let freeze three hours.[389]

DEEP SOUTH CUPCAKES
☛ Pour four tablespoonfuls of boiling water on one teaspoonful of saleratus, let it stand to dissolve, and then stir it into a large teacup of sour milk; add a cup of butter and two of sugar. Beat four eggs light, stir them into the batter, etc., alternately with four cups of flour; add a powdered nutmeg and a glass of mixed brandy and wine, beat it till quite smooth, and bake it in little buttered pans, or in one large one, which you choose.[390]

CONFEDERATE CUPCAKES
☛ Mix together one cup of butter, two of sugar, three of flour, four beaten eggs, a spoonful of cinnamon and a few spoonfuls of rose or lemon brandy. Commingle it very well, and bake it in small buttered pans with moderate heat.[391]

COTTAGE PUDDING
☛ 3 eggs (3 whites, 2 yolks),
1 quart of flour,
1 pint of sugar,
½ pint of butter (heaping),
1 cup of new milk,
1 teaspoon of cream of tartar,
½ teaspoon of soda.

Beat whites of eggs to stiff froth. Season all with fresh lemon or whisky. Bake in buttered gem molds and serve with rich sauce for cottage pudding.[392]

TAPIOCA PUDDING
☛ Three-fourths of a cup of tapioca, one and a half pints boiling water, little salt. Put on and let simmer an hour. Stir well with a fork to prevent

burning, and cook until clear. Strain the juice from a quart of canned fruit. Mix the fruit with the tapioca. Sweeten the whole to taste. (Raspberries are nice in it. Use half a jar.) Serve cold with whipped cream sweetened and flavored with vanilla.[393]

TAPIOCA CUSTARD PUDDING

☛ One quart of hot milk, three-fourths of a cup of tapioca, three eggs, one teaspoonful of salt, one tablespoonful of butter, two teaspoonfuls of vanilla, one cup of sugar. Cook the tapioca in the hot milk until transparent. Beat the eggs slightly; add the sugar and salt; stir it in the tapioca; then put in the butter and vanilla. Bake half an hour in a slow oven.[394]

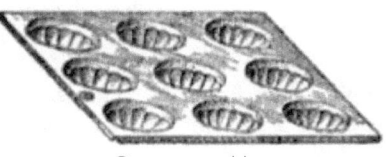

Gem pan molds.

TAPIOCA CREAM

☛ One pint of hot milk, one-third of a cup of tapioca, yolks of two eggs, half a teaspoonful of salt, teaspoonful of vanilla, whites of two eggs beaten stiff, half a cup of sugar. Stir the tapioca into the milk and let cook until transparent. Beat the yolks and sugar; add the salt and stir in the tapioca; add extract and fold in whites beaten dry. Delicious.[395]

VIRGINIA PUDDING

☛ Five eggs, reserving three whites for sauce; one pint of milk, one gill of cream or an ounce of butter, three tablespoonfuls of flour, a little salt; bake one half hour. Sauce: Beat the three whites to a froth with one half pound of sugar; flavor with wine or lemon. This is to be poured on the pudding just before serving. Serve cold.[396]

SPANISH CREAM

☛ ½ box of gelatine,
1 quart of milk,
Yolks of 3 eggs,
1 cup of sugar.

Soak the gelatine in the milk for an hour. Put on the stove and stir as it warms. Beat the yolks and sugar together and stir into the boiling milk. Flavor with vanilla. Pour into mold and serve with cream.[397]

CHOCOLATE MILK FLOAT

☛ 1 glass milk.
Chocolate sauce.
Vanilla ice cream.

Combine milk and chocolate sauce, add spoonful of ice cream to each glass and shake well.[398]

ALICE SNOW BALLS

☞ One pint of milk. Let come to a boil and stir in two full tablespoons of corn starch wet in a little cold milk, three medium sized tablespoons of sugar, little salt, stiff whites of three eggs. Cook the milk and corn starch thoroughly before adding eggs; then cook a moment longer. Pour out in cups. When cold turn out on a dish. Make a custard of the yolks to serve with it. Vanilla to flavor.[399]

SNOW PUDDING

☞ Dissolve ¼ box of gelatine in 2 cups of warm water. When cold, add ½ cup of sugar and grated peel and juice of 2 lemons. When it begins to harden, add whites of 5 eggs, well beaten. Beat thoroughly and turn into a mold. When cold, serve with a custard made of yolks of the eggs, 2 cups of milk, sugar, and flavoring to taste.[400]

SNOW FLAKES

☞ Grate a large cocoanut into a glass dish, and serve with cream, preserves, jellies or jams.[401]

LEMON PUDDING

☞ Grate the rind from six fresh lemons, squeeze the juice from three, and strain it; beat the yolks of sixteen eggs very light, put to them sixteen tablespoonsful of powdered loaf sugar, not heaped up—the same of melted butter; add the grated rind, and the juice, with four crackers finely pounded, or an equal quantity of rice flour; or for change, six ounces of corn meal, which is excellent—beat it till light, put a puff paste in your dish, pour the pudding in, and bake it in a moderate oven—it must not be very brown.[402]

Fluted cake pan.

CHERRY PUDDING

☞ Beat six eggs very light, add half a pint of milk, six ounces flour, eight ounces grated bread, twelve ounces suet, chopped fine, a little salt; when it is beat well, mix in eighteen ounces preserved cherries or damsins; bake or boil it. Make a sauce of melted butter, sugar and wine.[403]

PUMPKIN PUDDING

☞ Stew a fine sweet pumpkin till soft and dry; rub it through a sieve, mix with the pulp six eggs quite light, a quarter of a pound of butter, half a pint of new milk, some pounded ginger and nutmeg, a wine glass of brandy, and sugar to your taste. Should it be too liquid, stew it a little drier, put a paste round the edges, and in the bottom of a shallow dish or plate—pour in the mixture, cut some thin bits of paste, twist them, and lay them across the top, and bake it nicely.[404]

STEAMED WHITE PUDDING

☞ 1 pound of flour,
2 teaspoons of baking-powder, sifted with flour,
1 pound of raisins,
½ pound of butter,
½ pound of sugar,
4 eggs,
1 cup of new milk.

Flour raisins well with some of the 1 pound of flour. Season to taste and steam 3 hours.[405]

AMERICAN INDIAN BAKED PUDDING

☞ Stir into a cup of corn meal a little salt and two cups of boiling water. Beat until free from lumps. Beat light three eggs, one cup of molasses, one tablespoonful of softened butter, one teaspoonful of soda, ginger to taste. Stir in just enough mush to make a thick batter. Butter and heat a dozen patty pans; fill half full with the mixture; put a raisin on top of each; bake a nice brown. Turn out on a hot dish. Serve with hard sauce or with vanilla ice cream as sauce.[406]

AMERICAN INDIAN PUDDING

☞ Boil 1 cup of meal in 1 pint of milk till it thickens. Add ½ cup of sugar, ½ cup of molasses, 1 tablespoon of butter, 1 pint of cold milk, salt to taste. Steam and serve with hard sauce.[407]

EAST INDIAN PUDDING

☞ One cup of milk, three-fourths of a cup of flour sifted with a level teaspoonful of baking powder, three tablespoonfuls of butter, four eggs, four tablespoonfuls of minced preserved ginger, one tablespoonful of the syrup. Heat the milk, stir in the butter; when it boils stir in the dry flour, all at once.

Stir quickly to a smooth batter and turn out in a bowl to cool, quickly beating hard. When cold break in one egg at a time. Beat well before putting in another. Proceed until all the eggs are in. Dredge the minced ginger with flour before adding it. Last of all, put in the syrup. Butter a mold well, put in the batter and steam two hours. Serve with brandy sauce.[408]

ALMOND PUDDING

☞ Take three quarters of a pound of shelled sweet almonds, and two ounces of bitter ones, or peach kernels; scald and peel them, and throw them into a pan of cold water as you proceed.

Then pound them in a marble

Pudding molds.

mortar, adding a little orange flour, or rose water, to prevent them oiling or getting heavy; pound them to a perfect paste, removing them as you beat them.

Mix together three quarters of a pound of powdered sugar, half a pound of fresh butter, and beat it to a cream, adding a wine-glass of wine; then stir into it alternately and lightly the pounded almonds, and eight well beaten eggs.

Put the whole into a buttered dish, which has a broad, flat rim, lay round it, on the edge of the dish, a thin, narrow slip of puff paste, having one edge neatly serrated, notched or crimped; bake it in a moderate oven, and when cold, grate loaf sugar over it.[409]

TIPSY PARSON

☛ Moisten sponge cake with 1 cup of sherry wine. Make a custard of 1 pint of milk and yolks of 3 eggs. Pour over cake while hot.

Just before it goes to the table, stick it full of blanched almonds. Beat the whites to a stiff froth with 2 tablespoons of powdered sugar; then add 1 cup of sweet cream and pour over cake.

Before adding the last, stir in candied fruit, if desired.[410]

VIRGINIA PLUM PUDDING

☛ 1½ pounds best seeded raisins,
¾ pound finely chopped citron,
¼ pound conserved oranges,
1 pound finely shredded beef suet.
Sift over these ingredients
1½ pounds of flour, and mix thoroughly,
Beat 6 eggs very light with 1 pound of white sugar,
Add ½ grated nutmeg,
1 wineglass of brandy,
3 teacups bread-crumbs,
Enough sweet milk to make a batter,
Spices to taste.

Then add 2 teaspoons of baking-powder, and lastly all the fruit. Pour in a well-greased mold or pudding-bag and boil 6 hours.[411]

MRS. ABERCROMBIE'S PUDDING

☛ One cup of molasses, one cup of suet chopped fine, one cup of sweet milk, two cups mixed fruit, as raisins, currants, citron, chopped, two cups of flour, one teaspoonful of soda.

Boil four hours and serve with rich sauce.[412]

FEATHER PUDDING

☛ One cup of sugar, two cups of flour, half a cup milk, two eggs, half cup of butter, one teaspoonful of baking powder, one cup of raisins, nuts or preserves. Serve with sauce. Fine.[413]

JACK IN THE BOX

☞ 1 cup butter.
1 cup water.
½ pint whipped cream.
2 teaspoons Royal baking powder.
2 cups sugar.
3 cups flour.
3 eggs.
½ teaspoon vanilla.

Cream butter and sugar together; add eggs beaten; then add flour into which baking powder has been sifted. Mix well and bake in muffin pans and set aside after baking. The following day cut off top of cake, scoop out the inside and fill with whipped cream sweetened and flavored with vanilla. Replace the top and ice with heavy chocolate or caramel icing.[414]

BREAD PUDDING

☞ One cup fresh bread crumbs, two cups scalded milk, yolks of two beaten eggs with four tablespoons of sugar, grated rind of a lemon. Bake over hot water. When firm it is done. Beat the whites stiff, add two tablespoonfuls of sugar, two teaspoonfuls of lemon juice; drop it over the top with a teaspoon to form shells and brown in the oven lightly. Serve with sauce.[415]

CARROT PUDDING

☞ 1 cup carrots (ground).
1 cup sugar (scant).
1 cup Irish potatoes (ground).
½ teaspoon salt.
1 cup nuts (ground).
½ cup cloves.
⅔ cup suet (ground).
1 teaspoon nutmeg.
½ teaspoon cinnamon.
½ teaspoon soda.
1 cup dates (cut).
1 cup raisins (cut).
1 cup flour (scant).

Cream suet and sugar, add soda dissolved in water, then the other ingredients, turn into buttered molds and steam 4 hours. Serve with sea foam sauce, also hard sauce.[416]

GERMAN LAYER PUDDING

☞ Remove crust from a loaf of bread and cut in thin slices; butter these on both sides; dip each slice into milk; lay them on top of one another and set aside. Mix together half a cup of stoned raisins, three tablespoonfuls cleaned currants, two tablespoonfuls of finely cut citron, half a teaspoonful of cinnamon. Beat eight eggs to a froth and add one pint of milk. Butter a pudding form, sprinkle with crumbs, put in a layer of the sliced bread, sprinkle over some of the fruit and two tablespoonfuls of sugar, then another layer of bread, fruit and sugar until all are used; then pour over the milk and eggs. Boil one and a half hours. Sufficient for twelve persons. Serve with hard sauce.[417]

Charlotte princesse de galles.

SWEET POTATO PUDDING

☛ Boil and mash some sweet potatoes; weigh one pound; cream half a pound each of butter and sugar; add to the potatoes with six beaten eggs and one cup of milk. Season with wine, nutmeg, cinnamon, lemon extract. Bake till brown. Elegant.[418]

YAM PUDDING

☛ Press through a colander three quarters of a pound of roasted yam; mix with the pulp half a pound of butter, half a pound of sugar, half a pint of cream, a grated nutmeg, a teaspoonful of mace, a wine glass of wine and one of brandy. Beat them together till smoothly united, and then stir in six well beaten eggs. When the whole is well incorporated, put it into a buttered dish, and bake it in a moderate oven.[419]

SQUASH PUDDING

☛ Take three quarters of a pound of stewed squash, pass it through a colander, and stir it into a quart of rich sweet milk: put it into a pan and set it over the fire till it boils; then stir in six ounces of powdered sugar and four of butter; boil it up again, and set it by to cool; then stir in a glass of white wine, a teaspoonful of grated lemon, one of mace and half a grated nutmeg. Stir it till it is well intermingled, and then stir in very hard eight beaten eggs; pour it into a buttered dish, lay a rim of puff paste round it, and bake it in a moderate oven. Grate loaf sugar over it when cold.[420]

GINGER PUDDING

☛ One cup of butter and lard mixed, one cup of sugar, two cups of dark molasses, four cups of sifted flour, one cup of buttermilk, four eggs, two tablespoons cocoa, one teaspoon each soda, cloves, cinnamon, allspice, heaping of ginger, little salt. Bake in a square pan cut in squares.[421]

ENGLISH APPLE PUDDING

☛ Butter a deep pudding dish sprinkle with bread crumbs, line the sides with a rich pie crust, put a narrow strip around the bottom so as to leave the center uncovered. Fill the dish with finely cut apples sprinkle with sugar, little salt and bits of butter, cinnamon or nutmeg, cover with pastry and bake an hour. Turn out on plate, serve with hard sauce lemon flavored. Fine.[422]

COCOANUT PUDDING

☞ One pint milk, two full tablespoonfuls shredded cocoanut run through the chopper to make fine, or use the macaroon cocoanut, add two tablespoonfuls sugar stirred in the yolks of two eggs, one half cup cracker crumbs, pinch of salt, lemon extract. Bake about twenty minutes stirring once as it begins to stiffen, and again when about to sit off so the crumbs will not be solid at the bottom, as soon as firm remove and let stand while you make a meringue of the two whites and one half cup sugar, return to the oven to brown, serve cold.[423]

Cornstarch pudding molded in a ring mold and garnished and filled with white cherries.

RICE PUDDING

☞ Two tablespoonfuls of butter and sweeten to taste, one pint of rice boiled soft; thoroughly mix to this rice one pint of rich milk. Beat up two eggs very light, and add to the above also; well mix the whole. Flavor with the grated rind or peel of the half of an orange, and the juice of two oranges; mix well into pudding, and put into pan to bake.[424]

KENTUCKY CREAM

☞ Make a half gallon rich boiled custard, sweeten to taste, add two table-spoons gelatine dissolved in a half cup cold milk; let the custard cool, put it in freezer, and as soon as it begins to freeze, add one pound raisins, one pint strawberry preserves, one quart whipped cream; stir and beat well like ice-cream. Blanched almonds or grated cocoanut are additions. Some prefer currants to raisins, and some also add citron chopped fine.[425]

BLACKBERRY SPONGE

☞ Fill a bowl with small cakes of bread fitted in place, pour over blackberry juice, (berries cooked soft and mashed through a pure sieve,) then sweeten. Use all the juice it will absorb, set in a cool place, turn out serve with cream and sugar.[426]

GRATED SWEET POTATO PUDDING

☞ One pint of grated potatoes, two cups of sugar, one cup of molasses, three beaten eggs, one teaspoonful of ginger, some cinnamon, half a teaspoonful cloves, one quart of milk, grated peel of an orange, a large spoonful of butter. Bake in a slow oven, and when it crusts over stir it under and let crust again.[427]

CHOCOLATE PUDDING

☞ Melt one-fourth of a pound of sweet chocolate in one and a half cups of milk; then stir in one and a half cups grated bread crumbs. Remove from the stove and cool.

Beat in one by one the yolks of five eggs, one tablespoonful of butter softened, one cup of sugar, one cup sweet milk. Beat the whites stiff, add to the batter, flavor with vanilla and mix in some Maraschino cherries. Put in a pan and bake, setting it in a pan of hot water. When firm remove. Serve with cream or sauce.[428]

HOT CHOCOLATE SAUCE

☞ One cup of boiling water, one cup of sugar. Boil slowly without stirring ten minutes. Add one square of chocolate dissolved in a little boiling water. Flavor with vanilla and serve.[429]

BOILED CUSTARD

☞ Put to boil a quart of new milk, beat light four yolks and half a cup of sugar and one tablespoonful flour. Pour in the scalding milk and let thicken, stirring constantly. Beat the whites stiff, add half a cup of sugar, pour the hot custard over. Be sure to make this over hot water. Elegant. Fine for freezing.[430]

ONE-TWO-THREE-FOUR PUDDING

☞ One cup butter, two of sugar, three of flour, four eggs (beaten separately), one cup sweet milk, and two tea-spoons baking-powder; flavor with nutmeg, and bake in pudding or cake mold; leave in mold till next day, when steam for three-quarters of an hour over a kettle of boiling water and serve with hot sauce.[431]

CARAMEL CUSTARD PUDDING

☞ Put half a cup of sugar in a small saucepan. When it melts and browns add two tablespoonfuls of water. When dissolved stir it into a quart of warm milk.

Beat six eggs slightly, add the salt, a teaspoonful of vanilla and part of the milk. Strain in the remainder of the milk and pour in a buttered two quart pan. Set the pan in another pan of warm water and bake until firm. When a knife comes out clean it is done.

Serve with caramel sauce.[432]

SPLENDID PUDDING

☞ Four eggs, one tablespoonful of butter, six tablespoons flour, one cup of sweet milk, one cup of raisins, one teaspoonful of baking powder in flour. Boil three hours. Serve with sauce.[433]

CREAM MERINGUE PUDDING

☛ Mix four tablespoonfuls sifted flour, three tablespoonfuls of sugar and a little salt. Stir in this half a cup of sweet milk and rub the whole until free from lumps. Heat a quart of milk in a double boiler. When hot stir in the mixture and cook ten minutes. Have ready the beaten yolks of four eggs and white of one; stir into the hot custard and stir until thick. Flavor with vanilla and pour in a buttered dish. Make a meringue of the whites, pile roughly on the pudding and put in a cool oven to brown. Serve with foamy sauce or cream and sugar.[434]

ENGLISH PLUM PUDDING

☛ Beat eight eggs very light, add to them a pound of four sifted, and a pound of powdered sugar; when it looks quite light, put in a pound of suet finely shred, a pint of milk, a nutmeg grated, and a gill of brandy; mix with it a pound of currants, washed, picked, and dried, and a pound of raisins stoned and floured—tie it in a thick cloth, and boil it steadily eight hours.[435]

English plum pudding.

SOUFFLE PUDDING

☛ Four heaping tablespoons sifted flour, one and a half cups milk, two tablespoons sugar, one teaspoon butter. Mix flour and part of the milk to a smooth paste. Put the rest on to boil, pour in the butter while hot. Add four yolks and the four whites beaten stiff and folded in. Put in a pan set in another of hot water and bake until firm in a stove oven. Serve with sauce.[436]

VELVET CREAM

☛ 1 cup of wine,
½ box of gelatine,
1 lemon,
1½ pints of milk,
1 cup of sugar.

Dissolve gelatine in the wine over the fire. Add peel and juice of lemon, and when gelatine has dissolved, add sugar. Let it simmer, then strain. Add the milk and stir till cold. Mold and let congeal. Serve with whipped cream.[437]

WHIPPED CREAM

☛ Squeeze the juice from two large lemons and two oranges; put it into a bowl and mix with it a pint of white wine and eight ounces of powdered loaf sugar; set it by for three or four hours, and then beat it with rods or wires to a froth. Have ready some custard glasses, put in the bottom of each a coconut snowball or almond cones, pile on them the whipped cream, extending it as far above the top of the glass as possible, and drop over them at short intervals delicate spots of thick red or dark colored preserved juice.[438]

EGG CREAM

☞ Beat very well the yolks of half a dozen eggs, and stir them into a quart of rich sweet milk with half a pound of powdered loaf sugar: put it in a pitcher, set it in a pan of hot water, and simmer it till it gets thick, but do not suffer it to boil. Stir it all the time it is on the fire, and after it is set off, stir it occasionally till it gets cold, adding by degrees the juice of two fine oranges, and then put it in glasses.

Make a pint of sweet cream a little thick with powdered loaf sugar, flavor it with orange or lemon juice, color it a delicate yellow with saffron juice, beat it to a froth, and pile it high on the tops of the glasses.[439]

HONEY CAKES

The apiary.

☞ Dissolve a small teaspoonful of pearlash in four tablespoonfuls of boiling water; mix with it half a pint of sour milk, add six ounces of butter, a pint of strained honey and a grated nutmeg. Stir in flour till it gets too thick to stir with a spaddle; then lay it on your pasteboard, knead in more four till it is a good paste, and beat it slightly with a rolling-pin; after which roll it into a sheet about half an inch thick, cut it into small round cakes with a cutter, lay them on tin sheets, slightly buttered, and bake them briskly, but be sure you do not burn them, as honey cakes are very easily burnt.[440]

FLORIDA CAKE

☞ Mix together two pounds of flour, two pounds of sugar, a pound and three quarters of butter, and seventeen well-beaten eggs. Flavor with nutmeg and cloves, and a glassful of brandy, and stir in a pound of currants picked and washed and dredged with flour, and a pound of raisins, stoned, cut in halves, and floured.[441]

CHEESE CAKE

☞ Beat the yolks of ten eggs, the whites of two; then take one half pound sugar, one-half pound butter, work well together; beat in the eggs, flavor with nutmeg; bake the crust a little before putting in the custard; when the pudding is done, spread a layer of acid jelly over, and make an icing of the remaining whites; flavor with lemon, spread over, and brown slightly.[442]

SWEDISH PUDDING

☛ One and a half cups milk, two tablespoons flour, half tablespoon butter, three of sugar, three eggs, half teaspoon each vanilla and almond, three-fourths of a cup brandy peaches. Scald the milk, rub the flour to a paste with a little cold milk add the yolks and sugar, pour in the hot milk and cook ten minutes stirring all the while, add butter, when cool add the flavoring. Cover a dish with the brandy peaches cut small, pour over the above mixture. Make a meringue of the whites and three tablespoons sugar, put over the top and brown slightly. Decorate the top. Serve ice cold.[443]

RAISIN PUDDING

☛ Beat six eggs very light, and stir them into a quart of sweet milk, with a large spoonful of mixed mace and cinnamon, a grated nutmeg and a glass of white wine, adding by degrees enough flour to make it into a common pudding batter. Seed, cut and dust with flour a pound and a half of raisins; (Sultana raisins are preferable, having no seed;) stir them gradually into the other ingredients, giving all a hard stirring at the last. Put it into a pudding cloth, having first dipped it into boiling water, and dusted it with flour; tie a string firmly round the end of the cloth, leaving plenty of room for the pudding to swell, and dusting the tying place with a little dry flour, to secure it against the admission of the water, which would spoil the pudding, if suffered to approach it. Put it in a large pot of boiling water, and boil it gently and steadily for several hours, turning it over several times, and replenishing the pot with water from a boiling kettle. When it is done, turn it smoothly into a dish, sprinkle over it some preserved raisins, finely shred; grate on some loaf sugar, and eat it warm, with wine sauce, or white wine and sugar.[444]

Meringue top.

PEACH CHARLOTTE

☛ Butter a pudding dish, remove the crust from slices of bread, fit the bottom and sides of the dish with the bread, dip the slices lightly in milk, do not saturate. Fill the dish with peaches peeled and sliced, piling very high as they settle in baking, add bits of butter and a little salt. Cover with soaked bread, bake until the fruit is done, no longer. Turn out and serve with hot sauce.[445]

ALMOND MANDALINES

☛ 1½ cups of powdered sugar,
½ cup of butter,
¾ cup of milk,
4 eggs, or 8 yolks,

½ cup of cornstarch,
1½ cups of flour,
2 teaspoons of baking-powder,
1 teaspoon of vanilla.

Bake in 12 mandaline tins. When cold, cut off top with shell spoon, scrape out inside, fill with the following:

1 pint of whipped cream,
½ pound of almonds, grated,
½ cup of sugar,
½ teaspoon of vanilla.

Cover with top; frost with white icing.[446]

OLD DOMINION CAKE

☛ Cream one cup of butter and two cups of powdered sugar. Add stiffly beaten whites of six eggs, three cups of flour, in which has been sifted two teaspoonsful of baking powder, and one teaspoonful of vanilla. Bake in layers in moderate oven.

Filling: Put on two cups of white sugar with enough water to dissolve thoroughly and cook until it spins a thread. Then add one teaspoonful of vanilla and pour slowly over the whites of two eggs beaten stiff.

Beat until creamy and then spread on cake layers. Thickly strew the top of icing with raisins, English walnuts and blanched almonds.[447]

MARSHMALLOW CAKE

☛ Bake angel cake in a square pan and when two days old cut in slices across and spread a marshmallow filling between like a layer cake. Ice the top and sides with a soft icing, violet tint (pale). Serve with whipped cream around and candied violets scattered over the cake.[448]

MARSHMALLOW FILLING

☛ Make a boiled frosting; cut up marshmallows in it while hot and beat until stiff; flavor with almond, rose or violet.[449]

GENEVA CREAM

☛ Scald a pint of milk in a double boiler; beat all together three eggs, half cup sugar, turn into the hot milk and stir until thickened as a custard, then add half box Knox gelatine soaked in half cup cold water, put in the hot custard and stir until dissolved. When cold add a teaspoon vanilla, two tablespoons sherry, two oz. candied cherries, two oz. candied ginger cut fine, two tablespoon blanched and coarsely chopped pistachio nuts or almonds, stir occasionally.

Double layer strawberry cake.

After it becomes thick put in this fruit and stir to prevent its settling; pour in small wetted molds and turn out on lace paper on a fancy plate when they become hard.[450]

PRIDE OF KENTUCKY CAKE

☛ Four eggs,
Three cups of flour,
Two cups of sugar,
One cup of butter,
One cup of milk,
Two teaspoonsful of baking powder,
One teaspoonful of vanilla.
Separate eggs leaving out two whites for filling.
To beaten yolks, add butter and sugar creamed together, then the milk, flour, baking powder and vanilla and lastly whites of two eggs beaten stiff.
Bake in layers in moderate oven, and put together with any kind of filling desired.[451]

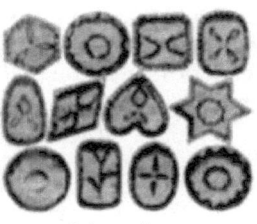

Cake cutters.

APRICOT CUSTARD PUDDING

☛ Make a soft boiled custard, with one pint of milk, two eggs, two-thirds cup sugar; add half box Knox gelatine after soaking in half cup cold water; put it into the hot custard and stir until dissolved, then strain.
Open a can of apricots, rub eight pieces through a sieve and mix the pulp smoothly with the custard; add a drop of almond extract. Pour in a wetted mold, when hard turn out and serve with cream.[452]

SNOW CREAM

☛ One quart cream, three-fourths cup sugar, one teaspoonful vanilla, two tablespoonsful sherry; whip and put in a bowl to drain.
Make a meringue of six whites of eggs beaten stiff, add six tablespoonfuls sugar, fold into the cream and serve with cake.[453]

NEW ORLEANS TEA CAKE

☛ Three pounds of flour, a pound and a half of sugar, three quarters of a pound of butter, two tablespoonfuls of caraway seed, one small teaspoonful of soda, and half a pint of milk.
Roll out, and bake in small cakes.[454]

KENTUCKY PUDDING

☛ Three fourths of a cup of butter, two and a half cupfuls of sugar, three eggs, one cup of cream, three tablespoonfuls flour.
Season with lemon, and bake in paste.[455]

ORANGE CREAM

☛ One cup cold water, one-third box Knox gelatine soaked in the water, then dissolved in one cup hot water. Add one cup orange juice and flavor with orange extract, put in a cup of sugar or more, set in ice water; when thick beat with a Dover until white, then add the whites of two eggs beaten stiff with two tablespoonfuls sugar, little salt.

Serve with whipped cream and angel cake.[456]

PINEAPPLE OMELET

☛ Melt two level tablespoonsful butter, cook in it two level tablespoonsful flour with a little salt, add a cup of grated pineapple juice and pulp, one-fourth cup of sugar and one tablespoonful lemon juice, stir and cook until the boiling point is reached, then remove and beat in the yolks of five eggs.

Then fold in the stiff whites beaten dry. Melt two tablespoonsful butter in a large omelet pan, pour in the mixture and let stand on top of stove to become set, then put on upper grate of oven, inside, and cook until a knife comes out clean; score entire across the center, fold at the scoring and turn out on a hot platter.

Sift powdered sugar over it and serve.[457]

CABIN CAKE

☛ To whites of eight eggs beaten stiff, add one cup of butter and two cups of sugar creamed together. Next add three-fourths cup of milk, three cups of flour, two teaspoonsful of baking powder and one teaspoonful of vanilla.

Bake in layers in moderate oven.[458]

PICKANINNY COOKIES

☛ Sift one quart of flour, make a hole in the center, put in two cups of sugar, one of lard, one beaten egg, and one cup of sweet milk, into which has been stirred a half teaspoonful of soda.

Work all together, roll thin and bake in a quick oven.[459]

ELECTION CAKE

☛ Take half a pint of lively yeast, mix with it half a pint of sweet milk and enough flour to make it a good batter; cover it, and set it by the fire to rise. This is called setting a sponge. Sift two pounds of four into a broad pan, cut up in it a pound of fresh butter, add a pound of powdered sugar, two grated nutmegs and six beaten eggs.

When the sponge is quite light, pour it on the flour, etc., make the whole into a soft dough, knead it well, and make it into small flattish loaves.

Sprinkle a shallow iron pan with flour, lay the rolls in it close together, put them at first in a very slow oven, that will permit them to rise, and when risen, bake them with moderate heat.[460]

JUMBALS
☛ Put one pound of nice sugar into two pounds of flour; add pounded spice of any kind, and pass them through a sieve; beat four eggs, pour them on with three quarters of a pound of melted butter, knead all well together, and bake them.[461]

BIRD'S NEST PUDDING
☛ Pare as many fine ripe pears as will fill your pudding dish, placing them side by side, and with a sharp penknife extract the cores, without cutting the pears in two. Fill the space whence the cores were taken with thin slips of fresh lemon peel, put them in the dish, strew over a little powdered cinnamon, and a handful of brown sugar; add a few spoonfuls of water, merely to keep them from burning, and bake them about half done, in a moderate oven.

Beat six eggs very light, stir them into a quart of sweet milk, with four ounces of powdered sugar, and pour it over the pears. Lay a puff paste round the pudding, on the edge of the dish, and bake it in a moderate oven. When done, grate loaf sugar over it, and eat it cold, or eat it warm with cream sauce. A similar pudding may be made of pippen apples.[462]

FIGS STEWED IN CLARET
☛ Take the best dried figs and cover with claret wine, let stew until tender, add sugar to taste. When the syrup has boiled thick and the figs tender set on ice to cool. Serve in tall frappe glasses topped with stiff whipped cream. Delicious.[463]

FRONTIER CAKE
☛ A pound and a half of sugar, half a pound of butter, two pounds of flour, and eight eggs beaten separately and light. Mix two teaspoonfuls of cream of tartar with the flour, and when all the ingredients are well beaten together, put in a teaspoonful of soda dissolved in a little hot water, and pour into your molds to bake.[464]

ORANGE BAVARIAN CREAM
☛ Soak one-third box gelatine in half cup cold water, then dissolve in half cup boiling water, add half cup sugar. When cool add two cups orange juice and the pulp. When beginning to set stir in gently one pint stiffly whipped cream. Beat until stiff enough to hold. Pour in a wetted mold. When ready to serve unmold and serve with cream.[465]

CHESTNUTS WITH WHIPPED CREAM
☛ Boil the large chestnuts and when perfectly tender press them through a colander in the center of a large chop plate. Dust them thickly with powdered sugar and heap around one pint of cream whipped to a stiff froth; flavor the cream with vanilla or sherry.[466]

GOOSEBERRY FOOL

The White Mountain Triple Motion Ice Cream Freezer.

☛ Pick three pints of gooseberries, stew them with half a pound of sugar and a very little water, merely to keep them from burning. When they get quite soft, mash them to a pulp, and set them by till cold; then stir them into a quart of cream custard, and put it in a glass dish or bowl. Make a pint of sweet cream a little thick with sugar; flavor it well with white wine, or lemon juice; color it a pale green with thick spinach juice, beat it to a froth, and pile it high on the gooseberries. Set it in ice for a few minutes before you send it to table.[467]

BETSY ROSS POUND CAKE

☛ One pound of flour,
Three-fourths pound of butter,
One pound of sugar,
Twelve eggs,

Cream butter and about two-thirds of the flour together. Beat whites of eggs to a stiff froth, beat yolks of eggs and sugar together until very light. Mix thoroughly all the ingredients, stirring in last the loose flour. Bake in a slow oven until done.[468]

CHOCOLATE BLANC MANGUE

☛ Soak a half box gelatine in half a cup cold water until soft. Warm a quart of new milk, stir in the gelatine with a cup of sugar; let it stand over the fire until the gelatine is thoroughly dissolved; remove, add three tablespoonfuls grated chocolate, stir until melted. Let it stand in a cold place, and when it commences to thicken flavor with vanilla, and with an egg beater commence to beat it. Add two tablespoonfuls Maraschino cherries cut fine. Pour into a wetted mold and put in refrigerator. When ready to serve turn out and surround with whipped cream studded with cherries.[469]

CRANBERRY PUDDING

☛ Beat six eggs very light, stir them into a quart of sweet milk, with as much finely grated bread as will make it into good batter. Add four ounces of melted butter, a grated nutmeg, a spoonful of mixed mace and cinnamon, and a glass of mixed brandy and wine; then stir in very hard a pound of preserved cranberries, continuing to stir it till well incorporated; after which put it in a buttered dish, lay round it a rim of puff paste, neatly serrated or scalloped, and bake it in an oven with moderate heat. Grate loaf sugar over it when cold. A boiled cranberry pudding may be made as directed for a cherry pudding, and eaten warm with wine sauce.[470]

CHOCOLATE SOUFFLE

☛ In making chocolate souffle melt one tablespoonful of butter in a double boiler, blend in two tablespoonfuls of flour and a cup of milk, half cup grated chocolate melted over steam. Stir until smooth and thick. Now add the yolks of four eggs and half a cup of sugar beaten together until very light. Cook until the yolks have had time to thicken; then stand away to cool. Half hour before serving add the whites of five eggs beaten very stiff and dry; put into a buttered baking dish and bake. Serve with any delicate sauce. Orange, lemon and vanilla are made the same way, leaving out the chocolate. Caramel is made by browning half a cup of sugar instead of other sweetenings.[471]

STRAWBERRY SAUCE

☛ One teaspoonful of cornstarch, three ounces of sugar; mix together and add one cup of water. Cook two minutes. Add the juice of half a lemon, one teaspoonful of butter, a few drops strawberry extract, the same of fruit coloring. [Use on souffles.][472]

CHOCOLATE SAUCE

☛ Boil one cup each of sugar and water five minutes. Melt six tablespoonfuls of chocolate by standing over hot water; add the boiling syrup and blend thoroughly. Now dissolve a tablespoonful of arrow root in two-thirds of a cup of milk, add to the sauce mixture, boil three minutes, strain, and add half a teaspoonful of vanilla.[473]

SOUFFLE FLOAT

☛ Souffle float is made by beating the whites of egg until very stiff, then adding half a tablespoonful of sifted powdered sugar for each white. Heap these beaten and sweetened whites into small flat bottomed cups and stand in a covered steamer over boiling water long enough to cook them. When done, turn gently from the cups, scoop out a teaspoonful from the top of each white mound, fill with a rich custard made from the yolks and pour more custard around the base. Orange makes a delicious flavoring for the custard. Serve ice cold.[474]

BANANAS AND WINE

☛ Sprinkle sugar on sliced bananas and pour over sherry wine.[475]

RICE CREAM WITH FRUIT

☛ Scald one and a half cups of milk in a double boiler; add one-fourth cup well washed rice, a pinch of salt, and cook until the milk is absorbed; then add three yolks beaten with half a cup of sugar, and one-fourth cup of milk. Stir gently until thickened, then put in half box gelatine dissolved in half a cup cold water; then set over hot water to dissolve. Set aside until cold and beginning to thicken. Now add one and a half cups of thick cream whipped to a solid froth. Flavor with one teaspoonful vanilla. Put in a mold until firm. Turn out, garnish with any variety of canned fruit, and serve.[476]

Cake cabinet.

HASTY PUDDING

☛ Boil a quart of entire sweet milk, and stir into it while boiling enough thin flour batter, made of milk and flour, to make the whole as thick as good pudding batter.

Add a little powdered cloves and cinnamon, a large spoonful of butter and two ounces of sugar. A handful of seeded raisins or cherries would improve it.

Stir it constantly till done, then serve it up in a bowl of suitable size, sprinkle a handful of brown sugar over the top, grating on a little nutmeg, and send it to table warm.[477]

VIRGINIA DOUGHNUTS

☛ Two eggs beaten light,
Two cups of sugar,
Three level tablespoonsful of melted butter,
One cup of sour milk (if sweet milk is used, add one teaspoonful of cream of tartar),
Four cups of flour,
One-half teaspoonful of soda,
One-half teaspoonful of cinnamon,
One-half teaspoonful of salt.

Mix in the order given adding the dry ingredients sifted together and enough more flour to make a dough just soft enough to handle. Have the board well-floured, and the fat for frying, heating. Roll out only a little at a time, cut into rings with an open cutter.

Do all the cutting before frying, as that will take your entire attention. The fat should be hot enough for the dough to rise to the top instantly.[478]

PLANTATION COOKIES

☛ 2 eggs,
1 cupful of sugar,
1½ cupfuls of oatmeal, or Rolled Oats,
⅔ cupful of cocoanut,
¼ teaspoonful of salt,
½ teaspoonful of vanilla,
2 tablespoonsful of butter.

Cream the butter and sugar together and add the well-beaten eggs. Add the remainder of the ingredients and drop on a well greased baking-pan. Bake in a moderate oven, from fifteen to twenty minutes.[479]

PRUNE PUDDING

☞ Stew a pound of prunes in a very little water till the stones will slip out; then extract them, spread the prunes on a large dish, and sprinkle them lightly with flour. Stir into a quart of rich sweet milk eight tablespoonfuls of flour, having first made it into a smooth batter, with some of the quart of milk. Add a glass of white wine and six beaten eggs alternately with the prepared prunes, stirring them in very hard; dip your pudding cloth into boiling water, spread it over a deep dish or pan, and dust it well with dry flour; pour in your pudding, tie it up securely, leaving plenty of room for it to expand, and dusting the tying place with a little dry flour. Put it into a pot, with a large quantity of boiling water, and boil it steadily till done. Send it to table very warm, accompanied with cold cream sauce, or butter and powdered sugar, worked together, and flavored with grated nutmeg, or lemon juice.[480]

MACAROONS

☞ Blanch a pound of sweet almonds, pound them in a mortar with rose water; whip the whites of seven eggs to a strong froth, put in one pound of powdered sugar, beat it some time, then put in the almonds mix them well, and drop them on sheets of paper buttered; sift sugar over, and bake them quickly. Be careful not to let them get discoloured.[481]

BROWN MANGE

☞ Soak half box gelatine in a cup of milk for three hours; stir into it a cup of sugar and a scant cup of scalding milk, not boiling. Add one-fourth of a cake of grated chocolate wet to a paste with milk. Stir over the fire just long enough to dissolve the gelatine and chocolate, but do not let it boil. Pour the hot milk on the stiff whites of four eggs. Turn the mixture into a bowl and set this in a pan of ice water while you beat the contents until it commences to thicken. Turn in a glass bowl and set on ice to form. When cold send to the table with great spoons of whipped cream on top of the brown meringue.[482]

MAROONS WITH WHIPPED CREAM

☞ Chop half a bottle of maroons and put a teaspoonful in each glass custard cup. Pour over them a little of the liquor in which they were put up, and fill the glass with whipped cream. Set in cracked ice until served.[483]

LADY FINGERS

☞ 9 yolks and 6 whites of eggs, ½ pound of sugar, ½ pound of flour. Beat the whites to a stiff froth; add the beaten yolks and sugar; beat over the fire until warm; then beat it until cool, and add the flour.

Lady finger pans.

When the flour is thoroughly mixed, mold with a spoon on paper, and bake them in a quick oven.[484]

BLANCMANGE

☛ Blanch and pound with a little rose water two ounces of sweet almonds and two of bitter ones. Boil a quart of water, and stir into it enough rice, white starch, first wetting it with a little cold water, to make it a thick jelly: then strain it into a clean pan, and stir into it the almond paste, with half a pound of powdered white sugar and the juice and grated rind of a lemon, or a few drops of the essence.

Stir it very well, simmer it a few minutes, cool it, and put it in molds to congeal, first wetting them with cold water. Accompany it with creams.[485]

QUEEN OF TRIFLES

☛ Half pound lady fingers, half pound macaroons, half pound almonds blanched, half pound crystalized cherries, one cup jelly, one cup wine, little rose water, one pint whipped cream, one pint milk made into a custard, using a tablespoonful of flour or corn starch to thicken the custard; vanilla to flavor. Spread the lady fingers and macaroons with jelly and dip in wine.

Put in your bowl in layers with a few cherries between. Continue until all are used. Cut up the almonds, flavor them with rose water, stir in the custard, and pour over the cake. Use only the yolks to make the custard, which should be quite thick, using the flour or cornstarch to thicken it.

Let it be cold before you pour it over the cake. Whip the whites stiff, sweeten the cream, flavor with vanilla, then whip solid. Fold the stiff whites into it and put over the top of the bowl.

Decorate with candied cherries or violets. Very fine.[486]

HEDGEHOG TRIFLE

☛ Lay an oblong sponge cake in a glass dish, soak with sherry wine. Stick blanched almonds in it in regular rows from end to end, half burying them in the cake. Now soak in warm boiled custard poured over it a little at a time, and when the custard is absorbed heap whipped cream at the base. Serve cold. Fine.[487]

PEACH TRIFLE

☛ Stew peaches soft and run through a colander. Sweeten to taste. Return to fire to get hot. Use a pint of this. Soak half a cup of gelatine in a cup of cold water for four hours. While the peach sauce is hot stir in the soaked gelatine. Remove from fire and let get cold, but before it sets stir in two cups whipped cream.

Wet a mold, fill with the mixture, set on ice. When firm turn out. You can use any canned or ripe fruit for the purpose.[488]

LEMON TRIFLE

☛ The juice of two lemons and grated peel of one, one pint of cream well sweetened and whipped stiff. Let sugar, lemon juice and peel stand together a couple of hours. Strain and whip gradually into the frothed cream. Serve immediately in small glasses lined with lady fingers.[489]

FRUIT TRIFLE

☛ One pint of cream beaten to a stiff froth, two tablespoonfuls each of sugar and raspberry jelly. Arrange the same as above.[490]

Glace oranges and grapes in paper boxes.

GRAPE TRIFLE

☛ Pulp through a sieve two pounds of ripe Concord grapes, add sugar to taste and the beaten white of one egg, a little gelatine soaked and added to the grape pulp is an improvement. Put into glasses and cover with whipped cream, flavored with vanilla. Serve very cold.[491]

APPLE TRIFLE

☛ Peel, core and quarter some astrakhan apples and stew them with one quince using only sufficient water to cover the bottom of the stew-pan. Add sugar in the proportion of one-half a pound to one pound of fruit; when cooked, press the pulp through a sieve. When cold pour over it one pint of whipped cream flavored with vanilla or lemon.[492]

MACAROON CREAM

☛ Soak a tablespoonful granulated gelatine in two tablespoonfuls cold water. Make a boiled custard with one and a fourth cups milk, two heaping tablespoonfuls of sugar, yolks two eggs. Add to the hot custard the soaked gelatine; stir until dissolved; set aside to cool. When quite thick add a teaspoonful of vanilla, eight stale macaroons pounded and a heaping cup of stiffly whipped cream. Turn into a wetted mold, and when you turn it out garnish with whipped cream.[493]

BISCUIT TORTONI

☛ One quart double cream beaten solid with an egg whip, make in a double boiler the egg preparation. Boil half cup water and half cup powdered sugar twenty minutes, beat the yolks of three eggs light and stir in the hot syrup. Cook and stir constantly five minutes, now set aside to cool. Chop fine one-fourth cup dried macaroons, one tablespoon blanched almonds, one tablespoon candied cherries; two tablespoons of sherry, a little almonds extract put in the egg preparation. Mix very gently the whipped cream, and egg mixture then sprinkle in the chopped fruit, use the surprise beater to mix in the fruit. Pack in ice and salt and let stand several hours, don't turn the freezer. Very fine.⁴⁹⁴

FREEZING CREAM
☛ The proportion of ice and salt for freezing cream is three parts ice to one of salt, beat the ice until as fine as the salt, put in a canvas bag and use a wooden mallet. Do not turn off the water until it is necessary, as heat is absorbed from the cream to warm the ice water. Turn the crank slowly at first.⁴⁹⁵

BISCUIT GLACE
☛ To half pint strawberry jam, put one pint of water and half cup sugar, juice of one or two lemons, stir until dissolved, soak half tablespoon gelatine in a little cold water then dissolve in hot water, and stir in the strawberry mixture freeze. Take a large cup of thick cream, sweeten and flavor with vanilla, beat with a Dover until very thick and stiff. Put in a mold surround with ice and salt, when hard put on the strawberry mixture, put a little melted butter around the rim of cover to prevent salt getting in and burry the mold in ice and salt let stand three hours to harden.⁴⁹⁶

Ice cream molds in brick forms and individual lead molds.

FRUIT ICE CREAM
☛ Canned or ripe fruit sweetened to taste and cut in very small pieces may be added to partly frozen cream giving many delicious varieties.⁴⁹⁷

PEPPERMINT ICE CREAM
☛ 1 pint milk.
1 lb. peppermint stick candy.
1 quart cream.
Crush candy and dissolve in milk; add cream and freeze. This is delicious.⁴⁹⁸

RASPBERRY ICE CREAM
☛ Make as for any other kind of fruit cream and add the fruit when half frozen. Mash and strain the berries and add a little lemon juice.⁴⁹⁹

PINEAPPLE ICE CREAM
☛ Take one large ripe pine-apple, pare it, cut it in very thin slices, mince them fine in a bowl, and sprinkle on a pound of powdered loaf sugar, stir them up, cover them, and set them by for two hours; then mash them fine and press it through a sieve: stir the juice into one quart of rich sweet cream, put it into the freezer, and when it has congealed,

which will probably be in two or three hours, put it into molds, and freeze it the second time as directed. Ice creams should always be accompanied with cake, and immediately followed by wine and cordials.[500]

GELATINE ICE CREAM

☛ Ice cream is richer and molds better when made with gelatine, but must be flavored highly to disguise the gelatine. Use one-fourth box Knox gelatine to two quarts custard. Soak in half cup milk; dissolve in the hot custard.[501]

GLACE CREAM

☛ Boil one cup sugar and half cup water to a soft ball. Pour slowly on the whites of three eggs beaten stiff, and beat until cool. Flavor and stir in any partly frozen cream made with much less sugar.[502]

FROZEN WATERMELON

☛ Make a plain cream by scalding 1 pint of milk. Mix
    1 tablespoon of flour,
    1 cup of sugar,
    ¼ teaspoon of salt,
    1 beaten egg.
Pour over this the scalded milk. In a double boiler cook until it thickens, stirring often. Cool and add 1 quart of cream. Flavor with 1 tablespoon of vanilla and 1 tablespoon of almond extract. Freeze.

Line a melon-mold that has been embedded in ice and salt with the frozen cream about an inch thick. Sprinkle over this raisins that have been soaked in brandy or wine 1 hour. Fill in the centre with whipped cream, which has been sweetened and flavored. Cover over the top with the frozen cream. Cover the mold with greased paper; fasten on top securely, and keep packed in ice and salt for 3 hours.[503]

ORANGE ICE CREAM

Compote of oranges garnished with candied cherries.

☛ Beat the yolks of eight eggs light, and stir them into a quart of rich sweet milk or cream, put it in a pitcher, set it in a pan of boiling water, and simmer it gently till it becomes thick, but do not let it boil, or it will curdle. Having stirred it all the time it was simmering, pour it into a bowl, and set it by to cool. Grate the yellow peel from four oranges, and squeeze out the juice, and when the cream is cold, stir them alternately into it with three quarters of a pound of powdered loaf sugar. Mix it very well, and freeze it. Cold orange cream makes a very fine ice when made sweeter.[504]

CHERRY ICE CREAM

☛ Get some fine ripe cherries, break them up, and squeeze out a pint of thick juice. Beat to a stiff froth the whites of six eggs, and mix it with the juice: put it in a porcelain skillet, set it over a few coals, and stir it till it raises the simmer.

Powder a pound of loaf sugar, put it in a bowl, pour over it while scalding the juice and egg, mix it well, and set it by to cool. Have ready a quart of entire sweet cream, and when the juice, etc. is cold, stir the cream gradually into it. Freeze it over twice as directed.[505]

CITRON ICE CREAM

☛ Slice very thin one pound of the finest citron melons, that are perfectly ripe. Powder a pound of loaf sugar, and put it in a bowl with the sliced citron, stratifying them, and set them by for several hours; then chop them small and press out all the juice you can through a sieve. Have ready a quart of rich sweet cream, stir the juice into it, and conglaciate it twice as directed.[506]

PEAR ICE CREAM

☛ Pare and slice some fine ripe pears, stew them till quite soft in a very little water; mash them to a pulp, press it through a sieve, and set it by to cool. Have ready a quart of sweet cream, mix with it the beaten yolks of four eggs, and simmer it over some coals till it becomes a little thick; stir into it three quarters of a pound of powdered loaf sugar, and then remove it from the fire. When it gets cold, stir hard into it a pint of the pear pulp. Add the grated rind of a lemon, or a few drops of the essence of lemon, and freeze it over twice.[507]

MARSHMALLOW ICE CREAM

☛ 1 quart thick cream, whipped stiff.
8 marshmallows.
Parched almonds.
Flavoring.
1 tablespoon gelatine.

Beat marshmallows into whipped cream, sweeten and flavor to taste; add gelatine to a little cold water, dissolve over hot water and beat into whipped cream last. Freeze. Serve with rolled parched almonds.[508]

ANGEL PARFAIT

☛ Three-fourths of a cup of sugar, one-third cup boiling water, boil until it will form a soft ball; pour in a fine stream on the stiff whites of two eggs, then fold in one cup double and one cup single cream beaten solid to the bottom. Flavor with wine and vanilla. Turn into a mold lined with paper, filling to overflow. Cover with paper. Bury in equal parts ice and salt; let stand three hours and serve with Kremette or Strawberry sauce.[509]

VANILLA PARFAIT

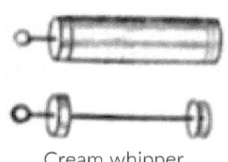
Cream whipper.

☛ Beat the yolks of eight eggs until light; add one cupful of syrup. Place the mixture on a slow fire and stir constantly until the eggs have thickened enough to make a thick coating on the spoon. Turn it into a bowl and beat it with a whip until it is cold; it will then be very light. If a vanilla bean is used for flavoring, infuse it with the syrup; if the extract is used add a teaspoonful of it to the custard when it is taken from the fire. When the custard is cold add a pint of cream whipped to a stiff froth. (If any liquid has drained from the cream do not let it go in.) Stir these lightly together; turn the mixture into a mold holding three pints. Pack in ice and salt for four hours. Make the joints of the mold very tight.[510]

MAPLE ICE CREAM

☛ Add yolks of four beaten eggs to a cup of maple syrup and let thicken as custard. Strain and set aside to cool. Beat solid a pint of cream, add the stiffly beaten whites to it. Beat the cool syrup until light; add to the cream and eggs and freeze.[511]

MAPLE PARFAIT 1

☛ One cup hot maple syrup, one pint double cream, the yolks eight eggs. Pour the hot syrup on to the beaten yolks, return to the fire and cook until the mixture coats the spoon. Beat until cold. Whip the cream until solid and fold it into the egg mixture. Pack in ice and salt and let stand four hours.[512]

MAPLE PARFAIT 2

☛ Beat a cup of double cream and a cup of cream from the top of a quart bottle of milk until thick to the bottom of the bowl and set aside to keep chilled. Boil one cup of maple syrup and one-eighth teaspoonful of cream of tartar until reduced a little. Beat the yolks of two eggs until thick, then pour the hot syrup over them in a fine stream, beating constantly meanwhile. Return the mixture to the fire and let cook over hot water until a little thick. Remove from the fire and beat until cold, then add to it a little of the cream. Cut and fold the two together; when the two are evenly blended add the remainder of the cream. Blend the two without breaking down the cream and pour in a quart mold. Spread a paper over the top, press the cover over the paper, and pack the mold in equal measures of ice and salt. Let stand three hours. When turned from the mold sprinkle with sliced pecan nuts.[513]

ALMOND ICE CREAM

☛ ½ gallon of cream,
1 cup of grated almonds,

3 or 4 bitter almonds,
7 oranges.

Sweeten the cream and freeze. When nearly stiff enough, beat the almonds and juice in and freeze well.[514]

APRICOT ICE CREAM

½ gallon of cream,
½ pint sugar,
1 can of apricots,
1 lemon,
1 tablespoon gelatine.

Make a syrup of the sugar and add the lemon juice. Mash and strain the apricots. When the syrup is cool, pour into the cream and put in the freezer. When half frozen, add the apricots and freeze quite hard.[515]

LEMON ICE CREAM

2 quarts milk,
4 eggs,
¾ pound sugar.

Beat the eggs together. Boil the milk and add 1 tablespoon gelatine. Beat the eggs and sugar and add to the boiling milk. When cool, add the juice of 5 lemons and 1 orange. Put in the freezer, and when half frozen, add 1 pint whipped cream.[516]

APPLE ICE CREAM

Ice cream molded in a ring mold; the center is filled with pink-colored whipped cream; the dish is garnished with real pink roses.

Select twelve medium sized perfect red apples. Cut a slice from the top of each and scoop out the meat. Drop the shells in water to prevent discoloration. Take the top slice, core, and meat, and put in a saucepan with a little water. Cook until the apples are soft, rub through a colander, sweeten to taste, and flavor with cinnamon. Put aside to become cold. Take a quart of cream, sweeten and flavor with sherry, put in freezer. When it becomes somewhat thick stir in the apples thoroughly. Continue the freezing until hard. When ready to serve fill the apple shells and garnish with candied cherries.[517]

ICE CREAM 1

One pint of milk, one cup of sugar, two small tablespoonfuls flour, one saltspoonful of salt, two eggs, one pint to one quart of cream, half to one cup of sugar, one tablespoonful flavoring extract. Boil the milk, mix the sugar, flour and salt, add the whole eggs, and beat all together. When well mixed turn into the double boiler and cook twenty minutes, stirring constantly until smooth; after that occasionally. When cool add the cream, flavoring and sugar to make it quite sweet. This is a delicious cream. A little black pepper added to vanilla ice cream greatly improves it.[518]

ICE CREAM 2
☛ One pint of cream, one pint milk, four eggs, one and a half cups sugar, butter the size of an egg. Make a custard of the milk, eggs, a tablespoonful of cornstarch and the sugar. When thick remove and add the butter. When cold add the cream. Makes three quarts. Flavor and freeze.[519]

ICE CREAM 3
☛ One tablespoonful of sea moss farina cooked in a quart of milk twenty minutes. Add a cup of sugar and a little lemon juice. When cool add one cup cream; flavor and freeze.[520]

ICE CREAM 4
☛ One quart of sweet cream and the whites of six eggs beaten to a light froth; then beat in the eggs half teacup of sugar. Beat the cream light, and add one teacupful of sugar to cream and beat again until light, flavor with one and a half tablespoonful of vanilla, and put the whole in freezer. Put at the bottom of freezer pail a layer of ice, cover with salt, set freezer in on it and fill in around freezer with ice and salt; a layer of ice and layer of salt until full to the top of freezer; let no salt get inside of freezer. Ten minutes will freeze it.[521]

PINEAPPLE SHERBET
☛ Cut in slices two pine apples, early in the morning, and lay them in one and one-half pounds of fine sugar for three hours. Squeeze all the juice from the apple and put to freeze like ice cream.[522]

PLUM PUDDING GLACE
☛ Scald a pint of milk with a small piece of stick cinnamon in a double boiler. Beat the yolks of six eggs with a cup of sugar until smooth and light. Stir the milk slowly when near boiling into the eggs and sugar. Return to double boiler and stir until it coats the spoon. Have ready four squares or less of chocolate melted over hot water. Add a little of the custard and stir until smooth, then add it to the rest of the custard, also one pint of cream. Strain into the freezer. Add a tablespoonful vanilla. When cold freeze. Cut candied fruit, as apricots, cherries, citron, sultana

Sugar thermometer (left), syrup gauge (right).

raisins, currants and figs, in small pieces. Boil in a syrup of half cup of sugar, same of water. When tender and plump drain, and when cold add to the frozen mixture in can. Mix thoroughly, pack in a mold, then in ice and salt for two or three hours. Surround with whipped cream sweetened and flavored. You can use four yolks and one tablespoonful of flour.[523]

MAPLE MOUSSE

☛ Whip 1 pint of cream; drain it well. Beat the yolks of 4 eggs light. Put into a saucepan a generous cup of maple syrup; stir in the beaten yolks, and place over the fire. Stir until the mixture becomes hot and the eggs thicken the syrup. Take from the fire at once and stand the pan in ice water, and beat the mixture with an egg-beater until it is light and cold; then gently mix with it the whipped cream, and mold for 4 or 6 hours, packed well in ice and salt.[524]

CHOCOLATE MOUSSE

☛ Put a three-quart mold in a wooden pail, first lining the bottom with fine ice and a thin layer of coarse salt. Pack the space between the mold and the pail solidly with fine ice and coarse salt, using two quarts of salt and ice enough to fill the space. Whip one quart of cream and drain it in a sieve. Whip again all the cream that drains through. Put in a small pan one ounce of chocolate, three tablespoonfuls of sugar and one of boiling water and stir over a hot fire until smooth and glossy. Add three tablespoonfuls of cream. Sprinkle a cupful of powdered sugar over the whipped cream.

Pour the chocolate in a thin stream, into the cream, and stir gently until well mixed. Wipe out the chilled mold and turn the cream into it. Cover and then place a little ice lightly on top. Wet a piece of carpet in water and cover the top of the pail. Set away for three or four hours; then take the mold from the ice, dip it in cold water, wipe, and then turn the mousse out on a flat dish.[525]

BANANA PUDDING

☛ 2 boxes vanilla wafers.
4 tablespoons flour.
6 large bananas.
1 tablespoon butter.
1½ cups sugar.
1 tablespoon vanilla.
2 egg yolks.
1 pint milk.

Mix flour and sugar, dissolve with milk, put in beaten yolks and butter. Cook in double boiler until thick. (Pineapple may be used instead of bananas.) Pour this over wafers and bananas which have been sliced lengthwise into pudding dish.[526]

FROZEN PUDDING

☛ Make a rich custard by any recipe and put in freezer. When beginning to freeze add
    ½ cup raisins,
    1 pound almonds, chopped fine,
    1 quart whipped cream.
Stir well to prevent fruit from going to bottom. Before the cream is too stiff, add seasoning of good whisky. Put the whisky last, as it prevents freezing.[527]

FROZEN GELATINE

Gelatine molds.

☛ One box of gelatine soaked in a tumbler of cold water; then pour over one quart boiling water, three cups of sugar, juice of five oranges and three lemons.
    Freeze. Fine.[528]

CARAMEL ICE CREAM

☛ One and a half cups sugar, yolks of seven eggs, one quart sweet cream, one tablespoonful orange flower water, or vanilla if you prefer. Boil half cup of sugar and one-fourth cup boiling water until it turns a light brown color.
    Add one-fourth cup boiling water, stir until the sugar is dissolved. Put in a saucepan with the cream the yolks beaten with a cup of sugar and stir over the fire until nearly boiling.
    When cold, flavor and strain and freeze.[529]

VANILLA ICE CREAM

☛ 2 quarts of rich cream, 1 pound of white sugar, whites of 4 eggs well beaten, and added. Flavor to taste, and freeze. If preferred, leave out the eggs.[530]

FINE VANILLA ICE CREAM

☛ Beat the yolks of eight eggs to a cream, add gradually one quart sweet cream which has been boiled and cooled; add three-fourths of a pound sugar, two teaspoonfuls of vanilla.
    Stir the whole over the fire until nearly boiling; remove and cool; strain into the freezer and freeze.[531]

GENERAL FORREST'S VANILLA ICE CREAM

☛ Boil a vanilla bean in a quart of rich sweet milk till the milk is sufficiently flavored; then take out the bean, and set the milk by to cool; after which stir into it the beaten yolks of half a dozen eggs, and simmer it again till a little thick, stirring it all the time.
    Add three quarters of a pound of sugar, and freeze it.[532]

SUGAR SYRUP

☛ Dissolve two pounds sugar in one pint of cold water, add in beaten white of an egg, stir until the sugar is dissolved, then simmer three minutes, skim well, strain and bottle for use.[533]

METROPOLITAN ICE CREAM

☛ 1½ gallons cream.
Take ½ gallon and color with chocolate and flavor with vanilla.
½ gallon of cream and color with cochineal and flavor with rose.
½ gallon and flavor with lemon.
Freeze each separately and then stack in a mold and put on ice and freeze again. Or take any other combination preferred and pack and freeze.[534]

GRAPE ICE CREAM

☛ Take the white English grapes when perfectly ripe, mash them fine, and press them through a fine wire sieve, that it may keep back the skins, etc. Mix with one quart of the juice, a pound of powdered loaf sugar. When it is completely dissolved, stir in a quart of sweet cream, and freeze it.[535]

PINEAPPLE MOUSSE

☛ Dissolve one ounce of gelatine (half box) in three-fourths of a cup cold water; after one hour add one cup hot water, three-fourths pound of sugar, the juice of a lemon and one can of grated pineapple. Stir until it begins to thicken, then add a cup of cream that has been whipped stiff. Put in mold and bury in salt and ice for three hours.[536]

COFFEE ICE CREAM

☛ Make a boiled custard. Whilst it is boiling, pour in 2 tablespoons of roasted coffee, in grains. Stir it for a little while; then strain off the grains and freeze the custard.[537]

French coffee pot and filter.

STRAWBERRY ICE CREAM

☛ One quart strawberries, one quart cream. If very rich use one pint cream and one pint milk. Wash and hull the berries, rejecting bad ones, add one pint of sugar and crush. Let the mixture stand two hours, then strain and squeeze, add the cream, color slightly and freeze. In freezing never drain off water which forms in tub. Turn crank slowly at first.[538]

TEA ICE CREAM

☛ Put two tablespoonfuls of good tea in a tea pot, pour on enough boiling water to cover it, and let it stand for half an hour to infuse. Stir into a quart of sweet cream the beaten yolks of eight eggs, and simmer it slowly till it becomes thick. Having strained the tea, stir it into the cream, and cool and freeze it as directed.[539]

FROZEN CUSTARD

☞ One quart of milk, yolks six eggs, one cup of sugar. Put the milk on to boil. Beat light the yolks and sugar, little salt. When milk boils, set off; in a few moments pour slowly on the eggs and sugar, stirring constantly. Set aside to cool. When ready to freeze beat the whites until foamy, and when you put in freezer flavor.

Put in some cream, if not more than half a cup. Should the custard curdle it will be smooth when frozen.[540]

CHOCOLATE ICE CREAM

☞ Melt two bars sweetened vanilla chocolate, with one or two tablespoons water, mix with a little cream, when smooth mix with the remainder of the cream. Flavor with teaspoon of vanilla and half teaspoon Ceylon cinnamon.[541]

PEACH ICE CREAM

☞ Select peaches that are very ripe and soft, peel them, extract the stones, and mash them to a marmalade.

Glace grapes in a nest of spun sugar.

Having one quart of peach pulp, mix with it one pound of powdered sugar, a grated nutmeg and a teaspoonful of powdered cinnamon; stir it into a quart of rich sweet cream, and freeze it as directed.

If cream is not to be had, substitute a quart of rich sweet milk, stir into it the beaten yolks of five or six eggs, simmer it till the eggs are sufficiently cooked, set it by till cold, and then stir into it the peaches, etc. as before directed.[542]

COCOANUT ICE CREAM

☞ Take a large cocoanut from the shell, pare off the dark skin, and grate the nutmeg fine. Have ready a quart of sweet cream and three quarters of a pound of loaf sugar. Stir into the cream two tablespoonfuls of rose water, and then stir in alternately the sugar and grated cocoanut. When it is very smooth, freeze it over twice by the directions.

If you serve it in glasses, pile it high on the top, and always accompany ice cream, whatever kind it may be, with some nice kind of cake: sponge-cake is generally preferred.

Send round your wines and cordials very soon after a course of cream and cake.[543]

SOUTHERN PUDDING

☛ 3 tablespoons corn starch.
5 eggs.
6 tablespoons sugar.
1 quart milk.
Canned peaches or preferred fruit.
Pinch salt.

Beat yolks of eggs light, add sugar and beat again until very light. Mix corn starch with a little cold milk and stir into 1 quart scalded milk. Add salt and stir until it thickens.

Pour into pudding dish, place in oven, let remain until it will bear icing. Place over top, layer of canned peaches or preferred fruit. (It improves to mix the syrup of fruit with custard.)

Beat white of eggs to stiff froth with 2 tablespoons of sugar to each egg. Spread on custard, brown evenly in oven. This is a very delicate pudding.[544]

GINGER SHERBET

☛ One-fourth pound Canton Ginger, cut in small pieces add to it four cups water, one cup sugar, boil ten minutes, add half cup orange juice and half cup lemon juice. Cooled, strained and frozen.[545]

BANANA SHERBET

☛ Put three cups water, one and a half cups sugar in a smooth saucepan, and boil five minutes, add the juice of one lemon and two oranges, and a little of the grated rind of each, and a cup of banana pulp run through a sieve.

Beat the syrup and fruit mixture until cold, then stir in three cups whipped cream, measured after whipping, or the whites of three eggs beaten stiff; if you have no cream, add half cup of sherry. Freeze until soft like mush. Serve in frappe glasses.[546]

GRAPE SHERBET

☛ Boil one quart of water and one pint sugar together a few minutes, add a teaspoon granulated gelatine that has been swollen, when cool add the juice of two lemons and a pint of grape juice. Freeze.[547]

LEMON SHERBET

☛ One quart water, one and a half cups of sugar, juice of four limes, one teaspoon gelatine softened in cold water, then dissolved in the hot syrup. May flavor with sherry.[548]

ORANGE SHERBET

☛ One tablespoon gelatine swollen in half cup cold water, then dissolve in half cup boiling water, add one cup sugar, and another cup cold water, add one pint orange juice, with a little lemon juice. Freeze.[549]

RASPBERRY SHERBET
☞ One pint raspberries, one pint sugar, one pint water, juice two lemons, one tablespoon gelatine dissolved.[550]

STRAWBERRY SHERBET
☞ Three quarts berries, wash, stem and sweeten with three cups sugar, mash to a pulp, then strain through a puree sieve, add the juice of two lemons, and three quarts water, make quite sweet and freeze.[551]

BOMBE GLACE
☞ Make a quart of sherbet, line the freezer around the bottom and sides, color the sherbet with a little pink and fill the center with the following filling.[552]

CHARLOTTE RUSSE FILLING
☞ Beat the white of an egg until dry, add one-third cup powdered sugar, one cup double cream, one teaspoon vanilla, two tablespoons wine or orange extract. Beat the cream with the flavoring until thick to the bottom of the bowl, fold the two mixture together, fill the center of the freezer with candied cherries. Sprinkled through the cream is very pretty. You may line the freezer with chocolate ice cream, and fill the center with charlotte russe filling, and filled with chopped candied fruit is one of the best. If pineapple sherbet is used, color a delicate green. Bury in ice and salt two or three hours.[553]

Charlotte russe with cake arranged in strips of two colors.

TUTTI-FRUTTI ICE CREAM
☞ 1 quart cream,
1 pint milk,
Yolks of 5 eggs,
3 cups sugar,
1 lemon,
1 glass whisky.
Crystallized fruit or candied fruit of any kind, cherries, raisins, currants, citrons, peaches, etc. Beat sugar and eggs together and add to the milk, which must be at boiling point. Boil 10 minutes. When cold, add the cream and freeze. When half frozen, add 1 pound fruit, which has been mixed with the lemon and whisky. Cover and freeze well.[554]

FROZEN MINT
☞ Make a quart of lemon ice, to two tablespoons water, add a teaspoon essence of peppermint, and stir into the ice with enough green color paste to make it a delicate green. Freeze and serve like a cordial in small glasses.[555]

CONFEDERATE PINEAPPLE ICE CREAM

☛ 2 quarts rich cream,
4 cups sugar,
2 cans of pineapple or two ripe pineapples.
Make a syrup of the sugar and add 1 tablespoon gelatine. Add juice of 1 lemon and boil. When cool, add half of the cream and put in the freezer. When it begins to freeze, add the pineapple, which has been chopped very fine, and after a few turns add the rest of the cream, which has been well whipped.[556]

BANANA ICE CREAM

☛ Peel and mash fine six ripe bananas with a silver knife, stir into two quarts of lemon ice cream, when half frozen beat the fruit in well and finish freezing. Freshly grated cocoanut may be used the same way.[557]

SOUTH CAROLINA CURDS

☛ Heat one quart of rich milk until lukewarm; stir into it one large spoonful of liquid rennet, and let it set. Drain off the whey and pour the curds into a perforated milk-pan or a clean basket to drip for twenty-four hours. Turn out on a platter and serve with powdered sugar, cinnamon, and very thick cream. Strawberry jam may be used instead of the cinnamon. If too dry, a little of the cream may be beaten into the curds.[558]

VIRGINIA DARE PUDDING

☛ Sift one quart of flour and into the flour put one pound of raisins, one pound of currants, one-half teaspoonful of salt, one pound of sugar, one grated nutmeg, one teaspoonful of ground spice. Beat four eggs and add after mixing the fruit well in the flour, and mix with enough water to make a stiff batter as for fruit cake. Boil or bake and serve with sauce. Cook for about two hours.[559]

ROMAN PUNCH

☛ Two quarts water, one pound sugar, five lemons, half pint Jamaica rum. Boil the sugar and water, when cold add the juice of the lemons, freeze, when half frozen add the rum. Let the punch stand two hours to ripen after freezing.[560]

GINGER ICE CREAM

☛ Use any plain ice cream, when half frozen stir in a cup of preserved ginger, minced very fine with two tablespoons of the syrup, from the preserves. Freeze until hard.[561]

GINGER ICE

☛ Is made by adding the minced ginger to two quarts lemon or pineapple ice.[562]

ORANGE ICE

☛ 1½ pints of orange juice mixed with ½ pint of cold water. Stir in ½ pound of loaf sugar; pare thin the rinds of 6 deep colored oranges. Cut the oranges in pieces, and lay in the bottom of a dish, over which pour the juice. Cover it, and let it stand 1 hour; then strain it into a freezer.[563]

RULES FOR CAKE MAKING

☛ In making cake accuracy in measuring the ingredients are absolutely necessary. Success follows those who give strict attention to details. The baking is usually the most difficult part. Eggs must be fresh, butter sweet, flour fine. Butter cakes, as pound, fruit and cup, must be baked in a very moderate oven; while layer cakes may be baked more quickly. Angel Food and Sunshine cake should be cooked in a very cool oven, the heat increased slowly for an hour, browning at the last. Use a wooden spoon to cream butter, and a yellow or white bowl to mix the cake in, but never tin. First measure everything before beginning; beat the eggs separately unless the receipt says otherwise. I find some cake [such] as pound [cake] are better to break in one egg at a time and beat with the butter and sugar. Beat the butter to a cream before adding the sugar, then beat the sugar and butter until light before adding the eggs. Usually, when a recipe calls for a teaspoonful it means a rounding spoonful, each teaspoonful may be replaced by half a level teaspoon soda and a rounding teaspoon cream of tartar sifted with the flour three or four times. Dried fruit as raisins and currents must be clean and well floured and added at the last moment to the batter; if the fruit sinks to the bottom of the cake, the cake is not sufficiently thick to hold it up, add more flour to the batter. Measuring cups hold half a pint. Never use butter to grease pans, suet is better, or lard. Have the oven ready as soon as the cake is made. Cookies and thin cakes require a moderately quick oven. Molasses cake a very moderate oven. If the oven becomes too hot put in a pan of cold water. Cakes baked too quick will come up in the center, crack and run over the sides of pan. Do not jar the stove or open the door until the cake is set. Do not cover a cake with paper; it burns and spoils the flavor of cake. If necessary to look at a cake while baking, do it as quickly as possible and open and close the door very carefully. Be sure the cake is done before you take it from the oven. Hold it to your ear; if it ticks loudly it is not done and will fall when removed. When it leaves the sides of pan, or when you press on it and it rebounds it is very apt to be done. Line the pans with paper, grease and sift over a little flour.

Different types of small cakes and the tins in which they were baked.

A good rule is to use two-thirds as much sugar as flour; if more is used it is apt to burn or fall. After creaming the butter the sugar is added gradually, then the eggs; then the flour, salt and baking powder is sifted together and added alternately with the milk or wetting. This is done to avoid curdling the butter by the cold liquid. Curdling always causes coarse texture. Fruit is always floured and added last.

Layer cakes and small cakes require a hotter oven than loaf cake; so cakes made with baking powder call for a higher temperature than do cakes made of soda and cream of tartar. You may use lemon juice with soda, or molasses with soda. Sponge and pound cake will bake at a lower temperature than cake lightened with soda or baking powder. Gold cake requires less heat than cake made from whites of eggs. Cake containing fruit must be baked slowly. Always use pastry flour for cake, and fine granulated sugar. Powdered sugar makes a close, dry cake, and coarse granulated sugar a very coarse grained cake. If yeast is used, bread flour is best to use. A pound cake is improved by a small quantity of baking powder.

Your hand is best to cream butter; the warmth of the hand is sufficient heat. But don't beat the yolks at all, just put them in. In cake mixtures with butter use a fork to beat in whites of eggs.

When baking cake in a gas stove, light both burners when cake is half made up to get just the right heat. Put a small pan of water in bottom and put the cake one-third from the bottom. If butter cake, decrease the heat after fully risen; if sponge, increase heat.

To tell when cake is done, put the pan to your ear; if you hear it crackle it is not done. Another very good test; when it leaves the side of pan all around; and if you press your finger on it and it rebounds, it is done.[564]

CONFEDERATE DAUGHTERS CAKE

☛ Cream one-half cupful of sweet butter with one and one-half cupfuls of sugar until very light; add one-half teaspoonful of almond flavoring and one cupful of milk, and mix carefully. Have ready, sifted together, three cupfuls of flour and two tablespoonfuls of Royal baking powder, and add. Last of all, fold in the whites of six eggs, beaten stiff. Bake in a moderate oven three-quarters of an hour. When it is cold take a strong linen thread and divide it into three layers, between which put the following mixture: Blanch five ounces of almonds; pound them in a mortar to a fine paste; add carefully to one pint of thick cream, sweeten, and beat until stiff, when it is ready for use. Decorate the top with the cream and halves of the almonds made to represent the petals of a flower, with one-half a candied cherry in the center of each.[565]

From a vintage ad.

MOCHA CAKE

☛ Beat three eggs well, whites and yolks separately; cream one cupful of granulated sugar with the yolks, one teaspoonful of vanilla extract, one tablespoonful of milk, and then one cupful of sifted flour, to which one teaspoonful of Royal baking powder has been added. When these have been well mixed, fold in the well-beaten whites of three eggs. Bake in a buttered tin in a moderate oven, and when cold divide into four layers with a strong linen thread. Brush each layer with some strong, black coffee, then fill with the following mixture.

Filling: Cream one-half pound of unsalted butter with one-quarter pound of sugar, stirring till smooth. Beat in, one by one, the yolks of three eggs, and then strong black coffee to taste. Spread between layers and on the top of the cake.[566]

French crullers.

CHOCOLATE LAYER CAKE

☛ Whites of 3 eggs,
1 cup of cream or rich milk,
3 cups flour, sifted with 2 teaspoons baking powder,
2 large tablespoons butter.

Cream the butter and sugar; then add flour and cream. Add the eggs last, and flavor with a little vanilla. Bake in jelly-pans, and when nearly cool put a filling between them and on top.

Filling:
2 cups brown sugar,
½ cake Baker's chocolate.

Cover with milk and add a tablespoon of butter. Cook till thick. Flavor with vanilla, and spread on cakes while warm.[567]

CRULLERS

☛ 1 cup of sugar,
½ cup of butter,
1 cup of sweet milk,
2 teaspoons of baking-powder,
Nutmeg, cinnamon, or rose water to taste,
3 eggs,
Flour enough to make a stiff dough.

Beat the yolks very light; add sugar, butter; then milk, with flour for stiff dough. Add seasoning and the whites well beaten. At the last, add baking-powder. Roll, cut in shapes, and fry rich brown in hot lard.[568]

MRS. BOYKIN'S FRUIT CAKE

☛ Make a pound cake of one pound brown sugar, one pound butter creamed, one pound of flour with three light teaspoonfuls of baking powder, twelve eggs beaten together, one cup sweet cream, one cup molasses, one teaspoonful each cloves, mace, allspice, nutmeg, one pint whiskey, one pound shelled almonds blanched and run through the food chopper, two pounds raisins, two pounds currants, one and a half pounds citron, one pound dates cut small. Flour the fruit with some of the pound of flour. Finest I ever ate.[569]

SOUTHERN BIRTHDAY CAKE

☛ 1 cup (½ lb.) butter.
1 teaspoon grated nutmeg.
2 cups (1 lb.) sugar.
1 teaspoon Royal baking powder.
4 eggs.
1 cup (½ pt.) milk.
4 cups flour.
1 cup (6 oz.) Sultana raisins.
1 wine glass brandy or fruit juice.
½ cup currants.
¼ teaspoon salt.
½ cup shredded citron.

Cream butter and sugar together. Add eggs, one at a time, and beat well. Add milk, fruit and brandy, also flour sifted with baking powder, salt and nutmeg. Pour into a well greased papered cake tin. Bake in a moderate oven two hours. Turn out, and when cool cover with white frosting. If desired, this cake may be decorated with tiny shamrocks and candles. This is sufficient for 14 to 16 persons.[570]

Southern birthday cake.

GENERAL ABE BUFORD'S CAKE

☛ One cup butter, two of white sugar, four of sifted flour, five eggs beaten separately, one cup sour milk, tea-spoon soda, pound seeded raisins chopped a little; beat the butter and sugar to a cream, add the yolks and milk, and stir in the flour with soda well mixed through it; then add the white of the eggs beaten to a stiff froth, and lastly the raisins dredged with a little flour; bake one and one-half hours. Use coffee-cups to measure. This makes a cake for a six quart pan.[571]

JUMBLE CAKE

☛ One teacup of butter, one and one-half teacups of sugar, one and one-half pints of flour; four eggs, two teaspoonfuls of cinnamon, one-half teacup of almonds chopped fine, two teaspoonfuls of yeast powder sifted in the flour. Beat the butter, sugar and eggs together, then add the flour.

Put cinnamon and almonds in and work the whole up well, then roll on the board to thickness of half an inch, and cut out a finger's length and join together at ends, so as to be round. Grease pans with butter and put to bake.[572]

MOBILE FRUIT CAKE

☞ One pound sugar, one pound flour, one dozen eggs, four pounds raisins, two pounds currants, one pound citron, half pound shelled almonds, one teaspoonful allspice, one teaspoonful each of mace and cloves, one tablespoonful cinnamon, little salt, one teaspoonful of soda in a glass of water, two wineglasses whiskey. Dredge your fruit with part of the flour. Elegant.[573]

EXCELSIOR FRUIT CAKE

☞ Ten eggs beaten together, one pound of butter, one pound of sugar, one pound flour, one pound citron, one and a half pounds raisins, spice with cinnamon and nutmeg, wineglass of wine, same of brandy, half teaspoonful of soda dissolved in the wine. Flour your fruit well. The batter should be stiff enough for the fruit not to settle. When the fruit is all through, it is the best cake made. Nice as patties.[574]

OLD VIRGINIA FRUIT CAKE

☞ 6 eggs.
 1 lb. citron.
 6 cups sifted flour.
 1 lb. nut meats.
 3 cups sugar.
 1 teaspoon each cloves and mace.
 1 cup black molasses.
 1 tablespoon cinnamon.
 1½ cups butter.
 1 wine glass brandy.
 3 lbs. raisins.
 1 teaspoon soda dissolved in.
 1 lb. currants.
 1 cup buttermilk.
 2 lbs. figs.

Cream butter and sugar together; add well beaten eggs. Stir spices into molasses and add to mixture; then pour in buttermilk. Cut fruit in pieces and dredge with flour. Stir in mixture; add remaining flour. Stir in brandy. Bake very slowly for 5 or 6 hours over large pan boiling water.[575]

NUT AND RAISIN CAKE

☞ Cream half a cup of butter and a cup of sugar, half cup of seeded and cut raisins, two eggs, half cup milk, one and three-fourths cups of flour, two and a half level teaspoonfuls baking powder, two squares of chocolate melted, half cup walnut meats cut small, a little salt, half teaspoonful of vanilla. Add the raisins to the butter and sugar. The chocolate and nuts are put in last. Frost with boiled frosting and decorate with nuts and raisins.[576]

MASON AND DIXON COOKIES

☞ One cup of brown sugar,
One-half cup of melted shortening,
One egg,
One-half cup of sweet milk,
One-half teaspoonful of soda sifted with flour,
One and one-half cups of flour,
One-half cup of chopped raisins,
One-half cup of chopped nuts,
One-half teaspoonful of salt,
Three squares of melted chocolate.
Mix in order given and bake in moderate oven.[577]

FRUIT CAKE

☞ One pound of butter, down weight, two pounds sugar, three pounds flour, twelve eggs, half pint molasses with the spices in it and heated gradually, one tablespoonful allspice, one teaspoonful of cloves, two tablespoonfuls cinnamon, two nutmegs, one tumbler of wine, nearly one pint of whiskey, one teaspoonful of soda in a little water, three good teaspoonfuls baking powder in the flour. Put all this in before you put in the fruit. Three pounds raisins, two pounds currants, one pound citron, half pound orange and lemon peel, one pound crystalized pineapple, one pound cherries, three pounds pecans in shells. Mix the fruit in a little of the flour and add last. Makes three nice cakes. Half makes one large cake. Fine.[578]

Spice box.

CONFEDERATE WHITE FRUIT CAKE

☞ Whites of twelve eggs beaten stiff, one pound sugar, one pound of flour with two teaspoonfuls baking powder in it, three-fourths of a pound of butter, one cup sweet milk, wineglass of wine, fruit, one pound desiccated cocoanut, one pound shelled almonds, one and a half pounds citron dredged in flour. Add half the sugar to the stiff whites. Cream the butter and add the rest of sugar, beat till light. Mix the flour and milk in alternately, now the white and sugar, a little rose water. Lastly the fruit and wine.[579]

ROBERT E. LEE JELLY CAKE

☛ Use any recipe for sponge layer cake and fill with the following:
Yolks of 3 eggs,
Juice and grated rind of 1 lemon,
¼ pound of butter,
½ pound of sugar.
Put in a skillet on the stove and stir till cooked; then put in the well-beaten 3 whites. As soon as it comes to a boil, take off and stir till cold. Put between layers of cake.[580]

SIMPLE WHITE CUP CAKE

☛ 5 eggs,
1 cup of butter,
1 cup of milk,
3 cups of flour after sifting,
2 cups of sugar,
2 teaspoons baking-powder.[581]

IMPERIAL CAKE

☛ Half pound butter, half pound sugar, half pound flour, five eggs, grated rind and juice of half a lemon, half pound raisins, half pound citrons, half cup of walnut meats, one-fourth teaspoonful soda. Add the whites beaten stiff to the creamed butter and sugar, then the flour with the soda in it, then the fruit cut fine and rubbed with some of the flour, then the lemon juice and grated rind. Elegant.[582]

NORFOLK TEA CAKE

☛ One pound of flour, the same quantity of sugar, half a pound of butter, and six eggs, with flavoring of lemon or vanilla.[583]

PALMETTO CAKE

☛ One pound of flour, the same of butter, a pound and a quarter of sugar, twelve eggs, two grated cocoanuts, and two pounds of citron sliced and floured as for fruit cake. Beat well and bake as pound cake, but it will require a longer time in the oven on account of the fruit.[584]

RICHMOND CAKE

☛ One tablespoonful of butter and one teacupful and a half of white sugar, beaten together to a cream, two eggs well beaten, one cupful of milk, with a teaspoonful of soda, dissolved in hot water and added to it, and a pint of flour with two teaspoonfuls of cream of tartar mixed in it. Beat all well together, and flavor to your taste.[585]

FRUIT CAKE FROSTING

☛ Mix four cups sugar with just enough water to spread without running. Flavor it. While moist sprinkle with all kinds chopped nuts, fruits and cocoanut, as crystalized fruits, raisins and citron.[586]

SILVER CAKE

☛ Half pound of butter, down weight, two cups sugar, one cup sweet milk, four light cups flour, one level teaspoonful of soda sifted with the flour two or three times, whites of eight eggs. After beating a little add two rounding teaspoonfuls cream of tartar and beat until stiff, but not too stiff. Almond extract or rose to flavor. First warm the sugar and cream the butter with it, then add flour, milk and whites alternately until it is all in, beat thoroughly, flavor and bake as a solid cake or layers.

Southern party cake.

The heat of the oven has everything to do with successful cake baking, and be careful not to let it get too hot. Your cake should first rise in the oven before it commences to brown on top. A cake made with soda and cream of tartar will not fall as one made with baking powder.[587]

EXCELLENT MARBLE CAKE

☛ White part:
    Whites of 7 eggs,
    3 teacups sugar,
    1 teacup of butter,
    4 teacups flour,
    1 teacup sour cream,
    ½ teaspoon soda in cream,
    1 teaspoon of cream of tartar in flour.

Cream sugar and butter. Add cream; then flour and eggs alternately. Flavor to taste and bake in layers.

    Dark part:
    Yolks of 7 eggs,
    2 teacups of brown sugar,
    1 teacup of molasses,
    1 teacup butter,
    5 teacups flour,
    1 teacup of sour cream,
    1 teaspoon soda in cream,
    Spices to taste.

Bake in layers, and stack alternate layers of dark and white together with white icing, flavored with lemon.[588]

ENGLISH WALNUT CAKE

☛ Make a batter as for white cake, bake in layers; put together with icing (into which has been stirred a teaspoonful of butter); and place

English walnuts in large pieces between each layer, icing the bottom of each layer of cake as well as the top. When it is stacked, ice and stick over the top the nuts, shelled carefully, breaking them in halves, placing the broken side down.[589]

PRIDE OF THE CONFEDERACY WHITE CAKE
☛ Whites of ten or twelve eggs, half pound butter, two cups sugar, three cups flour, two slightly rounding teaspoonfuls of baking powder sifted in the flour, three-fourths of a cup of sweet milk, one teaspoonful almond and vanilla mixed in milk.

To mix: Set your mixing bowl in a pan of hot water; put in your butter, and with a perforated spoon commence to cream it, and should it soften too much remove bowl from water; add a little sugar at a time, say a teaspoonful, until all the sugar is worked in. Use the bottom of spoon to blend with.

Next beat the whites stiff and set aside to dry. Now add the milk very slowly; after it is all in turn in some flour. Use the top of spoon to mix, alternating flour and whites, letting flour be last. Don't have any dry flour around the edges, or it will be tough; keep the edges wiped off.

Line your cake pan with paper, pour in batter, light both burners for five minutes, then turn both off half, put cake on middle shelf, cover over; in three-fourths of an hour remove cover and brown.

Top and side of bride's cake.

Should the batter get too thin it will be tough, or sugar in whites makes it tough. Try using one level teaspoonful of soda to three level teaspoonfuls of cream of tartar.[590]

KENTUCKY WHITE CAKE
☛ One and one half teacupfuls of butter, two and one half teacupfuls of sugar, three and one half teacupfuls of flour, twelve eggs (whites); heaping teaspoonful baking powder. Cream butter and sugar together, beating thoroughly. Beat the whites of the eggs to a stiff froth; add to the butter and sugar the flour and whites alternately. Beat well for fifteen minutes after all is mixed. Bake in a loaf in a moderate oven.[591]

BRIDE'S CAKE
☛ One cup of butter creamed with one cup of sugar, two cups of flour, whites of eight eggs, two level teaspoonfuls of baking powder; flavor with lemon, rose or almond extract.

Add part of the whites beaten stiff to the butter and sugar, then the flour sifted with the baking powder, the extract and remainder of the eggs. Bake in pan with tube in center.[592]

ELEGANT CAKE

☞ One cup butter, two of sugar, three and a half cups flour, half cup of milk, four level teaspoonfuls baking powder, whites of seven eggs. Bake in layers or one sheet.[593]

LEMON CHEESE CAKE

☞ 1 cupful butter.
1½ cupfuls sugar.
3 cupfuls flour.
2-3 cupful sweet milk.
1 teaspoonful baking powder.
5 eggs.
Filling:
2 large lemons.
1 teacupful sugar.
2 eggs.
1 tablespoonful butter.
Bake batter quickly in layer pans. Filling: Mix butter and sugar, add lemons, then eggs; cook over slow fire till well jellied. Then place between layers. Be careful not to burn.[594]

DELICATE CAKE

☞ Three-fourths of a cup of butter, two cups sugar, three cups of flour, half cup milk, two teaspoonfuls baking powder, whites of six eggs, little almond extract. Bake in loaf or layers. Perfectly delightful.[595]

WHITE MOUNTAIN CAKE

☞ Cream one cup of butter and three cups of sugar until light; now add four cups of flour sifted with two teaspoonfuls of baking powder alternately with one cup of milk, and the whites of twelve eggs beaten stiff; almond to flavor. Weighs three pounds.[596]

WHITE POUND CAKE

☞ One cup of butter, one cup of sugar, two cups flour, whites of eight eggs, one level teaspoonful of baking powder, half teaspoonful lemon extract.[597]

ANGEL CAKE

☞ The secret of good angel cake is, it must be baked very slowly. Put a drop of water in the oven; if it dries out slowly it is just right. One cup measured whites of eggs (about ten eggs), one and a half cups fine granulated sugar, one rounding cup of sifted flour, one level teaspoonful cream of tartar, very little salt, teaspoonful almond extract. Put the whites in an earthen bowl, break lightly with the surprise beater, sift in the cream of tartar and salt, and beat until the eggs will cling to the bowl, sift in the sugar gradually and the almond extract; lastly, sift in the flour.

Horn of plenty in nougat filled with glace grapes.

Use the surprise beater and combine as gently as possible. Put in an ungreased pan with a paper on the bottom, cover with a flat sheet, but do not exclude the air. In half an hour remove the cover, increase the heat a little and bake half an hour longer. Turn pan upside down to cool. Bake with one burner turned off one-half. If baked fast it will be tough.[598]

ANGEL FOOD CAKE

☛ Whites of 12 eggs,
10 ounces icing sugar,
3½ ounces flour,
1 teaspoon vanilla,
1 teaspoon cream of tartar.

Sift flour 5 times; add cream of tartar and sift again. Sift sugar 3 times. Beat eggs very light; add sugar, vanilla, and flour last, stirred in very lightly. Bake 50 or 60 minutes. When done, do not take out of mold till cold. The mold should be greased only on the bottom. When taken out of the oven it must be turned upside down on something to let the air to it.[599]

DEVILS FOOD CAKE

☛ 2 cups sugar.
3 eggs.
3 cups sifted flour.
¾ cup grated chocolate.
½ cup Snowdrift [shortening].
1 teaspoon soda.
1 cup sour milk.
1 teaspoon baking powder.
1 cup hot water.
¼ teaspoon salt.

Add sugar to Snowdrift, cream well, put in egg yolks, then chocolate dissolved in hot water, beat well. Dissolve soda in milk add to mixture, gradually sift in 2 cups of flour, beating well. Alternate last cup of flour and baking powder with well beaten egg whites. Add salt and favorite flavoring, bake in moderate oven, put together and ice with caramel.[600]

ARKANSAS ANGEL CAKE

☛ 1 dozen eggs (whites).
1 teaspoon vanilla.
1½ cups sugar.
1 teaspoon cream of tartar.
1 cup flour.

Sift sugar eight times, the last time into the beaten whites and stir until smooth. Sift cream of tartar into the flour and sift flour eight times, the last time into the mixture. Fold in gently, but do not beat. Put in ungreased pan and bake slowly 50 minutes. When done, the cake should be turned down on the edge of two cups until thoroughly cold before removing from pan.[601]

SUNSHINE CAKE

☛ Whites of seven eggs, yolks of five, one and a fourth cups of sugar, one cup of flour sifted before measuring, one-third teaspoonful cream of tartar in whites and beaten very stiff; beat the sugar in whites, beat yolks light, add a little salt and add to the whites and sugar, next the grated rind and juice of half a lemon, lastly a cup of flour folded in.[602]

GATEAU A LA WICKESSER

☛ A sponge cake, half pound fine granulated sugar, half pound of flour, thirteen yolks, nine whites of eggs, juice and rind of one lemon. Stir the sugar and yolks twenty-five minutes by the clock, then beat the whites stiff. Add the sugar and yolks slowly to the whites, beating constantly, then the lemon, and beat five minutes, then the sifted flour stirred in lightly. Butter a large round pan, dust it with flour, pour in the batter. Place the cake on a pan of salt and bake slowly. When done turn out on a board, dust with sugar and spread pineapple marmalade over the cake. Cover with the following glaze.[603]

SUGAR GLAZE

☛ One cup powdered sugar, two tablespoonfuls water, put over the fire and let get lukewarm, pour over the cake and decorate with crystalized fruit. Elegant.[604]

CONFEDERATE SPONGE CAKE

☛ Ten eggs, their weight in sugar, the weight of five in flour, juice of a lemon. Reject two yolks. Mix the lemon juice and two tablespoonfuls of the sugar with the yolks, beat with the Dover until very thick; now add a teaspoonful of lemon extract. Beat the whites very stiff, sift in the rest of the sugar, then pour in the yolk mixture; next, sift in the flour, a little at a time.

When it is all in stop at once; a little salt in the whites. Put in an ungreased pan. Cover and bake as angel cake. By measure two cups of sugar, two rounding cups of flour.[605]

JELLY ROLL

☛ Half pound sugar, nine ounces flour, one teaspoonful baking powder, half cup of milk, three eggs, half teaspoonful of lemon, pinch of salt. Sift flour, sugar and baking powder into a bowl and make a hollow in center; put in milk, eggs and lemon; mix all together.

Grease a large, shallow tin pan, cover with paper, spread on the mixture thin and evenly, bake in a slow oven. When done remove the pan, let stand a few moments to cool off, then turn upside down on a clean paper.

Remove the paper and spread with acid jelly over the surface. Roll the cake up like a music roll and let it lie until cold.[606]

BLACK CAKE

1 pound flour,
1 pound sugar, sifted,
1 pound butter,
12 eggs, beaten separately,
2 nutmegs,
1 small teacup of blackberry jam,
1 cup of dark molasses,
2 cups of brandy or whisky,
2 pounds raisins,
2 pounds currants,
½ pound citron,
1 tablespoon cloves,
2 tablespoons cinnamon,
1 tablespoon mace,
1 tablespoon allspice,
¼ pound figs, chopped fine,
½ cup of nuts,
1 small cup vinegar,
1 teaspoon soda,
½ pound candied orange.

Put the flour in a bread-pan and brown to a dark color. Do not burn it. Beat the eggs separately, then together. Cut the citron in very thin slices and dredge with flour. Dredge the fruits with flour and chop the figs and crush the nuts.

Beat the butter and sugar to a cream, and add eggs alternately with the flour. Add molasses, jam, brandy, and spices, and then the nuts.

Stir the fruits in lightly, and just before putting in the pan, add the vinegar, in which the teaspoon soda is stirred, and pour foaming into the mixture.

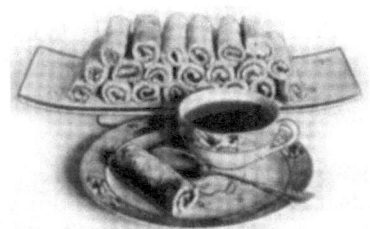

Little jelly rolls.

Put in a layer of the mixture, then sprinkle the citron over it, then another layer, and so on, but do not put any on top. Bake slowly for 4 hours or longer.

When cold, cover with icing flavored with a little citric acid.[607]

ROLLED SPONGE CAKE

☛ Beat until light four yolks of eggs with one cup of sugar; add four tablespoonfuls cold water and one cup of flour with a teaspoonful of baking powder in it; then fold in the stiff whites of four eggs. Bake in a square pan. Spread with jelly and roll. Serve with whipped cream or cocoanut foamy sauce. A pretty and delicious dessert.[608]

CARAMEL CAKE

☛ 5 eggs.
1½ teacupfuls sugar.
4 teacupfuls flour.
1 teacupful butter.
½ teacupful sweet milk.
2 teaspoonfuls baking powder.

Beat the yolks and half the sugar well; the butter and rest of sugar, cream together. Mix these and beat in the milk, then the flour with the baking powder well mixed in, and the whites of eggs, beaten to a stiff froth. Bake in layer pans.

Birthday party and cake.

For the caramel, brown half a cup of sugar in a flat pan; let it almost burn, then dissolve it, by pouring one cup of boiling water over it and letting it remain on the fire for fifteen minutes. When well dissolved, pour it over two cups of sugar and boil as for icing, stirring often. When it will fall from the spoon in short drops, add butter the size of a walnut; let boil five minutes, stirring all the time. Then take from the fire and beat until stiff enough to spread on the cakes. Use plain icing or the caramel for top and sides. Flavoring can be used, but is not necessary if the sugar is browned sufficiently.[609]

ROBERT E. LEE CAKE

☛ Bake a large white cake in layers. Filling: One lb. grated cocoanut, 1 lb. grated pineapple, 1 lb. blanched almonds; mix with icing and spread.[610]

IDEAL SPONGE CAKE

☛ Four eggs, one-fourth teaspoonful of salt, one cup of fine granulated sugar, three-fourths cup of flour, grated rind of half an orange or lemon, one tablespoonful of orange or lemon juice. Beat the whites with salt until dry; beat in half the sugar gradually. Beat the yolks the same length of time by the clock, and beat in the rest of sugar. Add the rind and juice and beat the two together. Now sprinkle the flour in, little by little, folding it under with a perforated spoon. Do not beat after any of the flour is added.[611]

STEAMED HUCKLEBERRY PUDDING

☞ 1 qt. berries.
1½ cups milk.
1 cup syrup (Georgia cane).
¾ teaspoon soda.
½ teaspoon salt.
Flour.

Wash and dry berries; flour them as if for fruit cake. Stir soda into syrup; add milk and salt; add flour sufficient to make very stiff batter. Carefully stir in berries—avoid breaking them; put in greased steamer or mold; steam three hours, and serve with hard sauce.[612]

AFRICAN SPONGE DROPS

☞ Bake some large sponge drops. When cold scoop the inside out. Coat them with chocolate icing. Fill them with stiff whipped cream and put two together and serve.[613]

VIRGINIA SPONGE CAKE

☞ Twelve eggs, the weight of eight eggs in sugar, and the weight of six eggs in flour. The juice of a lemon, or a tablespoonful of vinegar. Beat all well together. Put in the flour last.[614]

SCRIPTURE CAKE

☞ Four and one-half cups of I Kings 4:28, flour; one and one-half cups of Judges 5:25, butter, L. C.; two cups of Jeremiah 6:20, sugar; two cups of I Samuel 30:12, raisins; two cups of Nahum 3:12, figs; one cup of Numbers 17:8, almonds; two tablespoonfuls of I Samuel 14:25, honey; season to taste with II Chronicles 9:9, spices; six of Jeremiah 17:11, eggs; a pinch of Leviticus, salt; one and one-half cups of Judges 4:19, milk, L. C.; two teaspoonfuls of Amos 4:5, baking-powder. Follow Solomon's prescription for making a good boy by Proverbs 23:14—"thou shall beat him well with a rod"—and you will have a good cake.[615]

WHITE SUGAR COOKIES

☞ Three cups sugar, 1 cup butter, 1 cup sour cream, 3 eggs, 1 teaspoon soda, 1 nutmeg. Add just flour enough to mold out very soft.[616]

ALMOND WAFERS

☞ 1 tablespoonful of powdered sugar,
½ saltspoonful of salt.

Stir well together. Beat white of 1 egg just enough to break it; add enough flour to sugar to make it creamy. Flavor with a few drops of bitter almond essence. Grease the pan lightly and flour. Drop ½ teaspoonful of the paste on the pan, and with a wet finger spread into a thin round wafer. Bake in a moderate oven till the edges are lightly browned; then before removing from the oven door, lift each wafer and turn round a stick.⁶¹⁷

BROWN BETTY

☛ In a quart pudding-dish arrange alternate layers of sliced apples and bread-crumbs; season each layer with bits of butter, a little sugar, and a pinch each of ground cinnamon, cloves, and allspice. When the dish is full pour over it a half cupful each of molasses and water mixed; cover the top with crumbs. Place the dish in a pan containing hot water, and bake for three quarters of an hour, or until the apples are soft. Serve with cream or with any sauce. Raisins or chopped almonds improve the pudding.⁶¹⁸

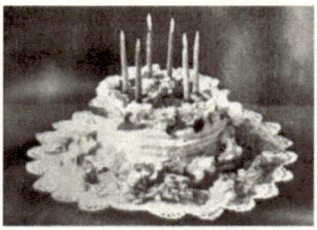

Scripture cake.

POUND CAKE

☛ One pound of sugar, one pound of flour, ten eggs, three-fourths of a pound of butter, one rounding teaspoonful of baking powder. Cream butter and sugar until you can't feel the grain of the sugar; then add the beaten yolks and flour alternately. This was soft and smooth as velvet. Lemon to flavor.⁶¹⁹

GRANDMOTHER'S POUND CAKE

☛ One cup butter packed solid, one and two-thirds cups granulated sugar, half teaspoonful mace, five unbeaten eggs, two cups sifted flour. Have a round pan greased and floured, the oven ready and ingredients measured, as the mixing must all be done by hand. Cream the butter, add the sugar, and work until very light; add mace and one egg at a time and stir with the hand until you can not see any yolk; then add another egg in the same way until all are used. Then mix in the flour and turn at once into the pan; bake slowly about one hour. The grain of the cake should be fine and close, and not tough or heavy, yet soft, light and velvety; this is obtained by the thorough blending of the butter and sugar, and not overbeating the eggs. Perfectly delightful.⁶²⁰

MOUNTAIN CAKE

☛ Take one pound of sugar, one-half pound of butter, one pound of flour, six eggs, the yolks and whites beaten separately, one cupful of sweet milk, three teaspoonfuls of baking-powder;-make a frosting of three eggs and lay the same as for jelly cake. Flavor the cake with lemon and the frosting with vanilla.⁶²¹

GOLD CAKE

☛ Five yolks and one whole egg. Cream half cup butter and two cups sugar, then add the well beaten eggs, three cups flour with two small teaspoonfuls of baking powder, three-fourths of a cup of milk. Beat half the sugar with the eggs, then add flour and milk alternately.[622]

GOLDEN CAKE
☞ Half cup of butter, one cup of sugar, yolks of eight eggs, half cup of milk, one and three-fourths cups of flour, four level teaspoonfuls baking powder, one teaspoonful orange extract. Bake in a tube pan. Cover with icing in which cocoanut has been stirred, dried or fresh. Fine.[623]

SNOW CAKE
☞ Whites of eight eggs, two cups of sugar, one cup of butter, one cup of corn starch, two cups of flour, two heaping teaspoonfuls of baking powder.[624]

PERFECTION CAKE
☞ Whites of sixteen eggs, one pound sugar, one pound flour, nearly a pound of butter, two rounding teaspoonfuls baking powder.[625]

POUND CAKE OF COTTOLENE
☞ Scant half pound cottolene, half pound sugar, half pound flour, six eggs, vanilla. Cream the cottolene and sugar until light, then beat in one egg at a time until they are all in, a little salt. Now sift in the flour, beating until a smooth light batter. Bake carefully. The French use the hand for beating cake. This is very nice indeed.[626]

DRIED APPLE CAKE
☞ Put three cups dried apples in soak over night; chop them fine the next morning and put on to boil in two cups of syrup; when tender remove, and when cool add one cup of butter creamed with one cup of sugar. Beat light four eggs, add with five cups of flour, two teaspoonfuls soda dissolved in a little boiling water. Put in a teaspoonful each of cloves, nutmeg, cinnamon and allspice, and one cup of raisins floured.[627]

PICNIC CAKE
☞ The ingredients needed for making two medium-sized cakes are: one and one-quarter pounds of flour, one-half pound of currants, the same of sugar, six ounces of butter, three eggs, four teaspoonfuls of baking-powder, six drops of essence of lemon (or small quantity of grated nutmeg) and one teacupful of milk. First well mix all the dry ingredients, lastly adding the eggs and milk; beat well for a few minutes and bake at once.[628]

WHITE LAYER CAKE
☞ 12 whites of eggs.
4 level cups of sifted flour.
½ cup cream.

1 teaspoon baking powder.
½ lb. butter.
3 cups sugar.

Cream butter with sugar, add cream. Stir in flour mixed with baking powder. Whites beaten thoroughly added last. Bake in layers in a moderate oven, and put together with any filling desired.[629]

CHRISTMAS PLUM PUDDING

☛ ¾ pound of suet chopped very fine; mix with it, while chopping, a tablespoonful of flour.

¾ pound of raisins seeded.
¾ pound of currants.
¾ pound of sugar.
¾ pound of fresh bread-crumbs.
Grated zest of one lemon.
¼ pound candied orange peel and citron cut into thin shavings.
1 teaspoonful each of ground cinnamon, cloves, nutmeg, and allspice.

Mix the dry materials together thoroughly, and then add six eggs, one at a time, and one half cupful of brandy; add another egg if too stiff, and more crumbs if too soft.

Wet a strong cloth in cold water, wring it dry, butter it, and dredge it well with flour; turn the mixture into the center and draw the cloth together over the top, leaving room for the pudding to swell a little, and tie it firmly; give it a good round shape.

Put it into a pot of boiling water, having it completely covered with water; cover the pot and boil four to five hours.

Do not let the water fall below the pudding, and in adding more let it be hot, so as to not arrest the boiling.

After it is removed from the water let it rest in the bag for ten minutes to harden a little, then cut the string and turn it carefully onto a dish. Cut a small hole in the top of the pudding and insert a paper bonbon case; trim it so it does not show.

Pour rum or brandy onto the dish and also into the paper box on top; place it on the table and touch it with a lighted taper. Serve with a brandy sauce. The amount given will serve twelve to fourteen persons.

The mixture may be divided and boiled in small puddings if it is too much to use at one time. It will keep for a long time, and the puddings can be warmed when used.

Slices of cold plum pudding may be steamed and served with a sauce; or they may be rolled in egg and crumbs and fried in hot fat, and be served as fruit croquettes.[630]

PRAIRIE CAKE

☛ One cupful of molasses, one-half cupful of brown sugar, one-half cupful of melted butter, one teaspoonful each of cloves and cinnamon, two teaspoonfuls of soda in one cupful of boiling water, two and one-half cupfuls of flour, yolks of four eggs well beaten and added last; for filling take ten tablespoonfuls of boiling water and two cupfuls of sugar; boil until it will hair, and pour over the beaten whites of four eggs and one cupful of chopped and seeded raisins; mix and spread at once over layers and on top. Try it. Excellent.[631]

SODA CAKES

☛ Dissolve half a pound of sugar in a pint of milk, add a teaspoonful of soda; pour it on two pounds of flour—melt half a pound of butter, knead all together till light, put it in shallow molds, and bake it quickly in a brisk oven.[632]

JAM CAKE

☛ Cream half cup butter and one cup of sugar, three eggs beaten separately, two cups of flour with two level teaspoonfuls baking powder, three tablespoonfuls milk or water, one teaspoonful each of cloves, cinnamon and nutmeg. After the batter is made put in a cup of blackberry jam. Delightful.[633]

CUP CAKE

☛ One cup of butter, two of sugar, three of flour, four eggs. Mix and bake the same as pound cake.[634]

GENOVESE CAKE

☛ Three eggs, their weight in butter, sugar and flour. Beat the sugar and butter until very light and creamy; add a little salt and half a teaspoonful of almond or vanilla or a little whiskey; then add the eggs one at a time, beating each one in well before adding the next. Beat the mixture fifteen or twenty minutes; then add the flour very lightly. Fill the pan two-thirds full or bake as snow balls. Bake slowly or they will be tough. Delightful.[635]

BLACKBERRY CAKE

☛ 3 eggs,
   1 cup of sugar,
   ¾ cup of butter,
   1½ cups of flour,
   1 cup of blackberry jam or preserves,
   3 tablespoons of sour cream,
   1 teaspoon of cinnamon,
   1 teaspoon of allspice,
   1 teaspoon of soda,

1 nutmeg.
Mix well and bake in layers, and spread white icing between.⁶³⁶

BLUE GRASS PLUM CAKE

☞ 1 pound of butter,
1 pound of granulated sugar,
1 pound of flour,
1 dozen eggs (white and yellows well beaten separately),
3 pounds of raisins (after seeding),
1½ pounds of currants (after cleaning),
1½ pounds of citron (cut very thin),
1 nutmeg (grated),
2 tablespoons of powdered cinnamon,
1½ pounds of blanched almonds (sliced),
1½ pounds of candied fruit (cut in small pieces), cherries, peaches, or apricots (do not cut cherries),
2 lemons (juice),
1 cup of golden syrup,
1 tumbler of mixed brandy, whisky, or rum.

Flour all the fruit with part of 1 pound called for, and do not add extra flour. Bake slowly in moderate oven for 5 or 6 hours.⁶³⁷

CHOCOLATE MARSHMALLOW CAKE

☞ Make a premium white or yellow cake, and bake in three square layers. Put in a pan in the warmer half of a pound of fresh marshmallows. Have ready a plain white icing, dissolve two tablespoonfuls of grated chocolate with a little boiling water, stirring until smooth, then mix this with the icing and add one-half teaspoonful of fresh butter, spread a layer of the cake with this, then quickly place on this half of the marshmallows, which should be light and fluffy; on the bottom of the next layer put a thin coat of icing and put in place; on top of this spread more icing

Plain cup cakes, iced and cored with a piece of angelica.

and the balance of the marshmallows; on bottom of top layer a thin coat of icing, and this put in place. Then ice all over with the balance of the icing, or, if preferred, with white icing.⁶³⁸

BLUE GRASS WHITE CAKE

☞ Whites of 12 eggs,
1 tumbler of butter,
2½ tumblers of sugar,
3½ tumblers of flour, after sifting,
⅓ teaspoon of soda, sifted with flour,

1 teaspoon of cream of tartar.
Bake in mold or bread-pan for 1 hour.[639]

CONFEDERATE MOUNTAIN CAKE
☛ Cream light half pound butter, add gradually a pound of sugar, yolks of six eggs; now add a pound of flour with a dessertspoonful of baking powder in it alternately with one cup of milk and stiff whites. This is nice for solid cake, layers, small cakes or sweet wafers. Fine.[640]

HICKORY NUT CAKE
☛ Half cup of butter creamed with one and a half cups sugar, two cups flour with one teaspoonful baking powder, three-fourths cup sweet milk added alternately with the flour, whites of four eggs; now add one cup of nut meats chopped. Reserve some of the whole pieces to put on top. Before baking sift a little sugar over the top. Bake slowly. You can use pecans or English walnuts. Fine.[641]

PARK STREET CAKE
☛ Half cup of butter, one cup of milk, two cups sugar, three cups flour, four eggs, one teaspoonful of baking powder, little vanilla and mace. Beat one cup of sugar with the butter, the other with the yolks; put in the butter mixture, then the flour and milk and whites beaten stiff. This is a very satisfactory cake as layers, loaf or small cakes.[642]

MOTHER'S CAKE
☛ One scant cup of butter, one and a half cups of sugar, three eggs beaten separately, one teaspoonful lemon or vanilla, little nutmeg, half cup milk, three cups flour, one full teaspoon of baking powder. Cream butter and sugar, add the yolks and flavoring, sift baking powder with the flour, put in batter, alternating with the stiff whites and milk. By adding one cup of currants you have currant cake. By adding dates cut small and floured you have date cake. By adding spices or chocolate to a little batter and putting in spots you have leopard cake. By using a full cup of butter, white mountain cake. Or split and fill with jelly or icing and fill with grated cocoanut, raisins and almonds chopped and one white of egg beaten stiff. Fine.[643]

BANANA CAKE
☛ Cream one-third of a cupful of butter with one cupful of sugar, add two well-beaten eggs, one half cupful of milk and one and three-quarters cupfuls of flour. Bake in layers. When baked spread between the layers a little boiled icing and sliced bananas; to be eaten while fresh.[644]

STRAWBERRY CAKE
☛ Three eggs, one cupful of sugar, two cupfuls of flour, one tablespoonful of butter, a heaping teaspoonful of baking-powder; beat

the butter and sugar together and add the eggs well beaten. Stir in the flour and baking-powder well sifted together and bake in deep tin plates. This quantity will fill four plates. With three pints of strawberries mix a cupful of sugar. Spread the fruit between the layers of cake. Cover the top layer of strawberries with a meringue made with the white of an egg and a tablespoonful of powdered sugar.[645]

COCOANUT CAKE
☛ Half cup butter, two and a half cups sugar, one cup milk, four and a half cups flour, whites of seven eggs, two teaspoonfuls cream of tartar, one small teaspoonful of soda, two small cocoanuts grated. Reserve a handful of cocoanut to sprinkle over frosting. This looks well sliced with fruit cake.[646]

CHOCOLATE CAKE
☛ One cup of butter, two and a half cups of sugar, four cups flour, five eggs, one cup milk, one cup broken chocolate melted over hot water, two teaspoonfuls baking powder, vanilla to flavor; white icing.[647]

ENGLISH BANBURY CAKE
☛ Take an equal quantity of clean, well-picked currants, granulated sugar and finely chopped lemon peel and mix it all together and then add a nice flavoring of ginger and cinnamon; now add good fresh butter, enough to form the whole into a nice paste. Take the best puff paste, roll it out in a sheet one-fourth of an inch thick; cut this in pieces two inches square and place a piece of the prepared butter, currants, etc., in the center of each; now take the two corners, the one nearest to you and the one opposite you, bring them up, press them together, and then with the palm of the hand press them down flat. This

Chocolate cake covered with chocolate icing.

makes the pieces oval in shape and leaves two ends which are folded together at liberty to rise; now wash the part that is not folded with water and add as much powdered sugar as you can get to remain on. Bake these in a slow heat. These are a little expensive, but are very fine and are the real English Banbury.[648]

NEAPOLITAN CAKE
☛ Roll out some puff paste one-eighth of an inch thick, cut it into strips five inches wide by ten inches long, moisten a large shallow tin pan with cold water, put in the strips, dust with powdered sugar, and bake in a medium hot oven. When done and cold cover with vanilla cream.

Put over this the second strip that has been spread with acid jelly. Lay over the third strip. Mix half a cup of powdered sugar, one tablespoonful of boiling water, a few drops of lemon juice. Pour over the cake.[649]

VANILLA CREAM

☞ Put one pint of milk in the double boiler over the fire; reserve a little to wet up two tablespoonfuls of flour; yolks of four eggs, one tablespoonful of butter, three tablespoonfuls sugar, pinch of salt.

Let come to a boil and cook until thick. When cold, put in one tablespoonful of vanilla, and use as directed. Grand.[650]

CONFEDERATE DELICATE CAKE

☞ One pound of sugar, three-fourths of a pound of butter, half pound flour, half pound corn starch, ten eggs, two teaspoonfuls baking powder. Cream the butter and sugar until light, then break in one egg at a time with the flour in which the powder is sifted. Flavor.

Bake in a square pan, cut in blocks and ice. Elegant.[651]

MARSHMALLOW CHOCOLATE CAKE

☞ Cream one cup of butter, gradually beat in one cup of granulated sugar, then a cup of brown sugar rolled and sifted, one cup of molasses, the beaten yolks of four eggs, two ounces of chocolate melted over hot water, one cup of sweet milk, alternating with four cups sifted flour, one teaspoonful of cream of tartar in the whites and half a teaspoonful soda in the last of the milk, one teaspoonful each of cinnamon and mace, half teaspoonful cloves.

Bake in a good sized tube pan. When done and cold invert and pour over the following frosting.[652]

MARSHMALLOW FROSTING

☞ Mix one and a half cups brown sugar, one-fourth cup butter, one-fourth cup boiling water. Boil until it forms a soft ball when dropped in cold water. Put in half a pound marshmallows cut, reserving some to decorate the top; beat until cold and thick, then pour over the cake. Decorate with marshmallows when partly set. As nice a cake as I ever ate.[653]

WHITE FRUIT CAKE

☞ One pound sugar, one pound flour, three-fourths of a pound of butter, ten eggs, two pounds almonds, two pounds citron, two pounds grated cocoanuts.

Have ready the almonds, blanched and pounded with a little rose water, adding this to the batter, then next the grated cocoanut, and then the citron; then add, last thing, tumbler of fine wine, Sherry or Madeira.

Bake slowly and evenly. Fine.[654]

LADY BALTIMORE CAKE

☛ One cup of butter, two cups sugar, three and a half cups flour, one cup sweet milk, whites six eggs, two level teaspoonfuls baking powder, one teaspoonful rose extract. Bake in three layers.[655]

FILLING FOR BALTIMORE CAKE

☛ Dissolve three cups granulated sugar in a cup of cold water; cook until it threads, then pour gradually on the stiffly beaten whites of three eggs, beating constantly. Add to this icing one cup of chopped raisins, one cup of chopped nuts and five figs cut in thin strips. Put between layers. Ice and emboss the top and sides of cake. Fine.[656]

CHOCOLATE NUT CAKE

☛ Beat to a cream half a cup of butter, gradually beat in one and a half cups sugar, then three-fourths of a cup of milk and two cups flour sifted with two level teaspoonfuls baking powder; add a cup of nut meats chopped fine and the whites of four eggs beaten stiff. Beat thoroughly. Bake in a shallow square pan and ice with the following frosting.[657]

CHOCOLATE FROSTING

☛ One cup sugar, half ounce chocolate, one-fourth cup water. Stir until the chocolate is dissolved without letting the syrup boil. Then cover it and let steam well. Remove cover and cook to a soft ball. Pour in a fine stream on the beaten white of an egg. Flavor and beat until cold. Pour over the inverted cake. Mark in squares with half a nut in each square. Fine.[658]

LEMON CHEESE FILLING

☛ 6 egg yolks.
¾ cups sugar.
½ cup water.
2 tablespoons butter.
2 tablespoons corn starch.
1 lemon (juice and rind).
1 orange (juice and rind).
2 cans cocoanut.
1 slice crystallized pineapple.
1½ cups crystallized cherries.

Cook yolks, sugar, water, and other ingredients together in double boiler until very thick. When cool enough to put between layers, add cocoanut (straining off all milk) and crystallized fruit (cut fine).[659]

WHITE ICING

☛ It is a very common way of making icing to allow five or six large teaspoonfuls of powdered loaf sugar to the white of egg; but the most correct way of proportioning it is to weigh it, and even then, when there

Confection cake.

is much made at a time, it requires some skill in proportioning, as the whites of some eggs are at least a third larger than others. Beat the whites of the eggs to a stiff froth, so much so that it will not fall from the dish in which it is beaten, when inverted. Powder some loaf sugar, pass it through a fine sieve, and mix it with the froth, allowing four ounces of sugar to one white of egg. Stir it in slowly, and but little at a time, and beat it till it looks quite smooth, adding as you proceed, a few drops of oil of lemon, or extract of roses, or the common lemon juice will answer; and you may also flavor it with orange juice, by adding a little more sugar.

Or you may make it with three ounces of sugar, one of starch, and the white of one egg, flavoring it as directed. If your cakes should be scorched, or rather brown, scrape them with a knife, and brush them neatly; then put the icing on the top and sides, making it very smooth and regular with a broad bladed knife, which for this purpose is preferable to any thing else; set them in a warm room to dry, where nothing can disturb them, and when the icing gets about half dry, put on the decoraments in the most adroit manner.[660]

ALMOND ICING

☛ Beat the whites of eggs to a stiff froth, flavor it with a little oil of lemon, and stir into it alternately till quite thick and smooth, equal portions of powdered loaf sugar and sweet almonds, that have been pounded to a smooth paste, and moistened with rose water as they were pounding, to make them white and light. Put it on the cakes as directed for other icing, only put it on some thicker.[661]

PINK ICING

☛ Prepare your egg and sugar as before directed, flavoring it in the same manner, or with any thing else you choose; add a little cochineal coloring, to make it a fine pink, beat it till it is very regularly mixed through the icing, put it on in the same manner as directed for the white icing, and if decorated at all, let it be with something white.

A dark red icing may be made by tinging it with tincture of saunders; and a very pretty icing for fruit cake may be made by coloring it with dark colored preserve juice, or with the juice of ripe cherries or strawberries, which will also give it a good flavor.[662]

YELLOW ICING

☛ Icing may be colored yellow, deep or pale, with saffron juice or turmeric; it may also be colored a very pretty pale yellow, by rubbing the sugar while in lumps, on the rind of a fine colored lemon, and also a beautiful yellow icing may be made by rubbing lumps of loaf sugar hard on deep colored orange peel, which will at the same time flavor it sufficiently, without the aid of any thing else; then pound it, and prepare the icing as before directed.[663]

CARAMEL ICING

☞ Two cups brown sugar, half cup of butter, half cup sweet milk, pinch of cream of tartar. Cook until it will form a soft ball when dropped in water, or spin a thread.

Remove, flavor with vanilla, and when cool beat. Put over or between cake very soon, or it will become too stiff. Chopped raisins and nuts are nice in icing.[664]

SUE'S SNOW BALLS

☞ One cup of butter, one cup of sugar, two cups unsifted flour, half cup of milk, four eggs, one teaspoonful baking powder. Bake in small tins and ice.[665]

FANCY CAKE

☞ For Sunday night or afternoon tea; is made by slicing pound cake, cutting it in circles, spreading with jelly or marmalade, then with a meringue which is dusted with sugar and crusted in a slow oven. Arrange on a plate and garnish with leaves.[666]

CHOCOLATE CREAM CAKE

☞ Cream one-fourth cup of butter with one cup of sugar, add half cup of milk and one and a half cups flour, two eggs, one teaspoonful baking powder; melt half cup of chocolate and add to the batter; vanilla to flavor. Bake in two layers.[667]

CREAM FILLING

☞ Two-thirds cup of milk, two cups granulated sugar; dissolve thoroughly; add tablespoonful butter; set in a saucepan of boiling water and stir until melted; then set on stove and boil five minutes or more, stirring constantly; flavor with vanilla. This icing should be smooth and cover two layers of cake. Fine.[668]

HARLEQUIN CAKE

☞ Cream one cup of butter with two cups sugar, yolks three eggs, one cup milk, three cups flour, one teaspoonful baking powder, lastly the stiff whites folded in. Mix in the order given. Divide the batter in four equal parts. Bake two parts the color of the batter; to the third, color pink; to the fourth, add melted chocolate.

When done lay first a light cake, then lemon jelly; then chocolate, then jelly; then light cake and jelly; then pink. Either ice the top or put over sugar.[669]

LEMON JELLY FOR HARLEQUIN CAKE

☞ Beat one egg, add a cup of water, the grated rind and juice of a lemon; pour this slowly on a cup of sugar mixed with two tablespoonfuls flour.

Cook in a double boiler until thick and smooth. Spread between layers. Fine.[670]

FEATHER CAKE

☞ One teacup of butter, two of flour, two of sugar. Cream the flour and butter together; two teaspoonfuls of yeast powder to one teacup of sweet milk.

Mix all with the flour and beat light with a large spoon. To be baked in round tins. Grease well and bake in a moderately hot stove.[671]

ICE CREAM CAKE

☞ Whites of twelve eggs, cream three-fourths cup rich butter with three cups sugar and three-fourths cup milk, three and three-fourths cups Swans Down flour, sift three times with three level teaspoons baking powder. Almond or rose to flavor.

After creaming the butter and part of the sugar, add flour and milk alternately. Add the remainder of the sugar to the stiff whites, then add the rest of the flour.

Bake in layers, or as a loaf cake.[672]

Cake board and rolling pin.

CREAM SPONGE CAKE

☞ Six eggs, their weight in sugar, weight of three in flour. Beat the yolks and sugar until very, very light, then add the stiff whites. Mix carefully and slowly sift in the flour.

Put one-fourth teaspoonful of soda in a tablespoonful of vinegar; when dissolved, stir quickly into the cake. Mix thoroughly and carefully and turn into a well greased shallow pan.

When done and cool, cut in half.[673]

ORANGE CAKE

☞ Whites of sixteen eggs, one pound sugar, one pound flour, half pound butter, down weight three small teaspoons baking powder, one cup sweet milk. Bake in four layers with the following orange cake filling.[674]

ORANGE CAKE FILLING

☞ Juice and grated rind of two oranges, juice of half lemon, two tablespoons water, two cups sugar.

Cook over hot water when scalding hot, stir in the yolks of two eggs, and the white of one slightly beaten.

When cold put between layers.[675]

ORANGE SOUFFLE

☛ Yolks of 4 eggs, well beaten,
1 pint (full) of orange juice,
1 pound of sugar,
½ box of gelatine,
1 quart of whipped cream.

Cover gelatine for 1 hour with ½ cup of cold water. Mix orange juice and sugar, add eggs, then beat in gelatine and let cool in ice water. When it begins to thicken, beat in lightly the whipped cream and freeze.[676]

BALLOONS

☛ Put a cupful of water in a saucepan; when it boils add one tablespoonful of butter; when the butter is melted add one cupful of flour and beat it with a fork or wire whip until it is smooth and leaves the sides of the pan. Remove from the fire and add three eggs, one at a time, beating vigorously each one before adding the next. Let it stand until cold. When ready to serve, drop a spoonful at a time into moderately hot fat and fry for about 15 minutes. Take out on a skimmer and dry on brown paper.

Iced cake decorated with candied cherries.

The batter will puff into hollow balls. If the fat is very hot it will crisp the outside too soon and prevent the balls from puffing. Fry only a few at a time, as they must be kept separated. Sprinkle with powdered sugar and pile on a folded napkin. Serve with lemon sauce made as follows.

Lemon sauce: Strain the juice of one and a half lemons; add one cupful of powdered sugar, then a half cupful of boiling water.[677]

KENTUCKY CAKE

☛ 12 eggs (whites)
1 pound of flour,
1 pound of sugar,
¾ pound of butter,
1 pound of raisins,
1 heaping teaspoon of baking-powder,
1 wineglass of whisky with a little nutmeg grated into it.

Wash butter and then cream it very light with sugar. Beat whites to stiff froth. Add alternately with the flour, reserving 1 small cup of flour to mix with baking-powder.

Next, put in whisky and raisins, and lastly, sift in the cup of flour and baking-powder.

Bake 2 hours in slow oven.[678]

JELLY CAKE

☛ For this cake make an orange marmalade and use in the place of jelly, as it makes a more delicious cake. Following are the directions: Half a dozen oranges to a teacup of granulated sugar; peel oranges and grate them, pick out the seed and pith, add sugar to oranges and stir well and put to cook; stir while cooking; twenty minutes will cook it. It must be made a day before using it for cake. For making the cake, one teacup of butter to two of sugar, three of flour and half a dozen eggs. Beat the

Jelly cake top.

whites and yolks of eggs separate, very light. Cream butter and sugar together, add the yolks of eggs to creamed sugar and butter, then add the whites, and add flour and stir till light. Sift two teaspoonfuls of best yeast powder with the flour. With the above directions the cake is made. Place it in the pans and put to bake; fifteen minutes will bake it. Spread marmalade over the cake after it is baked. Icing for the cake: Take the whites of four eggs and beat them very light indeed. Add three tablespoonfuls of powdered sugar, beat sugar and eggs together light, and spread on cake while cake is warm. Take one teacup of fine grated cocoanut and sprinkle over cake while icing is soft.[679]

SPIDERS

☛ Make a noodle dough, cut in shape, and fry it in hot lard. Sprinkle powdered sugar over them when done.[680]

CAROLAS

☛ Five eggs to two cups of sugar; break eggs into the sugar and beat the whole till perfectly light. Sift one quart of flour; take one-half teacup of sweet milk and put a level teaspoonful of soda in it, without lumps; one teaspoonful of salt. Flavor with the juice of one orange, the peel of half an orange, grated, and one teaspoonful of butter. Make the dough in the same way as for light bread; roll out dough as for biscuit. Cut them out five inches by two inches, slice them two inches in the middle and stretch open a little. Have your fat boiling hot, but do not let it burn. Put carolas in hot fat, shake skillet gradually till brown. As you take them out of the fat, lay them in a pan on clean paper, so as to drain grease from them.[681]

ROCHESTER JELLY CAKE

☛ Cream half cup butter, one and a half cups sugar, add two eggs, three-fourths cup milk, two heaping cups flour, one teaspoon cream tartar in flour, half teaspoon soda in the milk, put half the mixture in a layer cake pan, to the remainder add one teaspoon molasses, one-half cup chopped raisins or currents, with a tablespoon flour rub through, then season with cinnamon, cloves, allspice and little nutmeg, bake in the same sized pan and put together with any filling preferred.[682]

HARD TIMES CAKE

☛ Half a cup of butter, two of sugar, one of sour cream, three of flour, three eggs, half tea-spoon of soda; bake in layers and spread with jelly.[683]

OLD-TIME GINGER CAKE

☛ One pint molasses, one quart flour, one-half teacup brown sugar, one teacup butter, one tablespoonful cinnamon, two tablespoonsful ginger, one teacup sour milk.

With it mix a teaspoonful soda and three eggs. Cream butter and sugar together, then add molasses, then flour, then eggs, then milk, then ginger and cinnamon; stir thoroughly and put to bake in oblong pans.[684]

MRS. HENRY CLAY'S DROP CAKES

☛ 4 eggs,
6 ounces of butter,
8 ounces of sugar,
8 ounces of flour.[685]

BAKED BONBONS

☛ 1 egg.
Chopped hickory nuts.
Orange extract.
Pinch salt.
1¼ cups brown sugar.

Beat egg to a stiff froth, adding gradually brown sugar and salt. When smooth and creamy flavor with orange extract.

Stir in enough chopped nuts to form a stiff paste, spread in sheets on greased pans.

Bake about 20 minutes in a moderate oven.

Cut into squares when cold.[686]

Fondant and fondant bonbons.

FRUIT LAYER CAKE

☛ Cream one cup sugar, half cup butter, one and a half cups of flour, half cup wine, one cup raisins cut, two eggs, half teaspoon soda. Mix carefully bake in two or three layers with frosting between and over.[687]

PISTACHIO CAKE

☛ Make a white cake and bake in three layers, make a white mountain frosting, flavor with orange flower water, a little bitter almond to give the flavor of pistachio and color a delicate green.

Frost the top and sprinkle with chopped pistachio nuts or blanched almonds.[688]

PISTACHIO ICE CREAM

☞ Make a custard of
  1 pint of morning's milk,
  ½ pint of white sugar,
  Yolks of 2 eggs.
  Pound ½ of a vanilla bean and boil with the custard. When cold, color a delicate green with pure fruit coloring. Add 1 quart of rich whipped cream. Put in freezer, and when it begins to congeal add
  1 teacup of sweet almonds, and
  1 teacup of pistachio nuts, blanched and powdered.
  Freeze hard.[689]

FIG CAKE FILLING

☞ Steam one pound dried figs until soft, cut fine add a cup catuaba wine, one cup of sugar, a few walnuts cut small. Let stand some time; put between any layer cake.[690]

ALMOND CAKE

☞ Cream until light half cup butter and one cup sugar, two cups flour, two level teaspoons baking powder, half cup milk, whites five eggs beaten stiff, bake in layers.[691]

ALMOND CAKE FILLING

☞ Put in double boiler one pint milk, beat the five yolks and half cup sugar, one teaspoon flour, when the milk boils stir in slowly the eggs and sugar, let cook until thick when cool add half cup blanched almonds cut fine. Vanilla and lemon to flavor. Put between layers with sifted sugar over the top.[692]

FRUIT COOKIES

☞ Beat well together
  3 cups of brown sugar,
  1 cup of butter,
  1 cup of sour milk,
  1 teaspoon of soda,
  4 eggs, well beaten,
  1 teaspoon of cloves,
  2 teaspoons of cinnamon,
  1 teaspoon of nutmeg,
  2 cups of seeded and chopped raisins.
  Flour enough to make a stiff batter that will drop off a spoon. Bake in a quick oven. 1 teacup of nuts would be an improvement.[693]

GINGER COOKIES

☞ One teacup of molasses, one-half teacup of sugar, one tablespoonful of butter, one tablespoonful of lard, one quart of flour, two tablespoonfuls of ginger, one teaspoonful of cinnamon, one teaspoonful of allspice, two tablespoonfuls of yeast powder. Cream butter and sugar together and add molasses. Sift yeast powder and flour together and add to butter, sugar and molasses, then add lard and spices, etc., and work it up well. Roll out on a board, and cut them out and bake like you would a biscuit.[694]

GINGER BREAD

5 cups of flour, 4 eggs, 2 cups of molasses, 1 cup sugar, of butter, 1 cup of milk, 2 tablespoons of ginger, and 2 of allspice, 1 teaspoon of saleratus, dissolved in milk. Mix and bake as for pound cake, and add fruit if you wish. Put in the saleratus last.[695]

SOFT GINGER BREAD

1 large coffeecup of sugar,
1 large coffeecup of molasses,
1 large coffeecup of butter,
4 large coffeecups of flour,
1 large coffeecup of sour milk,
4 eggs,
½ teacup of ginger,
½ teaspoon of ground cloves,
½ teaspoon of cinnamon,
1 tablespoon of saleratus beaten into the sour milk, and poured in last.[696]

SOFT GINGER CAKE

Stir to a cream, one cup butter and half cup brown sugar, add two cups molasses, one cup sweet or butter milk, one tablespoon ginger, one teaspoon cinnamon, three eggs beaten separately, four cups flour, last one teaspoon soda in a little water. Butter and paper pan and bake slowly. Put half the flour in after the soda. Delicious.[697]

GINGER POUND CAKE

Three-fourth pound sugar, three-fourth pound butter, one pound flour, six eggs, one cup syrup, half cup sweet or sour milk, one tablespoon soda. Ginger, nutmeg and spices to taste, half makes a nice cake. Fine.[698]

Dessert cake.

GINGER SNAPS

One cup molasses, half cup sugar, one tablespoon ginger, one teaspoon soda, half cup creamed butter, flour to roll out very thin; heat the molasses, pour over the sugar, add the other ingredients, let stand awhile to get very cold. Roll as thin as a wafer cut and bake quick. None better.[699]

COFFEE CAKE

☞ Three eggs, one cupful of butter, one cupful of brown sugar, one cupful of molasses, one cupful of strong coffee, five cupfuls of flour, one cupful raisins, one level teaspoonful of soda, stirred into the molasses; nutmeg, allspice and cinnamon to the taste. Bake slowly. A little whisky improves it.[700]

QUEEN CAKE

☞ Sift into a pan a pound and a quarter of powdered loaf sugar, and cut into it one pound of fresh butter, having been washed thoroughly in cold water, to free it from salt; warm them a little by the fire, and beat them together till intimately united, and very smooth. Add to it a powdered nutmeg, a teaspoonful of cinnamon, one of mace, one of grated lemon, a wine glass of brandy, one of white wine, and one of rose water. Then stir in alternately eighteen ounces of superfine flour, and the whites of twenty-four eggs, having beaten them to a very fine froth; beat it hard for some minutes, put it in a large buttered pan, and bake it in a moderate oven.

When it is done, let it remain in the oven till it gets cold; then ice it very white, and when it gets about half dry, put around it a handsome decorament of tinsel leaves and flowers, put some small gilded leaves over the top, and elevate it considerably on the table. Cakes dressed in this manner are introduced only at large suppers, at which time, if you wish a splendid table, dress all your fine cakes in different attire, suitable to the names and materials of which they are made, and arrange them handsomely upon the table, that the company may see the different kinds of cake.[701]

PLAIN SPICE CAKE

☞ One egg, two-third cup sugar, two-third cup butter, two-third cup molasses, one cup milk, two and a half cups flour measured generously, one level teaspoon soda, one level teaspoon cream tartar, one tablespoon vinegar or lemon juice, one tablespoon mixed spices. Beat the egg, add the sugar, molasses, spices and creamed butter, mix the soda with the milk and add. Mix the cream tartar and flour and stir in butter and finally the vinegar. Bake in one cake or two layers. My favorite.[702]

LEMON FILLING

☞ 6 eggs, beaten separately,
3 lemons, grated rind of 2,
¾ teacup of ice water.

Sweeten to taste. Cook in vessel of hot water until thick. Spread on cake.[703]

CONFEDERATE MARSHMALLOW FILLING

☞ Use boiled icing, and when thick enough to spread flavor with marshmallows dissolved in the icing. Cut marshmallows into halves or quarters, and spread on each layer.

Pour icing over each. Place whole marshmallows on top and cover with icing.[704]

CONFEDERATE MARSHMALLOW FROSTING

☞ 1 cup sugar.
1 cup marshmallows cut fine.
⅓ cup water.
1 square chocolate.
1 egg white.

Candied plum cake covered in frosting, candied cherries, and sliced almonds.

Boil sugar and water until it spins a thread. Pour slowly on the egg-white, beating constantly with a wire whisk. Put in half of marshmallows at once and when dissolved spread first layer. Put in remainder of marshmallows beat a little longer; then spread on top layer.

Melt the chocolate and from a distance of one foot from cake shake the chocolate on gently.[705]

WHITE CREAM CARAMEL FILLING

☞ 3 cups of white sugar,
1½ cups of thick, sweet cream,
4 tablespoons of sweet butter,
1 teacup of almonds, blanched and grated.

Flavor with extract of almond. Stir well together and boil till it is thick. Take off the fire and let it stand for a few minutes. Beat till it is thick, and spread on cakes.[706]

DANDY CAKES

☞ Mix a pound of fresh butter with a pound of powdered loaf sugar, beat them till smooth, and add to them two powdered nutmegs, a teaspoonful of powdered cinnamon, the juice of an orange, and a glass of white wine.

Then add alternately and gradually fourteen ounces of flour, and ten beaten eggs. Beat it very well, put it in small scalloped pans that are well buttered, and take them in rather a brisk oven.

When they are done, being made of so little flour, they will shrink a little from the sides of the pans; then turn them out, ice them very white, spot them over with red sugar sand, and stack them on a large plate, having at least three stacks, and every two inverted.[707]

PLUM CAKE

☛ Prepare two pounds of currants and two of raisins in the usual manner.

Beat to a cream a pound of fresh butter and a pound of powdered brown sugar, and add to it a pint of molasses, a glass of brandy, one of wine, one of rose water, a spoonful of powdered cinnamon and three powdered nutmegs.

Confederate Christmas cake.

Beat very light one dozen eggs, sift a pound and a half of flour, and stir them also into the butter, etc.; then add alternately the fruits, stirring them in very hard. Bake it in a deep pan with moderate heat.

Do not remove it from the oven till it gets cold, and then ice it neatly, tinging the icing with preserve juice or cochineal.[708]

DATE BARS

☛ 4 cups dates.
Pinch of salt.
2 cups nuts.
2 eggs.
⅔ cups brown sugar.
⅔ cup of flour.
⅔ teaspoon baking powder.

Cream the sugar with yolks of eggs and add whites beaten light. Add the flour in which baking powder and salt have been mixed.

Stir in the dates and nuts, spread in a buttered pan and bake in a quick oven.

When cold, cut in squares.[709]

OLD VIRGINIA CHRISTMAS CAKE

☛ 12 eggs,
1 pound flour,
1 pound sugar,
1 pound butter,
1 nutmeg,
1 teaspoon each of mace and cinnamon,
3 pounds of raisins,
3 pounds currants,
½ pound citron,
1 pound each of cream nuts and almonds,
½ pint of brandy,
½ teaspoon soda in small cup of vinegar. Put in last.

Bake 3 or 4 hours. Cover with icing made of eggs and sugar. Flavor with acid.[710]

OATMEAL COOKIES

☛ One cup sugar, two eggs, little salt, one cup shortening, half butter and half lard, two and a half cups oatmeal, two and a half cups flour, four tablespoonfuls of sweet milk, one level teaspoonful of soda. Roll out quite thin and cut with a knife the size and shape of snow flake crackers. They are fine.[711]

HERMITS

☛ One and one-half cupfuls of brown or maple sugar, one cupful of butter, one-half teaspoonful of soda dissolved in two tablespoonfuls of hot water, three eggs, a little nutmeg, pinch of salt, one and one-half cupfuls of seeded and floured raisins, three and one-half cupfuls of flour in which one teaspoonful of cream of tartar has been sifted, and one-fourth cupful of buttermilk. Drop the dough from the spoon in disconnected cakes.[712]

CARAWAY COOKIES

☛ One and a half pounds flour, one heaping teaspoonful baking powder, one pound sugar, four beaten eggs, three-fourths pound of butter, one cup milk, two tablespoonfuls caraway seed. Make a hole in the center of flour, put in the butter, chopping it in with a knife, then put in the sugar and eggs and seed. Chop with a knife until well mixed, then add the milk. Knead the dough, set aside to get cold, then roll thin, cut and bake in a moderate oven.[713]

SUGAR COOKIES

☛ One cup of butter, two cups sugar, half cup sweet milk, two eggs, five cups flour, two teaspoonfuls baking powder. Roll thin and bake quick.[714]

MOLASSES COOKIES

☛ One cup sugar, one cup molasses, one cup butter or lard, half cup hot water, one teaspoonful each of soda, ginger, cinnamon; flour to roll out. Mark into cards, sprinkle with sugar, and bake.[715]

TEA CAKES

☛ Four eggs, two cups sugar, two tablespoonfuls butter, two scant teaspoonfuls soda, four of cream of tartar, lemon to flavor. Flour for a soft dough.[716]

ALLEGHENY TEA CAKES

☛ 1 pound butter,
1 pound sugar,
8 eggs,
1¼ pounds flour.
Rub butter and sugar together, and add by degrees the well-beaten

eggs and the flour. Flavor to taste. Drop with spoon on well-greased tin pans.[717]

JUMBLES

☛ 6 eggs,
1 pound sugar,
¾ pound butter.
Cream butter and sugar, beat the eggs into it with just enough flour to roll out. Take small quantity of dough and lay on board, and with a knife roll in sugar and flour.[718]

FRUIT SNAPS

☛ One cup butter, one and a half cups sugar, half cup molasses, three eggs, one teaspoonful soda, one cup cut raisins, two cups currants, one tablespoonful of ginger, same of cloves, same cinnamon and allspice. Mix with flour as soft as can be rolled. Mold in small cakes with the hands.[719]

ENGLISH TEA CAKES

☛ Cream six ounces butter, add half pound sugar, beat in four eggs and one pound flour, then add two ounces candied peel chopped fine, grated rind of a lemon, half pound currants. Drop in balls on a tin and bake until brown.[720]

MORAVIAN CAKE

☛ Sift a quart of fine flour, sprinkle into it a small spoonful of salt, two powdered nutmegs, a spoonful of cinnamon, one of mace, and four ounces of powdered sugar.
Rub in with your hands four ounces of butter and two beaten eggs; when they are completely saturated, add four table-spoonfuls of good yeast, and enough sweet milk to make it into a thick batter. Put it in a buttered pan, cover it, and set it by the fire to rise, but be sure you do not let it get hot, or the cake will be spoiled.
When it looks quite light, super-add four ounces of sugar, and a handful of four; sprinkle a handful of brown sugar over the top, and bake it in a moderate oven.[721]

A FINE COOKIE

☛ Cream three-fourths of a cup of butter, add gradually one and a half cups sugar, two beaten eggs, half cup of milk, a level teaspoonful each of soda and baking powder, and flour enough to roll out very thin. Any flavor preferred.[722]

COOKIES

☛ Cream one cup of butter, add two cups sugar and three eggs, one at a time, beating each in thoroughly before adding the next; then add a pinch of soda dissolved in a tablespoonful of cold water; about four cups of flour, enough to roll out, or use less flour, and drop from a tablespoon on a buttered dripping pan two inches apart and put nuts on top of each. They will run together, but can be cut apart before they are cold. Or, grease the inverted pan on bottom, sift over a little flour, spread the dough upon the pan with the rolling pin or knife very thin. Bake in a hot oven. Make a boiled icing and spread on cake while warm. Scatter candied caraway seed thickly over it. When cold cut in strips one and a half inches wide, or cut diagonally to form diamonds.[723]

HEALTH COOKIES

☛ One cupful of sugar dissolved in one cupful of sweet milk, three eggs beaten thick, and lemon color; four teaspoonfuls of baking-powder, one-half cupful of English currants, one-half teaspoonful of cinnamon, grating of nutmeg, one-half teaspoonful of salt and two and one-half tablespoonfuls of melted Ko-nut.

Sift dry the ingredients thoroughly together and add alternately with the beaten egg. To this add melted Ko-nut and currants, flour sufficient to support the mixing spoon upright in the dough. Drop by rounded teaspoonfuls into smoking hot Ko-nut. Observe level measurement.[724]

HONEY CAKE

☛ One cup strained honey, one cup sugar, one cup butter, half cup sour cream, half teaspoonful soda, pinch of salt, season with cinnamon or lemon, flour for a dough. Roll thin and bake in a hot oven.[725]

ALMOND MACAROONS

☛ Put a pound of almond paste in a large bowl. Beat the whites of five eggs only enough to break the stringiness. Chop the paste fine and work in the whites with the hands until quite soft and pliable.

Now add a portion of one pound of powdered sugar sifted in gradually until all in. The paste must be stiff enough to hold its shape when dropped lightly. Grease white paper and lay it on shallow pans. Drop the paste by half teaspoonfuls. Bake in a very moderate oven and be careful not to expose to draughts [drafts] while cooling or they will sink.

When cold wet the underside of paper and remove the macaroons.[726]

SAVORY CAKES OF OLDEN TIMES

☛ Beat eight eggs to a froth separately; then mix together, add a pound of powdered white sugar stirred in gradually. Beat the whole ten minutes, add the grated rind of a fresh lemon and half the juice, a pound of sifted flour and a couple of tablespoonfuls of coriander seed. Drop this mixture by the large spoonful, several inches apart, on buttered baking plates, sift white sugar over them and bake immediately in a quick, hot oven.

These cakes make a delicious addition to the afternoon tea table.[727]

COCOANUT MACAROONS
☛ Beat the whites of five eggs to a stiff froth, fold in carefully half pound fine sugar, one and a half cups grated or shredded cocoanut. Mix lightly and drop by teaspoonfuls on oiled paper. Bake very slowly.[728]

COCOANUT BALLS
☛ Grate a cocoanut, add to it half its weight in sugar, then stir in the whipped white of one egg. Roll the mixture into balls and bake in a moderate oven to a delicate brown. If the mixture is too soft to hold its shape without spreading add one tablespoonful flour.[729]

COCOANUT DROP COOKIES
☛ Sift together one and a half cups flour, one rounding teaspoonful baking powder. Beat an egg and half cup of sugar until light, add half cup grated cocoanut, a little grated lemon rind, then the flour and half cup of milk. Drop on little pats or pans which have been buttered and dusted with flour. Allow ample room for spreading. Sprinkle a little grated cocoanut over each cake and bake in a moderate oven.[730]

CONFEDERATE ALMOND WAFERS
☛ Half cup butter, one cup powdered sugar, half cup of milk, two cups flour, one teaspoonful vanilla, chopped almonds. Cream together the butter and sugar, add the milk, drop by drop, then the flour. Spread the mixture very thin on the bottom of dripping pans inverted and buttered. After scoring, sprinkle over the chopped almonds. Bake very quickly until delicately colored. Cut the wafers apart and roll in tabular shape. Roll either from side or corner, or over a broom handle.[731]

SOFT SPONGE GINGERBREAD
☛ A pint of molasses; a tablespoon of ginger; two spoonfuls of melted butter; two teaspoons of soda and flour sufficient to roll. Cut it about half an inch thick, and bake in a quick over.[732]

FAIRY GINGERBREAD
☛ Half cup butter, one cup powdered sugar, half cup of milk, one and a half cups flour, one tablespoonful ginger. Mix, bake and roll as almond wafers.[733]

KEWPIES
☛ 1 cup butter or Crisco.
1 level teaspoon soda.
1½ cups brown sugar.
2 cups nut meats.
3 eggs (beaten).
1 lb. raisins.
3 cups flour.

Mix together into a stiff batter. Drop by teaspoonfuls on a warm greased pan and bake. If Crisco is used, add 1 teaspoon salt to mixture.[734]

PFEFFERNUSS
("Peppernut")

☞ One pound sugar, one pound flour, grated rind of one lemon, half cup fine chopped citron, one tablespoonful cinnamon, half tablespoonful each of cloves, mace and nutmeg, two teaspoonfuls baking powder, five eggs. Pass the flour, spices and baking powder through the sieve, and the citron and lemon rind, and mix to a dough with the five eggs beaten together. With buttered hands shape into small balls the size of a hickory nut. Bake on buttered paper an inch apart. They resemble macaroons. Makes seventy cakes. Delightful.[735]

BROWNIES

☞ One-third cup each of butter, sugar and dark molasses, one beaten egg, one cup flour, one cup nut meats. Makes only a few, but they are nice. Mix in the usual way. Beat the eggs all together. Bake in small cake tins. Put half nut in top of each cake.[736]

Jelly cream cocoanut cake.

COCOANUT CAKES

☞ The grated meat of a cocoanut, its weight in sugar, half cup of flour, white of one egg. Shape into balls and bake twenty minutes.[737]

ROCKS

☞ One cup of butter creamed with one and a half cups sugar, three beaten eggs, a level teaspoonful of soda in a little water, one teaspoonful cinnamon, half teaspoonful allspice, two cups flour, or more if not very stiff.

Cut some dates in small pieces, and some chopped nuts.

Flour the fruit and add. Put on a buttered pan in little dabs, half a teaspoonful with a good space between. Bake in a hot oven.[738]

SAND CAKES

☞ Cream a scant cup of butter with one and a half cups light brown sugar. Beat two eggs, reserving the white of one, add to the butter and sugar. Mix two level teaspoonfuls baking powder with three and a half cups flour and half teaspoonful of cinnamon.

Stir this in the batter. It may need a little more flour to roll out. Roll as thin as possible, cut and lay on a paper, sift over some sugar mixed with cinnamon, then some blanched and split almonds. Bake in a quick oven.[739]

PECAN KISSES
☛ Whites of five eggs, ten tablespoonfuls of sugar, two cups broken pecan meats, pinch of salt. Do not beat the whites until you add the sugar, then beat until stiff; then add the broken nuts. Drop in tablespoonfuls on paper or a buttered tin. Bake very slowly. Dry out.[740]

PECAN CAKE
☛ 1½ pounds of brown sugar,
1 teacup of molasses,
1 pound of flour,
⅓ pound of butter,
6 eggs (beaten separately),
1 pound of pecans after they are shelled,
1½ pounds of raisins,
½ nutmeg, grated,
1 wineglass of whisky.
Bake about 3 hours.[741]

SWEET WAFERS
☛ One cup flour, one cup of milk, three tablespoonfuls sugar, one tablespoonful of butter. Cream butter and sugar, add flour and milk alternately until all used. Have wafer irons hot, put in a teaspoonful of batter. When done, roll while hot and sift over powdered sugar.[742]

TUXEDO WAFERS
☛ One cup of butter, two cups light brown sugar, one cup milk, three and a half cups flour, one teaspoonful ground ginger. Cream butter and sugar, add milk, ginger and flour.
Spread a thin coating of butter on a baking tin; when it is cold spread the paste over it no thicker than a card. Spread over pulverized nuts and bake in a slack oven. When done, cut about the size of a card and roll or bend over a broom handle.[743]

LEMON SNAPS
☛ 1 coffee cup sugar.
⅔ teacupful butter,
½ teaspoonful soda, dissolved in one tablespoonful of warm water.
1 teaspoonful lemon flavoring; flour enough to roll thin.[744]

DOUGHNUTS
☛ One egg beaten, add five-eighths cup of sugar, half cup milk, half level teaspoonful soda, two level teaspoonfuls cream of tartar, little salt and nutmeg. Put in enough flour to make a dough to roll out, roll thin, cut with a doughnut cutter and drop in very hot Wesson oil or other fat. Fry a light brown, turning often. Drain on soft paper. Sift over sugar. Serve for breakfast with coffee. Delicious.[745]

FRIED DOUGHNUTS

☛ Sift three pints of flour in a mixing bowl; make a well in the center, into which put a cup of sugar, half a cup sour milk, two eggs, two tablespoonfuls of butter, a level teaspoonful of soda, a little grated nutmeg. Mix these ingredients well together and work in flour for a dough sufficiently stiff to roll out half an inch thick. Cut any shape desired, fry in hot grease and drain, dust with powdered sugar. Sweet milk and baking powder may be used.[746]

KNOTS

Charlotte russe.

☛ Cream one-fourth cup of butter, scant measure, with three-fourths of a cup of sugar, one whole egg, yolk of another beaten without separating, add the grated rind of an orange or lemon, little mace or nutmeg, little salt, three and a half cups flour, two level teaspoonfuls cream of tartar, half of a level teaspoonful of soda sifted with the flour. Mix to a firm dough with half a cup of milk. Cut off bits of the dough, roll under hand until about the length and size of a lead pencil, tie in a loose knot, fry in deep fat, drain and dredge with sugar. Beautiful and delicious.[747]

NONDESCRIPTS

☛ Yolks of four eggs, little salt. Beat the yolks light. Enough flour to form a stiff dough. Beat the dough well and roll as thin as tissue paper; cut with a saucer and fold twice. Cut them in narrow strips, leaving them united at the ends. Fry in plenty of boiling lard or cottolene. When done sift thickly with powdered sugar.[748]

HOMEMADE BAKING POWDER

☛ One pound of bi-carbonate of soda, two pounds pure cream of tartar, ten ounces of starch, flour or cornstarch. Mix, sift five or six times, put in cans and fasten on cover tightly.[749]

FRIED CREAM FRITTERS

☛ Put a pint of milk in a double boiler with two inches of stick cinnamon. Beat together one tablespoonful of flour, one-fourth cup cornstarch, half cup sugar, pinch salt, one-fourth cup cold milk, yolks of three eggs. Blend the hot milk with this, return to the boiler and cook twenty minutes (remove the cinnamon), stirring often; add a teaspoonful each of butter and vanilla. Stir until the butter is absorbed, then pour in a well buttered shallow pan. When cold and firm, turn out carefully on a board sprinkled with fine bread crumbs. Cut in strips one inch wide and three inches long. Roll in bread crumbs, then in egg batter, then in crumbs again; let dry off and fry, in very hot fat, a golden brown. Drain on paper, dust with powdered sugar. Put a small spoonful of tart jelly on each fritter. Fine.[750]

FLOAT

☛ 3 eggs,
1½ pints of milk,
1 cup of sugar,
Heaping tablespoon of cornstarch.
Flavor with vanilla. Cook till thick. Serve in glasses.[751]

ORANGE ICING

☛ Put a cup powdered sugar in a bowl, put in the grated rind of an orange, two tablespoons orange juice and one tablespoon boiling water. Mix until the sugar is moist. Spread over the cake.[752]

FINE FROSTING

☛ Dissolve one cup granulated sugar in four tablespoons cold water, boil until the syrup spins a thread. Beat the white of an egg until frothy, add half teaspoon cream tartar, beat until stiff and cold. Enough for a cake.[753]

RAW ICING FOR DECORATING

☛ Don't beat your eggs at all until you put in some sugar allowing a full tablespoon for each white, put the sugar in slowly, one tablespoon lemon juice, use four whites to one pound sugar and a few drops acetic acid. Beat until very stiff.[754]

CONFEDERATE FRUIT CAKE FROSTING

☛ Use confectioners sugar with only enough water to make it spread without running, flavor, it is better without eggs, do not spread until the cake is cold. Sprinkle thickly while moist with chopped nuts, grated cocoanut, cherries, crystalized fruit. Fine.[755]

WHITE MOUNTAIN ICING

☛ One and a half cups granulated sugar, half cup boiling water, one-fourth teaspoon cream tartar, whites of two eggs beaten until foamy, lemon to flavor. Stir the sugar, cream tartar and water over the fire until the sugar dissolves, and the mixture reaches the boiling point, then cook until the syrup threads when dropped from the spoon, or 238 by thermometer. Pour the syrup in a fine stream on the whites of eggs, beaten until foamy. Set the saucepan on range and continue beating until the eggs look cooked, then set in cold water. Add the flavor and beat until cool enough to spread. Score for cutting as soon as spread. If your icing don't seem to be cooked enough, add some grated chocolate or chopped nuts.[756]

OATMEAL PUDDING

☛ Mix two ounces of fine Scotch oatmeal in a half teacup of sweet milk; add to it two teacups of boiling sweet milk. Sweeten to taste, and stir over the fire for ten minutes; then add two ounces of sifted bread crumbs; stir until stiff, then add one ounce of butter, and one or two well beaten eggs. Flavor with lemon or nutmeg, and bake in buttered dish slowly one hour.[757]

CHOCOLATE ICING

☛ One light cup butter, one cup milk, three cups sugar, one cup chocolate; cook to a ball, then beat. Vanilla. The best.[758]

CREAM ICING

☛ One cup milk to two cups sugar, cook to a very soft ball, then beat very hard. You may put a little melted chocolate in this.[759]

ORIENTAL ICING

☛ One pound sugar, one white of egg, one-fourth teaspoon glycerine, two drops acetic acid, half teaspoon vanilla, enough water to dissolve. Cook the sugar and water to 236 (soft ball) adding glycerine, when the sugar is dissolved, and the acid when it commences boiling, and be sure you wipe down sides and steam it by putting a cover over it, when cooked to 236 pour out on a platter or bowl, and let get cold.

Beat your egg white stiff, put it on the cold syrup and beat it, flavor. When you see it commencing to thicken, pour at once on the cake, in using this for layer cake ice the top layer first, or it may get rough before all used.[760]

SUGAR GLAZI

☛ One cup powdered sugar, two tablespoons water put over fire to get lukewarm, pour over the cake and put on the decorations, fruit juice or wine may be substituted for water.[761]

BOILED FROSTING

☛ Boil one cup of sugar, and one-third cup water to 238 or until the syrup spins a thread. Pour the syrup onto the white of an egg, beaten dry, in a fine stream beaten meanwhile with a Dover egg beater. Set the bowl in cold water and continue beating until the icing stiffens sufficiently to use.[762]

Cake layer tin.

PLAIN CHOCOLATE ICING

☛ Put in a shallow pan four tablespoons scraped chocolate, place it where it will melt, then stir in three tablespoons milk or cream, and one of water, mix and add one cup sugar, boil five minutes, when cool flavor and spread between and over cake. Nice for Eclairs.[763]

Dishes from the field and garden.

8. Dumplings

APPLE DUMPLINGS

☛ Roll out a large sheet of suet, potato, or common pie paste tolerably thick, and cut it up in circular pieces, sufficiently large to cover an apple. Pare and core, without cutting to pieces, some well flavored cooking apples, fill the space whence you extract the cores with brown sugar, and squeeze on each a little lemon juice. Put one apple in each piece of paste, closing it securely and smoothly round the apple on one side; dust them thickly with flour, put them in a pot of boiling water, and boil them steadily till done, which you may tell by piercing one with a fork. When they are done, serve them warm, in a covered dish, and accompany them with cream or cold sweet sauce. If you are not well experienced in the matter, tie them up separately in little cloths, and boil them as directed for puddings. This will secure them from all possibility of coming to pieces, though by proper management there is but little danger without the cloths.⁶⁴

Baked apple dumplings.

STRAWBERRY DUMPLINGS

☛ Get ripe strawberries, pick the stems and leaves carefully from them, put them into a dish, and strew over them a little sugar. Roll out a thick sheet of standing or common paste, cut out as many circular pieces as you wish to have dumplings, having them all of the same size, fill them up with the strawberries, making them about the size of a large apple, and closing them securely and neatly on one side. Having ready some little dumpling cloths, made of very thick linen, dip them into hot water and dredge them with flour; sprinkle the dumplings well with dry flour, put them separately in the cloths, and tie them up; put them into a pot of boiling water, and boil them steadily till done, which will only take a short time: then take them out of the cloths in which they are enveloped, put them into a covered dish, and send them warm to table with cream sauce. Blackberry and raspberry dumplings may be made in the same manner.[765]

CHERRY DUMPLINGS

☞ Roll out a thick sheet of suet paste, cut it into pieces about eight inches long and four wide. Extract the seeds from some fine ripe cherries, sprinkle them lightly with sugar, and put three large spoonfuls on one end of each piece of paste; turn the other end of the paste over the cherries, press the edges securely together, and crimp them nicely; dust them very well with flour, to make them look white and prevent them sticking together and coming to pieces; put them into a pot of boiling water, and boil them gently and steadily till done: then lift them carefully from the water with a perforated ladle, put them into a covered dish, and send them warm to table with cream or cold sweet sauce.[766]

BLACKBERRY DUMPLINGS

☞ 2 cups flour.
2 teaspoons baking powder.
½ teaspoon salt.
2 tbls. sugar.
2 cups shortening.
½ cup ice water.
2 tbls. brown sugar.
½ teaspoon butter.

Mix flour, salt, baking powder, sugar and water together making a dough. Roll out ¼ inch thick and cut into 4 squares. Place pastry in muffin pans and fill with blackberries. Brush with water and dust lightly with brown sugar and butter. Bake in moderate oven for 25 minutes. Serve with vanilla sauce.[767]

PEACH DUMPLINGS

☞ 2 cups flour.
½ cup sugar.
4 tbls. shortening.
1 teaspoon cinnamon.
¾ cup milk.
1 tbls. butter.
4 teaspoons baking powder.
Several peaches.
½ teaspoon salt.

Mix first 5 ingredients together. Roll ½ inch thick, cut into squares, put peaches in each square with cinnamon and sugar to taste. Take corners and pinch together. Place in greased pan, dot with sugar and butter. Bake in moderate oven until brown. Serve hot.[768]

CHICKEN DUMPLINGS

☛ 3 cups flour.
2 cups milk.
1 teaspoon baking powder.
1 teaspoon salt.
6 Irish potatoes.
Yolk of 1 egg.

Cut chicken as for frying, stew until tender with potatoes. Make a dough using one cup of milk, drop in large spoonsful into boiling pot, which should be about ½ full, cover closely and boil slowly for thirty-five minutes without lifting cover. Thicken gravy remaining in pot with yolk, one spoon flour and remaining cup of milk.

Dumplings should be light and spongy.[769]

CRANBERRY DUMPLINGS

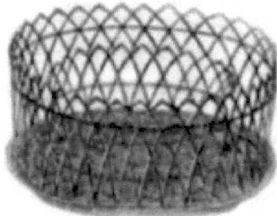

The Ford Dish Drain.

☛ Stir four beaten eggs into a pint and a half of sweet milk, make it into good batter with flour, and stir into it a pint of cranberries. Beat it very well, put it into buttered tea-cups, tie a little cloth over each, and boil them as you would a pudding.

When done, turn them out into a dish, sprinkle on them a large handful of brown sugar, and pour over a pint of rich sweet cream. Cranberry dumplings may also be made like apple dumplings.[770]

RICE DUMPLINGS

☛ Peel some nice cooking apples, and with a sharp knife extract the cores, excavating with it at least half of the apples, and fill the cavities with boiled rice, first sweetening it with brown sugar and flavoring it with nutmeg or cloves.

Take some suet or common pie paste, roll it out rather thick, and cut it into circular pieces sufficiently large for each to cover an apple; put your apples and rice into them, closing them firmly and smoothly on one side; sprinkle them well with flour, and tie them up separately in dumpling cloths, after dipping them into hot water and dredging them with flour.

Boil them as other dumplings or puddings till done, and eat them warm with cream sauce or butter and sugar, worked together and flavored with lemon.[771]

LIGHT DUMPLINGS

☛ Make up your dough exactly as for light bread, and let it set by the fire till it rises well: then flour your hands, make out the dough into balls the size of a goose's egg, dust them well with flour, tie them up in separate cloths, put them into boiling water, and boil them till done.

Eat them warm with butter, powdered sugar and grated nutmeg, or cream or wine sauce.[772]

SUET DUMPLINGS

☞ Mince very fine one pound of fresh hard lumps of suet, sprinkle it with a salt-spoonful of salt, rub it well into two pounds of sifted flour, and make it into good paste with cold water.

After kneading it thoroughly, make it into balls the size of a goose's egg, sprinkle them well with dry flour, drop them into boiling water, and boil them briskly till done; then serve them up with a perforated ladle, letting the water drain from them; put them into a covered dish, and eat them warm with molasses or wine sauce.

This kind of paste makes excellent dumplings to accompany fresh beef or mutton, for which purpose they should be rolled out about an inch thick and cut into small squares, or made into small round balls, very little larger than a hen's egg, and cooked with the meat which they are to accompany.[773]

INDIAN DUMPLINGS

☞ Sift a quart of fine Indian meal, mix with it a salt-spoonful of salt, a spoonful of butter, or two of finely chopped suet, two well beaten eggs and enough sweet milk to make it into good bread dough.

Work it well with your hands, make it into dumplings the size of a large biscuit, flour them well, drop them into a pot of boiling water, and boil them briskly till done.

Be very careful in serving them, lest you break them. Eat them warm with molasses. Indian dumplings are sometimes eaten with corned pork or bacon. In such cases they should be boiled with the meat with which they are served.[774]

BIRD DUMPLINGS

☞ Take any kind of nice small birds; pick and wash them clean and cut off their heads and feet, score the breasts, mash the joints, but do not cut them apart, fill them with a little grated bread and butter, seasoned with pepper and nutmeg, and moistened with white wine, and season them with salt and rub them over with butter.

Roll out a thick sheet of suet or standing paste; cut it into pieces sufficiently large to cover the birds, and put one into each piece of paste, close them up securely, dust them with four, tie them separately in pudding cloths, and boil them as other dumplings.

Eat them warm with melted butter and wine or highly seasoned gravy.[775]

Fish and shellfish.

9. Eggs

TO CHOOSE EGGS
☞ There are many rules for trying the soundness and freshness of eggs, one of which is to put them in a pan of fresh water; all that will sink readily to the bottom of the pan are good, and all that rise or float on the top, are certainly rotten. It is said that in proportion to the freshness of the egg its progress to the bottom of the pan will be.

There is another very good rule, though a singular one, that is, having washed and wiped the eggs clean, touch the large end with your tongue, and if, by holding it there a second or two, it feels warm to your tongue, it is good, but if it feels cold, it is a certain sign it is not good.[776]

TO KEEP EGGS
☞ Eggs will keep good for some time, buried in charcoal or wheat bran, after greasing them a little with mutton tallow; but I believe the general opinion of those who have tried it is, that to keep them in lime-water is the best way they can be preserved.

To half a bushel of water add little over a pint of unslaked lime, and as much coarse salt, and when the whole is dissolved, put in the eggs; be very particular that you do not put in one that is cracked, as it will spoil the whole; there should be plenty of water to cover them well; if the brine is too strong with the lime, it will eat the shells; this of course can be easily detected; if the eggs are fresh and whole, and water of the proper strength, it is said they will keep good for years.[777]

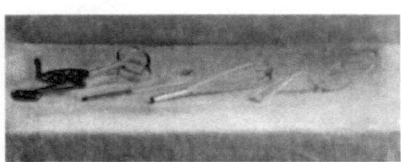

Egg utensils, L-R: Dover beater, wire spoon, wire whip, Daisy beater.

EGG BATTER

☞ Is made by beating an egg only enough to mix white and yellow, and adding a tablespoonful of hot water. Dip all articles that have to be crumbed in this.[778]

TO BOIL EGGS

☞ Have boiling water; drop in the eggs and let them remain three minutes, if you wish the whites congealed; if not, let them remain a shorter time. Silver spoons used in eating eggs should be put in water immediately.[779]

HARD BOILED EGGS

☞ Put egg in cold water and boil slowly half an hour.[780]

SOFT BOILED EGGS

☞ Put an egg in a pint of boiling water, cover closely and let remain twenty minutes (not over the fire). If four eggs are wanted three pints of water may be used. Only let them stand ten minutes.[781]

BAKED EGGS

☞ Cut some small slices from a loaf of light bread, toast them lightly, and put them in the bottom and round the sides of a small, deep dish. Grate fine some of the crust of the loaf, and mix with it four ounces of butter, broken up. Boil one dozen eggs till hard enough to slice, and peel and slice them. Put them in the dish on the toasts in alternate layers with the bread crumbs and butter, seasoning them with salt and pepper; pour in a cup of rich sweet cream, sprinkle on the top some grated bread and small bits of butter, and brown it in a Dutch oven.[782]

Molded eggs a la Polignac.

SCALLOPED EGGS

☞ Use six or eight hard boiled eggs. Make a white sauce of one-fourth of a cup each of flour and butter. Cook until it bubbles. Then add a pint of milk (cold), one teaspoonful of salt, one-fourth of a teaspoonful of pepper. Slice the eggs, pour the sauce over, sprinkle with crumbs and brown.[783]

CREAMED EGGS

☞ Make slices of toast, butter and dip in milk. Make a white sauce of one full tablespoon of butter, an even tablespoonful of flour, little salt. Cook until a little thick. Put slices of boiled eggs in the sauce and pour over the toast. Reserve one or two yolks. Put through the potato sieve over the whole.⁷⁸⁴

SCRAMBLED EGGS

☛ Six eggs, one teaspoonful of beef extract, three tablespoonfuls of cream, half a teaspoonful of butter, half a teaspoonful of salt, little pepper, two tablespoonfuls of grated cheese. Take thick slices of bread, cut in squares, hollow out the center, brush over with butter and crisp in the oven. Scramble the eggs and put in these cases.⁷⁸⁵

DROPPED EGGS

☛ Have the water in the saucepan boiling hard. Break gently the eggs, one at a time, into it, being very careful not to injure the yolks. With a spoon dip the hot water over them till a skin or crust has formed. Take them out with a skimmer, lay on a flat dish, slightly salting them, and garnish the platter with parsley.⁷⁸⁶

DRESSED EGGS

☛ Take any number of eggs; boil hard and cool them in water; peel and divide the whites carefully, cut the long way, lay, the pieces in pairs on a dish; mash the yolks with a small quantity of butter and minced ham; season highly with salt, pepper and mustard (add a very small quantity of onion); make the dressing into very small balls, place in the cavities of the whites and close very neatly as whole eggs.⁷⁸⁷

Egg poacher.

PICKLED EGGS

☛ Pint strong vinegar, half pint cold water, tea-spoon each of cinnamon, allspice, and mace; boil the eggs till very hard and take off the shell; put on the spices tied in a white muslin bag, in the cold water, boil, and if the water wastes away, add enough so as to leave a half pint when done; add the vinegar, and pour over the eggs; put in as many eggs as the mixture will cover, and when they are used, the same will do for another lot. Or, after boiling (hard) and removing shell, place in jar of beet pickles, and the white will be come red; cut in two in serving.⁷⁸⁸

HUNGARIAN EGGS

☛ A piece of butter the size of a walnut, small onion chopped fine, one pint of tomatoes strained, one-half pound of mild cheese, three eggs, salt, cayenne to suit taste. Place the butter in a pan (after having the water boil to heat the pan), let it melt, add onion and cook until soft. (If one does not care for the onion, only the flavor, it can be removed before adding the tomato.)

Now add the tomato, let it come to a boil, add cheese cut fine, stir until it is smooth; now break in the eggs and stir hard until the eggs are done.

Care should be taken to break the yolk in stirring, or it will result in a hard lump; serve on crackers or buttered toast.[789]

EGGS AND CHEESE

☛ Beat up eight eggs to a thick froth, put in a little salt, a half a teacup of grated cracker and three tablespoonfuls of grated cheese. Put into a frying-pan with some butter, and cook and serve as an omelet.[790]

OMELET

☛ 6 eggs beaten separately,
1 cup of milk,
1 tablespoon of butter.

Mix milk, yolks, butter, salt, and pepper, and add the whites last. Pour into a hot pan which has been well buttered, and cook quickly on top of oven.

When it begins to thicken, put inside the oven and brown. Cut in half and roll and serve hot at once. All omelets should be served immediately.[791]

PLAIN OMELET

☛ Melt two tablespoonfuls of butter in an omelet pan. Beat four eggs very little with four tablespoonfuls of water, little salt and pepper. Pour in the hot omelet pan.

When done fold. Milk makes a tough omelet. Sprinkle over a little salt when half done.[792]

OMELET SOUFFLE

☛ Break six eggs, beat the yolks and whites separately till very light, then mix them, add four tablespoonsful of powdered sugar, and a little grated lemon peel.

Put a quarter of a pound of butter in a pan; when melted, pour in the eggs and stir them.

When they have absorbed the butter, turn it on a plate previously buttered, sprinkle some powdered sugar, set it in a hot Dutch oven, and when a little brown, serve it up for a desert.[793]

Dutch oven.

TOMATO OMELET

☛ Make as for plain omelette; cut up 4 ripe tomatoes; drain off the water, and wipe the pieces dry on a coarse towel.

Then chop them fine, and add to the omelette just before baking.[794]

CORN OMELET

☛ Boil 1 dozen ears of young corn 10 minutes; when cooked and cold, grate fine and season with salt. Separate 5 eggs; beat the yolks till thick and add 1 gill of cream. After mixing well, stir it into the corn by degrees.

Beat the whites until stiff and dry; stir lightly through, ½ at a time; have ready in a frying pan equal quantity of lard and butter, boiling hot; pour in the mixture and cook rapidly. When done turn it out of the pan and send to the table at once.[795]

Wire egg stand.

SPANISH OMELET

☛ Fry a little garlic in sweet oil, in a tin or porcelain pan, having previously chopped it very fine; when the garlic is done, add some sliced tomatoes, sliced mushrooms, and smoked beef tongue; season well. Make a plain omelet; fry it in sweet oil and put the garlic, tomatoes, mushrooms, and tongue inside; cool and serve with a little tomato sauce.[796]

QUAKER OMELET

☛ Three eggs, ½ teacup milk, 1½ tablespoons corn starch, 1 teaspoon salt, 1 tablespoon butter.

How to do it: Put the omelet pan and a cover that will fit close on, to heat. Beat the yolks of the eggs, the corn starch and the salt thoroughly together. Beat the whites to a stiff froth, add the well-beaten yolks and corn starch, and add the milk. Now put the butter in the hot pan; when melted, pour in the mixture. Cover and place where it will brown but not burn; cook about 7 minutes, fold, turn on a hot dish. If the yolks and whites have been well beaten, the pan and cover hot, there will be no failure.[797]

SWISS EGGS

☛ Cover the bottom of a dish with two ounces of fresh butter and on this scatter grated cheese; drop the eggs upon the cheese without breaking the yolks; season to taste. Pour over the eggs a little cream and sprinkle with about two ounces of grated cheese; set in a moderate oven for about fifteen minutes.[798]

EGGS ON TOAST

☛ Put two quarts of water over the fire, and when it comes to a gentle boil add one-half teaspoonful of salt. Break in six eggs, taking care not to injure the yolks. Let them cook for five minutes. Have some toasted bread, slightly buttered, on a hot platter. Remove the eggs from the water with a skimmer and lay them on the toast and serve hot.[799]

MUSHROOM OMELET

☛ Four eggs, two tablespoonfuls of butter, four of chopped mushrooms, a generous half tablespoonful of flour, two-thirds of a cup of stock, a little water, salt and pepper to taste.

Put a tablespoonful of butter in a frying pan and let it get hot. Add the flour and stir until brown and smooth.

Gradually add the stock and after boiling up once add the mushrooms. Season with salt and pepper and simmer five minutes.

Beat the eggs rather light; add to them half a teaspoonful of salt and a tablespoonful of water.

Shirred egg (left); cocotte (right).

Put a tablespoonful of butter in a warm omelet pan and set on the stove; when hot put in the beaten eggs and shake vigorously until they begin to thicken.

Spread the mushroom and half the sauce upon the egg mixture, then fold and turn on a hot dish; pour the remainder of the sauce around it and serve at once. Garnish with croutons.[800]

FRENCH TOAST

☛ Use one egg to a cup of sweet milk; add salt and pepper and beat well. Dip slices of bread in this and fry quickly in boiling lard. Sift over this a half cup of sugar, with a teaspoonful of cinnamon.[801]

CONFEDERATE PICKLED EGGS

☛ To a quart of vinegar add one ounce of whole ginger, one teaspoonful of cloves, one blade of mace, and one teaspoonful of whole pepper. Boil the spices for five minutes in the vinegar and let stand three days; then strain the vinegar; boil the eggs to be kept for ten minutes, throw them into cold water and take off the shells; when they are cold put them into jars and cover with the vinegar.[802]

EGGS AND BEEF

☛ Chip some dried beef, and pour boiling water over it to freshen it. Pour off the water and put a little butter into the skillet with the meat. When it is hot stir in three or four eggs until they are well mixed with the meat; pepper, and send to the breakfast-table hot.[803]

SHIRRED EGGS

☛ Take 6 fresh eggs. Grease baking-dish with butter.

Do not beat the eggs, but break and pour them in the dish. Salt and pepper them and put in a hot oven and cook till the whites curl up.

Serve in baking-dish at once.[804]

EGG NOG
☞ Six eggs beaten separately very light, nine tablespoonfuls of sugar beaten with the yolks, nearly a cup of whiskey and rum mixed, the stiff whites folded in. A cup of cream or milk may be added. Grate nutmeg over.[805]

EGG ROLLS
☞ One quart of flour, half tablespoonful of butter, two eggs lightly beat, half tea-cup of sweet yeast, half teacup of water, one teaspoonful of salt. Mix as a sponge, about 10 o'clock at night, for breakfast; put to rise until morning. With dry flour knead the sponge, not too stiff; make off rolls, put to rise in baking pan, then have oven hot and bake slowly. When rolls are done, put them in a napkin until sent to table.[806]

POTTED EGGS
☞ Take the yolks of six hard-boiled eggs, one ounce of butter, one teaspoonful of anchovy sauce, a little salt and cayenne pepper. Pound the eggs and butter well together in a mortar, then add the salt and cayenne pepper, and lastly the anchovy sauce.[807]

WHIRLED EGGS

Stuffed eggs garnished with ribboned lettuce.

☞ One qt. of boiling water salted with a dessertspoon of salt; keep the water at a fast boil, stirring with a ladle or spoon in one direction until it whirls rapidly. Break the eggs one at a time, into a cup, and drop into the center or vortex of the whirlpool, which must be kept in motion until the egg is a round ball. Remove carefully with a perforated spoon, put it on a slice of buttered toast and place the dish in the oven to keep warm. Proceed in the same way with each egg, and when the desired number are cooked add a dash of pepper, a bit of butter and send hot to the table.[808]

CONVENT EGGS
☞ Peel and slice 4 hard boiled eggs, 1 onion cut up, 1 ounce of butter; when the butter is melted, add the onion, and fry white; add a teaspoon of flour; mix with these ½ pint of milk, until it forms a white sauce, ½ teaspoon of salt, and ¼ teaspoon of pepper. When nicely done, put the eggs, cut in 6 pieces each, into the saucepan. When they are hot through, serve them on toast.[809]

STUFFED EGGS
☞ Boil eggs very hard, put in cold water and remove the shell. Cut in half lengthwise and remove the yolk. Put some bread crumbs to soak in

milk, mash fine the yolks, season with salt, pepper and butter, Durkee salad dressing, a little olive oil, mustard and parsley chopped fine. Add the bread crumbs, fill the eggs with the mixture, fasten together with a toothpick and fry brown.[810]

EGG BUTTER
☛ To three well-beaten eggs add one pint of molasses, orleans or sorghum. Boil until it thickens. Excellent.[811]

EGG PIE
☛ Boil six or eight eggs hard, slice lengthwise, fill your plate with rich pastry, lay in the slices, sprinkle with salt, pepper and plenty of butter, pour over a cup of water, put on a top crust and bake.[812]

Curried eggs in a nest of rice.

FRIED EGGS
☛ Have plenty of fat, but not too hot, in a frying pan. Break the eggs one by one in a cup and turn them into the fat. If it bubbles it is too hot. With a spoon dip the fat over the eggs. When the yolks are covered with a film remove to slices of broiled ham, slices little larger than the egg.[813]

OYSTER OMELET
☛ Scald twenty-five oysters in their own liquor until they ruffle; remove oysters, and to each cup of liquor thicken with one tablespoonful each of flour and butter rubbed together. Put in the hot liquid and let thicken. Season with salt and pepper. Chop the oysters and add to the sauce, which must be quite thick. Beat four eggs separately. Add to the yolks one-fourth of a cup of water, little salt and pepper. Fold in stiff whites. Have a large omelet pan hot and greased, turn in the egg mixture, cook slowly. When a little brown underneath (shake while cooking) set the pan inside to cook the top or under the gas flame. Take out, make a crease in center, put in some of the mixture, fold and turn out on a hot platter. Put the rest of sauce around it. Garnish with croutons.[814]

EGGS IN TOMATO CUPS
☛ Scoop out the tomato after cutting a slice from the top, sprinkle over a little salt and pepper, let stand inverted half an hour, break in an egg, salt and pepper it. Bake and serve on toast. Sprinkle over fine cut parsley.[815]

CURRIED EGGS
☛ Slice two onions and fry in butter, add a table-spoon curry-powder and one pint good broth or stock, stew till onions are quite tender, add a cup of cream thickened with arrowroot or rice flour, simmer a few

moments, then add eight or ten hard-boiled eggs, cut in slices, and beat them well, but do not boil.[816]

STEAMED EGGS

☞ Break one-half dozen eggs into separate cups, and have ready a well-buttered dish, into which each egg should be placed carefully. Cover the dish to prevent the heat from escaping, and set it over a pan of boiling water, first putting small bits of butter lightly over the top of the eggs.

When they are set sufficiently, sprinkle them with a little salt and serve with fried ham or sausages. It takes four minutes to set.[817]

ROASTED EGGS

Eggs A L'aurore.

☞ Roll each egg in four layers of wet paper, brown, or newspaper; put down in the hot ashes and cover well; let stay until the outer layer is well scorched.

Let cool until it may be handled; then remove the paper. This is a pastime children delight in.[818]

DEVILED EGGS

☞ Grate a fourth of a pound of cheese fine; butter a shallow baking dish, spread the cheese in the bottom with bits of butter; sprinkle with salt and cayenne.

Break six eggs in a plate and slip on top of the dish; mix a teaspoonful of French mustard with half a cup of cream and pour over. Set in a hot oven for ten minutes and serve hot.[819]

EGGS WITH CHEESE

☞ For each person take a slice of bread, one-fourth of a cup of grated cheese and one egg. For four slices take a cup of milk and one egg, beat enough to mix and add the milk.

Dip each slice of bread in this and lay on a greased pan. Sprinkle over the cheese, dust with salt and pepper.

Break the eggs in a cup and slide carefully on the bread. Put in a hot oven until whites are set.[820]

SCRAMBLED EGGS

☞ Five eggs, two tablespoonfuls of butter, one-third of a cup of milk, half a teaspoonful each of salt and pepper. Put butter in an omelet pan. When hot, break in eggs, put in milk and seasonings. Serve on rounds of toast.

Garnish with parsley. Stir with a fork. The last cooking should be done by heat of pan. May be served in border of creamed potatoes.[821]

FRENCH OMELET
☞ Separate four eggs, stir yolks with a pinch of salt, dissolve a tablespoonful of flour in a cup of milk, add to yolks.

Lastly fold in the stiff whites. Cook as other omelets.[822]

EGGS AND BACON
☞ Cut twelve slices of bacon very thin, and fry until crisp; take them out and keep hot in the oven. Break six eggs separately into the boiling fat and fry until brown.

Serve with the eggs laid over the bacon, and small fried snippets of bread placed round. Hash can be used instead of bacon.[823]

ONION EGGS
☞ Boil six eggs hard, slice three of the eggs, white and yellow together; cut three onions in slices, fry in butter, lay them on a platter; place the sliced eggs over them, cover so as to keep hot; grate the three remaining eggs, mix them with a little salt and a trifle of cayenne pepper; boil up in a little cream and pour this over the eggs and onions; delicious.[824]

CELERY EGGS
☞ Six hard-boiled eggs, let cool and chop not very fine; one bunch of celery chopped fine, season with pepper and salt, add three rolled crackers and one cupful of milk; fry in hot butter.[825]

CONFEDERATE CREAMED EGGS
☞ Boil six eggs hard, cut in halves, arrange on a dish, pour over white sauce.[826]

CONFEDERATE TOMATO OMELET
☞ Beat six eggs separately; add a tablespoonful of bread crumbs to the yolks, then a half teacupful of sweet milk, and salt and pepper to taste. Cut two or three fine ripe tomatoes in half-inch blocks; add the whites, then the tomatoes. Cook quickly; butter and serve immediately.[827]

VEGETABLE OMELETS
☞ Half a teacupful of cold boiled Irish potatoes, chopped fine with parsley, or any vegetable liked, may be added to a plain omelet and fried, or baked.[828]

POACHED EGGS
☞ Grease an omelet pan, put half an inch of water and grease some muffin rings.

Drop the eggs in the rings and dip hot water over them. Salt and pepper.[829]

Poached egg.

EGGS A LA HAVANA

☛ Take eight eggs, two ounces of butter, two small Spanish onions, six tomatoes, one-half teacupful of bread-crumbs, one-half pint of stock. Boil the eggs ten minutes, cut them into slices, chop the onions and tomatoes, season with pepper and salt, and fry them with the crumbs in the butter. Add the stock and stir for ten minutes after it boils. Place the slices of eggs in the liquid and warm them through. [830]

Goodies for the lunch box.

10. Entrees

(These dishes may also be used as appetizers.)

CHICKEN CUTLETS
☞ Put a dressed chicken in boiling water with an onion and a little salt. Cook slowly until thoroughly done. Then remove skin and bones and chop rather fine.[831]

SAUCE FOR ENTREES
☞ Two tablespoonfuls of butter, three of flour, one cup of milk or the chicken stock. After the butter and flour cooks add the liquid and cook until thick. Remove, season with salt, pepper, parsley cut fine, and lemon juice. Add two cups of cut chicken. Spread on a platter to cool; then sprinkle your cutlet mold with fine bread crumbs; fill with the mixture, turn out on a bed of crumbs so every part is crumbed; dip in egg batter, then in crumbs again. Fry in very hot Wesson oil. Serve with the following mushroom sauce.[832]

MUSHROOM SAUCE
☞ Add a tablespoonful of lemon juice to a cup of white sauce, half a cup of cooked or canned mushrooms cut small.[833]

MEAT STEW ENTREE
☞ Cut your meat into inch pieces and put into a saucepan; season with salt, pepper, and butter or lard. Put one pint of water to a pound of meat. One hour will cook, unless very young, when less time is sufficient. Add onions if liked.[834]

SUPREME OF CHICKEN
☞ Chop the breast of a chicken in a meat chopper. To one cup of meat add one egg and beat until smooth; then add three more eggs, beating each one in well before adding the next season with a level teaspoonful

of salt and a dash of white pepper. Next add a pint of cream. Butter twelve Dariole molds, decorate with truffle and fill half full with the custard. Lay over a buttered paper and set them in a pan of boiling water. Poach twenty minutes. Serve with Bechamel sauce.[835]

CHICKEN CUTLETS

☛ Make a heavy white sauce of two tablespoonfuls of butter, three of flour. Cook together until it bubbles; then add a pint of cold milk or half chicken stock. Season with salt, pepper and Worcester sauce. Stir in gently two quarts of chicken chopped rather fine, Let get very cold; then mold as in other receipts. Let dry before using.[836]

Chicken timbale.

BROILED SWEETBREADS

☛ Select the throat sweetbreads, soak half an hour in cold water, place in boiling water, salted, with a teaspoonful of vinegar. Cook twenty-five minutes, but never let the water boil. Place in cold water, removing pipes and membranes. They are now ready for various dishes, but should only be heated. For broiling split and place in a fine wire broiler. When brown remove and spread with butter. Serve with lemon and toast points.[837]

CRÊME DE VOLAILLE

☛ 1 pound raw chicken, without bones, skin, etc.,
½ teaspoon onion juice,
2 teaspoons parsley.

Run through the grinder till very fine. Cream into this ¼ pound butter, with salt and pepper to taste. Break in 3 raw eggs, 1 at a time, then beat it well as you would a delicate cake.

Line a mold with this, leaving a hole for the following:

Stew half a can of champignons in their own liquor, thicken with butter and flour. Cover the hole with some of the meat and steam 5 hours. The other half of the champignons stew in cream and pour over the mold before serving. A small can of truffles is a great improvement. Pour the liquor from the truffles in the meat, slice them and stew one-half to go with the champignons in the hole, the other half with the champignons in the cream This is nice molded in individual molds.[838]

SWEETBREADS A LA BECHEMEL

☛ Wash and simmer the sweetbreads twenty minutes; remove the skin and fat and pick in small pieces. To each pint allow six mushrooms chopped fine, yolks of two eggs, salt and pepper. Make a white sauce of one tablespoonful each of flour and butter. When it bubbles add half a cup of white stock and half a cup of cream. Stir until it boils; then add the mushrooms and sweetbreads. Cook in double boiler. When ready to serve add the beaten yolks, salt and pepper. A tablespoonful of sherry's now added. Serve in individual paper cases. A calf brain may be parboiled, mashed and added to the sauce.[839]

BROILED SWEETBREADS
☛ After simmering twenty minutes, split when thick, season with salt and pepper, wrap in buttered paper, broil ten minutes. Spread with maitre d'hotel butter.[840]

SWEETBREADS A LA MONTEBELLA
☛ Put the cooked sweetbreads in a mold with a weight on top to cool; cut in small dice shaped pieces; serve in the following sauce.[841]

MONTEBELLO SAUCE
☛ Cook one tablespoonful of chopped onion, three of tarragon vinegar, twelve pepper corns coarsely pounded. Cook together until nearly dry; then add half a can of thick tomatoes. Season with salt and cayenne. Cook slowly ten minutes. Then rub the sauce through a sieve into a saucepan. Add the yolks of four eggs and half a wineglass white wine. Let get very hot; then set aside to cool. Stir four ounces of butter to a cream. Add slowly while stirring the tomato sauce. Put in a double boiler over the fire until hot. Add the sweetbreads. Garnish with red bell peppers cut in dice.[842]

GREEN PEPPERS STUFFED WITH CORN
☛ To 6 medium-sized peppers take 1 can of corn, or enough fresh corn to fill them. Boil the peppers with a little soda to soften them. Mix the corn; add pepper, salt, and butter to taste. Fill the peppers. Fill a baking-dish half full of water; put the peppers in and bake. Serve with a cream sauce.[843]

SWEETBREADS A LA CREAM
☛ Parboil the sweetbreads and pick them to pieces, rejecting the membranes; chop rather fine. Five mushrooms chopped very fine. Make a white sauce of one tablespoonful each of flour and butter. When it boils add a cup of cream. When it boils again add the sweetbreads and mushrooms; stir them over the fire five minutes; season with salt and pepper. Serve in paper cases.[844]

FRIED SWEETBREADS
☛ Cut the parboiled and cooled sweetbreads in slices. Egg and breadcrumb them. Fry in deep fat. Serve with sauce Tartare.[845]

HOW TO GARNISH SWEETBREADS
☛ After larding and baking your sweetbreads have some canned corn cooked in milk rather dry. Make a border of the corn around a chop

plate; sprinkle over some chopped red pepper; put sweetbreads in center.[846]

BOUDINS Á LA RICHELIEU

☛ 1 pound of raw turkey or chicken breast,
⅓ pound of panada,
½ pound of butter,
¼ pound of pickled pork,
3 eggs,
4 truffles,
Salt and pepper to taste.

Grind the turkey or chicken. Cream the butter with the panada and add the meat, having pork ground with the meat. Break in the eggs, one at a time, beating the mixture well. Slice a part of the truffles in this mixture, reserving the rest for the sauce.

Pour in the liquor from the truffles. Put this in the Boudin mold, place in bread-pan with water around, and boil ¾ of an hour. Serve with champignon sauce.[847]

BRAINS ON TOAST

☛ Boil the brains, remove membranes, cut in dice. Have some buttered toast, spread the brains over. Pour over drawn butter, flavor with Worcester sauce.[848]

SAUSAGE AND CABBAGE

☛ Brown two tablespoonfuls of butter with two of flour in a saucepan, add one pint of boiling water, one teaspoonful of salt, cayenne pepper, a bouquet of herbs, one carrot cut in rounds, one teaspoonful of onion juice, and one-half a small cabbage cut in four pieces. Simmer until the cabbage is nearly tender and the sauce has been somewhat reduced. Fifteen minutes before serving add one-half a pound of sausages and cook until done. Place the cabbage on a platter with the sausages in a row on top and pour over it the sauce. Brussels sprouts can be used instead of cabbage, but must not be cooked so long.[849]

FRIED BRAINS

☛ Prepare the brains as above, cut in squares, dip in egg and cracker crumbs, fry in hot fat. Serve with Mayonnaise, Tartare or Mushroom Sauce.[850]

STUFFED TOMATOES

☛ Cut off the tops of tomatoes, hollow the inside, and mix the inside that you take out with chopped up ham; to your bread crumbs or crackers powdered, butter, salt and pepper taste. Stuff the tomatoes full and replace the top close. Put them in a pan to bake in a hot oven for fifteen minutes.[851]

STUFFED EGGPLANT

☛ Take out the inside of the plant and boil it in just enough water to cover it for ten minutes, and then drain or press the water all out through a cullender. Chop some ham fine, take bread crumbs and butter (one tablespoonful to one egg plant), and have equal proportions of ham, cracker and bread crumbs to the inside of the plants. Season with salt and black pepper to taste and fry it brown. Then stuff the plants full and close and put them to bake. They will bake in ten minutes, but should not be put in the oven until just before table use. They are a delicious vegetable prepared in this manner. Use a hot oven.[852]

BRAINS WITH BROWN BATTER

Meat press.

☛ As soon as delivered drop the brains in a bowl of cold water, changing as often as discolored; then pull off as much of the tissue as you can without breaking the meat. Place in a saucepan with a little onion, salt, bit of bay leaf, teaspoonful of vinegar, and enough boiling water to cover. Simmer twenty minutes. No matter how the brains are to be served, the cooking is always the same.

Sauce: In a frying pan put two tablespoonfuls of butter, let heat gradually, and cook until brown; then add three tablespoonfuls of vinegar diluted and bring to the boiling point. Slice the brains and pour the sauce over. Season with Worcester sauce. Sift over some pepper. Delicious.[853]

CREAMED MUSHROOMS

☛ Three-fourths of a cup of mushrooms cut in quarters; cook them in two tablespoonfuls of butter four minutes; rub one and a half tablespoonfuls of flour in three-fourths of a cup of cream; add to the mushrooms; cook a little; remove and add salt and cayenne to taste, a tablespoonful of sherry.[854]

SCRAMBLED BRAINS ON TOAST

☛ Soak and cook the brains as directed above, drain and beat quite fine with a fork, season with salt and pepper. Add to them six beaten eggs and four tablespoonfuls of cream. Have ready some slices of hot buttered toast. Melt a tablespoonful of butter in a frying pan; turn in the prepared brains and stir over the fire until creamy and thickened; then spread over the toast; sprinkle with chopped parsley. Chopped mushrooms may be added to the brains.[855]

VIRGINIA HAM

☛ Soak a Smithfield ham in a tub of tepid water, skin side up. In the morning, scrub it well with a brush and trim off any imperfect places, then sew tightly in a strong piece of muslin, and weigh. Allow twenty minutes' boiling to every pound. Place the ham in a large boiler and fill up with cold water, throw in some whole spices and two or three bay leaves. Put on the back of the stove and heat very slowly, occasionally skimming. Simmer gently until it is nearly tender, then remove from fire, and as soon as it is cool enough to handle take off the cloth and skin. Trim away the brown, unsightly underside and place in a dripping pan. Paint the top with cream and cover with powdered cracker crumbs mixed with a little brown sugar. Stick whole cloves in at regular intervals and brown in a quick oven. Serve the following day with a good salad.[856]

BRAIN PATTIES

☛ For twelve patties get two sets of brains, one can of mushrooms. Boil brains until done, take off, put in clear water and lemon juice. Chop brains and mushrooms together. Make a sauce of a tablespoonful of butter, same of flour, and half a cup of cream. When a little thick remove; season with salt, pepper and nutmeg. Serve in patty cases heated.[857]

CREAMED DISHES

☛ Two tablespoonfuls of butter, four of flour; salt and pepper to season; two tablespoonfuls diced mushrooms, one tablespoonful fine cut parsley, one teaspoonful of grated onion, one of lemon juice, two cups of cream or milk. If you use milk, use four tablespoonfuls of butter. Prepare the sauce in the usual manner. If oysters are used they must be parboiled, and if large, cut in half. Fish must be flaked when hot, but meat cut in dice when cold. This sauce can be used for oysters, shrimp, lobster, chicken, sweetbreads, veal, fish, mushrooms, peas and asparagus tips.[858]

BREADED CALVES BRAINS

☛ Let the brains of two calves stand in cold water for half an hour; then remove the thin membrane that covers them. See that they are free from blood filled veins. Divide each set of brains in six parts and tie up each part in thin muslin. Drop all in a kettle of boiling water, just enough to cover them, and boil gently half an hour.

Take them up and put in cold water; when cool remove from the muslin, season with salt and pepper. Beat an egg with a tablespoonful of water, season with salt and pepper, dip the brains into it, roll in fine bread crumbs. Fry in boiling fat. Serve with the following cream sauce.[859]

CREAM SAUCE FOR CALVES BRAINS

☛ Put three tablespoonfuls of butter in a frying pan; when hot add a level tablespoonful of flour; stir the sauce until it bubbles, then add a pint of cold milk; stir until boils. Season with salt, pepper and onion juice. This sauce is nice for fish and potatoes with parsley in it.[860]

CHICKEN LIVER WITH WINE

☛ Cut your livers in pieces. Put two tablespoonfuls of butter in a pan. When hot put in the livers and one tablespoonful of flour; turn constantly and cook five minutes. Add a cup of stock and a cup of wine and a few stoned olives, salt and pepper. Simmer ten minutes and serve.[861]

CREAM SHRIMP IN CASES

☛ One pint of shrimp broken in small pieces. Make a white sauce of two tablespoonfuls of butter, three of flour, and a scant pint of cream. Season with salt, pepper and lemon juice. Add the shrimp, stir gently, and when very hot pour in cases.

To prepare the cases: Cut close grained bread in two inch slices; cut out with a large circular cutter and remove center with a smaller cutter. Spread with butter and brown in oven.[862]

CRABS OR SHRIMP BAKED IN BELL PEPPER

☛ Use one dozen bell peppers, one quart of picked shrimps, one teacupful of grated breadcrumbs, two tablespoonfuls of butter, one teaspoonful of mixed mustard, one-fourth teaspoonful of pepper, one-eighth teaspoonful of celery seed, one egg, salt, grating of nutmeg. Cut the stem end from the peppers; cut out the seed and veins; soak the peppers half hour in cold water. Cream the butter; add the egg and seasonings; next add the crumbs. Mix these ingredients well and add to the shrimps. Drain the peppers, stuff with the mixture, arrange in a pan open side up. Cook twenty minutes in a hot oven. Crabs may be prepared the same way. Serve as a fish course at dinner.[863]

VEAL OLIVES

☛ Having taken out the bone, cut several slices the full size of the leg; beat them lightly, and lay them for half an hour in sweet milk; then wipe them with a cloth, and spread them out smoothly on a table or board; spread thickly over them grated ham or minced oysters, sprinkle on some salt, pepper, grated nutmeg and powdered cloves; add some finely grated bread and bits of butter, and roll them up tightly, confining them with skewers.

Roast them before a clear but moderate fire, basting them with butter as they may require, and when done throughout, serve them up garnished with sliced oranges or lemons, and send to table with them a boat of drawn butter, flavored with nutmeg and orange juice. They may be introduced as a side dish at the dinner table.[864]

Dripping-pan with basting ladle.

CHICKEN PICANTE

☞ Cut up a chicken in small pieces. Cover with water, and stew until nearly tender; then add four medium-sized potatoes, cut in halves, and boil slowly. Half an hour before serving fry two sliced onions brown in two tablespoonfuls of hot lard; add the pulp of six large, sweet red peppers (soaked overnight and pressed through a colander); cook for two minutes, then add two tablespoonfuls of olive oil, and when very hot add one cupful of cheese, cut in small pieces. Stir until the cheese is melted, then pour over the chicken and potatoes and bring all to a boil, stirring to keep from burning. Serve very hot.[865]

CHICKEN PATES

Pate shells.

☞ Warm cold chicken, cut in dice in a sauce made of one cup of white stock, one cup of milk, one tablespoonful each of flour and butter, one teaspoonful of lemon juice, half a teaspoonful of salt, yolk of one egg, little white and cayenne pepper. Fill pate shells.[866]

DEVILED DISHES

☞ Season any of the creamed dishes highly with cayenne, onion juice, mustard and Worcester sauce.[867]

QUENELLES

☞ Mix 1 pound of cold turkey or chicken breast with
6 ounces of panada,
¼ pound of pickled pork,
¼ pound of butter,
½ teacup of cream,
Onion, salt, and pepper to taste,
1 lemon.

Shape 3 inches long. Roll in flour and drop in boiling water. Serve with champignon sauce.[868]

COQUILLE DE VOLAILLE

☞ Boil a chicken until very tender. When cold pick from the bone and cut in small pieces. Cook one tablespoonful of butter and two of flour until it bubbles; then add a cup of cream (not milk) and two tablespoonfuls of the water the chicken was boiled in; stir until smooth; season with a tablespoonful of chopped parsley, one tablespoonful of grated onion; salt and cayenne to season. Cut up a can of button mushrooms and two tablespoonfuls of the liquor; add to the mixture, also the chicken meat and a wineglass of sherry. Fill your baking dish, sprinkle bread crumbs over the top, set in the oven, let get thoroughly hot, and serve.[869]

CHICKEN A LA DREUSE

☞ For each pint of cold boiled chicken freed from skin and fat and cut very fine allow a tablespoonful of butter and two of flour, one cup of chicken broth, one-third of a cup of finely cut mushrooms, one large truffle chopped, three tablespoonfuls Madeira wine, two tablespoonfuls of fine chopped celery, salt, cayenne and white pepper to season. Make a thick sauce with the flour, butter and broth. Add the chicken, truffle, mushrooms and seasonings. Keep hot in the double boiler until ready to serve; then stir in quickly the wine and celery and serve in small paper cases, sprinkling over the top of each some finely chopped sweet red pepper or use a can of Spanish Pimentos.[870]

BRAIN TIMBALES

☞ One pair calf brains, whites of five eggs, twelve almonds, salt and pepper to season. Parboil the brains and pick fine, chop the almonds, stir in the brains, next the stiff whites. Fill greased timbale cups half full and steam. When done turn on a dish and pour over the following white sauce. Sauce: One tablespoonful of butter, two heaping spoonfuls of flour, six almonds chopped. Season with salt, pepper and Worcester sauce. Pour over timbales and serve.[871]

Hinged mold and individual timbale molds.

CHICKEN TERRAPIN

☞ One quart of cold cooked chicken cut in very small pieces, the cooked liver of one or two chickens, three hard boiled eggs, the yolks of two raw eggs, one cup of chicken stock, a cup of cream, a slight grating of nutmeg, a tablespoonful of salt, one teaspoonful of white pepper, four tablespoonfuls of sherry, three tablespoonfuls of butter, two of flour, one teaspoonful of lemon juice. Chop the liver and hard boiled eggs rather coarse, add them to the chicken with the salt, pepper and nutmeg. Cook the butter and flour together and stir until smooth and frothy; then add the stock. When it becomes smooth add the cream (not milk), stir for a moment, then add the chicken and seasonings. Beat yolks, add a little of the reserved cream, pour into the hot mixture. Taste to see if it needs more salt or pepper. Stir a moment. Remove, add Sherry and lemon juice, and serve.[872]

PRESSED CHICKEN

☞ Cover a grown fowl cut in joints with boiling water and let simmer until tender, together with a few slices of carrot, half an onion, a stalk of celery. When tender remove skin and bones. With the broth return it to the fire and simmer until reduced to a cup. Strain and set aside. Chop the chicken fine, remove the fat from the fire, reheat, and stir in the chicken, adding more seasoning if needed, Decorate a mold with slices of hard boiled egg. Dip in melted butter to have them stick. Pack in this the chicken, set aside to harden, cover with buttered paper bearing a weight and set aside until very cold. Slice thin and serve with tomato or potato salad.[873]

DEVILED SALMON

☛ Open a can of the best salmon, turn out its contents, remove skin and bone and break in small flakes. Make a sauce of one tablespoonful each of flour and butter. When it bubbles put in a cup of milk, and when smooth and thick add the yolks of three hard boiled eggs mashed fine. Season with salt, cayenne and a grating of nutmeg. When it comes from the fire add a teaspoonful of lemon juice, one tablespoonful of chopped parsley and the fish. Season highly to taste. Turn into a baking dish or individual shells. Sprinkle over buttered crumbs and brown. Serve with cucumber sauce.[874]

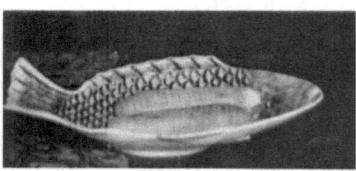
Cucumbers sliced in half lengthwise, to be served with fish.

DEVILED TOMATOES

☛ One quart of tomatoes. Put two tablespoonfuls of butter in a vessel. Put in the tomatoes that have been cooked and strained. Mash the yolks of two hard boiled eggs, two level teaspoonfuls of French mustard, two tablespoonfuls of vinegar, one teaspoonful of salt, little cayenne, two eggs beaten a little. Stir this into the cooked tomatoes and cook as thick as you wish. This is fine.[875]

PEPPER BASKETS

☛ Shave off the stem and cut a piece from the blossom. See that it stands steadily on a plate. Fill with hot minced chicken or fish seasoned to taste.[876]

RISSOLES

☛ ¼ pound of ground turkey heart,
3 sets of sweetbreads chopped,
¼ pound of butter,
¼ pound of flour,
1 pint of strong veal stock,
3 eggs.

Put the butter in a stew-pan; when it bubbles add the flour; let it cook, but do not let it boil; add the stock, then the turkey and sweetbreads, and when it is thick, add the eggs; cook the whole until it is as stiff as the panada for croquettes. Set it aside to cool, then add enough cream to make it soft, but not too wet. Make fine pastry thick as a biscuit, and cut with a biscuit cutter; then roll it out thin. Put a large spoonful in centre of each, and turn over like a turn-over pie; dip in eggs, roll in vermicelli, and fry a light brown.[877]

Biscuit cutters.

Fresh fruit dishes and preserves.

11. Fritters

FRITTER MAKING TIP

☛ In making fritters an essential to their success is, the fat in which they are fried should be very deep and boiling hot. Always test it by dropping in a small spoonful of batter. If this does not rise quickly to the surface, swell rapidly and acquire a light brown hue, it is too cool.[878]

Spiral egg beater: "cheaper though not so good as the "Dover."

ALABAMA RICE FRITTERS

☛ Four eggs beaten very light, one pint milk, one cup boiled rice, three tea-spoons baking powder in one quart flour; make into a batter; drop by spoonfuls into boiling lard. Sauce: One pound of sugar, one and a half cups water, stick of cinnamon; boil until clear.[879]

APPLE FRITTERS

☛ Two beaten eggs, one cup of milk, one teaspoonful of baking powder, enough flour for a drop batter, salt. Chop apples fine, add to the batter. Fry by spoonfuls in hot fat until brown.[880]

FRITTER BATTER

☛ Yolks of two eggs beaten, half a cup of milk or water, one tablespoonful olive oil, little salt, one cup of flour or enough for a drop batter. When ready to use add the stiff whites. If for fruit, add a teaspoonful of sugar; if for tripe, add a tablespoonful of vinegar.[881]

CORN FRITTERS

☛ To one dozen ears of corn add three eggs, half a teacupful of powdered crackers, one tablespoonful of sifted flour. Cut off the corn very lightly from the cob—say half of the grain—and then scrape the other half clean off with a knife. Add the crackers to corn and beat together light. Beat the eggs light and add with the flour and a quarter of a teacupful of sweet milk. Season to taste and beat the whole light. Have your lard or butter hot when you go to fry, and drip the batter into the hot fat from off the end of a spoon, letting it fry quick and brown. Have young and tender The fat ought to be hot enough to brown the fritters in two minutes.[882]

VIRGINIA CORN FRITTERS

☛ 1 can corn,
½ cup milk,
½ cup dried and sifted crumbs,
1 teaspoon salt,
1 teaspoon baking powder,
1 egg well beaten,
1 tablespoon flour.

Chop the corn, and add other ingredients in order given. Drop from a tablespoon into hot, deep fat and fry until brown.[883]

ORANGE FRITTERS

☛ Pare and quarter some oranges, remove the white skin and seed; mix the pulp with the fritter batter; drop by spoonfuls in hot fat.[884]

SAUCE FOR FRITTERS

☛ Cream two tablespoonfuls of batter with six of sugar; add the yolks of two eggs, half a cup of fine cut orange. Cook over hot water and serve with orange fritters.[885]

FRUIT FRITTERS

☛ Peel, core and slice two large tender apples, cover with sugar and a little brandy for half an hour, drain, dip each piece in juice, then in fritter batter. Fry and serve with sauce.[886]

SHRIMP FRITTERS

☛ Boil one pint of shrimps in salted water, remove the shells and chop fine; make a batter of two eggs, half teacup of sweet milk, teaspoonful of melted butter, and bread crumbs to make a good batter.

Stir in the shrimp and fry in rolls in boiling lard, and serve on a napkin.[887]

PINEAPPLE FRITTERS

☛ Boil two ounces of butter, two tablespoonfuls sugar, one cup of water; add five ounces of flour and stir until smooth. Cook until it leaves the sides of pan; remove and beat in four or five eggs, one at a time. Don't make batter too thin.

Drop by spoonfuls in boiling fat. Split each fritter and fill with pineapple marmalade or any stewed fruit.

Serve with sauce or whipped cream.[888]

BELL FRITTERS
☛ Put a tablespoonful of butter in a pint of water; let it boil; add a pint of flour; let cook until it leaves sides of pan. When cool beat in six eggs, one at a time. Fry in boiling lard. Never turn them, or they will be tough and flat. Fine.[889]

BREAD FRITTERS
☛ Cut your bread of a convenient size, pour on it some white wine, and let it stand a few minutes drain it on a sieve, beat four eggs very light, add four spoonsful of wine, beat all well together—have your lard boiling, dip the bread in the egg, and fry it a light brown; sprinkle sugar on each, and glaze them.[890]

CONFEDERATE APPLE FRITTERS
☛ Pare and core tart apples, cut in rather thick slices, put in a bowl of cool water. When ready for use, sprinkle with sugar, spice and lemon juice. Dip each slice in fritter batter and fry in hot lard. Drain and sprinkle with sugar.[891]

CLAM FRITTERS
☛ Take twelve large, or twenty-five small clams from their shells; if the clams are large divide them.

Mix two gills of flour, one gill of milk, half as much of the clam liquor, and one egg well beaten. Make the batter smooth, and then stir in the clams.

Drop the batter by tablespoonfuls in boiling lard; let them fry gently, turning them when done on one side.[892]

EGG PLANT FRITTERS 1
☛ Put your egg plant on unpeeled in plenty of boiling water. When done, peel and mash fine. Season with salt, pepper, butter, an egg, one tablespoonful of flour, one teaspoonful of baking powder.[893]

EGG PLANT FRITTERS 2
☛ Put the egg plant, whole, in boiling salted water with a tablespoonful of vinegar. Cook until tender; peel and mash fine. To two cups of egg plant add half a cup of flour, two beaten eggs, salt and pepper to season. Some like grated onion. Fry in small cakes on both sides in hot fat, browning well.[894]

SPINACH FRITTERS
☛ Boil spinach thoroughly, drain and mince it well; add some grated bread, one grate of nutmeg and a small piece of sugar. Add as much cream or yolks and whites of eggs as will make the preparation of the consistence of batter; drop the batter into a frying pan of boiling lard. When the fritters rise take out, drain and send to table.[895]

FISH FRITTERS

☛ The remains of any cold fish can be used here, and the same bulk of mashed potatoes as the fish. Pick the fish from the bones and skin, and pound it in a mortar with one onion, season with pepper and salt, then mix well with it the mashed potatoes, and bind together with a well-beaten egg. Flatten the mixture out upon a dish or pastry board, cut into small rounds or squares and fry in boiling lard to a light brown. Pile it in a napkin on a very hot dish, garnish with parsley and serve with any kind of fish sauce.[896]

SPANISH FRITTERS

☛ Make up a quart of four, with one egg well beaten, a large spoonful of yeast, and as much milk as will make it a little softer than muffin dough; mix it early in the morning; when well risen, work in two spoonsful of melted butter, make it in balls the size of a walnut, and fry them a light brown in boiling lard eat them with wine and sugar, or molasses.[897]

Luncheon table.

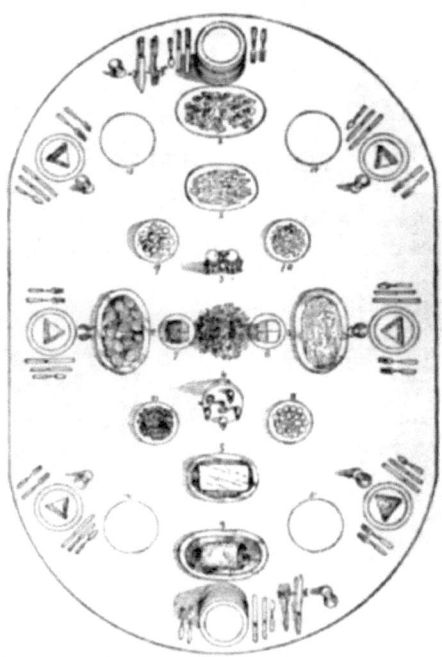

Summer lunch table setting for eight.

12. Fruits

TO BAKE APPLES

☞ Pare and core the apples, leaving them whole, rinse in cold water and place close together in a baking pan, the bottom of which has been greased with butter and sprinkled with granulated sugar. Sprinkle sugar over the apples and bake in a hot oven until they are a rich brown. Unless very tart, cover for ten minutes. Apples baked in this way are delicious served with the meat course; or, add more sugar and serve with cream for desert. If the seeds are removed and put in the dish with the apples, they flavor nicer than anything else.[898]

Fried apples.

FRIED APPLES

☞ Slice bacon thin and fry it crisp. Remove and put in thick slices of unpeeled apples. Fry until tender; drain and put in the center of a hot platter; sprinkle sugar over and lay the bacon around the edges. Serve for breakfast.[899]

SCALLOPED APPLES

☞ Butter a pudding dish and put in a layer of peeled and sliced apples; sprinkle with sugar, a little flour and cinnamon and bits of butter. Fill the dish in this manner and bake until done, covering the dish while baking. Serve hot or cold with meat.[900]

CRANBERRY SAUCE

☞ Wash and pick over two cups of cranberries, put in a small saucepan with half a cup of water, sprinkle over the top one cup of sugar, cover closely and cook ten minutes. Remove scum, but never stir them.[901]

BLACKBERRY DUMPLINGS

Whips with strawberries.

☞ One pint flour, one rounding teaspoonful baking powder, half a teaspoonful salt sifted together. Rub a tablespoonful of lard or butter into it with the tips of the fingers until fine. Make a soft dough with sweet milk. Knead the dough until smooth, roll out half an inch thick, cut it in four inch squares, put berries in center, pinch the edges together, put in steamer up side down, and steam until done. Serve with sauce.

Sauce: Cream two tablespoons of butter, work into it one cup of powdered sugar and some of the berries mashed fine. Work until light.[902]

PINEAPPLE PUDDING

☞ One can grated pineapple, one-fourth cup of butter, half a cup of milk, two tablespoonfuls corn starch, six beaten eggs.

Cream the butter and sugar until light; add the other things and bake until firm. Elegant.[903]

STRAWBERRIES WITH WHIPPED CREAM

☞ Prepare in layers as above, cover with one pint of cream, whites of three eggs and a tea-cup of powdered sugar, whipped together and flavored with strawberry juice.[904]

BLACKBERRY PUDDING

☞ One quart of blackberries, one pint of flour, one pint of molasses, half a teaspoonful of soda, a little salt, all kinds of spices. To mix, put half the molasses with the berries, stir the soda in the remaining molasses; then mix that with the fruit; next, put in the flour and spices. Boil three hours.

You will have a good plum pudding. Serve with hard sauce.[905]

FRUIT DUMPLINGS

☞ One cup of flour, one teaspoonful of baking powder, two level tablespoonfuls of lard, little salt, milk enough to form a dough. Divide in three pieces and roll out, not too thin. Put fruit in center. Either steam or bake. Serve with sauce.[906]

APPLE DUMPLINGS

☞ Peel and cut your apples; cook, but not real soft. Put a spoonful in each cup. Then make a thin batter of milk, flour, a little melted lard and baking powder; pour over the apples and steam half an hour.

Serve with the following sauce.[907]

DRAWN BUTTER SAUCE

☛ Two tablespoonfuls of butter, one of flour, one of cold water; mix and stir until smooth; add half a cup of water; let cook; then add one cup of sugar and flavoring.[908]

APPLE MERINGUE

☛ Pare and core the apples, fill the cavity with creamed butter and sugar, flavor with lemon or use lemon juice, bake until done, cover with a meringue. Take the yolks of the eggs, make a boiled custard, and make a meringue of three whites and three tablespoonfuls of sugar, put over apples and brown lightly.[909]

APPLES WITH WHIPPED CREAM

☛ Get medium sized apples; pare and core them. To six apples take a cup of sugar and half a cup of water. When it boils add a few apples at a time and cook, being very careful not to break them. When they are all fixed, arrange them in a circle on a flat glass dish. If the syrup isn't thick enough, boil down. When cold, pour over the apples; put a Maraschino cherry in center of each apple and surround with whipped cream sweetened and flavored with some Maraschino syrup; more flavoring if needed.[910]

Grapefruit served in the half peel.

PORCUPINE APPLES

☛ Select apples of equal size; pare, core and cook in syrup as above. Boil down the syrup; roll the apples in it. Stick almonds all over the apples. Fill the centers with jelly. Arrange on a chop plate with rolled sweet wafers around the edge of dish. Serve with cream.[911]

TO PREPARE APPLES

☛ To each pound of peeled, quartered and cored apples use a pound of sugar and a pint of water. Make a syrup, and while boiling drop in the apples; let cook until done, but not broken; remove and boil down the syrup. A sliced lemon or orange improves it. When thick pour over the fruit, and let get cold before serving.[912]

BAKED APPLES

☛ Peel and core your fruit. Make a heavy syrup. While boiling put in the apples, cook until tender; remove; boil the syrup until thick. Flavor with lemon and serve over the fruit. Serve cold.[913]

APPLE PUDDING

☛ Peel and core some apples, steam until tender; then fill the cores with chopped apples and nuts. Arrange in a baking dish. Pour a sponge cake batter around and over the apples. Bake and serve with sauce.[914]

APPLE SAUCE

☞ Take ripe acid apples, pare and slice them, put them into a pan with a little water, cover them and stew them till soft; add enough sugar to make them as sweet as you desire, mashing and stirring them till they become a smooth pulp and nearly dry. It is eaten with poultry, game and roasted pork.[915]

PRUNE PUDDING

☞ 1 pound prunes,
¾ pound sugar,
6 eggs.

Stew, seed, and chop the prunes very fine. Beat the whites of the eggs; add the sugar, and stir in the prunes, and bake in a buttered dish for 20 minutes.

Make a custard of the yolks of the eggs and 1 quart of milk. Sweeten and flavor to suit the taste.

Serve the pudding in the baking-dish, and after serving in small plates, use the custard as a sauce.[916]

PLUM PUDDING

☞ One pound of raisins cut small, half pound of butter, three ounces of flour, three ounces of bread crumbs, three eggs, four ounces of sugar, four ounces of citron, one cup of milk poured over the bread crumbs; season with mace, nutmeg, cinnamon, salt, orange peel cut fine. Serve with wine sauce. Elegant.[917]

Plum pudding.

THE QUEEN OF PLUM PUDDINGS

☞ Half a pound of butter, half a pound of suet run through the meat chopper or chopped fine, half a pound of sugar, one a fourth pounds of flour, one pound of raisins chopped and dredged with flour, one pound of currants, two ounces of citron cut fine, six eggs beaten separately, half a pint of milk, half cup of brandy, one grated nutmeg, a little mace and cloves.

Cream the butter and sugar; beat in the yolks, then the milk, then the flour with the beaten whites, then the brandy and spice; lastly the fruit dredged in flour. Mix all thoroughly.

Wring out your pudding bag in hot water; flour well inside; pour in the mixture and boil five hours. If not all eaten next day, slice and fry in butter.

This is a very fine plum pudding.[918]

FRIED BANANAS

☞ Peel and slice lengthwise, fry in butter, sprinkle with sugar, and serve. Thus prepared they make a nice dessert. The bananas must be ripe.[919]

APPLE AND PLUM PUDDING

☞ Three-fourths of a pound of tart apples pared and chopped, three-fourths of a pound of sugar, three-fourths of a pound of flour, half a pound of beef suet chopped fine, three-fourths of a pound of raisins chopped, six eggs, one teaspoonful each of salt, nutmeg and cloves, half a glass each of sherry and whiskey. Beat the yolks and sugar until light; then add the suet, apples and spice; next, the raisins dredged in flour; now the flour and liquor; lastly, the stiff whites.

Different ways of preparing oranges.

Bake in two molds in a moderate oven one and a half hours, or you may boil it.[920]

PLUM PUDDING CROQUETTES

☞ Heat a pint of milk blood warm; crumble into it sufficient stale bread to soak up all the milk, about a cup. Use no crusts. Cover and let stand where it will keep hot an hour, but not cook.

Add a beaten egg, two tablespoonfuls of sugar, little salt, nutmeg, cloves and cinnamon, one cup of mixed fruit, as currants, raisins and citron. Mix and set aside till cold. Flour the hands and make into tiny croquettes.

Dip in egg, then in bread crumbs. Fry in smoking hot fat. Serve with wine or vanilla sauce.[921]

DELICIOUS PLUM PUDDING

☞ One pound of raisins cut small, one pound of currants, one and a half pounds of suet run through the chopper, three-fourths of a pound of brown sugar, two ounces of lemon and orange peel, two ounces of citron, one-fourth of a pound of bread crumbs, half a pound of flour. Soften the crumbs with a little milk, eight beaten eggs, nutmeg. Steam four and a half hours.

Will serve a great many Chautauqua. Serve with sauce.[922]

VEGETARIAN PLUM PUDDING

☞ One heaping cup of bread crumbs, two cups of flour, one cup of molasses, one cup of raisins, half a cup of citron chopped fine, one cup of sweet milk, one teaspoonful each of salt, cloves, cinnamon, one level tablespoonful of soda.

Serve with wine or hard sauce.[923]

FLORIDA GRAPEFRUIT

☞ The fruit stores display a new clear-skinned lemon-colored fruit, about three times as large as an orange, and bearing a general resemblance to that fruit. Its flavor is sub-acid, but its juicy pulp is inclosed in a tough white membrane of intensely bitter taste; when this membrane is removed, the fruit is delicious. To prepare it for the table, cut the skin in sections and peel it off; separate the sections as you would those of an orange, and holding each one by the ends, break it open from the center, disclosing the pulp; tear this out of the bitter white membrane which covers the sections, carefully removing every part of it; keep the pulp as unbroken as possible, and put it into a deep dish with a plentiful sprinkling of fine sugar. Let it stand three or four hours, or over night, and then use the fruit. It is refreshing and wholesome, especially for a bilious temperament.[924]

Salpicon of fruits in orange-skin.

BOILED RAISIN PUDDING

☞ Three eggs, one cup of sweet milk, four tablespoonfuls sifted flour, half a pound of raisins seeded and cut, heaping tablespoonful of butter creamed with five tablespoonfuls of sugar, one full teaspoon of baking powder. Boil in a mold. Serve with wine sauce.[925]

FRUIT PUDDING

☞ Butter some slices of stale bread, remove crust, put a layer of bread in a serving dish and pour over hot stewed fruit, as cherries or blackberries. You can use canned fruit. Serve cold with cream. Good.[926]

FIG PUDDING

☞ Break in pieces size of a pea half a cup of beef suet; put it in a bowl with half a cup of flour, also half a cup of figs cut as fine as the suet. Mix with the flour a teaspoonful each of cinnamon and ginger, one-fourth teaspoonful of cloves, a little salt, half a cup of molasses, half cup of water, one egg beaten separately, one teaspoonful lemon juice with the yolk. Put a little soda in the molasses, stir in butter and one and a half teaspoons of baking powder; then the stiff whites. Put a greased mold half full and steam two hours. Serve with rich sauce.[927]

STRAWBERRY PUFF PUDDING

☞ One pint of flour, two teaspoonfuls of baking powder, salt. Enough sweet milk is added to make a thick batter. Put a layer in mold, then a layer of sweetened strawberries, then a layer of batter on top. Steam half an hour. Serve with sauce.[928]

ORANGE PUDDING

☞ 4 sweet oranges, sliced,
1 quart of milk,
1 cup of sugar,
2 tablespoons of cornstarch,
Yolks of 3 eggs.

Heat the milk; when nearly boiling add cornstarch (wet with a little cold water), the sugar, and eggs well beaten. Boil till thick as custard, and when cold pour over sliced oranges. Make a meringue of the whites of 3 eggs and small teacup of sugar. Spread on pudding and decorate with sections of orange.[929]

DRIED FRUIT

☞ Cherries, peaches, and damsons can be preserved by this receipt; stone them or not, as you please. To 4 pounds of fruit put 1 pound of brown sugar; let them boil well, and then spread them on dishes, and put them in the sun to dry; boil the syrup until thick and clear; pour it upon the fruit until it is dried. It will take 2 or 3 days to do it. Put in stone jars, with sugar between the layers, and tie down tightly.[930]

Stewed apples on a rice socle, garnished with candied cherries.

Picnics and luncheons.

13. Healing Recipes

REMARKS

☛ Whatever may be the disease of a person, if they are dangerously ill, whether they are under the influence of medicine or no, the strictest attention should be paid to their diet. Many a horrible disease has been driven from the system by such a course, and many others fed and nourished up, by indulging too freely in the luxuries of life. Not only a strict attention should be paid to the quality of their diet, but also to the quantity, as there is no one or two things that ever caused more dangerous relapses in sickness, than the indulgence of these two evils; therefore, they should both be carefully avoided, selecting only such articles of diet as may best agree with their situations, and giving it to them in proper proportions. There is very near as much depending on the understanding and management of the nurse as the physician.[931]

Bedridden.

CHICKEN SOUP FOR THE SICK

☛ Take an old chicken and put on with one gallon of water; boil down to half a gallon. Take the yolks of two eggs, tie them up in a clean cloth with a little thyme and put in the soup after you have strained the meat from it, and put back to boil till down to three pints. Dish up and send to table hot. Season with salt and pepper to taste.[932]

TONIC BITTER

☛ A Southern remedy for invalids. Take one ounce of cardamom seed, one ounce of Peruvian bark bruised, two ounces of Gentian root bruised, half ounce of dry orange peel, one ounce of aloes, and put the whole into half a gallon of best whiskey or brandy; let it come to a boil, then strain or filter it through a fine cloth or filtering paper. Dose half wineglassfull three times a day before meals. Will strengthen and produce an appetite.[933]

CORNMEAL GRUEL

☛ Three tablespoons of sifted cornmeal, moisten with a little cold water; pour it in a pint of boiling water; stir well; cook about ten minutes.[934]

BEEF JELLY

☛ Take a lean juicy piece of beef, 1 pound; cut it into small pieces; throw them into cold water, and let them soak for 1 hour. Then put it on the fire with 1 pint of water, and let it stew slowly until it is reduced ⅔; then strain it on a few blades of mace.

Salpicon of fruits in glass.

When you first put it on, season with pepper, salt, and a little celery seed. This is excellent for a person who is weak and needs nourishment. When it is used, always serve it hot.[935]

BEEF ESSENCE

☛ Take 2 pounds of juicy beef; put it into a stone jar, and set it on a pot of water; let the water boil around it for 4 or 5 hours; then take off the beef, and strain it; it will jelly when cold. A very little of this should be used at a time, as it is very strong.[936]

CHICKEN JELLY

☛ Take an old chicken; cut it up; wash and dry it with a coarse towel; cut off the meat, and wash the bones; put it into a jar, and set it in a pot of water; let the water boil for 5 hours; then strain the juices through a coarse muslin bag; only add a little salt. If the chicken is put back on the fire, and allowed to cook, it will make more jelly. When it cools, skim it.[937]

MUTTON BROTH

☛ Cut off the skin and fat of ½ pound of the scraggy neck part; put it into a stewpan, and cover it with cold water; let it stew gently for 1½ ours; skim off the grease; season to taste.[938]

MUSH

☛ Put 1 pint of fresh water in a stewpan; when it boils, stir in sifted cornmeal, a little at a time, until it is the proper consistency.

Stir it for 30 minutes, and then serve it with a little cream and salt.[939]

THICKENED MILK

☛ Make a powder, by beating the yolk of an egg, to which a pinch of salt has been added, very light, and mix it with sifted flour, until very stiff; after which, rub between the fingers, adding flour until perfectly dry. Continue the rubbing until the whole lump is reduced to a powder; then take as much milk as is desired (milk fresh from the cow), and put on the fire in a vessel in which it will boil quickly.

As soon as it boils throw on the surface a little of the powder, and let it remain there a moment before stirring down; continue this process until it seems thick enough.

This is eaten with either sugar or salt, and is extremely palatable and nourishing.[940]

TOAST WATER

☛ Take bread that is a little stale; slice it, and toast it a light brown; pour upon it boiling water. When it cools, it is ready to drink.[941]

PANADA

☛ Drop small pieces of stale bread into a little boiling water; sweeten to taste, and let it boil for 15 minutes; season with raisins, removing them before it is used, or with wine or lemon.[942]

"Life forces for the sick and convalescent."

OATMEAL COFFEE
☞ Mix common oatmeal and water to form cake; bake and brown it, powder it, and boil in water five minutes. Good for checking obstinate vomiting, especially in cholera morbus.[943]

HOT MILK FOR INVALIDS
☞ Toast snow-flake cracker until a golden brown, then pour over them hot milk; let stand a few minutes, then strain; add a little salt, and serve.[944]

SOFT BOILED EGGS FOR INVALIDS
☞ Boil one pint of water, and while boiling place in it two eggs; remove from the fire and let stand three minutes. The eggs will be thoroughly hot, but no part of them will be hard.[945]

RICE JELLY
☞ In preparing rice, pour on boiling water, and, when cool, rub it well between the hands several times. To a half pint of rice use one quart of boiling water; continue to add water until the liquid looks like starch, and then strain. Cook rapidly.[946]

A PREPARATION FOR THE SICK
☞ The white of one egg, three teaspoonfuls of sugar, half a glass of water, half a teaspoon of cracked ice, a few drops of peppermint, or a sprig of fresh mint.
Throw the ingredients from one tumbler into another, till the contents are thoroughly mixed.[947]

CORN MEAL GRUEL FOR INVALIDS
☞ Two tablespoonfuls of meal, sifted, four teacupfuls of boiling water, which has been placed in a stew pan, over the fire.
Stir in slowly, the meal. Boil one hour, stirring constantly the first fifteen minutes, then occasionally until done.[948]

A NOURISHING PREPARATION FOR INFANTS
☞ Half a pint of boiling water, three tablespoonfuls of new milk one teaspoonful of arrow root, a pinch of gelatine (dissolved in a little hot water); mix milk, arrow root and gelatine. Let it cook a few minutes together; take off and sweeten to taste.[949]

BLACKBERRY JELLY FOR SICKNESS
☞ Two quarts blackberry juice, one pound loaf sugar, half an ounce nutmegs, half an ounce cloves, half an ounce cinnamon, half an ounce allspice.
Pulverize the spices, if whole; boil all fifteen or twenty minutes. When cold, add one pint of brandy.[950]

Lemon squeezer.

BARLEY WATER
☛ Wash the barley, and put it to boil as you would rice. When the grains become soft, sweeten to taste, and flavor with lemon juice.⁹⁵¹

WINE WHEY
☛ 1 pint of boiling milk, ½ pint of good Madeira wine. Boil it until the curds form; pour off the whey; sweeten it, and serve.⁹⁵²

COUGH DROPS
☛ Take two ounces of slippery elm bark and break it into small pieces, put it into a bowl, add two ounces of flaxseed, and pour over it a half pint of water; cover and put aside for one hour, stirring occasionally, then strain through a fine sieve. Put one and a half pounds of brown sugar into a granite saucepan, add this mucilaginous water, stir over the fire until the sugar is dissolved, then boil for five minutes; add two tablespoonfuls of lemon juice and boil till brittle when dropped in cold water. Pour in square, greased tins, and when partly cold cut into square lozenges.⁹⁵³

BUTTERSCOTCH FOR A COLD
☛ Two cupfuls of sugar, two cupfuls of dark molasses, one cupful of fresh tried lard and the juice of two lemons. Boil over a slow fire until it hardens when dropped in cold water. Pour on tins well buttered and mark into little inch squares, before it cools.⁹⁵⁴

APPLE WATER
☛ Bake a juicy, tart apple, and pour over it boiling water; let it stand until cold. This water is very agreeable in sickness.⁹⁵⁵

ARROWROOT
☛ This may be made of either milk or water. Mix 1 tablespoon of arrowroot with enough cold water to make a paste; pour upon it, stirring all the time, ½ pint of boiling water; sweeten to taste, and put it in a saucepan; let it cook until it is clear. The milk should be fresh.⁹⁵⁶

SAGO JELLY
☛ Two tablespoonfuls sago to one quart of water; soak in cold water one hour, and wash thoroughly; let simmer with lemon peel and a few cloves; add wine and sugar when nearly done.⁹⁵⁷

SAGO CREAM
☛ 1 tablespoon of sago to 1 pint of water; let it boil well, and then add to it 1 teacup of milk; let them boil together for a few minutes, and then

pour it upon a well-beaten egg; stir it well, and season with loaf sugar and nutmeg. The white of the egg not to be used.[958]

LEMON FOR A COUGH
☛ Roast a lemon very carefully, without burning it; whilst it is hot, cut it and squeeze it into a cup upon 3 ounces of sugar, finely powdered. Take 1 spoonful of this mixture whenever the cough is troublesome. It is able to the taste, and seldom fails in giving relief.[959]

SOUP FOR AN INVALID
☛ Cut in small pieces 1 pound beef or mutton, or a part of both; boil gently in 2 qts. water; take off the scum and when reduced to a pint, strain it; season with a little salt, and take a tea-cup at a time.[960]

COUGH MIXTURE
☛ Take ½ pint of molasses, 1 tablespoon of butter, and 2 tablespoons of vinegar. Stew them all together until thick and smooth. Take 1 teaspoonful of this mixture every ½ hour until the cough is relieved, or if this be too often, as the sweet may disorder the stomach, use the mixture whenever the cough becomes troublesome.[961]

TAPIOCA JELLY
☛ Wash the tapioca two or three times; soak it five or six hours; let it simmer in the same water with bits of fresh lemon peel, until it becomes quite clear; then put in lemon juice, wine, and sugar. Three tablespoonfuls of tapioca to one quart water.[962]

FOR SEVERE COLD
☛ At night, take a very hot foot bath, drink a tumbler of hot, strong lemonade—a lemon to a tumbler of water and get immediately into bed. If the chest or throat is sore, rub with turpentine and bind around the throat, or place on the chest, a flannel cloth, on which sprinkle two tablespoonfuls of turpentine, melt two teaspoonfuls of mutton suet and sprinkle one of camphor.

Healthy food for the sick.

BEEF TEA
☛ Take a very nice, tender piece of fresh beef or veal; cut it into thin slices, and beat them tender. Season them as for eating with salt and pepper, and oil them till a light brown on a clean gridiron, over a bed of clear coals, turning them over once or twice; then cut them into small bits, put them in a bowl, pour on some boiling water, and cover them

with a plate. The nurse must be the judge as to the richness of the tea, knowing the situation of the patient. By the time it gets cold enough to drink, it will have imbibed a sufficient flavor of the steaks. This is a tea that may be used in most cases of sickness, where it is not too strong, and is generally liked.[963]

CHICKEN BROTH

☞ Take a small young chicken, clean it nicely, cut it into joints, and boil it very tender, leaving at least one quart of the liquor when done. If the chicken be half grown, it will make three pints of broth rich enough for a sick person. Beat up a large spoonful of flour in half a pint of entire sweet milk, and stir it gradually into the liquor. Boil it a few minutes longer, and take it from the fire, seasoning it lightly with salt and pepper; and if the patient is fond of the flavor, you may add a few sprigs of parsley. When you make broth of a grown chicken, only use half of it at one time.[964]

SQUIRREL SOUP

☞ Having cleaned a fat young squirrel, cut it into quarters, and boil it very tender, carefully removing the scum. If well boiled, it will make a quart of good soup. Mix up half a pint of stiff batter with half a beaten egg, sweet milk and flour; drop it into the liquor while it is boiling, dropping it from a dessert-spoon, that it may remain in lumps or small dumplings. Boil it till the dumplings are done, which will only take a few minutes, season it lightly with salt and pepper, as sick people are not generally fond of soups very highly seasoned, and if they were, they are not

"Enterprise" food chopper.

good for them. Add a little parsley, or thyme, if preferred by the patient, and serve it up moderately warm. Chicken, pheasant, partridge or rabbit soup may be made in the same manner.[965]

CHICKEN TEA

☞ Take a grown fowl, pick and clean it neatly, cut it into joints, and boil a small portion of it till tender, adding no seasonings, but barely enough salt to make it palatable. This will many times set upon a weak stomach when nothing else will.[966]

PARTRIDGE TEA

☞ You may make partridge tea as directed for chicken tea [above]; or you may broil the partridges neatly on a gridiron, seasoning them highly with salt water and pepper, and basting them lightly with butter; then cut them up into small bits, put them in a pitcher, and pour on some boiling water, allowing a pint to each partridge; add a little nutmeg and lemon juice, or grated lemon peel, and cover it with a plate, to keep in the steam. By the time it gets cool enough to sup, it will have extracted from the partridges the most of their juices. It may be taken warm or cold, but is generally preferred warm. Such teas are very nutritious, and principally designed for weak, debilitated patients, who are not able to take stronger nourishment.[967]

BROILED PARTRIDGES
☞ If the patient is allowed to eat a bit of meat for a relish, broiled partridges, and other small birds, are superior to any other kind of fresh meat. Clean them nicely, rinse them in cold water, and wipe them dry with a cloth. Broil them on a clean gridiron over clear coals, basting them with a little weak salt and water, and a small portion of pepper, until they are sufficiently seasoned, and at the last baste them slightly with fresh sweet butter. Squirrels and very small chickens may be broiled in the same manner. A chip of dried beef or venison is very good to give a relish to teas. They are generally preferred rare, but if not very dry, they may be slightly broiled, after washing the slices in hot water, and wiping them dry with a cloth, to take off the superfluous salt, which would be disgusting to a sick person. Such relishes are generally served with tea, and a bit of waffle, or batter cake, or dry toast.[968]

EGG NOG FOR THE SICK
☞ Scald one pint of new milk (but do not boil it), take three eggs, beat to a froth with one-fourth of a cupful of sugar, add one-half gill of best brandy and one tablespoonful of rum and a little nutmeg; when this is thoroughly beaten add the scalded milk.[969]

BATTER CAKES
☞ Batter cakes, or waffles, for a sick person, should be made with very little egg; one egg to a pint of milk is quite enough. Beat it light, mix in your milk and a little salt, and make it into a thin batter with flour; beat it well with a spoon, and strain it through a fine sieve, to get out all the little lumps of dry flour, which is very hard to break down in thin batter. Have your griddle hot, clean it nicely, and place it level over a bed of clear coals; grease it slightly with butter, merely enough to prevent the cakes sticking to it; put on your batter in very thin small cakes, turn them over as soon as the under side is a light brown and before they get hard; serve them up hot and slightly butter them. Cakes made in this manner generally agree with sick persons.[970]

PARTRIDGE PANADA
☞ Having cleaned your partridges neatly, rub them with salt and boil them very tender in a small quantity of water: then remove the skin, mince the meat fine from the bones, and pound one half of it in a mortar.

Return it to the liquor, which should be about half enough to make the whole as thick as common panada, or thick soup; add a small portion of butter, pepper and nutmeg, and serve it up with dry toasts. Chicken and squirrel panada may be made in the same manner.[971]

RICE
☛ Pick and wash your rice carefully, and boil it very soft in milk and water, mixed half and half: then drain it and mix in a small portion of butter, sugar and nutmeg. Or, if the patient is suffered to eat milk, boil the rice in clear water, season it lightly with salt, and eat it warm with cold sweet milk.[972]

RICE MILK
☛ Boil your rice quite soft, but do not mash it: mix it with sweet milk, making the whole about the consistence of thick soup; add a little water, lest it should be too rich, sweeten it to your taste, and boil it up again. Serve it warm, and grate a little nutmeg on the top.[973]

BOILED MILK
☛ Boil a pint of sweet milk with a little cinnamon till it has imbibed enough of the flavor. Beat very light half of one egg, mix with it a small portion of salt, a gill of sweet milk and enough flour to make it a stiff batter; drop it by spoonfuls into the boiling milk, that it may remain in lumps, and boil it till the dumplings are done. Season it with sugar and nutmeg, or butter and pepper.[974]

Puree sieve (left) and mortar and pestle (right).

CONFEDERATE COUGH SYRUP
☛ One ounce each of hoarhound and licorice, two ounces of gum arabic, one pint of molasses and one teacupful of vinegar. Boil the hoarhound in one quart of water; dissolve the licorice and gum arabic in a little water first. Strain the hoarhound before adding the other ingredients. Do not put in the vinegar until it is nearly done.[975]

MILK TOAST
☛ Boil a pint of sweet milk, and throw into it while boiling a small handful of light brown toasts, not larger than half a dollar: add a little sugar and nutmeg, and serve it up.[976]

MILK PORRIDGE
☛ Mix a large tablespoon heaping full of flour with a gill of sweet milk, beat it till smooth, and stir it into a pint of boiling sweet milk; boil it up again, stirring it all the time, add a little sugar, lemon juice and nutmeg, and serve it up with rusk or dry toast.[977]

RAISIN PORRIDGE

☛ Seed half a pint of raisins, shred them fine, and stew them tender in a small quantity of water, adding enough sugar to make them tolerably sweet: then stir in gradually enough sweet milk to make it the consistence of thick soup, boil it a minute or two longer, and remove it from the fire.[978]

HOTCH-POTCH

☛ Rub a large spoonful of butter in a small handful of flour till completely saturated, and stir it into a pint of boiling water.

Boil it till thoroughly done, stirring it occasionally; add a few spoonfuls of sweet milk, a little nutmeg or ginger, and sweeten with sugar.

If rightly proportioned, it will be tolerably thick and full of small lumps. It is excellent food for a sick person.[979]

CUSTARD

☛ Beat two eggs very light, stir them into three gills of sweet milk, with enough sugar to sweeten it, and bake it a light brown in cups.

Grate nutmeg on the tops. If the eggs are beaten sufficiently light, the custard will be perfectly harmless.[980]

CLOTTED MILK

☛ Beat one egg as light as possible, and stir it into a pint of cold milk; set it over a few coals, stir it till it comes to a boil, and then remove it from the fire.

Season it to your taste with spice, lemon and sugar, and serve it up with dry toasts.[981]

ARROWROOT JELLY

☛ Mix two spoonfuls of arrow root powder in a teacup of cold water, stirring it till quite smooth. When it is completely dissolved, stir it into a pint and a half of boiling water; add a little grated lemon and powdered loaf sugar, and boil it three or four minutes longer, stirring it all the time.

If the patient's system is in a relaxed state, a little wine and nutmeg may be added.

It is also very good made with sweet milk instead of water, but it is much richer, and does not always suit a weak stomach best.[982]

BREAD JELLY

☛ Take the crumb of a small light loaf, toast it brown, pour on enough boiling water to cover it well, and let it stand till completely saturated; then beat it smooth, add enough sweet milk to make it a little liquid, boil it a few minutes, and strain it into a bowl. Season it with grated lemon or nutmeg and loaf sugar.[983]

CONFEDERATE TAPIOCA JELLY
☛ After washing the tapioca in two or three waters, steep it for five hours in fresh water. Boil it in the same water with some bits of lemon peel till sufficiently thick and quite clear; then take out the lemon peel, and season the jelly with loaf sugar and lemon juice or a little wine, according to the taste and situation of the patient.[984]

CONFEDERATE RICE JELLY
☛ Mix up a cup of rice flour in a little milk: when smooth, stir it into a quart of boiling water, add a few slips of lemon peel, and boil it till it is a thick jelly; then strain it, and season it with loaf sugar and lemon juice, or nutmeg and wine.[985]

INDIAN GRUEL
☛ Mix up two large spoonfuls of fine Indian meal with as much water as will make it a smooth batter, and stir it into a pint of boiling water; boil it a few minutes till thoroughly done, stirring it all the time; add enough salt to make it palatable, and serve it up. It is generally taken warm, and is excellent to carry off medicine.[986]

LIME WATER
☛ Slack one-half cupful of lime with about one-half pint of water, slowly added; when slacked well add one quart of water and stir thoroughly, allow it to settle, decant closely and pour the water away, then add one gallon of fresh, clear, distilled or rain water to the washed lime; shake often for a day or two and let settle.[987]

CONFEDERATE APPLE WATER
☛ Bake some fine acid apples till very soft; then cut them up, and put them in cold water to steep, allowing two apples to each tumbler of water. Let them steep till the water becomes cold, and it will be ready for use. This water is excellent for a weak stomach, that cannot retain soup, etc.

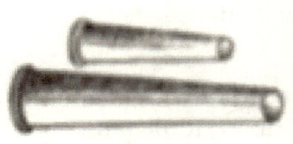

Apple corers.

Apple water is frequently made of raw apples, sliced up, and hot water poured over them, but I think it is not so good for the patient as when the apples are cooked.[988] [Similar healing drinks can be made from almost any fruit, including peach, apricot, plum, and lemon—the editor, L.S.]

COUGH SYRUP
☛ Take as much elecampane and comfrey roots as you can grasp between your thumb and finger; wash them clean, split them up, and put them in a skillet, with a quart of water. Add a small handful of horehound, and boil them together till the water is reduced to one half; then strain the liquid, rinse out the skillet, put in the liquor again, with

an equal portion of strained honey, and boil them gently together, till they form a thick syrup nearly as thick as the honey was before you mixed it with the liquid. Take a spoonful of it two or three times a day. It has been found an efficacious remedy for coughs nearly approaching to consumption.⁹⁸⁹

ORANGE AND LEMON JUICE

Cork pull.

☛ A fine preparation for an invalid is made of orange or lemon juice, strained and boiled with an equal weight of loaf sugar and then bottled and corked closely. It is an agreeable and valuable addition to gruel and other warm drinks. It takes fifteen minutes to boil. A dessert-spoonful of lemon juice must be added to one-half of a pint of gruel.⁹⁹⁰

Old South Southerners adopted and adapted recipes from every region around the world, including these: 1) Texas rice croquettes; 2) Michigan canned cherries; 3) Delaware pickled peaches; 3) California canned peaches; 4) New England mince pie; 6) Iowa doughnuts; 7) Montreal boneless turkey.

14. Jellies and Preserves

JELLY MAKING TIPS

☛ Fruit for jelly should never be fully ripe. It is important that the fruit should be used at the proper stage of ripeness. No amount of cooking will make jelly of over-ripe fruit, and if too green the flavor of the fruit is lost. It is necessary to use good sound fruit. As the fruit is cut, put it into clear water. Keep the kettle covered and steam the fruit until tender.

Jellies and jams.

When ready to strain, put in a jelly bag and let drip; don't squeeze. Always boil the juice about ten minutes before adding the sugar. Use a flat vessel and a quick fire, that the water may evaporate quickly. With most fruit use measure for measure. A pinch of powdered alum to each boiling of jelly clarifies it very much. Never cover jelly until perfectly cold.[991]

ORANGE JELLY

☛ ½ box of gelatine,
1 large cup of orange juice,
1 orange sliced thin,
1 lemon,
2 cups sugar,
1 pint hot water.

Put all in a kettle and let it come to a boil, and then strain and pour in mold to cool. Be sure to remove the seeds, as they are very bitter. Serve with whipped cream and cocoanut cake.[992]

ORANGE JAM

☛ Slice one dozen oranges, remove seeds and let stand over night in three quarts of water. Add six pounds of sugar. Boil till thick. Seal.[993]

PLUM JELLY

☛ Plums are best for jelly when half colored, and this point is very important. Put the plums in a granite kettle with barely enough water to cover. Cook until tender, but not a pulpy mass. Drain the juice, but do not squeeze the bag. Measure the juice and then measure an equal amount of sugar. Put four cups of juice in a large, flat bottom kettle and let cook rapidly fifteen minutes; then add an equal measure of sugar and cook from three to ten minutes, when the jelly will have formed. Have the tumblers warm, pour in the jelly. Drop a lump of paraffin on top of each tumbler while the jelly is hot. This will melt and act as a cover. Let it be cold before putting on tin tops. All jellies are made in exactly the same way.[994]

PEACH JELLY

☛ Take ripe soft peaches, pare, mash and stew them in a very little water. Put it in a jelly bag, which should be made of white flannel, squeeze out the juice, and to each pint allow a pound of loaf sugar. Break up and boil in a very little water, as many peach kernels as will flavor it well, and mix it with the jelly and sugar; put it in a preserving kettle, and boil it slowly till it is a thick jelly, stirring and skimming it as it may require. If you wish it a very stiff jelly, add a little dissolved isinglass, which will never fail to make it such, but I do not think the jelly keeps as well as when made without it. When it is done and quite cold, put it up in small glass jars, lay brandy papers on the tops, and cover them securely with folded white paper.[995]

Daisy design for aspic jelly forms: 1) yolk of hard-boiled egg; 2) white of hard-boiled egg; 3) parsley leaves; 4) parsley stems.

SYRUPS FOR PRESERVES

☛ To ten pounds of sugar add three pints of clear water, hot or cold. When it commences to boil skim the froth from it with a spoon, and let it boil until the froth ceases to collect, then the syrup is made.[996]

CRYSTALIZED CANTALOUPES

☛ Take young cantaloupes, after the seed are well-formed. Slice, peel and take out the inside. Put them in weak brine, or lime water for twenty-four hours. Then soak them until fresh in cold water. If salt water is used instead of lime water, the rinds will have to be soaked in weak, alum water until brittle. Soak them in cold water until the alum is out of the rinds. Have ready a tea made of white ginger, or whatever spice flavor is preferred; boil the rind in this until it is tender; take it out of the tea and drain on a cloth for a few minutes, then pack it in sugar, using three quarters of a pound of sugar to each pound of rind. Let it stand well covered until the sugar is dissolved, then boil until the syrup is thick. Put in jars, and in a day or two, boil it again.

If, at the last boiling, the syrup will not cover the rinds, boil half of the cantaloupe for half an hour, then spread on dishes and set in the sun, and boil the other rind in the same way. In a few days make a fresh syrup, just enough to boil a few of the rinds in at a time; as these are taken out spread on dishes and set in the sun, place the other rinds in the syrup to boil, then in the sun to dry; proceed in this way until all the rinds have been through the syrup. Dry them thoroughly in the sun, then pack, with oiled paper between each layer. This is nice to use in fruit cake in place of citron.[997]

PRESERVED ORANGES

☛ Peel ½ dozen oranges; cut a hole in one end, large enough to scoop out the inside part of the orange very carefully; put them in cold water to soak for 3 days, changing the water each day; then boil them slowly until the bitter is extracted, changing the water every ½ hour until the water no longer tastes bitter. To 1 pound of fruit put 1¼ pounds of sugar; clarify the sugar, and then put the oranges in, and let them boil slowly until transparent. They will take about 4 hours to boil, if the fire is well kept up.[998]

PRESERVED PEACHES

☛ Have cling peaches, peel them, cut them in half and take the kernels out. Put peaches in sugar, a layer of peaches, then a layer of sugar. Weigh peaches and sugar equally. Each layer of peaches should be about six inches deep; then cover with sugar. Keep repeating sugar and peaches in this manner until you get them all under sugar. Let them remain so one day and night. Next day take sugar and juice from the peaches and put on to boil, and when it comes to a boil, put the peaches in the syrup and let them boil ten minutes. Then take them out and put others in, and when the first lot gets cold put them back into syrup again, and keep repeating in this manner, letting them boil for ten minutes at a time, until preserved.

When the peaches look the color of gold coin they are preserved. When they are cold put them in jars, cover with syrup, seal or cork, and set away in a dark closet. Use the syrup they were preserved in; if you have not enough, make more. In preserving any kind of fruit, while cooking always keep the froth well skimmed off top of syrup, and don't neglect it.[999]

PRESERVED PINEAPPLE

☛ Take nice ripe pineapples; peel them and pick out the eyes, and put them upon a large dish. Take a silver fork and tear the pineapple apart, and put the pieces in jars that have hermetically sealed tops. Take the juice that came from the fruit, and allow ¼ pound of sugar to each quart jar; if not enough juice, add a little water; when the sugar has melted, fill the jars. Try and not make more juice than will fill the jars. Put the jars into a large flat bottom kettle; put a few sticks in the bottom to keep the jars from breaking. Pour cold water around the jars. Put on the glass tops, but not the India rubber pieces. When the water boils, take out the jars and seal them immediately. This manner of preserving pineapples retains the flavor and freshness of the fruit, and will keep for several years.[1000]

Preserves.

PRESERVED LIMES

☛ Put the limes in strong salt and water for 6 days; then slit them down the side, and take out the pulp; then soak out the salt with clear water, changing the water often; then boil them in alum water until they are green and tender; put them in a thin syrup, boiling hot; let them remain 24 hours; make a richer syrup of ½ pound of sugar to 1 pound of fruit; add it to the other syrup; boil until thick and clear, and then add to the limes. Put them all in a jar, and seal them.[1001]

PEACH PRESERVES

☛ For pickling, select large plum peaches that are ripe, but not the least soft. Wipe off the fuzz with a cloth, put them in strong salt and water, and let them stand for ten days; then soak them in fresh water two or three days, to draw out the salt, shifting the water every day. Put them in a jar, strewing between each layer a small handful of sugar, a few cloves, and a little powdered cinnamon, and cover them with the best vinegar. Firm clingstone peaches may be kept a year or two in strong brine, as directed for cucumbers, and pickled in the same manner. They look very pretty when pared, and colored pink with beet juice or cochineal.[1002]

PRESERVED PEARS

☛ The small pears are better for preserving than the large ones. Pare them and put 1 pound of sugar to the same of pears; make a syrup with a little water; leave the stem on, and stick a clove in the blossom end of each; stew them until perfectly transparent; skim off the scum; take out the pears, and let the syrup boil until clear and thick. Put in jars, and seal them.[1003]

FRUIT JELLY

☛ ½ box gelatine,
1 lemon,
1 pint wine,
2 cups sugar,
2 pints water.

Boil gelatine, lemon and sugar. Flavor when taking from the stove, and when it begins to congeal stir in ½ pound white grapes.[1004]

APPLE JELLY

☛ There is no flavor to apple jelly; it will take any flavor you choose to give it. If a rose geranium leaf is washed and held in the jelly a moment it will give a delightful flavor. It must not be held too long. Peach leaves will give the flavor of bitter almond. Extract of lemon flavors nicely.[1005]

APPLE BUTTER

☛ Cider for apple butter must be perfectly new from the press, and the sweeter and mellower the apples are of which it is made, the better will the apple butter be. Boil the cider till reduced to one half its original quantity, and skim it well. Do not use for this purpose an iron kettle, or the butter will be very dark, and if you use a brass or copper kettle, it must be scoured as clean and bright as possible, before you put the cider into it, and you must not suffer the butter to remain in it a minute longer than is actually necessary to prepare it, or it will

Small molds for aspic (left); mold with paper pasted over the top for coating the mold (right).

imbibe a copperish taste, that will render it not only unpleasant, but really unhealthy. It is best to prepare it late in the fall, when the apples are quite mellow. Select those that have a fine flavor, and will cook tender; pare and quarter them from the cores, and boil them in the cider till perfectly soft, having plenty of cider to cover them well. If you wish to make it on a small scale, do not remove the apples from the cider when they get soft, but continue to boil them gently in it, till the apples and cider form a thick smooth marmalade, which you must stir almost constantly towards the last. A few minutes before you take it from the fire, flavor it highly with cinnamon, nutmeg, ginger, and cloves, and when the seasonings are well intermixed, put it up in jars, tie folded paper over them, and keep them in a cool place. If made in a proper manner, it will keep good more than a year, and will be found very convenient, being always in readiness.

Many people who are in the habit of making apple butter, take it from the fire before it is boiled near enough. Both to keep it well, and taste well, it should be boiled long after the apples have become soft, and towards the last, simmered over coals till it gets almost thick enough to slice. If you wish to make it on a large scale, after you have boiled the first kettle full of apples soft, remove them from the cider, draining them with a perforated ladle, that the cider may fall again to the kettle, and put them into a clean tub.

Fill up the kettle with fresh apples, having them pared and sliced from the cores, and having ready a kettle of boiling cider, that is reduced to at least half its original quantity; fill up the kettle of apples with it as often as is necessary. When you have boiled in this manner as many apples as you wish, put the whole of them in a large kettle, or kettles, with the cider, and simmer it over a bed of coals till it is so thick, that it is with some difficulty you can stir it: it should be stirred almost constantly, with a wooden spaddle, or paddle, or it will be certain to scorch at the bottom or sides of the kettle. Shortly before you take it from the fire, season it as before directed, and then put it up in jars.[1006]

MAYPOPS

☛ Gather the Maypops when very green; take off a thin peeling, cut in halves and take out the seed. Drop them in lime water, made in the proportion of one teacup of lime to one gallon of water; let them stand twelve hours. Boil them fifteen minutes in weak alum water, then boil in fresh water until they are clear.

Take them out, drain well, and pack in granulated sugar using three-quarters of a pound of sugar to one of fruit. Let them remain twelve hours; then boil twenty minutes; flavor strongly with ginger or extract of lemon. If ginger is used, boil the root ginger with the preserves. When done put in jars and seal. These may be dried and crystalized just as are apricots and quinces.[1007]

GUAVA JELLY

☛ I find the strawberry guava makes the best jelly. Wash and cut the fruit with a silver knife, put in your kettle, cover with water and boil until soft. Drip it in a bag over night.

Next morning make the jelly as directed above. I add one or two teaspoonfuls citric acid in each boiling; helps to clear it. I prepare apple juice and mix with the guava; it can't be detected, and will make firmer jelly.[1008]

SCUPPERNONG JELLY

☛ Take the pulp and juice of half ripe scuppernongs. Boil a few minutes and strain through a flannel bag. Add one pound of white sugar to each pint of juice and boil until jellied. It will take from twenty to thirty minutes.[1009]

PIGS' FEET JELLY

☞ To one quart of stock take half a pound of loaf-sugar, one pint of wine, one wineglassful of brandy, the rind and juice of two lemons, a few sticks of cinnamon broken up, a little mace, and the whites of three eggs strained, not beaten, and the shells broken up; mix all these ingredients well together, and boil for forty minutes. Do not stir it. Then throw in a pint of cold water, and let it boil ten or fifteen minutes longer. Strain through a flannel bag with a thin layer of cotton at the bottom of it. If you have no lemons, use a part of a tumbler of strong white vinegar, and use the essence of lemon. If the stock has not kept well, boil it over, and strain it before making the jelly.[1010]

Jelly with a bunch of grapes molded in it.

BLACKBERRY JELLY

☞ Don't quite cover your berries with water; boil and strain as directed, and use a pint of sugar to each quart of juice. You will only make as much jelly as you use sugar. Too acid fruit is very difficult to jelly.[1011]

FLORIDA NECTARINE PRESERVES

☞ Pare, halve, stone and weigh the nectarines. Steam till tender. Make a syrup of three-fourths of a pound of sugar to every pound of fruit. Put sugar in granite pan, add just enough water to dissolve it and let slowly come to a boil. Add the fruit. Let come to a boil and with wooden spoon turn over the fruit. Put on top of stove and simmer slowly two hours. Set away to cool. Next day heat up syrup again to boiling point, add the fruit and when thoroughly heated seal.[1012]

EVAPORATED APPLE JELLY

☞ Wash a pound of evaporated apples. Put two and a half quarts of water in a kettle. When hot, put in the apples and cook until soft; then drip. You should have one quart of juice. After boiling this water about ten minutes, put in three cups of sugar and boil until it jellies. Lemon to flavor. It makes two and a half glasses of beautiful jelly.[1013]

WILD PLUM JELLY

☞ It's much nicer when mixed with apple juice. It is too acid to jelly nicely when pure.[1014]

PINEAPPLE JELLY

☞ Apples.
Sugar.
Pineapple.

Water.

Take tart apples, cut up without peeling and drop into water to prevent them turning dark. Add peeling and cores of one or two pineapples; boil all (covered with water) until apples are quite tender, strain juice through a jelly bag, add measure for measure of juice and white sugar. Boil quickly for ten minutes in shallow vessel. Put in glasses while hot.[1015]

APRICOT JELLY

☛ Peel almost ripe apricots; place in porcelain kettle and nearly cover with water; boil until perfectly done. Strain, and add one measure of sugar to each of juice. Boil thirty minutes, or until it jellies.[1016]

RASPBERRY JAM

☛ Weigh equal quantities of fruit and sugar; put the fruit into a preserving kettle; boil and mash it; let it boil very quickly, and stir constantly. When most of the juice is wasted, add the sugar, and boil it to a fine jam. Jam made in this way is of a finer color than when the sugar is put in first.[1017]

ORANGE PRESERVES

☛ To preserve oranges whole, cut a place out of one end large enough to take the pulps all out with a teaspoon. Then place the rinds in brine for twenty-four hours; then soak them in water until fresh; soak in alum water one night, and boil in clear water until tender. Don't boil many at a time, for fear of breaking or mashing them. Drain them on a cloth, place in jars. Make a syrup of one pound of sugar and place in jars. Make a syrup of one pound to each pound of fruit; let it boil ten minutes pour over the fruit and let it stand twenty-four hours. Then pour oranges and syrup into a kettle, boil for half an hour, put in jars, boil the syrup until there is just enough to cover the oranges, pour over them and seal.[1018]

ORANGE MARMALADE

☛ Remove the rind and seeds from the oranges. Cut the rind of ½ in fine strips and parboil in water till enough of the bitter has been removed and sufficient taste remains to flavor the pulp nicely. Cut up the pulp as fine as possible and mix with the rind. To every pound of fruit add 1 pound of granulated sugar.

Put into a preserving kettle and stir slowly all the time it is boiling. When it is a clear golden color, it is done.

This is delicious with ice cream, plain cream, or on pastry puffs.[1019]

QUINCE MARMALADE

☛ Pare, core, and cut into pieces the fruit. Put the skins and cores into a kettle; cover them with water, and boil thirty minutes, or until tender; strain off the water through a colander, and as much pulp as will pass without the skins. To this add the rest of the fruit and three quarters of a pound of sugar to each pound of fruit. Boil it until it becomes a jelly-like mass. Mash the fruit as much as possible. It may be colored red, if desired, with cochineal. Turn it into glasses, tin boxes, or wooden salt-boxes. It becomes solid, and is served cut into slices. The Russians cut it into inch squares, and serve it as a bonbon.[1020]

PEACH MARMALADE

☞ Take the ripest soft peaches (the yellow ones make the prettiest marmalade), pare them, and take out the stones; put them in the pan with one pound of dry light coloured brown sugar to two of peaches: when they are juicy, they do not require water: with a silver or wooden spoon, chop them with the sugar; continue to do this, and let them boil gently till they are a transparent pulp, that will be a jelly when cold. Puffs made of this marmalade are very delicious.[1021]

CHERRY PRESERVES

☞ Take any kind of fine, large cherries, that are full grown, but not soft. Be very careful in gathering them that you do not bruise them, remove the stones, and put the cherries in a glass jar. Mix a pound of sugar with three quarts of good vinegar; boil it in a covered vessel till reduced to two quarts, set it by till it gets perfectly cold, and then pour it over the cherries. Plums may be pickled in the same manner, and either of them makes a pretty garnish for fresh meats.[1022]

Pink jelly garnished with pink carnations.

FIG PRESERVES

☞ This receipt is for the small purple fig, which I like best. Cut the stems off quite close; weigh them, allowing pound for pound. Put the figs in a kettle and cover with water and very little soda; boil until tender; remove from the water and wash off in cold water; drain through the colander. Make a syrup of the sugar, put in the figs and boil until tender, and put in also some ginger tea. I then set the kettle in the sun for one or two days; then I cook again until syrup is thick enough to put up; then put in self sealing jars. I sometimes put in a few cloves; it flavors nicely.[1023]

CONFEDERATE FIG PRESERVES

☞ Gather fruit when fully ripe, but not cracked open; place in a perforated tin bucket or wire basket, and dip for a moment into a deep kettle of hot and moderately strong lye (some prefer letting them lie an hour in lime-water and afterwards drain); make a syrup in proportion of one pound sugar to one of fruit, and when the figs are well drained, put them in syrup and boil until well cooked; remove, boil syrup down until there is just enough to cover fruit; put fruit back in syrup, let all boil, and seal up while hot in glass or porcelain jars.[1024]

CONFEDERATE PEACH PRESERVES

☛ 1 pound sugar to 1 pound fruit.

Peel, stone, and halve peaches. Add enough water to the sugar to make a thick syrup, and boil till thick. Put in fruit and cook till clear and tender. A few stones added make a delicious flavor. Use firm peaches, as over-ripe ones lose their form and the under-ripe ones make dark preserves.[1025]

PEAR PRESERVES

☛ 8 pounds of pears, nearly ripe,
8 pounds of sugar,
4 lemons, peel very fine, and squeeze the juice,
¼ pound of green ginger,
1 tumbler of water.

Put all in a kettle together, and let boil ¾ of an hour, or until the syrup is the right consistency.[1026]

PEACH BUTTER

☛ Peach butter, when made in the proper manner, is cheap and really fine. Take rider just from the press, that has been made of the best of apples, boil it in a preserving kettle till reduced to one half its original quantity. Have ready some nice dried peaches, wash them clean, squeeze out the water, and put them in the cider. Boil them till they are very soft, stirring and washing them till they become a smooth pulp, and replenishing the kettle with fresh cider as it may require. Let it remain over a slow fire of coals till it gets hard enough to slice, but be careful to stir it almost constantly towards the last, lest it scorch. Flavor it highly with powdered cloves, ginger, cinnamon and nutmeg, put it up in stone or queen's ware jars, cover them securely by tying over the tops some folded paper, and keep them in a cool place. It will keep good a year, and will be found very nice and convenient.[1027]

PEACH JAM

☛ Pare, stone, and cut into thin slices half a peck of freestone peaches, and to each pound of fruit add three-quarters of a pound of sugar. Put them into a preserving kettle and let them cook until clear, which will probably require an hour. Then crack one-third of the peach stones, remove the kernels, blanch them in boiling water, cut them into thin slices, and add to the peaches. This should be done as soon as fruit is set on the fire, so that the kernels can cook with it. When done, put into glass jars. For use in small families the pint size is better than the quart.[1028]

SUGARED PEACHES

☛ Peel ripe cling-stone peaches, place in jar, using sugar between each layer until the jar is full; then seal and keep in a cool place. These will be ready for use when the sugar is thoroughly dissolved.[1029]

CONFEDERATE PRESERVED LIMES

☛ Get your limes as near the same size as possible, and preserve them in every respect as you would any citrus fruit. Lay on them pieces of paper dipped in brandy, and cut to fit in the tops of the jars; tie over the tops soft paper, that will fit closely round, and keep them in a cool place. Occasionally look to them, and if the syrup looks like fermenting, boil and skim it well, pour it over the limes, and when cold cover them as before directed.[1030]

PRESERVED LEMONS

☛ Select ripe thin rinded lemons, that are of equal size and without blemish: boil them in clear water till the rinds become tender, excavate a small portion of the stalk end of each, that the syrup may penetrate them easily, and spread them out on dishes to cool.

Make a plentiful syrup to cover them, allowing a pound of loaf sugar to each quart of water; boil it, skim it, and put in your lemons; simmer them a few minutes, put them with the syrup into an earthen jar, and set them by till next day: then turn off the syrup, boil it up, pour it hot over the lemons, and set them by till the second day.

Jelly molds, L-R: Charlotte molds, cylindrical mold, ring mold, a second type of ring mold.

Turn off the syrup again, add to it more loaf sugar, making in all a pound and a half to each pound of the lemons; mix with it the whites of eggs, allowing one to every five pounds of the sugar, and boil, skim it, scald your lemons in it a few minutes, drain and cool them, put them in a jar, and when you have boiled the syrup till thick, pour it over them while hot. Next day cover them securely.[1031]

STRAWBERRY JAM

☛ Must have fresh berries that are not running. Squeeze the juice from the berries through a clean linen cloth; then add one-half pint of sugar to every pint of juice and put on to boil in a porcelain kettle, and when it boils as thick as honey add the berries that you squeezed the juice from to the syrup and let it continue to boil until it gets as thick as mush, when it will be cooked enough.

You can put it up in glasses or jars; put paper on the top wet with brandy, and then cover and put in a dark place. Use granulated sugar.[1032]

RASPBERRY PRESERVES

☛ Raspberries should have one pound of sugar to one pound of fruit. Cook well.[1033]

MRS. ARRINGTON'S FIG PRESERVES

☛ Use large figs. Scrape them or peel with a knife; scald in weak alum water, then boil in ginger tea. Make a syrup, allowing pound for pound. Put figs in the hot syrup, cook fifteen minutes, then sun a day; then if the syrup is thick enough, heat, flavor with lemon and put up in self sealing jars.[1034]

TOMATO JELLY

☛ Get a can of the bright red tomatoes, cook with a cup of water; season with grated onion, one bay leaf, pepper corns, mace, cloves, salt. Cook all together and strain through a coarse strainer. Add two-thirds of a box of swollen gelatine; if it stands over night half a box will do. Rinse your mold out with white of egg to prevent its sticking. Put in the jelly and set in refrigerator.

You may put in a border mold to set, turn, fill the center with celery cut in straws and mixed with mayonnaise and surround with celery.[1035]

Tomato jelly molded in a ring and served with mayonnaise, lettuce, and curled celery.

PUMPKIN CHIPS

☛ Cut ripe pumpkin into one inch strips, peel and cut out the soft part next to the seed. Then chip into thin squares. Let stand in salt water over night; drain and boil in weak alum water for twenty minutes. Then soak in fresh water twenty-four hours.

Drain and pack in white sugar, three-quarters of pound to a pound of pumpkin. Slice a lemon into each half gallon when adding the sugar. Let it stand until the sugar is dissolved, then boil with the lemon in it until the pumpkin is clear. Place in jars a and seal. This retains the natural color and is very nice.[1036]

BLACKBERRY JAM

☛ Use blackberries, not dewberries, with small seed. Weigh them, wash your berries, mash as fine as you can, and put on to cook. In fifteen minutes put in the sugar, allowing pound for pound; cook a short while, then set the kettle in the sun until next day; then put on and cook until it almost jellies.

Put up in jars. Three quarts berries and three pounds sugar makes two quarts of jam.[1037]

CITRON PRESERVES

☛ Peel and weigh your cantaloupe or watermelon rind. Put a handful of lime in some water, dissolve it and let settle, strain over the rinds. Let them stand over night. Next morning put in clear water for twelve hours, changing the water often. Next boil in weak alum water, putting in very little green fruit coloring. Cover the vessel to keep in the steam; then soak over night again in clear water to extract the alum. Boil again in ginger tea while you make a syrup of one and a half pounds of sugar to each pound of rind. Cook in the syrup until clear. Set aside until next day, then boil until the syrup is thick. Lemon or pineapple to flavor.[1038]

PINEAPPLE PRESERVES

☛ Peel your pineapple, cut out the eyes, core and slice, weigh it and put in the preserving kettle. Cover with water and parboil until tender. Throw away this water, put the sugar over the pineapple allowing pound for pound, let them stand until next day, when they will have formed a syrup. Cook until the syrup is thick put up in quart jars. Fine.[1039]

WINE JELLY

☛ Soak ½ box of gelatine in ½ cup of water. Add ½ pound of sugar and 2½ cups of boiling water. Stir until gelatine is dissolved. Then add juice of 1 lemon, 1 orange, ½ cup of sherry, 1 tablespoon brandy, 1 tablespoon of Maraschino. Add last the beaten whites and crushed shells of 2 eggs. When it has boiled a few minutes, remove from the stove and strain into a mold and set on ice. Serve with whipped cream.[1040]

CRAB APPLE JELLY

☛ Put the apples to boil; one quart of water to one quart of apples and let them boil till soft; then mash the apples and put the apples and the water they were boiled in in a linen rag, and let all the juice drip into a vessel; measure the juice and take one quart of the dripped juice to one quart of sugar, and put on to boil for jelly.

Boil thirty minutes and then dip some into a saucer and set in the air to cool; if it is congealed when cool, it is done. Put up in glasses, first dipping the glasses into boiling hot water and letting them drain; put the jelly into the glasses hot, and then set to cool. Paper the same way you do currant jelly, and put away in a dark place. Use a porcelain kettle and granulated sugar.[1041]

STRAWBERRY PRESERVES

☛ Put your berries in a colander and let water run over them, cap and weigh them, allowing pound for pound. Put a layer of fruit then sugar, in your kettle, let stand to dissolve the sugar, then put on and cook twenty minutes. Put in dishes and set in the sun, stir often, in two days they will be a thick marmalade and are fine. Put them up in fair weather, I heat again to seal them.[1042]

PEAR JELLY

☛ Take half ripe pears, peel and cut them in slices, without removing the core. Keep them in clear water until all are cut; drain off the water, place in kettle, cover with clear water, cover and boil until quite tender; then drain off the juice, strain through a flannel bag, place on the fire, and boil ten or fifteen minutes. Measure, and add one pound of sugar to one pint of juice. Boil for thirty minutes, or until it jellies, which may be in less time.[1043]

FRENCH JAM

☛ The addition of one pound of raisins to each gallon of currant jam converts this into very fine French jam.[1044]

GUAVA MARMALADE

☛ Take all over ripe fruit, peel cut up and weigh, put in kettle with a little water, cook until you can mash smooth, then put in sugar, allowing pound for pound. Boil till thick.[1045]

WATERMELON PRESERVES

☛ Take small long melon, slice it round in half inch slices, pare, place in large earthen bowl and cover with brine, using one teacupful of salt to three quarts of water. Let it stand twelve hours, drain and cover with fresh water and let it remain until the salt is well out. Then soak in alum water until firm, using a teaspoonful of pulverized alum to one gallon of water. Take from the alum water and boil in fresh water until the rind is clear and the alum is well out of the melon. Drain and pack in white sugar, using one pound of sugar to each pound of melon. After the syrup is formed, return to the kettle, slice two lemons to each gallon, and boil until the melon is clear and the syrup thick; cover well and keep in a cool place. The meat of the melon will be a darker red than the natural color, but quite pretty. Leave the seed in.

Jelly molds, L-R: mold packed in ice for fancy molding, smaller mold that fits into the first for double molding.

To preserve the rind of melon, peel and take out the meat close; cut in any shape or size desired. Place in lime water, using half pint of lime to each gallon of water to be used; let the lime settle and drain off the water before putting in the rind. Let it stand twelve hours, then boil it in very weak alum water for thirty minutes. Drain, cover with fresh water and boil until the alum is all out and the rind is clear. The water

Rhubarb jelly and whipped cream.

will have to be changed if much alum has been used, as it must be well out of the rind before preserving. When fresh, drain well, pack in white sugar, using one pound of sugar to each pound of rind.

Let it remain in sugar twelve hours, then boil until the rind is clear. If the syrup is too thick add a little water; flavor with anything desired. If ginger is preferred, make a strong ginger tea, strain and boil the rind in it before packing in the sugar.[1046]

APPLE MARMALADE
☞ ¾ pound sugar to 1 pound of fruit.

Use tart apples. Add water and cook to a thick pulp. Measure and add ¾ pound of sugar to 1 pound fruit. Stir well all the time to keep from burning, and remove the scum as it rises. Flavor with cinnamon and lemon to taste. Put in stone jars and cover well.[1047]

DUNDEE ORANGE MARMALADE
☞ Slice unpeeled naval oranges thin. To five oranges use one lemon sliced thin. To every pound of fruit add three pints of cold water. Let stand twenty-four hours then place on stove and let boil briskly for forty-five minutes.

Time from the moment it commences to boil. Set aside for another twenty-four hours, then weigh, and to every pound allow one and a half pounds sugar and the juice of a lemon. Place fruit on stove as soon as it boils rapidly. Slowly add the sugar. Boil forty-five minutes. Put up in jelly glasses.[1048]

PRESERVED APRICOTS
☞ Weigh an equal quantity of sugar and apricots, or if you are going to preserve fifty pounds of apricots weigh fifty pounds of sugar, take the sugar and put it in a porcelain kettle the day before you buy the apricots, put two gallons of water at bottom of sugar in kettle, let it boil until thick as honey, seat off fire; next day you get the apricots, put the syrup again on the fire and have it boiling before you drop the apricots in; take the apricots out of boiling syrup every five minutes and put others in boiling syrup to remain boiling five minutes and take out before those last in; repeat the shifting of the apricots every five minutes for five hours when they will be preserved. If you want to preserve a less quantity you can do so; the only instructions needed is, to one pound of apricots one pound of sugar; make syrup the day before getting the apricots and set aside, the next day boil it and put apricots in while boiling. For making syrup, to one pound of sugar half pint of water.[1049]

TO CAN PEACHES

☛ Get yellow freestone peaches; peel and cut in half, wash them and put in kettle. Use no water. To twelve pounds of peaches put three pounds of sugar over the top. Cook until a little tender. Seal while hot.[1050]

PEAR AND QUINCE PRESERVES

☛ Made by parboiling until tender; then drain; put the sugar over; let stand over night; cook next day. Allow pound for pound. Flavor pears.[1051]

CONFEDERATE CRAB APPLE JELLY

☛ Cut the apples into quarters and cover with water and boil till tender. Strain through a flannel bag and add 1 pint sugar to 1 pint juice. Boil juice 20 minutes, at the same time melt the sugar in a kettle. Pour together and boil till it begins to jelly. Skim constantly. Fill glasses and set in dark closet.[1052]

CURRANT JELLY

Jelly with a rose molded in it and garnished with roses.

☛ Pick stems from currants and put in stone jar in kettle of boiling water and cook till skins break. Do not put water over them. Strain through a flannel bag and add 1 pint sugar to each pint juice. Boil the juice while the sugar melts and pour together and boil till it begins to jelly. Strain again and pour in glasses, which must be in hot water.[1053]

GRAPE JELLY

☛ Pick stems from grapes. Put in jar without water and set in kettle of hot water and cook till fruit bursts. Strain in flannel bag and to 1 pint juice add 1 pint sugar. Boil till it begins to jelly and pour in glasses. Cover with paper which has been dipped in brandy, which prevents mold, and set aside in dark place.[1054]

QUINCE JELLY

☛ Wash the quinces and rub them well with a rough cloth. Cut them in quarter pieces, keeping them in water until all are ready; drain off the water, put them in the kettle, cover with fresh water. Let them boil until very tender. Strain off the juice add one cup and a half of white sugar to two cups of juice. Let boil rapidly for twenty or thirty minutes. Have the molds dry, fill as quickly as possible without breaking the molds by heating too fast. Let cool, cover with paper dipped in alcohol and put on the tops.[1055]

CRANBERRY JELLY

☛ 1 quart cranberries.
1 pint sugar.
1 pint cold water.

Cook berries in water until soft, strain through sieve. Then add sugar and boil five minutes.[1056]

The delights of Christmas time.

15. Meats

TO CHOOSE MEATS AND FOWLS

☞ BEEF: Well-fed beef may be selected by the color and texture; the lean will display an open grain of deep coral red; the fat will be of a yellowish tinge, and present an oily smoothness. The suet firm and white. Of heifer beef, the lean is of a closer grain, of not so deep a red, and the fat whiter. Real yellow fat is not indicative of good beef, on the contrary, it is a test of meat of an inferior quality. In cow-beef, the older the cow, the closer the texture of the beef; and the meat is hard to the touch.

The animal, when slaughtered, should be bled very thoroughly. The care taken by the Jews in this, and other points, draws custom from other sects to their markets. The skin is tanned for leather, and the fat is used for candles and other purposes.

The tail is used for soups, and the liver, heart, and tripe are also used for cooking. The body is split into two parts through the backbone, and each half is divided as marked in the drawing.

Above: 1) The *head*; sometimes used for mince-pies; sometimes it is tied up for oil, and then the bones are used for fertilizers. 2) The *neck*; used for soups and stews. 3) The *chuck-rib*, or *shoulder*, having four ribs. It is used for corning, stews, and soup, and some say the best steaks are from this piece. 4) The *front of the shoulder*, or the *shoulder-clod*, which is sometimes called the *brisket*, or *rattleran*, used for soup and corning. 5) The *back of the shoulder*; used for corning, soups, and stews. 6) The *fore shin*, or *leg*; used for soups. 7) The *plate pieces*; the front one is called the *brisket* (as is also 4), and is used for corning, soups, and stews. The back plate piece is called the *flank*, and is divided into the *thick flank*, or *upper sirloin*, and the *lower flank*. These are for roasting and corning. 8) The *standing ribs*, divided into *first*, *second*, and *third cuts*; used for roasting. The second cut is the best of the three. 9) The *sirloin*, and is the best roasting piece. 10) The *sirloin steak* and the *porter-house steak*; used for broiling. 11) The *rump*, or *aitch-bone*; used for soup or corning, or to cook à la mode. 12) The *round* or *buttock*; used for corning, or for à la mode; also for dried beef. 13) The *hock*, or *hind shank*; used for soups.[1057]

VEAL: If the kidney be well surrounded by fat, the meat is of good quality. The whitest is not the best veal; but the flesh of the bull-calf is of a brighter color than that of the cow-calf. The fillet of the cow-calf is considered the best. A perceptible vein in the shoulder indicates the freshness of the meat; if bright red or blue, it is fresh, if any green or yellow spots are visible, it is stale. The suet will be flabby, and the kidney will smell. The calf should not be slaughtered until it is six weeks old. Spring is the best time for veal.

Above: 1. The *head*, sold with the *pluck*, which includes the *heart*, *liver*, and *sweet-breads*. 2) The *rack*, including the neck; used for stews, pot-pies, and broths; also for chops and roasting. 3) The *shoulder*. This, and also half the rack and ribs of the fore quarter, are sometimes roasted, and sometimes used for stews, broths, and cutlets. 4) The *fore shank*, or *knuckle*; used for broths. 5) The *breast*; used for stews and soups; also to stuff and bake. 6) The *loin*; used for roasting. 7) The *fillet*, or *leg*, including the hind flank; used for cutlets, or to stuff and boil, or to stuff and roast or bake. 8) The *hind shank*, or *hock*, or *knuckle*; used for soups. The *feet* are used for jelly.[1058]

MUTTON: The best is of a fine grain and bright color, the fat firm and white. The ram mutton may be known by the redness of the flesh, and the sponginess of the fat. The ewe mutton is not so bright in color, while the grain is closer. Mutton is better for being full grown.

Above: 1) The *shoulder*; for boiling or corning. 2) The *neck* and *rack*; for boiling or corning. 3) The *loin*; is roasted, or broiled as chops. 4) The *leg*; is boiled, or broiled, or stuffed and roasted. Many salt and smoke the leg, and call it smoked venison. 5) The *breast*; for boiling or corning.[1059]

LAMB: In the fore-quarter, if the vein is not blue, it is stale. In the hind-quarter judge by the kidney, its faintness of smell will prove it to be stale.

Lamb should be eaten very fresh. Mutton wrapped in a cloth wet with vinegar, and laid on the ground floor of a dry cellar, keeps well, and improves in tenderness.

VENISON: The choice of venison should be regulated by the appearance of the fat, which when the venison is young, looks bright, thick, clear, and close. By running a knife in the haunches, and then smelling the blade, you can tell if it be tainted.

PORK: In young pork the lean when pinched will break, the thickness and toughness of the rind is a proof of its being old. In fresh pork, the flesh is firm, smooth, a clear color, and the fat set. When stale it is clammy and flabby; if there be any kernels in the fat, it should not be eaten. Dairy fed pork is decidedly the best.

Above: 1. The *leg*, or *ham*; used for smoking. 2) The *hind loin*. 3) The *fore loin*. 4) The *spare-rib*; for roasting; sometimes including all the ribs. 5) The *hand*, or *shoulder*; sometimes smoked, and sometimes corned and boiled. 6) The *belly*, or *spring*, for corning or salting down. The *feet* are used for jelly, head-cheese, and souse.[1060]

BACON: Excellent young bacon may be known by the lean being of a bright color and tender, the fat firm and white, the rind thin, and the lean tender to the touch. Rusty bacon has yellow streaks in it.

TURKEY: The cock bird when young has a smooth black leg with a short spur. The eyes bright and full, and moist supple feet when fresh. The flesh very tender under the wings. The hen may be selected by the same rules, and is the most delicate.

CHICKENS: The young cock has a smooth leg, and a short spur, and may be selected by the same rules as are turkeys. Hens have smooth legs and combs when young. A good capon has a thick belly, and large rump, a full comb, and a swelling breast.

GEESE: In young geese the feet and bills will be yellow and free from hair. When fresh, the feet are pliable, and the skin tender.

DUCKS: May be selected in the same way as geese.

PARTRIDGES: Yellow legs, and a dark bill, are tests of a young bird; a rigid vent when fresh.

PHEASANTS: May be chosen the same as partridges and other birds.

HARES: When a hare is young and fresh, the cleft in the lip is narrow, the body stiff, the ears tear easily, and the claws are smooth and sharp.

LAST TIP: In hot weather where there is no ice, wipe meats dry; sprinkle on a little salt and pepper, and hang in a cellar. Or, still better, wrap it, thus prepared, in a dry cloth, and cover it with charcoal or wood ashes.[1061]

BEEF A LA MODE

☞ Take a ten-pound round of beef (have the butcher lard it), and tie it tight with a strong cord. Rub into the beef one and one-half tablespoonfuls of salt, one teaspoonful each of cayenne and black pepper. Have a pot of sufficient size and put the beef into it. Then slice thin four large carrots and two white turnips and lay them around the beef. Put in the pot about four sprigs of parsley, half a pint of good claret, and one small onion, sliced. Let it cook slowly five or six hours and send to table.[1062]

SPICED ROUND

☞ A twenty pound round of beef. Rub into this beef, one tea-cup of salt, two tablespoonfuls of cayenne and one of black peppers, quarter pound each of ground allspice and cloves rubbed into beef; then lay the round of beef into a vessel that will fit it and pour two quarts of vinegar on it and let it lay in vinegar one week, turning it over once every day, keeping it covered tight, so as to keep the flavor in it; after one week put it in a kettle to cook. First, tie it up tight in a clean cloth; put all the juice that lay around the beef in to cook with it, adding two quarts of water, and let it boil four hours and a quarter. Let it be cold when it is taken out of the cloth. Slice thin when it is served, as it is excellent for luncheons, parties, etc. The most delicious appetizer among meats.[1063]

Marrow bones served on slices of round toast.

BEEF STEAK PIE

☞ Butter a deep dish, and line it with rather a thick sheet of pie-paste. Cut some small thin slices from the thick part of a loin of fresh beef, and beat them tender, but do not tear nor break them to pieces; season them with salt and pepper, and put a layer of them on the paste in the bottom of the dish. Remove the hard part from an equal proportion of oysters to that of the steaks, and mince them fine; season them with a little pepper and nutmeg, and if they are fresh ones, add a little salt; put a layer of them over the steaks, dispersing among them some broken bits of butter, rolled in four, and some small thin squares of the paste. Do this till the dish is full, strain on a little of the oyster liquor, and fill the dish with water; then put a sheet of the paste over the top, notch and ornament it handsomely with paste leaves and flowers, and bake it in a moderate oven. Another mode is to substitute for the oysters fresh beet's marrow, or minced suet, and for the dumplings, white potatoes, neatly scraped and sliced.[1064]

BAKED HAM

☞ Never bake a ham under a year old. Rub the ham thoroughly and put to soak in cold water for 24 hours. Then cover with cold water in a boiler. When it begins to boil, set on back of stove and boil slowly till the bone is loose. (Twenty minutes to a pound is about the length of time required.) Then remove from stove and let stand in boiler till it is cool, over night or half a day. Put in a baking-pan and remove the skin and extra fat, being careful to keep the shape. Make a stiff batter of flour and water and cover the top. Set it in the oven and bake slowly for 2 hours. Then remove batter and with a knife make slight incisions all over the ham and sprinkle first with brown sugar, about 1 tablespoonful, then sprinkle thoroughly with black pepper. Make a dressing of grated bread or crackers, a little onion chopped fine, 1 tablespoon butter, pepper, salt, and mix with 1 egg and a little water. Cover the top with this dressing and put in oven to brown. Serve cold.[1065]

Cold ham covered in sauce with green garnishing.

RECIPE FOR CURING HAMS

☞ Kill your hogs when the wind is from the northwest. The night before you salt the meat take a string of red pepper and make a strong tea. (Let it remain on the stove over night.) Put in the tea 2 heaping tablespoons of saltpetre to every gallons. Take this strong tea and pour on the salt. Salt the meat lightly the first time to run off the blood. Let the meat lie packed 3 days longer, if the weather is very cold. Then overhaul the meat and put 1 teaspoon of pulverized saltpetre on the flesh side of each ham and rub in well. Then rub with molasses mixed with salt. Pack close for 10 days. After this overhaul again, rubbing each piece, and pack close again. Hang the meat in 3 weeks from the time the hogs were killed. Before hanging, wash each piece in warm water, and while wet roll in hickory ashes. Then smoke with green hickory wood, and tie up in cotton bags in February.[1066]

STUFFED HAM

☞ First boil the ham; then take the skin from it while boiling, put one tea-cup of vinegar to it; then take half pound of cooked veal, one tea-cup of powdered cracker; chop veal fine, mix both together, salt and pepper to taste; then make gashes about one-inch a part in the ham; stuff with veal and cracker, and put to bake; then pour one pint of sherry wine over ham and baste the ham while baking, until brown; while ham is baking grate one nutmeg over it, and sprinkle cracker powder over it.[1067]

PIGS IN A BLANKET
☞ Dry large fat oysters on a cloth, roll around each one a very thin slice of bacon and skewer with new tooth-picks. Fry in greased chafing-dish. Serve on rounds of toast.[1068]

FRIED HAM AND EGGS
☞ Cut the ham into slices and take care that they are of the same thickness in every part. Cut off the rind, and if the ham should be particularly hard and salt, it will be found an improvement to soak it for about ten minutes in hot water, and then dry it in a cloth. Put it into a cold frying-pan, set it over the fire, and turn the slices three or four times while they are cooking. When done, place them on a dish, which should be kept hot in front of the firs during the time the eggs are being poached; poach the eggs, slip them on to the slices of ham, and serve quickly.[1069]

CONFEDERATE PIGS IN A BLANKET
☞ Cut slices of breakfast bacon so thin one can almost see through them. Wrap an oyster in each slice of the bacon, and fasten it with a wooden tooth-pick. Light the lamp, having the wicks rather high and place the granite-ware dish over it. In a few seconds put in as many "little pigs" as will lie flat on the bottom of the pan. Turn constantly with a fork until they are brown on both sides; serve at once on slices of toast. With a dish of common size, six or eight can be cooked at a time.[1070]

BOILED MUTTON
☞ Put the mutton in just enough boiling water to cover it, and put on the lid of the pot. After fifteen minutes draw it aside, and let it simmer for the required time. Thirty minutes before removing the meat add some soup vegetables. They will give flavor to the meat, and

Ragout of mutton with farina balls and lettuce.

enrich the water, which may be used for soup the next day. Cut the carrot and turnip in half inch thick slices, and stamp with a fluted cutter, so the rims will be scalloped. Place the meat on a hot dish, and rub lightly over it enough of the white sauce (to be used for the caper sauce) to make the surface white and smooth. Sprinkle with chopped parsley or capers. Take the sliced vegetables, cut a hole in the center, and string them alternately on the bone, which will protrude at each end. This will give the effect of skewers, conceal the bone, and make the dish more presentable. Serve with caper sauce.[1071]

SAUCE FOR BOILED FISH OR BOILED MUTTON
☛ One and a half tablespoonfuls of flour, and one of butter rubbed together until creamed; boil one gill of sweet milk, then add it gradually to this creamed butter and flour, and stir it as you add it, until it is thoroughly mixed; season with pepper and salt to taste.

Boil four eggs hard and slice them in four pieces, lengthways, and put the eggs around the dish when you take up the fish to send to table, and also garnish the dish with parsley.[1072]

ROAST MUTTON
☛ Baste the meat with salt and water, and roast very slowly at first. Turn the spit, that it may be equally done.

Dredge over a little flour, and baste the meat with its own gravy about a half an hour before sending it to the table. Pour a glass of wine in the gravy. Let it boil up once, and pour in the sauce-tureen. Serve currant jelly with it.[1073]

Crown mutton roast filled with potatoes.

BEEFSTEAK PIE
☛ Take 2 pounds of tender beefsteak, and boil it in a little water until half done; have dish lined with paste; cut up the beef in small pieces, and put in the dish; add to the water that it was boiled in, 1 onion, pepper, salt, and it a ½ wineglass of wine; let it boil up, and pour upon the meat; cover it with a crust of paste.

Put a roll of paste around the edge of the dish. If beef is not tender, it can be improved by putting it upon a board and pounding it.[1074]

JAMBALAYA
☛ Take one chicken and cut it up, separating every joint, and adding to it one pint of cleanly-washed rice.

Take about half a dozen large tomatoes, scalding them well and taking the skins off with a knife. Cut them in small pieces and put them with the chicken in a pot or large porcelain saucepan. Then cut in small pieces two large pieces of sweet ham and add to the rest, seasoning high with pepper and salt.

It will cook in twenty-five minutes. Do not put any water on it.[1075]

BAKED CHICKEN

☛ Prepare young grown chicken 12 hours or more before using. Place the chicken flat in the pan. Add 1 pint water and cook till tender. Baste often with butter. Then make a dressing of butter, salt, pepper, a little onion and bread-crumbs and put around the chicken. Cook till chicken and dressing are a rich brown.[1076]

CHICKEN A LA KING

☛ 1 small can pimentos.
1 small can button mushrooms.
2 cups diced chicken.

Make a cream sauce, then add pimentos drained, mushrooms and chicken. Salt and pepper to taste. Serve on toast.[1077]

CHICKEN SALAD

☛ Take all the meat from the bones of a boiled chicken and chop it fine in a tray. Save out some of the breast meat so as to lay over the top of the salad when it is made. Chop fine half a bunch of white celery and add to chicken. Season the chicken with pepper and salt, using cayenne pepper to taste. Skim the oil from the boiling chicken to pour over the salad. Milanese sauce for chicken salad: Beat the yolks of three eggs a little, then add one pint of best sweet oil, beating a little sweet oil at a time into the eggs, so as to have it light, until the whole pint is added. Mix a teaspoonful of mustard thoroughly in strong vinegar and put in sauce with cayenne and black pepper to suit the taste. When you put the salad on the platter, pour this sauce all over it and set it in an ice box.[1078]

Chartreuse of chicken.

TO BARBECUE MEAT

☛ First, run a knife around the bone of the meat and salt it. Let stand an hour or two; then put it into a pan. Use no water and cook very slowly. Then make a dressing of vinegar, butter, catsup, Worcester sauce, Durkee's salad dressing, a little lemon peel. Set the sauce over the fire, covered closely; salt and pepper. When the meat is done pour over the dressing. For a large joint it takes a bottle of catsup and half a bottle of Worcester.[1079]

MINCE MEAT

☛ One pound of lean beef boiled and run through the meat grinder with a pound of apples, three-fourths of a pound of beef suet. Cut fine one pound each of raisins and citron, one pound currants, three-fourths of a pound butter, two pounds of sugar. Mix all together, put in a boiler, cover with water or the water the meat was boiled in and boil until the apples are cooked. Remove, and when nearly cold add three grated nutmegs and a quart of liquor; part rum flavors nicely.[1080]

MINCE MEAT FOR PIES

☛ 4 pounds of fresh tongue,
3 pounds of suet,
8 pounds of chopped apples,
3 pounds of currants,
4 pounds of seeded raisins,
6 pounds of white sugar,
2 pounds of citron, cut in small pieces,
4 lemons, grated rind and juice,
1 ounce of cinnamon,
¼ ounce of cloves,
¼ ounce of allspice,
4 nutmegs, grated,
1 quart of Madeira wine,
1 pint of cider,
1 quart of brandy or good whisky.

Boil the tongue in salted water until tender, and when cold, chop fine. Remove every particle of membrane from the suet and chop it fine, and mix with the tongue with enough salt to remove the fresh taste. To this, add the apples, sugar, fruit, spices and other ingredients. Mix all together and cover close. If too dry when ready for use, moisten with a little sweet cider.[1081]

PORK TENDERLOINS

☛ Tenderloins should be sliced crosswise and flattened, then fried or broiled, seasoned with salt and pepper. If desired, when done remove to platter and make a gravy by dredging a little flour into the hot fat; if not enough add a little butter, stir until browned, and add a little milk or cream, stir until it boils and pour over the dish.[1082]

BROILED BEEFSTEAK

☛ Should not be broiled until a few minutes before meal time: First, have the gridiron perfectly hot, then lay the steak on the iron while hot, the iron being over hot coals. Let the steak be on the iron about two minutes the first time you lay it on the iron, turning it over about once. In a minute remove from iron to a platter or pan and stick it through and through with a fork, so as to let the blood run out. Then place the steak back on the hot iron, turning it over as before; then take off iron, salt and pepper it and baste with butter; then lay it back on gridiron, turning it over for about two minutes; then lay in a dish, dress with butter and send to the table. A steak an inch and one-half thick may require twelve minutes to broil, turning it over every three minutes. A steak broiled in this style is very sweet and nice.[1083]

HUNTERS' BEEF
☛ Select a fine fat round weighing about twenty-five pounds, take three ounces saltpetre, one ounce of cloves, half an ounce of allspice, a large nutmeg, and a quart of salt; pound them all together very fine, take the bone out, rub it well with this mixture on both sides, put some of it at the bottom of a tub just large enough to hold the beef, lay it in and strew the remainder on the top, rub it well every day for two weeks, and spread the mixture over it; at the end of this time, wash the beef, bind it with tape, to keep it round and compact, filling the hole where the bone was with a piece of fat, lay it in a pan of convenient size, strew a little suet over the top, and pour on it a pint of water, cover the pan with a coarse crust and a thick paper over that, it will take five hours baking; when cold take off the tape. It is a delicious relish at twelve o'clock, or for supper, eaten with vinegar, mustard, oil, or salad. Skim the grease from the gravy and bottle it; it makes an excellent seasoning for any made dish.[1084]

ROAST LEG OF MUTTON
☛ Wash the meat nicely, and put it before the fire; baste it every 15 minutes with a little lard until the gravy is rich; then baste it with the gravy; turn the meat constantly, so that it will be done evenly through. If the meat is put in the oven, put a cupful of water in the dripping-pan, first baste with a little lard, and then with the gravy, and dredge the meat with flour. It will take 3 hours to cook. Before putting in the meat, sprinkle it with both salt and pepper.[1085]

Three kinds of mutton chops, L-R: a) English; b) French; c) boned and rolled.

MUTTON HASH
☛ Take the fat and lean of cold boiled mutton, and mince it fine; extract the gravy from the bones by stewing them in a little water; strain the liquid into a clean pan, put the mince into it, and if you have any cold potatoes, or any other nice vegetable, which have been boiled with the mutton, mince them fine, and put them in with the hash; it is an excellent way to save vegetables and small pieces of meat, that might otherwise be thrown away. Add one or two minced onions, a spoonful of four, a little salt and pepper, if needed, and a glass of sweet cream;

simmer it a few minutes, stirring it all the time, and serve it with the gravy, upon toast or sliced biscuit.[1086]

TO COOK A LAMB
☞ Roast the hind quarter, or if the lamb is small, roast the hind and fore quarters together without dividing them, that is, cut it down the back in two parts. It takes about an hour to roast lamb, and an hour and a half to boil it. If boiled, tie it up in a cloth, and pour cold water over it, and keep the pot tightly covered.[1087]

BAKED LAMB
☞ Cut the shank bone from a hind-quarter, separate the joints of the loin, lay it in a pan with the kidney uppermost, sprinkle some pepper and salt, add a few cloves of garlic, a pint of water and a dozen large ripe tomatoes with the skins taken off, bake it but do not let it be burnt, thicken the gravy with a little butter and brown flour.[1088]

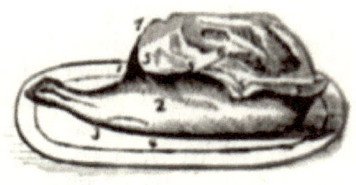

Leg of mutton showing the best cuts.

LAMB CHOPS
☞ The chops should be trimmed nicely and peppered well and rolled in butter. Broil nicely on both sides over clear fire. When done, put butter, pepper, and salt over them. Cover the ends with little white fluted papers and serve on dish with peas.[1089]

SADDLE OF MUTTON
☞ Wash it in soda water. Wipe dry, and then rub with soda, brown sugar, cayenne pepper, and salt. Grate a nutmeg over it. Make a dressing of
- Bread-crumbs,
- Brown sugar,
- Chopped celery,
- Tablespoon of butter,
- Salt and pepper,
- Teaspoon of powdered allspice.

Cook from 4 to 5 hours, according to size. Make a gravy of
- 1 pint of brown flour,
- 1 tumbler of brown sugar,
- 2 lemons,
- 1 teaspoon of allspice,
- 1 nutmeg,
- 1 tumbler of jelly,
- ½ teacup of butter,

Chopped celery,
Salt and pepper.[1090]

MUTTON CUTLETS
☞ Take the cutlets from a loin of mutton; beat them slightly; cover 2 cutlets with the yolks of 2 eggs well beaten, 1 pint of grated bread crumbs, mixed with thyme, parsley, nutmeg, salt, pepper, a little lemon peel, and roll the cutlets in it; fry them in butter, having tied them up. Take them out, and add to the butter they were fried in, a little water, some anchovy or catsup, and 2 spoonfuls of claret wine. When the gravy is done, pour it over the cutlets, and serve.[1091]

Tension chopping knife.

MUTTON CHOPS
☞ Cut the rack into chops with one bone in each, broil them, and when dished, pour over them a gravy made with two large spoonful of boiling water, one of mushroom catsup, a small spoonful of butter and some salt, stir it till the butter is melted, and garnish with horse-radish scraped.[1092]

ROAST OPOSSUM AND SWEET POTATOES
☞ 1 opossum.
1 dozen sweet potatoes.
Salt.
Black pepper.
Dress and place opossum (whole) in large pan with one and one-half gallons cold water; boil until tender. Drain and place in covered roaster—Surround with sweet potatoes (which have previously been peeled and boiled). Season with salt and pepper to taste. Put roaster in oven until both potatoes and possum are crisp and brown.[1093]

MEAT BALLS
☞ Chop the meat as fine as for sausage, then mix in some bread crumbs, 1 egg, and seasoning. Make up into balls, wash with beaten egg, roll in bread crumbs, and fry. Make a gravy of meat stock, and flavor with catsup. Good hot or cold.[1094]

IRISH STEW
☞ Cut the neck of mutton into pieces two and one half or three inches square. Put them into a saucepan with one tablespoonful of butter, and let them brown; stir frequently so they do not burn. When browned add enough water to cover them well, and two or three onions cut into pieces. Cover closely and let simmer two hours. Then add more water if necessary, some parboiled potatoes cut in two, and a few slices of

carrot, salt, and pepper to taste; cover and let cook one hour more. A teaspoonful of Worcestershire sauce is an improvement. The gravy must be quite thick, so too much water must not be used. The potatoes should be very soft, but not broken.[1095]

PORK CHOPS

☛ Should be broiled in the same way as the beefsteak recipe above, except that about eight to ten minutes should broil them, as pork must be well done.[1096]

CORNED SHOAT

☛ Shoat is the name given to very small, young hogs, for no other purpose than to distinguish their size, from pigs, or pork of a large size, they being of an intermediate size. When you merely wish to corn shoat, rub a very little saltpetre over it, with enough common salt to keep it from spoiling. Put it in a tub, cover it securely from flies, and keep it in as cool a place as possible. In extreme cold weather, it should be in salt for at least ten days, but in very warm weather, forty-eight hours will be long enough. Corned shoat should always be boiled with whatever vegetable it is to accompany.[1097]

Sirloin beef.

BRUNSWICK STEW

☛ Get a piece of stew meat free from bone, cut in small pieces, put on to cook about three hours before wanted. After cooking one hour add an onion cut fine, two Irish potatoes cut small, two tomatoes cut small after peeling or half a can, pod of red pepper, salt, and an hour before done put in one or two ears of corn cut from the cob.[1098]

HAMBURGER

☛ Use one pound from the round or the ends of steak. Put through a meat grinder or chop very fine. To it add:
   1 tablespoonful of onion juice.
   ¼ teaspoonful of pepper.
   1 beaten egg.
   1 teaspoonful of salt.
   Form into flat cakes, dredge with flour and saute in a little hot butter or drippings. Brown well on both sides. Remove to a hot platter, stir into the hot fat left in the frying pan one tablespoonful of butter. When brown, stir slowly into it one cup of stock or hot water. Season to taste with pepper and salt and add a few mushrooms or peas, or cubes of carrot that have first been cooked. Heat through and pour around the steaks.[1099] [Editor's note: Our Southern ancestors commonly referred to what we now call a hamburger as a "hamburger steak," or a "hamburg

steak"—the latter which was the original title of this recipe. Additionally, the hamburger bun was not invented until around 1916, which is why it does not appear in this 1903 recipe. L.S.]

BROILED STEAK
☞ Get a thick sirloin or Porterhouse steak, cut off the outer edge which is a tough skin; have a pan hot and lay it on it; turn often. When done lay it on a warm dish; put over a little salt and pepper and bits of cold butter. Set where it will keep warm until ready to serve.[1100]

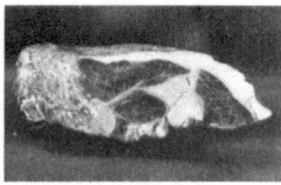
Porterhouse steak.

BEEFSTEAK WITH ONIONS
☞ Prepare a nice steak, salt, pepper and roll in flour; fry in hot lard. Take the steak from pan when done. Add to the gravy an onion chopped fine, salt, pepper and water enough to make a good gravy; pour in pan. When the onions are done put back the steak and let get hot and serve.[1101]

VENISON
☞ Put the venison to bake. Make a dressing of bread-crumbs highly seasoned with salt and pepper. When the meat is half done, turn it over and cut on either side places 2½ inches long, which fill with the dressing. Pour over the meat ½ cup of catsup. Take ½ cup black molasses, 1 tablespoon all-spice, and 1 tablespoon brown sugar. Put this too over the meat. Then crumble the light bread over. Baste often, for it burns easily. Just before removing from the fire put bits of currant jelly here and there.[1102]

ROAST VENISON
☞ First stuff the meat before roasting; make stuffing of bread crumbs browned; season stuffing with butter, salt, onions (grated), pork or ham chopped fine. When it is put into the oven, baste well with butter or lard, and while cooking notice and continue to baste until done. Two hours are sufficient, with a hot fire, to cook this roast. To make your gravy, brown a tablespoonful of flour in your pan from which you take the roast, add a little water, stir with spoon slowly until well done. You can make your gravy thick by the use of a very little water. If you do not like onions, use a little green or dry thyme.[1103]

BROILED VENISON
☞ Take nicely cut steaks and broil over hot coals. Remove and rub with butter. Broil a few minutes longer and place on a hot dish. Melt currant jelly and season with wine. Add a little more butter to hot steaks and pour wine and jelly over. Omit jelly and wine and serve as you would beefsteak, and serve with thin slices of lemon.[1104]

FROGS

☞ Frogs may be broiled, or made into a fricassee seasoned with tomato catsup.

The hind legs alone are eaten, and are a great delicacy [see following recipe].[1105]

FRIED FROGS' LEGS

☞ Boil in salt water for 3 minutes. Beat 2 eggs, 1 cup of milk, and salt and pepper, and dip first in egg, then in cracker-dust.

Put in frying-basket. Dip in skillet of boiling lard and fry rich brown and serve at once.[1106]

FRIED PIGS' FEET

☞ Mix well-beaten eggs with salt and pepper and dip the pigs' feet in it, then in the bread-crumbs, and let the egg dry.

Fry in skillet of hot lard till a rich brown.[1107]

CONFEDERATE HAMBURG STEAK

☞ 2 pounds lean meat,
2 teaspoons salt,
1 teaspoon pepper,
1 tablespoon onion juice.

Run the meat through a meat-chopper twice and add the seasoning and shape like a steak and broil. Serve hot with butter.

To get onion juice: Peel an onion and cut in pieces and squeeze through lemon squeezer.[1108]

MEAT POT PIE

☞ Cut veal, chicken, or beef into pieces; put them with strips of pork into boiling water and cook until tender; season with salt, pepper, and butter. There should be enough liquid to make a generous amount of gravy.

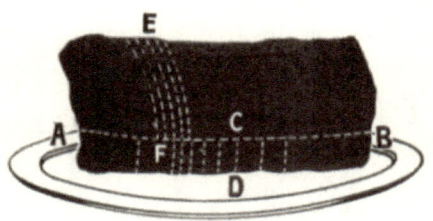
Breast of veal, with carving instructions.

When the stew is ready cook the dumplings, and place them on the same dish around the stew.

If suet dumplings are used, they must be placed in the pot as soon as it boils in order to cook them a sufficient length of time.

It is better to cook either kind of dumplings in a separate pot with plenty of water, and not remove them until the stew is dished and ready to be sent to the table.[1109]

CORNED BEEF HASH

☞ Take boiled corned beef and chop it very fine, four hot boiled Irish potatoes to one pound of beef, mash potatoes in the beef while hot, one slice of onion chopped with meat, half a teaspoonful of mustard mixed, two sprigs of parsley; then make into pones like a small loaf of bread, and bake brown. Season with black pepper to taste.[1110]

The Dover meat broiler.

BEEFSTEAK AND KIDNEY

☞ Cut your meat in pieces the size to eat. Use one kidney to two pounds of steak. Pour over a little boiling water, cover closely and cook two hours very slowly. About fifteen minutes before it is done put in an onion cut small, salt and pepper to season; thicken with a little flour. Pour the stew in a pan with a cup in center to hold up the crust. Make a rich pastry to put over the top and bake a nice brown.[1111]

BEEF KIDNEYS

☞ Kidney sliced thin will be tender after sauteeing in butter and then heating in a sauce. If boiled they will be so tough you can't eat them. Veal or lamb kidneys are best.[1112]

ROAST BEEF

☞ Should be well cooked outside and rare on the inside. The oven should bake on bottom and top. If it gets too hot on either top or bottom, shut the damper slightly off. A five-pound roast should cook in half an hour, and a ten-pound one in one hour.

Season roast with salt and pepper before putting it to cook, baste it with lard or butter before putting in stove, and while cooking baste with the juice that comes out of the meat every two or three minutes until done.[1113]

ROAST LAMB

☞ Prepare in the same way as the roast beef above, except the lamb should be well done. In a hot oven, one hour is necessary to cook the lamb. Mint sauce for roast lamb: Chop tender mint very fine, put cold water or vinegar, one tablespoonful of vinegar to three of water, and a little sugar according to taste.[1114]

ROAST SPARE-RIB

☞ Trim the ragged ends of a spare-rib neatly, crack the ribs across the middle, rub with salt and sprinkle with pepper. Fold it over, stuff with a turkey dressing, sew up tightly, place in dripping pan with a pint of water, baste frequently, turning it once or twice so as to bake both sides a rich brown.[1115]

IRISH MUTTON STEW

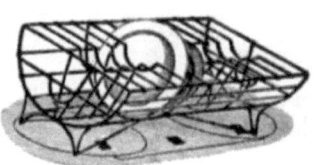

Dish warmer.

☛ Is made by cutting a loin of mutton into chops; put them in water and let stew for half an hour. Stir a cup of rich milk or cream in 12 Irish potatoes that have been boiled, peeled, and mashed while hot; put half the potatoes in a deep dish, and then put in the chops, and then the rest of the potatoes. Put them in the oven, and bake them a light brown. When ready to serve, pour over them a gravy made of the water in which the chops were stewed. Season it with pepper and salt, and an onion; let it stew for 20 minutes, and then thicken it with 1 tablespoon of butter rolled in 1 tablespoon of flour.[1116]

HAM OMELET

☛ 1½ tablespoons corn starch.
1 cup milk.
1 tablespoon butter.
3 eggs.
½ cup minced ham.

Stir corn starch in the milk, add beaten eggs and ham. Beat all together. Melt butter in omelet pan and cook. Serve hot.[1117]

FRIED LIVER AND BACON

☛ The bacon should be kept cold until ready to cook; then slices should be as thin as shavings. Cut the liver in slices quarter of an inch thick. If calf liver, simply wash in cold water; if beef liver, it should stand twenty minutes in cold water; then pour off, cover with boiling water, then drain and season with boiling water. Put the slices of bacon in a hot frying pan and turn constantly until crisp; then take up and keep hot. Reduce the heat under the frying pan, as rapid cooking ruins and hardens liver. Put the liver in the frying pan, cook eight minutes, turning frequently. Arrange the liver in center of a dish and garnish with the bacon.[1118]

TO BOIL A HAM

☛ Wash and scrape your ham, put it on in a pot, cover with cold water. Merely let it simmer three hours closely covered.[1119]

SHOAT STEAKS

☛ Cut as large steaks from the hindquarter as you can get, having first removed the skin; beat them very smooth, and broil them on a gridiron over a bed of clear coals. Turn them over occasionally till they are well done. They require a longer time to broil than beef steaks. As soon as they are done, place them in a dish, and season them immediately with salt and pepper, and pour over them a rich gravy, made of the skins and trimmings of meat, butter, flour and grated horseradish.[1120]

KENTUCKY BAKED HAM

☛ Take a good magnolia ham 1 or 2 years old and let it soak 36 hours. Make a stiff dough of flour and water and envelop the ham and put in a baking-pan. Add enough water to keep from sticking.

Baste frequently and cook till thoroughly done, or till the hock can be removed 5 or 6 hours.

When done, skin it and make an icing of brown sugar and yolk of 1 egg, and cover top and grate bread-crumbs over. Put in oven and brown.[1121]

SUGAR-CURED HAMS

☛ Let the hams lie in dry salt for 4 weeks after the killing. Then hang them up in the smoke-house and smoke them with dry hickory chips till they are a pretty light brown. Then rub them thoroughly with a pomatum made of New Orleans molasses, black and red pepper, using about 3 times as much black pepper as red. Mix the molasses and pepper in a large dish-pan, and if they do not mix easily, warm them by setting the pan on the stove.

When it is well mixed, have a man hold the ham by the hock with one hand, and with the other rub the mixture well into the ham on both sides. Make good strong sacks and tie each ham and hang up with the hock down, as the ingredients will be absorbed more readily.

They will be ready for use in about 8 or 10 months. Hams a year old are better than older hams, as they get too dry and strong when kept too long. In cooking the ham a handful of cloves dropped in the water while boiling gives it a rich flavor.[1122]

HAM PIE

☛ Having a fine young fowl cleaned and cut up in the usual manner, season it with salt and pepper, and stew it till nearly done in a small quantity of water. Cut some thin small slices from a boiled ham, and season them with pepper and mace.

Ham boiler.

Roll out a thick crust of standing or dripping paste; line the bottom and sides of a deep dish with it; roll out another sheet of the paste, cut it into small squares, and fill the dish with the slices of ham, fowl and dumplings, put in alternately; then put in the liquor in which the fowl was stewed, with four ounces of butter rolled in flour and broken up.

Put a paste over the top, ornament it round the edge with scalloped or crimped leaves of the same, and bake it in a moderate oven: it will not require but a short time to bake.[1123]

BOILED HAM

☞ Soak the ham overnight, and put it into cold water and let it cook slowly, very slowly, for four or five hours in a covered vessel. Skim it, leaving a small piece upon the knuckle, which carve handsomely, and serve with a paper frill tied around the knuckle-bone, or some fine bunches of curled parsley. If the ham is more than a year old, soak it well, and boil it for six or seven hours—changing the water three or four times.[1124]

DEVILED HAM

☞ To devil cold boiled ham, cut in slices one-third of an inch thick; season with cayenne pepper, and dip in mustard dressing. Broil a few minutes and serve.[1125]

FRENCH CHOPS

☞ Have the chops of medium thickness, scrape the bone; to be thoroughly cooked, put in a very hot oven for eight or ten minutes. Remove; egg and bread crumb them and fry in Wesson oil, not too hot or they will burn. Serve with a small spoonful of thick tomato sauce in center. Put a paper frill on the bone.[1126]

SPICED HAM

☞ Wash a ten pound ham in cold water. Put in a large boiler, and nearly fill with water; add two blades of mace, a dozen cloves, half a dozen pepper corns and a bay leaf. Set over a slow fire, let heat gradually; let simmer for an hour and a half, then boil gently, fifteen minutes to every pound. When done, let cool in the water in which it was boiled. Take up and skin. Brush over the fat with beaten egg, sprinkle with bread crumbs in which is mixed a tablespoonful of brown, or white sugar. Set in moderate oven to brown; baste with one pint of vinegar, in which is a tablespoonful of French mustard, a teaspoonful each of extract of celery, cloves and ginger. When brown, take up, lay on flat dish, stick whole cloves over thickly; set away twenty-four hours before using.[1127]

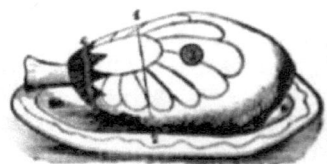

Ham, with diagram overlaid showing the three ways it can be carved.

MEAT CAKES

☞ Take any cold meat you may have, even if it is of different kinds, remove gristle and skin and chop fine, if dry beat an egg, add some water, and moisten your meat. If the meat is dry, add some butter. Salt and pepper to season. Make into rolls, balls or cakes; roll them in bread or cracker crumbs and fry in deep fat. Drain on paper.

Roast beef, lamb or mutton must not have a particle of salt or pepper put on it when put to roast, and if the skin is removed lamb and mutton is relieved of its strong taste.[1128]

BROILED LIVER

☛ Slice the liver. Let it soak in hot water a few minutes to draw out the blood. Dry it, rub it with butter, and broil five to eight minutes, turning it constantly. It should not be cooked until dry. When done, spread it with butter, and serve at once.[1129]

ROAST PIG

☛ Examine when it comes from the butcher and see that it is completely cleaned. The pig should be roasted the same way you would a turkey well done. For the stuffing take a loaf and one-half of baker's bread cut thin, fry the bread in butter or lard and mash it well; season it with salt and pepper according to taste, using a little red pepper. Then stuff the pig putting an apple in its mouth. Put it in the pan and baste with lard, then put it to roast, and while it is cooking keep basting it every five or ten minutes until it is cooked; you can tell when it is perfectly done by a fork passing through it easily. To make the gravy for the pig—After it is cooked, take about a tablespoonful of flour and put it in the pan where you cooked your roast and brown well on the stove, then add a little water; stir till it commences to get thick. A little onion in your stuffing is good.[1130]

Forequarter lamb.

SALT PORK

☛ Cut as many slices of pork as may be needed; if for breakfast, the night previous, and soak over night in a pint of milk and water, about one-half milk, either skimmed milk, sour milk or butter-milk; rinse till the water is clear, and roll in corn-meal and fry. It is quite as nice as fresh pork.[1131]

MEXICAN CHILE CON CARNE

☛ Can of tomatoes, 1 can red kidney beans. 1 stalk celery, 1 bay leaf, 1 onion, 1 clove of garlic, 1 pound beef, ¼ pound bacon, 1 teaspoon chili and 1 green pepper, salt. Cut beef and bacon in half-inch squares, fry until brown, in plenty of hot grease. Stew tomatoes, celery, onions, garlic, bay leaves until thoroughly cooked, strain and add balance of materials named in recipe. Cook altogether 20 or 30 minutes.[1132]

HOW TO MAKE COUNTRY PORK SAUSAGES

☛ Six pounds of lean fresh pork, three pounds of chine fat, three tablespoonfuls of salt, one and one-half tablespoonfuls of black pepper and four tablespoonfuls of pounded and sifted sage. Grind with a sausage grinder or a meat chopper the lean and fat pork finely, mix the seasoning in with the hands, taste to see that it has the right flavor, then make into flat balls or make long, narrow bags of stout muslin. Fill these with the meat and hang in a cold dark room. They can be used at once.[1133]

PORK ROAST

☛ The hind quarter of the hog makes the nicest roast, though the middling, when well cooked, is very good. It all depends on the cooking. With a sharp knife cut or score the ham in slices, just through the skin, half an inch apart. This makes it easier to carve and better absorbs the seasoning, when basting. Put into a roasting pan if convenient, if not, in an ordinary baking pan; pour in a quart of water, with a heaping tablespoonful of salt and as much cayenne pepper as is liked; now if in an ordinary pan, turn over it another pan, lifting to baste, every fifteen minutes; allow twenty minutes to the pound; when done, remove the cover and let it brown. Serve with hot tomato catsup, or Worcester sauce. Suspend the roast over the pan and steam, if preferred, basting as directed. The latter is the old-fashioned way.[1134]

Meat chopper.

BACON

☛ Cut bacon very thin. Lay the slices on a hot frying-pan. When clear turn them over. Tip the pan a little, so the fat will run to one side. If not wanted crisp and dry, turn the slices before they look clear, and remove before all the fat is tried out.[1135]

BAKED HASH

☛ Chop fine any cold meat you may have. Add to it about one-third as much bread crumbs, a tablespoonful of butter, some chopped onion, salt and pepper. Mix well, put in a pan, cover with milk. Let soak until bread is soft. Cover with bread crumbs and bits of butter and bake a nice brown.[1136]

DRIED LIVER

☛ Make a brine of salt and water that will bear an egg; let the liver remain in it for 3 weeks; then hang it up to dry for 6 weeks, in a dry cupboard. This is excellent for relish.[1137]

PORK AND BEANS

☛ Take 1 quart of white beans; wash and pick out the imperfect ones. Let the beans soak for 1 hour, in cold water; then put them to boil in water enough to cover them. When they come to a boil, pour off the water, and add fresh cold water; let them boil until nearly done; then pour off the water and put them in a deep pan. Have ready 1 pound of pickled pork, that has been soaked in cold water for 3 hours, and then stewed until tender. First gash the pork, and then put it in the dish with the beans; season with pepper and salt, and pour over the top 1 pint of the water that the meat was stewed in. Bake until the beans are soft and the meat is done.[1138]

A MEXICAN DISH

☛ Take a deep earthenware dish (always be sure to use earthenware, as even the finest metal imparts a poor flavor to the tomato), pour into it a cup of cream; having cut very thin slices—they must be cut as thin as wafers—of egg plant, salt them liberally and line the dish with them; next slice two large ripe tomatoes, and place a layer of these on the egg plant; next a layer of macaroni; sprinkle this with half a dozen lumps of good cheese about the size of a thimble; as many of sweet fresh butter; pepper it thickly; again cover this with more slices of tomato, and a top layer of egg plant and be sure that both of these latter are well salted and peppered. Now set your dish in a slow oven, let it cook gently for one hour and twenty minutes; take it out; pin it in a fringed napkin—for it must be served in the dish in which it has been cooked, and with a joint of beef, with roast lamb or veal, it will be found indeed a royal tasting compound.[1139]

The American broiler.

ROAST VEAL

☛ Use crackers for your stuffing. Slice an opening in the veal in five or six different places, and fill each one with the stuffing. Season the stuffing with salt, pepper, butter, and a little sage. You can tell when it is done by a fork passing through easily. Baste the roast while cooking with the essence that comes from the meat. Baste it with lard or butter when first put to cook. Use flour for making gravy, same as directed in other roasts.[1140]

ROAST VEAL FILLET

☛ Remove the bone, roll up the fat flap, confine it with skewers, and if practicable, let it lie in milk and water for an hour or two, turning it over several times. Fill the space whence the bone was taken with fresh sausage meat, grated ham, seasoned with pepper, sage and chopped parsley, or minced oysters, seasoned with pepper and nutmeg, and mixed with a small proportion of bread crumbs, butter and chopped parsley. Make numerous small, but deep incisions in the outside of the fillet, and fill them also with some of the stuffing. (A very nice filling is

Fillet of veal.

slips of ham, about half an inch wide, and long enough to put one end to the bottom of the incision, while the other end will be at least an inch above the surface of the fillet, and then confine the ends down with little skewers.) Roast it as directed, covering it with paper, to preserve the sat, and prevent its getting too brown, and baste it freely at the last with butter. When it is thoroughly done, and handsomely frothed, serve it up; garnish with sliced lemon, or lumps of fruit jelly, and accompany it with boiled ham, mashed potatoes, or boiled rice, and raw cucumbers, raw tomatoes, or cold slaugh. For gravy, use that of the dripping-pan; if it is too rich, skim it, and pour in a little boiling water, if not rich enough, add some melted butter; season it with pepper, brown flour, or grated bread and chopped parsley, or currant jelly and red wine, either is good.[1141]

VEAL CHOPS

☛ Cut veal chops about an inch thick; beat them flat with a rolling-pin, put them in a pan, pour boiling water over them, and set them over the fire for 5 minutes; then take them up and wipe them dry; mix a tablespoon of salt and a teaspoon of pepper for each pound of meat; rub each chop over with this, then dip them, first into beaten egg, then into rolled crackers as much as they will take up; then finish by frying in hot lard or beef dripping; or broil them.

For the broil have some sweet butter on a steak dish; broil the chops until well done, over a bright clear fire of coals; (let them do gently that they may be well done,) then take them on to the butter, turn them carefully once or twice in it, and serve. Or dip the chops into a batter, made of 1 egg beaten with ½ a tea-cup of milk, and as much wheat flour as may be necessary.

Or simply dip the chops without parboiling into wheat flour; make some lard or beef fat hot in a frying-pan; lay the chops in, and when one side is a fine delicate brown, turn the other. When all are done, take them up, put a very little hot water into the pan, then put it in the dish with the chops.[1142]

BROILED HAM AND EGGS

☛ Cut the ham very thin. If very salty, place it in boiling water for a few minutes. Then dry and broil it over hot coals for three or four minutes. Put a few pieces of salt pork into a frying pan. When tried out, add the eggs, one at a time, from a saucer. Baste the top of the eggs with fat from the pan. Let them brown a little on the edges, but not blacken, and serve them around the slices of ham. Boiled ham may be broiled. If so, cut it into thin, small pieces, and after broiling it, place on each piece a fried egg.[1143]

FRIED SALT PORK

☞ Cut in rather thin slices, and freshen by letting lie an hour or two in cold water or milk and water, roll in flour and fry till crisp (if in a hurry, pour boiling water on the slices, let stand a few minutes, drain, roll in flour and fry as before); drain off most of the grease from frying-pan, stir in while hot one or two table-spoons of flour, about half a pint new milk, a little pepper, and salt if not salt enough already from the meat; let boil and pour into gravy dish. This makes a nice white gravy when properly made.[1144]

VEAL CUTLETS

☞ If it is a large steak, take the yolks of 3 eggs, and after beating it for a short time, roll it in the yolks, and then in cracker dust. Put in the skillet 1 large tablespoon of lard; when it is boiling hot, put in the steak and let it fry a light brown; turn it so as to fry equally on both sides. Cut up and fry in one side of the skillet 2 onions, be careful not to let them burn; season with pepper, salt, and pour enough water into the skillet to cover the steak; cover it tight, and set it back on the stove to stew slowly for 1½ hours; the steam cooks it and makes the meat tender. Garnish the dish with parsley, and serve.[1145]

VEAL PIE

☞ Cut some small steaks from the leg, fillet or loin of a fresh veal, beat them tender, and season them with salt, pepper and nutmeg: stew the bones and trimmings of the veal in a small quantity of water, to extract the gravy; strain it into a sauce-pan, and stew the steaks in it till nearly done, adding a large lump of butter, rolled in flour. Line the bottom and sides of a deep dish with lard or dripping paste, and roll out another sheet for the top or lid, and one for dumplings, which should be cut into small squares and sprinkled with flour. Cut some small slices of boiled ham, and put them with the squares of paste and steaks in the dish, in alternate layers; pour in the liquor or gravy, and if it is not sufficiently rich, put in some bits of butter; put on the lid of paste, notching or girdling, it neatly round the edge, stick a bunch of paste leaves and flowers in the centre of the pie, and bake it in a moderate oven till a light brown.[1146]

TO ROAST BEEF

☞ Place the clean cut side of the meat upon a smoking hot pan. Press it close to the pan until seared and slightly brown. Reverse it and let the opposite side brown; then put it at once into the oven. The heat should be the same as for bread. Leave it undisturbed until cooked. If the oven is not too hot it will require no basting, but keep up a gentle

Beef sirloin.

sputtering in the pan. If on opening the door no sputtering is heard, more heat s required; or, if a smoke is discernable, decrease the heat. After it has been seared you must allow fifteen minutes for each inch in thickness. If a three inch roast, three-fourths of an hour will cook it rare. If you want it well cooked allow more time. After removing the roast from the pan pour off most of the grease and make the gravy from the glaze in pan. Season with salt and pepper, but put no salt on roast; it does not penetrate it, but makes it hard.

Serve with Mushroom Sauce: Cut a can of mushrooms in four pieces. Make a sauce of one-fourth of a cup each of flour and butter, little salt and pepper, two cups of stock, the mushrooms. Let cook five minutes; remove and add one tablespoonful of lemon juice.[1147]

CONFEDERATE ROAST BEEF

☞ Select choice fat rib roast; have bones removed; cut the edges to prevent it drawing up, and skewer into a round shape. When the oven is very hot place the meat on rack in a dripping pan. When the meat browns pour in a cup of hot water and dredge with flour, turning and adding flour when necessary. Reduce heat and finish cooking; if a gas stove, turn out one burner.[1148]

Rolled rib roast with potatoes.

GRAVY

☞ Make a gravy by browning a little flour in the drippings, and add some boiling water; season with salt, pepper and kitchen bouquet.[1149]

DUTCH PUDDING

☞ Boil the neck of the beef until perfectly tender, and the bones come out easily; take it up, on a tray, and pick it to pieces, just as you would souse meat; skim the grease off the liquor, and drain the liquor off; clean the vessel; return the meat and liquor; when it boils, thicken with sifted meal until like mush; cook till perfectly done; season with salt, pepper and sage; mold in pans, and slice and fry brown like sausage.[1150]

MISSISSIPPI SAUSAGE

☞ Eight lbs. lean tenderloin, 6 lbs. backbone fat, 4 teaspoons black pepper, 2 teaspoons salt, 1 teaspoon cayenne pepper, 7 tablespoons sage. Mix well after grinding.[1151]

WHITE PUDDING

☞ To one part of beef suet, chopped very fine, add two parts of flour; mix well, and season highly with salt and black pepper. This mixture may then either be put in skins or tied in strong cloth (enough for a dish in one cloth), allowing room to swell. It must then be put in boiling water, and boiled very vigorously for some time-perhaps an hour, or until the skins are tender when pricked with a fork. This pudding will keep many months. For breakfast, cut off what seems to be a sufficient portion. If in skins, broil it; if in a cloth, turn it into a pie-pan, and heat it. It is only good when very hot.[1152]

TO BONE A TURKEY

☛ Put the turkey on a cloth, after it is dressed. Cut the skin down the back with a sharp knife, dissecting to the wings and legs, and take out the bones carefully. Don't touch it with anything wet. Lay it open upon a cloth. Make rich forced meat of 1½ pounds of round of veal, and 2½ pounds of corned pork, grated cracker, and mix them together. Season them with butter, pepper, salt, mace, 1 onion and parsley. First stuff the legs, and the wings, and then the body, drawing it carefully into form, and sew it up, and tie carefully at both ends. Then tie closely in a cloth, and boil it. Have stock of calf's feet prepared, 3 quarts of it. Add to it 1 onion, 6 carrots, a bunch of celery, and 1 of parsley, cayenne pepper, salt, 5 tablespoons of vinegar, and 5 of white wine, whites of 4 eggs. Boil all together for an hour, and strain. Place the turkey breast downwards, and pour over it the jelly. When the turkey is cold, dip the dish in hot water, and turn it out.[1153]

Galantine of turkey under sauce, with truffles.

ROAST TURKEY

☛ First cleanse well and take the craw from the turkey. Make stuffing of light bread chopped fine, season with butter, pepper and salt; then stuff the body completely full, also where the craw was. Put in pan and baste with butter or lard, and put to roast. While cooking, keep basting it with the juice that comes from the turkey. When it is cooked take a tablespoonful of flour and brown it in the pan, then add a little water and stir for the gravy.[1154]

ROAST CHICKEN

☛ A roasted chicken may be stuffed or not. If stuffing is used it should only half fill the chicken. Truss it, or use skewers, doubling a cord across the back and around the ends of the skewers to hold them in place. A roasted or boiled chicken is not presentable, which has not been securely fastened into good shape before being cooked. Dredge the chicken with salt and pepper, and place it on slices of salt pork in a baking pan; add a very little water, and bake in hot oven, allowing fifteen minutes to the pound; baste frequently. White meat must be well cooked, but not dried. Fifteen minutes before it is done, rub it over the top and sides with butter, dredge it with flour, and replace it in the oven until it becomes a golden brown and looks crisp. Draw out the trussing cords, and garnish with parsley. Serve with it a giblet sauce. Do not use a tough chicken for roasting; one a year old is about right. A roasting chicken may be larded if desired.[1155]

CREAMED CHICKEN

☛ Boil a chicken until tender the usual way. When cold, or while hot, as you prefer, place the breast in the chafing dish in which a small lump of butter has melted and is just beginning to brown, heat thoroughly and add one cup of rich milk. Season, and when it comes to a boil, thicken slightly with flour rubbed until smooth in a little butter. As soon as it comes to a boil pour over squares of toast.[1156]

TO BOIL A TURKEY OR CHICKEN

☛ Clean the fowl, and prepare the same as for roasting; wrap or tie it up in a clean cloth, and put it in a pot deep enough to hold it; cover it with cold water, and let it boil slowly. Keep the pot tightly covered, and remove all scum that arises. When it is half done, turn it in the pot. When it has boiled for 2 hours, take it off, and cover the pot closely for half an hour, this will steam it, and make it white. This is the time for a turkey weighing about ten pounds. Serve with egg sauce. Use bread stuffing, if liked.[1137]

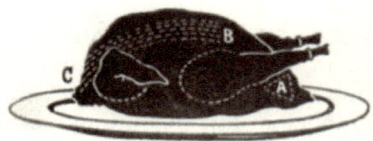

Turkey with carving instructions.

BEEFSTEAK WITH MUSHROOMS

☛ Buy Porter House steak cut at the hip bone one and a fourth inches thick. For roasts, three ribs from the short ribs. Broil your steak in the usual manner. Make a sauce of one tablespoonful each of flour and butter and the juice from the can of mushrooms. Season with a little thyme and cinnamon. Set the sauce off, put in the mushrooms, and pour over a broiled steak.[1158]

SCRAPPLE

☛ Clean a pig's head nicely and boil till meat leaves bones, and when cold remove grease and chop meat into small pieces. Heat the meat and liquor again, and stir corn meal in gradually till it is thick as mush. Season highly with pepper, salt, and sage. Mold in pans, and when cold slice thin, roll in meal, and fry in hot lard.[1159]

VEAL LOAF

☛ Get a pound of pork tenderloin; boil until done with a little salt in water; chop fine and add ten crackers rolled, four hard boiled eggs sliced, a teaspoonful of Worcester sauce, a little melted butter, a little cold ham chopped fine, nutmeg, salt and pepper to season. Make quite moist with milk. Make into a loaf and bake.[1160]

SPANISH FRIED STEAK

☛ Cut an onion very small and fry; remove; put in one or two potatoes cut small and fry brown; remove, beat and flour your steak, salt and pepper it, and fry. When done pour in a little water, put back the onion and tomato, let cook together. When brown remove to a dish. Sprinkle over fine cut parsley, pour the gravy around and serve.[1161]

HASH

☛ Use any cold meat you have chopped; cut fine an onion, fry until brown, sift in a little flour, let that brown. Now put in half a cup of water and the chopped meat, salt and pepper; let cook a short while and serve.[1162]

QUAILS

☛ When roasted, make nice toast, butter it nice and send quails to table on the toast. Do not forget to baste all game and fowls while cooking, so as to make them juicy. Make stuffing same as for chicken.[1163]

BROILED QUAILS

☛ Split them down the back. Broil over hot coals four minutes on each side. Baste them while broiling with a little butter. When they are done spread them with butter, salt, and pepper; place them on slices of slightly moistened toast, and stand them in the oven a few minutes to soak the butter.[1164]

Roast fowl.

CAMP STEW

☛ Take a hog or pig's head, cook in salted water until done and tender; take it up, cut in small pieces and return to the same water with some fine cut onion, Irish potatoes and tomatoes. When done season with Worcester sauce and Durkee's salad dressing. Thicken the gravy, if necessary, with flour.[1165]

POT ROAST

☛ Put a large spoonful of lard in a kettle. When hot put in your roast and let brown on all sides. Now a cup of boiling water, some fine cut onions and tomatoes, half a cup of vinegar, piece of stick cinnamon and some cloves, salt and pepper. Cook slowly until tender. Thicken the gravy with flour. Pour in some water if necessary.[1166]

DOMESTIC DUCK
☛ Bake or roast in the same manner you do a turkey, and have it well cooked. Make stuffing of bread, like that prepared for turkey, with salt, pepper, butter or lard. Baste while cooking.[1167]

ROAST DUCK
☛ When you have drawn the ducks, shred one onion and a few sage leaves, put them into the ducks with pepper and salt, spit and dust them with flour, and baste them with lard: if your fire be very hot, they will roast in twenty minutes; and the quicker they are roasted, the better they will taste. Just before you take them from the spit, dust them with flour and baste them. Get ready some gravy made of the gizzards and pinions, a large blade of mace, a few pepper corns, a spoonful of catsup, a teaspoonful of lemon pickle; strain it and pour it on the ducks, and send onion sauce in a boat.[1168]

STEWED DUCK
☛ Take one large fat duck, or two small ones; split each one into two, season them with salt and pepper, and stew them in a very little water with a few slices of ham, keeping the pan closely covered. At the last, add two or three minced onions, some flour, butter, cream and pepper. Serve the ducks warm, and pour the gravy round.[1169]

Boned birds in aspic.

WILD DUCK
☛ Should not be stuffed, but cleaned well and seasoned with pepper and salt, inside and outside, and put into a hot oven. Ten minutes will cook it.[1170]

ROASTED GROUSE
☛ Grouse, like all game, should not be too fresh. Wash them on the outside only, the same as you would for chicken. Put a little butter inside each bird and truss them into good shape. Roast them in a hot oven twenty-five to thirty minutes, basting them frequently with melted butter. Five minutes before removing them dredge them with flour. Boil the liver of the grouse, pound it with a little butter, pepper, and salt to a paste; spread it over hot buttered toast moistened with juice from the pan. Serve the grouse on the toast.[1171]

ROAST GOOSE

☛ Sprinkle with salt and pepper and put the goose in a roaster, and add water and baste frequently. Make a dressing of bread-crumbs, sage, butter, onion, salt and pepper, and mix together with an egg. Stuff the goose and cook for 2 hours. Make a gravy. Serve with apple-sauce.[1172]

GOOSE PIE

☛ Having a young, fat goose nicely cleaned, cut it into small pieces, rinse them in cold water, season them with salt and pepper, and stew them in a small quantity of water, with four ounces of butter, rolled in flour. Line a deep dish with a thick crust of standing or dripping paste. Peel and slice a fine smoked tongue, which has been boiled tender, and put it in the dish, in alternate layers, with the goose; add the gravy, and then put a paste over the top, ornamenting it handsomely round the edge with scalloped or crimped leaves of the paste, and bake it in an oven with moderate heat. A similar pie may be made of ducks.

Another way to make goose pie is to cut up, season and boil the goose as before directed; mix with it slices of cold boiled ham and boiled eggs, having them peeled, and each one cut in four, and baked in an oven, which is lined with a thick crust of lard, or dripping paste. Baked in this manner, you may have a greater quantity of gravy than you could possibly have if baked in a dish, of which the most of pie eaters are very fond.[1173]

MUTTON PIE

☛ A very good family pie is made with the remains of a cold leg, loin, or any other joint of mutton from which nice neat slices of rather lean meat can be cut. These should be put with a good seasoning, in alternate layers with thinly-sliced potatoes, into a pie-dish, commencing at the bottom with some of the meat, and finishing at the top with potatoes. Parsley, savory herbs, onion, or shallot, with a little mace, white pepper and salt may be used at discretion. A cupful of good gravy from the meat should be poured into the pie before the crust is put on. Suet is generally used for the crust.[1174]

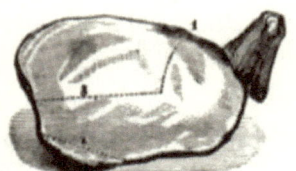

Shoulder of mutton.

MEAT PIE

☛ 1 cup diced cold meat.
1 teaspoon salt.
2 cups diced boiled potatoes.
½ teaspoon pepper.
1 can tomatoes.
2 tablespoons butter or stock.

Line sides only of a baking dish with good pie pastry. Beginning with meat at bottom, alternate with layers of meat, potatoes, tomatoes and seasoning to the top of the pan. Cover with pie crust, add enough hot water to cook thoroughly but without becoming dry. Bake until done about ¾ hour. It will make its own gravy. One or two onions may be added if desired.[1175]

SOUSE

☛ Take the head, feet and ears of a hog; remove the fat where there is too much, wash and scrape thoroughly. Soak over night; boil all to pieces; take out of the water, let cook, and remove all bone. Season with salt, pepper and sage, a teaspoonful each to a quart of meat. Place in a bowl or mold, to cool and jelly. It will be ready for use in ten hours. Serve cold with vinegar; or take from the vinegar, dip in egg, roll in bread crumbs and fry in boiling lard.[1176]

Skewers for meat and poultry.

LIVER CROQUETTES

☛ Made of lamb or veal liver. One pound of liver to a quarter of a pound of suet, part boil, chop both separately very fine; pick all strings out of suet, then add suet and liver together, a small piece of onion, grated, salt and pepper; season high. Beat one egg light and mix well with hand, roll in powdered cracker, fry in hot lard or butter, garnish dish with parsley and send to table.[1177]

ALICE'S MEAT IN INDIVIDUAL DISHES

☛ Chop cold meat rather fine. Make a white sauce of a tablespoonful each of flour and butter and one cup of milk; add and not cook too stiff one cup of meat. Put in a dish with bread crumbs and bits of butter over the top and brown in oven.[1178]

ALICE'S SCALLOPED MEAT

☛ Two cups of chopped meat, one cup of bread crumbs, half a cup of potatoes chopped fine, hot water enough to moisten, one teaspoonful of butter put over the top, salt and pepper. Sprinkle crumbs over and bake until brown.[1179]

MEAT SOUFFLE

☛ Make a smooth white sauce of two tablespoonfuls of butter, one heaping spoonful of flour. After it cooks add two-thirds of a cup of cold milk. Season with grated onion, chopped parsley, salt and pepper. While hot add the beaten yolks of two eggs, one cup of finely chopped cooked meat of any kind. Cook a moment. When cool fold in the whites of eggs beaten stiff. Bake in a buttered dish twenty minutes. Serve immediately with a sauce.[1180]

HASH FROM COLD MEAT

☛ Water and grease both spoil hash. Cold beef stock makes excellent hash. Remove skin and bone, cut the meat quite fine; cut some cooked potatoes coarser; wet with gravy or cream a little finely minced onion; then the meat and potatoes. Put in a frying pan and let brown. Fold as an omelet. Serve with apple sauce. Garnish with breakfast bacon.[1181]

Roast turkey ready for the carver.

HOW TO CORN BEEF

☛ 4 gallons of water,
5 pounds of salt,
2 ounces of saltpetre,
1 pounds of brown sugar.

Mix the above and boil 15 minutes, and skim well. The meat must have been rubbed well in salt and saltpetre, and packed for 3 days before. When mixture is cold, pour over meat and let it stand a week. This is excellent for tongues.[1182]

CORNED BEEF

☛ Should be cooked in plenty of cold water brought slowly to a boil; if very salt, the meat should be soaked over night; but if young and not too strongly brined this will not be necessary. It should be cooked sufficiently long to make tender, so that in a brisket or plate piece the bones may be readily removed.

Preserve the liquor in the pot, and if any of the meat remains after the first meal, return it and let it stand over night in the liquor so that it may absorb it.

If no meat remains to be returned to the liquor, the latter will make a good soup for next day's dinner if the beef was not too salt.[1183]

BOILED CORNED BEEF

☛ 1 piece of corned beef,
6 cloves (whole),
6 allspice (whole).

Soak for ½ hour in cold water. Then pour off and cover with fresh water. When it begins to boil, set back on range and add spices and let it simmer for 4 or 5 hours, skimming well. When done, put in small vessel. Put a plate on top and press down with heavy flat-iron. Let stand till next day.[1184]

CORN BEEF HASH

☛ Take cold corn beef, take out the gristle and little skinny pieces, chop fine, put in a round bottom kettle with little butter, let warm.

Take equal quantities of cold boiled potatoes chopped, mix with the meat, lifting up carefully with a fork to prevent being mushy, cover and let heat slowly. Season with salt and pepper. When hot serve.[1185]

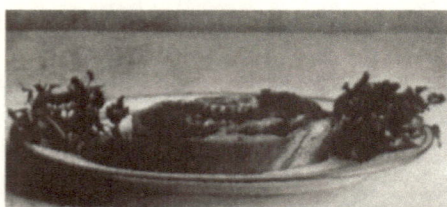
Tenderloin steak with watercress and lemon.

CHICKEN CROQUETTES

☛ Boil chicken very tender, pick to pieces, take all gristle out, then chop fine.

Beat two eggs for one chicken and mix into meat; season with pepper and salt; make into cakes oblong shaped; powder crackers and roll them into the powder, after dipping them into two eggs beaten moderately well. Then have your lard very hot, and fry just before sending them to the table.[1186]

RAGOUT OF BEEF

☛ Cut cold beef in very thin slices. Make this sauce: Put a tablespoonful of butter in a frying pan; when it browns add one tablespoonful of flour and mix well; now add one cup of hot water, let boil, season with Worcester sauce, one onion, one bay leaf, some tomato catsup. Put in the meat and simmer.

Put the meat in a baking pan, put over a little gravy, brown in oven. Dish and strain the gravy over it.[1187]

TOAD IN THE HOLE

☛ Mix one pint flour and one egg with milk enough to make a batter (like that for batter-cakes), and a little salt; grease dish well with butter, put in lamb chops, add a little water with pepper and salt, pour batter over it, and bake for one hour.[1188]

BOILED TRIPE

☛ Take it from the beef as soon as it is killed; empty it immediately of its contents, scrape and wash it clean, and let it lie in fresh water till next day; then scrape it again, wash it clean, soak it for twenty-four hours in weak brine; next day scrape it, and soak it again for twenty-four hours in water, with a handful of salt. By this time, if properly managed, it will be very white and nice. Cut it into several pieces, and boil it in a good quantity of water till nearly done, removing every particle of scum, and keeping the pot closely covered. It will take several hours to boil it tender: then put it into a stew-pan with some of the liquor in which it was boiled, and sweet milk, mixed in equal proportions; add a good lump of butter, rolled in flour, some black pepper, and several minced onions; stew them gently till all are well done, stir in a glass of sweet cream, and serve them together, putting the onions under the tripe and pouring on the gravy.[1189]

 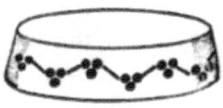

Forms made of rice and corn meal molded in tin basins and used to support various dishes.

PEPPER POT

☛ Boil two or three pounds of tripe, cut it in pieces, and put it on the fire with a knuckle of veal, and a sufficient quantity of water; part of a pod of pepper, a little spice, sweet herbs according to your taste, salt, and some dumplings; stew it till tender, and thicken the gravy with butter and flour.[1190]

MAMMY'S CHICKEN PATTIES

☛ One cup of cold diced chicken, two tablespoons of flour, one-half teaspoon of salt, cayenne pepper to taste, one cup of chicken stock.

Melt butter in sauce pan; stir in flour, add chicken stock, season and bring to boiling point. Add chicken and cook slowly for five minutes. Fill patty shells and serve at once.[1191]

SOUTHERN FRIED CHICKEN

☛ Dress a young chicken weighing 1½ to 2 pounds. Cut in pieces and wash in cold water. Drain and set in ice box or cool place from six to twelve hours. When ready to cook, salt and pepper to taste. Roll each piece of chicken in flour until covered nicely. Put in hot fat over moderate fire; turn once or twice until a golden brown. Place chicken on platter, drain off fat, leaving about two tablespoons. Into this sprinkle 1 tablespoons flour. Let brown, then add 1 cup of boiling water (with little milk added), stirring constantly. Cook 3 or 4 minutes, adding a little salt. Can be poured over chicken, but is usually put in a separate dish and served on rice cooked so each grain is separate.[1192]

FRIED CHICKEN 1

☛ Clean and cut up a nice fat chicken. Cover it for three hours with a mixture of lemon juice, olive oil, parsley, a bay leaf, salt and pepper. Now drain and dip each piece in egg batter and crumbs, or flour and fry a nice brown in deep fat. Have a sauce made of one cup of white stock, one cup of milk, the yolk of an egg and ten button mushrooms. Season and cook carefully and pour around the chicken. Add a little lemon juice and cut parsley to the sauce; if too thin, thicken with a little butter and flour rubbed together.[1193]

FRIED CHICKEN 2

☛ Wipe the chicken carefully, cut in pieces, rub over very little salt; then roll each piece in flour. Have lard in frying pan; when very hot lay in pieces and in a few minutes reduce the heat and cook slowly uncovered. After removing the chicken sift a little flour in the fat and let brown; add milk or water to the right consistency; season.[1194]

Frying-basket.

FRIED CHICKEN 3

☛ Nothing but a young, plump chicken will be good fried. The chicken should be killed several hours before using and kept in a cool place. Cut it up, and fifteen minutes before using lay it in salt and water, using a heaping teaspoonful of salt to a cup of water. Take out of the water and dry lightly. Have in a deep plate a cup of flour; dip each piece of chicken in this, being careful it is all well covered with flour. Fry in boiling lard enough to come up well on the edges of each piece. Do not move after it is placed in the lard until a nice brown, then quickly brown on the other side. Never crowd the chicken and fry quickly.[1195]

FRIED CHICKEN 4

☛ Cut the chicken up, separating every joint, and wash clean. Salt and pepper it, and roll into flour well. Have your fat very hot, and drop the pieces into it, and let them cook brown. The chicken is done when the fork passes easily into it. After the chicken is all cooked, leave a little of the hot fat in the skillet; then take a tablespoonful of dry flour and brown it in the fat, stirring it around, then pour water in and stir till the gravy is as thin as soup.[1196]

FRIED CHICKEN 5

☞ Prepare young chicken and sprinkle with salt and lay on ice 12 hours before cooking. Cut the chicken in pieces and dredge with flour and drop in hot boiling lard and butter equal parts salt and pepper, and cover tightly and cook rather slowly if it cooks too quickly it will burn. Cook both sides to a rich brown. Remove chicken and make a gravy by adding milk, flour, butter, salt, and pepper. Cook till thick, and serve in separate bowl.[1197]

FRIED CHICKEN 6

☞ Joint the chickens, and lay them in salt and water for 1 an hour; drain them, and wipe them perfectly dry with a coarse towel; sprinkle them with pepper and salt, and a little flour; put them in boiling lard, until they are of a light brown, being careful to turn them. Take them out, and put upon a dish; cover it and set near the fire; pour into the skillet a little water, and a cup of cream, stirring it briskly; garnish the chickens with parsley, and pour upon the gravy. Mush cut into thin slices and fried is an improvement, if added to the dish when served.[1198]

Frying kettle and basket.

FRIED CHICKEN 7

☞ Cut a tender chicken in pieces; dip the pieces in water; sprinkle them with salt and pepper, and roll them in flour; saute them in a tablespoonful of lard or butter, browning both sides; then remove and add to the pan a tablespoonful of flour; cook it for a minute without browning, stirring all the time, and add a cupful of milk or cream; stir until it is a little thickened; strain; mix into it a tablespoonful of chopped parsley. Place the sauce on the serving-dish and arrange the pieces of chicken on it.[1199]

FRIED CHICKEN AND CAULIFLOWER

☞ Use two chickens, one head of cauliflower, one pint of milk, half a pint of cream, one-fourth pound of clear salt pork, flour, salt and pepper. Cut the pork in thin slices and fry in a large frying pan. On taking up the pork lay the pieces of chicken that have been salted and peppered and rolled in flour in the hot bacon grease and fry slowly half an hour. Be careful to avoid burning. When brown on one side, turn and brown the other side. The cauliflower should stand one hour in cold water salted. Just before frying the chicken put the cauliflower in two quarts of boiling water and simmer half an hour. After cooking twenty minutes put in one tablespoonful of salt. Next, put a pint of milk in a double boiler; mix the cup of cream with two tablespoonfuls of flour, and when the milk boils thicken with this cream and flour. Cook ten minutes, stirring occasionally; then season with salt and pepper. When the cauliflower is done drain it; place in center of a large dish; pour half the white sauce over it. Arrange chicken at base of cauliflower. Pour all the fat from pan the chicken was fried in; put the rest of the white sauce in pan; put on the stove, stir well from the bottom. To give it more flavor, when it boils pour over the chicken.[1200]

TO BROIL A CHICKEN
☛ After dressing the chicken, split down the back and truss the wings. Put a slice of breakfast bacon under each wing and on the back. Put in a hot oven and after it commences to brown salt and pepper it; when done, put on some butter.[1201]

BROILED CHICKEN 1

Turkey with onions and potatoes.

☛ Prepare young chicken for broiling and spread with soft butter mixed with salt, pepper and a little lemon juice. Cook slowly under the gas flame for twenty minutes, basting and turning occasionally; then increase the heat and brown well. Place on a hot platter, spread with soft butter, pepper and minced parsley, and serve. If the chicken is large it is well to do the first part in the upper oven.[1202]

BROILED CHICKEN 2
☛ After dressing, split down the back and remove the backbone, truss the wings, lay open flat on a paper, lay a cloth over, and with a rolling pin flatten it. Put in a dry unheated pan, skin side up. Put on the middle rack and it will cook in twenty-five minutes. Turn over and brown the other side. Put on a warm platter, sift over salt and pepper, spread with softened butter. Stick the point of a knife about in places to let the seasonings penetrate.[1203]

STEAMED CHICKEN 1
☛ Put a nice fat hen in your stew pan with a dipper of water: cover closely. When done sprinkle over salt and pepper, some butter, two hard boiled eggs, one mashed in gravy and the other sliced and laid over the chicken. The gravy may have to be thickened with a little flour. Pour over the chicken and serve with rice.[1204]

STEAMED CHICKEN 2
☛ Rub the inside of a grown chicken with salt; put in the dressing; put it into a pot and simmer two hours; then take it out and rub with butter; sift over salt and flour; put in oven to brown. Thicken and season the water it was boiled in for gravy.[1205]

PRESSED CHICKEN
☞ Take one or two chickens, boil in a small quantity of water with a little salt, and when thoroughly done, take all the meat from the bones, removing the skin, and keeping the light meat separate from the dark; chop and season to taste with salt and pepper. If a meat presser is at hand take it, or any other mold such as a crock or pan will do; put in a layer of light and a layer of dark meat till all is used, add the liquor it was boiled in, which should be about one tea-cupful, and put on a heavy weight; when cold cut in slices. Many chop all the meat together, add one pounded cracker to the liquor it was boiled in, and mix all thoroughly before putting in the mold; either way is nice.[1206]

BONED TURKEY
☞ This is a difficult thing to attempt, but very nice when accomplished. Clean the fowl, as usual. Have a very sharp-pointed knife, begin at end of wing, pass the knife down close to the bone, cut all the flesh from the bone, leaving the skin whole. Pass the knife down each side of the breast bone and up the legs, keeping close to the bone. Split the back half way up, and carefully draw out the bones. Fill the places whence the bones are removed, with a stuffing restoring the fowl to its natural form, and sew up all the incisions made in the skin. Lay a few strips of fat bacon on the top, basting often with salt and water, and a little butter. A glass of port wine added to the gravy is liked by some. When serving carve across the fowl in slices, and add tomato sauce.[1207]

Corrugated spoon, used for beating eggs.

SOUTHERN HASH
☞ 4 raw potatoes,
¾ cup of water,
2 green peppers,
1½ cups cold chopped beef,
2 tomatoes,
Salt and pepper,
1 onion,
Toast points.

Put vegetables through the meat chopper, using coarse cutter; cook in the stock, covered, until tender; add beef, salt, and pepper, and when hot turn on a platter and garnish with toast points. If corned beef and stock are used, use salt with care.[1208]

MAMMY'S VEAL LOAF
☞ Mix well together three pounds of finely chopped veal, with one-half pound pork. Add to this one-half cup of grated bread crumbs, two beaten eggs, a little onion, salt and pepper to taste. Roll into a loaf and

pour the juice of a can of tomatoes over the loaf and two tablespoonsful of butter, cook in oven for one hour and half.[1209]

STEWED CHICKEN

☞ Use a fowl about a year old, weighing about five pounds; cut it into joints; wash carefully and dredge with salt, pepper and flour. Take about four tablespoonfuls of lard; when very hot put in the chicken and brown on both sides; then put in a stew pan. After browning all the meat, cut an onion fine and cook it slowly for five minutes, then add three tablespoonfuls of flour and stir until brown; then add three pints of water and stir until it boils. Next, add half a cup of stewed tomatoes and enough salt and pepper to season highly. Strain this liquor over the chicken. Now put the heart, liver and gizzard in the stew pan, put on the cover and set on a hot place on the stove. After it commences to boil reduce heat and only let it simmer for two hours. It should never be allowed to boil hard. When boiled meat is tough and dry, it has been cooked too rapidly; it should be cooked below the boiling point.[1210]

CHICKEN PIE

☞ Make a short biscuit dough, but not as short as pastry. Line the sides but not the bottom of pan. Cut up a young chicken; put a layer in pan with a layer of dumplings, half a cup of butter, salt and pepper to season, enough hot water to cover the chicken and dumplings; two layers of chicken to one of dumplings; then put on a top crust. When nearly done put in a cup of milk.[1211]

Chicken pie, Confederate style.

SOUTHERN CHICKEN PIE

☞ 1 chicken.
2 cups milk.
2 cups broth.
½ cup butter.
⅓ teaspoon black pepper.
2 level teaspoons salt.

Clean and dress young chicken from 1 to 1½ lbs. Cut in pieces, wash in cold water, drain and set in cool place a few hours. Cook chicken in boiling water until tender. There should be about 2 cups of broth when chicken is cooked. Make rich biscuit dough. Place ½ chicken in pan, pour in broth. Roll dough for dumplings very thin, cutting in 1 inch strips, tear off in 2 inch lengths. Place layer over chicken, adding some of butter, salt and pepper. Place over this balance of chicken, another layer of dumplings, butter, salt and pepper. Roll top crust. Cut in three strips. Place over top of pie. Moisten all over with about ¼ cup milk, placing small pieces of butter at intervals. Cook pie in moderately hot oven ½ hour until crust is rich golden brown. Raise crust and pour in remainder of milk. Cook a few minutes and serve.[1212]

CHICKEN PUDDING

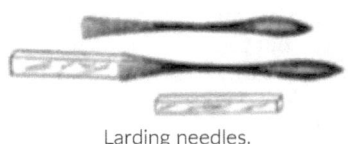
Larding needles.

☞ Stew 3 chickens until tender; remove from the liquor; put into a baking-dish and make a batter with flour, sweet milk, a tablespoon of butter, and 3 eggs beaten separately; beat all thoroughly and pour on the chicken; bake 1 hour; serve with gravy made of the liquor the chicken was boiled in; thicken with flour, add butter, salt, and pepper to taste.[1213]

CURRY POWDER FOR MEATS AND PASTAS

☞ 1 ounce of turmeric, 1 ounce of coriander seed, 1 ounce of cumin seed, 1 ounce of ginger, 1 ounce of nutmeg, 1 ounce of mace, 1 ounce of cayenne pepper; mix all together, and pass them through a fine sieve; bottle, and cork it well. 1 teaspoon is enough to season any made dish.[1214]

CURRIED CHICKEN

☞ Boil chicken tender; take out and lay on platter; take 1 teaspoon of curry and flour enough to make the liquor the thickness of good gravy; mix both together smooth with a little water, and stir into liquor the chicken was boiled in; then put back the chicken, and let all boil slowly for 15 minutes, stirring slightly.[1215]

BROWN FRICASSEE OF CHICKEN

☞ Cut up the chicken in joints, salt and pepper it, and fry in two tablespoonfuls of lard or oil. When nicely brown remove the pieces and add two tablespoonfuls of flour. Let that brown; then add one pint of stock made by boiling the liver, gizzard, neck, etc. Use that water; stir constantly until it boils; then add one slice of onion, one bay leaf, one tablespoonful of chopped carrot, salt and pepper. Put back the chicken, cover the pan and simmer slowly one hour. Dish it when done. Add the yolk of an egg beaten with two tablespoonfuls of milk; strain over the chicken and serve. Fry your chicken for fricassee in salt pork grease and only uses onion to season. Sprinkle over parsley cut fine.[1216]

WHITE FRICASSEE OF CHICKEN

☞ Cut up a chicken as for frying, put in a stew pan and partly cover with boiling water and set over a moderate fire and simmer until tender. When the chicken is done there should be no water left; if so, remove the cover from pan and cook until it evaporates. Dish the chicken. Put a tablespoonful of butter in a frying pan; when melted add two tablespoonfuls of flour; mix well, but do not brown. Now add one pint of cold milk, turn the whole in the stew pan in which it was cooked and stir constantly until it boils; season with salt and pepper; take it from the fire; add the beaten yolks of two eggs; pour it over the chicken in dish. Sprinkle with chopped parsley and serve with rice croquettes. Do not boil after adding eggs, or it will curdle.[1217]

CONFEDERATE CHICKEN PIE

☞ 2 hours before dinner, set on the fire, in a saucepan, 1 quart of water, with a little chopped parsley, onion, pepper, salt, and celery stalks. Cut up 2 chickens, and lay them on a dish in fresh water. An hour before dinner put them in the gravy, and put in 1 tablespoon of butter rolled in flour, and 1 teacup of cream or milk, and let stew for half an hour. Have a dish prepared with paste around it; have sliced 4 hard boiled eggs; put a layer of them in the bottom of the dish; then some chicken, and then egg, and so on until it is filled. Then fill up the dish with the gravy; put on the top a paste, and bake for half an hour.[1218]

OLD VIRGINIA CHICKEN PIE

☞ Line a deep pan with plain biscuit dough. Have two spring chickens cut in pieces; put in the pan with thin slices of fat bacon, a pint of cream, a teacup of stale bread crumbs, a pint of boiling water, three hard boiled eggs, salt and pepper. Cover with a top crust, and bake slowly for two hours.[1219]

CONFEDERATE ROAST TURKEY

☞ The secret of having a good roast turkey is to baste it often and cook long enough. Seven or eight pounds requires at least three hours; larger ones, four hours. After the turkey is dressed season inside with salt and pepper, stuff it, and tie in shape. Either lard the top or lay slices of bacon over. Wet the skin, and sprinkle with salt, pepper and flour. Let it stand sometime after stuffing before cooking. Pour a little boiling water in pan and bake slowly and baste often. Just before taking up, baste with butter and sift over more flour; it makes the skin crisp and brown.[1220]

TURKEY DRESSING

☞ Soak half a pound of bread in tepid water, squeeze dry; fry a minced onion in butter, add to the bread with a little parsley and thyme chopped fine, little grated nutmeg, salt and pepper, wine glass of stock. Stir over the fire until it leaves bottom and sides, then mix in two eggs. Poultry seasoning is fine in dressing.[1221]

TURKEY STUFFING
☞ 1 cup bread crumbs.
4 tablespoons butter (melted).
½ cup boiling water.
Salt and pepper.
Soak crumbs in boiling water, add butter and seasonings.[1222]

STUFFING FOR POULTRY
☞ Shredded wheat biscuit soaked in milk, then seasoned with butter, pepper, salt and poultry seasoning, makes a most delightful dressing for fowls.[1223]

QUAIL WITH TRUFFLES
☞ Broil delicately the breast of the quail, and cook truffles for ¾ hour in 1 pint of clear soup. Thicken with browned flour and 1 tablespoon of butter. Add wine to taste. Place quail's breast on dish. Scatter the truffles over it and pour the sauce over.[1224]

QUAIL ON TOAST
☞ Clean nicely. Cut open down the back; season, and dredge with flour. Crush them flat and put in a pan with butter and a little water. Cover, and put in a hot oven till nearly done. Then fry in hot butter till brown. Toast slices of white bread, butter lightly, and place the quails on the toast. Dish each separately. Thicken the gravy in the pan with flour, browned a little, and pour over the quails and toast. Serve very hot. Delicious.[1225]

Tenderloin roast: the choicest part of the beef.

ROASTED PHEASANT
☞ Roast as you would a chicken, and serve hot.[1226]

ROAST PIGEON
☞ When you have dressed your pigeons as before, roll a good lump of butter in chopped parsley, with pepper and salt, put it in your pigeons, spit, dust and baste them; if the fire be good, they will roast in twenty minutes; when they are through, lay round them bunches of asparagus, with parsley and butter for sauce.[1227]

PIGEON PIE
☞ Having picked and cleaned five pigeons, stuff them with a stuffing of grated cold ham, some salt, and grated cracker, some pepper and butter.

If asparagus is in season, the green tops may be substituted for the cracker. Pour milk and water into the dish until the pigeons are nearly covered. Put a lid of paste on the top, and bake an hour. If you wish the pigeons very tender, parboil them twenty minutes, and use the water in which they are boiled to make the pie.[1228]

BROILED PIGEON

☛ Prepare them; turn up the pinions, skewer up the legs to the bodies, and stuff them with chopped parsley, bread crumbs, butter and grated tongue or ham, seasoned with salt and pepper; dust them with flour, and put them into a stew-pan with a few slices of ham and a sufficiency of water to cover them: cover the pan, and boil them slowly till they are done. While they are boiling, cut up some asparagus about four inches long, tie it up in little bundles, and boil it in the nicest manner. When the pigeons are done, serve them up; place the bunches of asparagus on little buttered toasts, and lay round them. Season the gravy with butter, flour, chopped parsley, pepper and sweet cream, and serve it in a boat. Have stewed fruit to eat with them. Pigeons make a very good pie prepared like a chicken-pie, when they are young and fat; otherwise they are not good.[1229]

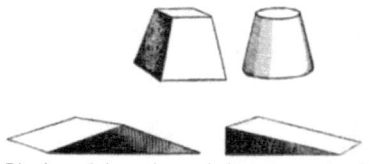
Blocks of bread used for support of meat, poultry, fish, game, etc.

RABBIT ROASTED

☛ Skin and dress the rabbit, cutting off the head and tail. Stuff with dressing of bread-crumbs, salt and pepper. Put in pan with water, and bake as you would chicken. Baste often with butter. Serve with apple-sauce and rice-cakes.[1230]

RABBIT PIE

☛ Cut a rabbit into eight pieces, soak in salted water one-half hour and stew until half done in enough water to cover it. Lay slices of pork in the bottom of a pie-dish and upon these a layer of the rabbit. Then follow slices of hard-boiled egg, peppered and buttered. Proceed until the dish is full, the top layer being bacon. Pour in the water in which the rabbit was stewed, and adding a little flour, cover with puff paste, cut a slit in the middle, and bake one hour, laying paper over the top should it brown too fast.[1231]

RABBIT STEW

☛ Cook them with a little chopped onion in a stewpan, with water enough to cover them, and butter and cream, pepper and salt, added when they are nearly done. Or add nothing but butter and wine to the gravy.[1232]

GRILLED RABBIT

☞ Take two fat young rabbits; case, clean and split them open on the backs, beat them flat with a roller, season them with salt, pepper, nutmeg and mace, and broil them on a gridiron till they are done and of a light brown, turning and basting them with butter as they may require. Have ready in a pan sour ounces of drawn butter, to which add a glass of sweet cream, two minced onions, two ripe tomatoes which have been peeled and sliced, a tea-spoonful of pepper and a small handful of grated bread; lay the rabbits in, let them simmer a minute or two, and serve up all together in a dish.[1233]

Jellied veal with lettuce and slices of hard-boiled eggs.

CRAB CROQUETTES

☞ Have crabs well boiled in salt and water, then pick them clean from the shell; chop fine; take the large end of a piece of celery and grate into the crab; chop with crab a small piece of onion fine; mix half a teacup of fine powdered cracker into crab; season with pepper and salt, also the least bit of fine red pepper, as crabs should be seasoned high to be nice. Have your lard hot, and fry just before wanted at table. Beat two eggs, dip croquettes in the egg, roll in powdered crackers before frying; make them oblong shaped.[1234]

BLUE GRASS RECIPE FOR ROAST QUAIL

☞ Rub the quail inside with pepper and put a slice of pickled pork on breast-bone of each, with salt and pepper. Baste often, and fill, when half done, with chestnut dressing as for turkey.[1235]

PARTRIDGE PIE

☞ Take 6 partridges, 1 dozen oysters, salt, pepper, nutmeg, and 1 tablespoon of butter, rolled in flour. Add some of the water that the partridges were boiled in, and put in a dish lined with paste. The partridges must be only parboiled. Cover the pie with a crust of paste, and bake for ½ an hour.[1236]

BROILED PARTRIDGES

☞ Open on back; if partridges are not tender, place in a small baking-pan with ½ inch hot water, and cover; 15 minutes is long enough if the oven is hot; dredge well with flour; lay on broiling-irons, breast down; make gravy of two tablespoons of flour in ½ cup of cold water, with pepper, salt, and butter; stir this into liquid in which birds are parboiled; always serve with toast and bacon, if preferred with this gravy. Slash birds in breast three times when done; put a little butter in each slash, also pepper and salt; place on toast, then pour liquor from pan over them.[1237]

BROILED PHEASANT

☞ If the pheasant is young, broil as you would young chicken. If full grown, cut into pieces, after having parboiled it, and add butter, salt, and pepper, and broil over a hot fire. Serve on thin slices of toast.[1238]

BROILED SQUIRREL

☞ If young and tender, broil as you would young chicken. If old, bake as you would chicken.[1239]

SQUIRREL PIE

☞ Cut them up, and parboil in water, with a little salt in it, for half an hour. Then proceed as in chicken pie.[1240]

DOMESTIC DUCKS

☞ These are best roasted. Clean them nicely, and prepare them like chickens; fill them with a rich stuffing made of grated bread crumbs, mixed with butter, pepper, salt, and a good deal of onion. Put them on a spit or in the oven; baste them constantly with a little butter and hot water, until there is enough gravy made to baste them with; turn them frequently. If put in the oven, put a little water in the bottom of the pan. Put a piece of middling on the top of each duck.[1241]

TO ROAST A GOOSE

☞ A goose is prepared the same as a turkey. Serve it with apple sauce; roast the liver, and serve with the gravy. A green goose is a goose not over 4 months old. It is not usual to stuff them, and they require less time to cook than a grown fowl. Truss the legs nicely. A green goose should be broiled; it will take longer to broil than a chicken, and will not require any butter to baste it. If put too near the fire it will burn without cooking.[1242]

ROASTED FOWLS

☞ Chickens, turkeys, ducks, or any kinds of birds, can be stuffed and baked in the following manner: Take some grated bread crumbs; mix with them some pepper, salt, and chopped onion, 3 leaves of sage, 1 sprig of pot marjoram, 1 dessertspoon of butter. Moisten them with a little water; stuff the fowl, and set them in a greased pan, and pour in 1 pint of water. Dust the fowl with flour, and put a piece of lard upon it; baste it constantly with the gravy. Then put in a saucepan, in a little water, the liver, gizzard, and heart, with pepper, salt, and onion, and add them to the gravy of the ducks when they are stewed. It will take

Boned birds in aspic around a bread platform.

about 2 hours to bake in a hot oven, or the same length of time if put on the spit before the fire. The fowl should be put in salt and water for 10 minutes before stuffed, and wiped perfectly dry with a coarse towel.[1243]

ROAST WOODCOCK AND SNIPE
☛ Birds should be picked soon after they are killed. Clean them and truss them; put them on the spit before the fire, and baste them constantly. Have ready a piece of toast, nicely browned and buttered. Serve each bird upon a piece of toast. Some persons cook these birds without removing the entrails. Allow 20 minutes to cook them.[1244]

PRAIRIE CHICKENS
☛ Clean them, and prepare the same as chicken, either to broil or roast. Stuff them, and serve with their own gravy. Put a large lump of butter in the craw of each.[1245]

Mrs. Joseph Heard, Sr., one of the recipe contributors to this book.

"Something new in cake-making!"

16. Pancakes and Waffles

PANCAKES

☛ Take 1 quart of sifted four, 3 eggs, beaten light, and enough snow or milk to make a batter about as thick as cream. This batter is thicker than that made for fritters. Put 1 tablespoon of lard into a heated skillet; and when the lard is boiling, put in a little of the batter, so as to make the cakes thin. When it is baked on one side, turn it; and when nicely browned, put it on a dish; do not serve more than three at a time, as they become clammy when allowed to stand any time. Each pancake can be folded over when served, or laid one upon another, according to taste. They should be eaten as soon as possible after being made. Serve with sugar and powdered cinnamon.[1246]

FRUIT PANCAKES

☛ Make a batter as above directed, and fry them in the same manner. Spread over them immediately a thin layer of some nice kind of marmalade or preserves; roll them as before directed, grate on a little loaf sugar, and eat them warm with cold cream sauce.[1247]

FRENCH PANCAKES

☛ 2 ounces of flour, 2 ounces of butter, 2 ounces of powdered sugar, 2 eggs, and 1 gill of milk. Cream the butter and sugar; add the eggs, beaten light, and then the milk, beating in the flour last. Bake in buttered saucers, half full, for 20 minutes, and serve them hot.[1248]

SWEET PANCAKES

☛ 3 eggs.
1 teaspoonful of sugar.

1 cupful of milk.
½ cupful of flour.
½ teaspoonful of salt.
½ tablespoonful of oil.

Some useful kitchen utensils.

Beat the yolks and whites of the eggs separately; mix them together and add the salt, sugar, and one half the milk; stir in the flour, making a smooth paste; then add the rest of the milk, and lastly the oil; beat well and let it stand an hour or more before using. Bake on a hot griddle in large or small cakes as desired; spread each cake with butter and a little jam or jelly, then roll them, sprinkle with sugar, and serve at once. Any pancake batter can be used. Those made of rice or hominy are good. The batter can be made of a consistency for thick or thin cakes by using more or less milk. Currant or tart jelly is better to use than a sweet preserve.[1249]

GENERAL BEAUREGARD BATTER CAKES

☛ Make a batter of one quart each of flour and sour milk, three eggs beaten separately, a table-spoon of butter, and two level teaspoons soda. Pulverize the soda very fine before measuring, then thoroughly mix with the flour. Add whites of eggs just before baking on the griddle. Sweet milk may be used; these may also be made without eggs.[1250]

GENERAL FORREST'S FLAPJACKS

☛ Take a pint of flour, a little salt, four well-beaten eggs, and milk enough to make a very thin batter, and beat well, and bake on a greased griddle, turning the cake so that both sides are browned nicely. Grease the griddle every few times.[1251]

CAROLINA FLAPJACKS

☛ One quart boiling milk, two cups white Indian meal, one small cup flour, one table-spoon each butter and brown sugar, one teaspoon soda dissolved in hot milk, one tea-spoon salt, two eggs; scald meal with the hot milk, cool a little, and add butter and sugar, and let stand until morning, covered closely; then add yolks of eggs, salt and flour. If batter is too thick, thin with cold milk before adding soda, and, last, lightly stir in the well-beaten whites.[1252]

BERLIN PANCAKES

☛ Roll out dough slightly sweetened and shortened, as if for very plain doughnuts; cut in circles like biscuit, put a tea-spoon currant jam or jelly on the center of one, lay another upon it, press the edges tightly together with the fingers, and fry quickly in boiling fat. They will be perfect globes when done, a little smaller than an orange.[1253]

WAFFLES FOR BREAKFAST

☛ Two eggs beat light, one pint of sour milk, to one and a half pint of flour, one teaspoonful of soda sifted with the flour, one tablespoonful of butter, teaspoonful of salt, well mixed, and then add the eggs. Always have your irons perfectly hot and well greased. In baking, melt butter before mixing in flour. Place them in a covered dish and butter them on sending to the table.[1254]

Waffle iron.

WAFFLES 1

☛ One pint of flour, one pint of sour milk, one teaspoonful soda, two beaten eggs. Have iron hot and well greased.[1255]

WAFFLES 2

☛ One pint of flour sifted with half a teaspoonful soda and a little baking powder, butter milk for a stiff batter, break in an egg, little salt; thin the batter with water. Don't fill irons too full; leave room to rise. The irons must be very hot.[1256]

WAFFLES 3

☛ 1 quart flour,
A little salt,
1 quart buttermilk,
1 pint melted lard,
1 heaping teaspoon soda,
1 egg.

As the success of the waffles depends on the mixing, the directions must be followed carefully. First, put the flour and salt in a pan and beat the buttermilk into it. Add the egg, which has been well beaten. Then add the hot lard. Beat the mixture thoroughly, and lastly add the dry soda. Add nothing after the soda is in. Beat all well and bake in hot waffle-irons that have been well greased. Use half this quantity for an ordinary sized family.[1257]

WAFFLES 4

☛ 1 quart of milk, 2 pounds of flour, ¼ pound of butter, 4 eggs, 4 teaspoons of good yeast. Mix at night; make the milk a little warm; melt the butter. First beat the eggs very light, add the milk and butter, and then stir in the flour; stir in the yeast last. Beat all well together until the bubbles rise to the top of the mixture. Set to rise over night; do not stir the mixture in the morning. The irons should be well heated before you commence to bake.[1258]

WAFFLES 5
☛ One pint of sour milk, one teaspoonful of soda; beat the whites of five eggs and the yolks of two, one large spoonful of butter, one tablespoonful of salt, one pint sweet cream mixed with the yolks. Put the soda in the buttermilk and pour on the yolks; after which add enough flour to make a light batter; and lastly, beat in whites of the eggs.[1259]

MARTHA WASHINGTON WAFFLES
☛ This is a recipe from Mrs. Washington's kitchen. Beat six eggs very light, sift in a quart of flour, add a teaspoonful of salt, a pint and a half of new milk and three tablespoonfuls of yeast. Beat well; set to rise over night, stir with a large spoon in the morning and bake in well greased waffle irons.[1260]

OLD FASHIONED WAFFLES
☛ Mix one quart of sweet milk with two and a half teacups of flour and one of meal; add a tablespoonful of salt and a tablespoonful of melted butter or lard. Add last, three eggs, well beaten. Bake at once in well greased irons.[1261]

QUICK WAFFLES
☛ Two pints sweet milk, one cup butter (melted), sifted flour to make a soft batter; add the well-beaten yolks of six eggs, then the beaten whites, and lastly (just before baking) four tea-spoons baking powder, beating very hard and fast for a few minutes.

These are very good with four or five eggs, but much better with more.[1262]

A gauffre or waffle iron.

CORN WAFFLES
☛ 1 quart of milk, 1½ pints of corn meal, 3 eggs, 1 tablespoon of butter, and 1 of lard. Pour the milk, boiling hot, upon the meal, mix in the butter and lard, beat the eggs, and add to them one teaspoon of salt, and bake immediately.[1263]

RICE WAFFLES
☛ One teacup of boiled rice, one teacup of meal, one teacup of buttermilk, one egg, well beaten two-thirds level teaspoonful of soda, sifted into the batter, level teaspoonful of salt; beat thoroughly; stir in last, one tablespoonful of melted lard. Bake in hot, well greased irons.[1264]

FEATHERY FLAPJACKS

☞ One quart of yellow corn-meal, one handful of wheat flour, three teaspoonfuls of baking-powder, one and one-half teaspoonfuls of salt, one pint of sour cream, one teaspoonful of soda and two eggs; add cold water enough to make a thin batter and fry on very hot pancake griddle with plenty of fat.[1265]

BUCKWHEAT CAKES

☞ Sift dry one pint of buckwheat flour and two teaspoonfuls of baking powder, and add a tablespoonful of brown sugar with water sufficient to make a batter.

Beat but lightly and bake at once on a hot griddle.[1266]

RICE GRIDDLE CAKES

☞ Take one-half of a teacupful of rice and boil; when cold mix with one quart of milk, the yolks of four eggs and two teacupfuls of flour sifted with two teaspoonfuls of baking-powder with a little salt; beat the whites of the eggs to a froth and add last. Bake on a griddle.[1267]

INDIAN GRIDDLE CAKES

☞ Sift and mix together two-thirds of a quart of corn-meal, one-third of a quart of flour, one teaspoonful of brown sugar, two heaping teaspoonfuls of baking-powder and a one-half of a teaspoonful of salt. Add two beaten eggs and one pint of milk, beating into a smooth batter. Brown nicely on a very hot griddle. Serve with syrup.[1268]

ENGLISH PANCAKES

☞ Sift together one teacupful of flour, one teaspoonful of baking-powder and a pinch of salt; beat two eggs with one tablespoonful of sugar and dilute with one pint of milk and one teacupful of cream; make thin batter with flour.

Pancake lifter.

Cook in hot frying-pan with melted butter, using sufficient batter to cover the pan.[1269]

RICE PANCAKES

☞ Set a pint of new milk over the fire and when scalding hot stir in two spoonfuls of ground rice which has been mixed smooth in one-quarter of a pint of cold milk. Let it thicken, but not boil. Cool it, adding gently one-quarter of a pound of butter.

When cold add white sugar, a little nutmeg, four eggs well beaten, and a little salt. Use as little lard as possible in frying these pancakes and make them light brown. Sift sugar over them, roll them to a round shape and cut slices of lemon to serve with them.[1270]

PRIDE OF TENNESSEE GRIDDLE CAKES

☛ 2 cups white or whole wheat flour.
1 cup meal.
1 teaspoon salt.
2 cups milk.
8 teaspoons baking powder (level).
1 teaspoon syrup.
Sift dry ingredients, stir in milk and cook in hot greased griddle. Condensed milk or water may be used.[1271]

CORN MEAL GRIDDLE CAKES

☛ One pint milk, 1 egg, ½ teaspoon salt, and corn meal to make a thin batter, 2 teaspoons baking powder, teaspoon sugar and 1 cup flour.[1272]

CONFEDERATE FRENCH PANCAKES

☛ Two cupfuls of flour, one heaping teaspoonful of baking-powder, three eggs, a pinch of salt and one cupful of milk. Beat thoroughly and fry on a hot griddle. Roll up and fill with any kind of cold meat, chopped fine and fried in butter.[1273]

SNOW PANCAKES

☛ Freshly fallen snow can be used instead of eggs in making batter for pancakes. Care must be had that the snow is as pure as possible. The batter should be made rather thick, and the snow mixed with each pancake, just before it is put into the pan. Two tablespoonfuls of snow will be equal to one egg. Graham gems can also be made by substituting snow for eggs, but putting three parts of snow to two of graham. Put into a hot oven and bake quickly.[1274]

BATTLE OF CHICKAMAUGA WAFFLES

☛ To a pint of milk put two eggs, two ounces of butter, one-half of a gill of yeast, a little salt, and flour enough to make a batter. The milk and butter are to be warmed together. Beat the eggs and mix with the flour. Add the salt and yeast. The iron must be heated on hot coals and buttered and one side filled with batter, then shut up and laid in the fire. After a few minutes turn it upon the other side.[1275]

OATMEAL GRIDDLE CAKES

☛ Take ½ pt. oatmeal, 1 pt. flour, 1 teaspoon sugar, 1 teaspoon baking powder, sifted in with the flour, a little salt, cold water enough to make a batter. Beat well, and bake quickly on hot griddle.[1276]

HOMINY WAFFLES

☛ One teacupful of cooked hominy, one egg, one tablespoonful of butter, a little salt, one pint of milk, one pint of flour, one heaping teaspoonful of baking-powder; beat the egg light, add butter, salt and hominy then add the egg, beat in the milk and sift in slowly the baking-powder and flour; beat all together and bake in a waffle-iron.[1277]

JOLLY BOYS

☛ Mix together thoroughly while dry one and one-half pints of rye-meal, one-half of a pint of four, one-half of a teacupful of corn-meal, two pinches of cinnamon, a little salt and two teaspoonfuls of baking-powder. Add one egg, well beaten; two tablespoonfuls each of molasses and sugar, and cold water enough to make a thick batter. Fry in hot lard a heaping tablespoonful at a time and cook until well browned.[1278]

Some meat dishes.

17. Pastas

HOW TO MAKE NOODLES
☛ Use one egg, one-half an eggshell of water, pinch of salt. Mix stiff with flour. Lay on napkin to dry; roll like jelly cake. Cut as thin as wafers.[1279]

HOW TO COOK MACARONI
☛ Boil 14 short sticks or 24 long ones in salt water for 20 minutes. Drain off water and mix with
½ pint of grated cheese (light measure),
1 pint of cream (or 1 pint of new milk with tablespoon of butter),
1 grated biscuit.
Place on top of stove and let it cook until it begins to thicken; then place in oven long enough to brown.[1280]

MACARONI
☛ 1 pound macaroni,
¼ pound butter,
¼ pound grated cheese.
Boil the macaroni till tender, and then put in a deep dish and spread over it pieces of butter and scatter the grated cheese. Put in another layer of macaroni, and so on. Put bits of butter on top, with salt and pepper, and bake well.[1281]

Perforated ladle.

BAKED MACARONI
☛ Take one-fourth a pound of maccaroni, break in three inch pieces and put into boiling salted water, boil about thirty minutes, drain in a colander, and pour cold water through to rinse off the gluten and keep them from sticking together. Cut into inch pieces. Butter a shallow pudding dish, put the macaroni in it and cover with a white sauce made

of one tablespoonful each of butter and flour to a cup and a half of milk, season with salt and pepper. Mix in the sauce one-fourth of a cup of grated cheese. Mix some grated cheese and bread crumbs and melted butter and sprinkle over the top. Let brown.[1282]

MACARONI WITH TOMATO SAUCE
☞ Break maccaroni in short lengths, put in a saucepan of boiling salt water. When tender drain and blanch in cold water for ten minutes. Cook a can of tomatoes with a bay leaf, bit of mace, onion, salt and pepper. Strain and thicken with two tablespoonfuls each of butter and flour rubbed together and cooked. Add the strained tomatoes, a little at a time. Drain the macaroni, pour in the tomato sauce, mix, and put in a baking pan. Cover with grated cheese and brown.[1283]

Macaroni timbale.

ITALIAN MACARONI SOUTHERN STYLE
☞ 1 can tomato soup.
1 can mushrooms.
1 cup grated American cheese.
2 cups cooked macaroni.
Melt cheese, stir in soup gradually. Put chopped mushrooms in, then macaroni. Season highly with red pepper, paprika, salt. Serve on crackers after cooked down.[1284]

PATRIOT'S MACARONI
☞ Put the macaroni into a pot of boiling water, with a little salt in it, and let it cook ten minutes. Then pour on fresh hot water and milk in equal quantities, and boil ten minutes. Then put it into a deep dish, with alternate layers of butter and grated cheese, until the dish is full, having macaroni on the top, with a little butter on it without cheese.[1285]

MRS. MATTHEWS' MACARONI
☞ Break in short lengths, put in boiling water, cover and let simmer, but never boil. Drain and pour over cold water. Break an egg; add a cup of milk; drain the macaroni, put in a baking dish, sprinkle over salt, cayenne, grated cheese and bits of butter. Pour the milk over, bake and serve.[1286]

MACARONI AND CHEESE
☞ Bake one-half of a package of macaroni, break into pieces two inches in length. Simmer twenty minutes in plenty of salted water. Drain, then put a layer in the bottom of a buttered baking-dish, then upon this put

a thin layer of grated cheese and bits of butter, then another layer of macaroni and so on till dish is full, leaving the cheese layer on top; sprinkle with cracker crumbs. Pour over the whole a cupful of cream or milk and bake a golden brown.[1287]

MACARONI PUDDING
☛ Simmer half a pound of macaroni in a plenty of water, with a tablespoonful of salt, till tender, but not broke—strain it, beat five yolks, two whites of eggs, half a pint of cream—mince white meat and boiled ham very fine, add three spoonsful of grated cheese, pepper and salt; mix these with the maccaroni, butter the mold, put it in, and steam it in a pan of boiling water for an hour—serve with rich gravy.[1288]

MACARONI A LA CREME
☛ 1 pint of cream, or rich milk, 4 tablespoons of flour, the rind and juice of 1 lemon. When the cream comes to a boil, stir in the flour smoothly; let it boil for 10 minutes. Then pour it on some macaroni that has been boiled in water, and drained. Pepper and salt. Bake it for ½ an hour, or serve it stewed.[1289]

MACARONI WITH EGGS
☛ One-half of a cupful of cold boiled macaroni, two tablespoonfuls of canned mushrooms cut in slices, three eggs, butter the size of a walnut and one-half cup of milk, salt and pepper to taste. Heat the milk in the chafing dish, add the butter, then the eggs, which have been well mixed together, then the macaroni, mushrooms and salt. Stir over the boiling water six or eight minutes. Serve with hot milk biscuits buttered.[1290]

Making pasta noodles from sheet paste.

VERMICELLI
☛ Beat two or three fresh eggs quite light, make them into a stiff paste with flour, knead it well, and roll it out very thin, cut it in narrow strips, give them a twist, and dry them quickly on tin sheets. It is an excellent ingredient in most soups, particularly those that are thin. Noodles are made in the same manner, only instead of strips they should be cut in tiny squares and dried. They are also good in soups.[1291]

SPAGHETTI
☛ For 4 persons, strain a can of tomatoes, add a suspicion of onion; stew 3 or 4 hours; add to the tomatoes a tablespoon of sugar and a little salt and a little butter. Boil macaroni 1½ hours; season with salt; pour

tomatoes over it; grated Parmesan cheese on top. Serve tomato dressing without sugar for chops.

ITALIAN SPAGHETTI

- 1 lb. beef.
1 can tomatoes.
1 pkg. spaghetti.
¼ lb. grated cheese.
1 large green pepper.
1 teaspoon salt.
1 teaspoon black pepper.
Dash of garlic.

Spaghetti timbales.

Cook beef very tender, season with salt, pepper, green pepper, onion and garlic. When beef is tender, add tomatoes and cook for about 15 minutes. Cook in another vessel 1 package spaghetti until tender. Place the cooked meat and tomatoes in baking dish or casserole, putting a layer of meat, then a layer of spaghetti, and last the grated cheese. Place in oven until cheese is melted. Serve in casserole.

MEXICAN SPAGHETTI

- 3 pork chops.
1 bell pepper.
1 can tomatoes.
1 onion.
¼ lb. cheese.
¼ teaspoon salt.
¼ package spaghetti.

Boil spaghetti in salty water until tender, then drain. Cut meat in small pieces and cook with tomatoes, onions and bell pepper. Place this in a baking dish, alternating with layers of spaghetti, the vegetable mixture and grated cheese. Season with pepper and salt. Bake 20 minutes. Serve hot.

NOODLES

- To three eggs (slightly beaten) mixed with two tablespoonfuls of water and a little salt, add enough flour to make a stiff dough; work it well for fifteen or twenty minutes, adding flour when necessary. When it is smooth and elastic, cut off a small piece at a time and roll it as thin as a wafer. It can be rolled very thin by placing a cloth under it. Sprinkle the thin sheet with flour, and roll it into a rather tight roll. With a sharp knife cut it, from the end, into threads, if for soup; if to use as a vegetable, into ribbons one quarter inch wide. Let them dry an hour or more. They will keep the same as macaroni.[1295]

NOODLES FOR SOUP

☞ Beat 1 egg light, and add to it enough flour to make a stiff dough. Knead it, and roll it out thin, and cut it into long narrow strips, and dry them in the sun or near the stove. Put them in the soup a short time before serving, or they will boil to pieces.[1296]

NOODLES SERVED AS A VEGETABLE

☞ Throw a few noodles at a time into boiling, salted water; boil them until they are done, separating them carefully with a fork to prevent their matting together. Skim them out when done, and keep them on a warm dish on the hot shelf until enough are cooked. Season with butter. Put them in the dish in which they are to be served, and sprinkle over them bread crumbs browned in hot butter to a golden color. This dish may be served with fish, with meat, or as a course by itself. Noodles may also be cooked like macaroni, with cheese.[1297]

Slitted wooden spoon.

NOODLE BALLS

☞ Take some of the noodle paste made as directed above. Roll it as thin as possible, then place it on a floured napkin and roll until it is as thin as paper; fold it double, and cut it into circles one quarter inch in diameter, using a small vegetable cutter or pastry bag tube. Fry them in smoking hot fat, tossing them in the frying basket so that they will color evenly. They will puff into balls and color in one minute. Drain and place them on paper on the hot shelf. Sprinkle them on the soup after it is in the tureen, or better pass them, as they soften very quickly.[1298]

FARCE FOR RAVIOLI

☞ Take one cupful of cold chicken, veal or fish, chop very fine and rub to a paste, with one calf or two sheep brains, parboiled; add one cupful of bread crumbs which have been soaked in milk and then squeezed dry, one teaspoonful of onion juice, one-half teaspoonful of salt, a grating of nutmeg, dash of cayenne and thyme, and rub well together. Have ready one cupful of spinach which has been boiled, drained and chopped; stir the spinach into the paste, add the yolks of two eggs, beat for two minutes.[1299]

RAVIOLI

☞ Make a paste of two cupfuls of flour, two eggs, one-half teaspoonful of salt, and water enough to make a stiff dough. Knead well and roll out into a sheet as thick as very thin cardboard. Cut it in half and proceed as follows: Place one teaspoonful of farce in regular rows on the paste two inches apart. Moisten the upper part of the paste and place carefully on top of the lower piece, pressing the two together with the fingers or with a ravioli rolling-pin, forming small cushions between. Cut through the rows down and across with a pastry knife in such a way as to leave pieces about two inches square. Place the ravioli on a board covered with a clean piece of muslin, near the stove, and dry thoroughly. When needed poach them, a few at a time, in clear bouillon for ten minutes. When all are done place in a tureen and pour the soup over the ravioli; add a few spoonfuls of grated Parmesan cheese, and serve.[1300]

Dinner table.

Sweetmeats for social gatherings.

18. Pastries, Pies, and Custards

PASTRY MAKING TIPS

☛ 1) Use winter wheat flour for pastry. 2) It takes half cup flour and half cup lard to make a double crust for one pie.[1301]

PASTRY FOR MAKING PIES OF ALL KINDS

☛ One pound of four nicely sifted to quarter pound of butter and one quarter pound of lard, one teaspoonful of salt, fine, mixed in flour while dry; then with your hands rub the butter and lard into the flour until thoroughly mixed, then add enough cold water and mix with your hands so as to make pastry hold together, be sure not have it too wet.

Sprinkle flour very lightly on pastry board, and roll pastry out to the thickness of an egg-shell for the top of fruit, and that for the bottom of fruit must be thin as paper.

In rolling pastry, roll to and from you; you don't want more than ten minutes to make pastry.[1302]

PREPARING THE FRUIT FOR PIES
☛ One gill of water to four pounds rhubarb; first peel the rhubarb; sweeten to taste while cooking, and put into pastry when cold. Prepare apples same way; season with cinnamon. Peaches the same way; season with cinnamon.[1303]

JEFFERSON DAVIS PIE
☛ Four eggs, 2 cups light brown sugar, 1 cup cream, ½ cup melted butter, 1 tablespoon flour, season with lemon and nutmeg; bake in bottom crust. For 2 pies.[1304]

JEFF DAVIS PIE
☛ Two eggs,
One cup of sour milk,
One cup of meal,
One-half cup of flour,
One teaspoonful of salt,
Two teaspoonsfuls of baking powder.
One tablespoonful of lard. Beat eggs separately. To yolks add salt, milk, melted lard, meal, flour and baking powder. Lastly put in the well beaten whites and bake in moderate oven.[1305]

JEFFERSON DAVIS CUSTARD
☛ Four eggs, beaten separately,
One cup of cream,
Two tablespoonsful of butter,
Two cups of sugar.
Flavor to taste. Pour the mixture on thin, rich crusts.[1306]

BLUE GRASS PASTRY
☛ 1 pound of best flour,
¾ pound of butter,
1 wineglass of ice water,
Whites of 2 eggs.
Take ¾ pound of flour and put in a bowl. Put the other in a plate. Beat the eggs very light and mix in the flour with the water so as to make stiff dough. Beat well with a rolling-pin for 10 minutes. Roll, adding the butter in four rollings and the ¼ pound of flour. Set the pastry on ice for 2 hours. This makes 3 pies.[1307]

SOUTHERN PASTRY
☛ One cup of flour,
One-fourth teaspoonful of salt,
One-fourth cup of lard or butter. Mix flour and salt, work lard lightly into the flour and mix with iced water to make stiff dough. Do not knead dough at all, just mix lightly together.[1308]

PUFF PASTE

☛ Half lb. each of flour and butter, half cup ice water; sift the flour in a bowl, add a little salt and ice water to make a smooth paste, work it thoroughly on a floured board, working and pounding until you can stretch it like India rubber (remember this has no butter in it.)

Put it in a covered box and set it in crushed ice, knead the butter well with your hand under ice water until it seems waxy then dry in a napkin or pat the water out.

Three pans arranged for chilling puff paste: the top and bottom ones are holding cracked ice, the center one is holding the paste wrapped in a napkin.

Now roll the paste out in a square, rather thin, pat your butter out and put in center of square, pull out the paste and fold loosely over the butter from the four sides.

Put in a tin box and put on ice twenty minutes, take out, turn the folded side under and roll quite thin, fold it in thirds, turn it around and roll out again quite thin (never let the butter break through); roll in thirds put again on ice as before.

Do this until the paste is rolled and folded six times, doing it twice between putting on ice each time. When ready to bake rinse out your pans but do not wipe them.

Always brush puff paste over with beaten egg before baking. Bake in a hot oven, most important part. Very fine.[1309]

A GOOD AND SIMPLE PASTE

☛ For one crust, three tablespoons flour, a little salt one tablespoon lard chopped in, put in a little ice water at a time until it will just stick together, flour your board and roll out.[1310]

PIE CRUST

☛ Sift together three cups of flour, half a teaspoonful of salt, half a teaspoonful of baking powder. With a fork or tips of fingers work in two-thirds a cup of lard.

When every little particle of fat is coated with flour add gradually enough cold water to make a paste that sticks together without adhering to knife or bowl.

Then turn out on a floured board, roll it in flour and pat out with rolling pin in a long strip. Roll it up like a jelly roll and use when desired. Will make two pies.

For a more flaky crust use half the lard in paste, the rest spread in layers after rolling out. Sift over flour and roll up as before.

Cut off pieces as needed for use.[1311]

PLAIN PASTE

☛ Three cups of pastry flour, one teaspoonful each of salt and sugar, half pound butter or lard, three-fourths of a cup ice water. Cut butter in flour with a knife or chopping knife; pour water carefully on the dry surface. Turn on a board as dry as possible. Lightly mix with pastry knife, fold and roll three times. Set on ice. Always make pastry in a cool room.[1312]

TO BAKE PUFF PASTE

☛ The most important part of all is the oven, for if the oven is not hot enough you have wasted your material. The paste should be ice cold when it is put in the oven, and the oven should be very hot. For patties the oven should have a strong under heat, allowing them to rise their full height before browning. Then put on the upper grate to brown. Should the oven be too hot and the paste begins to brown as soon as put in, open the draughts of the stove and stand a small basin of ice water in the oven.[1313]

EASY PIE CRUST

☛ Sift as much flour as you will require; a cup will make two crusts. Add a little salt and lard enough worked in so that when you crush a handful it will cling together and not crumble apart. Use only enough ice water to roll out; it takes very little.[1314]

LEMON PIES

☛ Take four eggs, one tablespoonful of butter to one and a half tea-cup of powdered sugar, rub butter and sugar together until a cream, then add the yolks of the eggs to butter and sugar, and beat until light; beat the white of the egg until perfectly light, and add to the others. Take two lemons, roll them with your hands, on board until soft, then grate peel of lemons and put into preparation, then squeeze juice of lemons into preparation. All articles in this preparation should be well mixed together and put in pastry, and baked immediately in a hot oven. Only one layer of pastry at bottom of pie plate.[1315]

Pastry bag and tubes.

CREAM APPLE PIE

☛ The best of apples to be used. To two pounds of apples use a gill of water; put on fire to steam till the apples will mash perfectly fine and soft; sweeten to taste and let them cool. Season with powdered cinnamon—one-half teaspoonful of the best. Have one crust of pastry only, and that at the bottom of plate; fill plate with the fruit, then bake quickly in a hot oven. Take one pint of fresh cream sweetened to taste; beat the white of five eggs light, and add to the cream; flavor with vanilla. Beat the cream lightly before adding the eggs, then with a spoon spread over pies on sending to table.[1316]

UNCLE JOHN'S PUFF PASTE

☛ One pound of flour, half a pound of butter and lard mixed, or all lard may be used, a little salt. Chop half the shortening into the flour until as large as a pea; then use a little ice water at a time until it will stick together. Use a fork to mix with. Then roll out and spread with some of the shortening; sift over flour; roll from both sides to the center; then fold the ends in. Roll out as before, spread with shortening, sift over flour, fold, and roll as before. Do this the third time. Handle as little as possible. Put on ice to chill before using. Put in a hot oven.[1317]

PINEAPPLE CUSTARD

☛ Beat together three yolks and the whites of one egg with two-thirds of a cup of sugar, little salt, half a cup grated pineapple, juice of half a lemon. Turn the mixture either in patty pans lined with paste or in a pie plate lined with paste. When baked make a meringue of the two whites and two tablespoonfuls sugar and put over. Let brown very slowly. You may use two whole eggs and no meringue for the custard. It is elegant.[1318]

Baked meringues.

STRAWBERRY CREAM CRUSTS

☛ Take some small common sauces, line them with nice pastry, put a narrow rim around them, crinkle the outer edge and bake a delicate brown. When baked slip from the saucers and let cool. Just before serving fill with a thin layer of strawberry jam and cover with a layer of cream whipped solid with the Dover. For a swell luncheon scatter brown macaroon crumbs over the cream.[1319]

APPALACHIAN BANANA PIE

☛ 3 bananas.
⅓ cup flour.
¾ cup sugar.
¾ cup boiling water.
1 tbls. butter.
¼ teaspoon vanilla.
2 eggs.
¼ teaspoon salt.
Cream sugar and butter, beat in yolks of eggs, add flour and boiling

water, cook until thick, stirring all the time. When cool add flavoring. Use whites of eggs for meringue for top as in lemon pies, also make pastry as in lemon pies. These proportions are sufficient for one pie. Slice bananas very thin, round and round, place on crust, cover with the custard and add meringue and brown lightly in oven. Bake pastry before putting in the filling. Delicious!¹³²⁰

ETHEREAL APPLE PIE
☛ Take eight large apples, bake and rub through a sieve into a large bowl. Add the whites of five beaten eggs, three-fourths of a cup of sugar. Chill the mass; then beat with a fork until thick and light colored. Put in a pudding dish and bake slowly twenty minutes. It should rise and brown on top. Serve with cream and sugar. These crustless pies are light and dainty.[1321]

SWEET WAFERS
☛ One teacup each of butter and sugar creamed together, one grated orange, four eggs, one tablespoonful of cinnamon. Add three pints of flour and make up stiff. Then roll out on a board and cut them out about the size of a biscuit, and roll again till thin as paper, and bake in a quick oven. Watch close while baking. You can roll them round on a fork handle while they are warm, if you like.[1322]

GOOSEBERRY AND CHERRY PIES
☛ Prepared the same way. Use one gill of water to two pounds of either fruit; sweeten to taste, leaving it a little tart. When it cools, put into plates for baking, having two crusts, top and bottom of plate. Bake quickly, and send to table cold.[1323]

CALEDONIAN CREAM
☛ 2 ounces of raspberry jam, or jelly, 2 ounces of currant jelly, 2 ounces of sifted loaf sugar, the whites of 2 eggs. Beat all together in a bowl for of ¾ an hour. This makes a very pretty cream.[1324]

RASPBERRY CREAM
☛ Rub a quart of raspberries through a sieve to take out the seeds, and then mix it well with some cream, and sweeten with sugar to your taste. Put it in a bowl and froth with a syllabub churn, taking off the froth as it rises. When you have as much froth as you want, put the rest of the cream into a deep glass bowl or dish, and put the frothed cream on it, as high as it will stand.[1325]

STRAWBERRY CREAM
☛ Make it in the same way as raspberry cream [above]. The coloring may be improved by using a little of the rose-coloring for ices and jellies.[1326]

TRANSPARENT CUSTARD

☛ Boil half a cup of water and one pound of sugar. Let boil five minutes and put in four ounces of butter. When it melts remove from the fire. You often have yolks left from making white cake. Beat ten yolks light; pour slowly into the syrup, beating until cool. Flavor with vanilla or anything preferred. By adding lemon juice you will have a lemon pie. Makes two custards. Fine.[1327]

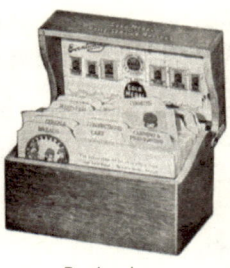

Recipe box.

MOLASSES CUSTARD

☛ Four well beaten eggs, one cup of sugar, one and a half cups molasses, one full tablespoon of flour, one tablespoonful of butter. Flavor with either lemon, orange peel, vanilla or mixed spices. For two pies.[1328]

LIGHT BREAD PIE

☛ Take stale bread and grate it. To one and one-half teacupfuls of the grated bread, add two teacupfuls of sweet milk, the juice of one orange, and half of the peel grated. Stir the yolks of four eggs beaten light into it. Take the whites of the four eggs beaten very light and meringue the pies after baking. Put half teacupful of sugar and one tablespoonful of butter to the prepared bread. Have one crust only, and that at the bottom of plate. Bake quickly.[1329]

CRACKER PIE

☛ To be made the same as light bread pie above, except flavor with one-half teaspoonful of ground cloves, one-half teaspoonful of ground cinnamon, and one tablespoonful of butter.[1330]

MINCE PIES

☛ One beef tongue boiled tender, then take the skin off; four pounds beef kidney suet, peel all the skin off it and chop very fire with the tongue; two pounds citron chopped fine, four pounds apples, four pounds raisins well seeded, four pounds currants well washed and dried with a towel, four oranges, the peel of two grated, and the fruit of all four grated into mince meat, two tablespoonfuls of ground allspice, one tablespoonful of cloves, two nutmegs grated, and two tablespoonfuls of ground cinnamon. Chop the whole very fine, and mix well together, then put in one-half gallon sherry wine, and one-half gallon brandy. Grate two lemons in the meat. Salt to your taste, also sweeten to your taste. Have bottom and top crust.[1331]

MOUNTAIN NECTAR

☛ Put six pounds of sugar, four ounces of tartaric acid, and two quarts of water; put all into a porcelain kettle, and let it come almost to a boil, but not quite to the boiling-point. Then take it off and stir in the whites of four well-beaten eggs. Strain it, and when it is cool, flavor it richly with essence of lemon. It will keep for months. Two tablespoonfuls of this mixture, and two-thirds of a glass of ice-water, to be put into a goblet, and when ready to drink, a small quantity of soda stirred in, which will make it effervesce finely.[1332]

WHIPPED CREAM PIE

☞ Sweeten with white sugar one tea-cup very thick sweet cream, made as cold as possible without freezing, and flavor with lemon or vanilla to taste; beat until as light as eggs for frosting, and keep cool until the crust is ready; make crust moderately rich, prick well with a fork to prevent blistering, bake, spread on the cream, and to add finish put bits of jelly over the top. The above will make two pies.[1333]

PUMPKIN PIE

Pumpkin pies.

☞ Stew pumpkin in just enough water to keep from burning. When soft, drain off water and stew about five minutes longer. Mash fine, strain through a sieve and measure one pint for one pie. Beat very light three eggs with half a cup of sugar and mix in the pumpkin; then add a teaspoonful of salt, one tablespoonful of brandy, one teaspoonful of cinnamon, one-fourth a teaspoonful each of ginger and nutmeg. After mixing, if not sweet enough add more sugar. Line a deep pie plate with crust, fill with mixture and bake in a very hot oven. Set Maraschino cherries over the top before bringing to table.[1334]

A KENTUCKY GIRL'S PUMPKIN PIE

☞ Cut pumpkin in halves, remove seeds, bake in a dripping-pan (skin side of pumpkin downward), with a slow fire, until pulp can readily be scraped from skin; mash fine, and while hot add to each quart pumpkin two table-spoons butter; when cold, sweeten to taste; add one pint cream or new milk, yolks of three eggs, well beaten and strained, cinnamon and allspice to taste (ginger, if preferred), one wine-glass of brandy; stir well, and just at the last add whites of eggs, well whipped. The brandy can be omitted and not injure recipe. Many like a table-spoon of lemon extract and less spice. If lemon is used, omit brandy. Bake in deep pie-plates in a quick oven.[1335]

CHAUTAUQUA PUMPKIN PIE

☞ One can of pumpkin will make three pies. Use three eggs, one and a half cups brown sugar, one pint milk, little salt, cinnamon and ginger to season. When in the pie plates grate over nutmeg. Fine.[1336]

APPLE OR SQUASH FANCHONETTES

☛ One cup of strained squash or apple, one-third cup of sugar, one tablespoonful melted butter, two eggs, one teaspoonful cinnamon, one teaspoonful ginger, one-fourth teaspoonful salt, one cup milk.

Line patty pans with pastry and fill with the mixture. At serving time put a spoonful of whipped cream on each fanchonette and serve.[1337]

Currant shortcake.

STRAWBERRY SHORTCAKE

☛ Rub 2 tablespoons of butter in
1 quart of flour, with
½ teaspoon of salt, and
2 teaspoons of baking powder,
Sweet milk enough for soft dough.

Mix lightly and put in pan the shape of Sally Lunn. Bake quickly. When done, split and butter while hot. In splitting any kind of hot bread, cut around the crust with a sharp knife and open carefully with a fork. Have fresh strawberries that have been well sweetened and spread over one-half; then lay on other half and spread with berries. Serve with whipped cream.[1338]

WHORTLEBERRY PIE

☛ Put your pastry on the pie plate, sift over some flour, put in the whortleberries, cover with sugar, sift over a little flour. Put on a top crust and bake.[1339]

APPLE PIE

☛ Pare and core six tart small apples, boil a cup of sugar and half a cup of water five minutes, put in a heaping teaspoonful of butter, lay in the fruit, cover and cook until tender.

Flavor the syrup with almond. Line a pie tin with paste; bake. Then lay in the apples and pour over the thick syrup. (Boil down if too thin.) Make a meringue of two whites and two tablespoonfuls sugar, spread over the top, sprinkle with blanched and shredded almonds. Dust over a little sugar and brown in a cool oven.[1340]

APPLE TARTS

☛ Ten apples, half a lemon, one cup of sugar, one teaspoonful of butter. Pare the apples. From four of the largest extract cores.

Place these in a small stewpan with half the sugar and half the lemon. Nearly cover with water and boil until done, keeping whole.

Cut the rest of the apples in small pieces and cook with the rest of the sugar and lemon juice. Make a marmalade, add the butter and mash fine. Fill the cores and put the rest around. Serve with cream.[1341]

SWISS CREAM

☞ 1 pint of rich cream, 6 ounces of sugar, the rind of 1 lemon, and the juice of 2, 1 drachm of cinnamon, 4 tablespoons of flour, 4 ounces of macaroons, 2 ounces of candied citron. Flavor the cream with the cinnamon and lemon rind; mix the flour with a little of the cream. When the cream comes to a boil, stir in the flour, cream, and sugar; season with lemon juice; cover a glass dish with the macaroons; put in the cream, then a layer of macaroons, and then the cream; ornament with the citron, cut in small pieces. Make the day before it is to be used.[1342]

ISINGLASS CREAM

☞ Use three quarts of new milk, one quart of water, with five ounces of isinglass dissolved in it (which when cool pour into the milk), sixteen yolks of eggs, two and a half pounds of sugar, one glass Madeira wine; mix them well, put through a jelly-bag, and mold.[1343]

IRISH POTATO PIE

☞ 1 pint mashed potatoes,
½ pint cream,
4 eggs,
¾ pound sugar,
1 orange,
1 cup of butter.
Cook and mash the potatoes. Beat the eggs together, add sugar and butter and beat well. Then pour in the cream and add the potatoes and stir well. Flavor with the juice of 1 orange. Bake in paste and cover with meringue of well-beaten whites of eggs and 2 tablespoons sugar.[1344]

Cherry pitter.

SLICED APPLE PIE

☞ Line a pie plate with paste, peel and core some apples and slice them; put a layer of apples, sprinkle over sugar, bits of butter, bits of sliced lemon, another layer of apples, butter, sugar and lemons. In all use a cup of sugar. Put on top crust and bake. Use no water. Fine.[1345]

SOUTHERN APPLE PIE

☞ 6 apples,
Grated rind and juice of one lemon,
½ cup of sugar,
1 teaspoon cinnamon,
2 macaroons rolled,
¼ teaspoon salt,
2 tablespoons butter,

2 eggs slightly beaten.

Pare and slice apples, add one-quarter cup of water; cook until soft, and rub through a sieve; add other ingredients in order given. Line a deep plate or patty tins with rich paste, fill, and bake about forty minutes. Cake crumbs may be substituted for macaroons.[1346]

CHERRY PIE

☛ Take a quart of cherries, stem and stone them. They should measure two cups. Put a cup of sugar and half a cup of water on to boil. After a few minutes put in the cherries and let cook. Mix two teaspoonfuls flour in a little cold water and pour in to thicken. Next put in a teaspoonful of butter. If thick enough, set off. Bake between two crusts.[1347]

Chocolate lemon pie.

LEMON PIE 1

☛ You often have a lot of yolks left from making white cake, if so make these custard. Beat lightly fifteen yolks and three cups of sugar, one-fourth of a lb. of softened butter, three full teaspoons of flour or corn starch, one cup water, juice of two or three lemons. Makes three pies.[1348]

LEMON PIE 2

☛ Beat light two eggs, add to them a cup of sugar, one tablespoon flour, one tablespoonful of butter, juice of one lemon, half cup of water. Fine.[1349]

LEMON PIE 3

☛ Yolks three eggs, one tablespoonful of butter, three-fourths a cup of sugar, one-third cup of water, one teaspoonful of flour, juice and grated rind of a lemon.

Mix all together, lastly put in water. Bake on single crust until firm. Cover with a meringue made of the three whites and three tablespoons of sugar. Fine.[1350]

LEMON PIE 4

☛ Cream together one lb. of sugar and one-fourth lb. butter, beat six eggs, add to the batter and sugar with the juice and grated rind of a lemon, little nutmeg, half wine glass of wine. Bake on single crust, makes two custards. This is a nice transparent custard.[1351]

LEMON PIE 5

☛ Beat all together three eggs, add to them one cup of sugar, one teaspoonful of flour, one desert spoon of butter, one desertspoonful of milk or water, grated rind and juice of one lemon. Put a layer of jelly or preserves on paste, then the custard.[1352]

LEMON PIE 6

☛ The yolks of eight eggs, add to them three-fourths a cup of sugar, one-fourth lb. of butter, the juice and grated rind of a lemon, makes two pies. Bake on single crust.[1353]

LEMON PIE 7

☛ 1 cup of buttermilk,
1½ cups sugar,
4 eggs,
1 tablespoon butter,
1 tablespoon cornstarch,
Juice and rind of 2 lemons.

Beat the yolks and reserve the whites for the meringue. Add the other ingredients and cook in a porcelain pan till thick. Fill the shells, spread the meringue on top and brown in the oven.[1354]

LEMON CHEESE PIE

☛ Boil the peel of two lemons until tender and chop them fine, take a cup of sugar and a cup of butter, cream it and add yolks of six eggs, stir all together and add the juice of the lemons.[1355]

LEMON CUSTARD

☛ Beat the yolks of 8 eggs until they are as white as milk; then put to them 1 pint of boiling water, the rinds of 2 lemons, grated, and the juice. Sugar to your taste; stir on the fire until thick enough; then add 1 wine-glass of good wine, and 1 glass of brandy. Give it all a good scald; put in cups, and set to cool; grate a little nutmeg over the top.[1356]

VANILLA CUSTARD

☛ Boil a vanilla bean in a quart of rich sweet milk till it is sufficiently flavored with the bean; then take it out and set it by to cool. Beat the yolks of eight eggs and the whites of four to a froth, mix them together, and when the milk is cold, stir them into it. Add six ounces of sugar, put it in a pitcher, set it in boiling water, and simmer it gently till thick and smooth, stirring it all the time; then remove it from the fire and set it by to cool; after which put it in cups or glasses, and grate nutmeg over the tops.[1357]

Ideas for chantilly custard.

BANANA CUSTARD

☛ ¾ cup sugar.
1 egg (well beaten).
2 cups milk.
1 teaspoon vanilla.

½ cup corn starch.
½ cup marshmallow whip.

Stir to dissolve ingredients mentioned in first column and then bring to a boil and cook slowly for 5 minutes. Add ingredients of second column. Rinse 6 small custard cups in cold water and then pour in custard. Set in ice box to chill. When ready to serve, unmold and cover the entire custard with thinly sliced bananas which have been dipped in sugar to make the bananas stick. Sprinkle with finely chopped nuts and top off with one teaspoonful marshmallow whip. Garnish with maraschino cherry. Then pour 1 teaspoon of the syrup from bottle of cherries over the custard.[1358]

Tart rings, along with crusts that were baked in them.

CHERRY TARTS

☞ Take fine ripe cherries, extract the seeds, saving all the juice, and sprinkle them thickly with brown sugar. Roll out as many sheets of plain paste as you want, rather thick, and allowing two to each tart. Butter some large scalloped patty-pans, spread over each a sheet of the paste, put in a thick layer of the cherries with some of the juice, sprinkle on each tart a small spoonful of flour, one of butter and a teacupful of water; then lay a paste over the tops, trim them smoothly round the edges, crimp them neatly with a sharp pen-knife, dipping the blade occasionally into dry flour, to prevent the paste sticking to it, and bake them in a moderate oven. They must be neatly iced with tart icing, and dried in the ovens, or have loaf sugar grated thickly over them. They are very fine, and should be eaten warm with cold sweet sauce or honey and sweet milk, boiled custard or some nice kind of cream.[1359]

CRANBERRY TARTS

☞ Prepare some plain paste as directed for the cherry tarts; butter some large scalloped pans, putting over each a sheet of paste, put in your cranberries, having first stewed them tender, and strew on at least half their weight in sugar, add to each a large spoonful of butter, rolled in one of flour and broken up, a wine glass of wine and a large teacupful of water, lay strips of twisted paste over the top, put round the edge a border of paste leaves, neatly notching and linking them together, and bake them in a moderate oven. Grate loaf sugar over them as soon as you take them from the oven, and eat them warm with rich sauce and boiled custard or cold cream.[1360]

STRAWBERRY TARTS

☞ Pick the stems and leaves from fine ripe English strawberries, put them whole into large scalloped shells of puff paste, and grate loaf sugar thickly over them, mash to a pulp some of the remaining berries, pass them through a sieve, stir enough of the pulp into some rich sweet cream to make it tolerably thick, beat it to a froth, and set it for a time in ice, to get a little firm, and then pile it on the tarts, forming a pyramidal heap. The real English raspberries may be converted into tarts in the same manner, and both of them are very nice.[1361]

PEACH TARTS

Apple tart pie (left), apricot tart pie with blanched almonds (right).

☞ Select the finest flavored freestone peaches that are very soft and farinaceous; pare and slice them from the stones, and mash them to a smooth marmalade, pressing them through a sieve; add to the pulp half its weight of powdered loaf sugar; make it a little more moist with sweet cream, and put it smoothly into large scalloped shells of puff paste; grate on a little nutmeg, and crown them handsomely with whipped cream. They are fine with iced milk, boiled custard, etc.[1362]

GRAPE TARTS

☞ Take the white English grapes, pick them from the bunch; stew them till tender in a very little water, and half their weight of sugar, press them through a sieve, and set them by to cool. Then put a thick layer of the pulp in large shells of puff paste, make them very smooth, grate on a little nutmeg, and make them white with powdered loaf sugar. They are introduced with boiled custards, cold creams, etc. No fruit should be put in shells of puff paste till shortly before they are sent to table.[1363]

FOOD FOR THE GODS

☞ One cup of sugar,
One-fourth pound of dates,
One-fourth pound of nuts,
Three tablespoonsful of cracker crumbs.

Beat whites of three eggs stiff and add one heaping teaspoonful of baking powder and the above ingredients. Cut the dates and almonds into small pieces. Put mixture in a pudding pan set inside of a pan of water and bake in oven one hour. Cover while cooking. Serve with cream.[1364]

GOOSEBERRY CUSTARD

☞ Stew 1 quart of ripe gooseberries in as little water as possible; mash them through a colander; stir in while the pulp is hot, 1 tablespoon of butter, and sugar sufficient to sweeten them. Beat 6 eggs very light; then simmer the pulp very slowly, and stir in the eggs gradually. When it comes to a boil, take it off; stir very hard, and set it to cool; serve cold, with nutmeg grated over the top.[1365]

ORANGE CHEESE PIE
☞ Is made just the same but change the water in boiling peel to extract the bitter, add the orange juice and a little lemon juice.[1366]

ORANGE PIE
☞ Cream together half lb. sugar and two ounces of butter, the grated rind and juice of an orange, one tablespoon of flour, one-fourth cup of water, yolks of five eggs, white of one egg, beaten very light and added. Make a meringue of two or three whites and put on top after it is baked, and put in a cool oven to brown. Makes one pie, but the very best.[1367]

ORANGE CUSTARD
☞ Six yolks beaten light, cream one cup each of sugar and butter, stir in the yolks, one tablespoon of flour one and a half tablespoons of milk or water, juice of two oranges, outside grated, little nutmeg. Two custards, you can put a meringue on top. Fine.[1368]

SYRUP CUSTARD
☞ Two eggs beaten, half cup sugar, three-fourths cup of any preserve syrup, one tablespoonful butter melted, one tablespoonful of flour. Bake on single crust. Elegant.[1369]

CARAMEL CUSTARD
☞ Put a cupful of granulated sugar into a small saucepan with a tablespoonful of water; stir until melted; then let it cook until a light brown color. Turn one half the caramel into a well-buttered mold which has straight sides and flat top, and let it get cold. Into the rest of the caramel turn a half cupful of hot water, and let it stand on the side of the range until the caramel is dissolved. This is for the sauce.

Stir four yolks and two whole eggs, with three tablespoonfuls of sugar, and one half saltspoonful of salt, to a cream, but do not let it froth; add a pint of scalded milk and a half teaspoonful of vanilla. Strain this into the mold onto the cold hardened caramel. Place the mold in a pan of hot water, and bake in a very moderate oven until firm in the center; test by running in a knife (see baked custard), and watch it carefully. The water in the pan must not boil, and the oven should be so slow that it will take at least an hour to cook the custard. It will then be very firm and smooth. Unmold the custard when ready to serve. It will have a glaze of caramel over the top, and some will run down the sides. Serve the caramel sauce in another dish. This dish is recommended.[1370]

Custard kettle.

CHOCOLATE CUSTARD

☞ The yolks of three eggs beaten with three-fourths of a cup of sugar, one tablespoonful of butter, one tablespoonful of flour, half cup of milk, two ounces melted chocolate, vanilla to flavor. Bake on single crust. Cover with a meringue. Delicious.[1371]

SYLLABUB

☞ Cream for this purpose must be perfectly sweet and very rich. Stir in gradually enough white wine to favor it, but not enough to curdle it; sweeten it with powdered loaf sugar, and put it into glasses. Make some cream very sweet with powdered loaf sugar, flavor it with lemon juice, whip it to a froth with rods or wires, and pile it high on the glasses.[1372]

CHOCOLATE PIE

☞ Line a deep pie plate with rich crust. Dissolve in a saucepan one-fourth of a pound of chocolate, half cup of milk. Beat yolks of three eggs with half a cup of sugar and stir in hot chocolate. Put the whole back on the stove; add a teaspoonful of butter and a tablespoonful of cornstarch wet in a little cold milk. Let come to a good boil. Remove and let get cold. Flavor with vanilla. Bake crust first. When the mixture is cold beat the whites stiff, add three tablespoonfuls of sugar to them. Put about one-third of whites in the chocolate mixture. Put in some Maraschino cherries or pineapple chopped fine; then put it on crust, bake and cover with a meringue. Sift sugar over and brown in a cool oven.[1373]

KENTUCKY BUTTERSCOTCH PIE

☞ 2 cups brown sugar.
2 cups milk.
3 tbls. flour.
1 teaspoon vanilla.
3 eggs.
1 tbls. butter.

Separate the eggs; mix the ingredients in order given, using egg yolks. Cook over double boiler till thick. Pour into crust already baked. Use egg whites and three tbls. sugar for meringue and brown in oven. Recipe makes two pies.

Recipe for crust:
1 cup flour.
3 level tbls. Snowdrift [shortening].
½ teaspoon salt.
3 tbls. ice water.

Sift flour and salt into a bowl, adding Snowdrift and three tbls. ice water.[1374]

RHUBARB PIE
☛ Take four stalks rhubarb, cut in short lengths and peel off the red skin. Pour over boiling water and let stand ten minutes. Mix a cup of sugar with a tablespoonful of flour, drain the rhubarb, put in your pie plate and sprinkle over the sugar with bits of butter and juice of half a lemon. Bake between crusts or only a top crust.[1375]

SWEET POTATO PIE 1
☛ Put through a strainer enough boiled or baked sweet potatoes to make two cups, add three-fourths of a cup of sweet milk, beat separately four eggs, cream three-fourths of a cup of butter and one cup sugar; then beat in the yolks, the potato and milk, half a nutmeg, half a cup of whiskey or fruit juice, and lastly fold in the stiff whites. Bake on single crust. Serve cold with powdered sugar sifted over. Makes two large pies. Elegant.[1376]

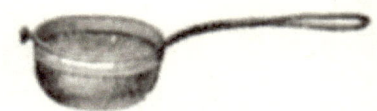
Handled strainer.

SWEET POTATO PIE 2
☛ Two pounds of potatoes will make two pies. Boil the potatoes soft; peel and mash fine through a colander while hot; one tablespoonful of butter to be mashed in with the potato. Take five eggs and beat the yolks and whites separate and add one gill of milk; sweeten to taste; squeeze the juice of one orange, and grate one-half of the peel into the liquid. One half teaspoonful of salt in the potatoes. Have only one crust and that at the bottom of the plate. Bake quickly.[1377]

SWEET POTATO PIE 3
(Famous Virginia Recipe)
☛ 1 pound boiled sweet potato.
¾ pound sugar.
¾ pound butter.
6 eggs.
1 lemon.
1 glass of brandy.

Rub the potatoes while hot through a colander. Cream the butter and sugar till very light and add to the potatoes. Beat 6 eggs till foamy and add to the mixture. Flavor with grated nutmeg, the juice and grated rind of 1 lemon, and add 1 glass of brandy. Line a pie-plate with rich pastry and pour the ingredients in and bake in a moderate oven. When done, sprinkle the top with sugar and cover with fine bits of citron.[1378]

SWEET POTATO CUSTARD
☛ Weigh a pound of sweet potatoes after boiling and running through a sieve. Cream half pound of sugar and one-fourth pound of butter; add

to potatoes with a small cup of milk and four beaten eggs; nutmeg and lemon to flavor, Bake on single crust. Makes two pies.[1379]

IRISH POTATO CUSTARD

☛ Boil some potatoes, mash and strain. Use two cups potatoes, one cup butter, one cup milk, two cups sugar, six beaten eggs. Flavor with wine and nutmeg. Bake on single crust or in a pudding dish.[1380]

CONFEDERATE CHOCOLATE CUSTARD

☛ 1 quart of milk.
4 eggs.
1½ bars of chocolate.
Sugar to taste.
Scald the milk and stir the chocolate in after it is grated. Beat the eggs and sugar together and stir into the milk, and let it cook till it is thick as boiled custard. Flavor with vanilla and pour into cups. Serve cold with whipped cream.[1381]

BAKER'S CUSTARD PIE

☛ Beat the yolks of three eggs. Stir thoroughly a tablespoonful sifted flour and four tablespoonfuls of sugar; this separates the flour. Add the beaten yolks, pinch of salt, little vanilla and nutmeg; next the beaten whites and a pint of scalded milk that has been cooled. Bake in a deep pie pan lined with paste. When cold, sift over sugar. Fine.[1382]

Colander.

MRS. MATTHEWS' CUSTARD PIE

☛ One pint of milk, three eggs beaten a little, two tablespoonfuls sugar, a little salt. Bake on a single crust. When done, grate over nutmeg. Fine.[1383]

CUSTARD PIE

☛ For two pies. Beat four eggs until you can take up spoonful; add half a teaspoonful of salt, two-thirds of cup of sugar; beat again, and when mixed add two and a half cups of milk. Turn into a deep plate lined with pastry. Bake in a slow oven. Grate nutmeg over the top.[1384]

SOUTHERN TOMATO PIE

☛ For one pie, peel and slice green tomatoes, add four table-spoons vinegar, one of butter, three of sugar; flavor with nutmeg or cinnamon; bake with two crusts slowly. This tastes very much like a green apple pie.[1385]

NUTMEG PIE

☞ 3 eggs beaten separately,
1 pint sugar,
1 medium-sized nutmeg,
Piece of butter the size of an egg.
Mix, adding the whites last. This will make pies.[1386]

NEAPOLITANS

☞ Make puff paste, using all butter, or they won't rise. After it is ice cold cut in strips one and a half by three inches. Bake in a hot oven, When done brush over with egg, sprinkle with chopped almonds; put back to toast the almonds. When cold split and fill with the following cream.[1387]

DATE PIE

☞ Soak one pound of dates over night in a little water and stew them in the same the next morning until soft enough to strain through a colander; add one quart of rich milk, three well-beaten eggs, a pinch of salt, butter size of a walnut and four or five gratings of nutmeg. Bake with an under crust. This quantity is sufficient for three pies. Icing may be made for the top.[1388]

ST. HONORE CREAM

Gateau St. Honore.

☞ One pint of milk, two-thirds cup of flour, one cup of sugar, grated rind of a lemon, little salt, six eggs beaten separately, the stiff whites added last. Mix the flour, half the sugar, salt with the hot milk. Cook in double boiler until thick. Beat the yolks and the rest of the sugar and add to the hot mixture. Stir until eggs are cooked. Stir in the stiff whites last. Cool and flavor. Chocolate may be added to part of the cream. Sift powdered sugar over them. Fine.[1389]

COCOANUT PIE

☞ Half pound grated cocoanut, three-fourths of a pound sugar, six ounces butter, whites of five eggs, wineglass of wine, nutmeg and a little extract of rose to flavor. Cream light butter and sugar, add flavor, cocoanut lightly stirred in, then the stiff whites. Sift sugar over the top when cold. Elegant.[1390]

COCOANUT CUSTARDS

☞ Beat light eight yolks, cream half pound sugar and half pound butter and add to eggs, six heaping tablespoonfuls grated cocoanut. Flavor with lemon and cover with meringue. Two pies. Two whites to a pie will make a meringue; three whites are better. Splendid.[1391]

DELICIOUS COCOANUT CUSTARDS
☞ Cream a full tablespoon of butter and three-fourths of a cup of sugar, add half a cup of milk or milk from cocoanut and half the meat from a grated cocoanut, two eggs beaten separately, lemon juice and vanilla to flavor. For one large pie.[1392]

PINEAPPLE MERINGUE CUSTARD
☞ For three pies use one quart boiled milk thickened with three tablespoonfuls flour wet in a little cold milk. When thick, set off; put in one tablespoonful of butter, one pound sugar, nine eggs beaten separately. Beat light the yolks and sugar, stir into the milk; then half a cup grated pineapple; lastly, the whites beaten stiff or make a meringue. Elegant.[1393]

Small custard cups.

BANANA CREAM PIE
☞ Line a pie pan with crust and bake in a hot oven. When done, cover the bottom with slices of banana cut lengthwise, very thin. (Two small bananas are enough for one pie.) Then fill the pan with a custard made in the following manner: Two glasses of milk, two tablespoonfuls of corn-starch dissolved in a little milk, yolks of two eggs and one teaspoonful of vanilla extract. Boil in a double boiler until it thickens; then pour it into the pie crust. Cover the top with the whites of the eggs beaten stiff and slightly sweetened. Place in the oven just long enough to give it a rich brown color.[1394]

CHESS CAKES
☞ Peel and grate a cocoanut. Boil a pound of sugar in a cup of water; stir in the grated cocoanut and boil fifteen minutes. While warm stir in one-fourth pound of butter, yolks of seven beaten eggs, wine and nutmeg to flavor. Makes two pies. If desiccated cocoanut is used take a cup of Macaroon cocoanut. Delicious.[1395]

PINEAPPLE MERINGUE TARTS
☞ Heat one can of grated pineapple and half cup sugar. When boiling thicken with two tablespoonfuls flour dissolved in one-fourth cup of water. Boil three minutes; add the juice of a lemon and two beaten egg yolks. Remove and cool. Bake your pastry over individual cake pans; fill with the mixture and cover with meringue made of the whites.[1396]

ORANGE MERINGUE PIE
☞ Cream half a cup of butter and a cup of granulated sugar, beat light the yolks of four eggs, mix them into the butter and sugar; add the juice

and a little grated peel of an orange, a teaspoonful of lemon juice and the stiff whites of two eggs. Line a pie tin with paste, turn in the mixture and bake until brown. Make a meringue of the two whites and two tablespoonfuls of sugar; spread over the pie, dust with sugar, and brown delicately.[1397]

CRANBERRY PIE

☞ 1 teacup of sugar,
1 teacup of cranberries, or cherries,
½ teacup of raisins,
1 tablespoon of butter,
1 tablespoon of flour.

Cream butter, add flour, then sugar and cranberries. Put mixture in raw crust and bake with top. Cook 30 minutes in slow oven.[1398]

CREAM PIE

☞ 1 quart of sweet milk,
2 eggs,
2 tablespoons of flour.

Mix the flour with some of the milk and let the remainder come to a boil. Beat the eggs light; put in the flour, and pour the boiling milk on these. Sweeten to taste and strain. Cook till thick as custard, stirring all the time. When cold, flavor with essence of lemon.

Bake a crust made of rich puff paste, and when cold, fill with the custard. The success of this depends on the cooking, and many good cooks slip a sharp knife under the crust here and there while it is cooking to make it light as possible.[1399]

Cranberry pie.

COCOANUT CREAM PIE

☞ One-half cup of prepared cocoanut soaked five minutes in two cups of milk, one egg, one small cup of sugar, butter the size of a walnut, one small tablespoonful of corn-starch. Put the milk and cocoanut over the stove in a double boiler and when hot stir in the sugar, then the butter and the yolk of the egg beaten in a little cold milk and one tablespoonful of corn-starch dissolved in milk. When cooked pour into a pie shell previously baked. Put a meringue on top.[1400]

CHOCOLATE CREAM PIE

☞ Heat one pint of milk to scalding, add one-third of a cake of Baker's chocolate, beat the yolks of four eggs with one coffee-cupful of sugar, then add the milk and the whites of the eggs last. Flavor with vanilla. A puff paste should be made for this and previously baked.¹⁴⁰¹

OLD-FASHIONED APPLE PIE

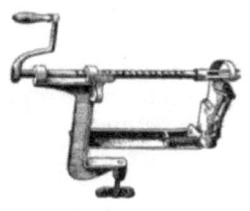
Apple parer.

☛ An old-fashioned apple pie that appeals to all tastes is made in the following manner: After making a nice light crust and covering a deep pie tin with it, wet the edge with cold water and lay a very thin strip all around to keep the juice in. Then pare, core and slice tart apples and lay them in the dish with plenty of sugar and any spice that may be preferred, such as cinnamon, ground cloves and grated lemon rind with the lemon juice. If the fruit is not juicy enough, the peelings and cores may be boiled in a little sugar and flavoring and then strained and added to the fruit. Bake in a quick oven.¹⁴⁰²

CONFEDERATE WHIPPED CREAM PIE

☛ Line a pie plate with rich crust, bake. When cool spread over a layer of jelly or marmalade. Whip a cup of sweetened and flavored cream until solid; pour it over the marmalade.¹⁴⁰³

BANBURY TARTS

☛ Make a nice paste, cut into pieces six inches square; in the center of each put a tablespoonful of jam, fold it in half and pinch the edges lightly together. Drop in a kettle of deep boiling cottolene.¹⁴⁰⁴

MARLBORO TARTS

☛ Quarter and stew twelve tart apples. To each cup of this pulp rubbed through a sieve add a cup of sugar, half cup melted butter, a cup of milk, juice and rind of a lemon, three eggs, half a nutmeg. Beat all together and bake in pastry. Very fine.¹⁴⁰⁵

CHEESE PIE

☛ One teacupful of sour milk curd slightly salted, two eggs, three-fourths of a cup of sweet milk, one-half cup of sugar and one-half cup of English currants well cleaned. Rub the curd thoroughly before mixing with the other ingredients. Bake in a deep pie tin lined with rich crust. Powder with cinnamon.¹⁴⁰⁶

SHORT CAKE

☛ Pick over your berries; if clean, never wash them. Put one cup of sugar to a box of strawberries; three-fourths of a cup of sugar to a quart of raspberries. For the short cake use two cups of flour, two teaspoonfuls baking powder, or half teaspoonful of soda to a rounding teaspoonful of cream of tartar; sift together, then add half a teaspoonful of salt. Chop in two rounding tablespoonfuls butter; two-thirds cup of milk added very gradually so as not to get it too soft. Don't tough the dough at all with the hands, but use a knife. Next, divide it into four equal parts. Make each part as round as possible. Have the board well floured and a little flour over the top.

Roll as round as possible; then make another piece the same size. Butter the lower cake and put the other on top. Let bake. Split, butter, mash the berries and sugar and spread between layers and over the top. Fix just before using, or it becomes soggy. You may serve some mashed berries as sauce, also cream.[1407]

ORANGE SHORT CAKE

☛ Remove the peel and white covering of three oranges, slice lengthwise and add the juice of half a lemon, sugar to sweeten. Put between layers as above.

Whip a cup of cream stiff, flavor with vanilla and put over the upper layer of oranges.[1408]

MARMALADE TART

☛ Line a pie plate with pastry, fill with apple or peach marmalade. Pare and core two or three apples, cut in rings, cover the top and sprinkle with sugar and bits of lemon. Bake until the apples are done. Serve with whipped cream or a slice of ice cream on top.[1409]

COCOANUT TARTLETS

☛ Put on to boil one cup of sugar and one cup of water. When it gets syrupy add half a pound desiccated cocoanut; boil a little longer.

Pie trimmer and marker.

Remove from the fire, add a little lemon juice and the grated rind, the yolks of three beaten eggs and two tablespoonfuls of cherries chopped fine. Line patty pans with paste, put in the cocoanut mixture and bake in a moderate oven. This makes ten tartlets.[1410]

HUCKLEBERRY PIE

☛ Pick out all the stems and wash one quart of berries; line a pie dish with paste, put in the berries two-thirds of an inch deep; cover with two-thirds of a teacupful of brown sugar; sprinkle a teaspoonful of flour over, a little salt; cover the pie, cut a slit in the center, press the two crusts together around the edge and bake in a quick oven for forty minutes.[1411]

BLACKBERRY PIE

☛ Wash a quart of berries, put on to cook; when soft, add a tablespoonful of flour and three-fourths to a cup of sugar.

Bake between crusts. Nice flavored with ginger and cinnamon.[1412]

CREAM PUFFS

☞ Half a cup of butter to one cup boiling water. (Lard or cottolene may be used.) When it boils stir in a cup of sifted flour, a little salt. Stir until the mixture leaves sides of pan. Turn into a bowl and beat in four eggs, one at a time, beating in each one thoroughly before adding the next one. Sometimes three eggs are enough. Shape the paste in rounds with a spoon, brush over the top with egg and milk, bake about twenty-five minutes or until quite firm. When cold, open the side and fill with whipped cream sweetened, crushed strawberries mixed with the cream, or a filling such as the following.[1413]

CREAM FILLING

☞ Scald a pint of milk in a double boiler. Sift together half a cup of sugar and half a cup flour, one-fourth teaspoonful salt. Dilute these with a little of the hot milk, then add to the rest of the milk and stir and cook until the mixture thickens; then cook fifteen minutes stirring occasionally. Beat two eggs or four yolks and one-fourth cup of sugar; stir in the hot mixture. Stir until eggs are cooked; then cool, flavor with vanilla and put in the cream puffs. Pour a little sherry over and sift over powdered sugar.[1414]

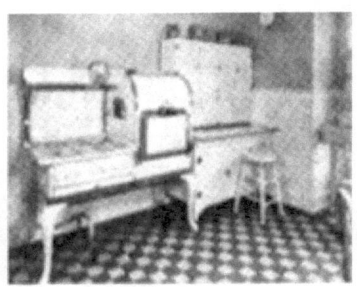

Vintage kitchen.

FRUIT FILLING

☞ 1 pound almonds in the shell,
½ pound raisins,
¼ pound citron,
¼ pound figs.

Blanch almonds and cut into 2 or 3 small pieces. Scald and clip raisins and cut figs and citron into small pieces. For icing, use 3 eggs and 3 cups sugar. Flavor with rose and stir in fruit. In making icing, put 3 cups of white sugar into pan and cover with water and let boil till thick, then pour over the well-beaten whites of three eggs, whipping all the time, and when thick put quickly between cakes.[1415]

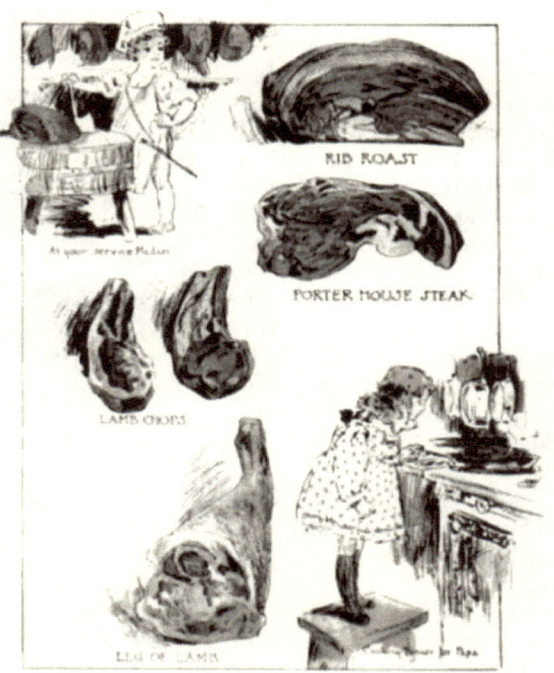

Various meats.

19. Pickling and Catsups

TO MAKE PICKLES

☛ As far as possible, it is well to boil the vinegar for pickles in stoneware jars, rather than in metal vessels. The hot vinegar dissolves the tin from the iron pans, and a portion of the substance from brass and copper ones, which is unwholesome. Stoneware jars, or glass bottles should always be used for keeping pickles, and never red glazed earthen jars.

These latter are glazed with lead, and this, when dissolved by the acid of the vinegar, is poisonous. It is essential that green pickles be well closed. Bottles are best corked and closed with wax, and for tying down jars, bladder; wash leather and gutta-percha tissue are good. Green pickle jars should be examined occasionally, and if mold is found to have accumulated, and the vinegar to have become insipid to the taste, it should be poured away, and new vinegar, which has been well boiled with a little spice, and allowed to cool, poured in. By attending to these directions, pickles may be kept good for many years, and will rather become better than worse.

Barbed pickle fork.

Walnuts especially always improve after several years keeping, and to be tasted in perfection should never be eaten new. It is important to keep pickles in a light dry place. Only the best cider vinegar ought to be used in making pickles. Yellow pickles and mango pickles are better for being kept several years.

Other kinds of pickle are better if used within the year in which they are made. Dissolve a small piece of alum in the salt and water that cucumbers are soaked in.[1416]

TO MAKE VINEGAR

☛ Have a barrel of good cider vinegar made in the summer or fall, and keep it until the next spring. Then take a tierce, and put in some good mother of vinegar, if you can get it; if not, put in 1 sheet of letter paper, some fermented preserves, 2 or 3 gallons of whiskey, and ½ gallon of molasses. This is an excellent receipt.[1417]

CIDER VINEGAR

☛ Mix with ten gallons of cider five quarts of strained honey; put it in a cask, and in six months you will have a vinegar too strong for common purposes, without diluting it with water.[1418]

TARRAGON VINEGAR

☛ Pick the leaves of the tarragon from the stalks just before it blooms; spread them out on a cloth, and let them lie for two or three days to dry a little; then put them into a jar of quality vinegar, close it and set it by for one week; then strain and bottle it. If you wish it very strongly flavored with the tarragon, fill it up the second time with fresh leaves and soak them in the same manner. Any kind of nice sweet herbs may be soaked in the same manner for the purpose of seasoning.[1419]

PLAIN PICKLES

☛ Any vegetable you want to pickle under this head, say small or large cucumbers, cabbage or green tomatoes, have them fresh and put them into a barrel, one layer of cucumbers, or other vegetable, about three inches deep, covering

Cucumber slicer.

thickly with salt, and repeating layers and salt until you have under brine all you desire to pickle. Let them remain under the brine, if you want to pickle right away, for twenty-four hours, which is long enough, but they will keep a long time by always having them well pressed down with a heavy rock. If you are going to pickle vegetables twenty-four hours after putting them in salt, let them lay in fresh water for two hours, so as to get the smell of the old brine off them. Take them out of the water and put to drain on a sieve made for that purpose of galvanized iron, square, three by four feet, or larger, if needed. Let them drain two or three days, then put in a clean keg or barrel and cover thoroughly with vinegar. Sprinkle over a keg of pickles two ounces of powdered alum while under the vinegar. Let them so remain twelve or twenty-four hours, then pour off the vinegar from the pickles into a large kettle and put to boil. Season while boiling, to five gallons of vinegar, one teacupful of allspice, one-fourth pound of ginger root, two ounces of cloves, one-half teacupful of black pepper, two tablespoonfuls of cayenne pepper. If you do not like pickles very hot, use one-half the quantity of peppers. When it boils with the seasonings twenty minutes, pour the boiling vinegar over the pickles. Make enough vinegar from these directions to cover well your pickles. They will keep a long time if under vinegar. Sprinkle over a five-gallon keg, when you put the vinegar on the pickles, two or three ounces of powdered alum, if you like pickles brittle.[1420]

SWEET PICKLES

☛ You can use cherries, damsons, peaches, or any other kind of fruit. Take off the stems and to seven pounds fruit, use three pounds sugar, one quart cider vinegar, one ounce of cinnamon, one half ounce of cloves. For two mornings vinegar and spices must be boiled and poured over the fruit; the third morning put all in the kettle and simmer a few minutes. Tie tightly and keep in a dark closet.[1421]

BLUE GRASS GREEN TOMATO PICKLE

☛ 1 peck of green tomatoes,
2 dozen onions,
2 tablespoons of mustard,
2 tablespoons of black pepper,
1 lemon,
2 tablespoons of turmeric,
3½ pounds of best brown sugar,
2 ounces of white mustard seed,
2 ounces of celery seed,
3 pods of red pepper,
3 pints of vinegar,
1 teaspoon of ground cloves,
1 teaspoon of allspice.

Slice tomatoes and onions and cover with salt and let stand over night. Squeeze well through a cloth; put in kettle and add ingredients, and boil till thick, stirring often to prevent sticking. Put in pint jars and seal.[1422]

GREEN PICKLE

☛ Put cucumbers, beans, small ears of corn, melons, etc., in brine strong enough to bear an egg. Let it stand 9 days or 2 weeks. When ready to make the pickle up, put them in kettle with grape or cabbage leaves and small lumps of alum. Cover with weak vinegar and simmer slowly till they are a fine green color. Drain them on a dish.

Bean pot.

½ ounce of mace,
1 ounce of cloves,

2 ounces of allspice,
1 ounce of cinnamon,
3 ounces of white mustard seed,
1 ounce of ground mustard,
2 ounces of whole grain black pepper,
1 ounce of race ginger,
1 ounce of celery seed,
½ pint of scraped horseradish.

Put spices in vinegar and pour boiling hot over pickle. Tie up closely in stone jars.[1423]

YELLOW PICKLE

☛ Take cabbage, cauliflower, nasturtium seed, asparagus, tender corn, and beans. Put into a kettle and pour over them boiling salt water and let stand 24 hours. Make this pickle on a clear day, and press the water from each piece and lay to dry on a cloth in the hot sun.

The cloth absorbs the moisture and the sun bleaches. By turning them often they become white and receive the turmeric better. One day of hot sun is enough to prepare them for the first vinegar. When dry, put in a jar and cover with cold plain vinegar, with a little turmeric.

Let stand 2 weeks and add spiced vinegar. Mix the turmeric smoothly before adding to the vinegar.[1424]

SPANISH PICKLE

☛ 2 dozen cucumbers,
½ peck of green tomatoes,
2 large green peppers, seeds taken out,
2 dozen white onions, sliced,
½ peck of beans.

Slice cucumbers thick, tomatoes thin, and sprinkle them with salt. Let stand 24 hours. Wash off the salt and let them drain well.

1 pint of grated horseradish,
1 pound of white mustard seed,
5 long red peppers,
15 cents' worth of cinnamon.

Make a paste of
1 pound of mustard (Colman's),
2 ounces of turmeric,
2 ounces of celery seed,
1 pint bottle of olive oil,
4 teacups of brown sugar,
1 handful of garlic.

Put vegetables in a large pan, mix spices and paste well together, and pour boiling vinegar over all enough to cover well.

Very fine. In place of tomatoes and beans, use cauliflower and celery.[1425]

CHOW CHOW 1

☞ One peck green tomatoes chopped fine, put in a bowl and mix in thoroughly a cup of salt. Let stand over night. The next morning put in a bag and drip; then chop fine six large onions, six large bell peppers; mix with the tomatoes and one tablespoonful of ground cloves, two of allspice, two of ground mustard, celery seed and sugar to taste. Cover well with vinegar and cook until done; then add one ounce of turmeric. Delightful.[1426]

CHOW CHOW 2

☞ Two gallons chopped cabbage, one gallon of green tomatoes sliced, one dozen onions sliced, one ounce of whole cloves, one ounce allspice, one ounce of ground ginger, half ounce white mustard seed, one ounce black pepper, two tablespoonfuls mustard, one ounce of celery seed, one cup of salt, two and a half pounds of brown sugar, one gallon of vinegar. Mix the salt with the cabbage and tomatoes, let stand over night, then drip all day in a bag; then put in the boiling vinegar with the spices and a teaspoonful of powdered alum, the sugar, and cook until tender; then add one ounce of turmeric. Fine.[1427]

Spice rack.

TAR HEEL CHOW CHOW

☞ Chop one head of cabbage, one gallon of green tomatoes, and one quart of onions. Add one-half cup of salt, put in a bag and let it drain for twenty-four hours.

Then put in kettle and add about two pounds of brown sugar, one cup of white mustard seed, and one-half cup of celery seed. Cover with good apple vinegar and cook until done, about three or four hours. To the above add one or two pods of chopped red pepper.[1428]

CHERRY CHUTNEY

☞ Get your cherries and seed them; to one gallon half dozen silver skin onions chopped fine; first put the onions to cook in half gallon of vinegar, 10 minutes, then add the cherries, season with two ounces of ground cinnamon, one teaspoonful of cayenne pepper and one of black pepper, two tablespoonfuls of salt, then let it continue to cook with a slow fire, twelve hours, stir it occasionally and keep from burning.[1429]

PLUM CHUTNEY

☞ 2 quarts plums (damsons).
¼ teaspoon each of ground mace, allspice, and cloves.
1 cup sugar to every 2 qts.

1 teaspoon ground cinnamon.
½ teaspoon salt.
1 grated lemon rind.
1 pint vinegar and water mixed.

Cook the plums in the liquid until they may be pressed through a sieve; add sugar and other ingredients. Simmer until thick as catsup. Keep in stone crock, or sealed in fruit jars.[1430]

SWEET MANGO PICKLES

☛ Use small musk melons or cantaloupes when quite tender. Cut a slit and put in strong brine for several days; take out, remove the seed and put in fresh water for twelve or twenty-four hours, changing water. Then scald in half vinegar and half water and a piece of alum. When green take out, wipe dry and let drain a few hours before stuffing.

Dressing: One pound each of black and white mustard seed, one and a half tablespoonfuls of cloves, one tablespoonful grain black pepper, two onions cut fine, one cup of celery seed, one ounce of mace, a little turmeric, some cucumbers cut small, five pounds brown sugar, one lemon to a dozen mangos. Before stuffing the mangos put a gallon of vinegar and most of the sugar on in a kettle; scald the melons in this syrup. Rub the inside of each melon with sugar, put in a small clove of garlic, then the stuffing; tie and place in your jar, slit side up. Put the sliced lemon between the layers; use two or three for a four gallon jar; more will make it bitter. This will stuff three dozen melons. Pour the vinegar over hot. In a few days look to see if more vinegar is needed; it soaks it up. If so, scald and sweeten vinegar enough to cover melons.[1431]

SWEET WATERMELON RIND PICKLE

☛ Take the melon rind and scrape all the meat from the inside, and then carefully slice all the outside of rind from the white part of the rind, then lay or cover the white part over with salt. It will have to remain under salt one week before pickling; the rind will keep in salt from year to year. When you want to pickle it, take it from the salt and put into clear water, change the water three times a day—must be changed say every four hours—then take the rind from water and dry it with a clean cloth. Have your vinegar boiling, and put the rind into it and let it scald four minutes, then take it off the fire and let it lay in vinegar four days; then take it from the vinegar, drain, and sprinkle sugar thickly over it and let it remain so one day. To make syrup, take the syrup from the rind and add eight pounds more sugar to it, and put to boil; boil till a thick and clear syrup. Weigh ten pounds of rind to twelve pounds of sugar; cover

Plums.

Strainer stand.

the rind with four pounds of it and make the syrup with the remaining eight pounds. While the syrup is cooking add one teacupful of white ginger root and the peel of three lemons. When the syrup is cooked, then put the rind into the boiling syrup, and let it cook till you can pass a fork through it with ease, then it is done. When cooled put in jar or bottles with one pint of vinegar to one quart of syrup, thus the pickle is made. See that they be well covered with vinegar and syrup as directed.[1432]

VIRGINIA YELLOW PICKLE

☛ Two and a half gallons of good vinegar, seven pounds of brown sugar, one pound of white mustard-seed, one of ginger, one half pound of white pepper, one quarter of a pound of turmeric, one box of mustard, and two ounces of nutmeg, mace, celery-seed, allspice, and grated horseradish. Mix the turmeric with a small portion of vinegar, as you do mustard, and add to the spiced vinegar, or tie it up in a thin bag. Slice and scald two dozen large onions; sprinkle them with salt, let them stand a day, then drain well, say for six hours, and wash them in vinegar, and throw into the jar of spiced vinegar with half a dozen lemons or limes sliced thin. Select firm heads of cabbage, split them in halves, or quarter them, scald them in brine that will bear an egg until they are half done, drain them, and squeeze the moisture out with a napkin, and lay in the sun for one day. Put them in plain vinegar for a fortnight, after which they must be drained and sunned another day, before they go into the spiced vinegar. This vinegar may be prepared at any season, and the cabbage added when you choose. One jar of vinegar will make three of pickled cabbage. The spices must all be pounded (but not finely) before putting into the vinegar. It will be ready for use in a week. Keep the jar covered tightly.[1433]

SWEET PEACH PICKLE

☛ Ten pounds of fruit to four pounds of sugar. Peel your peaches, put the sugar with them, and let stand over night. Next morning drain the syrup from them, put on to boil; put in a few peaches at a time and cook until a little tender. If much syrup is left, boil it down and then put in quart of vinegar, half ounce of mace, half ounce of cloves, half ounce of cinnamon. When this boils put back fruit and boil ten minutes. Put up in half gallon self sealing jars. Elegant.[1434]

PICKLED RED CABBAGE

☛ Select large, firm heads of red cabbage, cut each one in four, and slice them as for slaugh; put them in a vessel of strong salt-water, and let them lie in it for twentyfour hours; this will make them more brittle than to sprinkle dry salt on them; take them from the brine, and put them in a stone or earthen jar. Boil for a few minutes a sufficient quantity of the best vinegar to cover them well, with cloves, mustard seeds, and mace, proportioning them to suit your own taste; strain it, color it a fine pink with cochineal, and when it gets perfectly cold, pour it over the cabbage, stopping the jar closely with cork or leather.[1435]

TOMATO CATSUP 1

☛ Half bushel tomatoes, four ounces salt, three ounces ground black pepper, one ounce cinnamon, half ounce ground cloves, one drachm cayenne pepper, one gallon vinegar; slice the tomatoes and stew In their own liquor until soft, and rub through a sieve fine enough to retain the seeds; boil the pulp and juice down to the consistency of apple-butter (very thick), stirring steadily all the time to prevent burning; then add the vinegar with which a small tea-cup sugar and the spices have been mixed, boil up twice, remove from fire, let cool and bottle. Those who like the flavor of onions may add about half a dozen medium-sized ones, peeled and sliced, fifteen minutes before the vinegar and spices are put in.[1436]

TOMATO CATSUP 2

☛ Cut up your tomatoes and sprinkle with very little salt; put in a stone jar and let ferment, say three or four days; then cook and strain, To two gallons of juice put one quart of onions cut very fine, about six red bell peppers whole, a few cloves, a little allspice, some celery seed, some mustard, light brown sugar to sweeten to taste. Boil until it thickens; then add one and a half quarts of vinegar. Skim well before putting in seasonings. When it comes to a good boil, bottle. It may need more salt.[1437]

MUSHROOM CATSUP

☛ Gather fresh mushrooms and put alternate layers of salt and mushrooms in a jar and let them stand 24 hours. Stir them up and let them stand 2 days. Strain and put on the stove and let it boil.

To 1 quart of liquor add
1 ounce allspice,
1 ounce ginger,
2 teaspoons cayenne pepper,
1 teaspoon mace,
1 teaspoon cloves.
Boil till thick. While catsup is hot, bottle and seal. Nice for soups.[1438]

CUCUMBER CATSUP

☛ Grate the cucumbers, sprinkle with salt; to every three dozen cucumbers grate one half dozen large onions, a little horseradish; press the cucumbers till all the water is out. Save the water and measure it;

when dry, use the same quantity of good vinegar as there is of water; add sugar and a little turmeric; season with black and cayenne pepper, and white mustard seed; mix thoroughly, put in bottles and cork them tight.[1439]

CORN RELISH

☛ Ten cups of corn cut from cob, 10 cups chopped cabbage, 5 peppers, 3 green and 2 large red; 2½ pints vinegar, 1 tablespoon salt, 3 tablespoons granulated sugar, 2 tablespoons white mustard seed, 2 tablespoons celery seed, 1 bunch celery cut in small pieces. Mix well and cook ½ hour, put in pint jars and seal.[1440]

PICCALILLI

☛ One half peck green tomatoes fully grown. Chop well and add ½ pt. salt. Let them stand a day in cold water. Chop a large head of cabbage, 4 large onions, and 5 green peppers; cover with boiling vinegar. Let set four hours, then drain through a colander, add 1 cup molasses, 1 teaspoon each cloves, allspice, and white mustard seed. Cover with cold vinegar.[1441]

GAME SAUCE

☛ Take one peck of plums, half dozen silver skin onions and chop them very fine; put on the plums to cook. First seed plums; use a porcelain kettle; put the onions to stew in a pint of vinegar until thoroughly done, then add them to the plums; four pounds of granulated sugar to be added; season with one teaspoonful of cayenne pepper, one of black pepper, two ounces of cinnamon broke in five pieces; cook on a slow fire, stir frequently to avoid burning—one teaspoonful of table salt—it will take one whole day to cook; when cool cork in a tight jar and keep in cool closet—you will find it the best sauce in the world.[1442]

STUFFED CUCUMBERS

☛ Select one dozen large green cucumbers; cut a small piece from one end and remove the seed with a teaspoon. Put in strong salt water and let remain over night. Then chop very fine six heads of celery, six green tomatoes, one small cabbage, and three bell peppers; add one cup of sugar, half a cup of salt, two tablespoonfuls of mustard seed, and vinegar enough to mix together. Wash cucumbers in cold water and fill with the mixture; fasten the tops on with tooth picks, put in jars and cover with boiling spiced vinegar. Nice to serve with cold meats.[1443]

PICKLED EGGS

☛ Boil them till they are hard; throw them into cold water immediately while hot, which will make the shells slip off smoothly without breaking the eggs. Boil some red beets till very soft; peel and mash them fine, and put enough of the juice into some plain cold vinegar to color it a fine pink; add a very little salt, pepper, nutmeg and cloves; put the eggs into a jar, and transfuse the vinegar, etc., over them. They make a delightful garnish to remain whole, for poultry, game and fish, and still more beautiful when cut in ringlets.[1444]

GREEN MANGO PICKLES

☛ After having been in brine for several weeks, soak the mangoes in cold water for 2 days; then boil in vinegar, and let them stand in that vinegar for a week.

After that, take the seed from them and fill them with the following spices:

    1 pound of ginger, soaked in brine a day or two, or until soft enough to slice,
    1 ounce of grain black pepper,
    1 ounce of mace,
    1 ounce of allspice,
    1 ounce of cloves,
    1 ounce of turmeric,
    ½ pound of garlic, soaked for a day or two in brine, then dried,
    1 pint of grated horseradish,
    1 pint of black mustard seed,
    1 pint of white mustard seed.

Bruise all the spices and mix with teacup of olive oil. To each mango add 1 teaspoonful of brown sugar. This mixture will fill 4 dozen mangoes, having chopped up some of the indifferent ones to mix with the stuffing. Tie them up and pour over them best cider vinegar.

After a month, add 3 pounds of brown sugar. Keep closely covered, and don't eat for a year.[1445]

CAULIFLOWER PICKLES

☛ Choose such as are fine and of full size, cut away all the leaves, and pull away the flowers by bunches; soak in brine that will float an egg for two days, drain, put in bottles with whole black pepper, allspice, and stick cinnamon; boil vinegar, and with it mix mustard smoothly, a little at a time and just thick enough to run into the jars, pour over the cold cauliflower and seal while hot.

An equal quantity or less of small white onions, prepared as directed in recipe for onion pickles, may be added before the vinegar is poured over.[1446]

CUCUMBER PICKLES

☛ Take eighty-five cucumbers, put in salt water one day and night; one plate horseradish, two tablespoonfuls whole black pepper, two red peppers, two onions, one teaspoonful mace, same of cloves, three tablespoonfuls allspice, four tablespoonfuls mustard seed, three tablespoonfuls celery seed, one pound sugar, two pieces ginger.[1447]

WALNUT CATSUP

☛ Gather the nuts as for pickle. Crush them, put in a jar and sprinkle lightly with salt. Let stand five or six days, then strain off the juice. To every gallon of juice, add one pint of chipped onion, one tablespoonful mace, black pepper. Boil for thirty or forty minutes. Bottle, seal and keep in cool, dark place.[1448]

PICKLED BELL PEPPERS

☛ Get the large bell pepper while young and green, leave the stems on, cut a slit in one side, and carefully extract the seeds and cores, pour boiling salt and water on them, cover them, and keep them in a warm place for one week, repeating the process every day, and stirring them occasionally; then if they are not a good green, keep them still longer in the brine, repeating the same process every day till they are; after which fill them up with a stuffing, tie a pack thread round them, to prevent the stuffing from coming out, and put them in a jar of plain cold vinegar; add a small lump of alum to keep them firm, and close the jar.[1449]

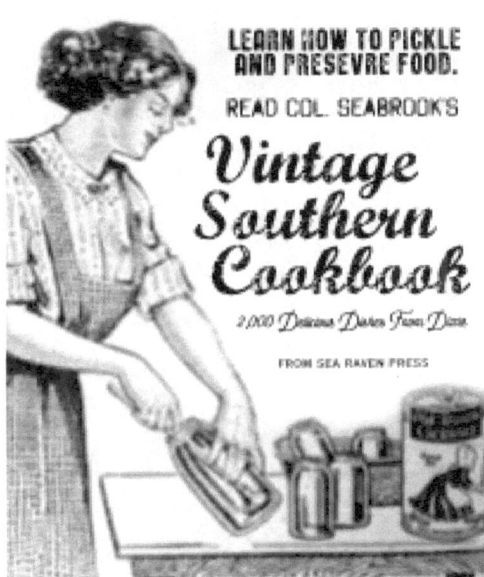

One of the finest cooks in the Old South: Marcellus of Kentucky (circa 1910), the master chef behind a number of the recipes in this book.

20. Salads

SALAD MAKING TIPS
☞ Salads are best marinaded for some time before you mix in the mayonnaise, which should be done at the last moment, as it liquefies if any moisture be in the meat.[1450]

TO MARINADE SALAD
☞ Make a sauce of three tablespoonfuls of vinegar to one of oil, one generous teaspoonful of salt, half a teaspoonful of white pepper. Add this to each quart of meat after it is cut. Set in refrigerator at least an hour or more. At serving time mix in half as much celery, and to this quantity drain and put in one cup of mayonnaise. The dressing must be suited to the material used. For French dressing use half as much acid as oil, and half as much pepper as salt. For Mayonnaise paprika is the favorite condiment. Tarragon vinegar is the flavoring that has precedence.[1451]

Lettuce salad.

RAW SALAD
☞ Gather your lettuce, tongue-grass, cress, etc., in the morning, while the dew is on; pick them nicely, and let them lie in a pan of cold water till dinner is nearly ready; then rinse them clean, drain them, put them in a plate, lay on the top a bunch of fine spring eschalots, having been nicely cleaned and the green ends split and curled; lay round them on the edge of the plate, some very small lumps of ice, and send it up immediately.[1452]

LETTUCE SALAD
☞ Place the prepared lettuce leaves in the salad bowl; sprinkle over it French dressing. Turn the leaves over and about until each leaf is covered with dressing. Serve on cold plates. Half a cup of dressing will serve six plates.[1453]

CAULIFLOWER SALAD

☞ Cook the cauliflower in boiling water till tender. Drop in cold water. Pull it apart and dry with a cloth. Serve with mayonnaise or French dressing.[1454]

From a vintage magazine ad for "Jell-O."

CELERY SALAD

☞ Cut crisp celery into short lengths and put on ice. When ready to serve, mix through it either mayonnaise or French dressing made of 2 tablespoons olive oil and 1 of vinegar, and salt and pepper to taste.[1455]

CELERY AND NUT SALAD

☞ Cut fine tender stalks of celery and some English walnut meat; mix with French dressing. Put in center with tender lettuce leaves and bits of curled celery.[1456]

PEACH SALAD

☞ Fill halves of canned California Crawford peaches with cherries and mixed nut meats. Serve on lettuce with a mayonnaise to which is added whipped sweet cream. Bartlett pears can be used instead of peaches.[1457]

FRUIT SALAD 1

☞ Put together in a bowl a small can of table peaches, small can each of apricots and pineapples sliced, six seedless oranges sliced. Sweeten and boil together the fruit juices. When cold add a cup of wine or maraschino. Pour over the fruit and serve cold.[1458]

FRUIT SALAD 2

☞ Cut oranges, bananas and pine apple in dice. Add to the mixed fruit some strawberries or canned cherries. To each one and a half pints allow a cup of sugar and half a cup of pineapple juice. Let the sugar and water boil ten minutes; set off to get cold; add some lemon juice. About an hour before serving pour over the fruit and set in refrigerator to get cold. Serve in sherbert glasses. Sherry wine improves it.[1459]

FRUIT SALAD 3

☞ Equal parts of fruit, Malaga grapes, celery, oranges, and nuts. Dressing of sugar, lemon juice, oil, and vinegar. Just before using, mix with whipped cream.[1460]

FRUIT SALAD 4

☞ 2 packages lemon Jell-O.
Mayonnaise.
1 can pears.

Lettuce.
1 can pineapple.
Follow directions on package for mixing Jell-O; when it begins to cool, put in cut pieces of pear and pineapple. When congealed serve with mayonnaise on lettuce.[1461]

SLAW
☛ One half head of good cabbage chopped finely, the yolks of two eggs, beat and put in a little vinegar, also some sour buttermilk if convenient; salt and butter to taste; boil thick and pour over the slaw.[1462]

COLD SLAW
☛ Select firm, fragile heads of cabbage, (no other sort being fit for slaw); having stripped off the outer leaves, cleave the top part of the head into four equal parts, leaving the lower part whole, so that they may not be separated till shaved or cut fine from the stalk. Take a very sharp knife, shave off the cabbage round-wise, cutting it very smoothly and evenly, and at no rate more than a quarter of an inch in width. Put the shavings or slaw in a deep china dish, pile it high, and make it smooth; mix with enough good vinegar to nearly fill the dish, a sufficient quantity of salt and pepper to season the slaw; add a spoonful of whole white mustard seeds, and pour it over the slaw, garnish it round on the edge of the dish with pickled eggs, cut in ringlets. Never put butter on cabbage that is to be eaten cold, as it is by no means pleasant to the taste or sight.[1463]

Salad of hard boiled eggs arranged on lettuce leaves.

WARM SLAW
☛ Prepare and cut cabbage up as for cold slaw; having put in a skillet enough butter, salt, pepper, and vinegar to season the slaw very well, put it into the seasonings; stir it fast, that it all may warm equally, and as soon as it gets hot, serve it in a deep china dish; make it smooth, and disseminate over it hard boiled yolks of eggs, that are minced fine.[1464]

BEEF SALAD
☛ Boil one pound of young, tender beef in enough boiling water, slightly salted, to cover. When perfectly tender, remove from the water and let it cool. Chip, shred or grind, as desired. Have ready three hard boiled eggs, chopped fine, two or three blades of celery and two cucumber pickles chopped fine. Mix these with the meat; season to taste with salt and pepper and last pour over it a teacupful of mayonnaise, mixing lightly with a fork.[1465]

BANANA SALAD

☛ Use red bananas, if possible, and slice them with silver knife. Shell English walnuts enough to make ⅓ quantity and chop fine. Mix fruit and nuts lightly and serve on lettuce with a mayonnaise dressing seasoned sharply with cayenne pepper.[1466]

EGG SALAD

☛ Take any number of hard-boiled eggs and remove the shells and cut in halves. Remove carefully the yellows and make a dressing of them with chopped ham, pepper, and salt, made mustard, butter, and a little cream. Mix well and fill the whites. Put on ice till ready to serve. Serve on lettuce leaves with French dressing or mayonnaise.[1467]

CUCUMBER SALAD

☛ Peel and slice cucumbers, not too thin; put on them crushed ice; cover closely and let stand half an hour; strain the water from them, add a little minced onion and a French dressing. Never sprinkle with salt; it toughens them.[1468]

CABBAGE SALAD

☛ Two quarts finely chopped cabbage, two level table-spoons salt, two of white sugar, one of black pepper, and a heaping one of ground mustard; rub yolks of four hard-boiled eggs until smooth, add half cup butter, slightly warmed; mix thoroughly with the cabbage, and add tea-cup good vinegar; serve with whites of the eggs sliced and placed on the salad.[1469]

Tomato salad.

CONFEDERATE CABBAGE SALAD

☛ Chop enough cabbage fine to fill a vegetable dish; heat a coffee cup full of strong vinegar, with a piece of butter in it the size of a small egg. Pepper and salt. When hot beat an egg very light and stir in, then pour it all onto the chopped cabbage.[1470]

TOMATO SALAD

☛ Slice tomatoes, place on a lettuce leaf, cover with mayonnaise and sprinkle with fine cut parsley.[1471]

HUNTER'S SALAD

☛ Cut cold wild ducks into thin slices and marinate in French dressing for several hours in a cold place. Shred a large head of celery into long strips, place in a salad-bowl and pile the meat in the center. Garnish with hard-boiled eggs chopped fine.[1472]

POTATO SALAD 1
☛ Use fresh boiled potatoes. Quarter them and cut slices across the grain. Season some cooked mayonnaise. Add a little minced parsley and grated onions; some whipped cream to make it light. Mix with the potatoes and garnish with hard boiled eggs cut in strips or parsley.[1473]

POTATO SALAD 2
☛ Boil and mash the potatoes fine, season highly with butter, pepper, salt, a little sweet cream, and then have ready about three hard boiled eggs to one quart of the mashed potato; take off the whites and chop fine; mash the yellows and mix them according to your taste with some made mustard, a little sugar, pepper, salt, and just enough vinegar to moisten the preparation; mix well these ingredients. Put a layer of the mashed potatoes in a flat pan, and with a spoon put the salad dressing in spots over the potatoes; another layer of potatoes, then the salad, and so on, putting potatoes on top. Smooth over nicely, and set in the stove to brown. A nice dish.[1474]

POTATO SALAD 3
☛ Boil the potatoes with the skins on; when cold remove the skins and cut them into slices three eighths inch thick, or into dice three quarters inch thick, or cut the potatoes into balls with a scoop; sprinkle them with a little grated onion and parsley, chopped very fine. Turn over them a French dressing. They will absorb a great deal. Toss them lightly together, but do not break the potatoes, which are very tender. A Mayonnaise dressing is also very good with marinated potatoes. A mixture of beets and potatoes with Mayonnaise is also used. Garnish with lettuce, chopped yolk of hard-boiled egg and capers. In boiling potatoes for salad, do not steam them after they are boiled, as they should not be mealy. New or German potatoes are best for salad.[1475]

OYSTER SALAD
☛ For a solid quart of oysters use this dressing: Beat well four eggs; add to them half a cup each of cream and vinegar, one teaspoonful of mustard, some celery seed or one pint of fresh celery cut small and added at serving time, one teaspoonful of salt, little cayenne, two tablespoonfuls of butter. Place in double boiler and cook until like soft custard, stirring constantly. Then add two tablespoonfuls rolled and sifted crackers. Scald the oysters in their own liquor; drain thoroughly, and add to them the dressing. Set in a cold place. At serving time add the celery.[1476]

CRAB SALAD
☛ Combine one pint of crab meat, two stalks of celery, cut fine; one hard-boiled egg chopped fine and one tomato cut into small pieces; season with salt, pepper and vinegar; thoroughly mix and place in

salad-bowl, garnishing it with crisp leaves of lettuce; dress with mayonnaise dressing.[1477]

BEET SALAD

☛ One can beets, French dressing, lettuce. Cut the beets into thin slices. Line the salad bowl with lettuce leaves; arrange on them the slices of beets; cover with French dressing and serve.[1478]

RUSSIAN SALAD

☛ One can tomatoes, 2 teaspoons chopped chives, 2 teaspoons chopped peppers, lettuce, mayonnaise dressing. Empty a can of tomatoes on a sieve and drain thoroughly. Spread lettuce hearts to form a nest, and fill the holes with large pieces of tomato. Serve with mayonnaise dressing and garnish with chives and peppers.[1479]

VEGETABLE SALAD

☛ Take nice fresh lettuce, separate the leaves; after washing thoroughly lay in cold water to crisp; when ready to use wipe dry and spread out on a flat dish.

Take some raw tomatoes, peel and slice thinly and lay over the lettuce; then a layer of cucumbers and over this another layer of tomatoes. Onion may be added if desired.

Dressing: Take the yolk of one egg and cook, stirring all the time to make a smooth paste; let cool; then take the yolks of two raw eggs and stir with the cooked one; add one-half teaspoonful of mustard, salt and sugar to taste. Stir in a tablespoonful or more of olive oil and into this stir the juice of one juicy lemon.

Just before serving pour the dressing over the salad and slice a lemon over the whole and serve. No vinegar. If pepper is added, use the red.[1480]

Vanderbilt salad.

CHICKEN SALAD

☛ Mix two parts of cold cooked chicken cut in dice to one part of celery cut small. Marinate and drain the chicken, add the celery dry, and mix with mayonnaise or boiled dressing. Arrange in nests of lettuce leaves and put a pimola in center of each nest.[1481]

SARDINE SALAD

☛ Wash the oil from a dozen sardines; remove the skin and bone. Put a head of crisp lettuce leaves in a salad bowl, chop up two hard boiled eggs, add the sardines to the lettuce, sprinkle with the egg, and pour over a plain salad dressing.[1482]

ANCHOVY SALAD

☛ Wash, skin and bone two anchovies, put in water to soak half an hour, drain, and dry them; then proceed as for sardine salad [above].[1483]

SALMON SALAD

☛ 1 can of salmon. Remove the skin and bones and pick into small pieces. Yolks of 6 hard-boiled eggs, 1 cup butter. Mash eggs and butter and add salmon with pepper and salt and 1 tablespoon made mustard. Serve on lettuce leaves.[1484]

WALDORF SALAD

☛ Pare and cut into quarter-inch dice the same amount of rich, tart apples that you do of celery cut in thin slices. Add to the apples and celery a generous handful of English walnuts or hickory nut meats and over all pour a rich mayonnaise dressing; serve on lettuce leaves with Long Branch wafers and toasted cheese.[1485]

Jell-O and its many uses.

SHRIMP SALAD

☛ Mix a pint of shrimps with a teacup of mayonnaise dressing. Arrange in the centre of a flat dish lined with lettuce leaves and put a row of peeled tomatoes around, showing the lettuce leaves around the edge of the dish. A few nasturtiums stuck in the centre add to the dainty look of the dish, and their colors harmonize with the red tomatoes and the pink shrimps. If the tomatoes are not uniform in size, they look better sliced.[1486]

FRENCH CHICKEN SALAD

☛ Cook the meats of English Walnuts in well seasoned chicken stock until tender; remove the brown skin and break in pieces. When cold mix with chicken salad it gives the flavor of truffles.

Blanched almonds cut and put in chicken salad is liked by many. One-fourth of a pound of almonds to each pint of cut chicken.

Cook a veal tongue in the water the chicken was cooked in; cut in dice and mix with the chicken. Also the ham of pork can be used the same way.

Fifteen good chicken hens will make enough salad for 125 people.

A pint of diced chicken meat, little less of celery, one and a half cups of mayonnaise will serve eight or ten people.[1487]

CHICKEN SALAD AND HOW TO BOIL IT

☛ The chicken should be especially boiled for salad and carefully seasoned while boiling. Put the chicken in a kettle of boiling water, add a chopped onion, one tablespoonful of chopped carrot, two bay leaves, one teaspoonful of pepper corns, half a teaspoonful of celery seed. Allow the chicken to boil rapidly for five minutes; then set back where the water will simmer until the chicken is tender. This will make the dark meat as white as the white. Remove the chicken when cold and take the flesh in large pieces from the bone, rejecting all fat and skin.

String bean salad.

Cut the meat in dice, measure it, then cut in the same sized pieces two-thirds as much celery. Sprinkle a tablespoonful of lemon juice over the chicken and set away. At serving time mix the chicken and celery.

Make a stiff mayonnaise dressing. To each quart add a teaspoonful of salt, half a teaspoonful of pepper and enough mayonnaise to cover each piece.

Line your bowl with lettuce leaves, turn in the salad, pour over a little extra dressing, garnish the center with heart of lettuce and sprinkle over a tablespoonful of capers drained dry.

Garnish with olives and celery tips. Some finely grated cocoanut sprinkled over this salad is a great improvement.[1488]

OYSTER AND CELERY SALAD

☛ Parboil the oysters in their own liquor, drain, and if large half. Marinate with French dressing, using lemon juice and oil. Dust with salt and pepper.

When ready to serve drain and add one-third as much celery cut in bits, one or two tablespoonfuls of capers. Mix with mayonnaise or a boiled dressing.[1489]

PORK SALAD

☛ Sprinkle a half teaspoonful of salt over one and one-half pounds of pork tenderloin. Place the meat in a vessel and cover with boiling water. Boil steadily until perfectly tender. When cold shave with a sharp knife and cut into inch squares.

Have ready three hard boiled eggs, sliced thin. Place in a salad dish a layer of meat and one of eggs until all is used; then pour over it one teacupful of mayonnaise, and toss lightly with a fork. Delicious.[1490]

RIPE OLIVE SALAD

☛ Prepare for this salad by putting some dice of stale bread in a jar with some bits of dried red peppers, several days before. Take two cupfuls of these crumbs, two cupfuls of ripe olives, and one-half cupful of young onions sliced thin.

Pour over all a cupful of mayonnaise, and serve on a bed of lettuce. If onions are disliked chopped cucumber pickle can be substituted.[1491]

STRING BEAN SALAD
☞ String young beans, break into half-inch pieces (or leave whole), wash and cook soft in salt water; drain well, add finely-chopped onions, pepper, salt and vinegar; when cool add olive oil or melted butter. The onions may be omitted.[1492]

DANDELION SALAD
☞ Select fresh white dandelion leaves and wash thoroughly in three waters; drain and place in a salad-bowl. Take a pinch of salt, one-half pinch of pepper and one tablespoonful of vinegar, adding one tablespoonful of oil. Mix thoroughly, pour over the salad, and serve.[1493]

PLANTATION SALAD
☞ Peel and cut very fine one large cucumber, one green onion, one punch of red radishes and shred one head of lettuce; mix all together with one teaspoonful of salt and one-quarter of a teaspoonful of pepper and one well-beaten egg. Brown a tablespoonful of bacon, cut into dice, in a pan over the fire, and add one-quarter of a cupful of cider vinegar with one-half cupful of water. Mix all together and serve.[1494]

LOBSTER SALAD
☞ Cut the lobster in good sized pieces and marinade with French dressing. Set aside until ready to serve. For each pint of lobster add one dozen olives cut in strips and half a cup of thick mayonnaise. Line the bowl with white lettuce leaves and on them heap the lobster. Mask with a thick coating of mayonnaise; on this arrange some capers, stoned olives, finely diced beets in some simple pattern. Serve as soon as possible.[1495]

IRISH POTATO SALAD
☞ Six potatoes boiled in salt water until done; let cool. Take one blade of celery, half a teacupful of mixed pickle, four hard boiled eggs; chop fine. Cut the potatoes in small blocks; salt and pepper each ingredient separately; then mix and pour over the salad one teacupful of mayonnaise dressing. Garnish with celery.[1496]

PINEAPPLE SALAD
☞ Use a slice of Hawaiian pineapple and place in ice several hours; serve on crisp lettuce with a French dressing.[1497]

HERRING SALAD
☞ Soak over night three Holland herrings cut in very small pieces; cook and peel eight medium potatoes, and when cold chop with two small cooked red beets, two onions, a few sour apples, some roasted veal, and three hard boiled eggs; mix with a sauce of 'sweet-oil, vinegar, stock, pepper, and mustard to taste. A table-spoon of thick sour cream

improves the sauce, which should stand over night in an earthen dish.[1498]

TONGUE SALAD
☞ Cut cold boiled tongue in blocks. Sprinkle over two tablespoonfuls of capers, one tablespoonful of Tarragon vinegar and a tablespoonful of chopped parsley. Over this turn a pint of finely cut celery. Cover the whole with mayonnaise and serve at once.[1499]

HAM SALAD
☞ Soak a tablespoonful of granulated gelatine in two tablespoonfuls of cold water; then dissolve in three-fourths of a cup of hot chicken stock. Strain over one cup of cooked ham chopped fine. When it commences to thicken fold in one cup of thick cream beaten stiff; salt and cayenne to season. Mold in a ring mold, turn out, fill center with a cup made of lettuce leaves and fill the cup with mayonnaise.[1500]

SWEETBREAD SALAD
☞ Cut celery in short lengths laid in ice water, then dried. Mix with sweetbreads picked up. Season with cooked mayonnaise.[1501]

SWEETBREAD AND CUCUMBER SALAD
☞ Parboil a pair of sweetbreads at a very low heat twenty minutes in slightly salted acidulated water. Cool and cut in cubes. Also the same quantity of cucumbers cut in dice and chilled in ice water and dried on a soft cloth. Drain the sweetbreads, dry the cucumbers, mix and put on lettuce leaves; salt and pepper to season the mixture. Press firm mayonnaise with a little dissolved gelatine in it in a bag with a star tube and make little stars over it.[1502]

WATERCRESS SALAD
☞ An excellent salad in the spring of the year is the watercress. Make as simple as possible. Select the best bunches, remove the heavy stalks, clean and dry in a napkin and place in a salad bowl. Dress with salt, pepper and lemon, or vinegar, instead of lemon. A little sugar if desired.[1503]

Watercress salad with "rose" radishes.

ARTICHOKE SALAD
☞ Select fresh young artichokes; wash and slice crosswise in a salad bowl. The thinner they are sliced the nicer they will be. Dress with vinegar, salt, pepper and oil. Delicious.[1504]

TOMATO AND ONION SALAD
☛ Take one-half dozen not over-ripe tomatoes and cut into thin slices; take one-half dozen small onions and cut up as fine as you can; sprinkle the onion over the tomato slices, add salt, pepper, and vinegar, and you will have a most appetizing relish.[1505]

BIRD NEST SALAD
☛ Rub a little green coloring into cream cheese, giving it a delicate color like bird eggs. Roll it into balls the size of bird eggs, using the backs of butter paddles. Arrange on a dish some well crimped lettuce leaves; group them to look like nests; moisten with French dressing and place five balls in each nest. You can fleck them with red or black pepper. You may make the nests of shredded lettuce.[1506]

ASPARAGUS SALAD
☛ Cut off a quart of asparagus tops and boil in salt water until tender; drain, throw in cold water and let stand half an hour; drain again, wipe dry, put in a salad bowl and pour over French dressing.[1507]

GRAPEFRUIT SALAD
☛ Grapefruit is among the most popular appetizers to be served at breakfast, or luncheon, and even finds its way to the dinner table. Remove the tops from 6 green peppers. Take out the seeds and refill with grapefruit pulp, fine cut celery and English walnut meats, mixed with mayonnaise dressing. To 1½ cups of the mixture add ¼ of a cup of heavy cream, beaten stiff, and tint a delicate green with vegetable color. For each pepper use 3 halves of walnut meats and half as much celery as grapefruit.[1508]

Grapefruit served in a basket made of the peel with a holly sprig tied to the handle.

FISH SALAD
☛ Pick the meat free from skin and bones; mix with some mustard pickle cut fine, especially onion, some hard boiled eggs chopped; season with cooked mayonnaise; mix all together. Garnish with lettuce and put in tomato cups set on a lettuce leaf.[1509]

ORANGE SALAD
☛ Take fresh, firm oranges and peel them carefully down to the pulp, removing all the white skin. Hold the orange with a fork and with a sharp knife cut down on each side of the section and remove the pulp, taking care to keep its shape. Go over the whole orange this way. Serve on lettuce leaves with a dressing of olive oil and lemon, using 2 tablespoons

of oil to 1 of juice. Add pecan nuts to the dressing.[1510]

SAUERKRAUT PREPARATION
☛ Take 6 heads of cabbage; cut off the stalks closely; sprinkle salt in the bottom of a cask, and put in the cabbage tightly, putting in layers of salt; keep covered with a heavy weight, and keep in a cold place. In 4 or 5 weeks the cabbage will have fermented, and is ready for use.[1511]

TO COOK SAUERKRAUT
☛ Soak it in water until fresh enough, and then put it on to boil with bacon, or pickled pork, or smoked sausage, or in water, salted. Boil it until tender; drain off the water, and serve it. When cold, it can be fried in either butter or lard.[1512]

Cover of an 1870 edition of *The Southern Farm and Home* magazine.

21. Salad Dressings

SALAD DRESSING
☛ Pound smooth the yolks of 2 hard-boiled eggs. Mix with 1 teaspoon of unmade mustard, 1 salt-spoon of salt; mix gradually with these either 1 cup of cream or the same quantity of olive oil. 2 tablespoons of vinegar. Add a little cayenne pepper.[1513]

BOTTLED SALAD DRESSING
☛ Beat yolks of eight eggs, add to them a cup of sugar, one tablespoon each of salt, mustard, and black pepper, a little cayenne, and half a cup of cream; mix thoroughly; bring to a boil a pint and a half vinegar, add one cup butter, let come to a boil.

Pour the melted butter upon the mixture, stir well, and when cold put into bottles, and set in a cool place. It will keep for weeks in the hottest weather, and is excellent for cabbage or lettuce.[1514]

MAYONNAISE
☛ Yolk of 1 egg,
½ teaspoonful of salt,
Dash of cayenne pepper,
1 cupful of salad oil,
½ teaspoonful of lemon juice.

Let the oil and egg be very cold before using. Also the plate must be on ice; let the yolk be entirely free from any white. Add salt and pepper to egg and mix well, then add oil, drop by drop.

The success depends on adding the oil slowly at first. Spend half of the time in incorporating the first 2 spoonsful of oil; after that, it can be added a little faster. After it is thick, alternate a few drops of lemon juice or vinegar with the oil. A little tarragon vinegar is nice.

If mustard is liked add ¼ teaspoonful of dry mustard with the salt at the beginning. Some like a hard-boiled egg added to the raw egg.[1515]

MAYONNAISE DRESSING 1

☞ In a bowl mix half a teaspoonful of salt, a dash of paprika, the raw yolks of two fresh eggs; then beat in two tablespoonfuls each of vinegar and lemon juice.

Add about one and a half cups of olive oil, one teaspoonful or more at a time, beating it in with the Dover. By adding all the acid before the oil the danger of curdling is eliminated and the oil can be added faster.[1516]

MAYONNAISE DRESSING 2

☞ No danger of curdling if the eggs are fresh and the oil added slowly. Everything must be cold. If the yolks don't thicken when beaten with the condiments, but spread over the bowl, they will not thicken when oil is added.

Take care and add a teaspoonful of acid to the yolks before dropping in the oil, as it is less liable to curdle. Use a Dover beater from the start.[1517]

MAYONNAISE DRESSING 3

☞ One teaspoonful each of mustard and sugar, half a teaspoonful of salt, little cayenne, yolks of two raw eggs, one pint of olive oil, two tablespoonfuls each of vinegar and lemon juice.

Have a small bowl ice cold, mix the first four ingredients, add the eggs; if it don't thicken commence over and add fresh eggs.

Mix with a Dover beater or fork. Add the oil in a very small stream until it thickens.

When stiff add a little lemon juice and oil alternately. When stiff enough to take up in a ball add the vinegar.

Should it curdle add a little white of egg. Do not mix with meat until ready to serve; it liquefies.[1518]

SLAW DRESSING

☞ 1 cup vinegar.
1 egg yolk.
1 teaspoon flour.
2 teaspoons sugar.
1 teaspoon butter.
1 teaspoon salt.
1 small teaspoon mustard.
Pinch of cayenne pepper.

Cream butter and all dry ingredients except sugar, then add egg yolk. Gradually beat in vinegar, cook in double boiler until thick. When cool add sugar.[1519]

MAYONNAISE DRESSING 4

☞ For one pint of dressing use one and a half cups of oil, yolks of two eggs, one teaspoonful of mustard, half a teaspoonful of salt, two tablespoonfuls lemon juice, two of vinegar, little cayenne, four tablespoonfuls of sweet thick cream. Have everything ice cold. Put the dry ingredients and yolks in a bowl and beat with a Dover until light and thick. Now add the oil, a few drops at a time. As soon as the mixture becomes thick and ropy add oil more freely. The vinegar may be added half a teaspoonful at a time. When it gets very thick again by the addition of the oil, add more vinegar until all is used; then add the lemon the same way. Whip cream stiff with a fork and fold in last.[1520]

COCOANUT FOR GARNISHING SALADS

☞ Grate cocoanut and sprinkle it over the top of salads. Especially nice over chicken, shrimp and fish; also on potato, tomato and egg salads. Grated cocoanut lends a handsome appearance to any salad.[1521]

FRENCH DRESSING 1

☞ Six tablespoonfuls of oil, two of vinegar, half a teaspoonful of salt, little pepper. Mix oil, salt and pepper; then add the vinegar.[1522]

FRENCH DRESSING 2

☞ Two tablespoonfuls of vinegar to four of oil, half a teaspoonful of salt, one-fourth a teaspoonful of pepper, ten drops of onion juice (grate the onion); or any prepared sauce can be added. Nice for cucumbers.[1523]

FRENCH DRESSING 3

☞ 4 tablespoons olive oil, 1 tablespoon of vinegar. Season to taste with pepper, salt, and a little garlic. The bowl in which the dressing is to be made rubbed with garlic will give sufficient flavor.[1524]

SIMPLE FRENCH DRESSING

☞ One tablespoonful of vinegar, three of oil, saltspoonful of salt, little mustard. Put the ingredients in a bowl and stir until thoroughly blended.[1525]

ROQUEFORT DRESSING

☞ 6 tablespoons Roquefort cheese.
¼ teaspoon paprika.
1½ tablespoons dry mustard.
1 tablespoon vinegar.
¼ teaspoon salt.
¼ cup salad oil.
¼ teaspoon pepper.

Cream cheese and olive oil, add seasoning. When smooth and thick, add 1 teaspoon Worcester sauce.[1526]

DRESSING FOR MEATS OR SALADS
☛ Mix a heaping teaspoon of mustard, 1 of salt, and 1 of sugar together. Add a little red pepper and enough vinegar to make a paste. Beat yolks of 5 eggs and add mustard, etc., ½ teacup of vinegar, 1 of rich cream, sour or sweet, and a piece of butter the size of an egg. Boil till thick, and let it cool. It can be bottled and kept in cool place, and used as needed.[1527]

BOILED DRESSING
☛ Beat separately three eggs. Mix two tablespoonfuls of sugar, one teaspoonful of mustard, two of salt, two tablespoonfuls of melted butter or oil, little cayenne, a cup of milk. Boil milk, stir in yolks and seasonings, let cook like custard over hot water; then pour over the stiff whites. Now add half a cup of hot vinegar. Let get very cold. Serve with lettuce, cauliflower, etc. Very fine.[1528]

COOKED MAYONNAISE
☛ Use two whole eggs or four yolks; beat with the Dover very light. Put in a small saucepan four tablespoonfuls of vinegar. When hot pour over the whipped eggs. Put back on fire and stir constantly back and forth until thick. Take off and put in a lump of butter. If it curdles the butter will smooth it. Season with salt, pepper and mustard for vegetables. Leave out mustard and use sugar for fruit.[1529]

WHITE DRESSING
☛ Drop a light yolk in a clean cold bowl; add a saltspoonful of salt and six tablespoonfuls salad oil very slowly. Now add slowly one tablespoonful of lemon juice. Now add six tablespoonfuls of cream beaten very stiff. It is as white as whipped cream.[1530]

THOUSAND ISLAND DRESSING
☛ 1 bottle small pickled onions.
Paprika.
1 box pimentos.
Salt.
8 eggs (hard boiled).
Cayenne pepper.
Grind eggs in meat chopper, slice pimentos and cut up onions fine. Mix all together, adding salt, paprika and cayenne to taste.
Prepare the mayonnaise:
Yolks of two eggs.
1 lemon (juice).
1 cup of chili sauce.
1 cup olive oil.

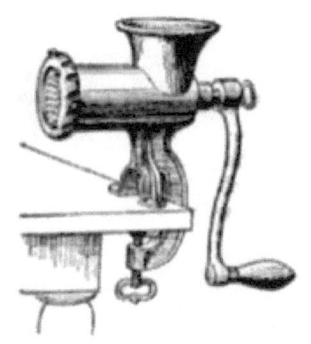

Meat chopper.

Beat egg yolks, add olive oil drop by drop; when it thickens add lemon juice, continue beating and adding oil until all oil is used. Add with the chili sauce to the above ingredients. Sliced green pepper improves this dressing.[1531]

Dishes loved by Southerners.

22. Sandwiches

SANDWICH MAKING TIPS

☞ Let the bread, free from crusts, be cut about one-eighth of an inch thick. Any bread twenty-four hours old is admissible. Sometimes two varieties of bread are combined in the same sandwich. Let the sandwich be small, and are best prepared just before serving. For large companies wrap in a damp cloth wrung as dry as possible; then in a dry cloth, or cover the sandwiches with a large bowl.

Cream the butter to insure its spreading nicely; avoid spreading the butter or filling over the edge. When slices of meat are used let it be as thin as a wafer, and use more than one in each sandwich. Sweet sandwiches are offered with tea or cocoa. Bread or lady fingers may be used with jams.

Jellies, marmalades, preserved ginger are the usual fillings. Better kept over night or some hours between layers of fresh violets or rose petals in a close receptacle. Used to spread sweet sandwiches is quite aesthetic.[1532]

White, brown, and graham bread-and-butter sandwiches.

REMOULADE SAUCE SANDWICHES

☞ Four hard boiled eggs chopped very fine, two cans of Underwood's deviled ham, a small pot of anchovy paste, a small bottle of capers chopped, pepper to season, also some butter and Tarragon vinegar. Cut bread and spread with creamed butter; then a thin layer of the mixture put between slices of buttered bread. This will spread about one hundred sandwiches. Fine.[1533]

GINGER SANDWICHES
☛ Bake a plain gingerbread in a thin sheet or make soft ginger cookies. When cold cut in oblong pieces and split carefully.

Spread with cream cheese and put a thin layer of preserved ginger in the center. Cover and press slightly and arrange on napkin.[1534]

MANLY SANDWICHES
☛ Chop fine a cup of pimolas, add half a teaspoonful of mustard, one and a half teaspoonfuls of thick tomato catsup, three drops of tabasco, half a teaspoonful celery salt, one cup of thick mayonnaise. Spread on thin slices of rye bread and put together in thin sandwiches.[1535]

HAM SANDWICHES
☛ Make a sauce of the yolks of four hard boiled eggs, mix with four ounces of butter, one raw yolk; add slowly two tablespoonfuls of tarragon vinegar, twelve anchovies that have been soaked in cold water, freed from skin and bone and mashed fine; also one or two teaspoonfuls of mustard, one teaspoonful of salt, half a teaspoonful of pepper, two tablespoonfuls of chopped capers, one tablespoonful of finely chopped shallot and the fine chopped whites of the eggs.

Mix all this with two pounds of ground ham. Dip some parsley in boiling water, instantly remove and chop fine; put one tablespoonful to the above mixture. Spread on thin slices of bread. This is elegant.[1536]

COTTAGE CHEESE SANDWICHES
☛ Cut slices of brown bread about ½ inch thick; do not remove the crusts. Rub ½ pint of cottage cheese to a smooth paste, then press it through a fine sieve.

Add 2 tablespoons melted butter, slowly beating the while, adding ½ teaspoon of salt and 2 tablespoons of thick cream. Spread each slice of bread thickly with the mixture. Cover with another thin slice of white bread, and on top of this another thin layer of cheese. Place a slice of brown bread on top and trim into shape.[1537]

RUSSIAN SANDWICHES
☛ Spread zepherettes with thin slices of cream cheese and cover with chopped olives mixed with mayonnaise. Place a zepherette over each and press together.[1538]

CELERY SANDWICH
☛ Butter bread on the loaf, first having creamed the butter. Cut away the crusts and starting at one corner of the slice, roll it tightly over two sticks of crisp celery. The butter will hold it together, but baby ribbon tied around each roll improves the appearance.

The celery should be broken into thin strips about the size of the smallest stalks towards the leaf end; also cut an appropriate length.[1539]

WATERCRESS SANDWICHES

Bread mold.

☞ Wash well and pick over fresh watercress, dry thoroughly with piece of cheese cloth, pressing out all the moisture. Pick leaves from stems, chop moderately, mix with hard boiled eggs finely chopped. Season with salt and pepper, moisten with mayonnaise dressing. Mix carefully with the other ingredients. There should be twice as much cress as hard boiled eggs. Spread between thin slices of bread spread with mayonnaise.[1540]

TOASTED CHEESE SANDWICH

☞ One-half pint milk, 1 teaspoon cornstarch, 1 egg, well beaten, piece butter size of egg, 1½ cups grated cheese, salt and pepper and paprika, moisten cornstarch with one tablespoon milk, heat the remainder of milk and butter, add egg and cook till it is thick as custard. Beat into it the cheese. Season well and spread ¼ inch thick on bread which has been buttered. Then toast, or put in a hot oven to brown.[1541]

CHEESE AND LETTUCE SANDWICHES

☞ Cut brown bread in thin slices, butter one side lightly, spread with cream cheese. On this lay a leaf of lettuce that has been dipped in French dressing.[1542]

PIMOLA SANDWICHES

☞ Cut slices or rounds of bread, spread with a stiff mayonnaise, slice your pimolas and lay thick over the surface. Cover with another round of bread that has been spread with mayonnaise. Fine.[1543]

LAYER SANDWICHES

☞ Remove the crust from bread and cut in thin slices, spread with deviled ham and make three or four layers high; then cut in any shape desired.[1544]

NUT AND CHEESE SANDWICHES

☞ Half a cup of blanched almonds, one-fourth a cup of English walnuts, one-fourth a cup of hickory nuts minced fine. Blend with one-fourth a cup of soft cheese. Season with salt and spread between buttered bread.[1545]

SUPPER CHEESE SANDWICHES

☞ Cut thin slices of bread in rounds with a biscuit cutter. Work grated Parmesan cheese to a paste with a little good stock, chicken if you have it. Season with salt and cayenne, butter your bread, spread with the paste, press firmly together and fry in hot drippings. These are very savory.[1546]

WALNUT AND CHEESE SANDWICHES
☛ Chop a cup of walnuts fine, mix with cream cheese grated, salt to season; spread between thin layers of buttered brown bread.[1547]

CHEESE SANDWICHES 1
☛ One hard boiled egg, one-fourth a pound of grated cheese, half a teaspoonful each of salt pepper and mustard, one tablespoonful of melted butter, one tablespoonful of vinegar or cold water. Mix and spread between slices of bread. Garnish with parsley.

Bread for sandwiches should be close grained and twenty-four hours old. Trim all the crust from a loaf and trim in good shape. Butter the bread before you cut the slice. Chop the meat fine for all sandwiches.[1548]

CHEESE SANDWICHES 2
☛ One pound of cream cheese grated, five eggs boiled hard and mashed fine, chicken stock or melted butter enough for a paste, salt, cayenne and white pepper. Worcester sauce to season.[1549]

LOBSTER SANDWICHES
☛ Pound the flesh of a freshly boiled lobster to a smooth paste, adding, while pounding, a sufficient seasoning of salt, pepper and pounded mace; moisten with a little warmed butter and mix thoroughly.

Spread the preparation between some small, daintily prepared croutons and mask the top with thick bechamel sauce.[1550]

LETTUCE SANDWICHES
☛ Sprinkle fresh crisp lettuce leaves with a little salt and lay them a few moments in a folded napkin, then lay them between slices of bread that have been buttered. Spread over a dressing of mayonnaise or not, as preferred.[1551]

BAKED BEAN SANDWICHES
☛ Beat one-half of a cup of baked beans to a smooth paste. Add one-half of a teaspoonful of chopped parsley and celery, one-quarter of a teaspoonful of onion juice and made mustard enough to just cover the end of a teaspoon. Spread between slices of graham or rye bread.[1552]

EGG SANDWICHES
☛ Boil six eggs ten minutes, throw them into cold water, take off the shells and cut them into slices; prepare thin slices of bread and butter, place the eggs between.

Season with salt, pepper, and a little dry mustard; trim and cut the sandwiches.[1553]

BEEF AND POTATO SANDWICHES
☞ Fry, slices of cold corned beef very lightly and spread on each side a heavy layer of mashed potatoes, press it down on the meat with a knife. Dip the whole in egg and bread-crumbs, fry them in drippings a very light brown and serve hot.[1554]

DUCK SANDWICHES
☞ These must be made of the smoked breasts of ducks cut in very thin slices. Cut hard-boiled eggs into thin rings, lay over the duck, squeeze a little lemon juice over them, a sprinkle of salt and pepper, and cover them with well-buttered slices of bread and butter.[1555]

CHICKEN AND HAM SANDWICHES
☞ Mince cold chicken and add a little minced cold ham. Stir in a cup of boiling gravy. Set the whole before the fire for a few moments. Cut slices of old bread with a round tin cutter and fry them. Spread a layer of the fowl and ham between two of them, add a small piece of cheese and butter made into a paste. Run the sandwiches in the oven, which should be pretty hot, for five minutes. Serve them hot on a folded napkin at tea-time.[1556]

Fancy sandwich cutters.

APPLE AND CELERY SANDWICHES
☞ Peel and chop very fine two large, tart apples and one-half of a dozen of the small inside stalks of celery; sprinkle lightly with salt; spread between thinly cut slices of buttered brown bread.[1557]

FISH SANDWICHES
☞ Cut bread and butter as for other sandwiches, place thin scallops of any fish on the slices, and instead of mustard use tartar sauce. Put a layer of finely-sliced lettuce on the top of the sauce, and cover with bread and butter. Serve cut into squares. Thin slices of hard-boiled eggs may be added.[1558]

DAINTY SANDWICH
☞ A dainty sandwich is made by frizzling the thinnest possible bacon till it can be crushed with a fork, then spread it between slices of bread and butter.[1559]

SANDWICHES A LA PARISIENNE
☞ These delicious little "tidbits" can be made with either fish, poultry, game, or ordinary meats, but we will suppose that the first named is being used. Free the fish from bones and skin, mince it finely, season rather highly with salt and cayenne, and put it into a basin with two hard

boiled eggs, finely chopped and sufficient sauce of some kind—"tartar" to be preferred—to moisten the whole. Mix all these ingredients well; then spread the preparation between slices of thinly cut brown or white bread and butter; stamp out in small rounds, squares, or finger shapes press together and butter the tops.

Sprinkle on half of the number of sandwiches a little very finely chopped mustard and cress, and hard boiled yolk of egg rubbed through a fine sieve; and on the other half, the mustard and cress and the white of the egg chopped very fine. Arrange the sandwiches in twos—one of each color—on tiny plates and garnish with a little tuft of mustard and cress at each corner.[1560]

PINEAPPLE CHEESE SANDWICHES
☞ Spread slices of bread with grated pineapple cheese, lightly mixed with chow chow sauce, the liquid part of chow chow pickle.[1561]

CONFEDERATE EGG SANDWICHES
☞ Chop hard boiled eggs fine, with cucumber pickles; add pepper and salt and a little mayonnaise. Rub smooth with a silver knife; spread between slices of buttered bread.[1562]

DEVILED HAM SANDWICHES
☞ Remove ham from can and rub enough to soften; then spread on bread cut thin, and just before putting the pieces together, pass over each one a knife, which has been dipped in chow chow, or mayonnaise.[1563]

LENTEN SANDWICH
☞ Chop the hard boiled yolks of four eggs, and the coral of a lobster; add a tablespoonful of butter, mix altogether into a paste; season with salt, cayenne and lemon juice. Slice light bread very thin, spread with the mixture, lay a crisp leaf of lettuce over each slice, cover with another slice of buttered bread, cut the sandwiches in halves, and serve on a napkin.[1564]

OYSTER SANDWICHES
☞ Take cold stewed oysters; put into chopping bowl which has been rubbed with onion (raw.) Chop oysters very fine; add pepper and salt, a pinch of powdered mace, and a small slice of cold boiled ham. Pour in sufficient of the liquor in which they have been cooked to reduce the mixture to a paste, adding a little lemon juice then with a silver knife spread each slice of bread with it.[1565]

CHICKEN SANDWICHES
☞ Grind your cooked chicken, season with a little onion juice, salt, pepper and melted butter, yolks of hard boiled eggs rubbed to a paste with a little milk. Delicious.[1566]

SARDINE CANAPES

☛ Spread circular pieces of toasted bread with sardines from which the bone has been removed, rubbed to a paste with a small quantity of creamed butter, season with Worcester and cayenne. Place in center of each a pimola. Around the edge arrange a border of very finely chopped whites of hard boiled eggs.[1567]

CLUB SANDWICHES 1

Rolling pin.

☛ Cut slices of bread in triangular shape and toast it, and while hot spread with butter and put between the slices a lettuce leaf or chopped lettuce, then a slice of cold chicken, then a few chopped olives and pickles, next a slice of hot broiled breakfast bacon, another lettuce leaf dipped in salad dressing, then a piece of toast.[1568]

CLUB SANDWICHES 2

☛ Have ready four triangular pieces of toasted bread, spread with mayonnaise dressing, cover two of them with lettuce, lay thin slices of cold chicken on the lettuce; over this arrange thin slices of hot breakfast bacon, then lettuce, and cover with the other triangle of toast. Spread with mayonnaise, trim neatly, arrange on a plate, and garnish with heart leaves of lettuce dipped in mayonnaise.[1569]

TONGUE SANDWICHES

☛ Get a box of tongue, chop fine, work in some softened butter, pepper, mustard mixed with vinegar and a little sugar, two or three hard boiled eggs chopped fine. A little grated onion, capers and tarragon vinegar season it nicely.[1570]

HOT OYSTER SANDWICHES

☛ Bring two dozen oysters to the boiling point in their own liquor, drain, and chop fine. Scald a cup of cream over hot water, add the chopped oysters, two tablespoonfuls of butter, a little salt, pepper, and some fine bread crumbs if too moist. Have ready rounds of hot toast, spread with butter, then the oyster mixture. Serve at once with olives or pickles. If you prefer, stir the oysters in a cream sauce.[1571]

CUCUMBER SANDWICHES

☛ 2 cucumbers.
Salt, pepper.
1 small onion.
Paprika.
1 slice of bacon.
Bread.
Grind and drain. Spread bread with mayonnaise then fill with

mixture. Cut bread in thin oblong slices.[1572]

SWEET SANDWICHES
☛ Cream some butter and sugar as for hard sauce, add some minced nuts and raisins; spread them between slices of bread, put two together and cut any shape desired.[1573]

NUT SANDWICHES
☛ Chop a cup of pecans with half a cup of grated cheese, then enough mayonnaise to spread. Slice bread very thin; cover with a lettuce leaf and the nut paste.[1574]

LADY FINGER SANDWICHES
☛ Add a tablespoonful powdered sugar and little vanilla to a cup of double cream and beat until solid. Spread lady fingers with strawberry jam or jelly; spread the other half with the whipped cream and put the two together. Put a lace paper on a plate and pile on the sandwiches.[1575]

Wedding table.

Making your own candy is fun and easy!

23. Sauces

CREAM SAUCE

☞ Melt a tablespoonful each of flour and butter, cook until it bubbles, add one cup of cold milk; when thick enough season with salt and pepper.[1576]

CHILI SAUCE

☞ 3 small green or red peppers,
12 tomatoes,
3 large onions,
2 tablespoons salt,
3 tablespoons sugar,
1 tablespoon cinnamon,
1 tablespoon black pepper,
3 cups vinegar,
1 tablespoon made mustard,
1 tablespoon mustard seed,
1 tablespoon mace,
1 grated nutmeg.

Peel tomatoes and onions and slice fine. Chop the peppers and add altogether with the other ingredients and boil till thick, about 2 hours. This is a good recipe, and will keep a long time if put in bottles and tightly corked. It may be made in the winter when ripe tomatoes can not be had by using 2 quarts of canned tomatoes in the place of the 12 ripe ones.[1577]

SAUCE TYROLIENNE

☞ Three-fourths of a cup of mayonnaise, half tablespoonful each of chopped capers, parsley and cucumber pickles, half a can of tomatoes stewed and strained. Using the same receipt, you may flour the oysters. Oysters prepared for frying may be broiled. You will find Wesson Oil much better for frying than any other fat.[1578]

SAUCE TARTARE 1
☞ One-fourth cup of chopped sour pickles, one-fourth cup of capers, half a cup of olives, half teaspoonful of salt, one teaspoonful of powdered sugar, half teaspoonful of mustard, one-eighth of a teaspoon of cayenne, yolks of two eggs.

These are to be blended together, and commence to use soft butter until you use a cup. Use a Dover beater to mix. Add two tablespoonfuls of lemon juice and two of parsley chopped fine.[1579]

SAUCE TARTARE 2
☞ Chop a tablespoonful of parsley very fine and rub to a paste; add to it a mayonnaise dressing; mix and add one tablespoonful of chopped capers, two or three olives chopped fine, a tablespoonful of chopped pickle and a teaspoonful of onion juice.

This sauce may be served with lobster cutlets, broiled or fried fish, deviled crabs or broiled tenderloin.[1580]

TARTARE SAUCE FOR FISH
☞ The yolks of 2 hard-boiled eggs,
The yolks of 2 raw eggs,
8 tablespoonfuls of olive oil,
3 dessertspoonfuls of vinegar,
1 teaspoonful of chopped onion,
1 tablespoonful of capers,
Salt and cayenne pepper to the taste.

Mash the hard-boiled eggs; add the raw eggs to them, and beat until perfectly smooth and light. Then beat in well the oil and vinegar alternately. Add the onion and capers; lastly the salt and cayenne pepper.

Serve cold in a sauce-boat.[1581]

LOBSTER SAUCE
☞ Boil a little mace, and whole pepper, long enough to take out the strong taste of the spice; then strain it off, and melt three quarters of a pound of butter in it.

Cut the lobster in very small pieces, and stew it till it is tender.[1582]

CHILLI SAUCE
☞ Peel, cut in half and press out the seed from six good sized tomatoes, chop the pulp very fine and drain in a sieve until dry; add a tablespoonful of grated onion, one-fourth teaspoonful of celery seed, two tablespoonfuls of Tarragon vinegar, half a teaspoonful of salt and a drop of Tabasco, or some sweet red pepper chopped fine and the seed removed.

Rub the mixing spoon with a clove of garlic. Serve with cold meats or a broiled lobster.[1583]

FOAMING SAUCE

☛ 1 cup of powdered sugar,
2 tablespoons of butter,
1 egg,
1 glass of wine.

Stir to a cream and add wineglass of wine grad-ually, and beat it hard till very light. Set the bowl over a teakettle of hot water till melted. Do not stir it.[1584]

HARD SAUCE

☛ 1 cup sugar,
½ cup of butter.

Cream together and flavor with lemon, wine, or brandy.[1585]

ABBIE'S SAUCE FOR MEATS

☛ Beat the yolk of an egg, add a small cup of vinegar, one dessertspoonful of sugar, little butter, put over the fire and let thicken; then remove and add a tablespoonful each of mustard and Worcester sauce; salt and pepper to season. Serve on slices of meat.[1586]

ASPARAGUS SAUCE

Saddle of lamb chops under sauce.

☛ Take the white tender stalks of asparagus, wash and scrape them neatly, tie them in little bundles, and boil them in water, with a little salt, till they are tender; then chop them small, season them with pepper, and put them into a sauce-pan, with equal portions of butter and cream; add a very little flour, boil it up, and serve it in a boat. There should be plenty of butter and cream, to make the sauce sufficiently liquid; a small handful of asparagus to a pint of the butter and cream, will be well proportioned. This is a delicious sauce for poultry and game.[1587]

WHITE SAUCE FOR FISH, MEAT, OR POULTRY

☛ One pint of milk, two tablespoonfuls of butter, two heaping tablespoonfuls of flour, half a teaspoonful of salt, little pepper, one slice of onion boiled in the milk.

Put the butter in a saucepan, when it bubbles add the dry flour and stir until well mixed. Pour in one-third of the milk cold, let it boil, then add another third, stir until smooth; then add the remainder of the milk. When smooth add salt and pepper to taste.[1588]

WHITE SAUCE

☛ Rub together one tablespoonful each of flour and butter, let bubble, then add one cup of cold milk; stir until boiling; take from the fire and add half a teaspoonful of salt and a little white pepper.

Serve with boiled mutton, potatoes, white meats or green vegetables.[1589]

HORSERADISH SAUCE

☛ 4 tablespoons of grated horseradish,
 1 teaspoon of sugar,
 1 teaspoon of salt,
 teaspoon of pepper,
 2 teaspoons of mixed mustard and vinegar,
 3 or 4 tablespoons of cream.

To serve with hot beef. Put in a jar, which place in a saucepan of boiling hot water. Do not allow it to boil, or it will curdle.[1590]

ONION SAUCE

☛ Peel the onions, and boil until tender; drain the water well from them; chop and pour on them drawn butter, together with a little rich milk; boil all up once. A turnip boiled with the onions makes them more mild.[1591]

CAPER SAUCE

☛ To one pint of cream sauce add three tablespoonfuls of capers, remove from the fire and add the yolk of an egg and juice of half a lemon.[1592]

MAPLE SUGAR SAUCE

☛ Melt over a slow fire, in a small tea-cup of water, half a pint maple sugar; let it simmer, removing all scum; add four table-spoons butter mixed with a level tea-spoon flour, and one of grated nutmeg; boil for a few moments, and serve with boiled puddings. Or, make a "hard sauce" of one table-spoon butter to two of sugar.[1593]

MINT SAUCE

☛ Four tablespoonfuls of chopped mint, two tablespoonfuls of sugar, half a cup of vinegar. Let stand one hour before using.[1594]

HOLLANDAISE SAUCE

☛ Four tablespoonfuls of vinegar, four pepper corns, half teaspoonful of salt. Let boil until reduced one-half. Let cool. Then add the beaten yolks of four eggs, four ounces of butter, little nutmeg.

Cook in double boiler until as thick as cream. Take from the fire and whip with a Dover until frothy. Add by degrees three tablespoonfuls of butter when light and smooth. It is delicious for fish.[1595]

TOMATO SAUCE

☛ Melt a tablespoonful of butter and a tablespoonful of flour and gradually add one cup of strained tomatoes, one clove, half a teaspoonful each of salt, sugar and pepper.[1596]

TRUFFLE SAUCE

☛ 1 pound can of truffles,
  1 pint of clear soup,
  1 tablespoon of butter,
  1 teaspoon of white flour,
  1 teaspoon of browned flour,
  2 tablespoons of sherry wine,
  Salt and pepper to the taste.

Chop the truffles and put them with their liquor into a saucepan with the soup. Boil steadily for ½ hour. Rub flour and butter together, stir in truffles, and simmer till thick; then add wine, salt, and cayenne pepper. Delicious for meats or entrees.[1597]

VIRGINIA SAUCE

☛ 1 cup mayonnaise.
  2 tablespoons mixed chow-chow pickle.
  1 teaspoon tomato catsup.

Blend ingredients and serve with fried soft crabs. This recipe is a famous one in Virginia.[1598]

TARTAR SAUCE

☛ 1 cup mayonnaise.
  2 teaspoons parsley.
  4 small cucumber pickles (sour).
  6 chopped olives.
  ½ teaspoon capers.
  ½ medium sized onion.

Cut up last five ingredients very fine and stir into the mayonnaise. Serve on meat.[1599]

MUSHROOM SAUCE

☛ Add one tablespoonful of lemon juice to one cup of white sauce, half a cup of cooked mushrooms cut in pieces or use brown sauce.[1600]

BROWN SAUCE

☛ Two tablespoonfuls each of butter and flour, one cup of brown stock, one-fourth of a teaspoonful each of salt and pepper.[1601]

GREEN TOMATO SAUCE

☛ Slice half gallon of tomatoes, boil in ginger tea until tender. Drain and add two pounds of sugar, one teaspoonful each of ground allspice and cinnamon, to each pint of vinegar. Boil fifteen or twenty minutes; bottle and seal.[1602]

SHRIMP SAUCE

☛ Wash half a pint of shrimps very clean—mince and put them in a stew-pan, with a spoonful of anchovy liquor, and a pound of thick melted butter; boil it up for five minutes, and squeeze in half a lemon. Toss it up, and put it in a sauce-boat.[1603]

CURRY SAUCE

☛ The powder for this sauce can be procured ready at most druggists. To make the sauce take one tablespoonful of butter, one tablespoonful of flour, one teaspoonful of curry-powder, a large slice of onion, a large cupful of stock, salt and pepper to taste.

Cut the onion fine and fry brown in the butter. Add flour and curry-powder. Stir a minute, add the stock, season with salt and pepper and simmer five minutes. Strain and serve. This sauce is designed for broiled meats or fish.[1604]

ANCHOVY SAUCE

Asparagus in cream sauce.

☛ Soak half a dozen anchovies in fresh water for two or three hours; then put them into a stew-pan with a quart of water, and simmer them till they are completely dissolved and the liquor reduced to half a pint: then strain it, return it to the pan, with half a pint of red wine and eight ounces of butter rolled in flour and broken up. Place the pan over a bed of clear coals; just let it raise the simmer, stirring it all the time, and serve it up. It is to accompany fresh fish.[1605]

PRAWN SAUCE

☛ Having boiled your prawns, mince half a pint of them, put them into a stew-pan with three quarters of a pound of butter rolled in flour and broken up, a few spoonfuls of vinegar and a tea-spoonful of pepper. Melt the butter slowly, stirring it all the time, and when it begins to boil, serve it up.[1606]

GARLIC SAUCE

☛ Grate a clove of garlic, and add the yolk of one egg; rub smooth, and add one tablespoonful of bread crumbs which have been soaked in milk and squeezed dry, a pinch of salt and cayenne pepper. Stir in from seven to eight spoonfuls of olive oil and the juice of one lemon. If it is too thick, add a little water.[1607]

CRAB SAUCE

☛ Having boiled your crabs, extract the meat from the shells, mince it fine, season it with salt, pepper and nutmeg; put half a pint of it into a stew-pan with three quarters of a pound of melted butter and a glass of white wine.

Just let it raise the simmer, and serve it in a boat. All these sauces are very good for fish.[1608]

DRAWN BUTTER

☛ Mix well together a quarter of a pound of butter, and one tablespoonful of flour. Put a pint of water into a rice-kettle, and when it boils stir in the flour and butter.

Season with salt and white pepper, and celery if in season, removing the stalks of celery before sending to the table. It will require but a few minutes' boiling, and must be stirred constantly.[1609]

MAITRE D'HOTEL BUTTER SAUCE

☛ Scald a bowl and cream one tablespoonful of butter; add one tablespoonful of lemon juice, one tablespoonful of chopped parsley, salt and pepper. Serve on broiled fish or steak.[1610]

PARSLEY SAUCE

☛ Make a thin white sauce of two tablespoonfuls of butter, one and a half tablespoonfuls of flour. When it bubbles add one cup of cold milk slowly.

Now season with salt and pepper and add one tablespoonful of chopped parsley.[1611]

SPANISH SAUCE

☛ Cook a slice of onion in two tablespoonfuls of butter until slightly colored; add two level tablespoonfuls of flour, and gradually one cup of stock or water and a cup of strained tomatoes.

Season with salt, pepper and half a teaspoonful of kitchen bouquet.[1612]

AGRA DOLCE

☛ Mix together:
 2 heaping tablespoonfulls of brown sugar,
 ¼ bar of grated chocolate,
 1 tablespoonful each of shredded candied orange and lemon peel,
 10 blanched almonds, cut,
 ½ cupful of currants,
 1 cupful of vinegar.

Let them soak for 2 hours, then pour over the cooked meat and simmer for 10 minutes. Nice for mutton, venison, sweetbreads, calf's head, etc.[1613]

CREOLE SAUCE

☞ One grated onion, two tablespoonfuls of butter, salt, pepper and a little mustard, small can of tomatoes, small bottle of Worcester sauce, some tomato catsup.

Cook and serve on beef.[1614]

CRANBERRY SAUCE 1

☞ Put a pint of washed cranberries in a granite sauce pan. On top of them put a cup of sugar, a wine glass of water; cover closely and cook ten minutes; never stir.

Remove scum. They will jelly when cold and are nice.[1615]

CRANBERRY SAUCE 2

☞ Wash and pick over one quart of cranberries, put in a granite saucepan with one pint of cold water, cover the saucepan and boil five minutes, press through a colander, add one pint of sugar, stir until dissolved, and turn out to cool.[1616]

CRANBERRY SAUCE FOR TURKEY

☞ Wash 1 quart of berries. Cover with water in a porcelain kettle and cook till the skins burst.

Mash and strain through a colander and return to fire. Add 1 cup of sugar and cook till thick. Mold in any shape and serve cold.[1617]

LEMON SAUCE

☞ 1 pint sugar,
1 tablespoon butter.

Pour over ½ pint hot water. Add the juice of 1 lemon. Let it boil, and add 1 tablespoon cornstarch. Strain and serve hot.[1618]

CUCUMBER SAUCE

☞ Pare and grate a cucumber, drain all the water from it, season with salt, pepper and grated onion, with a star of mayonnaise on top. Serve in lemon peel baskets with fish.[1619]

VERY RICH SAUCE

☞ Cream until light one cup of butter and two cups of sugar, half a cup of boiling water; let come to a boil.

Stir in two well beaten yolks. Stir rapidly to prevent curdling. Flavor to suit the pudding served.[1620]

SAUCE NOT SO RICH

☞ Cream half a cup of butter and two cups of sugar, mix in two whole eggs beaten light, and pour on slowly half a cup of boiling water. Just let come to a boil.

Lemon and nutmeg to flavor.[1621]

PUDDING SAUCE

☞ Cream half a pound of butter and half a pound of sugar, yolk of an egg, wineglass of sherry. Mix well. Stir constantly until it comes to a boil. Remove and serve with a pudding.[1622]

SAUCE FOR BLUE GRASS PUDDING

☞ ¼ pound butter,
2 cups of sugar,
2 eggs.
Mix and cook in saucepan with boiling water. Stir till it begins to thicken. When ready to serve, stir in 1 glass of brandy or whisky.[1623]

WINE SAUCE

☞ One-fourth of a cup of butter, one egg, one cup of sugar, one teaspoonful of flour, one wineglass of wine, one cup of boiling water; simmer ten minutes. Put in wine after it comes from the stove. Flavor.[1624]

CREAM SAUCE FOR FRUIT PIES

☞ One pint of cream, four tablespoonfuls of sugar, one teaspoonful of vanilla, little nutmeg. Serve over fruit pies.[1625]

CELERY SAUCE

☞ Take cream or rich milk, and boil with pieces of celery till the flavor is extracted. Remove it and season sauce with salt and pepper, and add butter, then a little flour to thicken it. Serve with vegetables.[1626]

EGG SAUCE

☞ Put a tumblerful of sweet milk on to heat. When boiling, stir in 1 tablespoon of butter, rolled in flour; stir until it is melted, to keep it from becoming oily; then stir in 1 tumblerful of cream. When the sauce is well heated, take it off. Have ready 4 hard-boiled eggs, cut in slices; put a few of the slices in the sauce, and garnish the dish of meat with the rest of them. To be served with boiled meat.[1627]

SUNSHINE SAUCE

☞ Moisten one tablespoonful of corn starch in a little cold water. Then pour in a pint of boiling water. Add half a cupful of sugar. Beat one egg until very light. Then pour over it gradually this hot corn starch, stirring all the while. Beat for just a minute. Add one teaspoonful of butter and dessertspoonful of vanilla.[1628]

MUSTARD SAUCE

☞ Beat yolks of two eggs, mix in them a glass of acid jelly, one teaspoonful black pepper, one tablespoonful of mixed mustard, one tablespoonful butter, one teacupful of vinegar, cook, stirring all the time; after it becomes cool, add a half tea cupful of catsup.[1629]

CARAMEL SAUCE

☛ Boil three-fourths of a cup of sugar, a small piece of stick cinnamon, two cloves, thin paring of lemon rind and a cup of boiling water ten minutes. Strain over one-fourth a cup of sugar cooked to the caramel degree, few grains of salt. Let cook a few minutes and keep hot till wanted. Flavor with sherry.[1630]

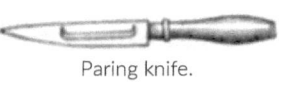

Paring knife.

BRANDY SAUCE FOR PLUM PUDDING

☛ Four tablespoonfuls of butter, one cup of powdered sugar, whites of two eggs, half a cup of brandy, half a cup of boiling water, Beat the butter to a cream; add gradually the sugar and beat until light and white; then add the whites, one at a time, beating all the while. When ready to serve add the brandy and boiling water. Stand the bowl in a basin of boiling water over the fire. Stir until light and creamy and it is ready to use.[1631]

BEE HIVE SAUCE

☛ Stir to a cream half a cup of butter and one and a half cups of sugar, one or two tablespoonfuls water or wine, juice of half a lemon, little nutmeg. Beat until light. Take out a small quantity; color the rest with red fruit coloring or chocolate; shape into a mound; put the uncolored in a cornucopia and wind in a ridge from base up; stick an almond on top.[1632]

FRUIT SAUCE

☛ Half a cup of raisins chopped fine, one tablespoonful of citron shredded, one tablespoonful of chopped almonds, half grated rind of a lemon, one teaspoonful of lemon juice. Pour a cup of boiling water on the fruit; cover and keep hot an hour. Cream a tablespoonful of butter with a cup of sugar and a teaspoonful of flour. Now add the fruit and water. Let boil as thick as you wish. Remove and flavor with wine. Serve on a batter pudding.[1633]

COCOANUT SNOW SAUCE

☛ Boil one cup of sugar and half a cup of water until it will form a thread between the fingers. Gradually pour on the stiff whites of three eggs as boiled icing. Then add a cup of freshly grated cocoanut. Lemon to flavor.[1634]

SAUCE FOR FRUIT ROLL

☛ One cup of brown sugar, one cup of water, two tablespoonfuls of butter, juice and grated rind of a lemon, one teaspoonful of flour or corn starch. Boil and add the beaten yolk of an egg. Season with nutmeg, mace, cloves and sherry.[1635]

OYSTER SAUCE

☞ Take 12 oysters; strain off the liquor, and wipe the oysters; strain the liquor, and put it in a saucepan; a little salt, and 1 blade of mace. When the liquor boils, stir in 1 tablespoon of butter that has been rolled in 1 teaspoon of flour.

When well mixed, stir in; pint of rich milk or cream; let it boil up and put in the oysters; let them stew until the gills are well turned, and then serve as sauce to boiled meats or fish.[1636]

FOAMY SAUCE

☞ Half a cup of butter, one cup of sugar, whites of two eggs, wineglass of boiling water, wineglass of sherry or vanilla. Cream light the butter and sugar; then add the unbeaten whites, one at a time, and beat very light.

At serving time add the water and wine. Stir over the fire until frothy, no longer. Serve at once.[1637]

LADY LEE PUDDING SAUCE

☞ 1 cup of white pulverized sugar,
½ cup of butter,
1 egg,
1 wineglass of Madeira wine.
Beat all together and set in the refrigerator for 2 or 3 hours.

Just before serving, set over teakettle of boiling water, but be careful not to stir it again.[1638]

SABAYON SAUCE

☞ Put in a double boiler twelve egg yolks and one pound of sugar; set on a slow fire and beat to a froth; add half a pint of sherry and whip until it thickens. Remove and serve.[1639]

CONFEDERATE HARD SAUCE

☞ Work to a cream three-fourths of a pound of butter and one pound of sugar; add the white of an egg and flavor to taste; work until very light. You may put it in a pastry bag with a large star tube and make roses on a clean pan. Set on ice to harden. You may color it a pretty pink. When serving place one of these roses on each plate.[1640]

DRAWN BUTTER FOR FOWL

☞ Melt ¼ pound butter and stir in 2 teaspoons flour. Mix thoroughly and add 6 teaspoons of cold water, a little at a time. Cook till smooth. Add salt and pepper to taste. If preferred, add oysters while mixture is simmering.[1641]

"Getting up steam." An old magazine ad for Cream of Wheat.

24. School and Business Lunches

PROPER EATING

☛ This day and time [1921] we keep well by proper eating, so every home maker, should be informed about food stuffs. It is an old subject, but always new, and as long as the world stands will be needed. Get away from medicines and learn how to prepare meals and lunches which will keep the family well. Does it pay? Your pay is rosy cheeked children, a well and happy family.

First, it is important to know something about the person for whom the lunch is being made, whether he is lean or fat, old or young, whether outdoor worker or inside. The man or woman who sits all day requires less and a different kind of lunch from the one who does not. The strong, fat, romping child would need a different lunch from the thin child who does not romp. The playing of children means to them what work does to the grown-ups and growing children require a good deal of food to build the body.

It is necessary for those carrying lunches to co-operate with the one who prepares them by eating all kinds of food, and thus keep the body well. Some folks pamper their appetites, eating just what they like, never getting a balanced meal, and then wonder why they have so many ailments. They do not stop to think that it could be improper eating. Some of their digestive organs are never exercised, while others are over-taxed.

We used to think we should have a balanced meal each time, but now many of our good specialists say if we get it in the three meals of the day it is just as well. This last method is easiest for the housewife. Consequently, you could fix for some a lunch entirely of fruit. Have cereals, milk, bread and butter for breakfast, and meat, vegetables, salads and desserts for dinner.

If you prefer, there can be a more general mixture in all meals—the person and occasion would determine this.

For fixing lunches, the first thing needed is the proper tools with which to work: a good sharp knife, waxed or white paper, rubber bands and the lunch box, which should contain a teaspoon, jelly glass with top, or the equivalent, a drinking cup and if soup or milk is ever carried, a small thermos bottle.

Next, the bread is considered—whether you are to make at home or buy, what kinds, white, whole wheat, graham or biscuit; brown or nut bread, too, occasionally.

Since sandwiches are the most convenient way of carrying lunches, the bread is an important part and the sandwiches we will put in two classes, meat or salad, and sweet.

The first kind is made of meat, eggs, cheese or nuts. If the person does not require much meat, a small portion chopped and shredded can be spread more evenly. Have your butter soft, so it can be readily spread—you cannot spread hard butter and to melt it gives an entirely different taste.

For grown folks and large children, a slice of pickle or mayonnaise may be added to the meat; in this case you can leave out these made of salad. Sandwiches of lean meat, eggs, cheese, fish (sardines), or nuts is protein food and for building and re-building the body.

The lunch is apt to have more of this particular food, so the lunch maker should see that cereals and all vegetables, particularly green or leaf ones, are given in the meals eaten at home. Vegetables and cereals give energy and heat and are just as important.

The sweet sandwiches made of jam, jelly, cottage cheese, raisins, nuts, fresh and dried fruit, give more heat and energy, as well as some minerals and some protein. Fat meat, butter, mayonnaise (oil) and nuts give still more and supply the fats for the body. You can readily see it is important to vary the lunch.

The breakfasts in many homes have become rather scant and I wonder if it is wise. The school teacher says "no," that the child who does not have a good, substantial breakfast and time to eat it is the one who becomes restless, tired and cannot study well and often is not the bright child.

From the above list, many lunches may be formed. A few additional lunch suggestions follow:

SCHOOL CHILD'S LUNCH

1 meat sandwich.
6 nuts, cracked, picked and wrapped in waxed paper.
1 jam or jelly sandwich.
1 apple or orange.
1 slice of cake or cookies.
2 or 3 pieces of candy or sweet chocolate.

BUSINESSMAN'S LUNCH

☛ 2 meat sandwiches or
1 jam or sweet sandwich and 1 cheese sandwich.
1 fruit tart or pie.

BUSINESSWOMAN'S LUNCH

☛ 2 meat sandwiches.
1 tasty or salad sandwich which contains pickle, celery or something pertaining to a salad mixture. Something sweet—stuffed dates, candy, slice of cake, sweet sandwiches (sliced pineapple with mayonnaise). The drink to be carried or bought.[1642]

"The turnpike road to people's hearts I find,
Lies through their mouths, or I mistake mankind."
Dr. Walcot

25. Seafoods

(Includes freshwater species)

TO CHOOSE FISH

☞ In selecting fish, take those that are firm and thick, having stiff fins and bright scales, the gills bright red and the eyes full and prominent. When fish are long out of water they grow soft, the fins bend easily, the scales are dim, the gills grow dark, and the eyes sink and shrink away. Be sure and have them dressed immediately; sprinkle them with salt; and if possible, use them the same day. In warm weather, put them in ice, or corning, for the next day.

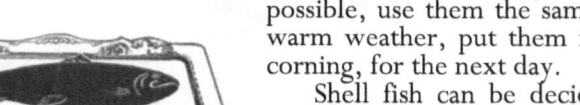

Use a fish trowel when serving fish.

Shell fish can be decided upon only by the smell. Lobsters and crabs are not good, unless alive, or else boiled before offered for sale. They are black, when alive, and red, when boiled. When they are to be boiled, they must be put alive into boiling water, which is the quickest and least cruel way to end life.

Oysters can be decided upon by the smell. If in the shell, it will open when the oyster is dead. Oysters that have been opened, and allowed to stand, will be slimy and flabby, if stale.[1643]

FISH COOKING TIPS

☞ Select perfectly fresh fish with firm flesh, bright eyes and gills. Serve potatoes with fish, and when in season cucumbers or lettuce with a French dressing.[1644]

BOILED FISH

☞ See that fish is well cleaned. Season inside and out with pepper and salt one or two hours before putting to boil, then have your boiler with one quart of luke-warm water to receive the fish, and let it remain on a quick fire twenty minutes; if it is a very large fish it will take thirty minutes to cook.¹⁶⁴⁵

BAKED FISH 1

☛ Fill the fish with stuffing, place it on its belly in a roasting pan and bake until nicely browned, basting with hot water and butter; place on a warm platter, garnish with parsley, celery or cress, or make gashes two inches apart and put slices of fat pork in the gashes. Bake in a quick oven three-fourths of an hour for a medium sized fish. Give it all the heat it will bear without burning. Dredge the fish with salt, pepper and flour and baste often.¹⁶⁴⁶

Fish chops.

BAKED FISH 2

☛ Butter the wires and lay fish on, skin side down; brush over with lard. If a gas stove, turn on both burners and put it as near the flame as you can without burning. When done use this sauce: Two tablespoonfuls of butter, one tablespoonful of fine chopped parsley, few drops of lemon juice or vinegar, salt and pepper to season.¹⁶⁴⁷

BAKED FISH 3

☛ Clean the fish thoroughly; make a stuffing of bread crumbs seasoned with onions chopped fine, little cayenne, salt, pepper and parsley cut fine, a few celery seeds. Stuff and sew up your fish; put in a pan. To a good sized fish put a pint of water; dredge with flour; add some butter; baste often. Bake slowly half an hour.¹⁶⁴⁸

BAKED FISH 4

☛ See that fish is well cleaned; then salt and pepper it inside and out, two or three hours before stuffing it or baking. For the stuffing, grate stale bread enough to fill the fish, then put it on fire in a skillet, and add one tablespoonful of butter and one of lard, chop fine one slice of onion and four sprigs of parsley; season with pepper and salt; let the stuffing stay five or ten minutes, stirring it to keep from burning; then stuff the fish until it is perfectly full. Sow it up with a needle and thread and put it to bake in a medium hot stove; pour about half a tea-cup of water in bottom of pan when you put fish on; while fish is baking, baste or spread a little butter on top of fish until it browns, when it will be ready for table.¹⁶⁴⁹

BROILED FISH

☛ Split and take out the backbone, lay on an oiled sheet, dust with salt, pepper and flour. Put on upper shelf of oven or under the gas flame.

Baste with butter before it goes in the oven and after it comes out.[1650]

STEAMED FISH
☛ Dust the fish with salt, pepper and flour, wrap in a napkin, put in a steamer, cover closely and let cook twenty minutes. Drawn Butter Sauce: One teaspoonful of butter, two of flour; when melted put in half a cup of water, when it comes off add another teaspoonful of butter, a teaspoonful of lemon juice or vinegar, salt and pepper; a hard boiled egg sliced.[1651]

FISH FILLETS
☛ Bone and skin a fish and cut it into strips, dip in a sauce of melted butter, onion and lemon juice; roll it up like a pin wheel and stick with an oiled toothpick and put it in a baking pan under the flame of a gas stove. When half done, salt and pepper it. Serve with New Potatoes (see Vegetables section for recipe).[1652]

Rolled fish fillets.

FISH A LA CREAM
☛ Cook a fish in boiling salt water with a tablespoonful of vinegar until the fish separates easily, drain, and when cool remove skin and bones and pick apart in flakes; sprinkle with salt and pepper. Put a layer of fish in a baking dish and cover with a rich white sauce; let the fish absorb all it will; then put another layer of fish and sauce. Moisten cracker crumbs with butter, put over the top and brown. You may mix grated cheese with the crumbs.[1653]

ANCHOVY CANAPES
☛ Cream two tablespoons butter and add one-fourth cup grated young American cheese and one teaspoon grape vinegar. Season with salt, paprika and mustard. Cut stale bread in one-fourth inch slices, and shape with a round cutter three inches in diameter. Toast on one side, and spread untoasted side with the prepared mixture. Garnish with filets of anchovies arranged lattice fashion, and pipe a border of the buttered mixture around each canape.[1654]

BAKED WHITE FISH
☛ Take out bone and then take off skin and cut fishing in pieces three inches long and two inches wide. Use two soup plates or two deep earthen dishes same size; butter thickly with cold butter, place in layer of fish, season with pepper and salt and a little butter, then another layer with plenty of butter on last layer; then butter inside of second soup dish

very thoroughly and turn it upside down over the fish; put in oven and bake twenty minutes or till flakes break. Those who use wine can pour over fish before baking a wine glass sherry or Madeira, using less butter.[1655]

FISH IN SHELLS

☛ Take a nice white fish and let it boil ½ hour; then pick it very fine, removing skin and bones. Make a dressing of 1 large cup of rich cream, 1 tablespoon of butter, a little flour, and put in saucepan and stir till thick. Add seasoning, salt and pepper and a little celery, and mix with the fish. Fill the shells. Sprinkle bread-crumbs and tiny pieces of butter on top, and put in oven and brown.[1656]

BOILED HALIBUT

Scalloped halibut.

☛ As halibut is seldom cooked whole, cut a piece from one the size you wish place it on the strainer of a fish kettle, fill it up with water, throw in a handful of salt, and boil it gently till it is done, skimming it well; then take it out carefully, score the back part, or outside of the piece, brush it with the yolk of egg, strew over some bread crumbs, with some broken bits of butter, place it on a trivet, before a brisk fire, and when it gets a little brown, serve it up, garnish with slices of lemon, and accompany it with a boat of drawn butter, a plate of lettuce, and a dish of mashed potatoes. Haddock may be dressed in the same manner. If there should be any of the halibut left from dinner, mince it fine from the bones, and set it by for breakfast; then put it in a stew-pan, with a little water, a good lump of butter, rolled in flour, a little salt and pepper, the juice of half a lemon, and two or three spoonfuls of lemon pickle. Let it get perfectly hot, and serve it up.[1657]

HALIBUT WITH CHEESE

☛ Cook a two pound steak of halibut, to which has been added two slices of onion, one sprig of parsley, a stalk of celery, a blade of mace, in boiling water until the flesh leaves the bone. Cool, drain and break into flakes. In a saucepan put a tablespoonful each of four and butter, half a teaspoonful of salt, little pepper; stir until mixed; then add half a cup of the water in which fish was boiled, half a cup of milk; stir until smooth and thick and let simmer five minutes, then remove and add the beaten yolk of one egg; season with salt and pepper. Place in a baking dish alternately layers of fish, sauce and grated cheese and chopped parsley, using a cup of cheese in all and a full tablespoon of parsley. Have the last layer sauce and buttered crumbs. Make a border of mashed potatoes around the dish. Brush with beaten egg and brown in the hot oven.[1658]

BAKED SHAD
☞ Clean, open, and take out the roe, if there is one. Wash carefully and scrape out the blood near the backbone. Lay in a pan long enough not to bend the fish with head on. Fill with seasoned breadcrumbs and sprinkle well in and out with pepper and salt. Gash the top about 2 inches apart and lay strips of fat bacon in the gashes. Bake in a hot oven, adding hot water enough to keep fish from drying and sticking to the pan. Bake from ½ to an hour, according to size. Serve with tomato catsup or Worcestershire sauce.[1659]

BAKED PICKEREL
☞ Scale, clean and wipe the fish leaving on the head and tail. Lay it on a buttered pan, dredge with salt and pepper, spread with soft butter and dredge with flour. Put in a hot oven, and when the four begins to brown, baste with butter and water. Bake forty minutes, and serve with oyster sauce.[1660]

FRIED OR SAUTEED FISH

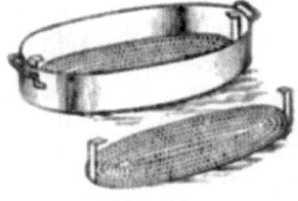

Fish kettle.

☞ Small fish or fish cut in pieces are fried. Wash and wipe the fish dry, season with salt and pepper, then roll in flour or sifted bread crumbs or corn meal. Cook in hot fat. Better if fried out of bacon or salt pork until a golden brown. Turn with a broad knife and cook the other side. There should be only enough grease to prevent its sticking to the pan.[1661]

BARBEQUED SHAD
☞ Split the fish open down the back, pepper and salt it, and then put it on a heated gridiron, the skin next the iron. Baste the upper side with butter, and keep it covered with a pewter plate to keep in the heat. Just before sending it to table, squeeze over it a little lemon juice. Take a small piece of butter, and brown it with a little flour, and when brown, add pepper, salt, and a little walnut catsup. Send it to table in a covered dish.[1662]

FISH PIE
☞ One can of salmon must be picked into small pieces, and put aside until the pap is made—thus: put one quart of fresh milk to boil; with a rolling-pin or mortar pulverize about ten cents worth of oyster crackers, with which thicken the milk, making it about the consistency of mush; when almost cool, stir into it a quarter of a pound of butter, and a little suet; fill your baking-dish with alternate layers of this pap and the fish,

beginning and ending with the pap; between each layer, grate a very little nutmeg; bake only until warm, for all of it has been cooked before.[1663]

CODFISH BALLS

☛ One cup of shredded codfish, pour over a cup of cold water, soak a moment, drain and squeeze; equal proportions of potatoes sliced and cooked; drain, put together and mash thoroughly, setting pan over the fire to dry it out and cook the fish; then add a spoonful each of cream and butter, a little sugar, pepper, one unbeaten white of egg; if too soft, a little bread crumbs. Fry in spoonfuls in deep fat or make in balls. Flour and fry. Drain on cheese cloth; lay on toast with a poached egg.[1664]

Sliced codfish, potato balls, and watercress.

CODFISH PIE

☛ Soak the fish, boil it and take off the skin, pick the meat from the bones, and mince it very fine; take double the quantity of your fish, of stale bread grated; pour over it as much new milk, boiling hot, as will wet it completely, add minced parsley, nutmeg, pepper, and made mustard, with as much melted butter as will make it sufficiently rich; the quantity must be determined by that of the other ingredients—beat these together very well, add the minced fish, mix it all, cover the bottom of the dish with good paste, pour the fish in, put on a lid and bake it.[1665]

CREAMED LAKE SALMON

☛ Scrape, clean and salt three or four pounds of fresh lake salmon; put in baking pan, with a teacup of boiling water, and one teaspoonful of fresh butter. Baste frequently, letting it cook ten minutes to each pound of fish, adding more water if necessary.

A few minutes before taking up, prepare the cream sauce thus: Scald one half teacup of sweet milk, same of sweet cream, small lump of butter; pour into it the gravy, stir, pour over the fish, let boil up once and serve. A little parsley or celery in the cream (chopped fine) adds to the flavor.

Use a cup of sweet milk if cream is not to be had and thicken the sauce with one teaspoonful of flour, mixed with water, and boil a few minutes.[1666]

TURBOT

☛ Steam 1 fish; pick to pieces and bone; sprinkle with salt and pepper in layers and set aside. Boil a little parsley and onion in a pint of milk; strain, set back on fire; stir in of a ¼ pound of flour, ¼ of a pound of butter, and boil till thick; set to one side until partially cold; beat up 2 eggs and stir in the mixture; butter a baking-dish and fill with alternate layers of fish and dressing; sprinkle top with bread-crumbs, and bake until it puffs up in centre.[1667]

BAKED PIKE

☛ Wash, scale and clean the fish, and dry it perfectly in every part. Fill it with forcemeat, and skewer it with its tail in its mouth. If the fish is not stuffed, sprinkle a little salt and cayenne in the inside, and place an ounce of butter there. Egg and bread-crumb it twice. Season the bread-crumbs with salt and cayenne, and mix with them a third of their quantity in shredded parsley. Pour clarified butter over the fish, and bake in a moderate oven. Lay a buttered paper over the dish. Any good fish sauce may be sent to table with pike dressed in this way.[1668]

BAKED BLACK BASS

☛ Eight good-sized onions chopped fine; half that quantity of bread-crumbs; butter size of hen's egg; plenty of pepper and salt; mix thoroughly with anchovy sauce until quite red. Stuff your fish with this compound and pour the rest over it, previously sprinkling it with a little red pepper. Shad, pickerel, and trout are good the same way. Tomatoes can be used instead of anchovies, and are more economical. If using them take pork in place of butter and chop fine.[1669]

FRIED FLOUNDER

☛ Having neatly cleaned your fish, season them with salt, pepper and mace, dredge them with flour, and fry them a light brown in boiling lard. Stir into the gravy a large spoonful of brown flour, and a cup of rich sweet cream; then stir in gradually the juice of half a lemon, pour it over the fish, and garnish with sprigs of parsley.[1670]

FISH CASSEROLE

Casserole.

☛ Line a mold or baking dish with seasoned mashed potato, first buttering it well. Fill up the mold with any kind of highly seasoned creamed fish, or fish that has been mixed with tomato sauce. Cover the top over with an inch layer of mashed potato, brush over with a beaten yolk of egg. Bake in a hot oven for fifteen minutes.[1671]

OYSTER PIE

☛ Make a rich pie-crust, and line a deep dish with it; put in it a folded towel, to support the upper crust; bake a light brown. Scald 3 quarts of oysters in their own juice; take out the oysters, and add to the liquor pound of butter, 1 teaspoon of black pepper, and 1 pint of water or milk. Let it boil up, and then put in the oysters. When the gills of the oysters have turned, pour them in the dish, first removing the top crust and the towel. Serve them immediately.[1672]

RAW OYSTERS

☛ Wash the shells, open, detaching the flat shell, loosen from the deep shell, but leave them in it, and serve half dozen on a plate, with a quarter of lemon in center. Eat with salt, pepper and lemon juice or vinegar. In serving them without the shells the most attractive way is in a dish of ice, made by freezing water in a tin form shaped like a salad bowl, or in a block of ice from which a cavity has been melted with a hot flat-iron. They should first be drained well in a colander, sprinkled with plenty of pepper and salt, and placed on the ice and let remain in a cool place for half an hour or until time of serving. A simpler and equally delicious way is to drain well, sprinkle with salt and pepper, and place the dish on ice or in a dish of cold water for half an hour before serving, adding bits of ice. Serve with horse-radish, Chili sauce, slices of lemon, or simply vinegar.[1673]

Creamed fish in clam shells.

FRICASSEED OYSTERS

☛ Make a white sauce of a tablespoonful each of flour and butter. When it bubbles add a cup of cold milk; season with salt and cayenne pepper. Wash fifty oysters scalded in their own liquor. When they ruffle add them to the white sauce; put in two beaten yolks; when done one tablespoonful of chopped parsley. Serve on rounds of toast with a sprig of parsley on top. Fine.[1674]

FRIED OYSTERS

☛ Select for frying the largest size oysters, drain in a colander and dry one by one. Do not lift out with a fork, but with the fingers. Season with salt and cayenne on both sides. Beat an egg just enough to break it; put in a tablespoonful of hot water; put it in a saucer; put some sifted bread crumbs on the board; season with salt and pepper; dip the oysters first in crumbs, then in egg, then in crumbs again, pressing with the hand. When your fat is smoking hot put in not more than six oysters. When a golden brown take out and drain on paper. Serve at once with cold slaw or pickle.[1675]

STEAMED OYSTERS

☛ Lay some oysters in the shell in some air-tight vessel, placing the upper shell downward so the liquor will not run out when they open. Set them over a pot of boiling water (where they will get the steam), and boil hard for twenty minutes; if the oysters are open they are done; if not, steam till they do open. Serve at once and eat hot, with salt and a bit of butter. Or, wash and drain one quart select oysters, put in pan and place in steamer over boiling water, cover and steam till oysters are plump with edges ruffled; place in heated dish with butter, pepper and salt, and serve.[1676]

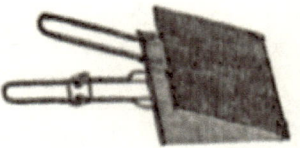

Oyster broiler.

WALLED OYSTERS

☛ Make a wall one and one-half inches high and three-quarters wide of one quart nicely mashed and seasoned potatoes, just inside raised edge of platter, glaze it by covering with beaten egg and placing in oven for a few minutes. Place the liquor from one quart oysters in porcelain kettle, let boil, skim well, then add oysters seasoned with salt, boil up once, skim out oysters (milk or water can be added to the liquor, then seasoned with butter and pepper, and served as soup), and add them to a cream dressing made by putting a tea-cup rich cream, butter size of half an egg, and a little pepper and teaspoon salt in a pan placed within a vessel of boiling water; when hot add two ounces of flour mixed smooth in some cream or milk, and let cook till thickened, then place oysters and dressing within the potato and serve immediately.[1677]

STEWED OYSTERS

☛ Separate the oysters from the liquor. Put the liquor in a stew-pan and add one pint water, a wine glass of cream, a lump of butter, size of hen egg; pepper, salt, bread crumbs to taste; let them boil together; then add oysters, and cook till thoroughly heated.[1678]

BROILED OYSTERS

☛ Dip your oysters in bread and cracker crumbs mixed, flatten with your hand, and broil on a well greased broiler two minutes on each side; then salt lightly. Serve on toast spread with maitre hotel butter sauce.[1679]

PANNED OYSTERS

☛ Put ½ tablespoon butter in pan; when it bubbles add oysters, salt, red pepper, Worcestershire sauce, tomato catsup, green pepper chopped.[1680]

BROILED OYSTERS ON GRIDIRON

☛ Use fat oysters. Dry with a towel. Season both sides with salt and cayenne. Have your griddle hissing hot. Test by a drop of water. If it hisses it is right. Stand a dish in a warm place; put in some butter. Now cover the griddle with oysters. As soon as brown on one side, turn and brown the other side. Put in a heated dish with butter or serve on buttered toast at once.[1681]

BROILED OYSTERS WITH BROWN SAUCE

☛ Take one pint of oyster liquor and put on to boil; skim it well. Put a tablespoonful of butter in a frying pan and set over the fire; when a nice brown add two full tablespoons of flour, mix well and brown; then add the oyster liquor and stir until it boils. Season with salt and pepper.

Keep hot, and when ready to serve add the broiled oysters. Serve on buttered toast.[1682]

ROAST OYSTERS

☛ Toast some slices of bread; wash some nice oysters and dry; spread as many as possible on each slice of toast; season with salt and pepper and bits of butter. Put in a hot oven until the edges of the oysters curl. Serve at once.[1683]

OYSTERS A LA POULETTE

☛ Twenty-five best oysters, one cup oyster liquor, one cup of milk or cream, yolks of three eggs, two tablespoonfuls of butter, four of flour; salt, cayenne and nutmeg to season. Scald the oysters until plump.

Put butter in a saucepan; when melted stir in flour; cook but not brown; stir in slowly the oyster liquor; when smooth add the cream and seasonings. Set off and when a little cool stir in the yolks.

Place on fire to thicken. Pour it over the oysters on a hot dish. Serve at once with croutons (toasted bread).

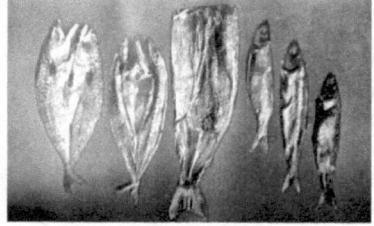
Three types of salted fish.

Do not add cream and egg to the mixture until ready to serve, or they will curdle, and are not good except hot. Serve with puff paste cakes; lemon juice if liked.[1684]

CREAMED OYSTERS 1

☛ For one pint of oysters make a sauce of two tablespoonfuls of butter, four of flour, one and a half cups of cream.

Add the drained oysters to the hot sauce. Cook until they ruffle. Season with salt, pepper and nutmeg. Serve in cases or on toast with brown bread sandwiches.[1685]

CREAMED OYSTERS 2

☛ To half a tablespoonful of butter melted in a saucepan, add a heaping tablespoonful of flour; cook a few minutes and stir in gradually one cup of milk. Season with salt, pepper and celery salt.

Wash and pick over one pint of oysters: scald them in their own liquor until plump; drain and pour over them the sauce.[1686]

CREAMED OYSTERS 3

☛ 1 tablespoon of butter in chafing-dish,
1 can of oysters or 1 dozen fresh oysters.
Drop in the hot butter and let cook till edges curl. Season with
Salt and pepper,
Juice of 1 lemon,
Yolks of 2 eggs beaten up with 2 tablespoons of cream.
Let cook till thick and serve on toast.[1687]

OYSTER LOAF

☛ 1 loaf of [uncut] bread,
1 quart of oysters fried,
½ teacup of tomato catsup,
½ dozen small pickles or 1 dozen olives.

Cut off one end of loaf and remove the soft inside, leaving a shell, which thoroughly butter and place in oven to toast.

Fill with a layer of hot fried oysters, a little catsup, and pickles or olives, another layer of oysters, till shell is filled. Fasten the top on, cut in slices, and serve very hot. A nice supper dish after theatre.[1688]

SCALLOPED OYSTERS

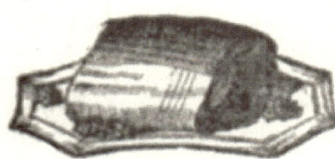

Middle cut of salmon.

☛ Drain one quart of oysters to a pint of bread crumbs, season with salt and pepper.

Mix the seasonings through the crumbs with a fork; then mix in half a cup of butter.

Take a baker not more than two inches deep. Put a layer of crumbs on the bottom, then cover with oysters, but not to overlap each other. Sprinkle with crumbs until nearly hidden from view; then another layer of oysters and crumbs; a heavy layer on top.

Never put but two layers in a dish and never add liquid of any kind. Put in a hot oven until crumbs are brown. The juice from the oysters will be sufficient moisture.[1689]

SALMON

☛ 1 pint can of salmon,
½ cup of crackers rolled coarse,
2 tablespoons butter,
3 well-beaten eggs,
Salt and pepper.

Steam one hour; serve with drawn butter poured over it, in which put chopped mushrooms a few minutes before taking from the stove. Chopped olives and capers are an improvement.[1690]

CREAMED SALMON

☞ One can of salmon minced fine; drain off the liquor and throw away. For the dressing boil one pint of milk, two tablespoonfuls butter; salt and pepper to season. Have a pint of bread crumbs; place a layer in the bottom of a dish, then a layer of salmon; until all is used; then pour over the dressing, having crumbs on top with bits of butter. Bake until brown.[1691]

BOILED SALMON

☞ The thick part of a fine salmon will require half an hour to boil. To 1 gallon of water, put 8 ounces of salt.

Do not allow the salmon to remain in the water after it is ready to be served. Send it to table in a napkin.

Have some sauce in a boat, made of melted butter, with cucumber or anchovy in it.

Jellied salmon.

Boiled salmon is eaten cold as a salad, when salad dressing is served with it.

Bake it as you would beef, and baste it with butter, and serve with sauce, flavored with catsup, or lemon juice.[1692]

BAKED BASS

☞ Make a filling of pounded cracker or crumbs of bread, an egg, pepper, clove, salt and butter. Fill it very full, an when sewed up, grate over it a small nutmeg and sprinkle it with pounded cracker. Then pour on the white of an egg, and a little melted butter. Bake it an hour in the same dish in which it is to be served.[1693]

BOILED FLOUNDER

☞ Lay the fish in a kettle, with salt and water in the proportion of six ounces of salt to each gallon, and a little vinegar. Let the water boil a minute or so, then remove it to the side to simmer till done.

The fish must not boil fast, or they will break. They should simmer fifteen minutes.[1694]

FRIED PERCH

☞ Clean the fish nicely, but do not take out the roes; dry them on a cloth, sprinkle some salt, and dredge them with flour, lay them separately on a board; when one side is dry, turn them, sprinkle salt and dredge the other side; be sure the lard boils when you put the fish in, and fry them with great care; they should be a yellowish brown when done. Send melted butter or anchovy sauce in a boat.[1695]

BAKED MACKEREL

☛ Wash and clean the mackerel, wipe it very dry, fill the inside with grated bread crumbs, seasoned with butter, pepper, salt, thyme and parsley; sew the fish up, and bake it, letting it be full length in the pan. Put a few pieces of butter on the top of it, and dredge the fish with flour. Let it bake for half an hour.[1696]

BROILED MACKEREL

☛ Clean your mackerel, split them open on the back, rinse them clean in cold water, wipe them dry with a cloth, rub a little salt on both sides of them, and broil them over a bed of clear coals, on a clean gridiron, the bars of which, having been greased, wiped with a cloth, and rubbed with a little chalk, or flour, to prevent the fish from sticking to them.

As soon as they are done, put over them pepper, butter and chopped parsley. Salted mackerel may be broiled and served in a similar manner, after soaking them for several hours in fresh water.[1697]

BROILED SMELTS

☛ Split the smelts down the back and remove the bone. Lay them on a hot broiler, which has been rubbed with suet, to prevent sticking. Broil over hot coals for two minutes on each side.

Put into a dish some Béchamel sauce, and lay the broiled fish on the sauce, or they may be spread with maître d'hôtel. Serve at once while very hot.[1698]

Smelts fried in rings.

OYSTERS A LA CREOLE

☛ Scald one hundred select oysters in their own liquor, remove and strain. Put in a saucepan one cup of butter and a full tablespoon of flour; let cook until it bubbles, but not brown.

Then add one cup each of milk and oyster liquor; let cook until it thickens; remove, season with one and a half tablespoonfuls Worcester sauce, salt and cayenne and nutmeg. Place the oysters in individual shells, pour over the sauce, cover with cracker crumbs, bits of butter and grated cheese.

Brown and serve hot. Fine.[1699]

BROOK TROUT

☛ Wash and drain in a colander a few minutes, split nearly to the tail, flour nicely, salt, and put in pan, which should be hot but not burning; throw in a little salt to prevent sticking, and do not, turn until brown enough for the table.

Trout are nice fried with slices of salt pork.[1700]

FISH CHOWDER

☞ 3 or 4 medium sized rock fish, or 1 large one; take about 8 slices of fat salt pork; fry them in the pot that the fish is to be cooked leave in the fat, but take out the slices; cut up the fish as for frying; put a layer of it in the pot; sprinkle it with salt, black pepper, chips in; of onion, and a slice of the sliced fried pork. Then put in a layer of raw potatoes, sliced, and season as you did the fish; then a layer of best Pilot bread, or Medford crackers. Continue this process until the pot is filled; when the potatoes are done, the chowder is ready to be served; be careful not to break the fish in dishing it. Should the chowder soak up the water too much in cooking, add sufficient to keep the pot filled. Some persons add, just before the chowder is done, 1 pint of cream or milk, but this is according to taste.[1701]

CLAM CHOWDER

☞ One quart each of water and clam juice, twenty-five clams chopped fine, three small onions chopped fine, seven chopped potatoes. Boil all together until potatoes are done; then add one-fourth of a cup of butter, one pint of cream, salt, pepper and thyme.[1702]

CODFISH CHOWDER

Codfish.

☞ Put in a deep stew-pan some slices of fat pork; mix with it sliced onions, and sweet herbs, and lay them on the pork; cut a fresh cod into thin slices, taking out all the bones; put them on the pork also; then cover with a layer of pork; add so on till the dish is nearly full, putting biscuit between the layers. Pour over it all a quart of water, and let it stew slowly for 4 hours. Season with pepper and salt.[1703]

TO PREPARE EELS

☞ Kill them by piercing the spinal marrow close to the back part of the skull. Skin them, and let them lie in salt and water until all slime is removed, then cook them in either way directed above.[1704]

FRIED EELS

☞ Skin them and wash clean; put a little pepper and salt upon them, cut them into pieces; roll each piece in corn meal, and fry them in boiling lard a dark brown. Serve them while hot.[1705]

BROILED EELS

☞ Prepare as above, and put them upon a heated gridiron or in the oven. If in the oven, put with them a little water. Baste with butter frequently.[1706]

STEWED EELS

☛ Clean them, and cut in pieces; if a large eel, put to it 1 onion and ½ pint of water. Let them stew slowly for 20 minutes; then pour in 1 pint of milk, and stir in 2 tablespoons of butter rolled in 1 tablespoon of flour.

Stir constantly until they are done.[1707]

BAKED STURGEON

☛ Take a piece of sturgeon and bake it in the same manner as a fillet of veal, by making incisions in it, and filling it with force meat.

When it is cold, serve it with lettuce and salad dressing.

Or it can be eaten while hot. Baste it constantly with its gravy while it is baking.[1708]

STURGEON CUTLETS

☛ The tail piece is the best; skin it and cut off the gristle, cut it into slices about half an inch thick, sprinkle over them pepper and salt, dredge them with flour, and fry them a nice light brown; have ready a pint of good gravy, seasoned with catsup, wine, and a little pounded cloves, and thickened with brown flour and butter; when the cutlets are cold, put them into the gravy and stew them a few minutes; garnish the dish with nice forcemeat balls and parsley fried crisp.[1709]

STURGEON STEAKS

☛ Prepare them, season them (as desired), and wrap them in separate pieces of white paper. Place a hot gridiron over clear coals, rub the bars clean with a cloth, to prevent them soiling the paper, broil them on the gridiron carefully, till thoroughly done, and send them warm to table with a boat of drawn butter and chopped parsley, flavored with lemon juice.[1710]

Boiled fish steaks and potato balls.

BOILED MUSSELS

☛ Brush the shells and wash the mussels in several waters, so they will be free from grit. Put them into a deep saucepan (without water) and sprinkle a little salt over them. Spread a napkin over them in the saucepan, put the lid on, and scald them over a sharp fire. Shake them about briskly, to keep them from burning.

When the shells open, take the saucepan off the fire, strain the liquor into a bowl, and take out the fish. Very carefully remove the little piece of weed which is found under the black tongue and throw it away.

If the mussels are left too long on the fire they will become leathery.[1711]

STEAMED CLAMS

☞ Scrub the required number of clams; place when clean in a saucepan over the fire without any water and heat until the shells open. Take out the clams and pour the liquor into a jar to settle. Remove the clams from their shells, pulling off the thin skin round the edge, and cutting off the black end with a pair of scissors. When the water has settled pour it into a saucepan, add the clams and heat but do not boil. Take out the clams and serve on brown bread.[1712]

DEVILED CRABS

☞ Twelve nice heavy crabs, one tablespoonful of butter, two of flour, one cup of cream, little grated nutmeg, salt and cayenne to season, chopped parsley, yolks of four hard boiled eggs. Make a white sauce of the butter, flour and cream.

When thick remove, add the seasoning, the yolks mashed fine and crab meat. Fill the shells, brush with beaten egg, cover with bread crumbs. Either fry in very hot fat or brown in the oven.[1713]

CRAB STEW

☞ ½ dozen crabs.
2 tablespoonfuls butter.
1 quart milk.
1 tablespoonful flour.
Yolks of 4 eggs boiled hard.
1 dessert spoonful mustard.
½ lemon.
½ teaspoonful salt.
1 nutmeg.
¼ teaspoonful red pepper.

Mash the hard-boiled yolks fine, and rub into them the butter, flour and mustard. Put the milk into a double boiler; when it is scalded stir in the mixture of egg, etc.; season, and just before serving stir in the crab meat, and add one cupful of sherry. Place in bottom of a deep dish a few thin slices of lemon and turn the stew over them.[1714]

POTTED CRAB

☞ Pick the meat from the shell and claws of a freshly-boiled crab. Pound it in a mortar with salt, cayenne, and pounded mace. Press it into small jars, cover it with butter, and bake it in a moderate oven for half an hour.

When cold, pour freshly-clarified butter over it. Set it aside until the butter becomes cold.[1715]

SOFT SHELL CRABS BROILED

☛ Dress carefully, season with salt, baste with oil or melted butter, and broil over a slow fire. Dress on a hot dish and cover with melted butter.[1716]

SOFT SHELL CRABS FRIED

☛ Dip the dried crabs in milk, then roll in flour and fry to a golden brown in deep fat.[1717]

ROASTED CLAMS

☛ Wash them and lay them on a gridiron over the hot coals. As soon as the shells open take off the top shell and place a little butter and pepper on them. Oysters may be done in the same way.[1718]

CLAM BAKE

☛ A party of twenty will require a bushel of clams, which should be gathered, if possible, the day before. Leave on the shell, place in a tub and cover with clean water. Into the water throw about one quart of Indian meal. This fattens them. When time to use wash thoroughly in two or more waters. Clean one fresh cod nicely, season with salt and pepper, and wrap in a clean cloth. Clean also a live lobster. Wash plenty of potatoes, cut off the ends, peel a generous lot of onions, husk some green corn (leaving on the inner husk to keep it clean) and all is ready for the oven.

Make the oven of flat stones placed together in the form of a square, about two and one-half feet each way; around the inside of this place other stones to form a bin. Fill this bin with small

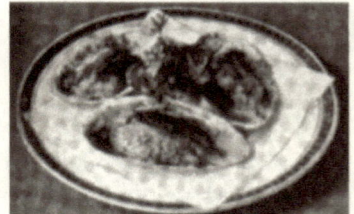

Baked clams.

sticks. On these pile larger sticks, crosswise, and on top of these a layer of stones. Start the fire, allowing it to burn down until the stones which are on top settle into the coals. Clean out quickly all the cinders with a poker, then cover the stones with a green seaweed about one and one-half inches thick. Have ready the clams, spread them on top of the seaweed, then the vegetables, then the fish and a live lobster. Cover the whole with a piece of cotton cloth to keep out dirt; then cover with seaweed until no steam can escape. Bake thirty-five minutes. Remove the covering from one corner at a time only-so that the rest may keep hot, and all hands take hold and help themselves.[1719]

HOW TO CURE AND SMOKE FISH

☛ Scale, slit the fish up the back and clean. Wipe with a damp cloth but do not wash. To twenty pounds of fish allow one pint of salt, one pint of brown sugar and one ounce of salt-peter. Mix well together and rub the fish well inside and out with this mixture. Put one fish over the other with a board on top, and on this place heavy weights to press them down. Allow them to remain so for sixty hours, then drain, wipe dry, stretch open and fasten with small pieces of stick. Smoke them for five days in a smokehouse or in a barrel over a smothered wood fire.[1720]

CLAM PIE

☛ Take 15 or 20 clams; cut off the gills and stew them in their own liquor slowly, with 2 sprigs of parsley, a small onion, a shallot, pepper and salt. Add a slice of bacon while stewing, and take it out before baking; then add 3 tablespoons of cream. Bake until the paste is done.

A few clams should be roasted, cut up, and gills taken off, and put in the pie just before baking. The clams should be nicely washed, put in a tub, and boiling water poured on them. Save the liquor to cook the clams in.[1721]

SHRIMP PIE

☛ To 2 quarts of peeled shrimps, put 1 cup of vinegar, 1 tumblerful of catsup, and 2 tablespoons of butter. Season with salt and pepper; scald together these ingredients, and then pour them in an earthen dish; strew bread crumbs over the top, and bake for 20 minutes.[1722]

SHRIMP GUMBO

☛ Salt and pepper.
Butter size of egg.
1 can tomatoes.
1 small onion.
Parsley.
1 green pepper.
Little celery.

Brown onion (minced) in butter, thicken with a little flour, then add tomatoes and other vegetables all minced fine and seasonings. Thoroughly wash shrimps, and add to mixture.[1723]

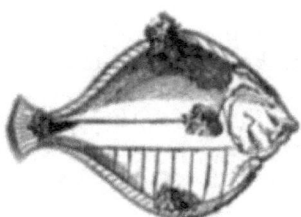

A European flatfish: the turbot.

SCALLOPS

☛ The heart is the only part used, dip them in beaten egg, then cracker crumbs and fry in hot lard; they can be stewed as oysters. Those sold in markets are generally ready for frying or stewing, but if bought in shell boil and take out hearts.[1724]

BAKED HERRING

☛ Soak salt herring over night, roll in flour and butter, and place in a dripping-pan with a very little water over them; season with pepper.[1725]

LOBSTER CUTLETS

☛ Make a thick white sauce of two tablespoonfuls of butter, one-fourth of a cup of flour, season with salt and pepper, one cup of milk or white stock, one egg, one teaspoonful of lemon juice, two cups of chopped lobster meat. Add the beaten egg to the thick sauce, the lobster meat and lemon juice; turn in a shallow dish, cover and set aside to become very cold. Sprinkle your mold with bread crumbs, fill with the lobster mixture, turn out on a bed of crumbs, egg and crumb again, let dry off and fry in very hot deep fat.[1726]

LOBSTER A LA DABNEY

☛ Pick the meat from good-sized lobsters, leaving with it some of the soft part. Put 1 quart of milk over boiling water, removing 1 gill to mix with 1 gill of flour. When the milk is scalding hot, stir this in. Season with red pepper and salt to taste. Stir until the flour is cooked; then pour it on the lobster and mix well.

It must be softer than for salad. Put in shallow pans or shells; cover with bread-crumbs; dot with butter and bake till brown. This can be prepared in the morning for tea.[1727]

Lobster farci.

LOBSTER A LA NEWBERG

☛ To one quart can of lobsters allow a full tablespoon of butter and a tablespoonful of flour, three hard boiled eggs, one and a half cups of milk, one or two tablespoonfuls of Sherry wine.

Cook the butter and flour together until they bubble, add the milk cold and let thicken; then add the eggs mashed very fine; now the lobster broken in pieces. Season with salt, cayenne and Sherry. Serve very hot with crackers.[1728]

STEWED CARP

☛ Gut and scale your fish, wash and dry them well with a clean cloth, dredge them with flour, fry them in lard until they are a light brown, and then put them in a stew pan with half a pint of water, and half a pint of red wine, a meat spoonful of lemon pickle, the same of walnut catsup, a little mushroom powder and cayenne to your taste, a large onion stuck with cloves, and a stick of horse-radish; cover your pan close up to keep in the steam.

Let them stew gently over a stove fire, till the gravy is reduced to just enough to cover your fish in the dish; then take the fish out, and put them on the dish you intend for the table; set the gravy on the and thicken it with flour, and a large lump of butter; boil it a little, and strain it over your fish; garnish them with pickled mushrooms and scraped horse-radish, and send them to the table.[1729]

PRAWNS

☛ Put your prawns in a kettle of boiling water, throw in a handful of salt, and boil them for fifteen or twenty minutes; then drain and set them by to cool. Make a plentiful dressing of vinegar, mustard, sweet oil, salt and pepper, preparing it in the same manner as for minced lobster. When the prawns are cold, arrange them neatly in a dish, lay round them small toasts, sliced crackers, or slices of bread and butter, and send with them to table the dressing, to be handed round to the company, and mixed by them in their plates, as their tastes may desire.[1730]

Lobster chops, served standing.

ROASTED OYSTERS

☛ Wash the shells well with a brush and cold water. Place them in a pan with the deep half of shell down. Put them into a hot oven, and bake until the shell opens. Remove the top shell carefully so as not to lose the liquor. Arrange them on plates, and on each oyster place a piece of butter and a little pepper and salt. If roasted too long the oysters will be tough.[1731]

OYSTER PATTIES

☛ Roll out puff paste a quarter of an inch thick, cut it into squares, cover ten patty pans, and put on each a crust of bread the size of a walnut. Roll out another layer of paste the same thickness, cut as above, wet edge of the bottom paste and put on top; pare them, so the edges will be even, notch them with the back of the knife, rub them lightly with the yolk of an egg, and bake them in a hot oven about a quarter of an hour. When done slice very thin off the top, remove the bread and the inside paste.

Filling: Parboil two dozen oysters in their own liquor, after boiling it down to half, cut the oysters in halves, put them in a pan with an ounce of butter rolled in flour, half a gill of cream and a little salt. Stir this mixture over the fire five minutes, fill the patties, put the cover on, and serve hot.[1732]

Examples of delightful and appetizing dishes for dinner.

26. Snacks

SALTED ALMONDS
☛ After blanching your almonds put in a bowl and pour over a little olive oil, let stand an hour and add a little fine salt. Put in shallow pans and set in the oven to brown, stirring occasionally. When done put in a paper sack and shake to remove surplus salt. Or, fry them a golden brown in olive oil.[1733]

CONFEDERATE SALTED ALMONDS
☛ Shell one pound of almonds; cover with boiling water; let stand five minutes; remove the skins and dry thoroughly. Put in a large pan a small piece of butter, and when melted, turn in the almonds, stirring rapidly until every nut is shining with butter. Then sprinkle over them a tablespoonful of salt, mixing so that every nut shall be coated. Then put the pan on the bottom of the oven, and let it remain (shaking and stirring frequently), until the nuts are a light yellowish brown, when they will be crisp and delicious.[1734]

SALTED PEANUTS
☛ The peanuts must be shelled and blanched. Put them in a pan with a little butter and fry them quickly. Remove them to a colander and sprinkle them with fine salt, shaking them constantly. They may be served in little trays at each plate.[1735]

SALTED PISTACHIO NUTS
☛ Pistachio nuts salted are so expensive an item, but such a picturesque addition to the table that one should learn how to prepare them at home. Take a cupful of the shelled nuts, blanch them and after removing the skins stir in some salt and a little sweet oil-perhaps a tablespoonful. Let the nuts stand for one-half hour, then put them in an oven to become crisp, but not too brown. They should be served in a tinted china dish that harmonizes with the color of the nuts, or in a bonbon basket of

filigree silver. A few chopped pistachios scattered thickly over a charlotte russe add to the appearance and flavor of the dessert.[1736]

POTATO CHIPS 1
☞ Slice your potatoes and put in water to soak over night, or sometime before cooking. When ready to fry, put in a basket and shake in order to dry as much as possible. Put in a kettle a good deal of the best lard. Have the lard quite hot, but not too hot; put some salt in it and put in the chips. Stir often while cooking. When done, shake well and sift over a little salt.[1737]

Dessert charlotte russe.

POTATO CHIPS 2
☞ Take nice smooth potatoes, peel them, and slice very thin with a machine for the purpose, or a cabbage-cutter. Throw in cold water. Pour boiling water on them till they are clear. Then pour ice water on them to crisp them. Wipe dry and drop one at a time into boiling lard and cook a pretty brown.[1738]

POTATO CHIPS 3
☞ Pare the potatoes, shave them very thin, soak for ½ hour in ice-cold salted water; drain in a colander, and spread upon a dry towel; fry a few at a time in very hot fat, 1 minute being sufficient to cook and brown them properly sprinkle lightly with salt, and when needed at table, heat quickly in the oven.[1739]

GUACAMOLE
☞ 2 alligator pear avocados.
1 teaspoon olive oil.
½ onion.
1 pinch cayenne.
1 clove of garlic.
1 sweet pomegranate.

Mash avocados and mix with crushed onion, cayenne and garlic. Have all perfectly smooth, then stir in seeds of pomegranate. Serve cold.[1740]

COLONEL SEABROOK'S POTATO CHIP NACHOS
☞ Aluminum foil a large cookie sheet. Spread the entire surface with potato chips one to two inches deep. Sprinkle one-fourth pound of shredded sharp cheddar cheese over the top of the chips; throw a handful of organic olives (sliced or whole), a quarter cup of diced bell peppers,

and a quarter cup of fresh chopped jalapeno peppers over the cheese. Bake for approximately seven minutes (or until done to your taste) on the middle oven rack. Serve with dipping bowls of warmed refried beans, guacamole, sour cream, Spanish rice, and salsa. These vegetarian nachos are both delectable and salubrious.[1741]

COLONEL SEABROOK'S FRITOS NACHOS
☞ Same as above recipe, but replace the potato chips with Fritos or any other corn chip of your preference.[1742]

SALSA
☞ Take a cupful each of tomatoes, onions and green peppers (from which the seeds have been removed); scald and skin the tomatoes, and skin the peppers by blistering on a hot stove. Chop all together, adding salt and enough olive oil to moisten. This can be eaten hot or cold on fish or cold meats.[1743]

POPCORN
☞ Drop the corn into boiling lard; cover it to keep it from popping out; when it is done popping, take it out and put it on a colander to drain. Have ready a rich syrup, flavored with orange or lemon juice; when it simmers, drop in the corn; take it out in large lumps, and lay it on buttered dishes to cool.[1744]

COLONEL SEABROOK'S HEALTHY BABY WHITE POPCORN
☞ Load air popcorn popper with proper amount of popcorn, using baby white popcorn kernels (organic if possible) and pop. Pour in large bowl. Season with organic cold pressed olive oil, nutritional yeast, and organic pink Himalayan sea salt. Note: *Baby white* popcorn is tastier, more delicate, more nutritious, and easier to digest than regular large yellow and white popcorn. Medium baby white popcorn is also very good.[1745]

CORN PUFFS
☞ One cup of cold mashed potatoes and 1 cup of milk, rubbed through a colander or sieve to work out all lumps; add the yolk of a well-beaten egg, and then stir in slowly, beating well as for breakfast puffs, one cup of corn meal; add lastly the white of the egg beaten to a stiff froth, and bake at once in heated gem-irons. A little salt may be added to the batter if desired. Wheat flour may be substituted for potato if preferred, in which case it should be mixed with the cornmeal before adding to the mixture.[1746]

"A delightful supper, a good night's sleep and a fine morning have often made a hero of the same man who, by indigestion, a restless night and a rainy morning would have proved a coward."

27. Soups

SOUP MAKING TIPS

☛ There are a few essential points in soup making which when once learned makes soup making easy.

First, cut the meat in small pieces and soak them in cold water before heating that every atom of nourishment may be extracted, cold water draws out and dissolves the meat juices, while hot water hardens the albumen on the outside of the meat, and prevents the juices escaping into the liquid.

Second, use a careful selection and preparation of meat bone and water, season judiciously so that no one flavor will predominate.

Third, use a steam tight kettle and simmer, never boil rapidly that the juice may be retained in the water and not wasted by evaporation.

Fourth, make the stock the day before using if possible that the fat may be removed easily.

Cook meats, odds and ends, beef bones, ham bones, chicken bones, can be made into soup to accompany a cold meat dinner, also an acid salad, as tomatoes, cabbage. Prepare the meat stock as above. Never wash a soup bone, place in cold water put in a kettle with a close fitting cover, to every gallon water one teaspoon salt. Let come to a boil then let it simmer. Never skim soup. Cook three or four hours.[1747]

TO MAKE SOUP

☛ The best soup is made of lean juicy beef that is fresh. It is poor economy to make soups of cooked meats; they impart a flat taste to the soup, the first cooking having greatly wasted the juices of the meat. Always put the meat in *cold* water to cook, having first washed it nicely in cold water. To each pound of meat allow 3 pints of water, and reduce by boiling to 1 quart. The soup-pot should always be kept covered; as the scum rises, it should be removed until the soup water is clear; then add the vegetables. If the soup becomes too thick after boiling for some time, add to it boiling water; a kettle of water should be kept boiling for the purpose. The water in which poultry has been boiled can be made into soup; but of course is not as rich as if the meat had been allowed to boil to pieces in the water.

If Irish potatoes are used in soup, they should be first boiled and then added to the soup; for the water in which Irish potatoes have been boiled is of a disagreeable taste, and thought by some persons to be poisonous.

For brown soups, before putting the meat in the pot, first put in a dessert-spoonful of butter; when it is hot put in the meat, and the herbs on the top of the meat; let the meat fry for a short time, and then pour in the water. It makes the soup of a richer flavor to prepare it in this manner.

Spices and herbs should always be tied in a muslin bag, and taken out of the soup before it is served.

Dip the cloth that the soup is to be strained through into cold water; it hardens the grease. White soup is clarified with egg; the whites of 2 eggs to ½ gallon of soup.

Soup should always be made the day before it is to be used; when cold, skim off all the grease. Soup should boil slowly and steadily. It requires from 3 to 5 hours to make.[1748]

DIXIE SOUP

☛ Cut up a chicken and put it, with a sliced onion, into a soup pot; fry it brown in a little hot butter or lard; then pour on it 3 quarts of water, and boil it slowly until the meat separates from the bones. Skim off all grease, and remove the bones; add 1 pint of oyster liquor, and boil for 30 minutes; then add 1 quart of oysters. When the gills turn, stir 1 tablespoon of butter, rolled in flour, to thicken the soup. Put some nicely toasted bread, cut in squares, into the tureen; pour upon them the soup, and serve. Knuckle of veal or rabbits can also be prepared in this manner.[1749]

DIXIELAND SOUP

☛ 4 potatoes,
3 pints of milk,
Piece of butter size of an egg,
Small piece of onion.

Take four large potatoes, boil until done and mash smooth, adding butter and salt to taste. Heat the milk in a double boiler, cook the onion in it a few minutes and then remove. Pour the milk slowly on the potato, strain, heat and serve immediately. Thicken with one tablespoonful of flour.[1750]

TOMATO SOUP

☛ 1 quart of peeled fresh tomatoes or canned. Let them stew till thoroughly cooked and add half a teaspoon of soda. Have ½ gallon of fresh milk boiling. Stir into the tomatoes 1 tablespoon of butter, 1 of flour, and red pepper and salt to taste. Pour tomatoes into milk and let it boil 15 minutes. Serve hot.[1751]

CARROT SOUP

☛ Put in soup-kettle a knuckle of veal, three or four quarts cold water, a quart finely-sliced carrots, one head celery; boil two and a half hours, add a handful rice, and boil an hour longer; season with pepper (or a bit of red pepper pod) and salt, and serve.[1752]

CORN AND TOMATO SOUP

☛ Take a fresh beef bone, put on to boil with one gallon of water, and when boiling skim the grease off. Cut corn from cob and scald tomatoes with boiling water. Skin them and put both vegetables into soup, the corn ten minutes before dinner. Cut tomatoes in small pieces and let them boil in soup at least one hour.[1753]

POTATO SOUP

☛ 1 quart of potatoes,
2 ounces of butter,
2 pints milk,
4 eggs.
Boil the potatoes soft, and smooth with a little boiling water until a thin batter. Stir the butter, pepper, and salt to taste into the milk. Beat the eggs and add to potatoes. When milk boils, pour over the potatoes and do not return to the fire.[1754]

BEEF SOUP

☛ 2 pounds of beef; put it on early in the morning; let it stew slowly for 3 hours. Skim it constantly; put in celery or celery seed, a small head of cabbage cut in quarters, some turnips, tomatoes and carrots, 3 of each; add a small handful of okra and any vegetable you please. When done, strain some of the meat and vegetables from the soup, or all of it as it may be liked.[1755]

GREEN PEA SOUP

☛ Make it exactly as you do the dried pea soup, only in place of the celery seed, put a handful of mint chopped small, and a pint of young peas, which must be boiled in the soup till tender; thicken it with a quarter of a pound of butter, and two spoonsful of flour.[1756]

MUTTON SOUP

☞ Put the shoulder part of mutton, after cutting it from the bones and cracking the bones, into a pot, and cover it with water. When it begins to boil, keep it skimmed; boil it slowly for 5 hours, taking off all grease. 2 hours before serving, put in 2 turnips, 2 carrots, and 1 onion, chopped fine, and a little parsley; salt to taste. Strain the soup before serving it; have small pieces of toasted bread in the tureen, and pour the soup upon it. Vermicelli is very good with this soup. Add it when you strain the soup, and let it boil until tender.[1757]

BOUILLON

☞ Take 8 or 9 pounds of beef, 6 quarts of water, 3½ ounces of salt, 6 carrots, 5 turnips, 3 stalks of celery; stick an onion with 4 cloves, 4 leeks, 1 teaspoon of whole black pepper, 1 large bunch of herbs. Let it simmer for 6 hours over the fire. This can be made and kept in a cool place for some time. It is excellent to use for gravies and for soups.[1758]

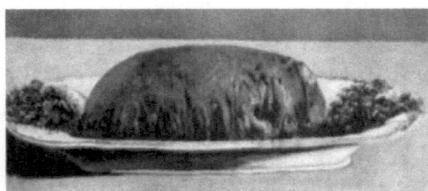
Stuffed shoulder of mutton.

GUMBO

☞ Get a large soup bone; cut deep gashes in the meat, but never wash it, and put on in a gallon of cold water; let come to a boil, then simmer five hours. Cut small two quarts okra, flour and fry in bacon grease or lard; in an hour put it in the soup pot; two hours later put two small cans tomatoes or two quarts fresh ones chopped fine, one large or two small onions chopped, six ears of corn cut from the cob, two or three Irish potatoes peeled and cut, salt to season, white and cayenne pepper. Let simmer two hours longer and serve. This is delicious. If any is left put it in refrigerator until next day.[1759]

CHICKEN GUMBO

☞ Salt and pepper chicken before frying it. Take a chicken, separating it from all the joints and breaking the bones, fry the chicken in one and a half tablespoonful of lard or butter. First well mix the chicken in dry flour, let the fat be hot, put chicken to fry until brown; don't burn chicken. After fried, put it on in soup kettle with half a gallon of hot water, one and a half quarts of green okra cut into thin pieces, throwing the end away, and let the whole boil to three pints; season with pepper and salt. Chop half of an ordinary sized onion fine, and fry it with chicken; chilli pepper chopped fine if added is nice when liked.[1760]

SOUTHERN GUMBO

☛ Put 2 quarts of ham liquor, after the fat has been removed, into a kettle and add ⅔ of a quart can of tomatoes. After cooking half an hour add a can of corn and a cup of cooked ham cut in small pieces. Let boil fifteen minutes, then add a can of okra about ten minutes before serving. Have a dish of hot boiled rice, and serve by putting a spoonful of rice into a plate and pouring the gumbo over it, or the rice may be added to the gumbo while cooking. This is an excellent way to utilize ham liquor.[1761]

SALSIFY SOUP

☛ 1 quart of salsify cooked in water till tender, 1 quart of new milk. Mash the salsify through sieve. Add to boiling milk 1 tablespoon flour and 1 large tablespoon butter. Pour all together and season with pepper and salt.[1762]

VEGETABLE SOUP

☛ Have your vegetables, peas, onions, carrots, cut in slender strips and cook in water. Salted beans and celery add to the soup stock; season with salt and pepper. Color with beef caramel. Make your soup out of beef stock. As the vegetables are sweet, add a slice of lemon to each serving.[1763]

REBEL VEGETABLE SOUP

☛ Three onions, three carrots, three turnips, one small cabbage, one pint tomatoes; chop all the vegetables except the tomatoes very fine, have ready in a porcelain kettle three quarts boiling water, put in all except cabbage and tomatoes and simmer for half an hour, then add the chopped cabbage and tomatoes (the tomatoes previously stewed), also a bunch of sweet herbs. Let soup boil for twenty minutes, strain through sieve, rubbing all the vegetables through. Take two tablespoons of best butter and one of flour and beat to a cream. Now pepper and salt soup to taste, and add a teaspoon of white sugar, a half cup of sweet cream if you have it, and last stir in the butter and flour; let it boil up and it is ready for the table. Serve with fried bread-chips, or poached eggs one in each dish.[1764]

CREAM OF ONION SOUP

☛ Salt.
White pepper.
2 cups onions.
1 cup milk.
1 cup of cold water.
2 tablespoons flour.

Place 2 cups of thinly sliced onions in sauce pan and add 1 cup of cold water. Cook until soft and then rub thru a fine sieve. Measure and return to sauce pan, and add 1 cup of milk for every cup of onion puree and 2 level tablespoons flour to every cup of milk. Stir to dissolve flour then bring to a boil and cook slowly for 5 mins. Season, using salt and white pepper. Serve, then add 1 tablespoon of butter to every quart of cream soup. Croutons or toasted strips of bread make a delicious accompaniment to the cream soup.

Method of preparing croutons: Cut slices of bread into one-inch blocks, and place on a baking sheet and bake until golden brown. Place in a tin box or jar and seal. When ready to use just reheat to crisp and then serve. Stale bread may be used for this purpose.[1765]

MUSHROOM SOUP

☛ Put 1 qt. milk into a double boiler, to this add ½ pt. cream and 2 bay leaves, thicken this with one small tablespoon flour dissolved in milk; after this boils strain and put back into the double boiler, then chop 1 can mushrooms very fine and stir into the soup; dissolve 2 tablespoons Armour's beef extract in ½ pt. boiling water, and stir into the soup; add salt to taste; serve in cups. This will be sufficient for 14 people.[1766]

RABBIT SOUP

☛ Cut up two hares, put them into a pot with a piece of bacon, two onions chopped, a bundle of thyme and parsley, which must be taken out before the soup is thickened, add pepper, salt, pounded cloves, and mace, put in a sufficient quantity of water, stew it gently three hours, thicken with a large spoonful of butter, and one of brown flour, with a glass of red wine; boil it a few minutes longer, and serve it up with the nicest parts of the hares. Squirrels make soup equally good, done the same way.[1767]

HARE SOUP

☛ Take a large hare, or two fine rabbits; case them, cut them into joints, and rinse them clean in cold water, but do not soak them in it; season them with salt and pepper, and put them into a pot with a few slices of ham and a good quantity of water. When it has boiled hard, remove the scum, put in a bundle of thyme, parsley, sweet marjoram, and a head of celery cut small,

Jugged hare.

and some onions and white potatoes, if you choose; cover the pot, and boil it gently till the meat is ready to drop from the bones, and there remain two quarts of the liquor. Then take up the meat, pass the liquid through a sieve, pressing the seasonings, to obtain all the essence you can; put it into a pan or pot, and set it again on the fire. Stir in two large spoonfuls of four, mixed in half a pint of sweet mills, with a large handful of force-meat balls, made about the size of a partridge's egg, dipped in the yolk of an egg and rolled in dry flour. Add a little powdered nutmeg, mace, and a glass of red wine. Just let it come to a boil, and serve it up on sliced crackers, toasts, or slices of light bread. Pick out some of the nicest pieces of the hare, and serve with the soup. Crown it with small sprigs of parsley, or green tops of asparagus, and send it to the table hot. If you choose, thicken the soup entirely with noodles, pounded crackers, biscuit, or boiled rice. Soup may be made in the same manner, of partridges, pigeons, pheasants, or grouse.[1768]

CHICKEN BROTH

☞ Salt and pepper.
1 fowl.
3 cupful of rice.
4 quarts of cold water.

Clean the fowl carefully; wash it with a wet cloth; cut it into pieces and remove the fat. Place the joints in a saucepan with a quart of water to each pound of fowl. Let it simmer until the meat is tender; then remove the breast; after four hours take it off and strain it through a sieve. Let the soup stand until the grease rises; then carefully remove it, and put the soup again in the saucepan; add the breast of the chicken, cut into dice, and the half cupful of rice; salt and pepper to taste, and cook until the rice is tender.[1769]

CLAM BROTH

☞ 12 large hard-shelled clams for 1 pint of broth.

Boil the clams and juice for twenty minutes; strain and let it stand to settle; strain it again carefully into a saucepan, and let it boil up once; season with butter and pepper—no salt—and serve in cups with whipped cream on top. To open the clams and obtain the juice, place the clams, after they have been carefully washed with a brush and clear water, in a saucepan; add two tablespoonfuls of hot water; cover and let them steam until the shells open; then strain off the liquor.[1770]

CREOLE SOUP

☞ Take three pints of bouillon, put on to boil, just before use chop four leaves of parsley fine, and put in. Brown a teaspoonful of brown sugar on a tin plate, add a sherry wine-glass of sherry wine to sugar, stir it well, then strain through a fine sieve; then stir three tablespoonfulls into soup. Beat two yolks of eggs into tureen and pour hot soup on it and send to table.[1771]

NOODLE SOUP

☞ Add noodles to beef or any other soup after straining; they will cook in fifteen or twenty minutes, and are prepared in the following manner: To one egg add as much sifted flour as it will absorb, with a little salt; roll out as thin as a wafer, dredge very lightly with flour, roll over and over into a large roll, slice from the ends, shake out the strips loosely and drop into the soup.[1772]

OX-TAIL SOUP

☞ Can be made in the following manner. Take two quarts of bouillon to two ox-tails; boil down to three pints. You can put in either okra or vermicelli.

Season with salt and pepper. Skim all grease off while boiling. Have the butcher unjoint the ox-tail.[1773]

CHICKEN SOUP

☞ Take two half-grown chickens, clean them nicely, and cut them up; rinse them clean, season them with salt and pepper, and boil them with a few slices of the lean of ham.

When it boils hard, skim it; then cover it and boil it slowly till the chickens are about half done. Have ready some noodles, or vermicelli, made in the usual manner, or small white potatoes, or onions neatly prepared and sliced; put them with the chicken, and boil them till tender, and the soup reduced to two quarts.

Stuffed celery.

Then take out the meat and stir in two spoonfuls of flour, mixed with a little sweet milk, till smooth; add a cup of sweet cream, a handful of chopped parsley or thyme, and serve it up with toasts.

Partridge or pheasant soup may be made in the same manner.[1774]

CREAM OF CHICKEN SOUP

☞ Cook together one tablespoonful of butter and two of flour in a small sauce pan, then strain in as much chicken broth as you want soup; cook it well and add some celery broth to flavor. Put in as much milk as you have broth; salt to season. Heat to boiling point and serve.[1775]

CREAM OF CELERY SOUP

☞ Cut your celery in very small pieces; cook until very tender in clear water; strain and make as chicken soup.[1776]

CREAM OF PEA SOUP

☞ One pint of canned peas, one pint of cream, one tablespoonful of butter, salt and white pepper, to taste. Strain and mash the peas in a pan; fill the can with boiling water; pour on the peas, place over the fire and let come to a boil.

Pour in the cream, and stir in the butter, salt and pepper.

Serve with whipped cream, and squares of toast.

If preferred, the soup may be strained.[1777]

GUMBO SOUP

- 1 chicken,
2 pints okra,
1 pint tomatoes,
1 tablespoon butter.

Fry the chicken and pour over ½ gallon of boiling water and cook till the meat drops from the bones. Remove bones. Prepare the vegetables and add to the soup and boil. Then add thickening and season to taste, or as for any other soup. Before pouring off add the butter. Add hot water as it boils down. Serve hot, with rice boiled dry.[1778]

CREAM OF TOMATO SOUP

- 1 can tomato soup.
½ pint cream, whipped.
1 pint milk.
Salt.

Combine soup and milk, add seasoning, and heat. Drop spoonful of whipped cream on each serving, and sprinkle paprika over top.[1779]

DIXIE LENTIL SOUP

- Take four carrots, two sliced onions, a chopped lettuce head, two ounces of butter, two pints of lentils, the crumbs of two French rolls and two quarts of stock. Put the vegetables, with the butter, into a stew-pan, and let them simmer five minutes; add the lentils, which should be soaked in cold water for two hours previous and a pint of the stock, and stew gently for one-half hour. Now fill up with the remainder of the stock, let it boil another hour and put in the crumbs of the rolls. When these are well soaked rub all through a wire sieve or tammy cloth. Season to taste with pepper and salt, boil up once more, and serve. Water may be used in the place of the stock, if desired; but in that case a cupful of milk, thickened with corn-flour, should be added just before the final boil.[1780]

PRIDE OF THE SOUTH MACARONI SOUP

- Take five or six pounds of fresh beef or veal; cut several deep gashes in it, and soak it four or five hours in fresh water, to draw out the blood, changing the water two or three times; then break the bone in several places, boil it till the meat is ready to drop to pieces, adding a sufficiency of salt and pepper, and strain the liquid into a soup-pan. Have ready a pound of the best macaroni; cut it up, and boil it in the soup till tender; then take it out, mash half of it very fine and smooth, return it to the liquor, and boil and stir it occasionally, till it is well mixed with the soup, which should be at least five pints. Then put in the remaining half of the macaroni, with four ounces of the best cheese, grated fine; let it simmer a minute or two, stirring it all the time, and pour it into a tureen. You may make this soup with entire sweet milk, instead of broth, season it tolerably high with butter, and reserve the cheese to be served on a plate. You may also make it of poultry broth, by soaking the fowls in water after they are cut up, to draw out the blood.[1781]

CALF'S HEAD SOUP

☞ Let the butcher open the head wide. Take the brains from it and lay into clean water with a little salt. Leave the tongue in the head when put on to boil; when the tongue is tenderly boiled or done, take it out of the pot and let it get cold for making tongue salad. Two gallons of water to a calf's head; boil to one gallon; strain it off clear for soup to one dozen guests. Take two quarts of this liquid and put to boil; two tablespoonfuls of flour and brown it; one tablespoonful of butter; rub into the brown flour till it comes to a cream, then add to the soup gradually, and stir well while adding. Season with salt and pepper, and a little red pepper. While cooking, boil a small piece of thyme and the half of an ordinary sized onion tied tight in a clean linen rag, and to be taken out of soup when done. One teaspoonful of mustard mixed with one tablespoonful of wine, to be put into the tureen before pouring in the soup hot, also one glass of sherry wine. Pick all skin from brains; beat two eggs light and add to the brains, then beat the eggs and brains together to a batter; take one-quarter tea cup of powdered cracker, one tablespoonful of flour added to the brains and egg batter well beaten together. Then make this brain batter in cake the size of a hickory nut, and fry them brown in hot fat just before taking up soup, and send to table on separate dish. Serve them with the soup, two cakes to a plate of soup. Chop parsley very fine, and boil it into the soup. You will find the calf's head soup the most delicious soup in the cookery. Study the recipe and remember it well.[1782]

CATFISH SOUP

☞ An excellent dish for those who have not imbibed a needless prejudice against these delicious fish. Take two large or four small white catfish that have been caught in deep water, cut off the heads, and skin and clean the bodies; cut each in three parts, put them in a pot, with a pound of lean bacon, a large onion cut up, a handful of parsley chopped small, some pepper and salt, pour in a sufficient quantity of water, and stew them till the fish are quite tender but not broken; beat the yolks of four fresh eggs, add to them a large spoonful of butter, two of flour, and half a pint of rich milk; make all these warm and thicken the soup, take out the bacon, and put some of the fish in your tureen, pour in the soup, and serve it up.[1783]

SPINACH SOUP

☞ Wash half a peck of spinach, put it on to cook without adding water—there is enough that clings to the leaves to cook it—one teaspoonful salt, a small onion sliced. When tender, mash through a strainer or puree sieve. Scald two cups of milk in double boiler, melt in sauce pan two tablespoonfuls of butter, stir into it one of flour. When blended, stir it into the hot milk. Cook ten minutes, then add one cup of the spinach pulp and the yolk of one egg diluted with a half cup of cream. Cook ten more minutes. Season with salt and pepper.[1784]

Chartreuse of spinach.

CREAM OF SPINACH SOUP WITH STOCK
☞ Take one pint of cold cooked spinach, chop and pound into a soft paste. Put it into a stew-pan with four tablespoonfuls of butter and a teaspoonful of salt.

Cook and stir it about fifteen minutes. Add to this one quart of stock and one pint of boiling water; let boil up, then rub through a strainer. Set it over the fire again, and, when boiling, add a tablespoonful of butter, and a teaspoonful of sugar.[1785]

OYSTER SOUP
☞ Take 2 quarts of oysters; wash them in their liquor, and strain the liquor. Put on the liquor, with a slice of lean bacon, pepper and salt, and thicken with a tablespoon of butter, rolled in flour. Just before serving, pour in a pint of cream and milk mixed. Keep stirring constantly for a few minutes, and then serve. It will burn if it is not stirred. The oysters are put in the liquor when it comes to a boil. When the gills of oysters turn, they are cooked enough.[1786]

CREAM OF OYSTER SOUP
☞ Scald one quart of milk, half a small onion and two sprigs of parsley, half cup celery leaves and stalks over hot water; stir one-fourth cup of flour with cold milk to pour; then stir it into the scalding milk. Continue stirring until the mixture thickens; then cover and cook twenty minutes. Pour a cup of cold water over a quart of oysters; look them over carefully to remove bits of shell; strain the oyster liquid and heat to the boiling point; add the oysters and bring again to the boiling point; skim and add the thickened and flavored milk; season with salt, cayenne and white pepper and stir in little by little one-fourth of a cup of butter. Will serve six people. Delicious.[1787]

SWISS SOUP
☞ Five gallons water, six potatoes and three turnips sliced; boil five hours until perfectly dissolved and the consistency of pea soup, filling up as it boils away; add butter size of an egg, season with salt and pepper, and serve.

A small piece salt pork, a bone or bit of veal or lamb, and an onion, may be added to vary this soup.[1788]

OYSTER GUMBO SOUP

☛ Take an old chicken, cut into small pieces, salt and black pepper. Dip it well in flour, and put it on to fry, over a slow fire, till brown; don't let it burn. Cut half of a small onion very fine and sprinkle on chicken while frying. Then place chicken in soup pot, add two quarts water and let it boil to three pints.

Have one quart of fresh oysters with all the liquor that belongs to them, and before dishing up soup, add oysters and let come to a boil the second time, then stir into soup one tablespoonful of gumbo quickly. Dish up and send to table. Have parsley chopped very fine and put in tureen on dishing up soup. Have dry boiled rice to go to table with gumbo in separate dish. Serve one tablespoonful of rice to a plate of gumbo.[1789]

GAZPACHO

☛ Put some soft biscuit or toasted bread in the bottom of a salad bowl, put in a layer of sliced tomatoes with the skin taken off, and one of sliced cucumbers, sprinkled with pepper, salt, and chopped onion; do this until the bowl is full; stew some tomatoes quite soft, strain the juice, mix in some mustard, oil, and water, and pour over it; make it two hours before it is eaten.[1790]

CRAB SOUP

☛ Boil a quart of milk, and thicken it with a tablespoon of flour, rolled in butter, pepper and salt. Boil and pick 8 crabs, and when the milk comes to a boil put in the crabs. Just before serving, stir in a cup of cream. Let the soup boil for 20 minutes after adding the crabs.[1791]

GERMAN CABBAGE SOUP WITH MEAT STOCK

☛ Take one sound white cabbage, wash and trim off the outer leaves, chop fine and put it in a stew-pan with a quart of water. Let boil until tender. Add a quart of beef broth, salt and pepper to taste, and boil once more. Before serving stir in a lump of butter and two small lumps of sugar. Serve hot.[1792]

RICE SOUP

☛ Pick and wash a pint of rice, boil it till quite soft, drain the water from it, and put it in tea-cups to congeal, filling them about half full. Make a rich broth of a piece of fresh beef, veal, mutton, poultry, or game; pass it through a sieve into a soup-pan, season it with salt, pepper and nutmeg, and thicken it with flour, butter and sweet cream. Just let it boil up, and no more.

When the rice has congealed and taken the shape of the cups, turn them smoothly into a tureen, pour the soup boiling over them, and send it immediately to table. Barley soup may be made in the same manner.[1793]

CREAMED VEGETABLE SOUPS
(Asparagus, peas, string beans, spinach, corn, celery)

☛ These soups are very delicate, and are much esteemed. They are all made in the same way. The vegetable is boiled until soft, and is then pressed through a sieve. A pint of the vegetable pulp is diluted with a quart of stock (the stock may be veal, beef, or chicken broth). It is thickened with a roux made of one tablespoonful of butter and two tablespoonfuls of flour, seasoned with pepper and salt, and is then strained again, so it will be perfectly smooth. It is replaced on the fire, a cupful or a half cupful of cream added, and the whole beaten with an egg-whip to make it light, and is served at once very hot. The French thicken cream soups with egg-yolks. In this case two yolks would be used for the above quantity. The beaten yolks are diluted with the cream, and cooked only just long enough to set the egg. It would curdle if allowed to boil. Butter is needed for seasoning, and where eggs are used it should be added in small bits before the cream and eggs. Where roux is used for thickening, there is enough butter in the roux.[1794]

ORANGE SOUP

☛ The juice of six oranges and one lemon, sweeten slightly, add a little sherry wine if desired. Chill. Serve with chipped ice.[1795]

MILK SOUP

☛ Boil two quarts of entire sweet milk with a stick of cinnamon, a few cloves and a vanilla bean, till sufficiently flavored; then strain it, and return it to the pan. Beat the yolks of six eggs very light, mix them with half a pint of milk, and stir it gradually into the boiled milk; add four ounces of butter, rolled in flour, a grated nutmeg, and sugar to your taste. Just let it come to a boil, stirring it all the time, and remove it instantly from the fire, or it will curdle. Then stir in very gradually the juice of a lemon, and serve it immediately in a tureen on some baked apples, small bits of toasted bread, rusk, or pounded crackers.[1796]

CHESTNUT SOUP

☛ 2 quarts of Spanish chestnuts,
  2 quarts of chicken stock,
  1 pint of rich cream,
  Salt, nutmeg, and cayenne pepper to taste.

Shell the chestnuts, put them in a pan and cover with cold water. Let them scald until the inner skin can be taken off. Put them on a sieve to allow the hot water to drain off, and while draining, pour on some cold water, so as the skins can be removed with the hand. When they are well skinned put them into a saucepan with the chicken stock, and let them simmer until perfectly tender. Then mash through the sieve into the same stock. Season with nutmeg, salt, and cayenne pepper to the taste. Put it into a saucepan with hot water underneath, stirring all the time until it begins to simmer; then pour in the pint of cream, and after stirring 5 minutes longer, serve.[1797]

WHITE SOUP WITH MACARONI

☛ Put in a pot, 3 or 4 pounds of meat, or a chicken, a slice of lean bacon, an onion, celery stalks or seed, parsley, thyme, pepper, and salt; pour on 2 quarts of water; let it boil to 1 quart.

When ready to serve, strain it, and thicken with a dessertspoon of butter, rolled in flour, and add pint of milk or cream. If the soup is made of beef, it will take 6 hours to boil; if of chicken, 3 or 4 hours. Soup is always better if made the day before and set aside to skim. 1 hour before serving, add 1 teacup of macaroni broken into small pieces.[1798]

BARLEY SOUP

☛ Put on three gills of barley, three quarts of water, a few onions cut up, six carrots scraped and cut into dice, an equal quantity of turnips cut small; boil it gently two hours, then put in four or five pounds of the rack or neck of mutton, a few slices of lean ham, with pepper and salt; boil it slowly two hours longer and serve it up. Tomatoes are an excellent addition to this soup.[1799]

SOUP STOCK OF BEEF

☛ 1 large shin-bone,
4 quarts of water,
2 pounds of lean beef,
4 carrots,
3 onions,
4 turnips,
1 bunch of parsley,
1 teaspoonful of celery seed,
Salt to the taste.

Put the bone, which has been previously cracked in 3 pieces, into the soup-pot, with the water, and beef cut into pieces the size of an egg, and some salt. Boil slowly for 1 hour, skimming well until all of the grease is taken off. Scrape the carrots, peel the onions and turnips, then quarter, and, with the celery seed, add to the soup. Let this boil slowly for 4 hours; take off, strain into a stone jar, and keep in a cool place. Veal stock can be made in the same way, by getting a large knuckle of veal and adding 2 pounds of the meat.[1800]

FISH SOUP

☛ Clean and trim any kind of fish—fresh or salt water. Boil the fish with a head of celery, a small quantity of parsley, two onions, a bay-leaf, and five cloves. Use water, and cover the saucepan closely. When the contents have boiled one hour, add as much water as will be required to make the soup. Strain and stir in a cup of cream. Season with salt and white pepper. Lay in the tureen some eggs, nicely fried in butter; allow one for each person. Pour the soup over, and serve with toasted bread.[1801]

SQUIRREL SOUP

☞ Take two fat young squirrels, skin and clean them nicely, cut them into small pieces, rinse and season them with salt and pepper, and boil them till nearly done. Beat an egg very light, stir it into half a pint of sweet milk, add a little salt, and enough flour to make it a stiff batter, and drop it by small spoonfuls into the soup, and boil them with the squirrels till all are done.

Then stir in a small lump of butter, rolled in flour, a little grated nutmeg, lemon and mace; add a handful of chopped parsley and half a pint of sweet cream; stir it till it comes to a boil, and serve it up with some of the nicest pieces of the squirrels.[1802]

POTATO CHOWDER

☞ 6 good-sized potatoes.
1 pint milk or cream.
¼ lb. salt pork.
1 pint water.
1 onion.
1 tablespoonful chopped parsley.
1 tablespoonful butter.
1 teaspoonful salt.
1 tablespoonful flour.
½ teaspoonful pepper.

Cut the potatoes into dice, cut the pork into small pieces, and put it with the sliced onion into a frying pan, and fry until a light brown. Put into a kettle a layer of potatoes, then a layer of onions and pork, and sprinkle with salt, pepper, and chopped parsley. Repeat this until all the potatoes, pork, onions, and parsley are in. Pour over them the grease from the pan in which the pork and onions were fried. Add one pint of water, cover, and let simmer twenty minutes

Scald the milk in a double boiler, and add it to a roux made of the flour and butter. Add this to the pot when the potatoes are tender, and stir carefully together, so as not to break the potatoes. Taste to see if the seasoning is right. Serve very hot.

This is a good dish for luncheon, or for supper in the country.[1803]

CORN SOUP

☞ 1 can of corn,
1 quart of boiling milk,
Butter, salt, and pepper to taste.

Press the corn through the colander and add to the quart of boiling milk, and season to taste. Serve hot with toast in squares.[1804]

CORN CHOWDER

☛ One quart raw sweet corn, 1 pint potatoes diced, ¼ cup butter, 2 tablespoons flour, 1 pint milk, 2 hard boiled eggs, salt and pepper. Score each row of kernels and scrape raw corn from cobs. Boil cobs twenty minutes in water to cover, pour boiling water over potatoes, dice them, drain it off, remove cobs, add potatoes, salt and pepper. When potatoes are nearly done add corn and milk, cook five minutes. Cook flour in the hot butter, stir into chowder, add the eggs, whites chopped fine and yolks rubbed through a sieve; serve with crackers.[1805]

CREAM OF CORN SOUP

☛ Put a can of corn, one tablespoonful of grated onion, a bay leaf, a level teaspoonful of salt, a saltspoonful of pepper in the double boiler; rub together two table spoonfuls of butter, three of flour; add to the hot mixture and stir constantly until the water boils in the outer vessel; press through a colander, reheat and serve with croutons.[1806]

LIMA BEAN SOUP

☛ One can Lima beans, 2 cups milk, 1 sliced onion, 2 cups water, 2 tablespoons flour. Drain liquor from beans and add water; cook twenty-five minutes and rub through strainer. Cook onion five minutes in butter and add with milk. After thoroughly heating, remove onion, stir in flour, with salt and pepper to taste.[1807]

BARLEY BROTH

☛ Put two pounds shin of beef in one gallon of water. Add a teacup of pearl barley, three large onions cut up fine, a small bunch of parsley minced, three potatoes sliced, a little thyme, and pepper and salt to taste. Simmer steadily three hours, and stir often, so that the meat will not burn. Do not let it boil. Always stir soup or broth with a wooden spoon.[1808]

TURTLE SOUP

☛ 1 turtle weighing 4 or 5 pounds,
1 gallon cold water,
1 onion,
4 cloves,
2 tablespoons butter,
Salt and pepper to taste,
½ tablespoon flour,
1 glass of claret or Madeira wine,
2 lemons.

Boil the turtle in the water till the meat drops from the bones; 3 or 4 hours will be required. Add the seasoning and boil 30 minutes. Roll butter and flour together and add just before taking from the fire. Pour in tureen and add wine and lemons thinly sliced. Serve at once.[1809]

GREEN TURTLE SOUP

☛ To two pounds of turtle add two quarts of water, put to boil an a slow fire and cook down to three pints. Season while boiling with pepper and salt to taste.

Take three hard boiled eggs, slice very thin and lay in tureen; slice one-fourth of a lemon and put in tureen also. Then pour in tureen one gill of sherry wine. Then pour on hot soup and send to table.

The above quantity will make soup for one dozen guests. If there are more to serve, increase the quantity.[1810]

SPAGHETTI SOUP

☛ Boil two pounds of beef, cut as for beef tea, and a slice of ham, in two quarts of water.

When it has cooked for two hours add one cupful of white beans, previously boiled, two sliced onions, four chopped Spanish red peppers, one-half lemon sliced.

Simmer all together until everything is soft, then mash through a colander. Add salt and one-half pound of spaghetti, and thicken with one tablespoonful of butter well mixed with one-half tablespoonful of flour. Simmer until the spaghetti is tender, then serve.[1811]

VENISON SOUP

☛ Your venison must be quite fresh, as it is not fit for soup after the first five days. If it is a small one, take a whole shoulder, but if large, half a one will do. Chop it into several pieces, rinse them clean, and season them well with salt and pepper.

Slice up a pound of ham, put it with the venison into a porridge pot; pour in enough water to cover the meat, add one or two sliced onions and a bunch of parsley, and boil it fast for a few minutes till scum rises; then remove the scum, cover the pot, and boil it gently till the meat is done very tender; after which take out the meat, reserve some of the nicest pieces to serve whole with the soup; mince from the bones a small portion of the other venison, and pound it in a mortar to a paste, adding a teaspoonful of celery seeds, one of mace, lemon and cloves, half a one of cayenne, and by degrees a glass of red wine.

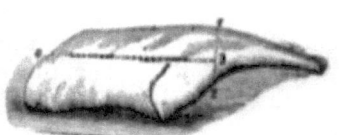

Haunch of venison.

Strain the liquid into a soup-pan, and put in two ounces of butter, rolled in flour; mix the beaten yolks of two eggs in half a pint of entire sweet milk, and stir it in the soup; add the venison paste, stirring it by degrees; and before it comes to a hard boil, serve it up; put in a few small pieces of the reserved venison, and send it hot to table, with a plate of dry toasts and a dish of boiled rice, as both are much liked with venison soup.[1812]

VEAL SOUP

☛ Take 2 pounds veal and 1 gallon of water; let it boil until tender; add [into] pot marjoram, thyme, chopped onions, pepper and salt. To brown it, take a tablespoon of butter, and 2 of flour; mix with a little of the broth; roll the butter in the flour, and let it stew in the broth; then add to the soup. Just before serving, add a wine-glass of wine, a few cloves, spice, and cayenne pepper. Cut and slice 3 hard boiled eggs.[1813]

KENTUCKY BURGOUT

☛ 6 squirrels,
6 birds,
1½ gallons of water,
1 teacup of pearl barley,
1 quart of tomatoes,
1 quart of corn,
1 quart of oysters,
1 pint of sweet cream,
¼ pound of butter,
2 tablespoons of flour,
Season to taste. Boil the squirrels and birds in the water till tender and remove all the bones. Add barley and vegetables and cook slowly for 1 hour. Ten minutes before serving add the oysters and cream with butter and flour rubbed together. Season and serve hot.[1814]

EEL SOUP

☛ Take 6 eels; cut them in pieces, and pour boiling water upon them—3 quarts. First put in the pot 1 tablespoon of butter; fry in it, to a light brown, 2 onions; then fry the eels slightly before adding the boiling water. Season with a little thyme, parsley, allspice, pepper, and salt. Cover the soup and let it boil for 2 hours, being careful to remove all the scum as it rises. Strain the soup, and then put it back in the pot, and thicken it with 1 tablespoon of butter stirred in 2 tablespoons of browned flour. Some of the pieces of eel may be fried a light brown, and put in the soup.[1815]

ONION SOUP

☛ Chop up twelve large onions, boil them in three quarts of milk and water equally mixed, put in a bit of veal or fowl, and a piece of bacon with pepper and salt. When the onions are boiled to pulp, thicken it with a large spoonful of butter mixed with one of flour. Take out the meat, and serve it up with toasted bread cut in small pieces in the soup.[1816]

CONSOMME

☛ 4 lbs. lower part round of beef.
2 sprigs of parsley.
4 lbs. knuckle of veal.

15 peppercorns.
2 tablespoonfuls of butter.
3 cloves.
6 quarts of cold water.
1 inch square of cinnamon.
1 large onion.
A little thyme.
½ carrot.
A little marjoram.
3 stalks of celery.
A little summer savory.
1 tablespoonful of salt.
2 bay-leaves.

Cut the beef into pieces one inch square. Remove the veal from the bone, and cut it also into small pieces. Put one tablespoonful of butter into a very clean soup-pot with the pieces of meat, and stir over a hot fire until the meat is browned, care being taken that it does not burn; then add one quart of water, and let it cook until a glaze has formed on the bottom of the kettle, which will take about one hour.

Then add five quarts of cold water and let it come slowly to the boiling-point. Set the soup-pot back on the fire and let the soup simmer for six hours. Remove the scum from time to time as it rises.

One hour before the time for removing the soup add to it the vegetables, which have been cut fine and browned in one tablespoonful of butter. Add also the herbs and spices, and one tablespoonful of salt. When it has simmered six hours, strain it through a fine cloth, laid on a sieve, into an earthen bowl, and let it cool without covering. A fowl added to this receipt will give the soup a more delicate flavor.

If used it should be put in the pot at the time the five quarts of water are added.

The veal-bone may also go in at this time, but the soup will not be so clear if the bone is used.

If a chicken is used it may be removed from the stock when tender and used for other purposes.

(Note: This receipt gives a perfectly clear brilliant soup after it is clarified. If no bones are used it can be boiled slowly without injury instead of being simmered. The stock will not always jelly.)[1817]

SOUP JULIENNE

☛ Add all kinds of cooked green vegetables to hot consomme and serve.[1818]

OKRA SOUP

☛ Take ½ gallon of beef stock, 1 quart of tomatoes, and 1 quart of okra, and pepper and salt to taste and boil ½ hour. Thicken with 1 tablespoon of flour.[1819]

OKRA GUMBO

☞ Get a beef shank, have it cracked and put to boil in one gallon of water. Boil to half a gallon, then strain and put back on fire. Cut okra in small pieces and put in soup; don't put in any ends of okra. Season with salt and pepper while cooking. Stir it occasionally and keep it from burning.

To be sent to table with dry boiled rice. Never stir rice while boiling. Season rice always with salt when it is first put on to cook, and do not have too much water in rice while boiling.[1820]

TURKEY SOUP

☞ Place the remains of a cold turkey and what is left of the dressing and gravy in a pot, and cover it with cold water. Simmer gently four hours, and let stand until the next day.

Take off what fat may have arisen, and take out with a skimmer all the bits of bones. Put the soup on to heat until at boiling point, then thicken slightly with flour stirred into a cup of cream, and season to taste. Pick off all the meat from the bones, put it back in the soup, boil up and serve.[1821]

BROWN STOCK

☞ Brown in a soup kettle two tablespoonfuls of butter, to which add, cut into small pieces, two pounds of lean beef and an equal amount of the meat from a knuckle of veal. Stir over the fire five minutes, when cover closely and stew gently for half an hour. Add two quarts of cold water to this, and let the whole simmer for four hours. Cut an onion, a small carrot and a stalk of celery into dice and add these and a sprig of parsley, to the stock, and cook very slowly for an hour longer. Strain through a fine sieve, and when cold remove the fat which will have caked upon the top.

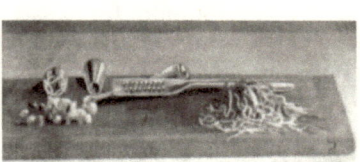
Preparing julienne soup vegetables.

To prepare for serving, let the stock come to a boil, add salt and pepper to taste and the beaten white and shell of one egg, thoroughly mixed with a cup of cold water; boil hard for ten minutes. Throw in another half cup of cold water, let the soup boil again for five minutes, strain into a heated tureen and serve with very small squares of toasted bread.[1822]

WHITE SOUP STOCK

☞ Take four pounds of knuckles of veal and cut the meat in small pieces, crack the bone and put in soup kettle; add two onions cut small, two stalks celery, one level tablespoonful of salt, six pepper corns; cover with three quarts cold water. Set where it will heat slowly. Let simmer five or six hours, strain, and when cold remove the fat. This is the foundation for velvet and cream soups.[1823]

CLAM SOUP

☛ 24 clams,
½ gallon water,
2 tablespoons butter,
2 onions,
Salt and pepper to taste.

Chop the clams and use the meat and liquor and add the water. Do not boil, but cook gently till it begins to thicken. Season, and just before taking from the stove add 1 pint cream or rich milk. Pour in tureen, add a little parsley, and serve at once.[1824]

SCOTCH BROTH

☛ Boil four pounds of lean mutton in four quarts of water, stir into it half a pound of Scotch barley. Keep it well mixed until the water boils, and skim the surface carefully while simmering, as fast as the scum rises. Cut up a couple of carrots, a turnip and an onion; add these, with a quart of green peas, a few sprigs of parsley, and a dessert-spoonful of pepper and salt, mixed. The vegetables should not be allowed to boil a longer time than is required to cook them. Scotch broth may be made of beef or veal.[1825]

LOBSTER SOUP

☛ Take a fresh knuckle of veal, break the bone in several places, rub it well with salt and pepper, and boil it till the meat is ready to drop from the bone, leaving about two quarts of the liquor, which must be strained into a soup pan. Having boiled two common sized lobsters tender, extract the meat from the bones and claws. Pound the coral, with an equal proportion of the meat, to a smooth paste, seasoning it with mace, cayenne pepper, cloves and grated lemon. Divide it into two equal portions; reserve one half to thicken the soup, and make the other half into little balls, the size of a partridge's egg; dip them in the yolk of egg, and roll them in dry flour. Cut the remaining part of the meat into small bits, and put them into the veal liquor, with two ounces of butter, divided and rolled in two spoonfuls of flour. Boil them together eight or ten minutes, and stir in the coral paste, and then drop in the balls; boil all together a minute or two, add a cup of sweet cream, gradually stirred in, and pour it boiling into a tureen. Grate a nutmeg on the top, lay on some light sprigs of parsley, and accompany it with slices of light bread, dry toasts, sliced crackers, or bread and butter.[1826]

CONFEDERATE TOMATO SOUP

☛ Boil a small piece of meat with cabbage, parsley, celery, pepper and salt, onions, allspice. When they are well boiled, add a good quantity of tomatoes, and a dessertspoon of butter, rolled in flour; strain all through a colander, and serve with small squares of toasted bread.[1827]

TOMATO BISQUE
☛ Melt two tablespoonfuls of butter in a saucepan and add one and a half tablespoonfuls of flour; rub together until smooth; when it bubbles add one quart of milk and cook until thickened.

Cook half a can of tomatoes in half a cup of water, half a bay leaf and two cloves together for five minutes; strain and add while hot to the thickened milk. Season with salt, pepper and a tablespoonful of sugar. Serve at once.[1828]

OLD FASHIONED TURNIP SOUP
☛ Take two pounds veal bones to half a gallon of water, and boil to one quart. Put turnips and bones on to boil together, then strain the liquor off and send to table hot. Season while cooking with pepper and salt.[1829]

ASPARAGUS SOUP
☛ 3 bunches of asparagus,
1 quart of cream or rich milk,
1 tablespoon of butter,
½ tablespoon flour.

Boil the asparagus in 1 quart salt water till tender. Drain water off, then add cream. Rub butter and flour together and add before taking from the stove. Add salt and pepper to taste. Serve with toasted bread or crackers.[1830]

CREAM OF ASPARAGUS SOUP
☛ Cut the tips from a bunch of asparagus and steam until tender; cut the stalk in inch pieces and simmer in water until it can be mashed through a puree sieve. Cook two tablespoonfuls of butter and three of flour until it bubbles; add one quart of cold milk; when hot add the asparagus pulp and tips; cook in double boiler ten minutes; season with salt and pepper and serve.[1831]

CLEAR SOUP OR BOUILLON
☛ Cut up the lean of coarse beef into small pieces.
1 good-sized onion (peel and cut up before using),
1 good-sized carrot (peel and cut up before using),
1 good-sized turnip (peel and cut up before using).
Salt, nutmeg, and cayenne pepper to taste,
4 whole cloves.

Fry with 1 tablespoon of butter in soup-kettle. When it begins to look whitish, pour over it the stock from 1 chicken. Boil the chicken in 1 gallon of water in early morning, and make stock in afternoon. Boil 1 hour, strain and put away till next day for aspic or bouillon. For bouillon, beat an egg and let it come to a boil in the bouillon, and strain before serving.[1832]

BLACK BEAN SOUP

☛ 2 cupfuls of black beans.
Egg balls.
Brown stock.
Thin slices of lemon.
Brown roux.
Force-meat balls.
Bouquet of herbs, made of a sprig of parsley, a sprig of thyme, one clove.
White of hard-boiled egg.
¼ cupful of sherry or red wine.
4 peppercorns, 1 onion.
Salt and pepper to taste.

Soak two cupfuls of black beans over night. Put the soaked beans into a saucepan with a bouquet of herbs, and cover them with cold water. Let them boil slowly until tender, which will take several hours, adding more water if necessary. When the beans are very soft remove the bouquet, drain off the water, and pass the beans through a purée sieve. Add to the pulp enough brown stock to make a soup of the consistency of thin cream. Place it again on the fire and add a brown roux made of one tablespoonful of butter and one tablespoonful of flour, cooked together until brown; dilute it to smoothness before adding and cook it with the soup for five minutes. This will prevent the soup from separating. Season with salt and pepper. Strain it through a sieve into the tureen; then add thin slices of lemon, egg balls, and force-meat balls, allowing one of each to each portion of soup; add also the white of one hard-boiled egg cut into small dice, and one quarter of a cupful of sherry or red wine.[1833]

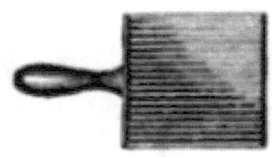
Butter roller.

BEEF BROTH

☛ Cut an onion, a carrot, one turnip, one parsnip, and a stalk of celery into small dice. Fry them in butter and as soon as brown add two pounds of the rump of beef which has also been cut up very small, and fry. Wash half a cup of barley. Season with salt and pepper, and add two quarts of water. Boil two hours. Brown small squares of bread in the oven, and serve with the broth.[1834]

PEA SOUP

☛ Two pints of shelled peas, ½ chicken; put on with 1½ gallons of water, some thyme, parsley, salt and pepper. When the peas are done, take them out, then return them to the water in the mashed state. Add ¼ pound of butter rolled in flour. Before sending to table add ½ pint of cream.[1835]

SPLIT PEA SOUP

☛ Make a broth of some water that corned beef or salt pork has been boiled in, and some beef bones. Do not let it be too salty; in that case use half water. Put 1 quart of split peas in enough of the water to cover them; when they have stewed soft, mash them through a colander, and then mix with them 2 quarts of the broth in which the bones have been boiling; add 1 onion, and 1 turnip, chopped up, and 1 carrot, grated. Just before serving, put small pieces of toast in the soup.[1836]

ARTICHOKE SOUP

☛ 1 quart of Jerusalem artichokes, first peeled, and then boiled very soft; 1 tablespoon of butter rolled in 2 tablespoons of flour; mix them and make drawn butter of them. Pour upon it 1 quart of broth that has been prepared in French style, a strong essence of meat, with plenty of celery, cayenne pepper and salt, having taken all grease off it whilst it was boiling, the broth to be made of chicken, beef, or veal. Let the broth and drawn butter boil, and then add the artichokes, having first passed them through a sieve. Be careful to stir it well, so as not to let them lump. Pour the broth upon them; then stir in a quart of milk to prevent its turning. The French prepare artichokes, after boiling them, by forcing them through a thin, coarse towel, one person holding each end of the towel and another person mashing them through with a strong spoon. It makes them finer and smoother. They must be prepared whilst the broth is making.[1837]

Victorian cooking class.

Food furnished by the sea, lakes, and rivers.

28. Vegetables

VEGETABLE COOKING TIP
☞ All vegetables must go over the fire in boiling water uncovered, except potatoes, and cooked at the boiling point. When done, drain carefully and add a well made sauce.[1838]

TO CLEAN VEGETABLES
☞ If vegetables, with leaves to them, are put into a strong brine for an hour before they are cooked, it will kill any bugs or insects that may be in them, and draw them out.[1839]

MASHED POTATOES

"Better is a dinner of herbs where love is, than a stalled ox and hatred therewith" (Proverbs 15:17 KJV).

☞ When the potatoes are thoroughly boiled, drain and dry them perfectly, pick out every speck, and rub them through a colander into a clean stew-pan; to a pound of potatoes put half an ounce of butter, and a tablespoonful of milk; do not make them too moist; mix them well together. When the potatoes are getting old and specked, and in frosty weather, this is the best way of dressing them—you may put them into shapes, touch them over with yolk of egg, and brown them very slightly before a slow fire.[1840]

CONFEDERATE MASHED POTATOES
☞ Pare and boil till done, drain, and mash in the kettle until perfectly smooth; add milk or cream, and butter and salt; beat like cake with a large spoon, and the more they are beaten the nicer they become. Put in a dish, smooth, place a lump of butter in the center, sprinkle with pepper; or add one or two eggs well-beaten, pepper, mix thoroughly,

put in baking dish, dip a knife in sweet milk, smooth over, wetting every part with milk, and place in a hot oven twenty minutes.

To warm over mashed potatoes, season with salt and butter, and a little cream or milk, place in a buttered pie-pan, smoothing and shaping the top handsomely, and making checks with a knife; brown in a stove or range oven; place tin on a second dish and serve on it.

Or, add a little cream or milk to cold mashed potatoes, press evenly in a basin, set away, and in the morning slice and fry.[1841]

BOILED IRISH POTATOES

☛ Select potatoes of medium size, yellowish white color; cook unpeeled. Put them on with just enough boiling water to cover them; place over a moderate fire to boil slowly until nearly done; then throw in half a cup of cold water to chill the surface; it will render them mealy. Cook closely covered until done, then drain off the water, sprinkle over salt and leave uncovered to dry out.[1842]

DIXIE POTATOES

☛ 4 or 5 baked potatoes,
1 pint of milk,
½ teaspoonful of salt,
Butter, the size of a walnut.

Pare the potatoes and cut into small pieces. Put them on the stove, in an agate dish, salt and cover with milk. Let them cook fifteen or twenty minutes, then thicken with one tablespoonful of flour, stirred with half a cupful of water; put in the butter and serve hot.[1843]

SOUTHERN CREAMED SWEET POTATOES

☛ To two cups of mashed sweet potatoes add one teaspoonful of cinnamon, one cup of sweet milk, one-half cup of sugar, one-half cup of seeded raisins and butter size of an egg.

Cook in buttered baking dish and when done, cool, spread the top with marshmallows and brown in oven.[1844]

RICED POTATOES

☛ Pass through a ricer eight boiled potatoes, add three tablespoonfuls of butter, half a teaspoonful of salt and about half a cup of hot milk or cream.

Beat thoroughly with a perforated cake spoon.

Beat until very light and puffy and pile irregularly in a serving dish, putting a bit of butter here and there in the depressions.[1845]

POTATO CAKES

☞ Shape mashed potatoes left from dinner into small flat cakes, dip in sifted flour, and saute first on one side and then the other in hot salt pork fat.[1846]

TEXAS BAKED IRISH POTATOES

☞ Boil some good Irish potatoes; when done, mash, season with salt, pepper and butter; mince a large onion fine, mix well through the potatoes, put in oven and brown nicely.[1847]

BOILED POTATOES

☞ Put potatoes in plenty of boiling water slightly salted; if watery, add a little lime water.[1848]

FRIED POTATOES

☞ Take the pulp of common mashed potatoes, make it in small balls or cakes, dip them in the beaten yolks of eggs, flour, and fry them brown in lard or butter; the fat or butter should be boiling when they are put in, or they will soak it up, and become soft, and break to pieces. These are also often eaten for breakfast. Potatoes may be boiled till about half done, then peeled, sliced, seasoned with salt and pepper, floured, and fried brown in lard or butter.[1849]

Potato slicer.

BAKED SWEET POTATOES

☞ Wash, and wipe them nicely. Put them in the oven. They will take 1 hour to roast, if medium size.[1850]

FRENCH FRIED POTATOES

☞ Pare the potatoes and cut in eighths lengthwise; let stand in water until they are all ready; then dry between towels. Fry in a basket, and but few at a time. Drain on soft paper and sprinkle with salt. Serve at once.[1851]

POTATO CHIPS

☞ Slice your potatoes and put in water to soak over night, or sometime before cooking. When ready to fry, put in a basket and shake in order to dry as much as possible. Put in a kettle a good deal of the best lard. Have the lard quite hot, but not too hot; put some salt in it and put in the chips. Stir often while cooking. When done, shake well and sift over a little salt.[1852]

POTATOES BAKED IN THEIR JACKETS

☞ After washing and drying potatoes, put them in a pan and set in oven for an hour or more. Remove when the skins break easily. If greased with either lard or butter they will bake quickly. If mashed with the hands on taking from the oven they will be very mealy. Wrap in a napkin. Serve hot.[1853]

POTATOES AU GRATIN
☛ Boil three Irish potatoes. When well done, peel and cut in dice shape. Put in a baking dish and mix with a dressing made of a cup of milk, two tablespoonfuls of flour, one of butter, which is a white sauce; salt and pepper. Grate cheese over and bake fifteen minutes.[1854]

STEWED POTATOES
☛ Pare, cut in dice, and soak in cold water ½ hour; stew in enough hot salted water to cover them; before taking up, and when they are breaking to pieces, drain off the water, and pour in a cup of rich milk and butter the size of a hen's egg; boil 3 minutes, stirring well; roll the butter in flour, add a little salt and pepper, boil up well, and turn into a hot dish.[1855]

Potatoes cut to look like roses.

ROASTED POTATOES
☛ Take smooth white potatoes, no other sort being nice to send to table with the skins on. Wash them clean, wipe them dry, and roast them before rather a brisk fire in a tin toaster. When they are done clear through, send them warm to table with salt and a plate of firm butter. They are generally eaten at supper with cold meat, etc.[1856]

STUFFED POTATOES
☛ Take large potatoes, bake until soft; cut a round piece off the top of each; scrape out the inside very carefully so as not to break the skin, and set aside the empty cases; mash the inside very smoothly, working into it while hot some butter and cream, about a teaspoon of each for every potato; season with salt and pepper, with a good pinch of cheese grated for each; work it very soft with cream and put into saucepan to heat, stirring hard to prevent burning; when scalding hot, stir in one well-beaten egg for six large potatoes; boil up once; fill the skins with the mixture and return them to the oven for 3 minutes; arrange in pretty napkin with caps uppermost; cover with fold of napkin; stand them up in something while heating.[1857]

BROWN HASHED POTATOES 1
☛ Put four medium sized Irish potatoes in boiling water and cook twenty-five minutes. When cold, chop rather fine. Fry a tablespoonful of onion chopped very fine. When done add a full tablespoonful of flour;

let cook a few minutes, then add a cup of broth, milk or water; salt and pepper.

When it boils add the potatoes and cook five minutes. Have a large frying pan; put in a spoonful of lard (bacon grease is better) and turn in the potato mixture, spreading it over the bottom; let cook until the bottom is brown, then fold as an omelet. Season to taste with salt and pepper. Fine.[1858]

BROWN HASHED POTATOES 2
☞ Make a white sauce, season with salt and pepper and pour over minced cooked potatoes. Stir lightly with a fork to prevent mashing. Put in a pan with clarified butter. The pan must be cold, but butter warm so it will not stick. Set inside the stove to brown the bottom. Keep the top covered. When brown on the bottom, fold and turn on a warm dish.[1859]

BAKED POTATOES
☞ Place the potatoes in an oven of moderate temperature and gradually increase the heat until the inside is thoroughly cooked.

Stuffed baked potatoes.

Another way: Put the potatoes in boiling water, boil rapidly fifteen or twenty minutes, then bake in a hot oven.

When done, make a gash an inch long lengthwise, then press the ends together to widen the gap and let the steam escape. Serve in a deep dish with a napkin thrown over.[1860]

SCALLOPED POTATOES
☞ Take cold boiled potatoes and chop; put in layers with bread crumbs, butter, salt and pepper. Cover with milk. Have crumbs on the top. Bake brown.[1861]

CONFEDERATE FRENCH FRIES
☞ Peel the potatoes, slice them lengthwise in slices one-quarter inch thick, drop them in cold water for one hour, then take them out and dry them with a cloth, and fry them in hot lard. If you wish them to puff up, remove them with a skimmer before quite done, drain, and again return to the hot lard to continue frying until done. Sprinkle with fine salt and serve hot.[1862]

FLAKED POTATOES
☞ Take large, perfect potatoes, boil in their skins in salt water, drain well, peel and rub them through a coarse sieve on a hot dish before the fire, without touching them, to keep as flaky as possible, sprinkle with fine salt and melted butter, and serve hot.[1863]

TO BOIL RICE

☞ Rice should be quickly cooked in unsalted water. Wash a cup of rice through several cold waters. Have ready a large kettle partly filled with rapidly boiling water. Sprinkle in the rice slowly so as not to stop the boiling. Boil rapidly in an uncovered vessel half an hour. If the grains taste done, drain the rice in a colander; pour through it quickly a quart of cold water; stand the colander on a plate inside the oven, or, set the colander, closely covered, over boiling water to steam dry; now and then toss it with a fork over and over; sprinkle salt over; turn into a dish and serve. [Add raw or cooked vegetables as desired.]^{1864}

STEWED TOMATOES

☞ First scald the tomatoes in boiling water and then peel the skin from them, then cut them up in small pieces, cutting also one slice of onion fine in them; add no water; bread crumbs, one tablespoonful of butter, pepper and salt to taste. To one dozen of tomatoes, half a tea-cupful of bread crumbs.^{1865}

STUFFED TOMATOES

☞ Tomatoes cut open, the centers filled with butter, pepper and salt, and the halves pressed together and baked in a hot oven, form an appetizing entree for dinner.^{1866}

TURNIPS

☞ Peel and slice them thick; put them into cold water until ready to cook them. Then put them into boiling water, with a little salt; and if young, boil them for ½ an hour; but a longer time is required if they be old. Serve them either in slices, or mash them through a colander, after having drained the water from them; return them to a clean stewpan, and stew them with a little butter, pepper, and salt.^{1867}

Stuffed tomatoes with celery and mayonnaise standing on lettuce leaves.

RUTABAGA

☞ Rutabaga is one of the oldest vegetables we serve. They are much more solid than the other turnips, but may be cooked and served according to the recipe given for turnips [above], except to add more cream.^{1868}

NEW GREEN PEAS

☞ If you cook green peas long they become hard. Put in boiling water, cover closely and cook twenty minutes. Add salt when nearly done.^{1869}

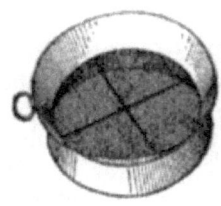
Vegetable sieve.

CARROTS STEWED

☞ Parboil the carrots; then cut them in slices; put them into a stewpan, with a dessertspoon of butter, rolled in flour, 1 cup of milk, pepper, salt, and 1 teaspoon of powdered sugar, a little nutmeg.

This is for 6 large carrots. Stew for ½ an hour, and serve.[1870]

PARSNIPS FRIED

☞ Boil them soft; take them out of the water, and let them drain; cut them in slices, and sprinkle them with pepper, and salt; fry them a pale brown, and have the butter that they are to be fried in quite hot.[1871]

JERUSALEM ARTICHOKES

☞ They should be nicely peeled; pour boiling water upon them, and keep covered; let boil for 1½ hours; then steam them in a steamer or colander, and put them on the top of a pot of boiling water.

Artichokes are always served whole, with drawn butter sauce.[1872]

CUCUMBERS STEWED

☞ Peel cucumbers, and cut them as for table; stew them in a little water, with butter, pepper, salt, and 1 onion. Let them stew for ½ an hour, and serve.[1873]

ASPARAGUS

☞ Tie the asparagus in bunches and boil in salted water till tender. Drain, untie and place on toasted bread. Make a sauce of cream, butter, salt, pepper, a little flour, and boil a few minutes and pour over the asparagus.[1874]

CREAMED ASPARAGUS

☞ Cook the asparagus until tender, lay on toast, and pour over this White Sauce: Mix a tablespoonful each of flour and butter, rub together until smooth; add gradually a cup of water the asparagus was cooked in; then add one tablespoonful of lemon juice; season with salt and pepper. When smooth and thick pour over the toast.[1875]

ASPARAGUS FILLING FOR PATTIES

☞ Canned asparagus is far superior to the fresh for all purposes. Make a white sauce of three level tablespoonfuls of butter and flour, half a cup of chicken or veal broth and the water from the asparagus can.

Add the beaten yolks of two eggs, one teaspoonful of lemon juice, salt and pepper, a can of asparagus tips cut in pieces and heated in the sauce.

Heat patty cases and fill.[1876]

CARROT SOUFFLE

☛ ¼ cup butter.
1 cup cooked carrots rubbed through a sieve.
⅓ cup cream.
¼ cup flour.
3 eggs (yolks.)
3 eggs (whites.)
⅓ cup water in which carrots are cooked.

Salt and pepper. Melt butter, add flour, and pour on gradually cream and water; add carrots, yolks of eggs beaten until thick and lemon-colored, and fold in whites of eggs beaten until stiff; then add seasonings. Turn in a buttered baking-dish and bake in a slow oven.[1877]

SEA KALE

☛ Is tied up in bundles, and dressed in the same way as asparagus [previous page].[1878]

EGG PLANT 1

☛ Cut the slices quarter of an inch thick and do not cut until ready to fry them. Put two tablespoonfuls of butter in a frying pan on stove and have it hot; sift flour on one side of egg plant liberally, brown on lower side; sift flower on upper side and turn over; let brown on that side, stick a fork in it, and when done and tender put on a warm dish with plenty of salt, pepper and butter, and don't pile one on the other, it toughens it; and never put in water before cooking. Cook slowly.[1879]

A double-boiler.

EGG PLANT 2

☛ Peel and slice the egg plant, lay in salt and water, let stand. Make a thick batter of egg, sweet milk, flour, a little baking powder, salt and pepper. Lay slices of egg plant in the batter, then in very hot lard.[1880]

BAKED EGG PLANT

☛ Do not peel the plant, but parboil it till tender, and then throw it into cold water. Then peel and cut it open and remove the seed and fill with a dressing made of bread-crumbs, a little chopped onion, butter, salt, and pepper. Put in a pan with a little water and bake a rich brown.[1881]

FRIED EGG PLANT

☛ After peeling the plant cut in slices and lay in salt water. Steam till tender. Make a batter of
  2 eggs beaten separately,
  1 teacup of sour cream,

1 teaspoon salt,
1 teaspoon soda,
Flour enough to thicken.
Dip the egg plant in the batter and fry a rich brown. Serve hot.[1882]

FRIED CUCUMBERS
☞ Slice the cucumbers lengthwise, lay in salt water a while, drain and roll in corn-meal, and fry in hot lard; salt and pepper to taste.[1883]

TOMATO FRICASSEE
☞ Cook together half a can of tomatoes and one tablespoonful of butter; season with salt and pepper. When the tomatoes are very soft, add a pinch of soda.

When the foam passes, add three beaten eggs; stir, and remove as soon as they begin to thicken.[1884]

SCALLOPED CORN AND TOMATOES
☞ Mix together a pint of raw corn scraped from the cob, one pint of tomatoes skinned and chopped fine, one and a half teaspoonfuls of salt, a little pepper, two tablespoonfuls of butter, one teaspoonful of sugar. Pour this in a buttered dish; cover the top with buttered crumbs; bake slowly half an hour.[1885]

Brinly's hand-operated garden plow.

BAKED TOMATOES
☞ Peel the tomatoes and make a hole in the centre of each and fill with bread-crumbs, salt, pepper, butter, and a little sugar. Put in dish and bake hours.[1886]

BROILED TOMATOES
☞ Place on a griddle smooth, flat tomatoes, the stem side down; when brown, turn, and cook thoroughly. Serve with butter, pepper, and salt.[1887]

FRIED TOMATOES
☞ Cut fresh tomatoes in thick slices. Fry ½ hour in little butter and take out of frying-pan. Stir into what is left in frying-pan 1 teaspoon of flour moistened in milk.

Add a little milk. When consistency of cream sauce, pour over tomatoes.[1888]

FRIED GREEN TOMATOES
☞ Slice green tomatoes and lay them in salt water. Drain and sprinkle with sugar. Roll in corn meal and fry in hot lard. Salt and pepper to taste.[1889]

OLD SOUTH FRIED GREEN TOMATOES
☛ Cut six large green tomatoes in slices one-eighth of an inch in thickness. Beat the yolk of one egg with a tablespoonful of cold water, sprinkle salt and pepper over the tomatoes. Dip first in the egg, then in fine bread-crumbs. Fry in butter quite brown on both sides and serve with a gravy made as follows: Rub one tablespoonful of flour with two tablespoonfuls of butter. When well creamed brown in a pan, add one-half pint of boiling milk, stir steadily till it begins to thicken, then add salt-spoonful of salt and pour over the tomatoes.[1890]

Bean pot.

SCALLOPED TOMATOES
☛ Peel and slice the tomatoes. Grate bread-crumbs on them and season highly with sugar, butter, cayenne pepper, and salt. Alternate the layers of tomatoes and bread-crumbs and bake in a dish for 2 hours.[1891]

PRESERVED TOMATOES
☛ Pick off the stems of green tomatoes, and weigh them; to 1 pound of tomatoes put 1 pound of sugar. First stew the tomatoes in a strong ginger tea, for 2 hours, made of green ginger; take them out of the ginger, and put them in the syrup; when it boils, also put in the pieces of ginger used for the tea; let them cook until tender and clear, and then take them out, and put in jars; let the syrup boil until it is thick, and then pour it upon the tomatoes. Secure the jars, and keep them in a dry place.[1892]

BAKED BEANS
☛ Put 1 pint of dry beans and 1 quart of water to soak over night. Wash well and add 3 pints of water and boil till tender, about 2½ hours. Drain off the water and put in baking dish, season with salt, pepper, tablespoons molasses or brown sugar, and lay a few slices of thin bacon on the top. Bake for an hour till a rich brown. Serve warm or cold with tomato catsup.[1893]

NEW POTATOES
☛ Scrape the potatoes and drop in boiling water salted. When done put the [fish] fillets in a circular dish with the potatoes in the center of the dish [see Meat section for recipe]; pour over drawn or melted butter and serve with Hollandaise Sauce. This sauce can't stand, and must be made at the moment of serving.

Yolks of two eggs and half a cup of butter, little salt and pepper. Set the saucepan over boiling water and add half a cup of hot water with the eggs and butter; cook until it thickens; then add the juice of half a lemon. Have it as thick as mayonnaise. Fine.[1894]

CREAMED POTATOES
☛ One pint of cold Irish potatoes sliced very thin, one tablespoonful of butter, one heaping teaspoonful of flour, three gills of milk, one teaspoonful of salt and one-fourth full of white pepper. Put the butter in the granite dish over the lamp, when it melts add the four and stir until smooth and frothy, then the milk slowly; season with salt and pepper. When the sauce boils up, add the potatoes and boil five minutes stirring once or twice; have lamp wicks low.[1895]

BROCCOLI
☛ Select the hard heads; peel the stalks; wash them, and put them in boiling water that has a little salt in it; let them boil in an open vessel for 20 minutes, or until tender. Drain off the water from them, and serve them with drawn butter.[1896]

SPINACH
☛ Wash through several waters, and put in boiling water with a small piece of pork. Boil quickly, and when done season with butter, salt, and pepper, and serve with poached eggs.[1897]

Spinach served in bread boxes.

CREAMED SPINACH
☛ Put in boiling water and boil till tender. Drain and chop fine and season highly with butter, salt, and pepper. Serve on toast.[1898]

CELERY
☛ Celery is sometimes chopped small and mixed with a dressing made as directed for lettuce; but the usual way of preparing them is to scrape and wash them clean, and let them lie in cold water till just before they are to be sent to the table; then wipe them dry, split the ends of the stalks, leaving on a few of the green leaves, and send them to table in celery glasses. Celery should be kept in a cellar, aud the roots covered with tan to keep them from wilting.[1899]

RADISH
☛ Radish should be eaten fresh, as the taste is not only impaired by lying a day or two after they are drawn, but tough and heavy, which makes them hard of digestion, and of course renders them unhealthy. Trim off the roots, cut off the tops, leaving on about one inch of the green part; wash them, lay them in a pan of cold water with a lump of ice till shortly before they are sent to table, which will make them more tender and fragile: then take off a thin paring, cleave the large end of each in four, arrange them handsomely in a glass dish, with the large ends pointing out from the centre of the dish, and send them to table to be eaten with salt

only. The round turnip radish has much the mildest taste, but it is not so nice to look upon.[1900]

FRIJOLES

☛ Wash well one pint of small red beans, cover with two quarts of cold water and bring to a boil slowly. Drain the beans and cover again with cold water, and boil, and then again. The third time, add only enough water to cover the beans about one inch. Add two large tablespoonfuls of lard or dripping, one pounded clove of garlic (if liked), one large Spanish onion sliced, two Chile peppers broken, with some of the seeds removed (unless it is desired to have the beans very hot), and five slices of bacon. Simmer slowly on the back of the stove all day, stirring occasionally with a wooden spoon to thicken the gravy. When done it should be of the consistency of mush, with the beans partly broken. Half an hour before serving pour the desired quantity into a Mexican earthenware pot. Pour over it one teaspoonful of Sierra Madre olive oil and simmer until needed. If you cook the beans rather dry and let them get cold, you can cover spoonfuls with batter and fry in hot lard.[1901]

SUCCOTASH

☛ Take ½ gallon of beans, string them carefully, and break into short pieces. Add ½ pound bacon and cover with water. Put in a kettle and boil for 2½ hours, or till nearly dry, when add the corn cut from 6 cobs. Season with salt, pepper, 1 cup of cream, 1 tablespoon flour, and let it boil ½ hour.[1902]

BROILED MUSHROOMS

☛ Take fresh mushrooms, and after peeling them lay them in salted water for a few minutes. Wipe dry and season with salt and pepper, and dip in butter and broil over a hot fire. Serve with crisp toast.[1903]

STEWED MUSHROOMS

☛ Peel fresh mushrooms. Put butter in saucepan and let it get hot. Put mushrooms in and stir till they become tender. Season with salt and pepper, and add 1 cup of cream and half a spoonful of flour. Let it simmer. Serve in a dish or on toast.[1904]

SWEET POTATOES

☛ Take those that are nearly of the same size, that they may be done equally—wash them clean, but do not peel them—boil them till tender, drain the water off, and put them on tin sheets in a stove for a few minutes to dry.[1905]

CANDIED YAMS

☛ Boil sweet potatoes until done, slice and put in a pan, turn over the top a cup of sugar and bits of butter. Pour in the pan a little water; pour it around the edge in order not to wet the sugar.

Grate over nutmeg or cinnamon, if you like, and brown in the oven. Sift over a very little flour to thicken the gravy.[1906]

BAKED SWEET POTATOES IN HALF SHELL

☛ Select shapely sweet potatoes of even size, wash nicely, bake, and cut in half lengthwise, remove the pulp and pass it through a ricer.

Season with salt, butter and cream; beat until smooth and refill the skins. Dust the tops with sugar and cinnamon and reheat.[1907]

ONIONS FOR BREAKFAST

☛ Take good-sized onions, peel and slice them and boil till tender. Put a layer of onions in a pan and cover with bread-crumbs, salt, pepper, and butter; then another layer of onions, and so on till pan is full. Pour over it a cup of cream and bake till brown.[1908]

STEWED ONIONS

☛ Boil the onions in clear water. Change the water several times, and boil them till tender.

Drain and season with butter, flour, salt and pepper, and cream. Let simmer till thick. Serve hot with sauce poured over onions.[1909]

Radishes cut to imitate roses.

LIMA BEANS

☛ Shell and wash 1 quart of lima beans and cook in salt water till tender. Drain and add 2 ounces butter, a cup of cream, with salt and pepper to taste.[1910]

CORN

☛ Remove the silk, and drop into boiling water with a little salt in it, for half an hour. If it is old, it will take an hour. Lay a napkin on a dish, put in the corn, and fold the napkin over, to keep it hot.[1911]

CORN ON THE COB

☛ Strip off the outside husks, leaving enough of the husks to completely cover the ear, tie a string around the end of each ear to hold the husk. Cook in boiling unsalted water for ten or fifteen minutes, according to the age of the corn. Salt would harden the hull. Before boiling remove all the silk from the ear, then replace the husk.[1912]

INDIAN CORN

☛ Get the large white corn, when nearly full grown, but very tender and full of milk; strip off the shucks in which the ears are enveloped, pick off the silks carefully, and boil them in plenty of water till they are done;

then drain the water from them, cut off the grains close to the cobs, season them with salt, pepper and butter, and serve them in a deep dish. The sugar or rare-ripe corn is sufficiently small and nice to send to table whole; therefore it should not be cut from the cobs, but trimmed nicely and sent to the table, to be handed round with butter, pepper and salt.[1913]

CORN OYSTERS

☞ One cup of corn, one beaten egg, two tablespoonfuls of flour, salt and pepper to season, one tablespoonful of milk, one-fourth a teaspoonful of baking powder. Mix all together and drop by tablespoonfuls on a greased griddle. Fry brown on both sides.[1914]

FRIED CORN

☞ Take a can of corn, stew it in a little sweet milk or water and a tablespoonful of butter until done; then turn out into a frying pan with just enough lard to prevent burning or sticking. Take two eggs to each can of corn, beat them a little and turn into the corn. When the eggs are done, serve. Season with salt and pepper.[1915]

STEWED CORN

☞ Cut your corn down the center, then cut the grains in half and scrape the cob. Put a dessertspoon of lard in your frying pan; when hot, put in the corn and some hot water. Cook at first fast, then set back and cook slowly, keeping closely covered all the time. When done, put in salt and a tablespoonful of butter; should it become too stiff, add a little water or milk. Never cook corn long, it makes it hard.[1916]

TO BOIL CORN

☞ Have water salted and boiling before putting in the corn. Cook from five to ten minutes and serve immediately. If cooked long it destroys the flavor and becomes hard.[1917]

GENERAL PICKETT CORN PUDDING

☞ One pint of fresh corn,
    or
One can of corn,
Two eggs,
One cup of sweet milk,
One cup of sugar,
Butter the size of an egg,
Little salt,
One tablespoonful of flour,
One-fourth teaspoonful of baking powder.
Mix well together, leaving out whites for meringue. Pour into baking dish and cook in hot oven. When cool, beat whites of eggs stiff,

sweeten and flavor, spread on top of pudding and bake a delicate brown.[1918]

TO COOK BUTTER BEANS
☞ Put to cook in hot water salted. When done, slip off the outer skin and season with butter, pepper and more salt, if needed. Serve hot.[1919]

SWEET AND SOUR BEANS
☞ Split string beans and put in boiling water, salted. Cook until done. Put in your frying pan some lard; when hot, sift in a little flour and let brown; then pour in half a cup of syrup and a little sugar, cinnamon, some vinegar and water, half a cup.

Drain beans, put in the sauce and cook until thick. A slice of lemon may be used.[1920]

POTATO SOUFFLE
☞ Two cups of smooth, well-seasoned, and quite moist mashed potatoes add the yolks of two eggs. When a little cool stir in lightly the whites of two eggs beaten very stiff. Put the whole into a pudding-dish, and brown it in a quick oven.[1921]

FRENCH PEAS
☞ Open a can of French peas and turn them into a strainer. Rinse thoroughly by pouring cold water over them. Put in a flat bottom pan and add very little water, only enough to prevent burning, a tablespoonful of butter, a teaspoonful each of salt and sugar. Cook uncovered until hot. Serve at once.[1922]

Extension strainer.

SORREL
☞ Is dressed as the spinach; and if they be mixed in equal proportions, improve each other.[1923]

FRIED SQUASH
☞ Slice your squashes, sprinkle with salt and pepper, let stand awhile; then drain, roll in meal and fry brown.[1924]

STEWED SQUASH
☞ Take the large part of the squash that contains the seeds, split it, peel it, and cut it in small pieces. Stew them in plenty of water till they get soft, and then stew and mash them to a pulp, stirring them frequently; add a large slice of butter, some salt, pepper and cream; continue to stir it till nearly dry, and serve it up; it will be found very nice with meat.[1925]

SUMMER SQUASH

☛ Are good only when young, fresh and tender. Wash and cut in small pieces, leaving on the skin and seed. Cook in boiling water, salted, until tender. Place the squash in a colander to drain, then mash thoroughly; season with salt, pepper and butter. Heat before serving.[1926]

WINTER SQUASH

☛ The crooked neck of this squash is the best part. Cut it in slices an inch thick, take off the rind, and boil them with salt in the water; drain them well before they are dished, and pour melted butter over serve them up very hot.

The large part, containing the seeds, must be sliced and pared—cut it in small pieces, and stew it till soft, with just water enough to cover it; pass it through a sieve, and stew it again, adding some butter, pepper, and salt; it must be dry, but not burnt. It is excellent when stewed with pork chops.[1927]

BAKED CORN

☛ Fill a baking dish with corn, cut and scraped from the cob; cover the corn with sweet milk, season with salt, pepper and a teaspoonful of butter to each quart of corn, and bake half an hour.[1928]

ROASTED CORN

☛ Shuck, silk and put in the oven, and brown. Then salt and eat; or roll in wet, brown paper, and put down in the ashes, covering well. When the paper begins to burn, the corn is generally done.[1929]

STRING BEANS

☛ 2 quarts beans.

String carefully and put in a saucepan and boil 20 minutes. Drain the water from them and replace with 2 quarts boiling water. Add a piece of bacon or middling and boil 1½ hours. Instead of the bacon a dressing of 1 pint of cream, a lump of butter, a little flour, salt, and pepper may be used. Serve hot.[1930]

CABBAGE

☛ Select a small heavy cabbage, cut in quarters and remove the hard centers. Cook in an open vessel in plenty of boiling water, salted, and a piece of red pepper. When tender, drain, cut or chop fine and serve with white sauce, using three tablespoonfuls of butter, two of flour, one cup of water. Pour over the cabbage and put buttered crumbs over the top and bake until the crumbs are brown.[1931]

BAKED CABBAGE

☛ Take one head of cabbage and remove the outside leaves and split in four sections. Boil in salt water till tender. Drain through a colander. Put in a baking dish and pour over it 1 cup of cream. Add a small piece of butter, with salt and pepper to taste. Break an egg over the centre. Put in oven and bake till brown. Serve hot.[1932]

BOILED CABBAGE

☞ Take off the outer leaves of the cabbage; cut in quarters, and let it lie in salt and water for 20 minutes. Pour boiling water over it, and let it stand for 1 minute, and then put it in cold water to cook. Boil it slowly for 1 hour; and if cooked by itself, put some salt in the water, and serve it with drawn butter sauce.[1933]

Ideas for cutting and arranging vegetables (left) and truffles (right) for decorating molds and various dishes.

SOUTHERN CABBAGE

☞ Chop or slice one medium-sized cabbage fine, put it in a stew pan with boiling water to well cover it, and boil fifteen minutes; drain off all water, and add a dressing made as follows: Half teacup wine-vinegar, two-thirds as much sugar, salt, pepper, half teaspoon mustard, and two tea-spoons salad oil; when this is boiling hot, add one tea-cup cream, and one egg stirred together; mix thoroughly and immediately with the cabbage, and cook a moment. Serve hot.[1934]

BRUSSEL SPROUTS

☞ Remove any wilted leaves from the outside of the sprouts, and let them stand in cold salted water from fifteen to twenty minutes, so that any insects there may be in them will come out. Put the sprouts into salted, rapidly boiling water, and cook uncovered fifteen or twenty minutes, or until tender, but not until they lose their shape. Drain them thoroughly in a colander; then place them in a saucepan with butter, pepper, and salt, and toss them until seasoned; or mix them lightly with just enough white sauce to coat them.[1935]

CONFEDERATE CAULIFLOWER

☞ Trim off the outside leaves, cut the stalk even with the flower, let it soak upside down in cold salted water for half an hour to draw out any insects, cook the same way as cabbage. Serve with white, Hollandaise, Bechamel sauce or drawn butter; or serve in any of the ways as directed for cabbage.[1936]

TO COOK CAULIFLOWER

☞ Select those that are of a common or middle size, and very close and white; trim off the outside leaves and stalk, split the flower, or white part in four, and let them lie in water for an hour or two before they are boiled; tie the head together again, to prevent its coming to pieces, put it in a pot of boiling water, with a handful of salt, and boil it gently till done, skimming it well; then take it up immediately, as, if suffered to remain in the water a few minutes longer would spoil it, drain it well, and send it to table with a boat of melted butter.[1937]

Specialized utensils for vegetables, such as knives, scoops, cutting boards, and a potato press.

BAKED CAULIFLOWER

☞ 1 fresh cauliflower,
1 ounce of grated Parmesan cheese,
1 ounce of cracker powder,
1 tablespoon of butter,
1 dessertspoon of flour,
White pepper and salt to taste.

Put cauliflower, top down, in salt and water, and let it stand for 1 hour. Put in pot of salted boiling water and boil 20 minutes. Mix butter and flour and add to boiling water, and stir till it thickens. Add salt and pepper. Put cauliflower in baking dish, pour sauce over it, and sprinkle with cheese and cracker-powder. Brown and serve hot.[1938]

PUMPKIN

☞ Select a large, deep colored pumpkin, as such are generally sweetest. Split it in two, take out the seeds and stringy fibres, but do not scrape off any of the firm part of the pumpkin, as that which is next to the seeds is much the sweetest part. Cut the pumpkin in slices of convenient thickness, peel them, cut them up small, and boil them in a large quantity of water till quite soft; then do not drain them from the liquor, but stew them gently in it, till they form a thick pulp, stirring it frequently at the last, to prevent its scorching. This is much the best way of cooking pumpkin, as by stewing down the liquor, you retain all its

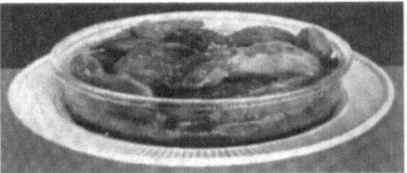

Candied sweet potatoes.

sweetness, and take off the raw taste that the pumpkin otherwise would have. To prepare it for table, put it in a pan, with some rich, highly seasoned gravy, or salt, pepper and butter; the former is preferable. Fry it a few minutes over hot coals, stirring it all the time; when it gets nearly dry, serve it up; it is eaten with fresh beef or pork.

Pumpkin is sometimes stewed with pork, but the receipt I have just given is far superior to any other way it can be dressed; it requires so long a time to cook it well, that it would not be more than half boiled, when the meat would be perfectly tender, and to cook them separately, and then put the pumpkin in the gravy, you would have the flavor and essence of the meat as much as when cooked with it.

They will keep well through the winter, put up as directed for squash and potato pumpkin; they are sweetest after taking a few light frosts in the fall of the year, which will not injure their preservation through the winter.[1939]

HOMINY PUFFS

- 1 quart of cold boiled hominy,
  4 heaping tablespoons of flour,
  3 teaspoons of baking powder,
  1 coffeecup of sweet milk,
  1 teaspoon of salt, 4 eggs.

Take thoroughly cooked hominy when cold and stir in the well-beaten yolks, then flour, milk, and salt alternately with the baking-powder. Add last the whites of eggs beaten to a stiff froth and stirred in slowly. Have lard boiling and drop the mixture in with a spoon, and fry rich brown.[1940]

GEORGIA HOMINY PUFFS

- 1 teacup pearl grits, boiled until soft and perfectly done.
  Scant tablespoon butter.
  ½ cup cold sweet milk.
  1 teaspoon sugar.
  1 egg, well beaten.
  ½ teaspoon salt.

Stir the mixture well, put in a pan, bake in moderately hot oven about half hour.[1941]

MAMMY'S CANDIED SWEET POTATOES

☞ Boil 6 small sized sweet potatoes, peel them and lay on a shallow plate or pan. Put a teaspoon butter on each potato, sprinkle on them ½ cup of brown sugar, 2 tablespoons water in pan, cook slowly and baste as you would meat. Cinnamon, cloves, nutmeg, and lemon peel improve the flavor.[1942]

STEWED LETTUCE

☞ Wash the lettuce carefully to remove the dust and any insects. Take off the wilted leaves, and cut the root even with the head. Tie the top together. Lay the heads side by side in a baking-pan; add enough stock to cover the pan one and a half inches deep. Cover, and place in a moderate oven to simmer for one half hour, or until the lettuce is soft; renew the stock if necessary.

Lift the lettuce out with a fork, putting it under the middle; let it drain, and lay it double, as it will be over the fork, in a row on a hot dish. Season the gravy in the pan with, butter, salt, and pepper; thicken it with cornstarch, or with a beaten egg, and serve it with the lettuce.[1943]

SQUASH

☞ Select those that the outside skin can be easily punctured; peel and slice them; put them in water until ready to cook; put them in boiling water that has a little salt in it, and let them boil for ¾ of an hour; keep the vessel covered.

When tender, empty them into a colander, and press the water out; mash them, and return them to a clean stewpan; season them with butter, pepper, and salt, and a little cream. When they have thickened, serve them.[1944]

CARROTS

☞ Let them be well washed and scraped—an hour is enough for young spring carrots; grown carrots will take from an hour and a half to two hours and a half. The best way to try if they are done enough, is to pierce them with a fork.[1945]

STUFFED PEPPERS

☞ One onion, finely chopped, 2 tablespoons butter, 4 tablespoons chopped mushrooms, 4 tablespoons left-over ham minced fine, ⅓ cup brown sauce, 3 tablespoons fine bread crumbs, salt, pepper, cayenne, 6 green peppers.

Cook onion in butter 3 minutes, add mushrooms, ham, and cook 1 minute. Moisten with brown sauce, add bread crumbs, and season to taste. Cut a slice from the stem end of peppers, remove the seeds and veins, parboil peppers 8 minutes, drain and fill with the ham mixture. Cover top of each with buttered crumbs, and bake in buttered gem cups 10 minutes. Serve on rings of toast.[1946]

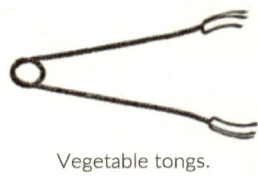
Vegetable tongs.

PARSNIPS

☞ Are to be cooked just in the same manner as carrots; they require more or less time, according to their size; therefore match them in size, and you must try them by thrusting a fork into them as they are in the water; when this goes easily through, they are done enough: boil them from an hour to two hours, according to their size and freshness. Parsnips are sometimes sent up mashed in the same way as turnips.[1947]

BEETS

☞ Beets should be boiled in plenty of water for 6 hours. When done, slice them into a saucepan with a small lump of butter, a little salt, ½ a teaspoonful to a common-sized dish, 2 tablespoons of vinegar, and 1 teaspoon of brown sugar. Let them simmer for ½ an hour before serving. A dust of flour to thicken the gravy.[1948]

RED BEET ROOTS

☞ Are not so much used as they deserve to be; they are dressed in the same way as parsnips, only neither scraped nor cut till after they are boiled; they will take from an hour and a half to three hours in boiling, according to their size; to be sent to the table with salt fish, boiled beef, etc. When young, small and juicy, it is a very good variety, an excellent garnish, and easily converted into a very cheap and pleasant pickle.[1949]

DANDELIONS

☞ They are fit for use until they blossom. Cut off the leaves, pick over carefully, wash in several waters, put into boiling water, boil one hour, drain well, add salted boiling water, and boil two hours; when done, turn into a colander and drain, season with butter, and more salt if needed, and cut with a knife; or boil with a piece of salt pork, omitting the butter in the dressing.[1950]

ONIONS

☞ Put them in salted boiling water, and cook until tender; drain, and pour over them a white sauce, or melted butter, pepper, and salt. If browned onions are wanted for garnishing place them, after they are boiled tender, in a pan; sprinkle with salt, pepper, and a little sugar; and put them in a hot oven to brown.[1951]

SOUTHERN STYLE SWEET POTATOES

☞ Cut cold, baked or boiled sweet potatoes in quarter-inch slices, cover the bottom of a baking dish with a layer of the potato spread quite thickly with pieces of butter, and scatter over a little sugar and salt, season each layer in this way, having the sugar on top. Bake in the oven until heated through and browned slightly.[1952]

PEAS
☛ Put 1 peck of shelled peas in a saucepan; pour over them 1 gallon of boiling water, and let them boil for 20 minutes; strain off the water, and put them into a dish, with small pieces of fresh butter, and serve. Boil a little salt in the water.[1953]

CONFEDERATE LIMA BEANS
☛ These are prepared similar to peas, except when strained from the water; they should be returned to the saucepan, and stewed for 10 minutes. 1 cupful of butter to 1 quart of beans.[1954]

CONFEDERATE STRING BEANS
☛ String beans should always be young and tender. They are called snap beans because when doubled over they will snap, if right for use. Carefully remove the string on either side of the bean, and cut it down the middle in two strips, and then crosswise, making 4 pieces of each bean. Cover them with boiling water, and put a little salt in the water; let them boil for 20 minutes; take them out and strain them; return them to the saucepan with butter, pepper, salt, and a little milk; let them stew for 15 minutes, and serve.[1955]

CAYENNE PEPPER
☛ Take ripe chillies, and dry them perfectly in the sun, or before a slow fire, taking care not to scorch them, which would in a great degree spoil their flavor. Grind or pound them to a perfect powder, mixing with them one eighth of their quantity of fine salt. Put it up in small dry bottles, securing the corks with leather. It will keep its strength, and a very small portion of it will give a fine flavor to gravies, soups, etc.[1956]

MUSTARD
☛ The most common way of preparing mustard for the table is to add to the best flour of mustard a very little salt and a sufficient quantity of boiling water to dilute it to the proper consistence, mashing and stirring it with a spoon till it becomes quite smooth. Some people make use of vinegar instead of water, and others, preferring it very mild, substitute for the water and salt, sweet-milk and sugar.[1957]

The End

480 ~ VINTAGE SOUTHERN COOKBOOK

Notes

1. See my book, *Everything You Were Taught About the Civil War is Wrong, Ask a Southerner!*, for more information on this and related topics.
2. Gregory, p. 339.
3. Gregory, p. 339.
4. Ronald, p. 534.
5. Fox, pp. 288-289.
6. Gregory, p. 326.
7. Randolph, p. 143.
8. Fox, p. 281.
9. Fox, p. 282.
10. Fox, p. 289.
11. McLaren, p. 56.
12. Randolph, p. 144.
13. Fox, p. 282.
14. Fox, p. 285.
15. Kirtland, p. 1.
16. Wilcox, p. 141. The title of this recipe is my creation, the author-editor, L.S.
17. McKinney and McKinney, p. 23.
18. Barringer, p. 108.
19. Gregory, pp. 341-342.
20. Ladies, pp. 495-496.
21. Kirtland, p. 1.
22. McKinney and McKinney, p. 25.
23. Kirtland, p. 1.
24. Kirtland, p. 3.
25. Fox, pp. 183-184.
26. Bryan, p. 386.
27. Bryan, p. 387.
28. Bryan, p. 387.
29. McKinney and McKinney, p. 23.
30. Tyson, pp. 353-354.
31. Kirtland, p. 3.
32. Kirtland, p. 4.
33. Fox, p. 291.
34. Randolph, p. 174.
35. Bryan, p. 390.
36. Fox, pp. 291-292.
37. Gregory, p. 343.
38. Bryan, p. 400.
39. Fox, p. 292.
40. Kirtland, p. 17.
41. Tyson, p. 350.
42. Tyson, p. 350.
43. Tyson, p. 351.
44. Gregory, p. 344. The title of this recipe is my creation, the author-editor, L.S.
45. Kirtland, p. 29.
46. Fox, pp. 286-287.
47. Bryan, p. 408. The title of this recipe is my creation, the author-editor, L.S.
48. Ronald, p. 557. The title of this recipe is my creation, the author-editor, L.S.
49. Berdan, p. 48.

50. Carlisle, p. 82. The title of this recipe is my creation, the author-editor, L.S.
51. Barringer, p, 109. The title of this recipe is my creation, the author-editor, L.S.
52. Fox, pp. 184-185. The title of this recipe is my creation, the author-editor, L.S.
53. Fox, p. 283.
54. Ladies, p. 502.
55. Dillon, p. 837. Note: This is an American rather than a specifically Southern recipe of "America's favorite beverage."
56. Dillon, p. 837. Note: This is an American rather than a specifically Southern recipe of "America's favorite beverage."
57. Dillon, p. 837. Note: This is an American rather than a specifically Southern recipe of "America's favorite beverage."
58. Dillon, p. 837. Note: This is an American rather than a specifically Southern recipe of "America's favorite beverage."
59. Gregory, p. 349.
60. Gregory, p. 349.
61. Barringer, p. 105.
62. Bryan, p. 404.
63. Dennis, p. 57.
64. Kirtland, p. 137.
65. Kirtland, p. 155.
66. Kirtland, p. 202.
67. Fox, p. 295.
68. Bryan, p. 392.
69. Kirtland, pp. 202-203.
70. Fox, p. 183.
71. Fox, p. 185.
72. Fox, p. 185.
73. Bryan, p. 407.
74. Fox, p. 186.
75. Fox, p. 186.
76. Fox, p. 187.
77. Kirtland, p. 203.
78. Kirtland, p. 203. The title of this recipe is my creation, the author-editor, L.S.
79. Kirtland, p. 203.
80. Berdan, p. 54.
81. Randolph, p. 170.
82. Fox, p. 284.
83. Ronald, p. 554.
84. Bryan, p. 379.
85. Bryan, pp. 379-380.
86. Ronald, p. 557.
87. Fox, p. 296.
88. Dennis, p. 329.
89. Fox, p. 296.
90. Bryan, p. 396.
91. Bryan. p. 399.
92. Bryan, pp. 397-398.
93. Bryan, p. 398.
94. Bryan, pp. 398-399.
95. Tyson, p. 239.
96. Tyson, p. 241.
97. Kirtland, p. 68.
98. Fox, p. 21.
99. Tyson, pp. 60-61.

100. Fox, p. 13.
101. Tyson, pp. 58-59.
102. Wilcox, p. 34. The title of this recipe is my creation, the author-editor, L.S.
103. McKinney and McKinney, p. 3.
104. Kirtland, p. 8.
105. Tyson, p. 59.
106. Dennis, p. 108.
107. Fox, pp. 3-4.
108. McKinney and McKinney, p. 13. The title of this recipe is my creation, the author-editor, L.S.
109. McKinney and McKinney, p. 1.
110. Barringer, p. 41. The title of this recipe is my creation, the author-editor, L.S.
111. Gregory, p. 148. The title of this recipe is my creation, the author-editor, L.S.
112. Gregory, p. 145. The title of this recipe is my creation, the author-editor, L.S.
113. Gregory, p. 249. The title of this recipe is my creation, the author-editor, L.S.
114. Dennis, p. 110.
115. Fisher, p. 9.
116. Tyson, p. 35.
117. *American Cookery*, December 1924, Vol. 29, No. 5, pp. 380, 382. The title of this recipe is my creation, the author-editor, L.S.
118. Fox, p. 13.
119. Fox, p. 11.
120. Bryan, p. 306.
121. Bryant, p. 62.
122. Bryan, pp. 306-307.
123. McKinney and McKinney, p. 1.
124. Bryan, p. 307.
125. Kirtland, pp. 68-69.
126. Stefferud, p. 471. The title of this recipe is my creation, the author-editor, L.S.
127. Gregory, p. 149.
128. Fox, p. 10.
129. Barringer, p. 53. This recipe comes from a relative of General Washington.
130. Gregory, p. 139.
131. Bryan, p. 309.
132. Bryan, p. 312.
133. Carlisle, p. 40.
134. Dennis, p. 125.
135. Bryant, p. 75.
136. Bryan, p. 313.
137. Dennis, 103.
138. Norton, p. 6.
139. Bryan, pp. 317-318.
140. Norton, p. 11.
141. Gregory, p. 153. The title of this recipe is my creation, the author-editor, L.S.
142. Carlisle, p. 48.
143. Fisher, p. 11.
144. Wilcox, p. 46.
145. Dennis, p. 111.
146. Tyson, p. 44.
147. Kirtland, p. 69.
148. McKinney and McKinney, p. 113.
149. Kirtland, p. 69.
150. Norton, p. 15. The title of this recipe is my creation, the author-editor, L.S.
151. Dennis, p. 104. The title of this recipe is my creation, the author-editor, L.S.
152. Tyson, p. 54.

153. Fox, p. 14.
154. Dennis, p. 122.
155. Tyson, p. 55.
156. Fox, pp. 1-2.
157. Tyson, p. 58.
158. Carlisle, pp. 41-42.
159. Wilcox, p. 43.
160. Fisher, p. 71.
161. Fisher, pp. 11-12.
162. Fox, p. 12.
163. Wilcox, p. 38.
164. Ladies, p. 271.
165. Fisher, p. 64.
166. Carlisle, pp. 45-46.
167. Ladies, p. 275.
168. Tyson, pp. 53-54.
169. Gregory, p. 146.
170. Carlisle, p. 28.
171. Fisher, p. 64.
172. Kirtland, p. 69.
173. Fox, p. 14.
174. Wilcox, p. 45.
175. Tyson, p. 47.
176. Ladies, p. 284.
177. Ladies, p. 285.
178. Carlisle, pp. 46-47.
179. Fisher, p. 11.
180. Kirtland, p. 70.
181. Fox, p. 7.
182. Kirtland, p. 70.
183. Berdan, p. 60.
184. Gregory, p. 143.
185. Tyson, p. 41.
186. Fox, p. 16.
187. Kirtland, p. 70.
188. Tyson, p. 52.
189. Dennis, p. 95.
190. Dennis, pp. 95-96.
191. Kirtland, p. 70.
192. Kirtland, pp. 70-71.
193. Dennis, p. 113.
194. Gregory, p. 144.
195. Tyson, p. 42.
196. Tyson, p. 49.
197. Kirtland, p. 71.
198. Fisher, p. 10.
199. Tyson, p. 49.
200. Tyson, p. 41.
201. Kirtland, p. 71.
202. Tyson, p. 50.
203. Presbyterian Church, p. 49.
204. Fox, p. 4.
205. Kirtland, p. 72.
206. Fisher, p. 11.

207. Dennis, pp. 96-97.
208. McKinney and McKinney, p. 5.
209. Tyson, p. 42.
210. Presbyterian Church, p. 57.
211. Kirtland, p. 72.
212. Dennis, p. 92.
213. Fox, pp. 18-19.
214. Kirtland, p. 100.
215. Randolph, p. 142.
216. Randolph, p. 139.
217. Randolph, p. 139.
218. Tyson, p. 50.
219. Fox, p. 7.
220. Fox, pp. 19-20.
221. Dennis, p. 94.
222. Tyson, p. 43.
223. Tyson, p. 43.
224. Kirtland, pp. 209, 210. (Editor's note: The measurements in the original recipe were not clear. Please use caution and good judgment. L.S.)
225. Kirtland, p. 210.
226. Kirtland, p. 210. (Editor's note: The measurements in the original recipe were not clear. Please use caution and good judgment. L.S.)
227. Kirtland, p. 210.
228. Kirtland, p. 210.
229. Kirtland, pp. 210-211. (Editor's note: The measurements in the original recipe were not clear. Please use caution and good judgment. L.S.)
230. Ladies, p. 509.
231. Kirtland, p. 211.
232. Wilcox, p. 114.
233. Kirtland, p. 211.
234. Kirtland, p. 211.
235. Kirtland, p. 211. (Editor's note: The measurements in the original recipe were not clear. Please use caution and good judgment. L.S.)
236. Fox, pp. 344-345.
237. Kirtland, pp. 211-212.
238. Kirtland, p. 212. (Editor's note: The measurements in the original recipe were not clear. Please use caution and good judgment. L.S.)
239. Kirtland, p. 212.
240. McKinney and McKinney, p. 57.
241. Kirtland, pp. 212-213.
242. Fox, p. 339.
243. Ronald, pp. 521-522.
244. Kirtland, p. 213.
245. Ladies, p. 511.
246. Gregory, p. 329.
247. Gregory, p. 329.
248. Gregory, pp. 329-330.
249. Fox, p. 343.
250. Kirtland, p. 213. The title of this recipe is my creation, the author-editor, L.S.
251. Kirtland, p. 213.
252. Carlisle, pp. 128-129.
253. Kirtland, p. 213.
254. Fox, p. 345.
255. Fox, pp. 345-346.

256. Kirtland, p. 213.
257. Ronald, p. 520-521.
258. Kirtland, pp. 214-215.
259. Fox, p. 339.
260. Kirtland, p. 215.
261. Kirtland, p. 215.
262. Kirtland, p. 215.
263. McKinney and McKinney, p. 53.
264. McKinney and McKinney, p. 55.
265. Kirtland, p. 215.
266. Fox, p. 341.
267. Ronald, p. 523.
268. Gregory, p. 331.
269. Fox, p. 147.
270. Wilcox, p. 341.
271. Dennis, p. 121.
272. Carlisle, p. 37.
273. Randolph, p. 84.
274. Randolph, p. 227.
275. Dennis, pp. 124-125. The title of this recipe is my creation, the author-editor, L.S.
276. Dennis, p. 125.
277. Dennis, p. 125.
278. Randolph, pp. 227-228.
279. Randolph, p. 228.
280. Dennis, p. 122.
281. Browne, February 1870, p. 144.
282. McLaren, p. 31.
283. Randolph, p. 228.
284. Tyson, p. 215.
285. Ladies, p. 306.
286. Bryan, pp. 380-381.
287. Bryan, pp. 381-382.
288. Bryan, p. 382.
289. Bryan, p. 383.
290. Kirtland, pp. 74-75.
291. Kirtland, p. 76.
292. Kirtland, pp. 76-77.
293. Tyson, p. 214.
294. Kirtland, p. 76.
295. Carlisle, p. 56.
296. Kirtland, p. 77.
297. Dennis, p. 349.
298. Fox, p. 349.
299. Fox, pp. 349-350.
300. Dennis, p. 109.
301. Dennis, p. 109.
302. Dennis, p. 109. The title of this recipe is my creation, the author-editor, L.S.
303. Dennis, p. 109.
304. Dennis, p. 351. The title of this recipe is my creation, the author-editor, L.S.
305. Fox, p. 350.
306. Fox, p. 350.
307. Kirtland, p. 77.
308. Kirtland, p. 78.
309. Tyson, pp. 212-213.

310. Kirtland, pp. 53-54.
311. McKinney and McKinney, p. 75.
312. Ladies, p. 236.
313. Carlisle, p. 55.
314. Ladies, pp. 382-383.
315. Berdan, p. 25.
316. Dennis, p. 345.
317. Kirtland, pp. 31-32.
318. Kirtland, pp. 32-33.
319. Kirtland, p. 33.
320. Kirtland, pp. 33-34.
321. Kirtland, p. 34.
322. Kirtland, p. 34.
323. Fox, p. 81.
324. Kirtland, p. 34.
325. Kirtland, pp. 34-35.
326. Kirtland, p. 35.
327. Kirtland, p. 36.
328. Kirtland, p. 36.
329. Kirtland, p. 36.
330. Kirtland, p. 35.
331. Wilcox, p. 98.
332. Wilcox, p. 98.
333. Fox, pp. 223-224.
334. Barringer, p. 80.
335. Wilcox, p. 82.
336. Fox, p. 226.
337. Barringer, p. 82. The title of this recipe is my creation, the author-editor, L.S.
338. Barringer, p. 82. The title of this recipe is my creation, the author-editor, L.S.
339. Ladies, pp. 451-452.
340. Fox, p. 227.
341. McKinney and McKinney, p. 99.
342. Wilcox, p. 67. The title of this recipe is my creation, the author-editor, L.S.
343. Wilcox, p. 78.
344. Wilcox, p. 78.
345. Barringer, p. 82.
346. McKinney and McKinney, p. 111.
347. Kirtland, p. 2. The title of this recipe is my creation, the author-editor, L.S.
348. Kirtland, p. 2.
349. Ladies, p. 314.
350. Fox, p. 190.
351. Bryan, p. 338.
352. Fisher, p. 10.
353. Tyson, p. 279.
354. Bryan, p. 292.
355. Fisher, pp. 65-66.
356. Gregory, p. 216.
357. Wilcox, p. 79.
358. Dennis, pp. 279-280.
359. Ladies, p. 433.
360. Kirtland, p. 79.
361. Randolph, p. 82.
362. Dennis, p. 276.
363. Kirtland, pp. 94-95.

364. Ladies, p. 455.
365. Fox, p. 193.
366. Fox, p. 189.
367. Ladies, p. 418.
368. Bryan, pp. 285-286.
369. Fox, pp. 231-232.
370. Gregory, p. 218.
371. Dennis, pp. 284-285.
372. Wilcox, pp. 72-73.
373. Kirtland, p. 100.
374. Barringer, p. 80.
375. Barringer, p. 81.
376. Kirtland, p. 101.
377. Ladies, p. 424.
378. Randolph, p. 97.
379. Fisher, p. 63. The title of this recipe is my creation, the author-editor, L.S.
380. Fox, p. 136.
381. Barringer, p. 63.
382. Barringer, p. 66.
383. Dennis, p. 287.
384. Fox, p. 220.
385. Fisher, pp. 29-30.
386. Fox, p. 217.
387. Randolph, p. 119.
388. Fox, pp. 217-218.
389. Dennis, p. 288.
390. Bryan, p. 297. The title of this recipe is my creation, the author-editor, L.S.
391. Bryan, p. 297. The title of this recipe is my creation, the author-editor, L.S.
392. Fox, pp. 222-223.
393. Kirtland, p. 101.
394. Kirtland, p. 101.
395. Kirtland, p. 101.
396. Randolph, p. 91.
397. Fox, p. 195.
398. Carlisle, p. 82.
399. Kirtland, pp. 101-102.
400. Fox, p. 232.
401. Wilcox, p. 165.
402. Randolph, pp. 123-124.
403. Randolph, p. 125.
404. Randolph, p. 127.
405. Fox, p. 232.
406. Kirtland, p. 102.
407. Fox, p. 226.
408. Kirtland, pp. 102-103.
409. Bryan, p. 235.
410. Fox, p. 234.
411. Fox, pp. 234-235.
412. Kirtland, p. 103.
413. Kirtland, p. 103.
414. Carlisle, p. 241.
415. Kirtland, pp. 103-104.
416. Carlisle, p. 27.
417. Kirtland, p. 104.

418. Kirtland, p. 105.
419. Bryan, p. 238.
420. Bryan, pp. 238-239.
421. Kirtland, p. 106.
422. Kirtland, p. 106.
423. Kirtland, p. 107.
424. Fisher, pp. 69-70.
425. Wilcox, p. 179.
426. Kirtland, p. 107.
427. Kirtland, p. 107.
428. Kirtland, p. 108.
429. Kirtland, p. 108.
430. Kirtland, p. 109.
431. Wilcox, p. 234.
432. Kirtland, p. 110.
433. Kirtland, p. 111.
434. Kirtland, p. 111.
435. Randolph, pp. 119-120.
436. Kirtland, p. 115.
437. Fox, p. 196.
438. Bryan, p. 326.
439. Bryan, p. 326.
440. Bryan, p. 299.
441. Barringer, p. 78.
442. Randolph, pp. 72-73.
443. Kirtland, p. 115.
444. Bryan, pp. 241-242.
445. Kirtland, p. 116.
446. Fox, p. 215.
447. McKinney and McKinney, p. 31.
448. Kirtland, p. 133.
449. Kirtland, p. 133.
450. Kirtland, p. 133.
451. McKinney and McKinney, p. 37.
452. Kirtland, pp. 133-134.
453. Kirtland, p. 134.
454. Barringer, p. 77.
455. Randolph, p. 74.
456. Kirtland, pp. 134-135.
457. Kirtland, p. 136.
458. McKinney and McKinney, p. 37.
459. McKinney and McKinney, p. 39.
460. Bryan, pp. 299-300.
461. Randolph, pp. 130-131.
462. Bryan, pp. 242-243.
463. Kirtland, p. 136.
464. Barringer, p. 78.
465. Kirtland, p. 136.
466. Kirtland, p. 137.
467. Bryan, p. 329.
468. McKinney and McKinney, p. 41.
469. Kirtland, p. 138.
470. Bryan, p. 246.
471. Kirtland, pp. 139-140.

472. Kirtland, p. 140.
473. Kirtland, p. 140.
474. Kirtland, p. 140.
475. Kirtland, p. 140.
476. Kirtland, p. 141.
477. Bryan, p. 249.
478. McKinney and McKinney, p. 45.
479. McKinney and McKinney, p. 45.
480. Bryan, pp. 251-252.
481. Randolph, pp. 130-131.
482. Kirtland, p. 142.
483. Kirtland, p. 143.
484. Tyson, p. 291.
485. Bryan, p. 333.
486. Kirtland, pp. 143-144.
487. Kirtland, p. 144.
488. Kirtland, p. 144.
489. Gregory, p. 307.
490. Gregory, p. 307.
491. Gregory, p. 307.
492. Gregory, p. 307.
493. Kirtland, pp. 144-145.
494. Kirtland, pp. 148-149.
495. Kirtland, p. 149.
496. Kirtland, p. 149.
497. Kirtland, p. 149.
498. Carlisle, p. 173.
499. Fox, p. 179.
500. Bryan, p. 339.
501. Kirtland, p. 150.
502. Kirtland, p. 150.
503. Fox, pp. 180-181.
504. Bryan, p. 342.
505. Bryan, p. 342.
506. Bryan, p. 342.
507. Bryan, p. 343.
508. Carlisle, p. 173.
509. Kirtland, pp. 150-151.
510. Ronald, pp. 503-504.
511. Kirtland, p. 151.
512. Kirtland, p. 151.
513. Kirtland, pp. 151-152.
514. Fox, p. 165.
515. Fox, pp. 165-166.
516. Fox, p. 170.
517. Kirtland, p. 152.
518. Kirtland, p. 152.
519. Kirtland, p. 152.
520. Kirtland, p. 153.
521. Fisher, p. 52.
522. Fisher, p. 53.
523. Kirtland, p. 153.
524. Fox, p. 171.
525. Gregory, p. 300.

526. Carlisle, p. 177.
527. Fox, p. 169.
528. Kirtland, p. 153.
529. Kirtland, pp. 153-154.
530. Tyson, p. 217.
531. Kirtland, p. 154.
532. Bryan, p. 343. The title of this recipe is my creation, the author-editor, L.S.
533. Kirtland, p. 154.
534. Fox, p. 172.
535. Bryan, p. 343.
536. Kirtland, p. 154.
537. Tyson, p. 216.
538. Kirtland, p. 154.
539. Bryan, p. 344.
540. Kirtland, pp. 154-155.
541. Kirtland, p. 155.
542. Bryan, pp. 341-342.
543. Bryan, p. 341.
544. Carlisle, p. 179.
545. Kirtland, p. 155.
546. Kirtland, pp. 155-156.
547. Kirtland, p. 156.
548. Kirtland, p. 156.
549. Kirtland, p. 156.
550. Kirtland, p. 156.
551. Kirtland, pp. 156-157.
552. Kirtland, p. 157.
553. Kirtland, p. 157.
554. Fox, pp. 173-174.
555. Kirtland, p. 157.
556. Fox, pp. 178-179. The title of this recipe is my creation, the author-editor, L.S.
557. Kirtland, p. 157.
558. McLaren, p. 45.
559. McKinney and McKinney, p. 115.
560. Kirtland, pp. 157-158.
561. Kirtland, p. 158.
562. Kirtland, p. 158.
563. Tyson, p. 218.
564. Kirtland, pp. 158-160.
565. McLaren, p. 53.
566. McLaren, p. 53.
567. Fox, pp. 249-250.
568. Fox, p. 250.
569. Kirtland, pp. 160-161.
570. Carlisle, pp. 113-114. The title of this recipe is my creation, the author-editor, L.S.
571. Wilcox, p. 66.
572. Fisher, p. 33.
573. Kirtland, p. 161.
574. Kirtland, p. 162.
575. Carlisle, p. 115.
576. Kirtland, p. 162.
577. McKinney and McKinney, p. 49.
578. Kirtland, pp. 162-163.
579. Kirtland, p. 163. The title of this recipe is my creation, the author-editor, L.S.

580. Fox, pp. 264-265.
581. Fox, p. 265.
582. Kirtland, pp. 163-164.
583. Barringer, p. 83.
584. Barringer, p. 83.
585. Barringer, pp. 84-85.
586. Kirtland, p. 164.
587. Kirtland, p. 165.
588. Fox, p. 253.
589. Dennis, p. 254.
590. Kirtland, pp. 165-166.
591. Dennis, p. 261.
592. Kirtland, p. 166.
593. Kirtland, p. 166.
594. Dennis, p. 257.
595. Kirtland, pp. 166-167.
596. Kirtland, p. 167.
597. Kirtland, p. 168.
598. Kirtland, p. 168.
599. Fox, pp. 243-244.
600. Carlisle, p. 104.
601. Carlisle, p. 17.
602. Kirtland, p. 168.
603. Kirtland, p. 169.
604. Kirtland, p. 169.
605. Kirtland, p. 169. The title of this recipe is my creation, the author-editor, L.S.
606. Kirtland, pp. 169-170.
607. Fox, pp. 244-245.
608. Kirtland, p. 170.
609. Dennis, p. 258.
610. Ladies, p. 359.
611. Kirtland, p. 170.
612. Carlisle, p. 16.
613. Kirtland, p. 170.
614. Barringer, p. 86.
615. Gregory, pp. 220-221. (Note: I do not advocate hitting children, even if the Bible says to. I have merely copied the recipe verbatim from the original 1902 source—the editor, L.S.)
616. Ladies, p. 366.
617. Fox, p. 243.
618. Randolph, p. 429.
619. Kirtland, p. 171.
620. Kirtland, p. 171.
621. Gregory, p. 230.
622. Kirtland, p. 172.
623. Kirtland, p. 172.
624. Dennis, p. 243.
625. Kirtland, p. 172.
626. Kirtland, pp. 172-173.
627. Kirtland, p. 173.
628. Gregory, p. 231.
629. Carlisle, p. 108.
630. Ronald, p. 437.
631. Gregory, p. 234.
632. Randolph, p. 136.

633. Kirtland, p. 173.
634. Kirtland, p. 173.
635. Kirtland, p. 173.
636. Fox, pp. 246-247.
637. Fox, pp. 247-248.
638. Dennis, p. 260.
639. Fox, p. 248.
640. Kirtland, pp. 173-174. The title of this recipe is my creation, the author-editor, L.S.
641. Kirtland, p. 174.
642. Kirtland, p. 174.
643. Kirtland, p. 174.
644. Gregory, p. 238.
645. Gregory, p. 238.
646. Kirtland, p. 175.
647. Kirtland, p. 175.
648. Wilcox, p. 375.
649. Kirtland, p. 175.
650. Kirtland, p. 175.
651. Kirtland, pp. 175-176. The title of this recipe is my creation, the author-editor, L.S.
652. Kirtland, p. 176.
653. Kirtland, p. 176.
654. Kirtland, p. 176.
655. Kirtland, pp. 176-177.
656. Kirtland, p. 177.
657. Kirtland, p. 177.
658. Kirtland, p. 178.
659. Carlisle, p. 118.
660. Bryan, p. 301.
661. Bryan, pp. 301-302.
662. Bryan, p. 302.
663. Bryan, p. 302.
664. Kirtland, p. 178.
665. Kirtland, p. 178.
666. Kirtland, p. 178.
667. Kirtland, p. 180.
668. Kirtland, p. 180.
669. Kirtland, p. 183.
670. Kirtland, p. 184.
671. Fisher, p. 29.
672. Kirtland, p. 184.
673. Kirtland, p. 185.
674. Kirtland, p. 186.
675. Kirtland, pp. 186-187.
676. Fox, pp. 177-178.
677. Randolph, p. 428.
678. Fox, pp. 259-260.
679. Fisher, pp. 30-31.
680. Gregory, p. 248.
681. Fisher, p. 31.
682. Kirtland, p. 187.
683. Wilcox, p. 85.
684. Fisher, p. 32.
685. Fox, p. 261.
686. Carlisle, p. 125.

687. Kirtland, p. 187.
688. Kirtland, pp. 187-188.
689. Fox, p. 179.
690. Kirtland, p. 188.
691. Kirtland, p. 188.
692. Kirtland, p. 188.
693. Fox, p. 256.
694. Fisher, pp. 32-33.
695. Tyson, p. 292.
696. Fox, p. 257.
697. Kirtland, p. 189.
698. Kirtland, p. 189.
699. Kirtland, p. 189.
700. Randolph, pp. 110-111.
701. Bryan, pp. 277-278.
702. Kirtland, p. 191.
703. Fox, p. 277.
704. Fox, p. 277. The title of this recipe is my creation, the author-editor, L.S.
705. Carlisle, p. 119. The title of this recipe is my creation, the author-editor, L.S.
706. Fox, pp. 278-279.
707. Bryan, p. 278.
708. Bryan, p. 282.
709. Carlisle, p. 120.
710. Fox, p. 261.
711. Kirtland, pp. 191-192.
712. Gregory, p. 251.
713. Kirtland, p. 192.
714. Kirtland, p. 192.
715. Kirtland, p. 192.
716. Kirtland, p. 192.
717. Fox, p. 266.
718. Fox, p. 258.
719. Kirtland, p. 192.
720. Kirtland, p. 193.
721. Bryan, p. 285.
722. Kirtland, p. 193.
723. Kirtland, p. 193.
724. Gregory, pp. 254-255.
725. Kirtland, p. 193.
726. Kirtland, pp. 193-194.
727. Dennis, p. 266.
728. Kirtland, p. 194.
729. Kirtland, p. 194.
730. Kirtland, p. 194.
731. Kirtland, p. 195. The title of this recipe is my creation, the author-editor, L.S.
732. Browne, February 1870, p. 144.
733. Kirtland, p. 195.
734. Carlisle, p. 123.
735. Kirtland, p. 195.
736. Kirtland, p. 196.
737. Kirtland, p. 196.
738. Kirtland, p. 196.
739. Kirtland, pp. 196-197.
740. Kirtland, p. 197.

741. Fox, p. 262.
742. Kirtland, p. 197.
743. Kirtland, p. 197.
744. Dennis, p. 266.
745. Kirtland, p. 198.
746. Kirtland, p. 198.
747. Kirtland, pp. 198-199.
748. Kirtland, p. 199.
749. Kirtland, p. 199.
750. Kirtland, pp. 199-200.
751. Fox, p. 225.
752. Kirtland, p. 200.
753. Kirtland, p. 200.
754. Kirtland, p. 200.
755. Kirtland, p. 200. The title of this recipe is my creation, the author-editor, L.S.
756. Kirtland, pp. 200-201.
757. Dennis, p. 125.
758. Kirtland, p. 201.
759. Kirtland, p. 201.
760. Kirtland, p. 201.
761. Kirtland, pp. 201-202.
762. Kirtland, p. 202.
763. Kirtland, p. 202.
764. Bryan, p. 252.
765. Bryan, pp. 252-253.
766. Bryan, p. 253.
767. Carlisle, p. 183.
768. Carlisle, p. 183.
769. Carlisle, p. 184.
770. Bryan, p. 253.
771. Bryan, pp. 253-254.
772. Bryan, p. 254.
773. Bryan, p. 254.
774. Bryan, pp. 254-255.
775. Bryan, p. 255.
776. Bryan, p. 224.
777. Bryan, pp. 224-225.
778. Kirtland, p. 15.
779. Presbyterian Church, p. 67.
780. Kirtland, p. 27.
781. Kirtland, p. 27.
782. Bryan, pp. 226-227.
783. Kirtland, p. 27.
784. Kirtland, pp. 27-28.
785. Kirtland, p. 28.
786. Gregory, p. 178.
787. Presbyterian Church, pp. 67-68.
788. Wilcox, p. 149.
789. Gregory, p. 179.
790. Barringer, p. 13.
791. Fox, p. 25.
792. Kirtland, p. 28.
793. Randolph, p. 86.
794. Tyson, p. 62.

795. Berdan, p. 27.
796. Fox, p. 26.
797. Ladies, p. 238.
798. Gregory, p. 183.
799. Gregory, p. 182.
800. Kirtland, p. 28.
801. Dennis, p. 110.
802. Gregory, p. 180. The title of this recipe is my creation, the author-editor, L.S.
803. Barringer, p. 14.
804. Fox, p. 28.
805. Kirtland, p. 29.
806. Fisher, p. 9.
807. Gregory, p. 181.
808. Ladies, p. 240.
809. Tyson, p. 66.
810. Kirtland, p. 29.
811. Gregory, p. 177.
812. Kirtland, p. 29.
813. Kirtland, p. 30.
814. Kirtland, p. 30.
815. Kirtland, p. 30.
816. Wilcox, p. 147.
817. Gregory, p. 176.
818. Dennis, p. 220.
819. Dennis, p. 220.
820. Kirtland, p. 31.
821. Kirtland, p. 31.
822. Kirtland, p. 31.
823. Gregory, p. 185.
824. Gregory, p. 185.
825. Gregory, p. 185.
826. Kirtland, p. 31. The title of this recipe is my creation, the author-editor, L.S.
827. Dennis, p. 222. The title of this recipe is my creation, the author-editor, L.S.
828. Dennis, p. 222.
829. Kirtland, p. 31.
830. Gregory, p. 177.
831. Kirtland, p. 36.
832. Kirtland, pp. 36-37.
833. Kirtland, p. 37.
834. Fisher, p. 16.
835. Kirtland, p. 37.
836. Kirtland, p. 37.
837. Kirtland, pp. 37-38.
838. Fox, p. 69.
839. Kirtland, p. 38.
840. Kirtland, p. 38.
841. Kirtland, p. 38.
842. Kirtland, pp. 38-39.
843. Fox, p. 146.
844. Kirtland, p. 39.
845. Kirtland, p. 39.
846. Kirtland, p. 39.
847. Fox, p. 64.
848. Kirtland, p. 39.

849. McLaren, p. 21.
850. Kirtland, p. 39.
851. Fisher, pp. 64-65.
852. Fisher, p. 65.
853. Kirtland, pp. 39-40.
854. Kirtland, p. 40.
855. Kirtland, p. 40.
856. McLaren, p. 23.
857. Kirtland, p. 40.
858. Kirtland, p. 41.
859. Kirtland, p. 41.
860. Kirtland, p. 41.
861. Kirtland, pp. 41-42.
862. Kirtland, p. 42.
863. Kirtland, p. 42.
864. Bryan, p. 62.
865. McLaren, p. 25.
866. Kirtland, p. 42.
867. Kirtland, p. 42.
868. Fox, pp. 71-72.
869. Kirtland, p. 43.
870. Kirtland, p. 43.
871. Kirtland, pp. 43-44.
872. Kirtland, p. 44.
873. Kirtland, p. 45.
874. Kirtland, p. 45.
875. Kirtland, p. 45.
876. Kirtland, p. 46.
877. Fox, p. 72.
878. Kirtland, p. 116.
879. Wilcox, p. 49.
880. Kirtland, p. 116.
881. Kirtland, p. 116.
882. Fisher, pp. 62-63.
883. McKinney and McKinney, p. 5.
884. Kirtland, p. 116.
885. Kirtland, p. 117.
886. Kirtland, p. 117.
887. Dennis, pp. 149-150.
888. Kirtland, p. 117.
889. Kirtland, p. 117.
890. Randolph, p. 130.
891. Kirtland, p. 117. The title of this recipe is my creation, the author-editor, L.S.
892. Gregory, p. 92.
893. Kirtland, p. 88.
894. Kirtland, p. 88.
895. Gregory, p. 472.
896. Gregory, p. 76.
897. Randolph, p. 130.
898. Kirtland, p. 86.
899. Kirtland, p. 86.
900. Kirtland, p. 86.
901. Kirtland, p. 87.
902. Kirtland, p. 95.

903. Kirtland, p. 111.
904. Wilcox, p. 165.
905. Kirtland, p. 95.
906. Kirtland, p. 96.
907. Kirtland, p. 96.
908. Kirtland, p. 96.
909. Kirtland, pp. 96-97.
910. Kirtland, p. 97.
911. Kirtland, p. 97.
912. Kirtland, p. 97.
913. Kirtland, p. 97.
914. Kirtland, pp. 97-98.
915. Bryan, p. 175,
916. Fox, p. 230.
917. Kirtland, p. 98.
918. Kirtland, pp. 98-99.
919. Wilcox, p. 162.
920. Kirtland, p. 99.
921. Kirtland, p. 99.
922. Kirtland, pp. 99-100.
923. Kirtland, p. 100.
924. Wilcox, p. 166.
925. Kirtland, p. 100. The title of this recipe is my creation, the author-editor, L.S.
926. Kirtland, p. 103.
927. Kirtland, p. 110.
928. Kirtland, p. 110.
929. Fox, p. 228.
930. Tyson, p. 316.
931. Bryan, p. 412.
932. Fisher, p. 23.
933. Fisher, p. 67.
934. Randolph, p. 152.
935. Tyson, p. 371.
936. Tyson, p. 371.
937. Tyson, p. 372.
938. Tyson, p. 372.
939. Tyson, p. 372.
940. Randolph, p. 152.
941. Tyson, p. 372.
942. Tyson, p. 373.
943. Gregory, p. 508.
944. Dennis, p. 220.
945. Dennis, p. 220.
946. Randolph, p. 153.
947. Randolph, p. 153.
948. Dennis, p. 124.
949. Randolph, pp. 153-154.
950. Randolph, p. 154.
951. Tyson, p. 373.
952. Tyson, p. 373.
953. Dennis, p. 372.
954. Gregory, p. 338.
955. Tyson, p. 373.
956. Tyson, p. 373.

957. Randolph, p. 153.
958. Tyson, p. 374.
959. Tyson, p. 374.
960. Ladies, p. 111.
961. Tyson, p. 374.
962. Randolph, p. 153.
963. Bryan, pp. 412-413.
964. Bryan, p. 413.
965. Bryan, p. 413.
966. Bryan, p. 412.
967. Bryan, pp. 413-414.
968. Bryan, p. 414.
969. Gregory, p. 510.
970. Bryan, pp. 414-415.
971. Bryan, p. 415.
972. Bryan, p. 415.
973. Bryan, p. 415.
974. Bryan, pp. 415-416.
975. Gregory, p. 533.
976. Bryan, p. 416.
977. Bryan, p. 416.
978. Bryan, p. 416.
979. Bryan, p. 416.
980. Bryan, p. 416.
981. Bryan, p. 417.
982. Bryan, p. 417.
983. Bryan, p. 417.
984. Bryan, p. 417.
985. Bryan, p. 417. The title of this recipe is my creation, the author-editor, L.S.
986. Bryan, pp. 419-420.
987. Gregory, p. 509.
988. Bryan, p. 420. The title of this recipe is my creation, the author-editor, L.S.
989. Bryan, p. 427.
990. Gregory, p. 514.
991. Kirtland, p. 204.
992. Fox, p. 199.
993. Gregory, p. 359.
994. Kirtland, p. 204.
995. Bryan, p. 348.
996. Fisher, pp. 45-46.
997. Dennis, p. 54.
998. Tyson, pp. 308-309.
999. Fisher, p. 46.
1000. Tyson, p. 300.
1001. Tyson, p. 311.
1002. Bryan, p. 184.
1003. Tyson, p. 311.
1004. Fox, p. 198.
1005. Kirtland, pp. 204-205.
1006. Bryan, pp. 375-377.
1007. Dennis, pp. 50-51.
1008. Kirtland, p. 205.
1009. Dennis, p. 60.
1010. Barringer, p. 97.

1011. Kirtland, p. 205.
1012. Gregory, p. 354.
1013. Kirtland, p. 205.
1014. Kirtland, p. 205.
1015. Carlisle, p. 101.
1016. Dennis, p. 37.
1017. Tyson, p. 315.
1018. Dennis, p. 63.
1019. Fox, p. 330.
1020. Randolph, p. 542.
1021. Randolph, p. 156.
1022. Bryan, p. 182.
1023. Kirtland, pp. 205-206.
1024. Wilcox, pp. 246-247. The title of this recipe is my creation, the author-editor, L.S.
1025. Fox, p. 331. The title of this recipe is my creation, the author-editor, L.S.
1026. Fox, p. 331.
1027. Bryan, pp. 348-349.
1028. Dennis, pp. 39-40.
1029. Dennis, p. 45.
1030. Bryan, p. 359. The title of this recipe is my creation, the author-editor, L.S.
1031. Bryan, pp. 358-359.
1032. Fisher, p. 48.
1033. Randolph, p. 151.
1034. Kirtland, p. 206.
1035. Kirtland, p. 54.
1036. Dennis, pp. 53-54.
1037. Kirtland, pp. 206-207.
1038. Kirtland, p. 207.
1039. Kirtland, p. 208.
1040. Fox, p. 200.
1041. Fisher, pp. 49-50.
1042. Kirtland, p. 208.
1043. Dennis, p. 47.
1044. Wilcox, p. 189.
1045. Kirtland, p. 208.
1046. Dennis, pp. 51-52.
1047. Fox, p. 327.
1048. Kirtland, pp. 208-209.
1049. Fisher, p. 51.
1050. Kirtland, p. 209.
1051. Kirtland, p. 209.
1052. Fox, p. 336. The title of this recipe is my creation, the author-editor, L.S.
1053. Fox, p. 336.
1054. Fox, pp. 336-337.
1055. Dennis, p. 49.
1056. Carlisle, p. 101.
1057. Tyson, pp. 119-121.
1058. Tyson, pp. 121-122.
1059. Tyson, p. 122.
1060. Tyson, p. 123.
1061. Tyson, pp. 123-125.
1062. Fisher, p. 55.
1063. Fisher, pp. 55-56.
1064. Bryan, pp. 40-41.

1065. Fox, pp. 97-98.
1066. Fox, p. 98.
1067. Fisher, p. 56.
1068. Carlisle, p. 79.
1069. Ladies, pp. 178-179.
1070. Dennis, p. 359.
1071. Ronald, pp. 163-164.
1072. Fisher, p. 57.
1073. Barringer, p. 19.
1074. Tyson, p. 131.
1075. Fisher, pp. 57-58.
1076. Fox, p. 85.
1077. Carlisle, p. 78.
1078. Fisher, p. 58.
1079. Kirtland, pp. 55-56.
1080. Kirtland, p. 128.
1081. Fox, pp. 208-209.
1082. Gregory, p. 128.
1083. Fisher, p. 12.
1084. Randolph, pp. 31-32.
1085. Tyson, p. 134.
1086. Bryan, p. 83.
1087. Tyson, p. 136.
1088. Randolph, p. 44.
1089. Fox, p. 105.
1090. Fox, p. 107.
1091. Tyson, p. 138.
1092. Randolph, p. 47.
1093. Carlisle, p. 21.
1094. Ladies, p. 159.
1095. Ronald, p. 165.
1096. Fisher, p. 12.
1097. Bryan, p. 95.
1098. Kirtland, p. 56.
1099. Norton, pp. 61-62.
1100. Kirtland, p. 56.
1101. Kirtland, p. 56.
1102. Fox, p. 115.
1103. Fisher, p. 13.
1104. Fox, p. 103.
1105. Wilcox, p. 201.
1106. Fox, p. 103.
1107. Fox, p. 104.
1108. Fox, p. 104. The title of this recipe is my creation, the author-editor, L.S.
1109. Ronald, pp. 169-170.
1110. Fisher, p. 67.
1111. Kirtland, pp. 56-57.
1112. Kirtland, p. 57.
1113. Fisher, p. 13.
1114. Fisher, p. 14.
1115. Gregory, p. 128.
1116. Tyson, pp. 139-140.
1117. Carlisle, p. 53.
1118. Kirtland, p. 57.

1119. Kirtland, p. 57.
1120. Bryan, p. 99.
1121. Fox, pp. 99-100.
1122. Fox, pp. 100-101.
1123. Bryan, p. 110.
1124. Barringer, p. 18.
1125. Dennis, p. 330.
1126. Kirtland, p. 57.
1127. Dennis, pp. 157-158.
1128. Kirtland, p. 58.
1129. Ronald, p. 172.
1130. Fisher, pp. 14-15.
1131. Gregory, p. 127.
1132. Berdan, p. 37.
1133. Gregory, p. 129.
1134. Dennis, p. 160.
1135. Ronald, p. 178.
1136. Kirtland, p. 58.
1137. Tyson, p. 365.
1138. Tyson, pp. 143-144.
1139. Dennis, p. 344.
1140. Fisher, p. 15.
1141. Bryan, pp. 53-54.
1142. Ladies, pp. 163-164.
1143. Ronald, p. 178.
1144. Wilcox, p. 204.
1145. Tyson, pp. 148-149.
1146. Bryan, p. 65.
1147. Kirtland, pp. 58-59.
1148. Kirtland, p. 59. The title of this recipe is my creation, the author-editor, L.S.
1149. Kirtland, p. 59.
1150. Presbyterian Church, p. 21.
1151. Ladies, p. 176.
1152. Presbyterian Church, p. 21.
1153. Tyson, p. 157.
1154. Fisher, p. 15.
1155. Ronald, p. 184.
1156. Gregory, p. 194.
1157. Tyson, p. 155.
1158. Kirtland, p. 59.
1159. Fox, p. 110.
1160. Kirtland, pp. 59-60.
1161. Kirtland, p. 60.
1162. Kirtland, p. 60.
1163. Fisher, p. 16.
1164. Ronald, p. 198.
1165. Kirtland, p. 60.
1166. Kirtland, p. 60.
1167. Fisher, p. 16.
1168. Randolph, pp. 70-71.
1169. Bryan, p. 126.
1170. Fisher, p. 16.
1171. Ronald, pp. 197-198.
1172. Fox, p. 91.

1173. Bryan, p. 116.
1174. Gregory, pp. 121-122.
1175. Carlisle, p. 153.
1176. Dennis, p. 162.
1177. Fisher, p. 18.
1178. Kirtland, p. 61.
1179. Kirtland, p. 61.
1180. Kirtland, p. 61.
1181. Kirtland, p. 61.
1182. Fox, p. 113.
1183. Gregory, p. 114.
1184. Fox, p. 114.
1185. Kirtland, pp. 61-62.
1186. Fisher, p. 17.
1187. Kirtland, p. 62.
1188. Wilcox, p. 199.
1189. Bryan, p. 48.
1190. Randolph, p. 81.
1191. McKinney and McKinney, p. 73.
1192. Carlisle, p. 142.
1193. Kirtland, p. 62.
1194. Kirtland, p. 62.
1195. Kirtland, pp. 63-64.
1196. Fisher, pp. 19-20.
1197. Fox, p. 88.
1198. Tyson, p. 162.
1199. Ronald, p. 187.
1200. Kirtland, p. 63.
1201. Kirtland, pp. 64-65.
1202. Kirtland, p. 64.
1203. Kirtland, p. 64.
1204. Kirtland, p. 65.
1205. Kirtland, p. 65.
1206. Wilcox, p. 281.
1207. Gregory, p. 98.
1208. McKinney and McKinney, p. 79.
1209. McKinney and McKinney, p. 79.
1210. Kirtland, p. 65.
1211. Kirtland, p. 66.
1212. Carlisle, p. 142.
1213. Fox, p. 86.
1214. Tyson, p. 357.
1215. Fox, p. 87.
1216. Kirtland, p. 66.
1217. Kirtland, p. 67.
1218. Tyson, pp. 161-162. The title of this recipe is my creation, the author-editor, L.S.
1219. Dennis, p. 187.
1220. Kirtland, p. 67. The title of this recipe is my creation, the author-editor, L.S.
1221. Kirtland, p. 67.
1222. Carlisle, p. 141.
1223. Kirtland, p. 68.
1224. Fox, p. 94.
1225. Ladies, p. 200.
1226. Fox, p. 95.

1227. Randolph, p. 77.
1228. Barringer, pp. 26-27.
1229. Bryan, pp. 131-132.
1230. Fox, p. 95.
1231. Gregory, p. 109.
1232. Barringer, p. 25.
1233. Bryan, p. 134.
1234. Fisher, p. 17.
1235. Fox, p. 93.
1236. Tyson, p. 168.
1237. Fox, pp. 93-94.
1238. Fox, p. 94.
1239. Fox, p. 94.
1240. Barringer, p. 26.
1241. Tyson, p. 165.
1242. Tyson, pp. 165-166.
1243. Tyson, p. 166.
1244. Tyson, p. 170.
1245. Tyson, p. 171.
1246. Tyson, p. 270.
1247. Bryan, pp. 256-257.
1248. Tyson, p. 298.
1249. Randolph, p. 426.
1250. Wilcox, p. 53.
1251. Barringer, p. 53. The title of this recipe is my creation, the author-editor, L.S.
1252. Wilcox, p. 53.
1253. Wilcox, pp. 96-97.
1254. Fisher, p. 10.
1255. Kirtland, p. 71.
1256. Kirtland, p. 71.
1257. Fox, p. 20.
1258. Tyson, p. 37.
1259. Presbyterian Church, p. 46.
1260. Dennis, p. 107.
1261. Dennis, pp. 107-108.
1262. Wilcox, p. 44.
1263. Tyson, p. 38.
1264. Dennis, p. 106.
1265. Gregory, p. 149.
1266. Gregory, p. 149.
1267. Gregory, p. 149.
1268. Gregory, p. 150.
1269. Gregory, p. 150.
1270. Gregory, p. 150.
1271. Carlisle, p. 204. The title of this recipe is my creation, the author-editor, L.S.
1272. Berdan, p. 59.
1273. Gregory, p. 151. The title of this recipe is my creation, the author-editor, L.S.
1274. Gregory, p. 152.
1275. Gregory, p. 152. The title of this recipe is my creation, the author-editor, L.S.
1276. Ladies, p. 294.
1277. Gregory, p. 152.
1278. Gregory, p. 152.
1279. Gregory, p. 51.
1280. Fox, p. 141.

1281. Fox, p. 140.
1282. Kirtland, p. 75.
1283. Kirtland, p. 75.
1284. Carlisle, p. 78.
1285. Barringer, p. 39. The title of this recipe is my creation, the author-editor, L.S.
1286. Kirtland, p. 75.
1287. Gregory, p. 173.
1288. Randolph, pp. 127-128.
1289. Tyson, pp. 209-210.
1290. Gregory, p. 190.
1291. Randolph, p. 85.
1292. Fox, p. 141.
1293. Carlisle, p. 197.
1294. Carlisle, p. 242.
1295. Ronald, p. 93.
1296. Tyson, p. 94.
1297. Ronald, p. 93.
1298. Ronald, pp. 93-94.
1299. McLaren, p. 33.
1300. McLaren, p. 33.
1301. Kirtland, p. 118.
1302. Fisher, p. 24.
1303. Fisher, p. 24.
1304. Ladies, p. 399.
1305. McKinney and McKinney, p. 17.
1306. McKinney and McKinney, p. 101.
1307. Fox, pp. 201-202.
1308. McKinney and McKinney, p. 15.
1309. Kirtland, p. 118.
1310. Kirtland, p. 118.
1311. Kirtland, pp. 118-119.
1312. Kirtland, p. 119.
1313. Kirtland, p. 119.
1314. Kirtland, p. 119.
1315. Fisher, pp. 24-25.
1316. Fisher, pp. 25-26.
1317. Kirtland, p. 120.
1318. Kirtland, p. 120.
1319. Kirtland, pp. 120-121.
1320. Carlisle, p. 190. The title of this recipe is my creation, the author-editor, L.S.
1321. Kirtland, p. 121.
1322. Fisher, p. 33.
1323. Fisher, p. 26.
1324. Tyson, p. 223.
1325. Barringer, p. 101.
1326. Barringer, p. 101.
1327. Kirtland, p. 121.
1328. Kirtland, p. 121.
1329. Fisher, p. 27.
1330. Fisher, p. 27.
1331. Fisher, pp. 27-28.
1332. Barringer, pp. 102-103.
1333. Wilcox, p. 216.
1334. Kirtland, p. 122.

1335. Wilcox, p. 224.
1336. Kirtland, p. 121.
1337. Kirtland, p. 122.
1338. Fox, p. 211.
1339. Kirtland, p. 122.
1340. Kirtland, p. 122.
1341. Kirtland, p. 123.
1342. Tyson, pp. 227-228.
1343. Randolph, p. 124.
1344. Fox, p. 206.
1345. Kirtland, p. 123.
1346. McKinney and McKinney, p. 103.
1347. Kirtland, p. 123.
1348. Kirtland, p. 123.
1349. Kirtland, pp. 123-124.
1350. Kirtland, p. 124.
1351. Kirtland, p. 124.
1352. Kirtland, p. 124.
1353. Kirtland, p. 124.
1354. Fox, p. 207.
1355. Kirtland, p. 124.
1356. Tyson, p. 232.
1357. Bryan, p. 324.
1358. Carlisle, p. 168.
1359. Bryan, p. 263.
1360. Bryan, pp. 263-264.
1361. Bryan, p. 265.
1362. Bryan, p. 265.
1363. Bryan, p. 265.
1364. McKinney and McKinney, p. 95.
1365. Tyson, p. 232.
1366. Kirtland, p. 125.
1367. Kirtland, p. 125.
1368. Kirtland, p. 125.
1369. Kirtland, p. 125.
1370. Ronald, p. 396.
1371. Kirtland, p. 126.
1372. Bryan, p. 325.
1373. Kirtland, p. 126.
1374. Carlisle, p. 185.
1375. Kirtland, p. 126.
1376. Kirtland, pp. 126-127.
1377. Fisher, p. 26.
1378. Fox, pp. 212-213.
1379. Kirtland, p. 127.
1380. Kirtland, p. 127.
1381. Fox, pp. 219-220.
1382. Kirtland, p. 127.
1383. Kirtland, p. 127.
1384. Kirtland, p. 127.
1385. Wilcox, p. 222.
1386. Fox, p. 210.
1387. Kirtland, p. 128.
1388. Gregory, p. 209.

1389. Kirtland, p. 128.
1390. Kirtland, p. 128.
1391. Kirtland, p. 129.
1392. Kirtland, p. 129.
1393. Kirtland, p. 129.
1394. Gregory, 206.
1395. Kirtland, p. 130.
1396. Kirtland, p. 130.
1397. Kirtland, p. 130.
1398. Fox, pp. 204-205.
1399. Fox, p. 205.
1400. Gregory, p. 206.
1401. Gregory, p. 208.
1402. Gregory, p. 205.
1403. Kirtland, p. 130.
1404. Kirtland, p. 130.
1405. Kirtland, p. 131.
1406. Gregory, p. 213.
1407. Kirtland, p. 131.
1408. Kirtland, p. 131.
1409. Kirtland, pp. 131-132.
1410. Kirtland, p. 132.
1411. Gregory, p. 207.
1412. Kirtland, p. 132.
1413. Kirtland, p. 132.
1414. Kirtland, pp. 132-133.
1415. Fox, p. 276.
1416. Tyson, pp. 323-324.
1417. Tyson, pp. 342-344.
1418. Bryan, p. 411.
1419. Bryan, p. 179.
1420. Fisher, pp. 42-43.
1421. Presbyterian Church, p. 40.
1422. Fox, pp. 297-298.
1423. Fox, p. 305.
1424. Fox, p. 310.
1425. Fox, pp. 314-315.
1426. Kirtland, p. 72.
1427. Kirtland, pp. 72-73.
1428. McKinney and McKinney, p. 83.
1429. Fisher, p. 36.
1430. Carlisle, p. 96.
1431. Kirtland, p. 73.
1432. Fisher, pp. 40-41.
1433. Barringer, pp. 40-41.
1434. Kirtland, p. 74.
1435. Bryan, p. 186.
1436. Wilcox, p. 130.
1437. Kirtland, p. 74.
1438. Fox, p. 324.
1439. Presbyterian Church, p. 27.
1440. Berdan, p. 55.
1441. Ladies, p. 205.
1442. Fisher, pp. 36-37.

1443. Dennis, p. 74.
1444. Bryan, p. 187.
1445. Fox, pp. 304-305.
1446. Wilcox, p. 258.
1447. Presbyterian Church, p. 32.
1448. Dennis, p. 82.
1449. Bryan, p. 189.
1450. Kirtland, p. 46.
1451. Kirtland, p. 46.
1452. Bryan, pp. 220-221.
1453. Kirtland, p. 53.
1454. Fox, p. 151.
1455. Fox, p. 151.
1456. Kirtland, p. 55.
1457. Berdan, p. 22.
1458. Kirtland, p. 55.
1459. Kirtland, p. 55.
1460. Fox, p. 154.
1461. Carlisle, p. 66.
1462. Presbyterian Church, p. 62.
1463. Bryan, pp. 192-193.
1464. Bryan, p. 193.
1465. Dennis, p. 213.
1466. Berdan, p. 21.
1467. Fox, pp. 153-154.
1468. Kirtland, p. 54.
1469. Wilcox, p. 289.
1470. Browne, February 1870, p. 144. The title of this recipe is my creation, the author-editor, L.S.
1471. Kirtland, p. 54.
1472. McLaren. p. 41.
1473. Kirtland, p. 53.
1474. Presbyterian Church, p. 43.
1475. Ronald, p. 378.
1476. Kirtland, pp. 18-19.
1477. Gregory, p. 199.
1478. Berdan, p. 23.
1479. Berdan, p. 23.
1480. Gregory, p. 482.
1481. Kirtland, p. 49.
1482. Dennis, p. 215.
1483. Dennis, p. 215.
1484. Fox, p. 157.
1485. Gregory, p. 478.
1486. Fox, p. 157.
1487. Kirtland, p. 50.
1488. Kirtland, pp. 50-51.
1489. Kirtland, p. 51.
1490. Dennis, p. 163.
1491. McLaren, p. 40.
1492. Wilcox, p. 289.
1493. Gregory, p. 482.
1494. Gregory, p. 481.
1495. Kirtland, p. 51.
1496. Dennis, p. 211.

1497. Berdan, p. 21.
1498. Wilcox, p. 291.
1499. Kirtland, pp. 51-52.
1500. Kirtland, p. 52.
1501. Kirtland, p. 52.
1502. Kirtland, p. 52.
1503. Gregory, p. 486.
1504. Gregory, p. 486.
1505. Gregory, p. 486.
1506. Kirtland, p. 52.
1507. Dennis, p. 210.
1508. Berdan, p. 21.
1509. Kirtland, p. 53.
1510. Fox, p. 156.
1511. Tyson, p. 208.
1512. Tyson, p. 208.
1513. Tyson, p. 205.
1514. Wilcox, p. 293.
1515. Fox, p. 162.
1516. Kirtland, p. 47.
1517. Kirtland, p. 46.
1518. Kirtland, p. 47.
1519. Carlisle, p. 74.
1520. Kirtland, pp. 47-48.
1521. Kirtland, p. 47.
1522. Kirtland, p. 48.
1523. Kirtland, p. 48.
1524. Fox, p. 161.
1525. Kirtland, p. 48.
1526. Carlisle, p. 75.
1527. Fox, p. 161.
1528. Kirtland, p. 48.
1529. Kirtland, p. 49.
1530. Kirtland, p. 49.
1531. Carlisle, p. 18.
1532. Kirtland, p. 78.
1533. Kirtland, pp. 78-79.
1534. Kirtland, p. 79.
1535. Kirtland, p. 79.
1536. Kirtland, pp. 79-80.
1537. Berdan, p. 57.
1538. Berdan, p. 57.
1539. Berdan, p. 58.
1540. Berdan, p. 58.
1541. Berdan, p. 58.
1542. Kirtland, p. 80.
1543. Kirtland, p. 80.
1544. Kirtland, p. 80.
1545. Kirtland, pp. 80-81.
1546. Kirtland, p. 81.
1547. Kirtland, p. 81.
1548. Kirtland, p. 81.
1549. Kirtland, p. 81.
1550. Dennis, p. 197.

1551. Gregory, p. 161.
1552. Gregory, p. 161.
1553. Gregory, p. 162.
1554. Gregory, p. 163.
1555. Gregory, p. 163.
1556. Gregory, p. 164.
1557. Gregory, p. 164.
1558. Gregory, p. 165.
1559. Dennis, p. 197.
1560. Dennis, pp. 197-198.
1561. Dennis, p. 198.
1562. Dennis, p. 198. The title of this recipe is my creation, the author-editor, L.S.
1563. Dennis, p. 199.
1564. Dennis, p. 199.
1565. Dennis, p. 199.
1566. Kirtland, p. 81.
1567. Kirtland, p. 82.
1568. Kirtland, p. 82.
1569. Kirtland, p. 82.
1570. Kirtland, p. 82.
1571. Kirtland, pp. 82-83.
1572. Carlisle, p. 71.
1573. Kirtland, p. 83.
1574. Kirtland, p. 83.
1575. Kirtland, p. 196.
1576. Kirtland, p. 35.
1577. Fox, p. 322.
1578. Kirtland, p. 15.
1579. Kirtland, p. 22.
1580. Kirtland, p. 22.
1581. Fox, p. 128.
1582. Randolph, p. 92.
1583. Kirtland, p. 22.
1584. Fox, pp. 237-238.
1585. Fox, p. 238.
1586. Kirtland, p. 22.
1587. Bryan, p. 170.
1588. Kirtland, p. 23.
1589. Kirtland, p. 23.
1590. Fox, p. 124.
1591. Presbyterian Church, p. 23.
1592. Kirtland, p. 23.
1593. Wilcox, p. 241.
1594. Kirtland, p. 23.
1595. Kirtland, p. 23.
1596. Kirtland, p. 24.
1597. Fox, p. 130.
1598. Carlisle, p. 157.
1599. Carlisle, p. 157.
1600. Kirtland, pp. 24-25.
1601. Kirtland, p. 25.
1602. Dennis, p. 69.
1603. Randolph, p. 92.
1604. Gregory, p. 389.

1605. Bryan, p. 165.
1606. Bryan, p. 165.
1607. McLaren, p. 12.
1608. Bryan, p. 165.
1609. Barringer, p. 14.
1610. Kirtland, p. 25.
1611. Kirtland, p. 25.
1612. Kirtland, p. 25.
1613. Fox, p. 117.
1614. Kirtland, p. 25.
1615. Kirtland, p. 26.
1616. Kirtland, p. 26.
1617. Fox, p. 121.
1618. Fox, p. 238.
1619. Kirtland, p. 26.
1620. Kirtland, p. 92.
1621. Kirtland, p. 92.
1622. Kirtland, p. 92.
1623. Fox, p. 239.
1624. Kirtland, p. 92.
1625. Kirtland, p. 92.
1626. Fox, p. 119.
1627. Tyson, p. 186.
1628. Dennis, p. 323.
1629. Presbyterian Church, p. 24.
1630. Kirtland, pp. 92-93.
1631. Kirtland, p. 93.
1632. Kirtland, p. 93.
1633. Kirtland, p. 93.
1634. Kirtland, pp. 93-94.
1635. Kirtland, p. 94.
1636. Tyson, p. 186.
1637. Kirtland, p. 94.
1638. Fox, pp. 240-241.
1639. Kirtland, p. 94.
1640. Kirtland, p. 94.
1641. Fox, p. 122.
1642. Carlisle, pp. 223-224. The title of this entry is mine (the editor, L.S.).
1643. Tyson, pp. 95-96.
1644. Kirtland, p. 10.
1645. Fisher, p. 57.
1646. Kirtland, p. 12.
1647. Kirtland, p. 11.
1648. Kirtland, p. 13.
1649. Fisher, pp. 56-57.
1650. Kirtland, p. 11.
1651. Kirtland, p. 12.
1652. Kirtland, p. 12.
1653. Kirtland, p. 13.
1654. Berdan, p. 13.
1655. Wilcox, p. 379.
1656. Fox, p. 51.
1657. Bryan, pp. 145-146.
1658. Kirtland, pp. 13-14.

1659. Fox, p. 52.
1660. Gregory, p. 66.
1661. Kirtland, p. 14.
1662. Tyson, pp. 98-99.
1663. Presbyterian Church, p. 8.
1664. Kirtland, p. 14.
1665. Randolph, pp. 64-65.
1666. Dennis, p. 146.
1667. Fox, p. 53.
1668. Gregory, p. 68.
1669. Ladies, p. 126.
1670. Bryan, p. 145.
1671. Norton, p. 43.
1672. Tyson, pp. 111-112.
1673. Wilcox, pp. 302-303.
1674. Kirtland, p. 14.
1675. Kirtland, pp. 14-15.
1676. Wilcox, p. 303.
1677. Wilcox, p. 303.
1678. Presbyterian Church, p. 10.
1679. Kirtland, p. 15.
1680. Ladies, p. 139.
1681. Kirtland, p. 16.
1682. Kirtland, p. 16.
1683. Kirtland, p. 16.
1684. Kirtland, pp. 16-17.
1685. Kirtland, p. 17.
1686. Kirtland, p. 17.
1687. Fox, p. 56.
1688. Fox, p. 59.
1689. Kirtland, p. 18.
1690. Fox, p. 52.
1691. Kirtland, p. 18.
1692. Tyson, p. 101.
1693. Gregory, p. 71.
1694. Gregory, p. 71.
1695. Randolph, p. 60.
1696. Tyson, p. 101.
1697. Bryan, p. 146.
1698. Ronald, p. 118.
1699. Kirtland, pp. 19-20.
1700. Wilcox, p. 155.
1701. Tyson, pp. 368-369.
1702. Kirtland, p. 20.
1703. Tyson, p. 102.
1704. Tyson, p. 104.
1705. Tyson, p. 104.
1706. Tyson, p. 104.
1707. Tyson, p. 105.
1708. Tyson, p. 106.
1709. Randolph, p. 57.
1710. Bryan, p. 142.
1711. Gregory, p. 90.
1712. Gregory, p. 91.

1713. Kirtland, p. 20.
1714. Ronald, p. 144.
1715. Gregory, p. 90.
1716. Kirtland, p. 21.
1717. Kirtland, p. 21.
1718. Gregory, p. 92.
1719. Gregory, p. 405.
1720. Gregory, p. 80.
1721. Tyson, p. 116.
1722. Tyson, p. 116.
1723. Carlisle, p. 134.
1724. Wilcox, p. 378.
1725. Wilcox, 157.
1726. Kirtland, p. 21.
1727. Fox, p. 51.
1728. Kirtland, p. 21.
1729. Randolph, pp. 67-68.
1730. Bryan, p. 157.
1731. Ronald, p. 133.
1732. Gregory, p. 82.
1733. Kirtland, p. 80.
1734. Dennis, p. 348. The title of this recipe is my creation, the author-editor, L.S.
1735. Gregory, p. 448.
1736. Gregory, p. 448.
1737. Kirtland, p. 84.
1738. Fox, p. 144.
1739. Ladies, p. 222.
1740. Carlisle, p. 65.
1741. Lochlainn Seabrook.
1742. Lochlainn Seabrook.
1743. McLaren, p. 12.
1744. Tyson, p. 377.
1745. Lochlainn Seabrook.
1746. Ladies, p. 298.
1747. Kirtland, pp. 4-5.
1748. Tyson, pp. 73-74.
1749. Tyson, pp. 92-93.
1750. McKinney and McKinney, p. 131.
1751. Fox, p. 45.
1752. Wilcox, p. 312.
1753. Fisher, p. 23.
1754. Fox, p. 41.
1755. Tyson, p. 76.
1756. Randolph, p. 17.
1757. Tyson, pp. 93-94.
1758. Tyson, p. 77.
1759. Kirtland, p. 5.
1760. Fisher, pp. 68-69.
1761. Berdan, p. 7.
1762. Fox, p. 43.
1763. Kirtland, p. 5.
1764. Wilcox, p. 318. The title of this recipe is my creation, the author-editor, L.S.
1765. Carlisle, p. 131.
1766. Ladies, p. 107.

1767. Randolph, p. 18.
1768. Bryan, pp. 12-13.
1769. Ronald, p. 95.
1770. Ronald, p. 95.
1771. Fisher, p. 61.
1772. Wilcox, p. 315.
1773. Fisher, p. 20
1774. Bryan, p. 11.
1775. Kirtland, p. 6.
1776. Kirtland, p. 6.
1777. Dennis, p. 133.
1778. Fox, pp. 34-35.
1779. Carlisle, p. 132.
1780. Gregory, p. 425. The title of this recipe is my creation, the author-editor, L.S.
1781. Bryan, p. 23. The title of this recipe is my creation, the author-editor, L.S.
1782. Fisher, pp. 20-21.
1783. Randolph, p. 19.
1784. Norton, pp. 35-36.
1785. Gregory, p. 63.
1786. Tyson, p. 84.
1787. Kirtland, p. 7.
1788. Wilcox, p. 316.
1789. Fisher, p. 22.
1790. Randolph, p. 89.
1791. Tyson, p. 84.
1792. Gregory, p. 62.
1793. Bryan, p. 26.
1794. Ronald, pp. 106-107.
1795. Norton, p. 37.
1796. Bryan, p. 26.
1797. Fox, p. 31.
1798. Tyson, p. 79.
1799. Randolph, pp. 16-17.
1800. Fox, p. 44.
1801. Gregory, pp. 60-61.
1802. Bryan, pp. 13-14.
1803. Ronald, p. 110.
1804. Fox, p. 33.
1805. Berdan, pp. 6-7.
1806. Kirtland, p. 8.
1807. Berdan, p. 4.
1808. Gregory, p. 54.
1809. Fox, p. 45.
1810. Fisher, p. 22.
1811. McLaren, p. 4.
1812. Bryan, p. 14.
1813. Tyson, p. 80.
1814. Fox, pp. 37-38.
1815. Tyson, p. 91.
1816. Randolph, p. 19.
1817. Ronald, p. 98.
1818. Kirtland, p. 8.
1819. Fox, p. 38.
1820. Fisher, pp. 22-23.

1821. Gregory, p. 54.
1822. Dennis, p. 128.
1823. Kirtland, p. 8.
1824. Fox, p. 32.
1825. Gregory, p. 57.
1826. Bryan, pp. 17-18.
1827. Tyson, p. 88.
1828. Kirtland, p. 8.
1829. Fisher, p. 23.
1830. Fox, p. 29.
1831. Kirtland, pp. 9-10.
1832. Fox, pp. 32-33.
1833. Ronald, pp. 102-103.
1834. Gregory, p. 56.
1835. Fox, p. 40.
1836. Tyson, p. 90.
1837. Tyson, pp. 89-90.
1838. Kirtland, p. 86.
1839. Tyson, pp. 204-205.
1840. Randolph, p. 98.
1841. Wilcox, pp. 336-337. The title of this recipe is my creation, the author-editor, L.S.
1842. Kirtland, p. 83.
1843. McKinney and McKinney, p. 137.
1844. McKinney and McKinney, p. 139.
1845. Kirtland, p. 83.
1846. Kirtland, p. 84.
1847. Wilcox, p. 339.
1848. Kirtland, p. 84.
1849. Bryan, p. 195.
1850. Tyson, p. 193.
1851. Kirtland, p. 84.
1852. Kirtland, p. 84.
1853. Fox, p. 144.
1854. Kirtland, p. 84.
1855. Fox, p. 145.
1856. Bryan, p. 197.
1857. Fox, p. 145.
1858. Kirtland, pp. 84-85.
1859. Kirtland, p. 85.
1860. Kirtland, p. 85.
1861. Kirtland, p. 85.
1862. Gregory, p. 458.
1863. Gregory, p. 458.
1864. Kirtland, pp. 85-86.
1865. Fisher, p. 69.
1866. Dennis, p. 239.
1867. Tyson, pp. 208-209.
1868. Gregory, p. 464.
1869. Kirtland, p. 87.
1870. Tyson, p. 201.
1871. Tyson, p. 202.
1872. Tyson, p. 202.
1873. Tyson, p. 202.
1874. Fox, p. 133.

1875. Kirtland, p. 87.
1876. Kirtland, p. 87.
1877. Bryant, p. 28.
1878. Randolph, p. 101.
1879. Kirtland, pp. 87-88.
1880. Kirtland, p. 88.
1881. Fox, pp. 137-138.
1882. Fox, p. 138.
1883. Presbyterian Church, p. 65.
1884. Kirtland, p. 88.
1885. Kirtland, p. 88.
1886. Fox, p. 148.
1887. Presbyterian Church, p. 60.
1888. Fox, p. 149.
1889. Fox, p. 149.
1890. Gregory, pp. 463-464. The title of this recipe is my creation, the author-editor, L.S.
1891. Fox, p. 149.
1892. Tyson, p. 318.
1893. Fox, p. 133.
1894. Kirtland, pp. 12-13.
1895. Dennis, pp. 358-359.
1896. Tyson, p. 191.
1897. Fox, p. 148.
1898. Fox, p. 148.
1899. Bryan, p. 221.
1900. Bryan, p. 221.
1901. McLaren, pp. 31-32.
1902. Fox, p. 148.
1903. Fox, pp. 141-142.
1904. Fox, p. 142.
1905. Randolph, pp. 108-109.
1906. Kirtland, p. 89.
1907. Kirtland, p. 89.
1908. Fox, p. 143.
1909. Fox, pp. 143-144.
1910. Fox, p. 134.
1911. Barringer, p. 34.
1912. Norton, p. 137.
1913. Bryan, p. 222.
1914. Kirtland, p. 89.
1915. Kirtland, p. 89.
1916. Kirtland, pp. 89-90.
1917. Kirtland, p. 90.
1918. McKinney and McKinney, p. 137.
1919. Kirtland, p. 90.
1920. Kirtland, p. 90.
1921. Ronald, p. 202.
1922. Kirtland, p. 90.
1923. Randolph, p. 109.
1924. Kirtland, p. 91.
1925. Bryan, p. 214.
1926. Kirtland, p. 91.
1927. Randolph, pp. 110-111.
1928. Dennis, p. 238.

1929. Dennis, p. 238.
1930. Fox, p. 134.
1931. Kirtland, p. 91.
1932. Fox, p. 134.
1933. Tyson, p. 194.
1934. Wilcox, p. 332.
1935. Ronald, p. 214.
1936. Norton, p. 129. The title of this recipe is my creation, the author-editor, L.S.
1937. Bryan, p. 206.
1938. Fox, p. 135.
1939. Bryan, p. 215.
1940. Fox, p. 140.
1941. Bryant, p. 63.
1942. McKinney and McKinney, p. 143.
1943. Ronald, p. 219.
1944. Tyson, p. 196.
1945. Randolph, p. 103.
1946. Berdan, p. 31.
1947. Randolph, p. 102.
1948. Tyson, p. 196.
1949. Randolph, p. 102.
1950. Wilcox, p. 332.
1951. Ronald, p. 219.
1952. Norton, p. 127.
1953. Tyson, p. 197.
1954. Tyson, p. 197. The title of this recipe is my creation, the author-editor, L.S.
1955. Tyson, pp. 197-198. The title of this recipe is my creation, the author-editor, L.S.
1956. Bryan, p. 161.
1957. Bryan, p. 162.

Waiting . . .

Bibliography

AND SUGGESTED READING

American Cookery (magazine). Boston, MA: The Boston Cooking School Magazine Co., 1924.

Barringer, Maria Massey. *Dixie Cookery: Or How I Managed my Table for Twelve Years - A Practical Cook-Book for Southern Housekeepers*. Boston, MA: A. K. Loring, 1867.

Berdan (and Company, pub.). *Chef Cook-Book*. Toledo, OH: Berdan and Co., 1912.

Browne, William M. (ed.). *The Southern Farm and Home* (magazine). November 1870, Vol. 2, No. 1. Macon, GA: J. W. Burke and Co., 1870.

Bryan, Mrs. Lettice. *The Kentucky Housewife*. No city, KY: self-published, 1839.

Bryant, Mrs. Annie Mae Wood (ed.). *Athens Woman's Club Cook Book*. Athens, GA: Athens Woman's Club, 1922.

Carlisle, Mrs. J. A. (committee chair). *Atlanta Women's Club Cook Book*. Atlanta, GA: Atlanta Women's Club, 1921.

Dennis, Annie E. *The New Annie Dennis Cook Book: A Compendium of Popular Household Recipes for the Busy Housewife*. Atlanta, GA: Mutual Publishing Co., 1901.

Dillon, John J. (ed.). *The Rural New-Yorker: A Journal for the Suburban and Country Home* (magazine). Vol. 71, No. 4162, August 3, 1912.

Fisher, Abby. *What Mrs. Fisher Knows About Old Southern Cooking, Soups, Pickles, Preserves, etc*. Mobile, AL: self-published, 1881.

Fox, Minnie C. (ed.). *The Blue Grass Cook Book*. New York: Duffield and Co., 1911.

Gregory, Annie R. *Woman's Favorite Cook Book*. Chicago, IL: Monarch Book Company, 1902.

Kirtland, Mrs. A. E. *New Southern Cook Book*. Montgomery, AL: self-published, 1906.

Ladies of Position and Influence (contributors). *The "Home Queen" Cook Book: Two Thousand Valuable Recipes on Cookery and Household Economy, Table Etiquette, Toilet, etc*. Chicago, IL: M. A. Donahue and Co., 1893.

McKinney, Emma, and William McKinney. *Aunt Caroline's Dixieland Recipes: A Rare Collection of Choice Southern Dishes*. Chicago, IL: Laird and Lee, 1922.

McLaren, Linie L. (ed.). *High Living: Recipes From Southern Climes*. San Francisco, CA: Paul Elder and Co., 1904.

Norton, Caroline Trask. *The Rocky Mountain Cook Book*. Denver, CO: self-published, 1903.

Presbyterian Church of Paris, Kentucky (The Ladies of the). *House-Keeping in the Blue Grass: A New and Practical Cook Book Containing Nearly a Thousand Recipes*. Cincinnati, OH: George E. Stevens and Co., 1875.

Randolph, Mary. *The Virginia Housewife; or, Methodical Cook*. Baltimore, MD: Plaskitt, Fite and Co., 1838.

Ronald, Mary. *The Century Cook Book*. New York: The Century Co., 1895.

Seabrook, Lochlainn. *The McGavocks of Carnton Plantation: A Southern History - Celebrating One of Dixie's Most Noble Confederate Families and Their Tennessee Home*. 2008. Franklin, TN, 2011 ed.

———. *Everything You Were Taught About the Civil War is Wrong, Ask a Southerner!* 2010. Franklin, TN: Sea Raven Press, revised 2019 ed.

———. *A Rebel Born: A Defense of Nathan Bedford Forrest*. 2010. Franklin, TN: Sea Raven Press, 2011 ed.

———. *The Quotable Jefferson Davis: Selections From the Writings and Speeches of the Confederacy's First President*. Franklin, TN: Sea Raven Press, 2011.

———. *Honest Jeff and Dishonest Abe: A Southern Children's Guide to the Civil War*. Franklin, TN: Sea Raven Press, 2012.

———. *The Old Rebel: Robert E. Lee As He Was Seen By His Contemporaries*. Spring Hill, TN: Sea Raven Press, 2012 Sesquicentennial Civil War Edition.

———. *The Quotable Stonewall Jackson: Selections From the Writings and Speeches of the South's Most Famous General*. Spring Hill, TN: Sea Raven Press, 2012 Sesquicentennial Civil War Edition.

———. *The Alexander H. Stephens Reader: Excerpts From the Works of a Confederate Founding Father*. Spring Hill, TN: Sea Raven Press, 2013.

———. *Jesus and the Law of Attraction: The Bible-Based Guide to Creating Perfect Health, Wealth, and Happiness Following Christ's Simple Formula*. Spring Hill, TN: Sea Raven Press, 2013.

———. *Everything You Were Taught About African-Americans and the Civil War is Wrong, Ask a Southerner!* Spring Hill, TN: Sea Raven Press, 2016.

———. *Nathan Bedford Forrest and African-Americans: Yankee Myth, Confederate Fact*. Spring Hill, TN: Sea Raven Press, 2016.

———. *Women in Gray: A Tribute to the Ladies Who Supported the Southern Confederacy*. Spring Hill, TN: Sea Raven Press, 2016.

———. *Rise Up and Call Them Blessed: Victorian Tributes to the Confederate Soldier, 1861-1901*. Spring Hill, TN: Sea Raven Press, 2017.

———. *The God of War: Nathan Bedford Forrest as He Was Seen by His Contemporaries*. Spring Hill, TN: Sea Raven Press, 2018.

———. *Heroes of the Southern Confederacy: The Illustrated Book of Confederate Officials, Soldiers, and Civilians*. Spring Hill, TN: Sea Raven Press, 2021.

Stefferud, Alfred (ed.). *The Yearbook of Agriculture 1965* (U.S. Dept. of Agriculture). Washington, D.C.: United States Government Printing Office, 1965.

Tyson, M. L. *The Queen of the Kitchen: A Collection of Southern Cooking Receipts*. Philadelphia, PA: T. B. Peterson and Brothers, 1886.

Wilcox, A. G. (pub.). *The Dixie Cook-Book: Carefully Compiled From the Treasured Family Collections of Many Generations of Noted Housekeepers: Largely Supplemented by Tested Recipes of the More Modern Southern Dishes, Contributed by Well-Known Ladies of the South*. Atlanta, GA; L. A. Clarkson and Co., 1885.

Williams, Robert F. *Food and Diet in Health and Disease*. Philadelphia, PA: Lea brothers, and Co., 1906.

Index

BEVERAGES

Acorn Coffee	25
Alexander H. Stephens Egg Nog	32
Almond Milk	41
Apple Wine	24
Beer	23
Black Coffee	24
Black Currant Wine	41
Blackberry Cordial	36
Blackberry Wine	38
Blockade Coffee	25
Blue Grass Apple Toddy	23
Bonnie Blue Egg Nog	32
Bourbon Whisky Punch	24
Brandy Peaches	35
Carolina Pineapple Punch	23
Champagne	30
Champagne Ice	36
Cherry Shrub	33
Chocolate Coffee	25
Claret Punch	28
Cocoa	38
Confederate Army Coffee	24
Confederate Brandy Peaches	37
Confederate Coffee	24
Confederate Egg Nog	31
Confederate Frozen Egg Nog	33
Confederate Milk Shake	31
Corn Beer	34
Cranberry Punch	26
Dandelion Wine	38
Drinking Water	21
Egg Nog	31
Elderberry Wine	41
Filtered Water	21
Frozen Egg Nog	32
Frozen Punch	35
Fruit Juices	22

Fruit Nectar 34
Fruit Punch 28
Gadsden Flag Egg Nog 32
Ginger Ale 30
Ginger Beer 31
Ginger Pop 30
Ginger Wine 38
Grape Fruit Cocktails 35
Grape Ice 36
Grape Wine 40
Hot Chocolate 38
Iced Tea 26
Lemon Brandy 27
Lemon Cordial 29
Lemonade 27
Louisiana Coffee 25
Madeira Ice 36
Mead 35
Milk 39
Milk Shake 39
Mint Cordial 36
Mint Julep 22
Mint Punch 26
Old-Fashioned Kentucky Toddy 23
Orange Ice 37
Orange Wine 40
Orange-Ade 27
Oyster Cocktail 30
Pineapple Julep 23
Punch 23
Raisin Wine 41
Raspberry Cordial 37
Raspberry Ice 37
Raspberry Wine 40
Rice Milk 41
Root Beer 1 33
Root Beer 2 33
Root Beer 3 33
Root Beer 4 33
Root Beer 5 34
Sangaree 37

Sassafras Mead 34
Scuppernong Wine 35
Sherry Cobbler 28
Southern Negus 40
Southern Tea 26
Strawberry Cordial 29
Strawberry Ice 37
Strawberry Wine 40
Swannee Fruit Punch 27
Tea 26
To Keep Cream 38
To Make Apple Cider 28
Tom and Jerry 29
Very Fine Egg Nog 31
Vienna Hot Chocolate 29
Wild Plum Cordial 36
Xalapa Punch 30

BREADS
Abby's Flannel Cake 64
Alabama Hoe Cake 53
Apple Rolls 58
Aunt Sally's Crackling Bread 61
Bannock 52
Batter Bread 61
Beaten Biscuit 59
Blueberry Muffins 51
Boiled, Baked or Steamed Roll 67
Bran Bread 62
Bread Cakes 66
Bread Making Rules 43
Breakfast Corn Bread 61
Buckwheat Cakes 67
Buttermilk Cakes 64
Buttermilk Muffins 64
Cheese Biscuits 58
Cheese Straws 60
Cheesed Crackers 47
Cinnamon Toast 45
Clabber Cakes 54
Confederate Cinnamon Rolls 46
Confederate Crackers 46

Confederate Graham Crackers	47
Confederate Wafers	54
Confederate Zwieback	54
Corn Bread	61
Corn Cakes	62
Corn Egg Bread	65
Corn Muffins	60
Cream Scones	52
Croutons	45
Crumpets	67
Dixie Biscuits	45
Drop Muffins	60
Dry Toast	45
Dry Yeast	43
Egg Bread	64
Egg Crackers	48
Elegant Rolls	49
English Muffins	60
Flannel Cakes	64
French Rolls	67
George Washington's Breakfast Cakes	50
Georgia Hoe Cake	53
Graham Bread	47
Graham Muffins	61
Hanover Rolls	57
Hoe Cake	53
Hominy Cakes	63
Hominy Muffins	63
Hot Corn Bread	63
Hot Cross Buns	56
How to Make Bread	44
How to Make Yeast	43
Indian Bread	50
Indian Flappers	51
Indian Muffins	51
Johnny Cake	50
Johnny Reb Cake	46
Kentucky Batter Bread	67
Kentucky Buttermilk Biscuits	51
Kentucky Corn Dodgers	48
Laplands	48

Light Bread	57
Light Indian Bread	52
Light Rolls	55
London Crumpets	60
Louisiana Rice Pone	59
Mammy's Graham Muffins	65
Maryland Beat Biscuit	47
Milk Biscuit	49
Milk Toast	45
Mrs. Matthews' Batter Cakes	64
Mt. Airy Beaten Biscuits	55
Muffins	59
Mush Cakes	68
New Orleans Nut Bread	54
Norwegian Sweet Bread	56
Nut Bread	54
Nut Cakes When We Were Children	65
Oatmeal Muffins	51
Old South Biscuits	45
Old Virginia Corn Batter-Bread	57
Old Virginia Loaf Bread	66
Owenden Bread	63
Parker House Rolls	68
Pizza of the Confederacy	50
Plantation Corn Bread	53
Pone Corn bread	65
Popovers	63
Potato Bread	67
Premium Crackers	52
Pretzels	50
Quick Muffins	64
Rice Bread	55
Rice Cakes	62
Rice Muffins	63
Rolls	55
Rusks	58
Rye Bread	62
Sally Lunn	66
Sally Lunn Bread Cake	66
Salt Rising Bread	62
Salt-Rising Bread	66

Sauce for Apple Rolls 59
Scottish Scones 53
Secession Wheat Crackers 46
Second Amendment Cinnamon Rolls 47
Soda Biscuit 49
Soda Biscuits 64
Sour Milk Biscuits 54
South Carolina Biscuits 57
Southern Beaten Biscuit 58
Southern Brown Bread 59
Southern Buttered Toast 44
Southern Corn Bread 53
Southern Sweet Potato Biscuits 49
Spoon Bread 62
Steam Pone 68
Sweet Rolls 55
Tea Biscuit 48
To Toast Bread 44
Vienna Rolls 56
Virginia Batter Bread 61
Washington Breakfast Cakes 68
Wheat Gems 63
Whole Wheat Bread 52
Yorkshire Pudding 57

CANDIES
Alice Chocolate Candy 72
Alice Molasses Candy 71
Alice Peanut Candy 71
Alice Sugar Candy 72
Brown Taffy 74
Butterscotch 72
Candied Orange and Lemon Peel 78
Candy Making Tips 70
Caramel Candy 77
Chocolate Caramels 71
Chocolate Drops 78
Chocolate Fudge 73
Cocoanut Balls 76
Cocoanut Brittle 78
Cocoanut Candy 73
Cocoanut Drops 75

Cocoanut Kisses 73
Confederate Cocoanut Drops 75
Cream Candy 76
Crystalized Popcorn 75
Divinity Candy 78
Egg Kisses 75
French Fondant 70
Fudge 72
Ground Pea Candy 71
Lemon Drops 75
Mammy's Peanut Candy 78
Maple Candy 79
Marshmallows 74
Molasses Taffy 76
New Orleans Pralines 72
Nut Creams 70
Nut Fritters 71
Old Virginia Molasses Taffy 73
Peanut Brittle 76
Peanut Brittle 1 77
Peanut Brittle 2 77
Peppermint Candy 76
Peppermint Drops 75
Peppermints 77
Pinochi 74
Popcorn Balls 76
Salt Water Taffy 74
Sugar Plums 79
Sugared Almonds 77
White Candy 71
CEREAL GRAINS
   Confederate Oatmeal 82
   Corn Meal Short Cake 84
   Cornmeal Mush 84
   Cracked Wheat 83
   Cream of Wheat 82
   Delicious Way to Cook Rice 81
   Hominy 84
   Oatmeal Fried 83
   Oatmeal Porridge 83
   Polenta 82

Risotto 82
Rolled Oats 83
Samp 84
South Carolina Rice 82
Southern Rice 81
Spanish Rice 84
Steamed Rice 84
CHEESE DISHES
Cheese and Egg Toast 90
Cheese Balls 89
Cheese Blocks 92
Cheese Chips 92
Cheese Fondu 1 88
Cheese Fondu 2 88
Cheese Fondue 3 88
Cheese Macaroni 88
Cheese Mousse 92
Cheese Omelet 89
Cheese Pudding 89
Cheese Ramequins 92
Cheese Salad 89
Cheese Souffle 89
Cheese Sticks 90
Cheese Straws 90
Cheese Toast 90
Cheese Toast With Milk 90
Confederate Cheese Pie 89
Confederate Cheese Toast 90
Frozen Cheese 91
Grated Cheese 88
Massa's Cheese Croquettes 91
Mexican Enchiladas 92
Rebel Cheesed Crackers 90
Sardine Rarebit 91
To Make Cheese 86
To Make Cottage Cheese 87
To Make Cream Cheese 87
Welsh Rarebit 1 91
Welsh Rarebit 2 91
CROQUETTES
Cheese Croquettes 96

Chicken Croquettes 95
Croquette Making Tips 95
Croquettes 95
Egg Croquettes 96
Fish Croquettes 97
Ham Croquettes 97
Oyster Croquettes 97
Plain Rice Croquettes 98
Potato Croquettes 1 97
Potato Croquettes 2 97
Potato Croquettes Stuffed 98
Sweetbread and Chicken Croquettes 96
Sweetbread and Mushroom Croquettes 96

DESSERTS
A Fine Cookie 183
African Sponge Drops 161
Alice Snow Balls 114
Allegheny Tea Cakes 182
Almond Cake 177
Almond Cake Filling 177
Almond Ice Cream 137
Almond Icing 171
Almond Macaroons 184
Almond Mandalines 123
Almond Pudding 115
Almond Wafers 161
American Indian Baked Pudding 115
American Indian Pudding 115
Angel Cake 156
Angel Food Cake 157
Angel Parfait 136
Apple Ice Cream 138
Apple Trifle 133
Apricot Custard Pudding 125
Apricot Ice Cream 138
Arkansas Angel Cake 157
Augusta Pudding 110
Baked Bonbons 176
Balloons 174
Banana Cake 167
Banana Ice Cream 146

Banana Pudding	140
Banana Sherbet	144
Bananas and Cream	110
Bananas and Wine	129
Bavarian Cream With Almonds	107
Betsy Ross Pound Cake	128
Bird's Nest Pudding	127
Biscuit Glace	134
Biscuit Tortoni	133
Biveau Cream	104
Black Cake	159
Black Pudding	111
Blackberry Cake	165
Blackberry Sponge	119
Blanc Mange	132
Blue Grass Corn Pudding	110
Blue Grass Plum Cake	166
Blue Grass Pudding	111
Blue Grass White Cake	166
Boiled Custard	120
Boiled Frosting	190
Bombe Glace	145
Bread Pudding	117
Breakfast Cream Cake	104
Bride's Cake	155
Brown Betty	162
Brown Mange	131
Brownies	186
Buttermilk Ice Cream	106
Cabin Cake	126
Cake Pyramid	104
Caramel Cake	160
Caramel Custard Pudding	120
Caramel Ice Cream	141
Caramel Icing	172
Caraway Cookies	182
Carolas	175
Carrot Pudding	117
Charlotte Russe Filling	145
Charlotte Russe Pudding	109
Cheese Cake	122

Cheese Ice Cream	107
Cherry Ice Cream	136
Cherry Pudding	114
Chestnuts With Whipped Cream	127
Chocolate Bavarian Cream	107
Chocolate Blanc Mangue	128
Chocolate Cake	168
Chocolate Cream Cake	172
Chocolate Eclairs	111
Chocolate Frosting	170
Chocolate Ice Cream	143
Chocolate Icing	190
Chocolate Layer Cake	149
Chocolate Marshmallow Cake	166
Chocolate Milk Float	113
Chocolate Mousse	140
Chocolate Nut Cake	170
Chocolate Pudding	120
Chocolate Sauce	129
Chocolate Souffle	129
Chocolate Syrup for Vanilla Ice Cream	106
Christmas Plum Pudding	164
Citron Ice Cream	136
Cocoanut Balls	185
Cocoanut Cake	168
Cocoanut Cakes	186
Cocoanut Drop Cookies	185
Cocoanut Ice Cream	143
Cocoanut Macaroons	185
Cocoanut Pudding	119
Coffee Cake	179
Coffee Ice Cream	142
Confederate Almond Wafers	185
Confederate Cakes	100
Confederate Cupcakes	112
Confederate Daughters Cake	148
Confederate Delicate Cake	169
Confederate Fruit Cake Frosting	189
Confederate Jumbles	100
Confederate Marshmallow Filling	180
Confederate Marshmallow Frosting	180

Confederate Mountain Cake	167
Confederate Pineapple Ice Cream	146
Confederate Sponge Cake	158
Confederate White Fruit Cake	152
Cookies	183
Cottage Pudding	112
Cranberry Pudding	128
Cream Boulet	109
Cream Filling	172
Cream Icing	190
Cream Meringue Pudding	121
Cream Sponge Cake	173
Crullers	149
Cup Cake	165
Dandy Cakes	180
Danish Pudding	106
Date Bars	181
Deep South Cupcakes	112
Delicate Cake	156
Devils Food Cake	157
Dixie Cream Cakes	101
Dixie Pudding	100
Doughnuts	187
Dried Apple Cake	163
East Indian Pudding	115
Egg Cream	122
Election Cake	126
Elegant Cake	156
English Apple Pudding	118
English Banbury Cake	168
English Christmas Pudding	107
English Plum Pudding	121
English Tea Cakes	183
English Walnut Cake	154
Excellent Marble Cake	154
Excelsior Fruit Cake	151
Fairy Gingerbread	185
Fancy Cake	172
Feather Cake	173
Feather Pudding	116
Fig Cake Filling	177

Figs Stewed in Claret	127
Filling for Baltimore Cake	170
Fine Frosting	189
Fine Vanilla Ice Cream	141
Float	189
Florida Cake	122
Flummery	111
Freezing Cream	134
Fried Cream Fritters	188
Fried Doughnuts	188
Frontier Cake	127
Frozen Custard	143
Frozen Gelatine	141
Frozen Mint	145
Frozen Pudding	141
Frozen Watermelon	135
Fruit Cake	152
Fruit Cake Frosting	153
Fruit Cookies	177
Fruit Ice Cream	134
Fruit Layer Cake	176
Fruit Snaps	183
Fruit Trifle	133
Gateau A La Wickesser	158
Gelatine Ice Cream	135
General Abe Buford's Cake	150
General Forrest's Vanilla Ice Cream	141
General Lee Jelly Cake	104
General Stonewall Jackson Jumbles	101
Geneva Cream	124
Genovese Cake	165
German Layer Pudding	117
Ginger Bread	178
Ginger Cookies	177
Ginger Ice	146
Ginger Ice Cream	146
Ginger Pound Cake	178
Ginger Pudding	118
Ginger Sherbet	144
Ginger Snaps	178
Glace Cream	135

Gold Cake	162
Golden Cake	163
Gooseberry Fool	128
Grandmother's Pound Cake	162
Granola Cake	103
Grape Ice Cream	142
Grape Sherbet	144
Grape Trifle	133
Grated Sweet Potato Pudding	119
Hard Times Cake	176
Harlequin Cake	172
Hasty Pudding	130
Health Cookies	184
Hedgehog Trifle	132
Hermits	182
Hickory Nut Cake	167
Homemade Baking Powder	188
Honey Cake	184
Honey Cakes	122
Hot Chocolate Sauce	120
How to Make Frosting	105
Ice Cream 1	138
Ice Cream 2	139
Ice Cream 3	139
Ice Cream 4	139
Ice Cream Cake	173
Iced Chocolate	103
Ideal Sponge Cake	160
Imperial Cake	153
Italian Cream	104
Jack in the Box	117
Jam Cake	165
Jeff Davis Pudding	101
Jefferson Davis Jumbles	101
Jelly Cake	175
Jelly Roll	158
Jumbals	127
Jumble Cake	150
Jumbles	183
Kentucky Cake	174
Kentucky Cream	119

Kentucky Pudding	125
Kentucky White Cake	155
Kewpies	185
Knots	188
Ladies' Cake	109
Lady Baltimore Cake	170
Lady Fingers	131
Lady Lee Pudding	101
Lemon Cheese Cake	156
Lemon Cheese Filling	170
Lemon Filling	179
Lemon Ice Cream	138
Lemon Jelly for Harlequin Cake	173
Lemon Pudding	114
Lemon Sherbet	144
Lemon Snaps	187
Lemon Trifle	133
Macaroon Cream	133
Macaroons	131
Mammy's Sweet Potato Pudding	103
Maple Ice Cream	137
Maple Mousse	140
Maple Parfait 1	137
Maple Parfait 2	137
Maroons With Whipped Cream	131
Marshmallow Cake	124
Marshmallow Chocolate Cake	169
Marshmallow Filling	124
Marshmallow Frosting	169
Marshmallow Ice Cream	136
Mason and Dixon Cookies	152
Metropolitan Ice Cream	142
Mobile Fruit Cake	151
Mocha Cake	149
Molasses Cookies	182
Molasses Pie	106
Montgomery Pudding	110
Moravian Cake	183
Mother's Cake	167
Mountain Cake	162
Mrs. Abercrombie's Pudding	116

Mrs. Boykin's Fruit Cake	149
Mrs. Henry Clay's Drop Cakes	176
Nashville Pepper-nuts	100
Neapolitan Cake	168
New Orleans Tea Cake	125
Nondescripts	188
Norfolk Tea Cake	153
North Carolina Jumbles	103
Nut and Raisin Cake	151
Oatmeal Cookies	182
Oatmeal Pudding	190
Old Dominion Cake	124
Old Virginia Christmas Cake	181
Old Virginia Fruit Cake	151
Old-Time Ginger Cake	176
One-Two-Three-Four Pudding	120
Orange Bavarian Cream	127
Orange Cake	173
Orange Cake Filling	173
Orange Cream	126
Orange Ice	147
Orange Ice Cream	135
Orange Icing	189
Orange Sherbet	144
Orange Souffle	174
Order of Confederate Rose Sponge Pudding	109
Oriental Icing	190
Palmetto Cake	153
Park Street Cake	167
Peach Charlotte	123
Peach Cobbler	105
Peach Ice Cream	143
Peach Trifle	132
Pear Ice Cream	136
Pecan Cake	187
Pecan Kisses	187
Peppermint Ice Cream	134
Perfection Cake	163
Pfeffernuss	186
Pickaninny Cookies	126
Picnic Cake	163

Pineapple Ice Cream 134
Pineapple Mousse 142
Pineapple Omelet 126
Pineapple Sherbet 139
Pink Icing 171
Pistachio Cake 176
Pistachio Ice Cream 177
Plain Chocolate Icing 190
Plain Spice Cake 179
Plantation Cookies 130
Plum Cake 181
Plum Pudding Glace 139
Pound Cake 162
Pound Cake of Cottolene 163
Prairie Cake 165
Pride of Kentucky Cake 125
Pride of the Confederacy White Cake 155
Prune Pudding 131
Pumpkin Pudding 114
Queen Cake 179
Queen of Trifles 132
Raisin Pudding 123
Raspberry Ice Cream 134
Raspberry Sherbet 145
Raw Icing for Decorating 189
Rice Cream With Fruit 129
Rice Pudding 119
Richmond Cake 153
Robert E. Lee Cake 160
Robert E. Lee Jelly Cake 153
Rochester Jelly Cake 175
Rocks 186
Rolled Sponge Cake 160
Roman Punch 146
Rules fo Cake Making 147
Sand Cakes 186
Savory Cakes of Olden Times 184
Scotch Cake 109
Scotch Cakes 107
Scotch Pudding 108
Scripture Cake 161

Silver Cake	154
Simple White Cup Cake	153
Snow Cake	163
Snow Cream	125
Snow Flakes	114
Snow Pudding	114
Soda Cakes	165
Soft Ginger Bread	178
Soft Ginger Cake	178
Soft Molasses Cookies	106
Soft Sponge Gingerbread	185
Sons of Confederate Veterans Bluegrass Cake	102
Souffle Float	129
Souffle Pudding	121
South Carolina Curds	146
Southern Birthday Cake	150
Southern Fruit Cake	108
Southern Heritage Corn Pudding	110
Southern Pudding	144
Southern Rights Cake	102
Southern Seed Cake	103
Spanish Cream	113
Spiders	175
Splendid Pudding	120
Sponge Cake	111
Squash Pudding	118
Steamed Huckleberry Pudding	161
Steamed White Pudding	115
Stonewall Jackson Pudding	101
Strawberry Cake	167
Strawberry Ice Cream	142
Strawberry Parfait	112
Strawberry Sauce	129
Strawberry Sherbet	145
Strawberry Short Cake	105
Sue's Snow Balls	172
Sugar Cookies	182
Sugar Glaze	158
Sugar Glazi	190
Sugar Syrup	142
Sunshine Cake	158

Swedish Pudding 123
Sweet Potato Pudding 118
Sweet Wafers 187
Tapioca Cream 113
Tapioca Custard Pudding 113
Tapioca Pudding 112
Tea Cakes 182
Tea Ice Cream 142
Tennessee Cake 105
Thanksgiving Fruit Cake 108
Tipsy Parson 116
Tutti-Frutti Ice Cream 145
Tuxedo Wafers 187
United Confederate Veterans Chocolate 103
United Daughters of the Confederacy Pudding ... 102
Vanilla Cream 169
Vanilla Ice Cream 141
Vanilla Parfait 137
Velvet Cream 121
Virginia Dare Pudding 146
Virginia Doughnuts 130
Virginia Plum Pudding 116
Virginia Pudding 113
Virginia Sponge Cake 161
Whipped Cream 121
White Charlotte 108
White Cream Caramel Filling 180
White Fruit Cake 169
White Icing 170
White Layer Cake 163
White Mountain Cake 156
White Mountain Icing 189
White Pound Cake 156
White Sponge Cake 110
White Sugar Cookies 161
Yam Pudding 118
Yellow Icing 171

DUMPLINGS
   Apple Dumplings 192
   Bird Dumplings 195
   Blackberry Dumplings 193

Cherry Dumplings 193
Chicken Dumplings 194
Cranberry Dumplings 194
Indian Dumplings 195
Light Dumplings 194
Peach Dumplings 193
Rice Dumplings 194
Strawberry Dumplings 192
Suet Dumplings 195

EGGS
   Baked Eggs 198
   Celery Eggs 206
   Confederate Creamed Eggs 206
   Confederate Pickled Eggs 202
   Confederate Tomato Omelet 206
   Convent Eggs 203
   Corn Omelet 201
   Creamed Eggs 198
   Curried Eggs 204
   Deviled Eggs 205
   Dressed Eggs 199
   Dropped Eggs 199
   Egg Batter 198
   Egg Butter 204
   Egg Nog 203
   Egg Pie 204
   Egg Rolls 203
   Eggs A LA Havana 207
   Eggs and Bacon 206
   Eggs and Beef 202
   Eggs and Cheese 200
   Eggs in Tomato Cups 204
   Eggs on Toast 201
   Eggs With Cheese 205
   French Omelet 206
   French Toast 202
   Fried Eggs 204
   Hard Boiled Eggs 198
   Hungarian Eggs 199
   Mushroom Omelet 202
   Omelet 200

Omelet Souffle 200
Onion Eggs 206
Oyster Omelet 204
Pickled Eggs 199
Plain Omelet 200
Poached Eggs 206
Potted Eggs 203
Quaker Omelet 201
Roasted Eggs 205
Scalloped Eggs 198
Scrambled Eggs 199, 205
Shirred Eggs 202
Soft Boiled Eggs 198
Spanish Omelet 201
Steamed Eggs 205
Stuffed Eggs 203
Swiss Eggs 201
To Boil Eggs 198
To Choose Eggs 197
To Keep Eggs 197
Tomato Omelet 200
Vegetable Omelets 206
Whirled Eggs 203
ENTREES
  Boudins A La Richelieu 212
  Brain Patties 214
  Brain Timbales 217
  Brains on Toast 212
  Brains With Brown Batter 213
  Breaded Calves Brains 214
  Broiled Sweetbreads 210, 211
  Chicken A La Dreuse 217
  Chicken Cutlets 209, 210
  Chicken Liver With Wine 215
  Chicken Pates 216
  Chicken Picante 216
  Chicken Terrapin 217
  Coquille De Volaille 216
  Crabs or Shrimp Baked in Bell Pepper 215
  Cream Sauce for Calves Brains 214
  Cream Shrimp in Cases 215

Creamed Dishes 214
  Creamed Mushrooms 213
  Creme De Volaille 210
  Deviled Dishes 216
  Deviled Salmon 218
  Deviled Tomatoes 218
  Fried Brains 212
  Fried Sweetbreads 211
  Green Peppers Stuffed With Corn 211
  How to Garnish Sweetbreads 211
  Meat Stew Entree 209
  Montebello Sauce 211
  Mushroom Sauce 209
  Pepper Baskets 218
  Pressed Chicken 217
  Quenelles 216
  Rissoles 218
  Sauce for Entrees 209
  Sausage and Cabbage 212
  Scrambled Brains on Toast 213
  Stuffed Eggplant 213
  Stuffed Tomatoes 212
  Supreme of Chicken 209
  Sweetbreads A La Bechemel 210
  Sweetbreads A La Cream 211
  Sweetbreads A La Montebella 211
  Veal Olives 215
  Virginia Ham 213
FRITTERS
  Alabama Rice Fritters 221
  Apple Fritters 221
  Bell Fritters 223
  Bread Fritters 223
  Clam Fritters 223
  Confederate Apple Fritters 223
  Corn Fritters 221
  Egg Plant Fritters 1 223
  Egg Plant Fritters 2 223
  Fish Fritters 224
  Fritter Batter 221
  Fritter Making Tip 221

Fruit Fritters 222
Orange Fritters 222
Pineapple Fritters 222
Sauce for Fritters 222
Shrimp Fritters 222
Spanish Fritters 224
Spinach Fritters 223
Virginia Corn Fritters 222

FRUITS
Apple and Plum Pudding 230
Apple Dumplings 227
Apple Meringue 228
Apple Pudding 228
Apple Sauce 229
Apples With Whipped Cream 228
Baked Apples 228
Blackberry Dumplings 227
Blackberry Pudding 227
Boiled Raisin Pudding 231
Cranberry Sauce 226
Delicious Plum Pudding 230
Drawn Butter Sauce 228
Dried Fruit 232
Fig Pudding 231
Florida Grapefruit 231
Fried Apples 226
Fried Bananas 230
Fruit Dumplings 227
Fruit Pudding 231
Orange Pudding 232
Pineapple Pudding 227
Plum Pudding 229
Plum Pudding Croquettes 230
Porcupine Apples 228
Prune Pudding 229
Scalloped Apples 226
Strawberries With Whipped Cream 227
Strawberry Puff Pudding 231
The Queen of Plum Puddings 229
To Bake Apples 226
To Prepare Apples 228

Vegetarian Plum Pudding 230

HEALING RECIPES

A Nourishing Preparation for Infants 237
A Preparation for the Sick 237
Apple Water 238
Arrowroot 238
Arrowroot Jelly 243
Barley Water 238
Batter Cakes 241
Beef Essence 235
Beef Jelly 235
Beef Tea 239
Blackberry Jelly for Sickness 237
Boiled Milk 242
Bread Jelly 243
Broiled Partridges 241
Butterscotch for a Cold 238
Chicken Broth 240
Chicken Jelly 235
Chicken Soup for the Sick 234
Chicken Tea 240
Clotted Milk 243
Confederate Apple Water 244
Confederate Cough Syrup 242
Confederate Rice Jelly 244
Confederate Tapioca Jelly 244
Corn Meal Gruel for Invalids 237
Cornmeal Gruel 235
Cough Drops 238
Cough Mixture 239
Cough Syrup 244
Custard 243
Egg Nog for the Sick 241
For Severe Cold 239
Hot Milk for Invalids 237
Hotch-Potch 243
Indian Gruel 244
Lemon for a Cough 239
Lime Water 244
Milk Porridge 242
Milk Toast 242

Mush 236
Mutton Broth 235
Oatmeal Coffee 237
Orange and Lemon Juice 245
Panada 236
Partridge Panada 241
Partridge Tea 240
Raisin Porridge 243
Remarks 234
Rice 242
Rice Jelly 237
Rice Milk 242
Sago Cream 238
Sago Jelly 238
Soft Boiled Eggs for Invalids 237
Soup for an Invalid 239
Squirrel Soup 240
Tapioca Jelly 239
Thickened Milk 236
Tonic Bitter 235
Wine Whey 238
JELLIES AND PRESERVES
  Apple Butter 251
  Apple Jelly 251
  Apple Marmalade 261
  Apricot Jelly 254
  Blackberry Jam 258
  Blackberry Jelly 253
  Cherry Preserves 255
  Citron Preserves 259
  Confederate Crab Apple jelly 262
  Confederate Fig Preserves 255
  Confederate Peach Preserves 256
  Confederate Preserved Limes 257
  Crab Apple Jelly 259
  Cranberry Jelly 263
  Crystalized Cantaloupes 248
  Currant Jelly 262
  Dundee Orange Marmalade 261
  Evaporated Apple Jelly 253
  Fig Preserves 255

Florida Nectarine Preserves 253
French Jam 260
Fruit Jelly 251
Grape Jelly 262
Guava Jelly 252
Guava Marmalade 260
Jelly Making Tips 247
Maypops 252
Mrs. Arrington's Fig Preserves 258
Orange jam 248
Orange Jelly 247
Orange Marmalade 254
Orange Preserves 254
Peach Butter 256
Peach Jam 256
Peach Jelly 248
Peach Marmalade 255
Peach Preserves 250
Pear and Quince Preserves 262
Pear Jelly 260
Pear Preserves 256
Pigs' Feet Jelly 253
Pineapple Jelly 253
Pineapple Preserves 259
Plum Jelly 248
Preserved Apricots 261
Preserved Lemons 257
Preserved Limes 250
Preserved Oranges 249
Preserved Peaches 249
Preserved Pears 250
Preserved Pineapple 250
Pumpkin Chips 258
Quince Jelly 262
Quince Marmalade 254
Raspberry Jam 254
Raspberry Preserves 258
Scuppernong Jelly 252
Strawberry Jam 257
Strawberry Preserves 259
Sugared Peaches 257

Syrups for Preserves 248
To Can Peaches 262
Tomato Jelly 258
Watermelon Preserves 260
Wild Plum Jelly 253
Wine Jelly 259
MEATS
   A Mexican Dish 287
   Alice's Meat in Individual Dishes 296
   Alice's Scalloped Meat 296
   Bacon 286
   Baked Chicken 273
   Baked Ham 270
   Baked Hash 286
   Baked Lamb 276
   Beef A La Mode 269
   Beef Kidneys 281
   Beef Steak Pie 269
   Beefsteak and Kidney 281
   Beefsteak Pie 272
   Beefsteak With Mushrooms 292
   Beefsteak With Onions 279
   Blue Grass Recipe for Roast Quail 309
   Boiled Corned Beef 298
   Boiled Ham 284
   Boiled Mutton 271
   Boiled Tripe 299
   Boned Turkey 303
   Broiled Beefsteak 274
   Broiled Chicken 1 302
   Broiled Chicken 2 302
   Broiled Ham and Eggs 288
   Broiled Liver 285
   Broiled Partridges 309
   Broiled Pheasant 310
   Broiled Pigeon 308
   Broiled Quails 293
   Broiled Squirrel 310
   Broiled Steak 279
   Broiled Venison 279
   Brown Fricassee of Chicken 305

Brunswick Stew	278
Camp Stew	293
Chicken A La King	273
Chicken Croquettes	298
Chicken Pie	304
Chicken Pudding	305
Chicken Salad	273
Confederate Chicken Pie	306
Confederate Hamburg Steak	280
Confederate Pigs in a Blanket	271
Confederate Roast Beef	290
Confederate Roast Turkey	306
Corn Beef Hash	298
Corned Beef	297
Corned Beef Hash	281
Corned Shoat	278
Crab Croquettes	309
Creamed Chicken	292
Curried Chicken	305
Curry Powder for Meats and Pastas	305
Deviled Ham	284
Domestic Duck	294
Domestic Ducks	310
Dried Liver	286
Dutch Pudding	290
French Chops	284
Fried Chicken 1	300
Fried Chicken 2	300
Fried Chicken 3	300
Fried Chicken 4	300
Fried Chicken 5	301
Fried Chicken 6	301
Fried Chicken 7	301
Fried Chicken and Cauliflower	301
Fried Frogs' Legs	280
Fried Ham and Eggs	271
Fried Liver and Bacon	282
Fried Pigs' Feet	280
Fried Salt Pork	289
Frogs	280
Goose Pie	295

Gravy	290
Grilled Rabbit	309
Ham Omelet	282
Ham Pie	283
Hamburger	278
Hash	293
Hash From Cold Meat	297
How to Corn Beef	297
How to Make Country Pork Sausages	285
Hunters' Beef	275
Irish Mutton Stew	282
Irish Stew	277
Jambalaya	272
Kentucky Baked Ham	283
Lamb Chops	276
Liver Croquettes	296
Mammy's Chicken Patties	299
Mammy's Veal Loaf	303
Meat Balls	277
Meat Cakes	284
Meat Pie	295
Meat Pot Pie	280
Meat Souffle	296
Mexican Chile Con Carne	285
Mince Meat	273
Mince Meat for Pies	274
Mississippi Sausage	290
Mutton Chops	277
Mutton Cutlets	277
Mutton Hash	275
Mutton Pie	295
Old Virginia Chicken Pie	306
Partridge Pie	309
Pepper Pot	299
Pigeon Pie	307
Pigs in a Blanket	271
Pork and Beans	286
Pork Chops	278
Pork Roast	286
Pork Tenderloins	274
Pot Roast	293

Prairie Chickens	311
Pressed Chicken	303
Quail on Toast	307
Quail With Truffles	307
Quails	293
Rabbit Pie	308
Rabbit Roasted	308
Rabbit Stew	308
Ragout of Beef	298
Recipe for Curing Hams	270
Roast Beef	281
Roast Chicken	291
Roast Duck	294
Roast Goose	295
Roast Lamb	281
Roast Leg of Mutton	275
Roast Mutton	272
Roast Opossum and Sweet Potatoes	277
Roast Pig	285
Roast Pigeon	307
Roast Spare-Rib	281
Roast Turkey	291
Roast Veal	287
Roast Veal Fillet	287
Roast Venison	279
Roast Woodcock and Snipe	311
Roasted Fowls	310
Roasted Grouse	294
Roasted Pheasant	307
Saddle of Mutton	276
Salt Pork	285
Sauce for Boiled Fish or Boiled Mutton	272
Scrapple	292
Shoat Steaks	282
Souse	296
Southern Chicken Pie	304
Southern Fried Chicken	299
Southern Hash	303
Spanish Fried Steak	293
Spiced Ham	284
Spiced Round	269

Squirrel Pie	310
Steamed Chicken 1	302
Steamed Chicken 2	302
Stewed Chicken	304
Stewed Duck	294
Stuffed Ham	270
Stuffing for Poultry	307
Sugar-Cured Hams	283
To Barbecue Meat	273
To Boil a Ham	282
To Boil a Turkey or Chicken	292
To Bone a Turkey	291
To Broil a Chicken	302
To Choose Meats and Fowls	265
To Cook a Lamb	276
To Roast a Goose	310
To Roast Beef	289
Toad in the Hole	299
Turkey Dressing	306
Turkey Stuffing	307
Veal Chops	288
Veal Cutlets	289
Veal Loaf	293
Veal Pie	289
Venison	279
White Fricassee of Chicken	305
White Pudding	290
Wild Duck	294

PANCAKES AND WAFFLES

Battle of Chickamauga Waffles	318
Berlin Pancakes	314
Buckwheat Cakes	317
Carolina Flapjacks	314
Confederate French Pancakes	318
Corn Meal Griddle Cakes	318
Corn Waffles	316
English Pancakes	317
Feathery Flapjacks	317
French Pancakes	313
Fruit Pancakes	313
General Beauregard Batter Cakes	314

General Forrest's Flapjacks ... 314
Hominy Waffles ... 318
Indian Griddle Cakes ... 317
Jolly Boys ... 319
Martha Washington Waffles ... 316
Oatmeal Griddle Cakes ... 318
Old Fashioned Waffles ... 316
Pancakes ... 313
Pride of Tennessee Griddle Cakes ... 318
Quick Waffles ... 316
Rice Griddle Cakes ... 317
Rice Pancakes ... 317
Rice Waffles ... 316
Snow Pancakes ... 318
Sweet Pancakes ... 313
Waffles 1 ... 315
Waffles 2 ... 315
Waffles 3 ... 315
Waffles 4 ... 315
Waffles 5 ... 316
Waffles for Breakfast ... 315

PASTAS
Baked Macaroni ... 321
Farce for Ravioli ... 325
How to Cook Macaroni ... 321
How to Make Noodles ... 321
Italian Macaroni Southern Style ... 322
Italian Spaghetti ... 324
Macaroni ... 321
Macaroni A La Creme ... 323
Macaroni and Cheese ... 322
Macaroni Pudding ... 323
Macaroni With Eggs ... 323
Macaroni With Tomato Sauce ... 322
Mexican Spaghetti ... 324
Mrs. Matthews' Macaroni ... 322
Noodle Balls ... 325
Noodles ... 324
Noodles for Soup ... 325
Noodles Served as a Vegetable ... 325
Patriot's Macaroni ... 322

Ravioli	325
Spaghetti	323
Vermicelli	323
PASTRIES, PIES, AND CUSTARDS	348
A Good and Simple Paste	330
A Kentucky Girl's Pumpkin Pie	335
Appalachian Banana Pie	332
Apple or Squash Fanchonettes	336
Apple Pie	336
Apple Tarts	336
Baker's Custard Pie	345
Banana Cream Pie	347
Banana Custard	339
Banbury Tarts	349
Blackberry Pie	350
Blue Grass Pastry	329
Caledonian Cream	333
Caramel Custard	342
Chautauqua Pumpkin Pie	335
Cheese Pie	349
Cherry Pie	338
Cherry Tarts	340
Chess Cakes	347
Chocolate Cream Pie	348
Chocolate Custard	343
Chocolate Pie	343
Cocoanut Custards	346
Cocoanut Pie	346
Cocoanut Tartlets	350
Confederate Chocolate Custard	345
Confederate Whipped Cream Pie	349
Cracker Pie	334
Cranberry Pie	348
Cranberry Tarts	340
Cream Apple Pie	331
Cream Filling	351
Cream Pie	348
Cream Puffs	351
Custard Pie	345
Date Pie	346
Delicious Cocoanut Custards	347

Easy Pie Crust	331
Ethereal Apple Pie	333
Food for the Gods	341
Fruit Filling	351
Gooseberry and Cherry Pies	333
Gooseberry Custard	341
Grape Tarts	341
Huckleberry Pie	350
Irish Potato Custard	345
Irish Potato Pie	337
Isinglass Cream	337
Jeff Davis Pie	329
Jefferson Davis Custard	329
Jefferson Davis Pie	329
Kentucky Butterscotch Pie	343
Lemon Cheese Pie	339
Lemon Custard	339
Lemon Pie 1	338
Lemon Pie 2	338
Lemon Pie 3	338
Lemon Pie 4	338
Lemon Pie 5	338
Lemon Pie 6	339
Lemon Pie 7	339
Lemon Pies	331
Light Bread Pie	334
Marlboro Tarts	349
Marmalade Tart	350
Mince Pies	334
Molasses Custard	334
Mountain Nectar	334
Mrs. Matthews' Custard Pie	345
Neapolitans	346
Nutmeg Pie	346
Old-Fashioned Apple Pie	349
Orange Cheese Pie	342
Orange Custard	342
Orange Meringue Pie	347
Orange Pie	342
Orange Short Cake	350
Pastry for Making Pies of All Kinds	328

Pastry Making Tips 328
Peach Tarts 341
Pie Crust 330
Pineapple Custard 332
Pineapple Meringue Custard 347
Pineapple Meringue Tarts 347
Plain Paste 331
Preparing the Fruit for Pies 329
Puff Paste 330
Pumpkin Pie 335
Raspberry Cream 333
Rhubarb Pie 344
Short Cake 349
Sliced Apple Pie 337
Southern Apple Pie 337
Southern Pastry 329
Southern Tomato Pie 345
St. Honore Cream 346
Strawberry Cream 333
Strawberry Cream Crusts 332
Strawberry Shortcake 336
Strawberry Tarts 340
Sweet Potato Custard 344
Sweet Potato Pie 1 344
Sweet Potato Pie 2 344
Sweet Potato Pie 3 344
Sweet Wafers 333
Swiss Cream 337
Syllabub 343
Syrup Custard 342
To Bake Puff Paste 331
Transparent Custard 334
Uncle John's Puff Paste 332
Vanilla Custard 339
Whipped Cream Pie 335
Whortleberry Pie 336

PICKLING AND CATSUPS
Blue Grass Green Tomato Pickle 355
Cauliflower Pickles 362
Cherry Chutney 357
Chow Chow 1 357

Chow Chow 2 357
Cider Vinegar 354
Corn Relish 361
Cucumber Catsup 360
Cucumber Pickles 362
Game Sauce 361
Green Mango Pickles 362
Green Pickle 355
Mushroom Catsup 360
Piccalilli 361
Pickled Bell Peppers 363
Pickled Eggs 361
Pickled Red Cabbage 359
Plain Pickles 354
Plum Chutney 357
Spanish Pickle 356
Stuffed Cucumbers 361
Sweet Mango Pickles 358
Sweet Peach Pickle 359
Sweet Pickles 355
Sweet Watermelon Rind Pickle 358
Tar Heel Chow Chow 357
Tarragon Vinegar 354
To Make Pickles 353
To Make Vinegar 354
Tomato Catsup 1 360
Tomato Catsup 2 360
Virginia Yellow Pickle 359
Walnut Catsup 363
Yellow Pickle 356

SALAD DRESSINGS
  Boiled Dressing 381
  Bottled Salad Dressing 378
  Cocoanut for Garnishing Salads 380
  Cooked Mayonnaise 381
  Dressing for Meats or Salads 381
  French Dressing 1 380
  French Dressing 2 380
  French Dressing 3 380
  Mayonnaise 378
  Mayonnaise Dressing 1 379

Mayonnaise Dressing 2 379
Mayonnaise Dressing 3 379
Mayonnaise Dressing 4 380
Roquefort Dressing 380
Salad Dressing 378
Simple French Dressing 380
Slaw Dressing 379
Thousand Island Dressing 381
White Dressing 381
SALADS
Anchovy Salad 371
Artichoke Salad 374
Asparagus Salad 375
Banana Salad 368
Beef Salad 367
Beet Salad 370
Bird Nest Salad 375
Cabbage Salad 368
Cauliflower Salad 366
Celery and Nut Salad 366
Celery Salad 366
Chicken Salad 370
Chicken Salad and How to Boil It 371
Cold Slaw 367
Confederate Cabbage Salad 368
Crab Salad 369
Cucumber Salad 368
Dandelion Salad 373
Egg Salad 368
Fish Salad 375
French Chicken Salad 371
Fruit Salad 1 366
Fruit Salad 2 366
Fruit Salad 3 366
Fruit Salad 4 366
Grapefruit Salad 375
Ham Salad 374
Herring Salad 373
Hunter's Salad 368
Irish Potato Salad 373
Lettuce Salad 365

Lobster Salad 373
Orange Salad 375
Oyster and Celery Salad 372
Oyster Salad 369
Peach Salad 366
Pineapple Salad 373
Plantation Salad 373
Pork Salad 372
Potato Salad 1 369
Potato Salad 2 369
Potato Salad 3 369
Raw Salad 365
Ripe Olive Salad 372
Russian Salad 370
Salad Making Tips 365
Salmon Salad 371
Sardine Salad 370
Sauerkraut Preparation 376
Shrimp Salad 371
Slaw 367
String Bean Salad 373
Sweetbread and Cucumber Salad 374
Sweetbread Salad 374
To Marinade Salad 365
Tomato and Onion Salad 375
Tomato Salad 368
Tongue Salad 374
Vegetable Salad 370
Waldorf Salad 371
Warm Slaw 367
Watercress Salad 374

SANDWICHES
  Apple and Celery Sandwiches 387
  Baked Bean Sandwiches 386
  Beef and Potato Sandwiches 387
  Celery Sandwich 384
  Cheese and Lettuce Sandwiches 385
  Cheese Sandwiches 1 386
  Cheese Sandwiches 2 386
  Chicken and Ham Sandwiches 387
  Chicken Sandwiches 388

Club Sandwiches 1 389
Club Sandwiches 2 389
Confederate Egg Sandwiches 388
Cottage Cheese Sandwiches 384
Cucumber Sandwiches 389
Dainty Sandwich 387
Deviled Ham Sandwiches 388
Duck Sandwiches 387
Egg Sandwiches 386
Fish Sandwiches 387
Ginger Sandwiches 384
Ham Sandwiches 384
Hot Oyster Sandwiches 389
Lady Finger Sandwiches 390
Layer Sandwiches 385
Lenten Sandwich 388
Lettuce Sandwiches 386
Lobster Sandwiches 386
Manly Sandwiches 384
Nut and Cheese Sandwiches 385
Nut Sandwiches 390
Oyster Sandwiches 388
Pimola Sandwiches 385
Pineapple Cheese Sandwiches 388
Remoulade Sauce Sandwiches 383
Russian Sandwiches 384
Sandwich Making Tips 383
Sandwiches A La Parisienne 387
Sardine Canapes 389
Supper Cheese Sandwiches 385
Sweet Sandwiches 390
Toasted Cheese Sandwich 385
Tongue Sandwiches 389
Walnut and Cheese Sandwiches 386
Watercress Sandwiches 385

SAUCES
Abbie's Sauce for Meats 394
Agra Dolce 398
Anchovy Sauce 397
Asparagus Sauce 394
Bee Hive Sauce 401

Brandy Sauce for Plum Pudding	401
Brown Sauce	396
Caper Sauce	395
Caramel Sauce	401
Celery Sauce	400
Chili Sauce	392
Chilli Sauce	393
Cocoanut Snow Sauce	401
Confederate Hard Sauce	402
Crab Sauce	398
Cranberry Sauce 1	399
Cranberry Sauce 2	399
Cranberry Sauce for Turkey	399
Cream Sauce	392
Cream Sauce for Fruit Pies	400
Creole Sauce	399
Cucumber Sauce	399
Curry Sauce	397
Drawn Butter	398
Drawn Butter for Fowl	402
Egg Sauce	400
Foaming Sauce	394
Foamy Sauce	402
Fruit Sauce	401
Garlic Sauce	397
Green Tomato Sauce	396
Hard Sauce	394
Hollandaise Sauce	395
Horseradish Sauce	395
Lady Lee Pudding Sauce	402
Lemon Sauce	399
Lobster Sauce	393
Maitre D'Hotel Butter Sauce	398
Maple Sugar Sauce	395
Mint Sauce	395
Mushroom Sauce	396
Mustard Sauce	400
Onion Sauce	395
Oyster Sauce	402
Parsley Sauce	398
Prawn Sauce	397

Pudding Sauce	400
Sabayon Sauce	402
Sauce for Blue Grass Pudding	400
Sauce for Fruit Roll	401
Sauce Not So Rich	399
Sauce Tartare 1	393
Sauce Tartare 2	393
Sauce Tyrolienne	392
Shrimp Sauce	397
Spanish Sauce	398
Sunshine Sauce	400
Tartar Sauce	396
Tartare Sauce for Fish	393
Tomato Sauce	396
Truffle Sauce	396
Very Rich Sauce	399
Virginia Sauce	396
White Sauce	395
White Sauce for Fish, Meat, or Poultry	394
Wine Sauce	400

SCHOOL AND BUSINESS LUNCHES

Businessman's Lunch	406
Businesswoman's Lunch	406
Proper Eating	404
School Child's Lunch	405

SEAFOODS

Anchovy Canapes	410
Baked Bass	419
Baked Black Bass	414
Baked Fish 1	409
Baked Fish 2	409
Baked Fish 3	409
Baked Fish 4	409
Baked Herring	425
Baked Mackerel	420
Baked Pickerel	412
Baked Pike	414
Baked Shad	412
Baked Sturgeon	422
Baked White Fish	410
Barbequed Shad	412

Boiled Fish	408
Boiled Flounder	419
Boiled Halibut	411
Boiled Mussels	422
Boiled Salmon	419
Broiled Eels	421
Broiled Fish	409
Broiled Mackerel	420
Broiled Oysters	416
Broiled Oysters on Gridiron	416
Broiled Oysters With Brown Sauce	417
Broiled Smelts	420
Brook Trout	420
Clam Bake	424
Clam Chowder	421
Clam Pie	425
Codfish Balls	413
Codfish Chowder	421
Codfish Pie	413
Crab Stew	423
Creamed Lake Salmon	413
Creamed Oysters 1	417
Creamed Oysters 2	417
Creamed Oysters 3	418
Creamed Salmon	419
Deviled Crabs	423
Fish A La Cream	410
Fish Casserole	414
Fish Chowder	421
Fish Cooking Tips	408
Fish Fillets	410
Fish in Shells	411
Fish Pie	412
Fricasseed Oysters	415
Fried Eels	421
Fried Flounder	414
Fried or Sauteed Fish	412
Fried Oysters	415
Fried Perch	419
Halibut With Cheese	411
How to Cure and Smoke Fish	424

Lobster A La Dabney 426
Lobster A La Newberg 426
Lobster Cutlets 426
Oyster Loaf 418
Oyster Patties 427
Oyster Pie 414
Oysters A La Creole 420
Oysters A La Poulette 417
Panned Oysters 416
Potted Crab 423
Prawns 427
Raw Oysters 415
Roast Oysters 417
Roasted Clams 424
Roasted Oysters 427
Salmon 418
Scalloped Oysters 418
Scallops 425
Shrimp Gumbo 425
Shrimp Pie 425
Soft Shell Crabs Broiled 424
Soft Shell Crabs Fried 424
Steamed Clams 423
Steamed Fish 410
Steamed Oysters 415
Stewed Carp 426
Stewed Eels 422
Stewed Oysters 416
Sturgeon Cutlets 422
Sturgeon Steaks 422
To Choose Fish 408
To Prepare Eels 421
Turbot 413
Walled Oysters 416

SNACKS
Colonel Seabrook's Fritos Nachos 431
Colonel Seabrook's Healthy Baby White Popcorn 431
Colonel Seabrook's Potato Chip Nachos 430
Confederate Salted Almonds 429
Corn Puffs 431
Guacamole 430

Popcorn 431
Potato Chips 1 430
Potato Chips 2 430
Potato Chips 3 430
Salsa 431
Salted Almonds 429
Salted Peanuts 429
Salted Pistachio Nuts 429

SOUPS
   Artichoke Soup 456
   Asparagus Soup 454
   Barley Broth 448
   Barley Soup 446
   Beef Broth 455
   Beef Soup 435
   Black Bean Soup 455
   Bouillon 436
   Brown Stock 452
   Calf's Head Soup 442
   Carrot Soup 435
   Catfish Soup 442
   Chestnut Soup 445
   Chicken Broth 439
   Chicken Gumbo 436
   Chicken Soup 440
   Clam Broth 439
   Clam Soup 453
   Clear Soup or Bouillon 454
   Confederate Tomato Soup 453
   Consomme 450
   Corn and Tomato Soup 435
   Corn Chowder 448
   Corn Soup 447
   Crab Soup 444
   Cream of Asparagus Soup 454
   Cream of Celery Soup 440
   Cream of Chicken Soup 440
   Cream of Corn Soup 448
   Cream of Onion Soup 437
   Cream of Oyster Soup 443
   Cream of Pea Soup 440

Cream of Spinach Soup With Stock 443
Cream of Tomato Soup 441
Creamed Vegetable Soups 445
Creole Soup 439
Dixie Lentil Soup 441
Dixie Soup 434
Dixieland Soup 434
Eel Soup 450
Fish Soup 446
Gazpacho 444
German Cabbage Soup with Meat Stock 444
Green Pea Soup 435
Green Turtle Soup 449
Gumbo 436
Gumbo Soup 441
Hare Soup 438
Kentucky Burgout 450
Lima Bean Soup 448
Lobster Soup 453
Milk Soup 445
Mushroom Soup 438
Mutton Soup 436
Noodle Soup 439
Okra Gumbo 452
Okra Soup 451
Old Fashioned Turnip Soup 454
Onion Soup 450
Orange Soup 445
Ox-Tail Soup 440
Oyster Gumbo Soup 444
Oyster Soup 443
Pea Soup 455
Potato Chowder 447
Potato Soup 435
Pride of the South Macaroni Soup 441
Rabbit Soup 438
Rebel Vegetable Soup 437
Rice Soup 444
Salsify Soup 437
Scotch Broth 453
Soup Julienne 451

Soup Making Tips	433
Soup Stock of Beef	446
Southern Gumbo	437
Spaghetti Soup	449
Spinach Soup	442
Split Pea Soup	456
Squirrel Soup	447
Swiss Soup	443
To Make Soup	433
Tomato Bisque	454
Tomato Soup	435
Turkey Soup	452
Turtle Soup	448
Veal Soup	450
Vegetable Soup	437
Venison Soup	449
White Soup Stock	452
White Soup With Macaroni	446

VEGETABLES

Asparagus	464
Asparagus Filling for Patties	464
Baked Beans	467
Baked Cabbage	473
Baked Cauliflower	475
Baked Corn	473
Baked Egg Plant	465
Baked Potatoes	462
Baked Sweet Potatoes	460
Baked Sweet Potatoes in Half Shell	470
Baked Tomatoes	466
Beets	478
Boiled Cabbage	474
Boiled Irish Potatoes	459
Boiled Potatoes	460
Broccoli	468
Broiled Mushrooms	469
Broiled Tomatoes	466
Brown Hashed Potatoes 1	461
Brown Hashed Potatoes 2	462
Brussel Sprouts	474
Cabbage	473

Candied Yams	469
Carrot Souffle	465
Carrots	477
Carrots Stewed	464
Cayenne Pepper	479
Celery	468
Confederate Cauliflower	475
Confederate French Fries	462
Confederate Lima Beans	479
Confederate Mashed Potatoes	458
Confederate String Beans	479
Corn	470
Corn on the Cob	470
Corn Oysters	471
Creamed Asparagus	464
Creamed Potatoes	468
Creamed Spinach	468
Cucumbers Stewed	464
Dandelions	478
Dixie Potatoes	459
Egg Plant 1	465
Egg Plant 2	465
Flaked Potatoes	462
French Fried Potatoes	460
French Peas	472
Fried Corn	471
Fried Cucumbers	466
Fried Egg Plant	465
Fried Green Tomatoes	466
Fried Potatoes	460
Fried Squash	472
Fried Tomatoes	466
Frijoles	469
General Pickett Corn Pudding	471
Georgia Hominy Puffs	476
Hominy Puffs	476
Indian Corn	470
Jerusalem Artichokes	464
Lima Beans	470
Mammy's Candied Sweet Potatoes	477
Mashed Potatoes	458

Mustard	479
New Green Peas	463
New Potatoes	467
Old South Fried Green Tomatoes	467
Onions	478
Onions for Breakfast	470
Parsnips	478
Parsnips Fried	464
Peas	479
Potato Cakes	460
Potato Chips	460
Potato Souffle	472
Potatoes Au Gratin	461
Potatoes Baked in Their Jackets	460
Preserved Tomatoes	467
Pumpkin	475
Radish	468
Red Beet Roots	478
Riced Potatoes	459
Roasted Corn	473
Roasted Potatoes	461
Rutabaga	463
Scalloped Corn and Tomatoes	466
Scalloped Potatoes	462
Scalloped Tomatoes	467
Sea Kale	465
Sorrel	472
Southern Cabbage	474
Southern Creamed Sweet Potatoes	459
Southern Style Sweet Potatoes	478
Spinach	468
Squash	477
Stewed Corn	471
Stewed Lettuce	477
Stewed Mushrooms	469
Stewed Onions	470
Stewed Potatoes	461
Stewed Squash	472
Stewed Tomatoes	463
String Beans	473
Stuffed Peppers	477

Stuffed Potatoes 461
Stuffed Tomatoes 463
Succotash 469
Summer Squash 473
Sweet and Sour Beans 472
Sweet Potatoes 469
Texas Baked Irish Potatoes 460
To Boil Corn 471
To Boil Rice 463
To Clean Vegetables 458
To Cook Butter Beans 472
To Cook Cauliflower 475
To Cook Sauerkraut 376
Tomato Fricassee 466
Turnips 463
Vegetable Cooking Tips 458
Winter Squash 473

Interviewing the cook, 1893.

Col. Seabrook's Vintage Southern Cookbook
Appendices

"The more man follows nature, and is obedient to her laws, the longer he will live; the further he deviates from these, the shorter will be his existence."

Christoph Wilhelm Hufeland
GERMAN PHYSICIAN
(1762-1836)

Appendix A
Vintage Weights & Measures

General

4 tablespoons = 1 wineglass.
4 cups sifted flour = 1 lb.
4 wineglasses = 1 cup.
9 large eggs = 1 lb.
2 cups = 1 pint.
2 cups granulated sugar = 1 lb.
4 cups = 1 quart.
2½ cups powdered sugar = 1 lb.
3 teaspoons liquid = 1 tablespoon.
2 tablespoons butter (level) = 1 oz.
1 gill = ½ cup.
4 level tablespoons flour = 1 oz.
16 tablespoons liquid = 1 cup.
2 cups butter (solid) = 1 lb.
3 tablespoons grated chocolate = 1 oz.
1 quart sifted corn meal = 1 lb. 1 oz.

Quart and pint measures.

Avoirdupois Weight

16 drams make 1 ounce.
16 ounces make 1 pound.
28 pounds make 1 quarter of a hundred.
4 quarters, or 112 pounds, make 1 hundred.
20 hundred make 1 ton.

Liquid Measure

4 gills make 1 pint.
2 pints make 1 quart.
4 quarts make 1 gallon.
63 gallons make 1 hogshead.
2 hogsheads make 1 pipe or butt.
2 pipes make 1 ton.

Dry Measure

1 saltspoonful equals ¼ teaspoon.
2 pints make 1 quart.
8 quarts make 1 peck.
4 pecks make 1 bushel.
1 quart of flour weighs 1 pound.
1 quart of cornmeal weighs 1 pound 2 ounces.

1 quart of soft butter weighs 1 pound 1 ounce.
1 quart of loaf sugar weighs 1 pound.
1 quart of powdered sugar weighs 1 pound 1 ounce.
1 quart of brown sugar weighs 1 pound 2 ounces.
10 eggs weigh 1 pound.
1 gallon is ½ of a peck.
2 gallons make 1 peck.
4 gallons make ½ of a bushel.
8 gallons make 1 bushel.

Liquid Measure

16 tablespoonfuls make 1 half of a pint.
8 tablespoonfuls make 1 gill.
4 tablespoonfuls make ½ of a gill.
1 common sized tumbler holds ½ of a pint.
1 common sized wine-glass holds ½ of a gill.
1 common sized tablespoonful of salt is one ounce.

A set of accurate scales and a set of aluminum measuring spoons is an absolute necessity in the kitchen.

Appendix B
Things to Remember

EGGS

A dash of salt added to the whites of eggs makes them whip better.

Not a speck of the yolk must get into the whites which are to be whipped.

Fold the whipped whites into any mixture rather than stir them in, as the latter method breaks the air cells.

Break eggs one at a time into a saucer, so any can be rejected if necessary and the mixture not be spoiled.

Add a tablespoonful of water to an egg used for crumbing in order to remove the stringiness.

MILK

Use a double boiler for milk.

Milk is scalded when the water in the lower pan boils.

A pinch of bi-carbonate of soda mixed with tomato before milk or cream is added prevents the milk from curdling.

With sour milk, or molasses, use soda instead of baking powder.

BUTTER

Milk and butter should be kept in closely covered vessels, as they readily absorb flavor and odor from other articles.

Butter added slowly in small bits to creamy mixtures, or sauces, prevents a greasy line forming.

CRUMBS

Crumbs grated directly from the loaf give a more delicate color than dried crumbs to fried articles.

Dried crumbs absorb more moisture, and are better for watery dishes.

Crumbs spread over the tops of dishes should be mixed evenly with melted butter over the fire; this is a better method than having lumps of butter dotted over the crumbs after they are spread.

When the sauce bubbles through the crumbs on top of a scallop dish, the cooking is completed.

MEATS

Meat should not be washed. It can be cleaned by rubbing with a wet cloth, or by scraping with a knife.

Drippings are better than water for basting meats.

Meats should not be pierced while cooking.

Soak salt fish with the skin side up over night. Change the water several times.

To skim sauces, draw the saucepan to the side of the fire, throw in a teaspoonful of cold water, and the grease will rise so that it can be easily taken off.

A few drops of onion juice improve made-over meat dishes; not enough need be used to give a pronounced onion flavor.

DRIPPINGS

The skimming from soups, drippings from any beef roasts, and trimmings from any beef, serve the same uses as lard, cottolene, or butter.

ONION JUICE

To extract onion juice, press the raw surface of an onion against a grater, move it slightly, and the juice will run off the point of the grater.

CHOPPING SUET

Chop suet in a cool place, and sprinkle it with flour to prevent its oiling and sticking together. Remove the membrane before chopping it.

CHOPPING OR POUNDING ALMONDS

Add a few drops of rose-water to almonds to prevent their oiling when chopped or pounded.

To loosen grated peel, or other articles, from the grater, strike the grater sharply on the table.

MIXING

When mixing a liquid with a solid material, add but little liquid at a time and stir constantly to prevent lumping.

When adding cornstarch, arrowroot, or any starchy material to hot liquid, first mix it with enough cold water, or milk, to make it fluid; pour it in slowly and stir constantly until it becomes clear.

GELATINE

Soak gelatine in a cool place for an hour in cold water or milk. It will then quickly dissolve in hot liquid and have no odor. If jellied dishes do not stiffen, add more gelatine; boiling down will not effect the purpose.

MOLDS

Grease molds evenly with butter or oil, using a brush. Lumps of butter on the side of molds leave an uneven surface on the article cooked or molded in them. Molds for jellies are not greased.

Invert a dish over a mold before turning it, so that the form will not break; also, place it in exactly the right spot before lifting off the mold.

STRAINERS

It is desirable to pass all liquid mixtures through a strainer to make them perfectly smooth.

KEEPING DISHES WARM

To keep dishes warm until time of serving, place the saucepan in a pan of hot water.

FLAVORING

Any flavoring is added after the mixture is cooked, excepting for baked dishes. Wine increases the taste of salt, therefore, where wine is used for flavoring, very little salt should be put in until after the wine is used, when more can be added if necessary.

Dishes which are to be frozen need an extra amount of sweetening

RAISINS

Flour raisins before adding them to a mixture in order to prevent their settling to the bottom.

BAKING

Never slam the oven door, or jar any rising material while it is baking.
Anything being cooked for the second time needs a hot oven.

(From *The Century Cook Book*, 1895)

Appendix C
Table Etiquette

A host or hostess should never allude to the quality of the dishes or contents—either is in poor taste. The guests will discover their excellence without assistance.
If a guest does not care for a certain article do not press it upon him.
Do not, in serving, overload the plates.
Do not finger knife, fork, dishes or anything on the table.
Do not overload the fork.
Do not leave the knife and fork crossed on the plate when you have finished, but leave them parallel on the plate, the tines of fork down, the knife to the right and the sharp edge next to the fork.
Do not, under any circumstances, put the knife in the mouth.
Do not drink from the saucer.
Do not rise from the chair to reach anything.
Do not tip the soup-plate, or put the end of the soup-spoon in the mouth, except when eating oyster-soup.
Soup should be eaten from the side of the spoon and taken from the further side of the plate by moving the spoon from you.
Close the mouth when chewing.
Never make a hissing sound when eating soup.
Never cut bread, but break it, buttering each piece as it is eaten.
Never reach across others.
Bread should be buttered on the edge of the plate, never in mid-air.
Olives should be taken with the fingers.
The fork should be used for croquettes, patties and most made dishes, and must be used equally well in either hand. Never eat anything with a spoon that can be eaten with a fork.
Do not hesitate to take the last piece.
Do not move the chair, but seat yourself quietly.
Look into, not over, the cup or glass when drinking.
Never quite fill the spoon, it is bad form.
A lady, if in a restaurant or hotel, rises when another stops to speak to her, even though she is seated at the table.
A gentleman half unfolds his napkin and places it over the left knee. Do not mop the face with the napkin.
Napkins should be unfolded below the level of the table and as unobtrusively as possible.
Never tuck the napkin under the chin or in the waistcoat.
Soft cheese may be put on the cracker with a knife. Hard cheese is taken in the fingers.
If the host is carving, at a family table, it is not necessary to wait until all

are served before beginning to eat.
The spoon is used for berries and cream, stewed fruit, peaches and cream and soft desserts.
Crackers or bread should not be broken into the soup, but eaten from the fingers.
Strawberries served with the stem, are eaten with the fingers.
The fork should be raised laterally and not in such a fashion as to bring it at right angles to the mouth.
The smaller knife, of two at the plate, should be used for fish. Never use a steel knife for fish.
Side dishes of vegetables should be placed at the left and eaten with a fork.
Never smear the meat with mustard or sauce of any kind; place it at the side.
Never transfer the fork from one hand to the other.
Never drink with the spoon in the cup.
Do not leave the spoon in the cup after stirring coffee or tea, but place it in the saucer.
Do not rest the elbow on the table.
The knife should be taken by the handle only, resting the forefinger on the upper part of the blade.
The fork should be used for mashing and eating potatoes. Never touch potato with a knife, except to butter it.
Ice cream may be eaten with either a spoon or ice-cream fork.
Pass anything which you see is desired, even to a stranger.
When through dinner the napkin should be left unfolded, unless at home.
Ladies should always be served before gentlemen.
Never place toothpicks on the table and never use a toothpick at the table.
Never talk with the mouth full.
Never take a piece of bread with a fork.
Never put glasses on the table with the stems up.
Never blow on soup or coffee to cool it.
Never smack the lips.
Never leave the table with food in the mouth.
Never put salt on the table-cloth.
Always eat slowly.
Gentlemen should seat ladies first.
Do not bend over the plate for each mouthful.
Carry food to the mouth with an inward, not an outward, curve of the fork or spoon.
Do not spread the elbows in cutting meat.
Knives, forks and spoons should be placed on the table for all the courses except the dessert.
Finger-bowls are filled one-third full of tepid water, and are placed on

the table only when fruit is eaten, and after a meal. The finger-tips only should be dipped in the finger-bowl.
The handles of the knife and fork should rest in the palms of the hands.
Do not tip up the glass or cup too much when drinking, but keep it at a slight angle.
Do not ask any one whether he wishes more potato, etc., but some potato.
Do not reach after a knife, fork or spoon that is dropped but ask for another.
Do not oblige the carver to make a selection for you when asked what part of the fowl you prefer, but answer promptly, giving your preference.
Do not eat onions or garlic unless intending to remain alone.
Do not eat after passing a plate for another to the carver, until the plate has been returned.
Do not twist the feet around the legs of the chair.
A crumb knife or fresh napkin should be used in brushing crumbs from the table.
Never shove dishes on the table; always pass them.
Never shove yourself from the table.
Never touch the face or head at the table or fuss with the hands.
Never suck an orange.
Never spit seeds of fruit on the plate, but take them out of the mouth with a spoon and lay them on the plate.
Never take a larger mouthful than will allow you to speak with ease.
Never hold the spoon so that the handle rests in the palm of the hand.
Never loll back in your chair or lean against the table, but sit upright.
Never make introductions after the guests are seated.
Never lift a glass by the rim; take goblets by the stem and tumblers near the bottom.
Never ask whether any one will have *some* meat, but whether he will have roast beef, beefsteak, or whatever kind of meat is served.
When asking for anything at the table mention the party's name when you speak.
Do not give any one at the table the trouble of waiting upon you if there be a servant in the room.
Do not, when at a private table, leave until all have finished.
Gentlemen remaining for cigars, rise when the ladies do, and remain standing until they have left the room.
Gentlemen allow the ladies to pass out first *en masse*, if all leave the dining-room.
Wear evening dress at a formal dinner party.
Wear gloves and do not take them off until seated at the table.

(From *Woman's Favorite Cook Book*, 1902)

Appendix D
French Words in Cooking

Aspic—Savory jelly for cold dishes.
Baba—A sweet French yeast cake.
Bechamel—Rich white sauce made with stock.
Bisque—White soup made of shell fish.
Blanch—To remove skin by plunging in boiling water. To bring any article to a boil, and then plunge in cold water; to whiten poultry, vegetables, etc.
Bouillon—A clear soup, not so strong as consomme.
Braise—Meat cooked in closely covered stew pan, so as retain flavor of meat and whatever is cooked with it.
Cannel—Stuffed rolled up meat.
Consomme—Bouillon or clear soup boiled down till very rich.
Croquettes—A mince of various articles made with sauces into shapes and fried.
Entree—A small dish, usually served between courses at dinner.
Fondant—Boiled sugar beaten to a creamy paste.
Mayonnaise—A salad dressing.
Meringue—White of egg and sugar beaten to sauce.
Piquance—Sauce of several flavors, acid predominating.
Purse—Very thick soup, for which the ingredients have been rubbed through a sieve.
Quenelles—Forcemeat with bread, yolks of eggs, highly seasoned, made oval shape with a spoon; then poached and used as a dish by themselves, or to garnish.
Ragout—A rich, brown stew, with mushrooms, vegetables, etc.
Rissole—A mince of fish or meat, rolled in thin pastry and fried.
Roux—A mixture of butter and flour, cooked, for thickening stews and soups.
Sauter—To toss meat, etc., over the fire, in a little fat.
Souffle—Very light, much whipped-up pudding or omelet.
Timbale—A sort of pie in mold.

(From *The "Home Queen" Cook Book*, 1893)

A 1912 Hudson Motor Car, the "Torpedo"; price: $1,600.

Appendix E
Housekeeper's Alphabet

Apples—Keep in dry place, as cool as possible without freezing.
Brooms—Hang in the cellar-way to keep soft and pliant.
Cranberries—Keep under water, in cellar; change water monthly.
Dish of hot water set in oven prevents cakes, etc., from scorching.
Economize time, health, and means, and you will never beg.
Flour—Keep cool, dry, and securely covered.
Glass—Clean with a quart of water mixed with table-spoon of ammonia.
Herbs—Gather when beginning to blossom; keep in paper sacks.
Ink Stains—Wet with spirits turpentine; after three hours, rub well.
Jars—To prevent, coax husband to buy the *Vintage Southern Cookbook*.
Keep an account of all supplies, with cost and date when purchased.
Love lightens labor.
Money—Count carefully when you receive change.
Nutmegs—Prick with a pin, and if good, oil will run out.
Orange and Lemon Peel—Dry, pound, and keep in corked bottles.
Parsnips—Keep in ground until spring.
Quicksilver and white of an egg destroys bedbugs.
Rice—Select large, with a clear, fresh look; old rice may have insects.
Sugar—For general family use, the granulated is best.
Tea—Equal parts of Japan and green are as good as English breakfast.
Use a cement made of ashes, salt, and water for cracks in stove.
Variety is the best culinary spice.
Watch your back yard for dirt and bones.
Xantippe was a scold. Don't imitate her.
Youth is best preserved by a cheerful temper.
Zinc-lined sinks are better than wooden ones.

Reminder: regulate the clock by your husband's watch,
and in all apportionments of time remember the Giver.

(From *The Dixie Cook-Book*, 1885)

Appendix F
How to Cook Husbands

A GOOD MANY HUSBANDS ARE ENTIRELY spoiled by mismanagement in cooking, and so are not tender and good. Some women go about it as if their husbands were bladders and blow them up. Others keep them constantly in hot water. Others let them freeze by their carelessness and indifference. Some keep them in a stew by irritating ways and words. Others roast them. Some keep them in pickle all their lives. It can not be supposed that any husband will be tender and good managed in this way. Turnips wouldn't, onions wouldn't, cabbage heads wouldn't, and husbands won't; but they are really delicious when properly treated. In selecting your husband, you should be guided not by the silvery appearance, as in buying mackerel; not by the golden tint, as if you wanted salmon. Be sure to select him yourself, as tastes differ. And, by the way, do not go to the market for him, as the best is always brought to the door. It is far better to have none unless you will patiently learn how to cook him. A preserving kettle of the finest porcelain is the best, but if you have nothing but an earthenware pipkin it will do, with care.

Late 19th-Century cooking stove, Macon, Georgia.

See that the linen in which you wrap him is nicely washed and mended, with the requisite number of buttons and strings nicely sewed on. Tie him in the kettle by a strong silken cord called Comfort, as the one called Duty is apt to be weak. Husbands are apt to fly out of the kettle and be burned and crusty on the edges, since, like crabs and lobsters, you have to cook them while alive. Make a clear, strong, steady fire out of Love, Neatness, and Cheerfulness. Set your husband as near this as seems to agree with him. If he sputters and fizzles do not be anxious. Some husbands do this until they are quite done. Add a little sugar in the form of what confectioners call kisses, but no vinegar or pepper on any account. A little spice improves him, but it must be used with judgment. Do not stick any sharp instrument into him to see if he is becoming tender. Stir him gently; watch, the while, lest he lie too flat and close to the kettle, and so become inert and useless. You can not fail to know when he is done. If thus treated, you will find him very digestible, agreeing nicely with you and the children, and he will keep as long as you want, unless you become careless and set him in too cold a place.

(From the *Athens Woman's Cook Book*, 1922)

Appendix G

CONTRIBUTORS TO THE
Vintage Southern Cookbook

(PARTIAL LIST)

Abbott, Miss Nannie
Adair, Mrs. R. M.
Addison, Mrs. Walter E.
Alexander, Mrs. A. J.
Alexander, Miss Kate
Alexanders, Mrs. C.
Allin, Mrs. B. T.
Armstrong, Mrs. H.
Arnold, Mrs. L. J.
Arrington, Olivia
Bannister, Mrs.
Barclay, Mrs.
Barnes, Mrs. L. D.
Barnes, Mrs. M.
Bashford, Mrs. Allen
Bashford, Mrs. James
Bashford, Miss Mary
Battaille, Miss
Batterton, Mrs.
Beaujean, Mrs.
Beckie, Miss
Bedford, Cornelia
Beers, Mrs.
Bell, Mrs. William
Berryman, Mrs. J. C.
Berryman, Mrs. Charles
Bigelow, Mrs.
Black, Mrs.
Blanton, Mrs. L. H.
Blanton, Kate
Blanton, Mr. Baker
Blythe, Mrs. Jas.
Bragg, Mrs. D.
Brent, Mrs. C. S., Sr.
Brent, Mrs. C.
Brent, Mrs. Chambers
Brent, Mrs. J. H.
Brock, Mrs.
Brooks, Mrs. S.
Brown, L.
Buckner, Mrs. H. C.
Buckner, Mrs. B. F.
Buckner, Mrs. Henry C.
Buckner, Mrs. W. T.
Buckner, Mrs. W. T.
Bullitt, Mrs.

Burnley, Mrs.
Cabell, Mrs. C. Ellet
Carrington, Campbell
Cassidy, Mr.
Castleberry, Mrs.
Chapline, Mrs. M.
Cheny, G.
Clark, Mrs.
Clay, Mrs. Brutus J.
Clay, Mrs. Cassius M.
Clay, Mrs. James E.
Clay, Mrs. Frank
Clay, Mrs. Ezekiel
Clay, Mrs. Green
Clay, Mrs. Sam
Clay, Mrs. Brutus J.
Clay, Mrs. Amanda
Clay, Miss Mattie
Clay, Mrs. C. F.
Cochran, Mrs.
Conway, Mrs. Sara
Cook, Sallie
Cook, Miss Jennie
Cooke, Mrs.
Crawford, Mrs.
Crossland, Mrs.
Crossland, Miss Kate
Croxton, Miss Virginia
Croxton, Miss Belle
Cunningham, Mrs. Mary
Dabney, Miss, Bothwell
Davidson, Mrs. H.
Davies, Mrs. Wm.
Davis, Mrs. Geo. W.
Dearing, Mrs.
Deigman, Mrs.
DeLong, Mr.
Dennis, Annie
Dodge, Mrs. D. M.
Donaldson, Mrs.
Dougherty, Mrs. C. A.
Dowling, Mrs.
Dudley, Mrs.
Duncan, Mrs. Garnett
Duncan, Mrs. Mary
Durr, Lucy

Edmiston, Miss
Edwards, Mrs.
Elbert, Miss Sue
Ewing, E. P.
Farley, Mrs. Lewis
Farmer, Miss
Farnham, Mrs.
Faunce, Mrs.
Fisher, Mrs. Abby
Fisher, Mrs. W. W.
Fithian, Mrs. Wash
Fithian, Mrs. Washington
Ford, Mrs. J. C.
Fox, Minnie C.
Fox, Mrs. John W.
Frederick, Mrs.
Garrard, Mrs.
Garrett, Mrs. Alice
Gass, Mrs. Morris
Gayle, Mrs.
Geddes, Lucy
Gill, Mrs. W. W.
Glass, Mrs.
Goddard, Mrs. Mary E.
Goff, Mrs. Strauder
Goodloe, Mrs. David
Gorton, Mrs. Francis
Graddy, Miss Lucy
Graves, Mrs.
Green, Mrs. M. L.
Green, Miss
Gregrey, Mrs.
Hall, Dr. W. W.
Halleck, Miss
Halliday, Mrs.
Hamilton, Mrs.
Hannon, Pauline
Hanson, Mrs. R. H.
Hanson, Miss
Hanson, Mrs. Col.
Hanson, Mrs. R. H.
Harland, Marion
Harland, Marvin
Harrison, Miss Ella
Haseworth, Mrs.
Hatchings, Annie
Hawes, Hon. R.
Hawes, Siss
Hazzard, Mrs. J. C.
Heard, Mrs. Joseph, Sr.
Hedges, Mrs. John T.
Hegman, Mr. C. E. F.
Henderson, Mrs. Senator
Henry, Lizzie
Hibler, Mrs. Geo.
Higgins, Mrs. V.
Hill, Mrs. Ambrose Powell
Hill, Janet M.

Hogan, Mrs. Dr.
Holt, Mrs. Joseph
Holt, Miss Bettie
Holt, Mrs. J. H.
Howerton, Mrs. J. A.
Hughes, Mrs. James
Hughes, Mrs.
Humphrey, Mrs. Dr.
Hunt, Mrs. A.
Ingles, Mrs. J.
Jackson, Martha
Jaynes, Miss
Johnson, Mrs. W. A.
Johnson, Mrs. L.
Johnston, Mrs. L.
Johnston, Mrs. Dave
Johnston, Mrs. Jack
Jones, Mrs. William
Jones, Mrs. Lawrence
Jones, Mrs. J. M.
Jordan, John
Justice, Mrs.
Kellar, Mrs. Georgia
Kenney, Miss Hattie
Kenney, Mrs. Dr.
Kinkead, Mrs. W. B.
Kirtland, Mrs. A. E.
Kohn, Frances
Lee, Jennie
Leek, Mary
Lemcke, Mrs.
Lenicke, Mrs. Gesne
Ligon, Mrs. S.
Lowry, Mrs.
Lowther, E.
Lyle, Miss Annie
Lyle, Miss Daisy
Lyle, Mrs. E.
Marks, Mrs. Sam
Martin, Mrs. N. T.
Massie, Mrs. W. W.
Massie, Mrs. Frank
Mathews, Penny
May, Susie
McCarney, Mrs. J.
McCarney, Miss Iva
McCarthy, Ella
McCombs, Annie
McCormick, Mrs. Francis
McCormick, Mrs. Cyrus
McCoy, Mrs.
McDougall, Mrs.
McDowell, Mrs. H. C.
McMannus, Mrs.
Meister, John
Miller, Miss
Minor, Mrs.
Mitchell, Annie

Mitchell, Miss Belle
Mitchell, Miss Ella
Mitchell, Mrs. T. H.
Mitchell, Mrs. Mollie
Moore, Mrs. A.
Moritz, Mrs.
Morrow, Mrs. Robert
Myers, Mrs.
Neely, Mrs. J.
Neely, Mrs. Robert J.
Nippert, Mr. P.
Northcutt, Mrs.
Oppenheim, Mrs.
Owen, Mrs.
Owens, J.
Parloa, Miss
Patterson, Mrs. Dr.
Paul, Bettie
Payne, J. B.
Payne, Mrs. Walter
Payne, Mrs. Richard
Payne, Mrs. John B.
Pease, Mr.
Pease, Mrs., Sr.
Peers, Mrs.
Pope, Mrs. Patrick
Powell, Mrs. Dr.
Randolph, Mary
Randolph, Mrs. Col.
Ray, Mrs. John
Redmon, Miss M.
Rion, Mrs. N. B., Jr.
Rives, Mattie
Rogers, Mrs. Johnson
Rogers, Mrs. M. L.
Ronald, Mary
Rorer, Mrs.
Rosser, Mrs. Thomas L.
Rucker, Mrs.
Russell, Mrs.
Ryland, Mrs. Anne
Scott, Mrs. M. T.
Seabrook, Lochlainn
Seelye, Mrs.
Semple, Mrs.
Sewel, Mrs.
Sheehan, Maggie
Shoemaker, Mrs.
Short, Mrs. J.
Short, Miss F.
Shropshire, Miss Fannie
Simms, Mrs. William E.
Simms, Mrs. W. E.
Simms, Col. W. E.
Sinege, Mrs.
Smedley, Mrs. L. J.
Smith, Rev. Green Clay
Snow, Martha
Spears, Mrs. Henry
Spears, Mrs. Woodford
Spears, Miss R. Keith
Spears, Miss Kate
Spratt, Mrs. G.
Squire, Miss
St. Nicholas Hotel (Cincinnati, OH)
Stevens, Mrs. K.
Stone, Mrs.
Stoner, Mrs. R. G.
Stratford, Mrs.
Stringfellow, Miss
Stump, Mrs.
Sweat, Mrs.
Talbott, Mrs. W. G.
Taylor, Mrs.
Taylor, Mrs. W.
Taylor, Mrs Ed.
Taylor, Bill
Thomas, Mrs. F.
Thompson, Mrs.
Thornton, Mrs. Carrie Preston
Thornton, Mrs. Richard
Thornton, Mrs. Belle
Turney, Mrs. Amos, Sr.
Turney, Mrs. Mat.
Turney, Mrs. Amos, Jr.
Tyson, M. L.
Walker, Ella
Walker, Mrs. Sallie
Warfield, Mrs. E.
Washington, Mrs. B.
Watson, Mrs.
Webb, Mrs. M.
Webb, Mrs. Mary
Wentz, Mrs. Daniel B.
White, Miss Annie
White, Miss Elise
White, Mrs. Mary
Whiting, Mrs.
Wiley, Mrs.
Williamson, Carrie
Wilson, Dr.
Wing, Mrs.
Withrow, Mrs. C.
Wood, Miss Phebe
Woodford, Mrs. B.
Wornall, Mrs. Perry
Worswick, Edith
Wyles, Mrs. Tom R.
Wynn, Mrs.
Young, Mrs. Dr.
Young, Rev. D. P.

MEET THE AUTHOR

NEO-VICTORIAN SCHOLAR LOCHLAINN SEABROOK, a descendant of the families of Alexander Hamilton Stephens, John Singleton Mosby, Edmund Winchester Rucker, and William Giles Harding, is a 7th generation Kentuckian and the most prolific pro-South writer in the world today. Known by literary critics as the "new Shelby Foote" and by his fans as the "Voice of the Traditional South," he is a recipient of the prestigious Jefferson Davis Historical Gold Medal. As a lifelong writer he has authored and edited books ranging in topics from history, politics, science, religion, and biography, to nature, music, humor, gastronomy, and the paranormal; books that his readers describe as "game changers," "transformative," and "life altering."

One of the world's most popular living historians, he is a 17th generation Southerner of Appalachian heritage who descends from dozens of patriotic Revolutionary War soldiers and Confederate soldiers from Kentucky, Tennessee, North Carolina, and Virginia. A proud member of the Sons of the Confederate Veterans, he is a true Renaissance Man. Besides being an accomplished and well respected author-historian and Bible authority, he is also a Kentucky Colonel, eagle scout, screenwriter, nature, wildlife, and landscape photographer, artist, graphic designer, songwriter (3,000 songs), film composer, multi-instrument musician, vocalist, session player, music producer, genealogist, former history museum docent, and a former ranch hand, zookeeper, and wrangler.

His (currently) 76 adult and children's books contain some 60,000 well-researched pages that have earned him accolades from around the globe. His works, which have sold on every continent except Antarctica, have introduced hundreds of thousands to vital facts that have been left out of our mainstream books. He has been endorsed internationally by leading experts, museum curators, award-winning historians, bestselling authors, celebrities, filmmakers, noted scientists, well regarded educators, TV show hosts and producers, renowned military artists, esteemed heritage organizations, and distinguished academicians of all races, creeds, and colors. Colonel Seabrook holds the world record for writing the most books on Southern icon Nathan Bedford Forrest: 12.

Of northern, western, and central European ancestry, he is the 6th great-grandson of the Earl of Oxford and a descendant of European royalty. His modern day cousins include: Johnny Cash, Elvis Presley, Lisa Marie Presley, Billy Ray and Miley Cyrus, Patty Loveless, Tim McGraw, Lee Ann Womack, Dolly Parton, Pat Boone, Naomi, Wynonna, and Ashley Judd, Ricky Skaggs, the Sunshine Sisters, Martha Carson, Chet Atkins, Patrick J. Buchanan, Cindy Crawford, Bertram Thomas Combs (Kentucky's 50th governor), Edith Bolling (second wife of President Woodrow Wilson), Andy Griffith, Riley Keough, George C. Scott, Robert Duvall, Reese Witherspoon, Lee Marvin, Rebecca Gayheart, and Tom Cruise.

A constitutionalist and avid outdoorsman and gun advocate, Colonel Seabrook is the author of the international blockbuster, *Everything You Were Taught About the Civil War is Wrong, Ask a Southerner!* He lives with his wife and family in beautiful historic Middle Tennessee, the heart of the Confederacy.

For more information on author Mr. Seabrook visit
LOCHLAINNSEABROOK.COM

LOCHLAINN SEABROOK ~ 587

If you enjoyed this book you will be interested in Colonel Seabrook's popular related titles:

☞ ABRAHAM LINCOLN WAS A LIBERAL, JEFFERSON DAVIS WAS A CONSERVATIVE
☞ EVERYTHING YOU WERE TAUGHT ABOUT THE CIVIL WAR IS WRONG, ASK A SOUTHERNER!
☞ ALL WE ASK IS TO BE LET ALONE: THE SOUTHERN SECESSION FACT BOOK
☞ EVERYTHING YOU WERE TAUGHT ABOUT AMERICAN SLAVERY IS WRONG, ASK A SOUTHERNER!
☞ CONFEDERATE FLAG FACTS: WHAT EVERY AMERICAN SHOULD KNOW ABOUT DIXIE'S SOUTHERN CROSS
☞ LINCOLN'S WAR: THE REAL CAUSE, THE REAL WINNER, THE REAL LOSER

Available from Sea Raven Press and wherever fine books are sold

  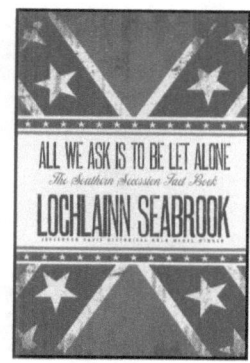

ALL OF OUR BOOK COVERS ARE AVAILABLE AS 11" X 17" COLOR POSTERS, SUITABLE FOR FRAMING

SeaRavenPress.com

www.ingramcontent.com/pod-product-compliance
Lightning Source LLC
Chambersburg PA
CBHW030513230426
43665CB00010B/601